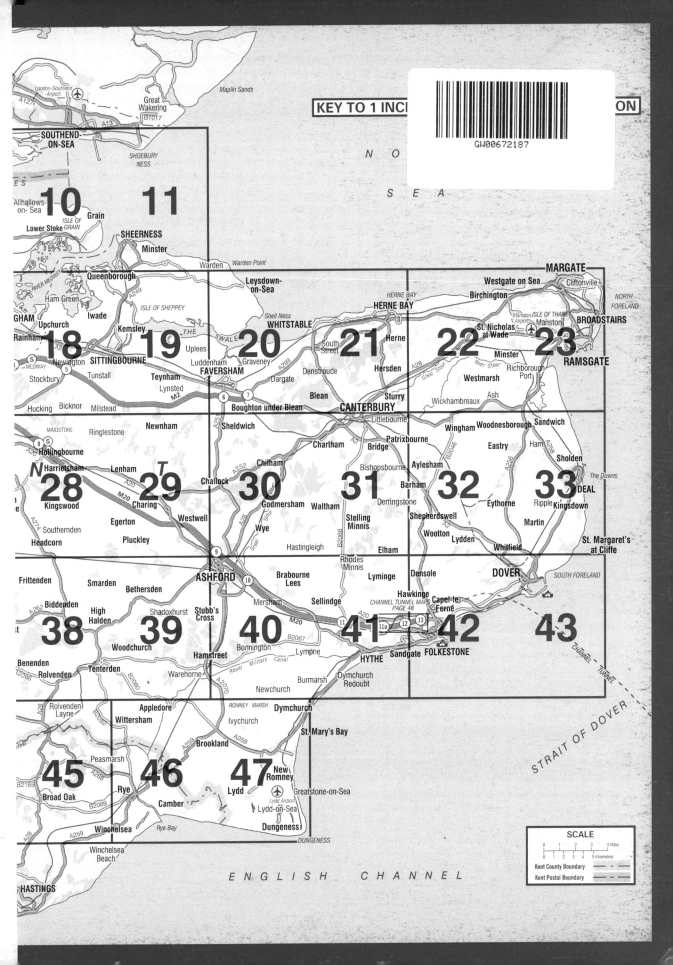

REFERENCE TO 1 INCH TO 1 MILE STREET MAP SECTION

Motorway	**M2**
Motorway Junction Numbers	
Unlimited Interchange **4**	Limited Interchange **3**
Motorway Service Area	**S** **MEDWAY**
Mileages - between Motorway Junctions	*4*
Primary Route	**A2**
North & South Circular Roads	
Primary Route Destination	**DOVER**
A Road	A274
B Road	B2162
Other Selected Roads	
Dual Carriageway	
Red Route (Priority Clearway)	
Primary Route	
North & South Circular Roads	
A Road	
One Way Road	
(Motorway, Primary Route & A Road only - Traffic flow indicated by a heavy line on the driver's left)	
Tunnel	
Major Road Under Construction	
Major Road Proposed	
Junction Name	**KESTON MARK**
Toll	TOLL
Ferry	

Railway and Croydon Tramlink	
Level Crossing and Tunnel	
Railway Station	SEVENOAKS
London Underground Station	ROTHERHITHE
D.L.R. Station and Tramlink Stop	SOUTH QUAY
Local Authority Boundary	
Posttown Boundary	
Postcode Boundary	
within Posttown	
Map Continuation	
for 1 Inch to 1 Mile Street Mapping (Blue Pages)	**5**
to 3 Inches to 1 Mile Street Mapping (Red Pages)	**89** or **223**
Airport	LONDON - BIGGIN HILL AIRPORT
Airport Runway	
Built-up Area	
National Grid Reference	⁵80
Place of Interest	• *Chartwell*
River or Canal	

Sporting Venues		
Cricket	Stadium	
Football	Horse Racing	
Golf Course	Motor Racing	
18 Hole 9 Hole	Rugby	
	Tennis	

Tourist Information Centre

Open all year	**i**	Open Summer only	**i**
Viewpoint		180°	360°

Wood, Park, Cemetery, Etc.

SCALE

1 Inch (2.54 cm) to 1 Mile
1.58 cm to 1 Kilometre

0 ½ 1 2 Miles
0 1 2 3 Kilometres

1:63,360

The following features are shown only in those areas of Kent not covered by 3 Inches to 1 Mile Street Mapping (Red Pages)

Building	☐	Hospital	**H**
Car Park - selected	**P**	Police Station	▲
Church or Chapel	†	Post Office	★
Fire Station	■	Toilet	▽
		with facilities for the Disabled	♿

AZ KENT

CONTENTS

Geographers' A-Z Map Company Ltd.

Head Office : Fairfield Road, Borough Green, Sevenoaks, Kent TN15 8PP Telephone : 01732 781000 (General Enquiries & Trade Sales)

Showrooms : 44 Gray's Inn Road, London WC1X 8HX Telephone 020 7440 9500 (Retail Sales)

www.a-zmaps.co.uk

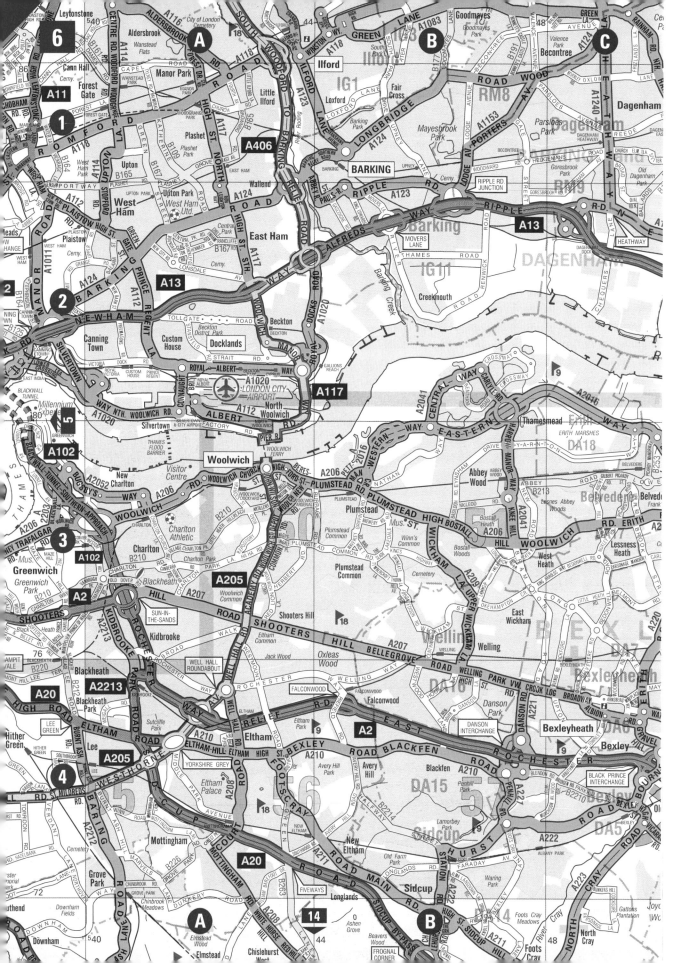

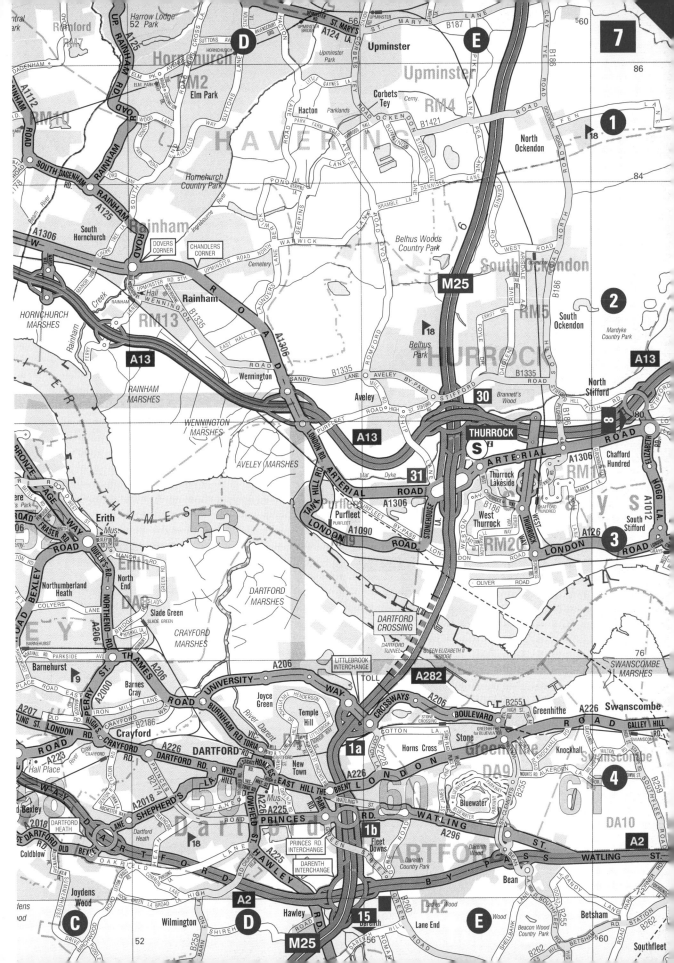

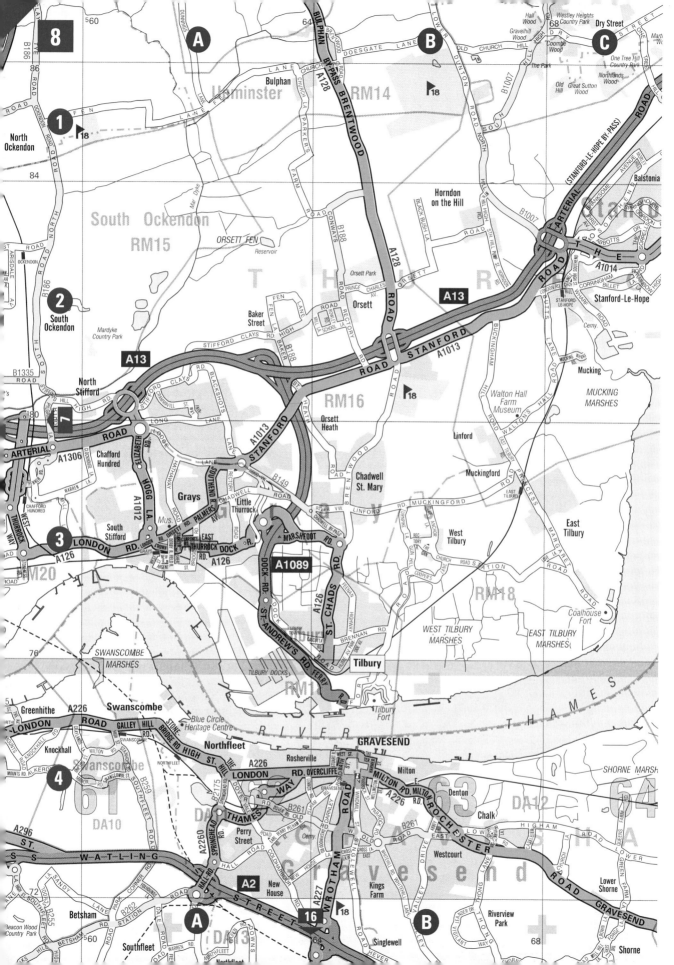

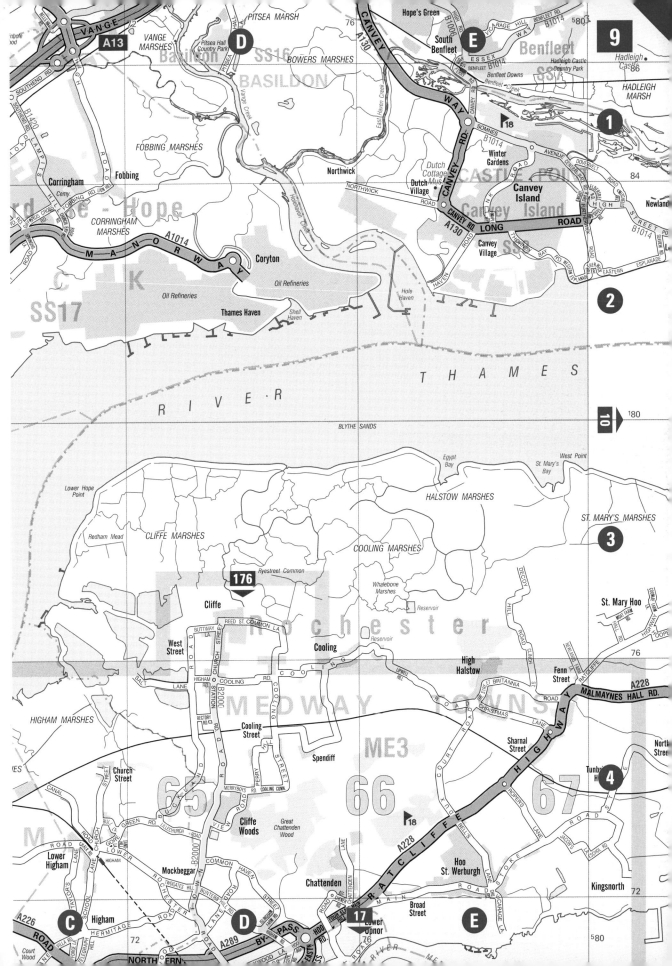

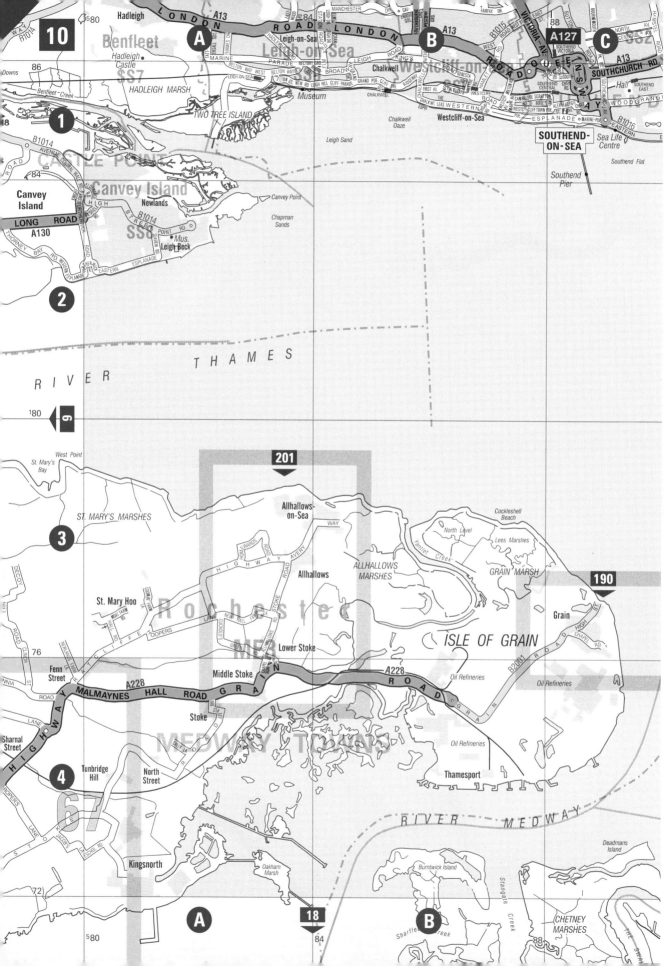

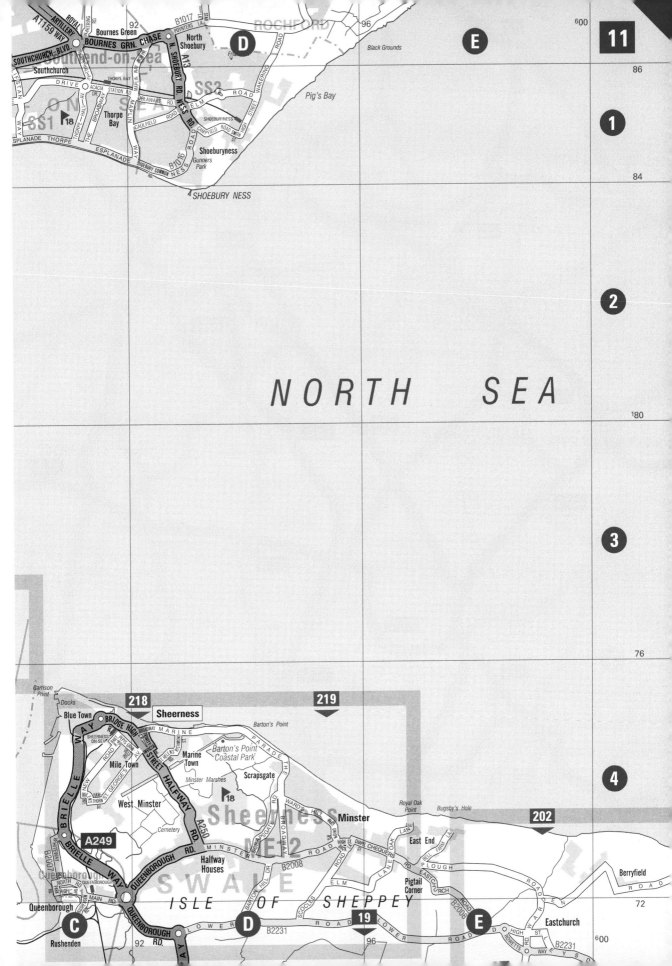

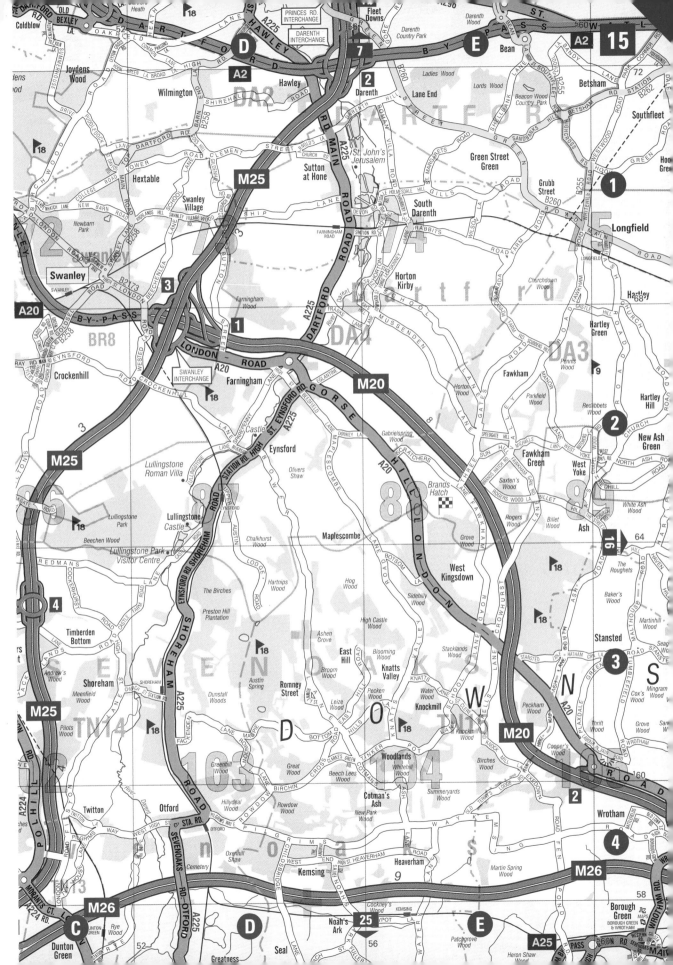

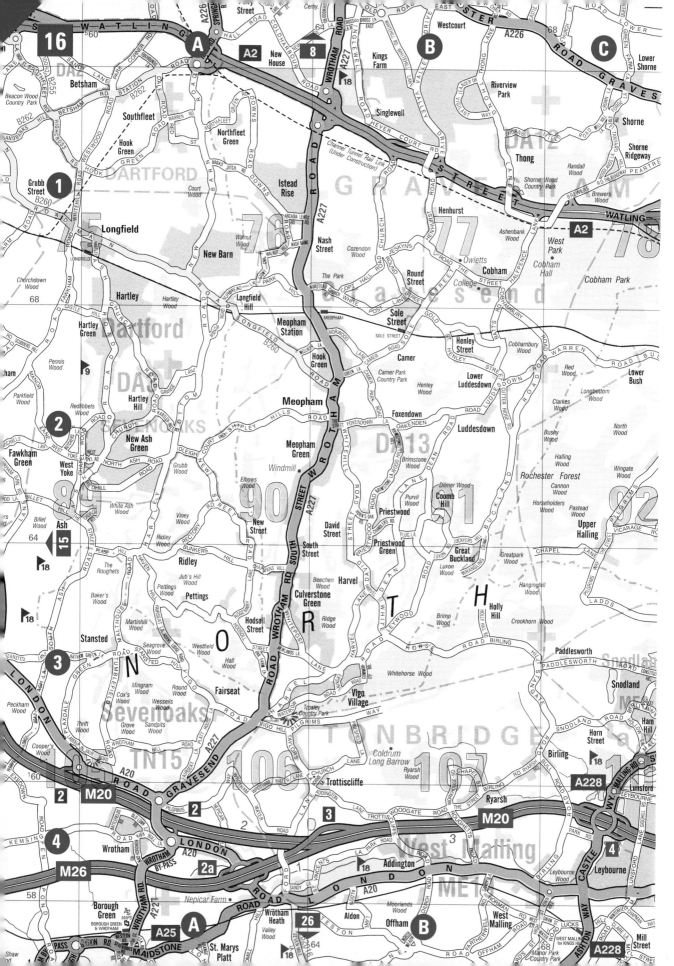

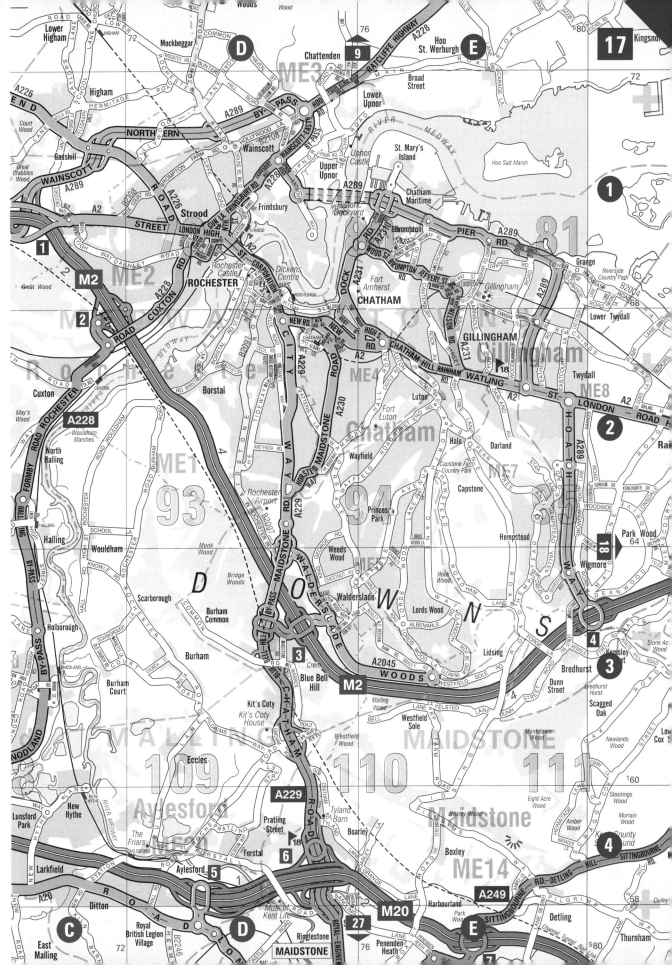

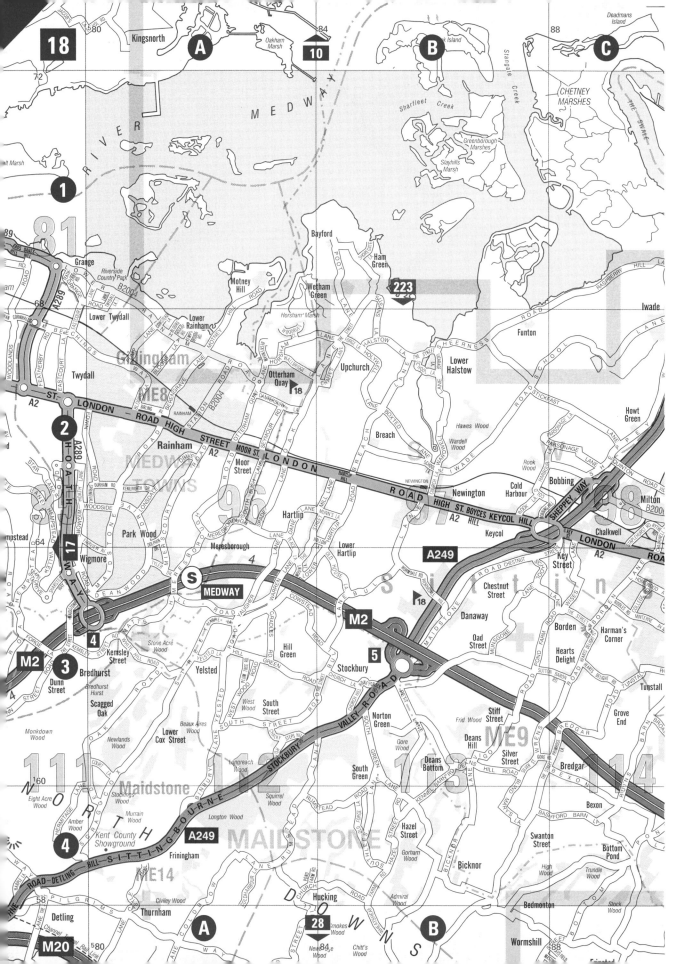

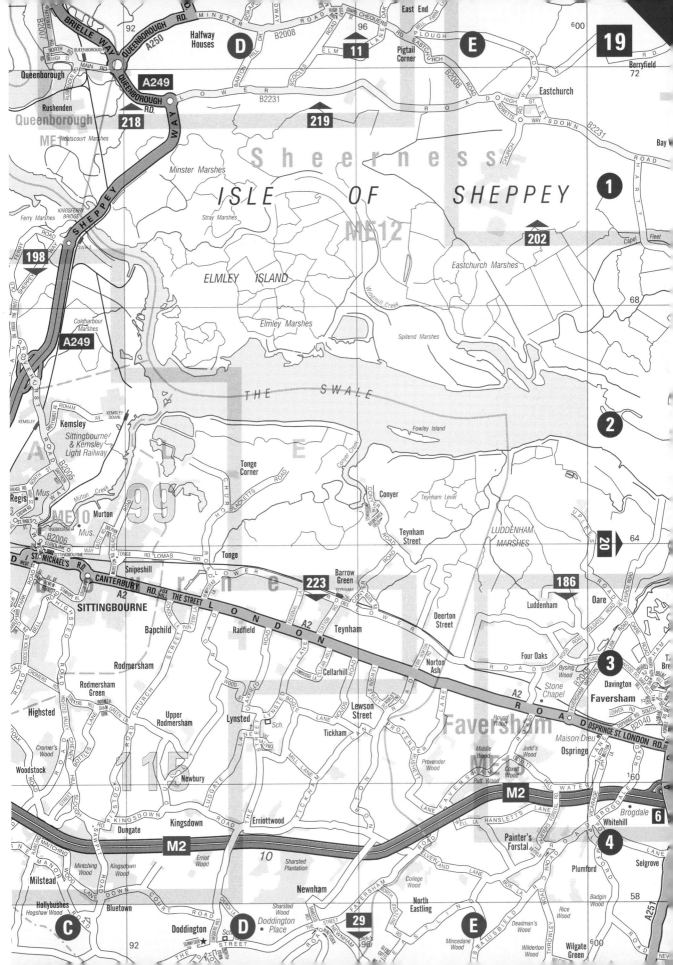

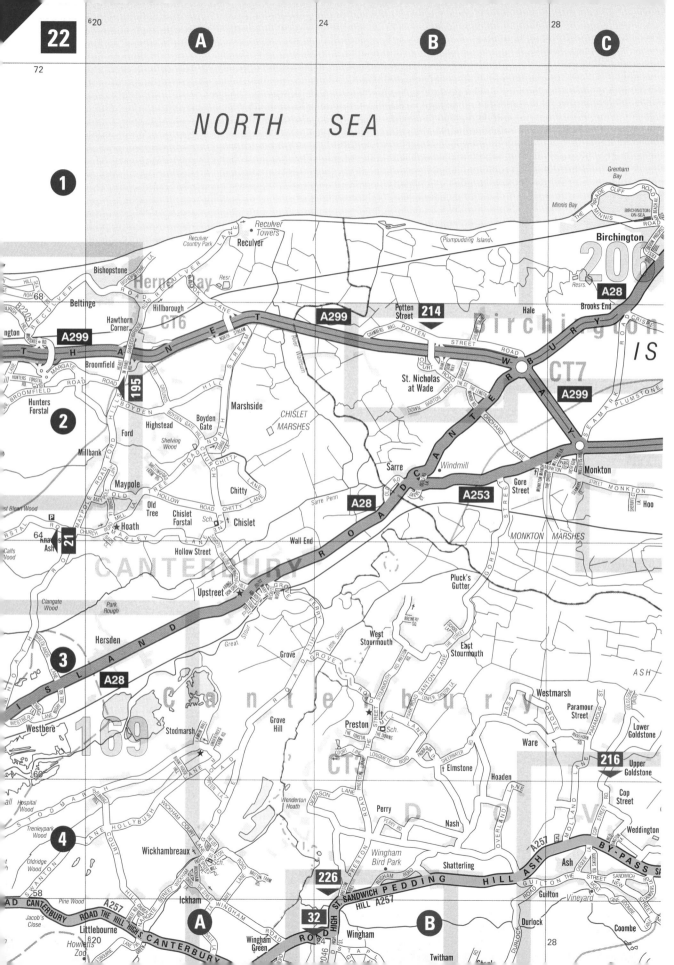

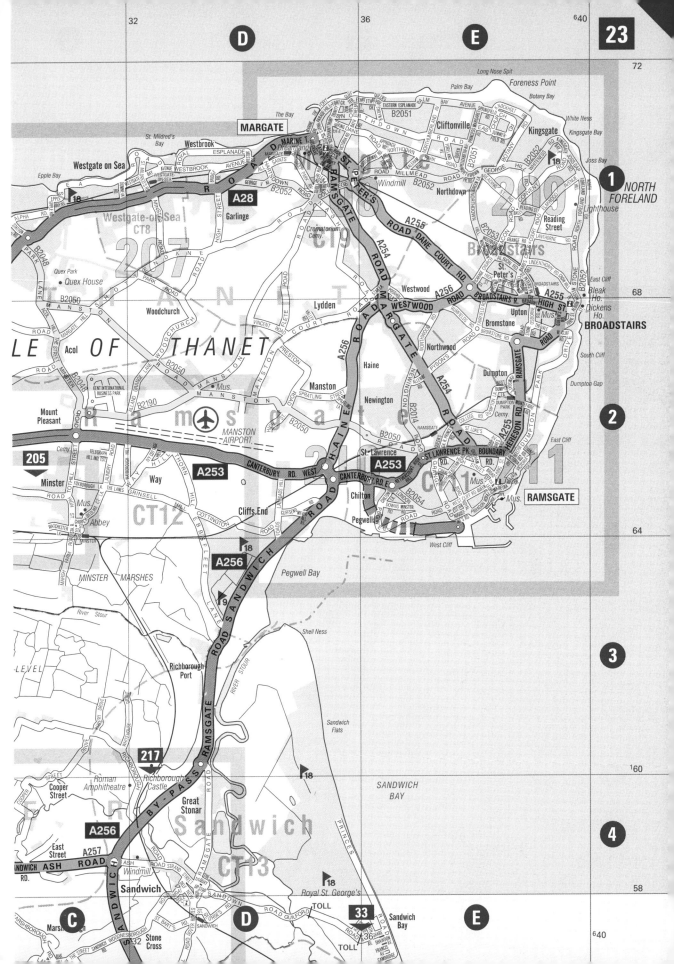

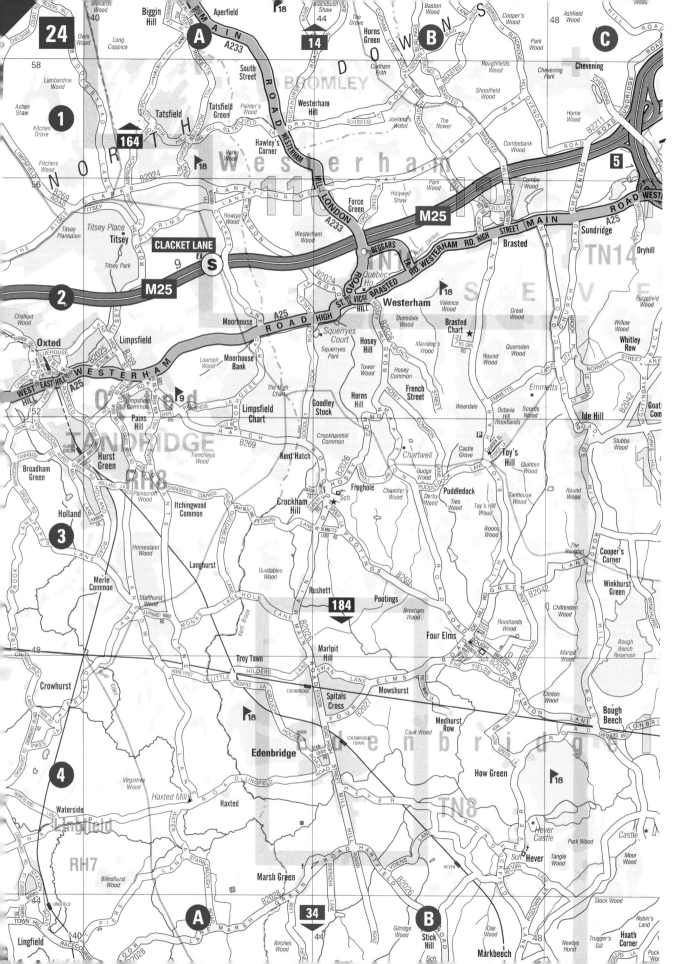

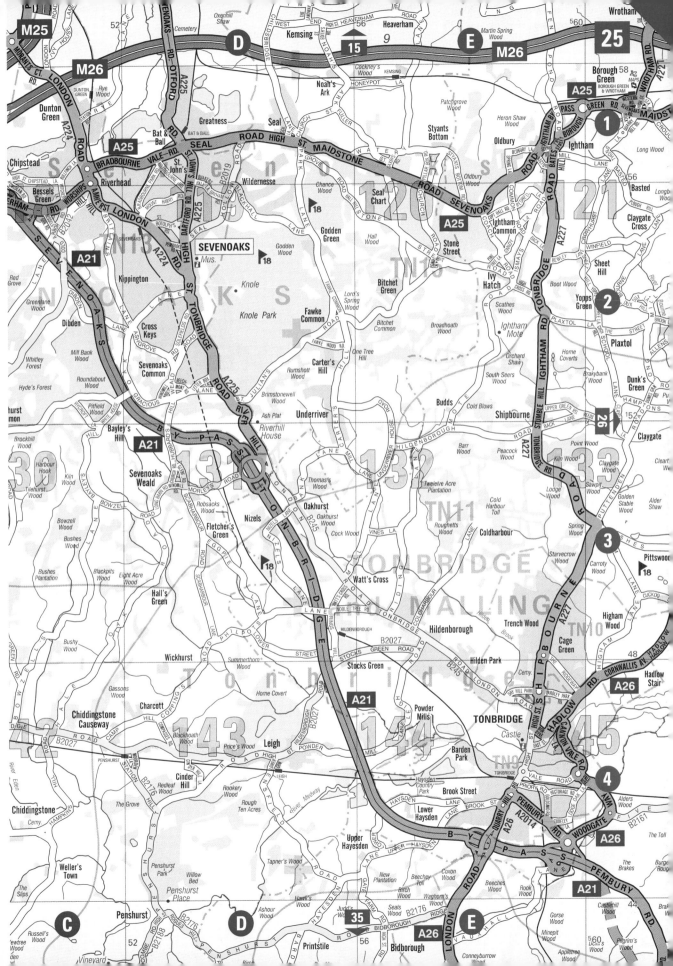

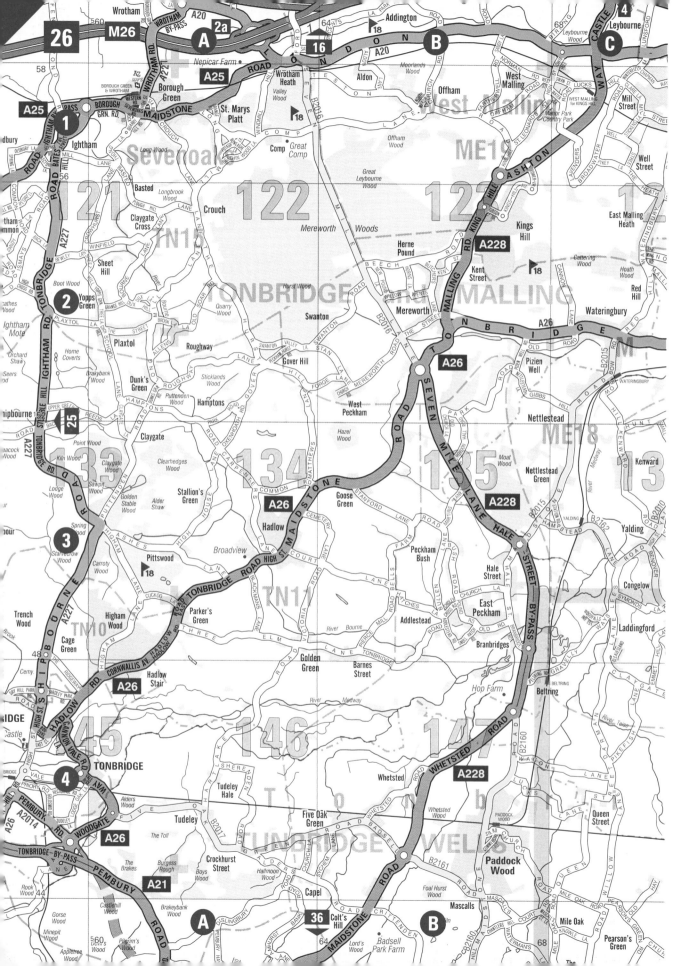

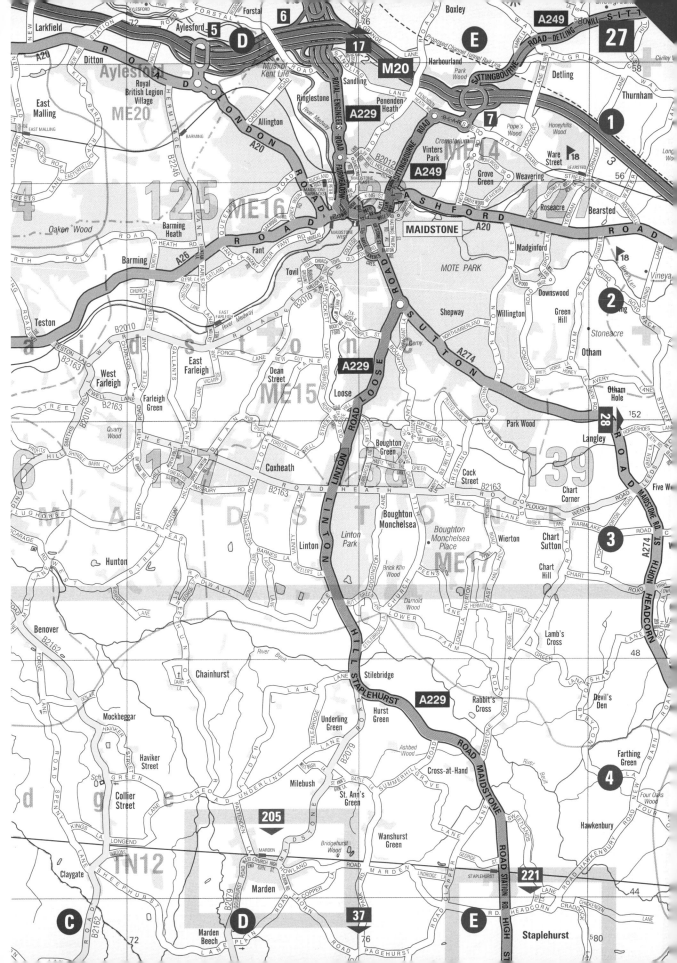

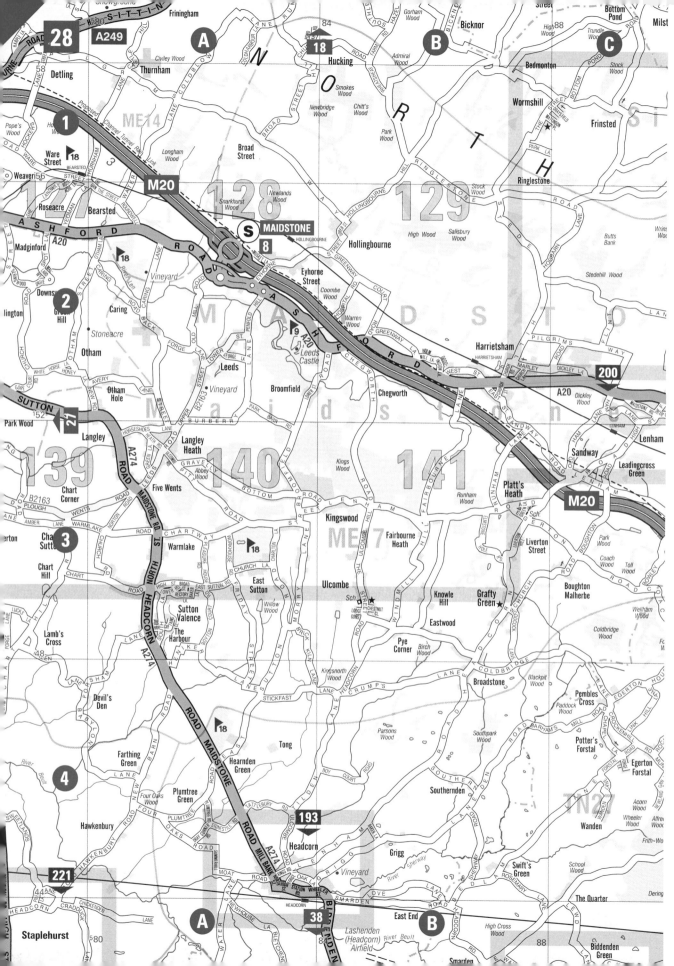

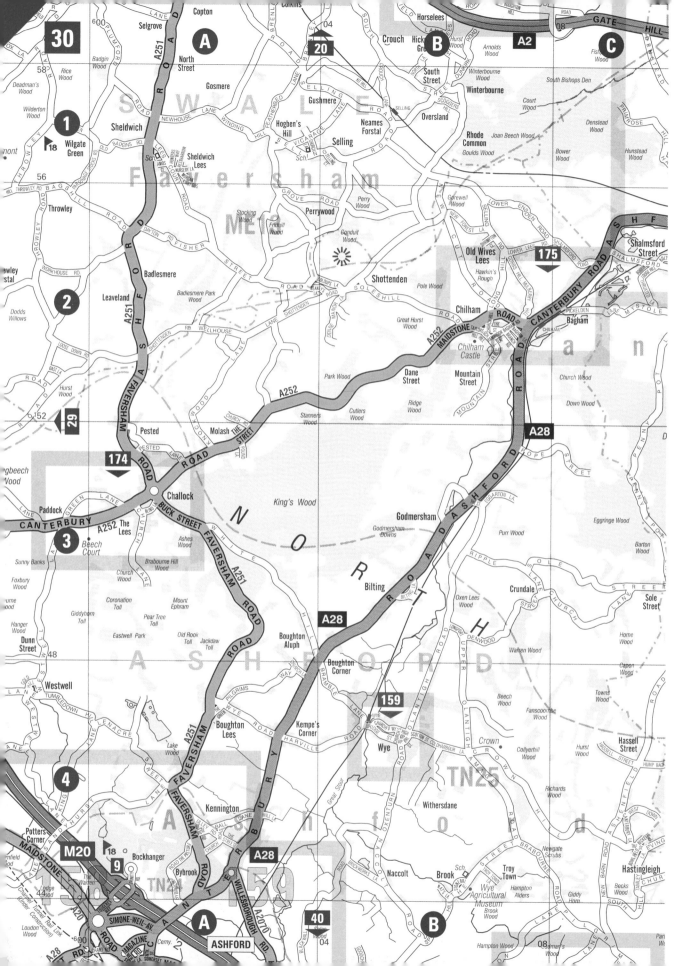

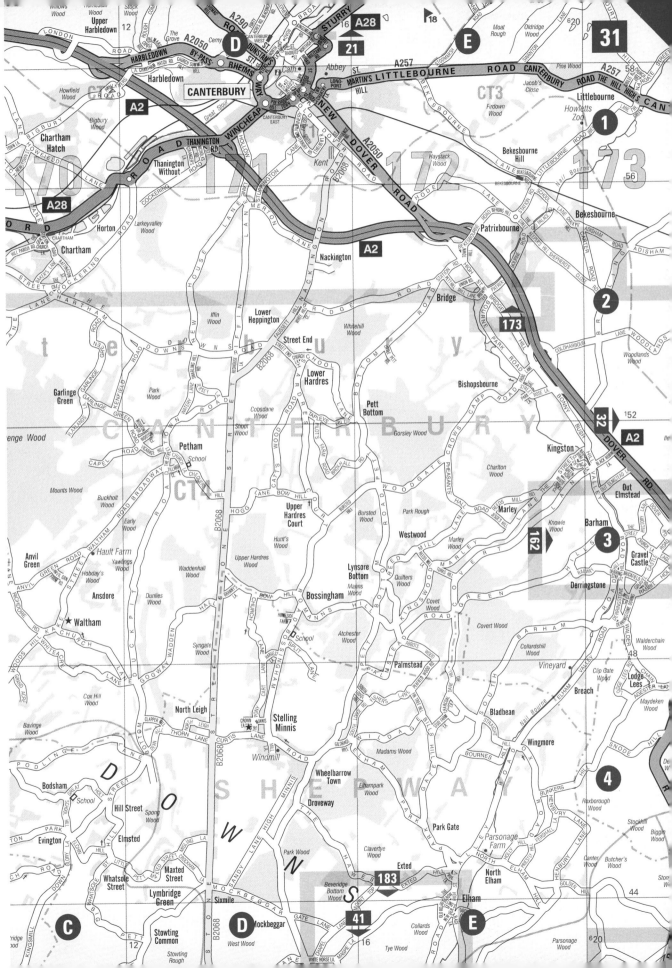

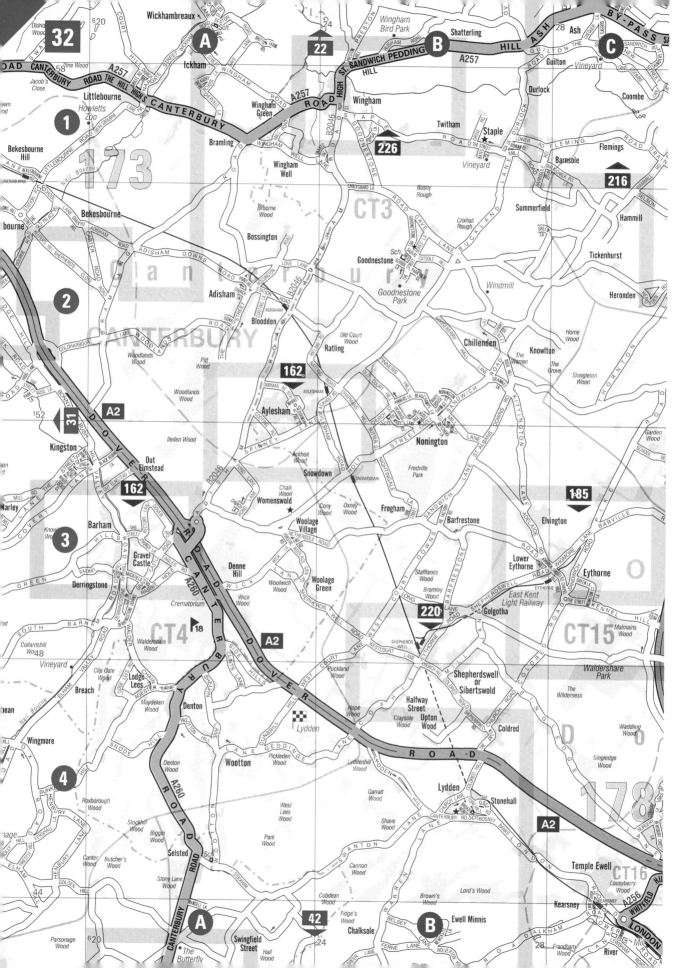

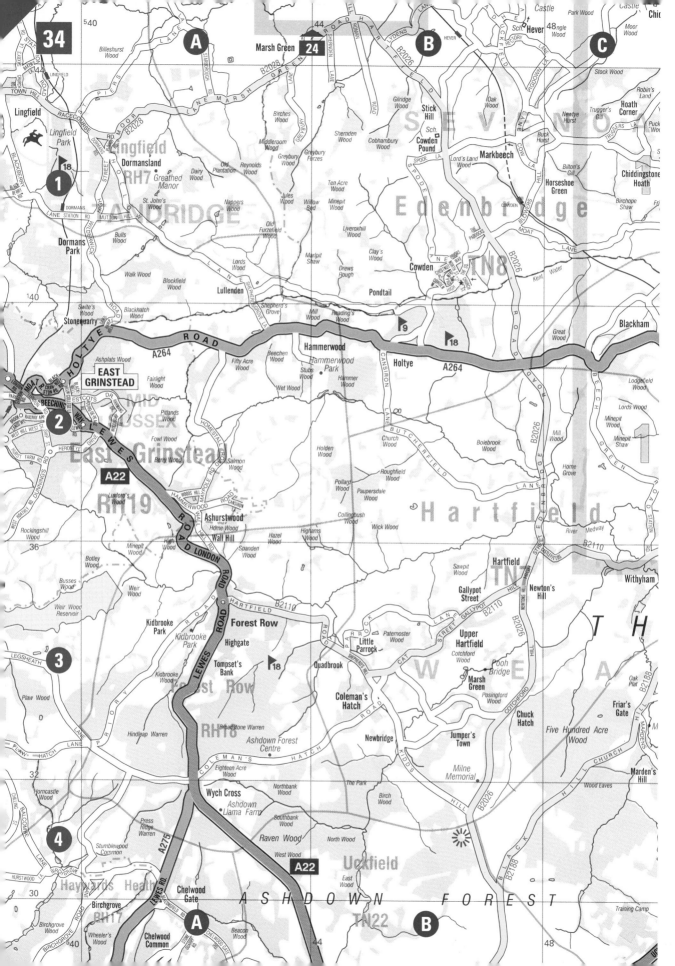

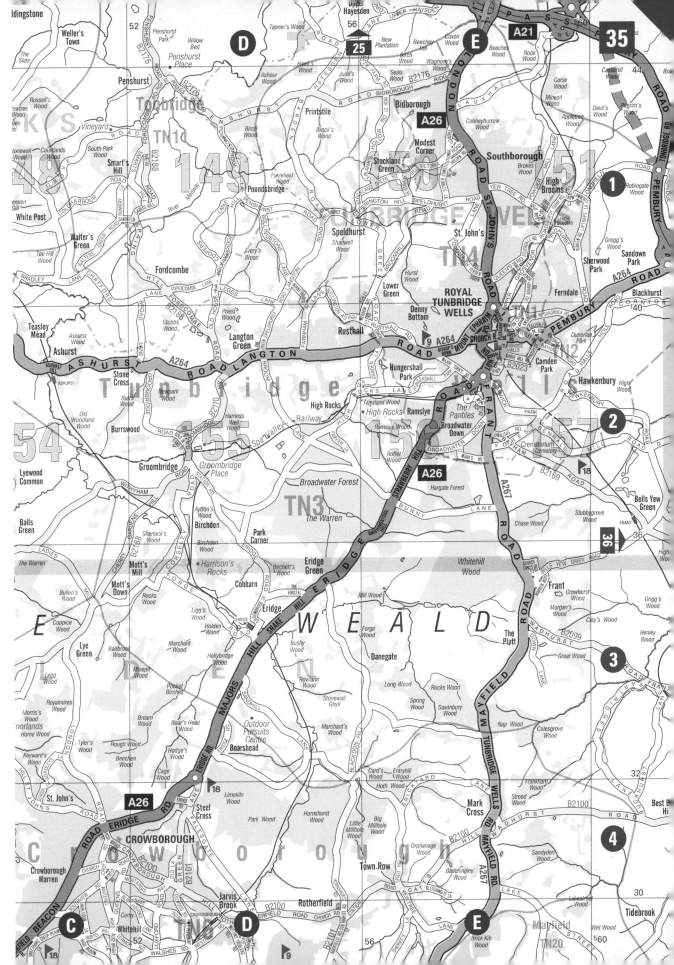

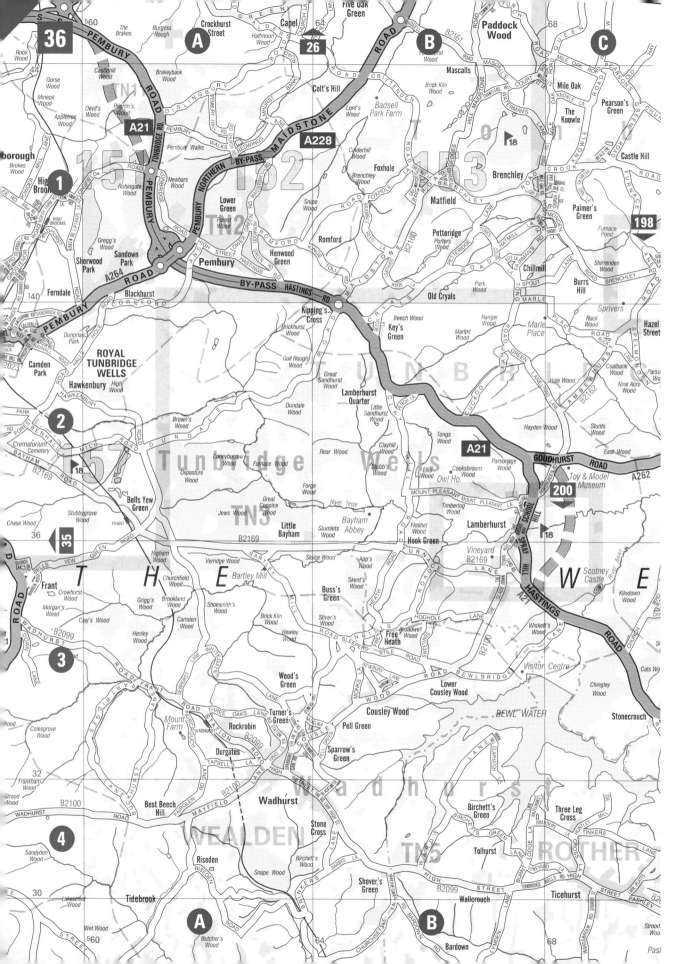

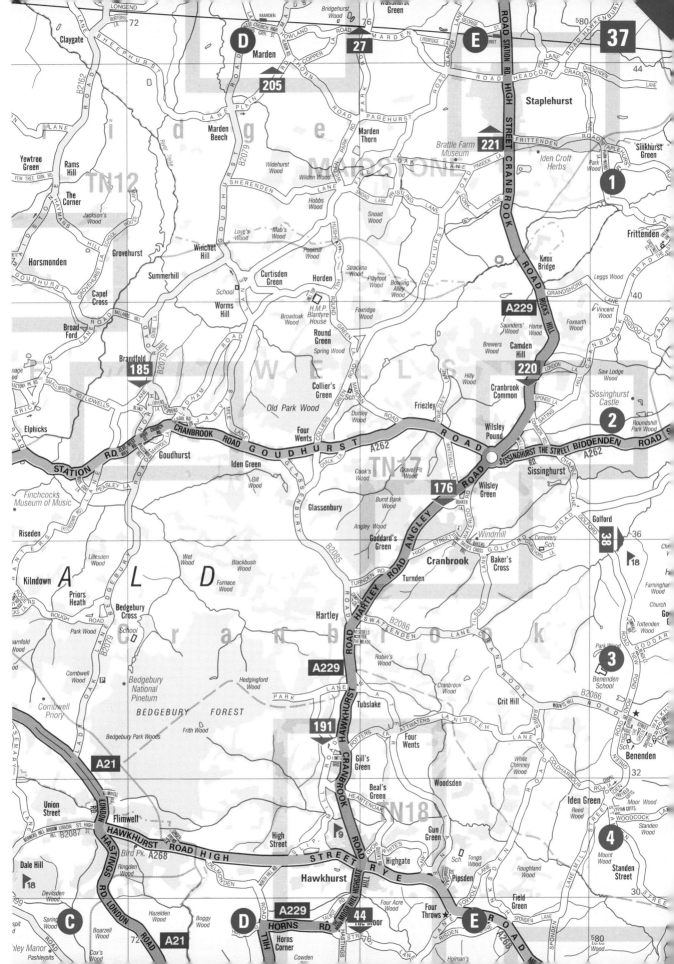

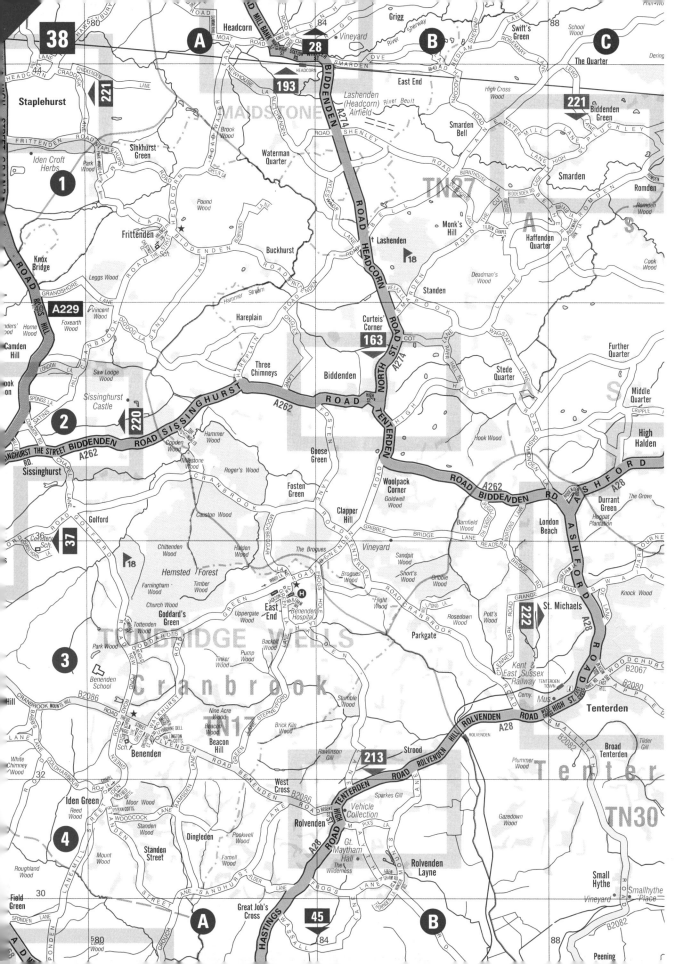

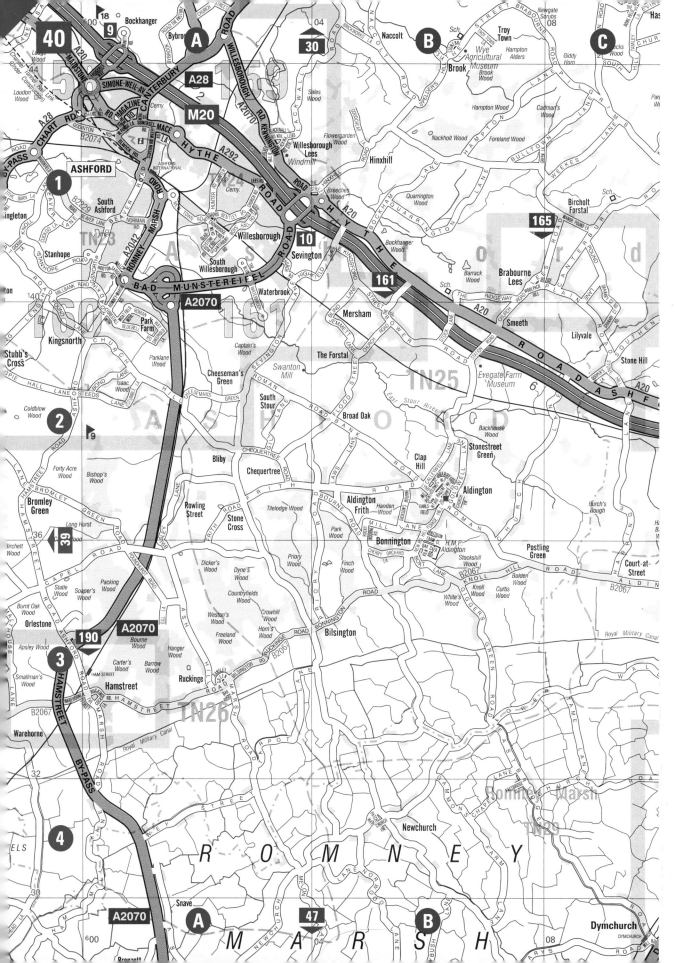

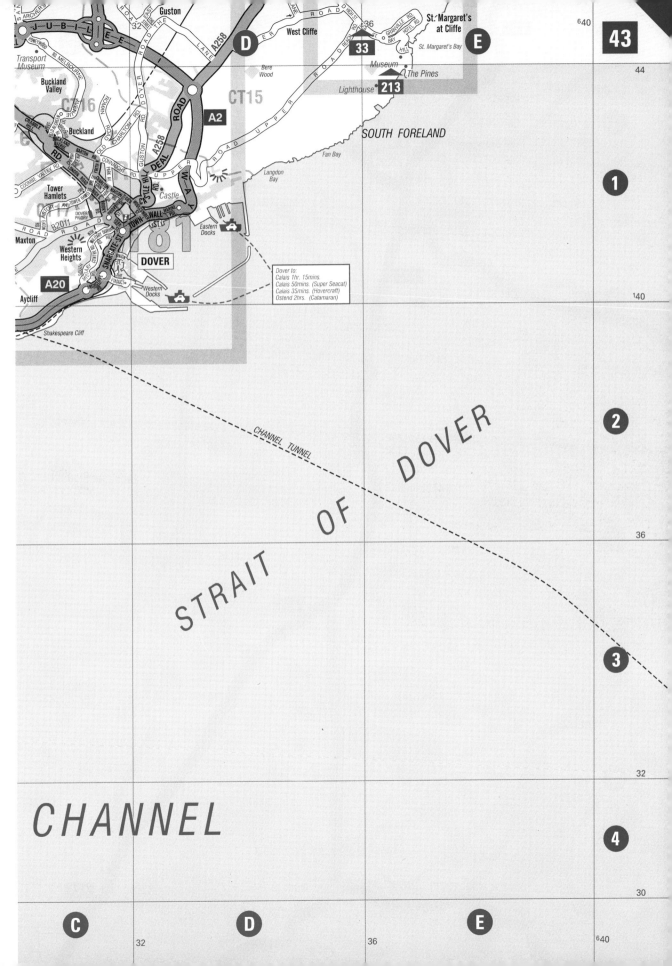

Guston

West Cliffe

St. Margaret's
at Cliffe

33

St. Margaret's Bay

D

E

Museum

The Pines

Lighthouse 213

Transport
Museum

44

Buckland
Valley

CT16

SOUTH FORELAND

Buckland

CT15

A2

A258

Fan Bay

1

Tower
Hamlets

Castle

Langdon
Bay

RD

CASTLE HILL

DOVER PRIORY

Maxton

B2011

Eastern
Docks

Western
Heights

DOVER

140

Ayclliff

A20

Western
Docks

Dover to:
Calais 1hr. 15mins.
Calais 50mins. (Super Seacat)
Calais 35mins. (Hovercraft)
Ostend 2hrs. (Catamaran)

Shakespeare Cliff

CHANNEL TUNNEL

2

OF DOVER

STRAIT

36

3

32

CHANNEL

4

C

D

E

640

32

36

640

30

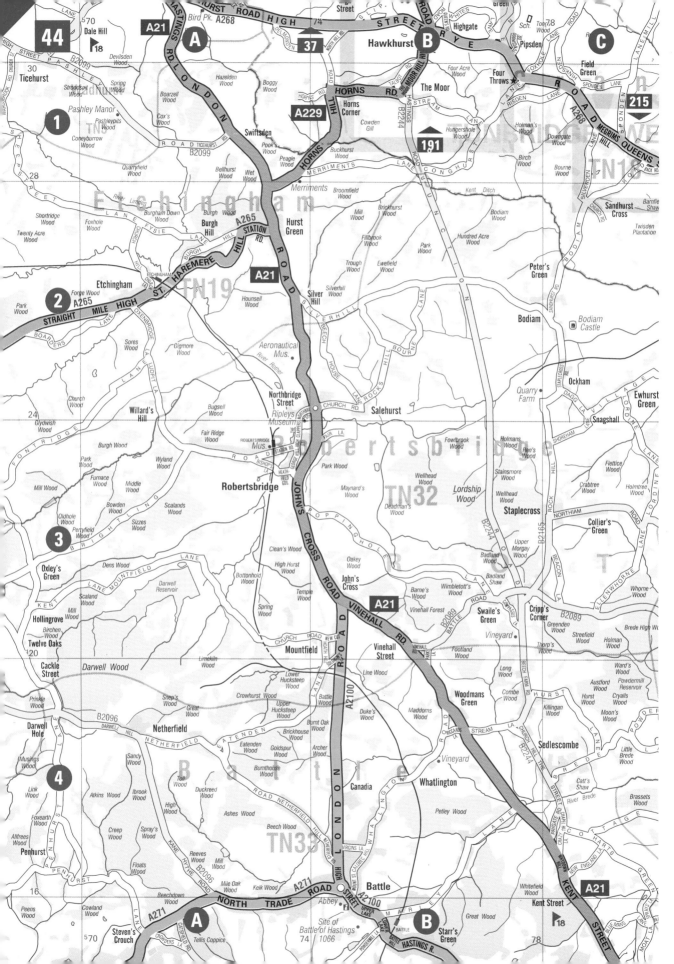

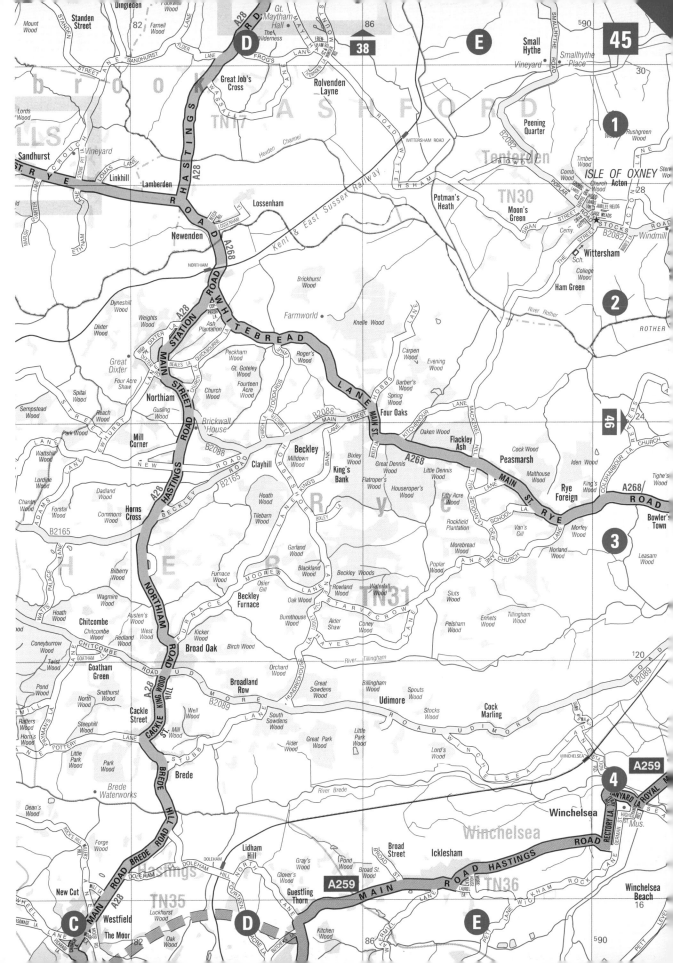

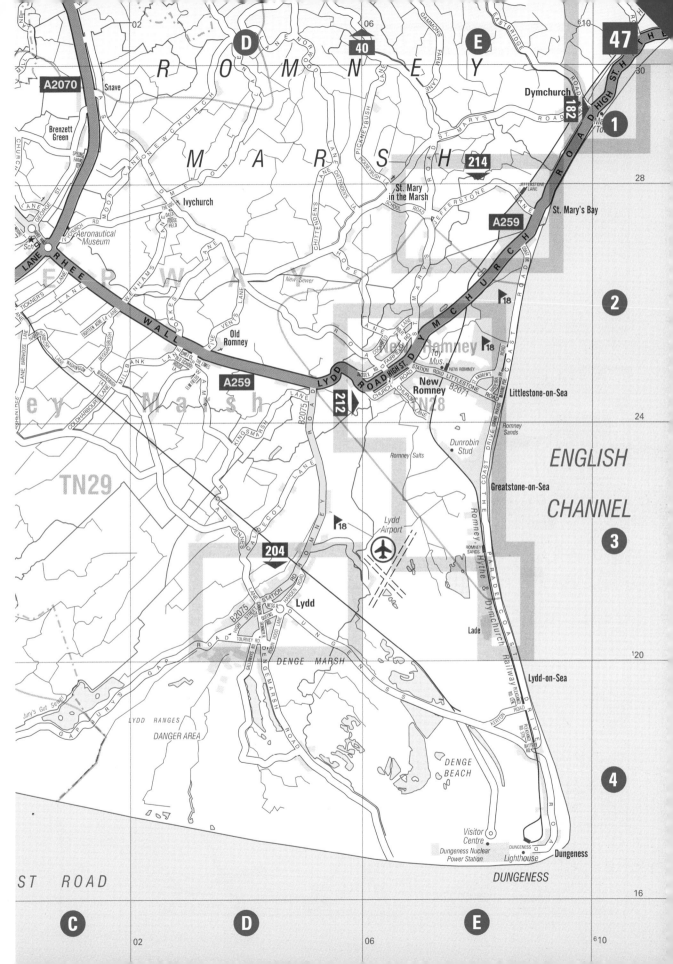

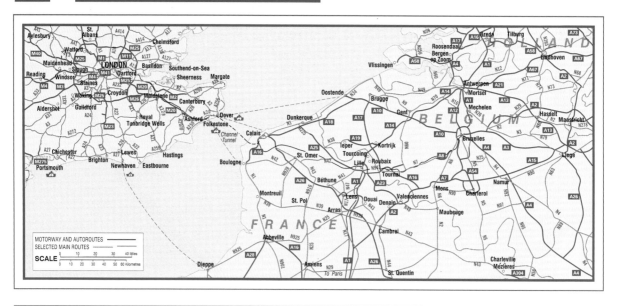

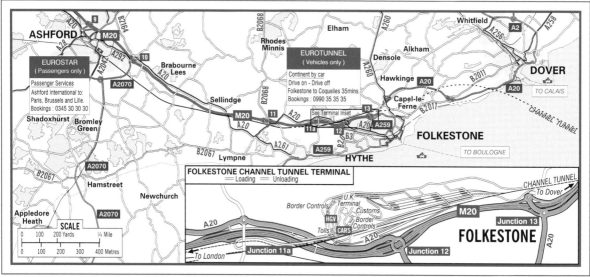

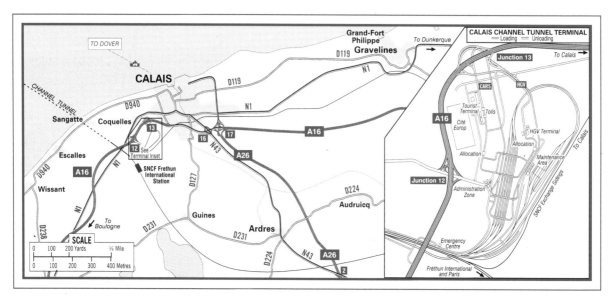

REFERENCE TO 3 INCHES TO 1 MILE STREET MAP SECTION

Motorway	M2
A Road	A2
Under Construction	
Proposed	
B Road	B2068
Dual Carriageway	
Tunnel	A299
One Way Street Traffic flow on A Roads is indicated by a heavy line on the driver's left	→
Junction Names	SWANLEY INTERCHANGE
Pedestrianized Road	
Restricted Access	
Track and Footpath	
Residential Walkway	
Railway	Tunnel Station Level Crossing
Croydon Tramlink The Boarding of Tramlink trains at stations may be limited to a single direction, indicated by an arrow.	Tunnel Stop
Built Up Area	HIGH STREET

Local Authority Boundary	·—·—·—·—
Posttown Boundary	
Postcode Boundary Within Posttown	———
Map Continuation For 3 Inches to 1 Mile Street Mapping (Red Pages)	110
Map Continuation To 1 Inch to 1 Mile Street Mapping (Blue Pages)	20
Car Park Selected	P
Church or Chapel	†
Cycle Route	⊚o
Fire Station	■
Hospital	H
House Numbers A & B Roads only	51 19 22 48
Information Centre	i
National Grid Reference	535
Police Station	▲
Post Office	★
Toilet	▼
with facilities for the Disabled	♿
Viewpoint	180° ⋇
	360° ✳

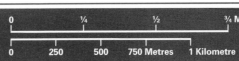

SCALE approx. 3 Inches (7.94 cm) to 1 Mile

0 ¼ ½ ¾ Mile
0 250 500 750 Metres 1 Kilometre

1:20,267 or 4.93 cm to 1km

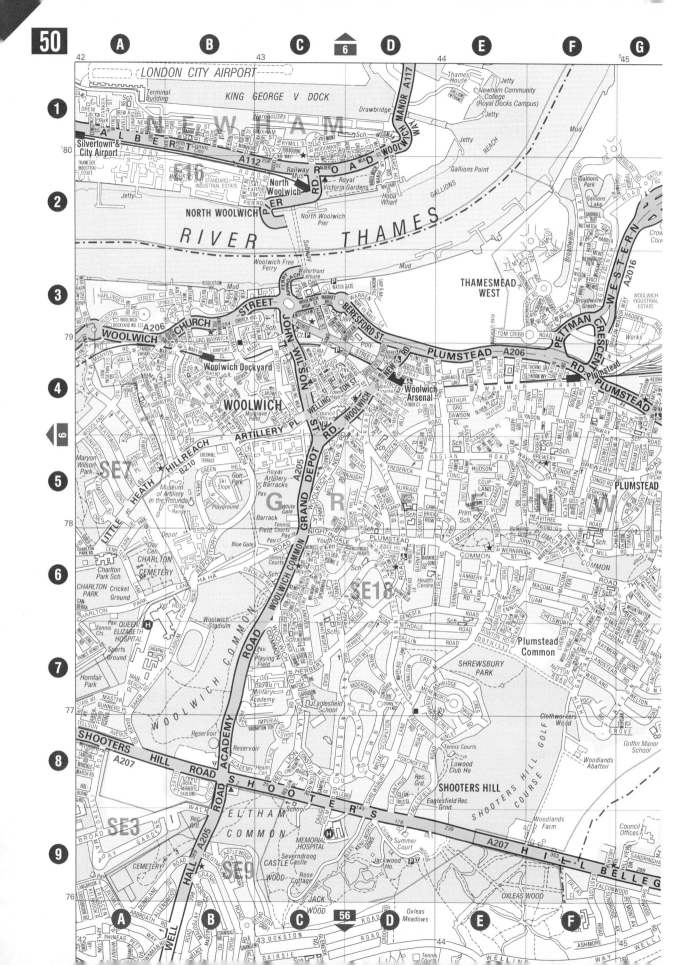

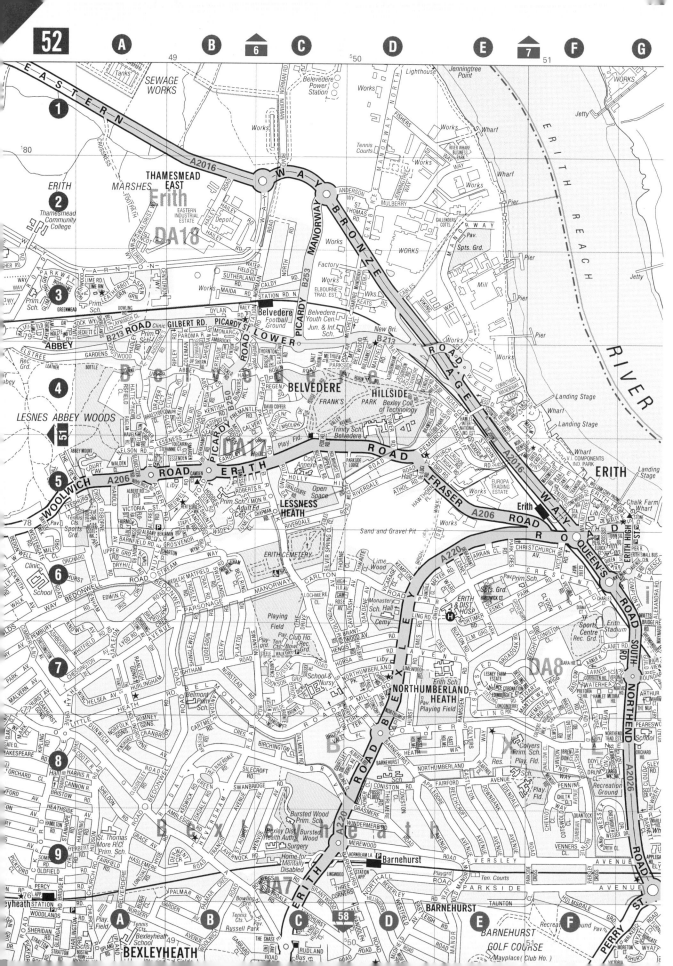

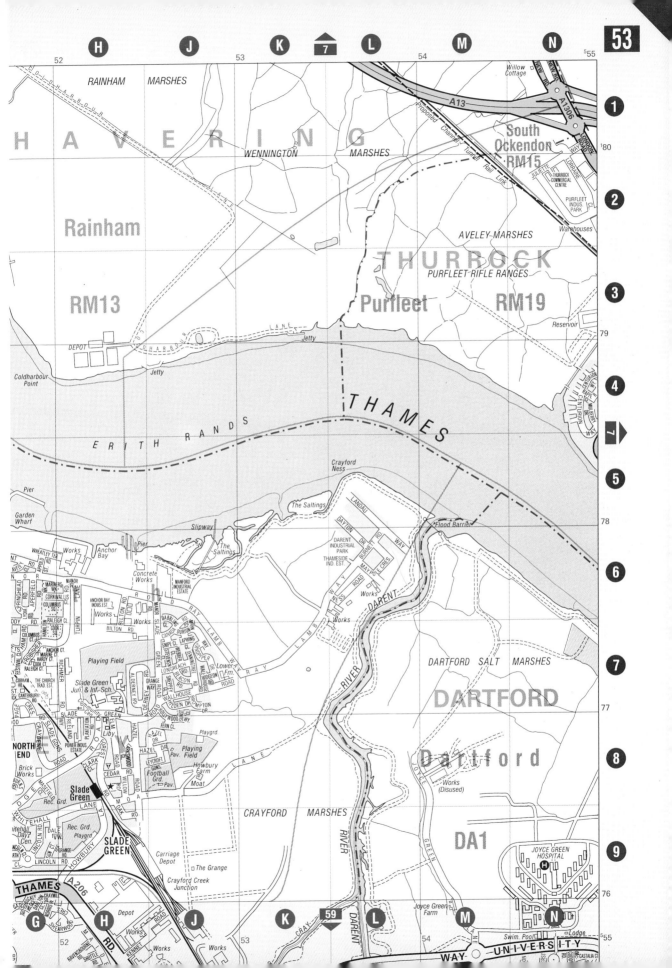

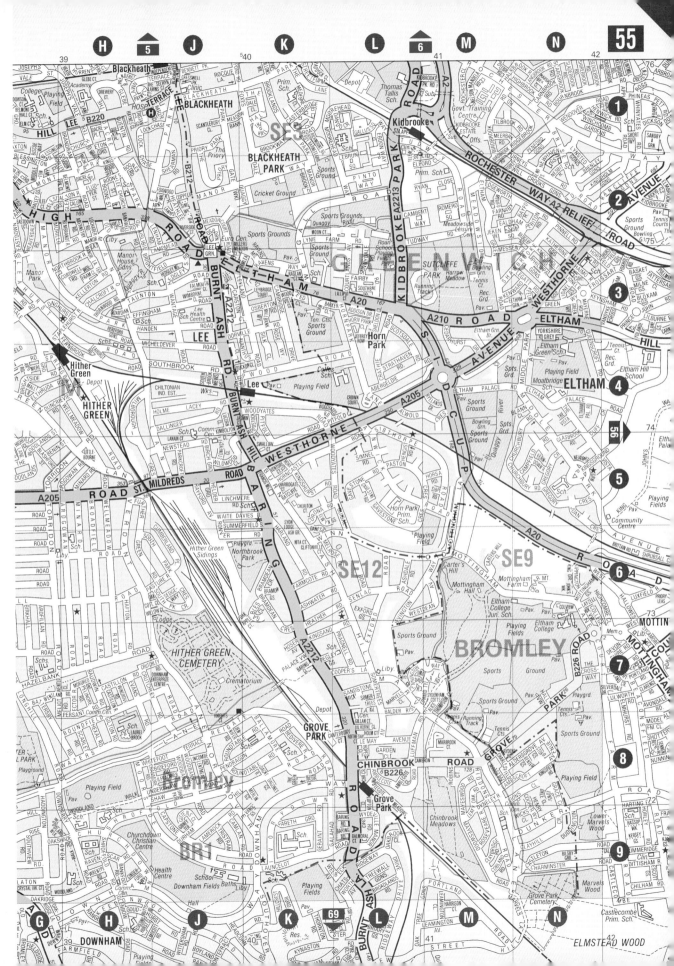

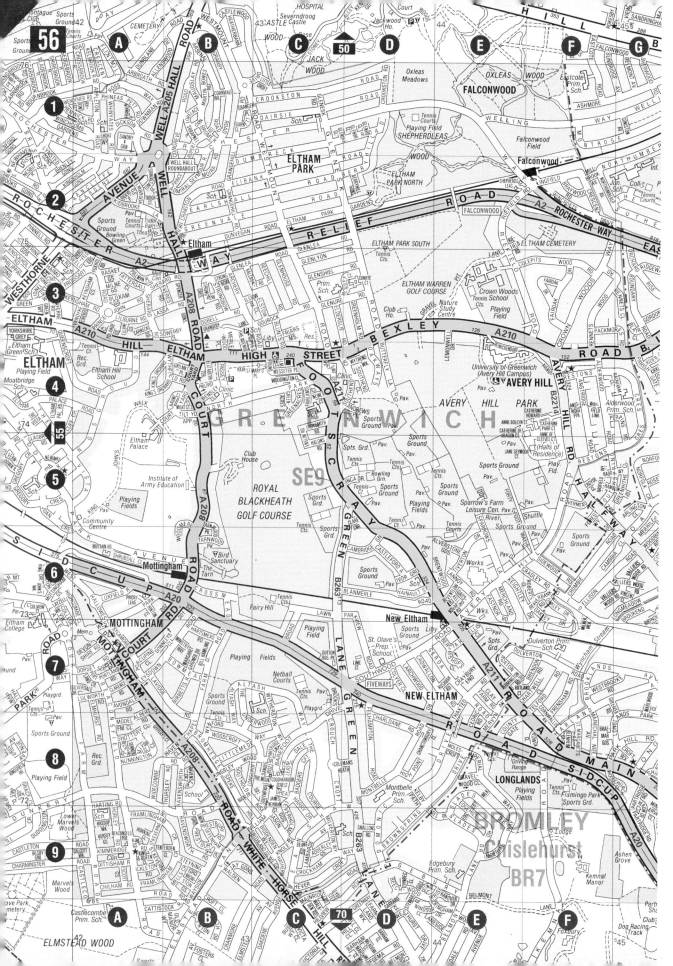

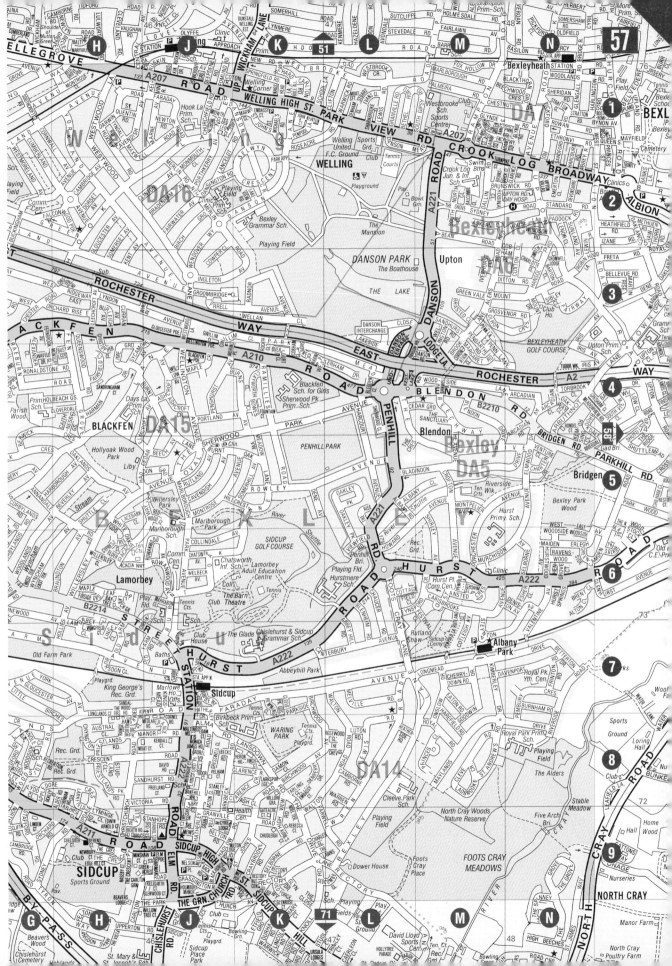

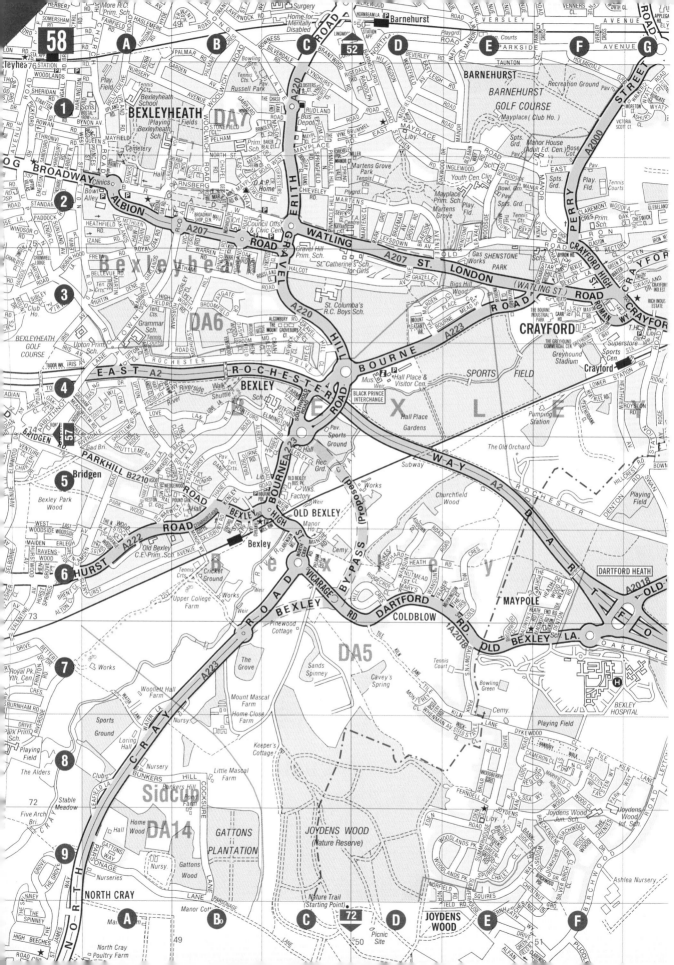

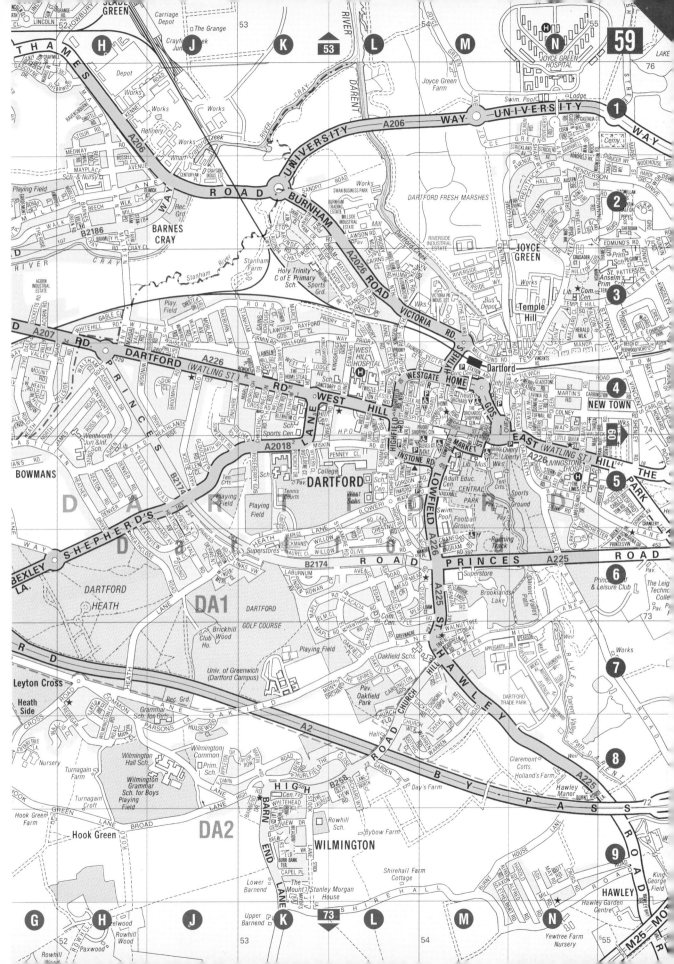

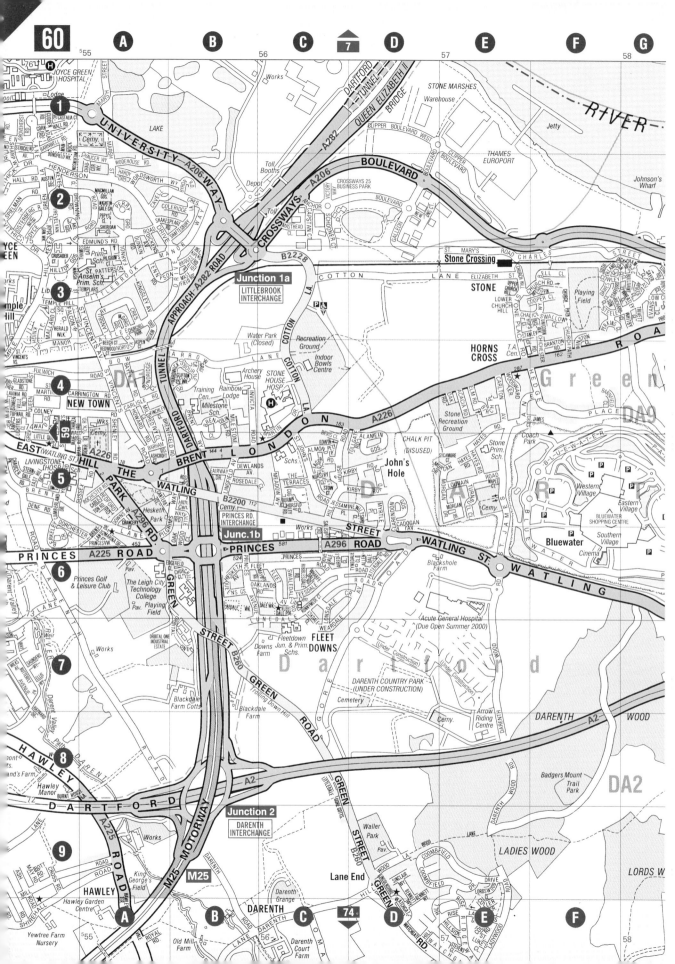

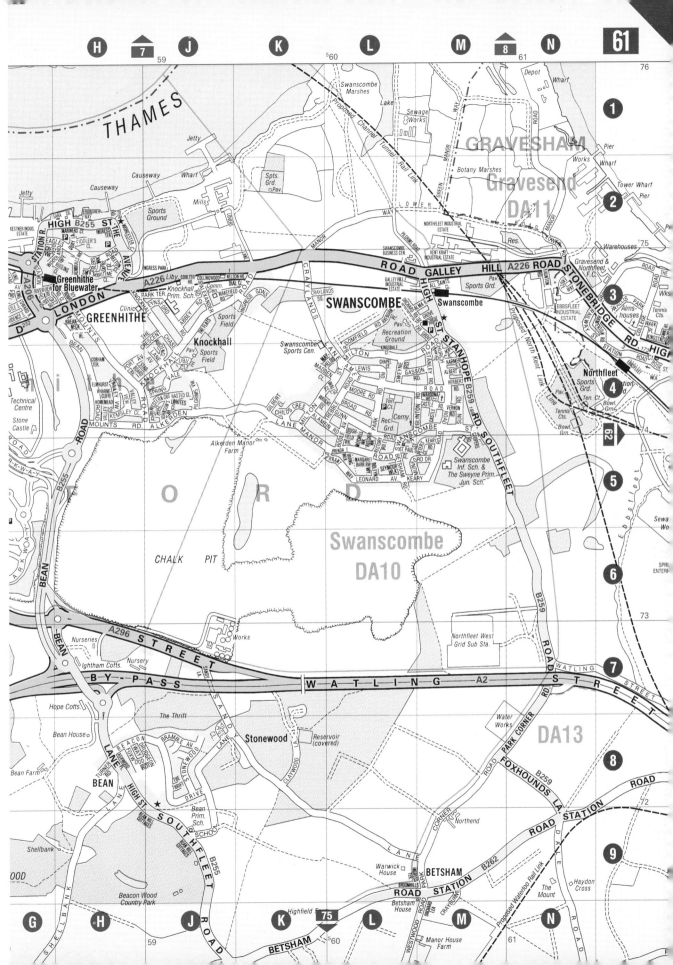

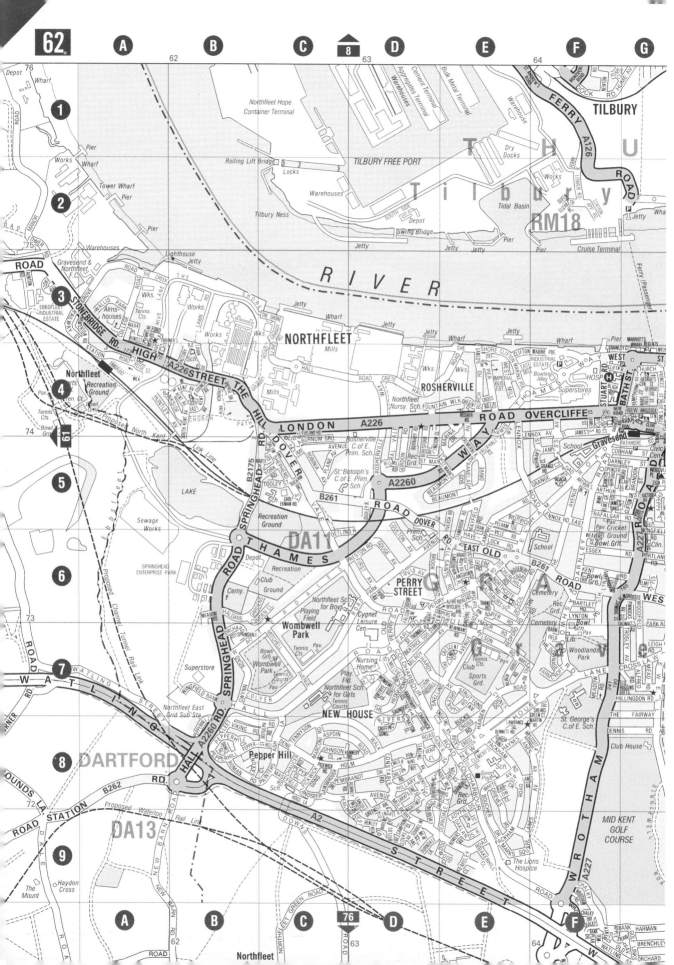

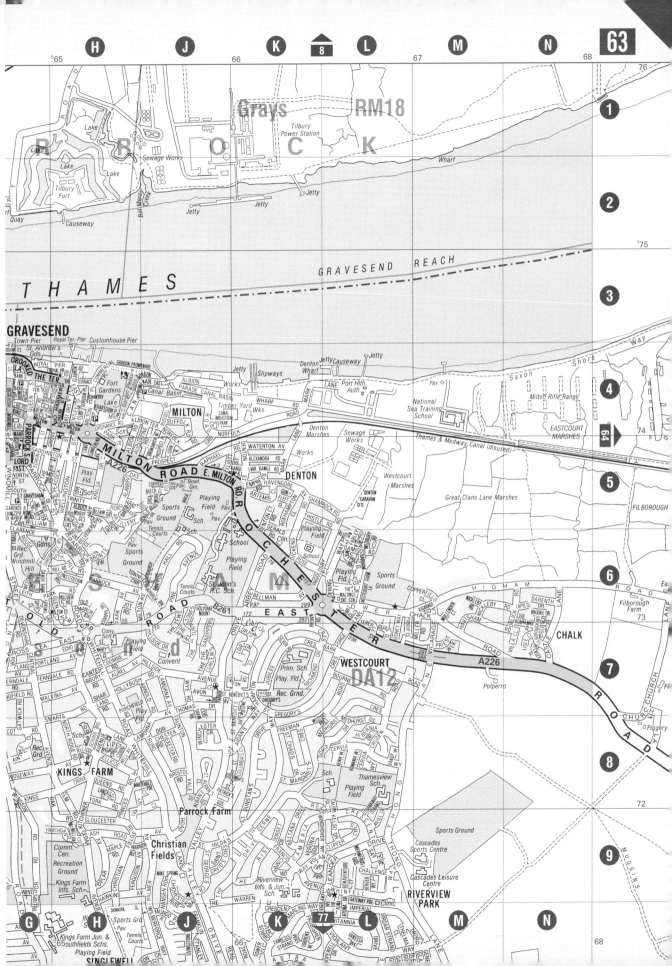

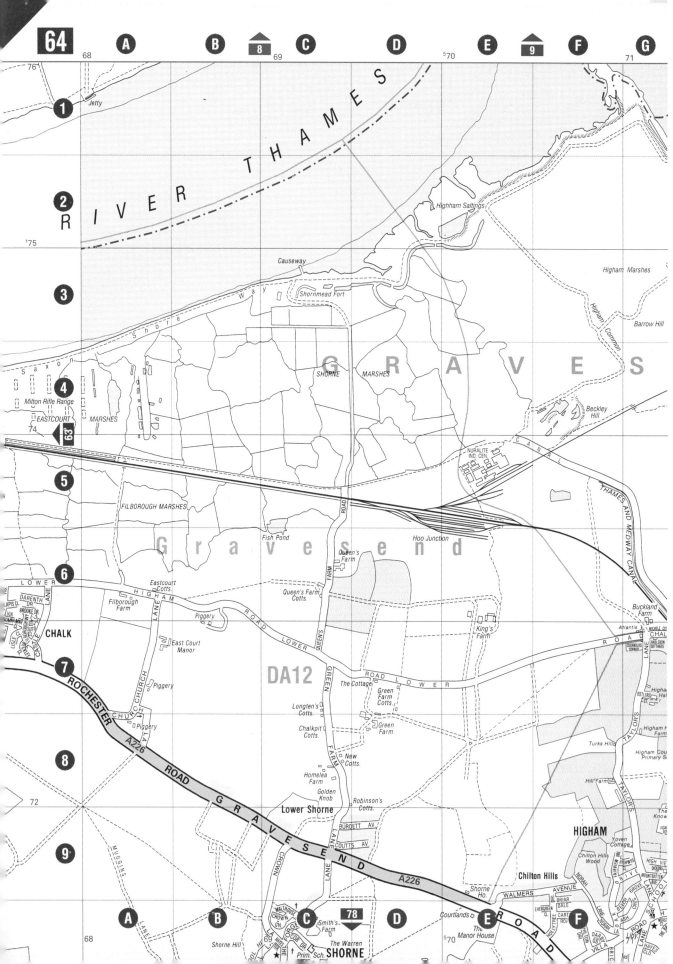

¹76

1   Jetty

R I V E R   T H A M E S

2   R

Higham Saltings

¹75

Causeway

Higham Marshes

3

Shornmead Fort

Higham Common   Barrow Hill

Shore   Way

G R A V E S

SHORNE   MARSHES

Saxon

Beckley Hill

CANAL

4   Milton Rifle Range

EASTCOURT   MARSHES

74

63

NURALITE IND. CEN.

THAMES AND MEDWAY CANAL

5   FILBOROUGH MARSHES

Fish Pond

Hoo Junction

G r a v e s e n d

Queen's Farm

6   LOWER   Eastcourt Cotts.

DARENTH DR.   Filborough Farm

LAPIS CL.   BROOKS DR.   VIA ROMANA

HIGHAM

Piggery

Queen's Farm Cotts.

King's Farm

Buckland Farm

Atlantis X

CUCKNOLDS CORNER   CHAL

MICHELE COTT   HASLEDON COTTAGES

CHALK

East Court Manor

LOWER   ROAD

GREEN   FARM   LANE

QUEEN'S   LANE

ROAD   LOWER

The Cottage

Green Farm Cotts.

Higha   Hal

OSTLERS L

7   ROCHESTER

CHURCH LA.

Piggery

DA12

Longten's Cotts.

Chalkpit Cotts.

Green Farm

Higham H Farm

A226

Piggery

New Cotts.

Turks Hill

Higham Cou Primary S

TAYLORS

8

72

Homelea Farm

Golden Knob

Robinson's Cotts.

Hill Farm

The Know

HIGHAM

ROAD   GRAVESEND

Lower Shorne

BURDETT AV.

COUTTS AV.

A226

Yoven Cottage

VICAR RO

MUGGINS LANE

CROWN LANE

CROWN   FARM   LANE

Chilton Hills Wood

Chilton Hills

HIGH VIE

9

MALTHOUSE   CROWN GN.

JACOB DR.

Smith's Farm

78

Courtlands

Shorne Ho.

The Manor House

WALMERS   AVENUE

EVERGREEN   BRIAR   DALE

HOLLY TREE

CART RO

DARBY   HAYES   VILLA

Shorne Hill

The Warren   Prim. Sch.

SHORNE

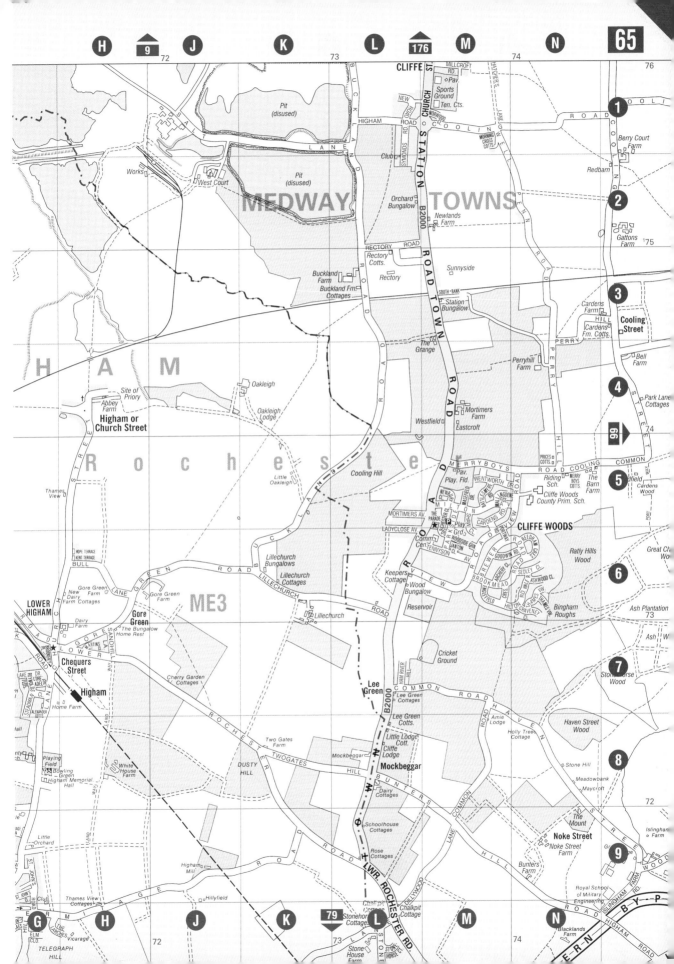

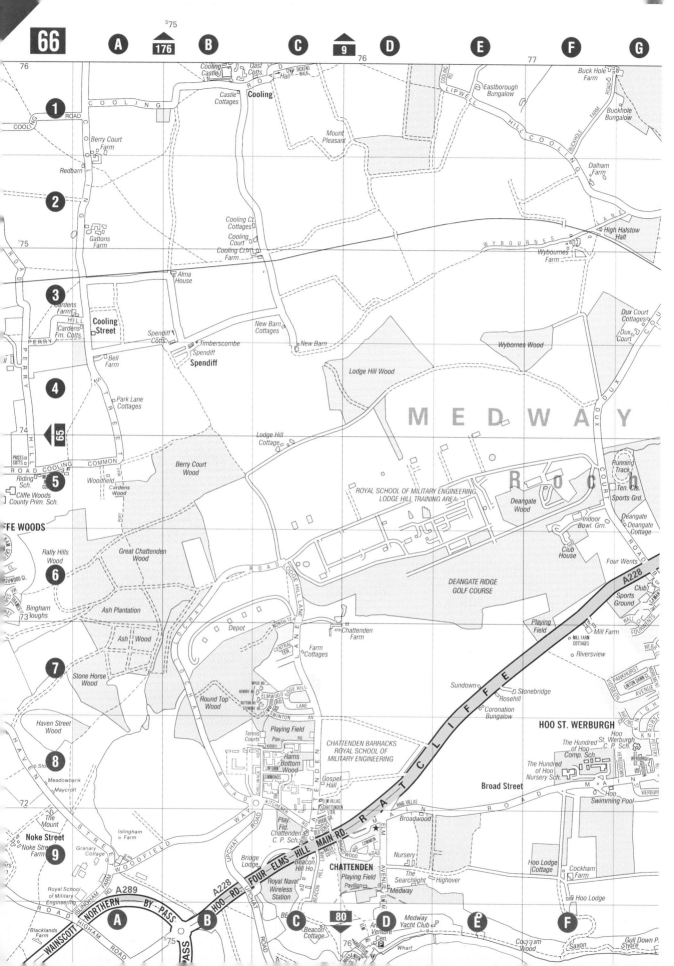

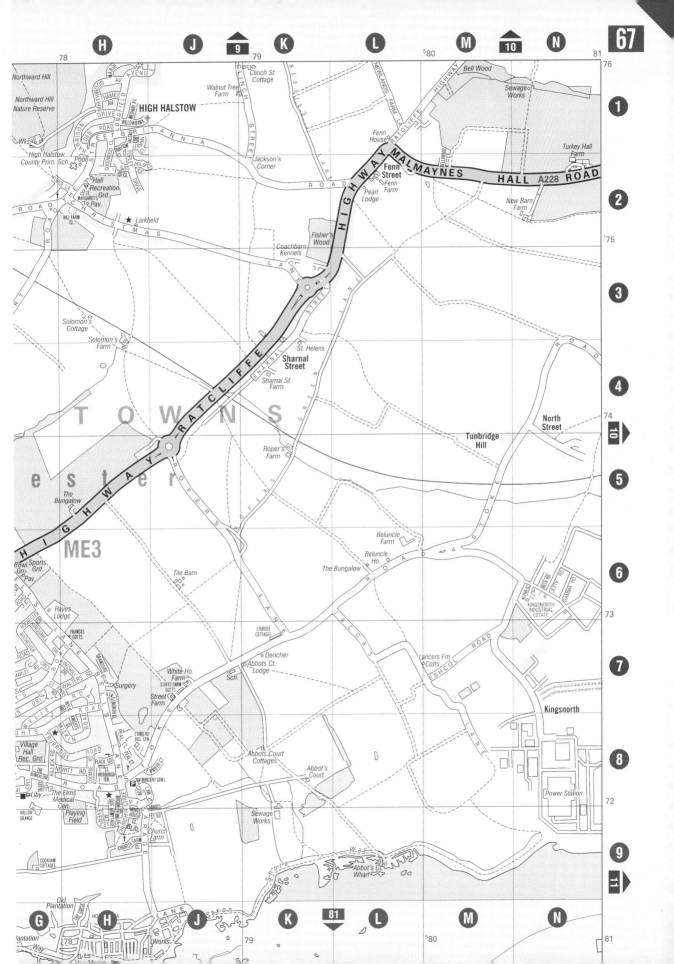

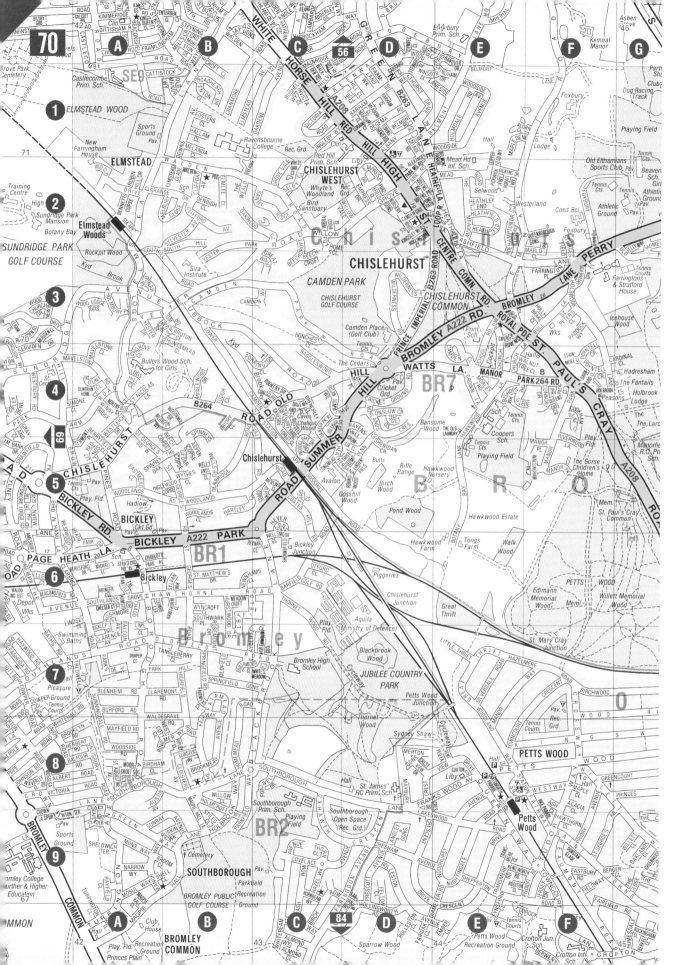

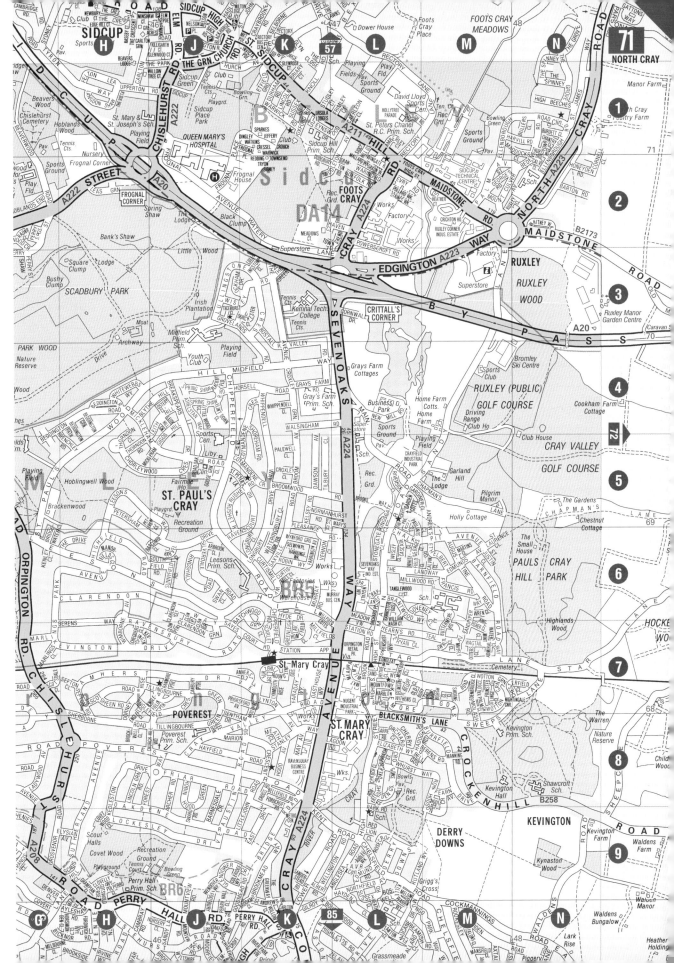

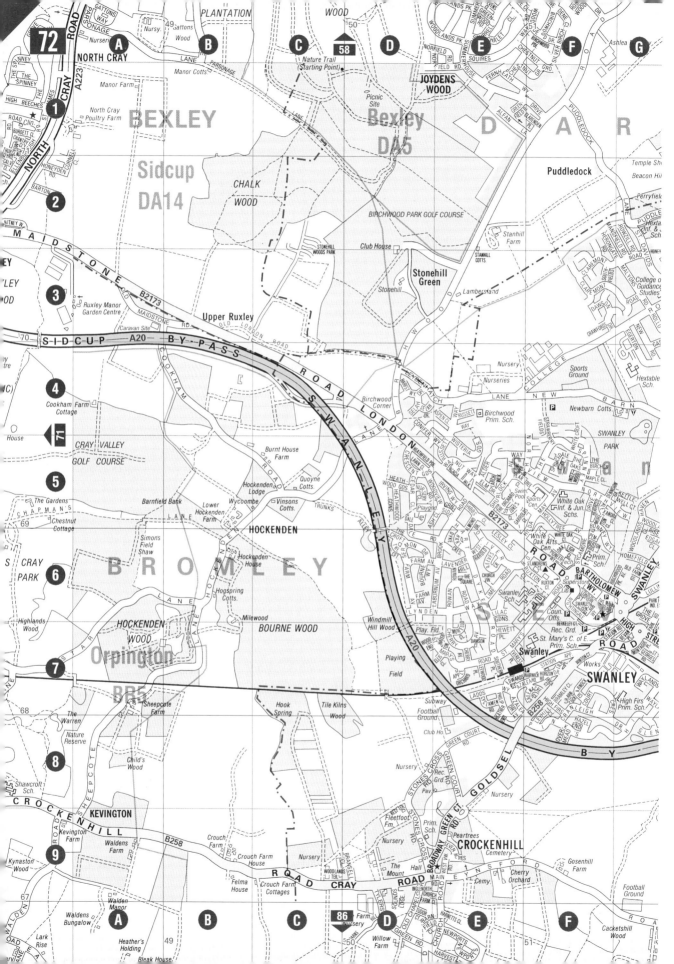

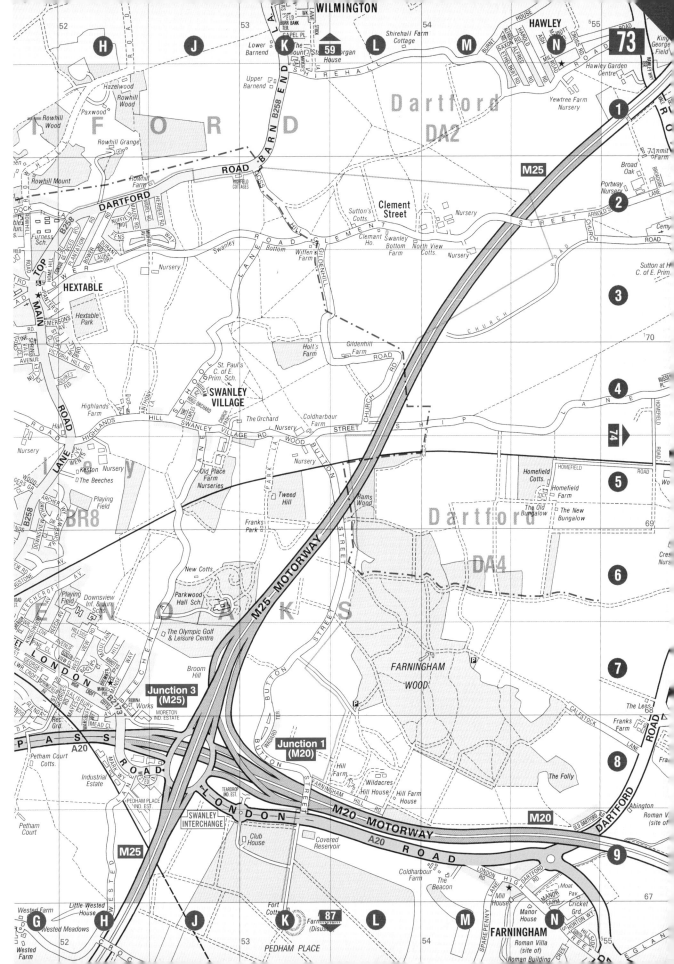

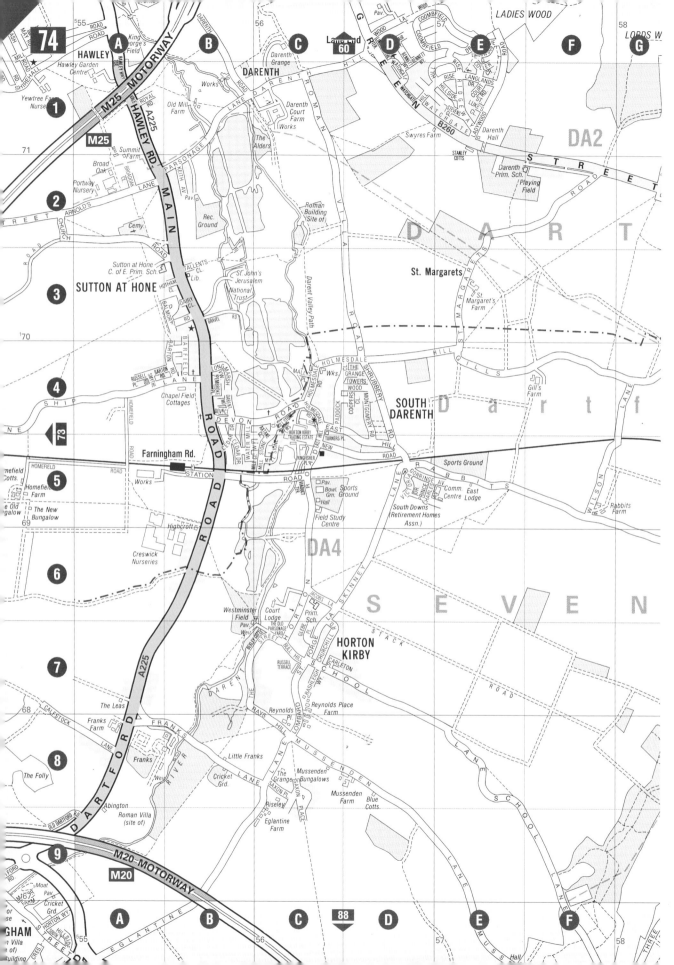

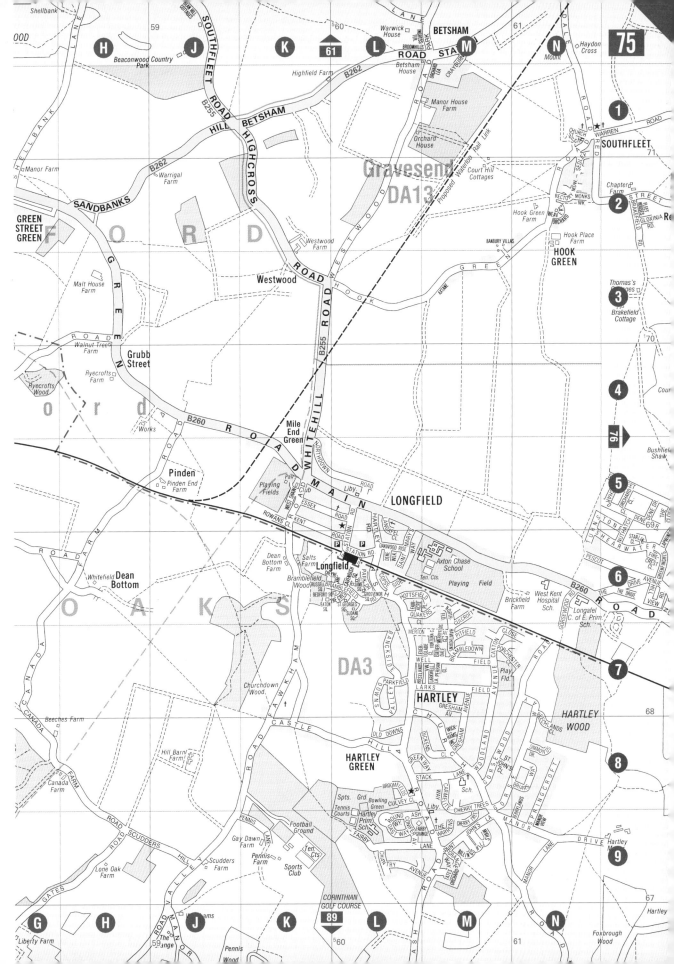

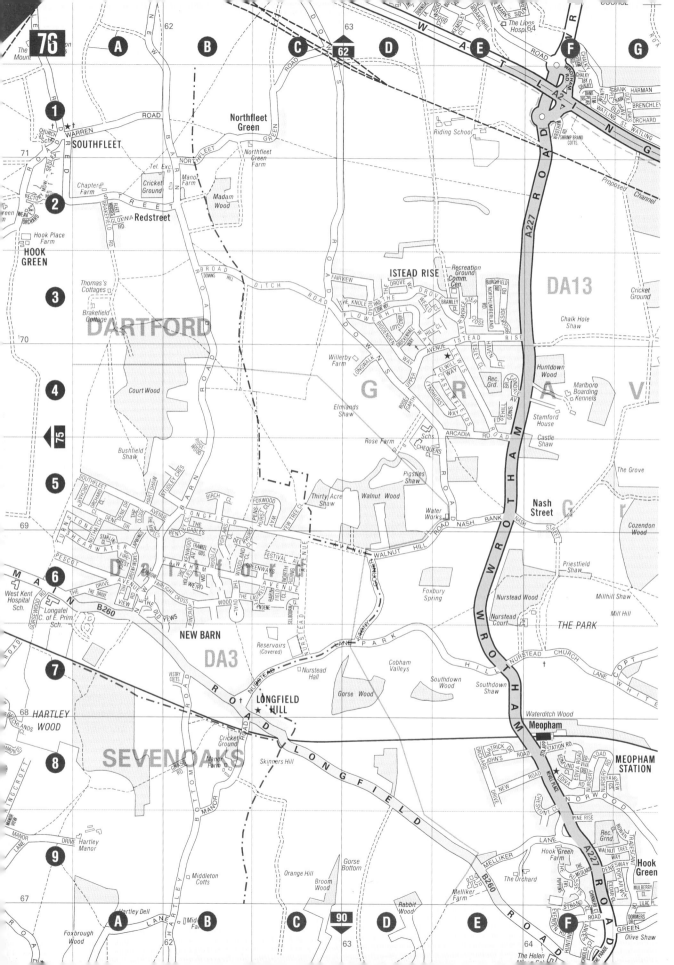

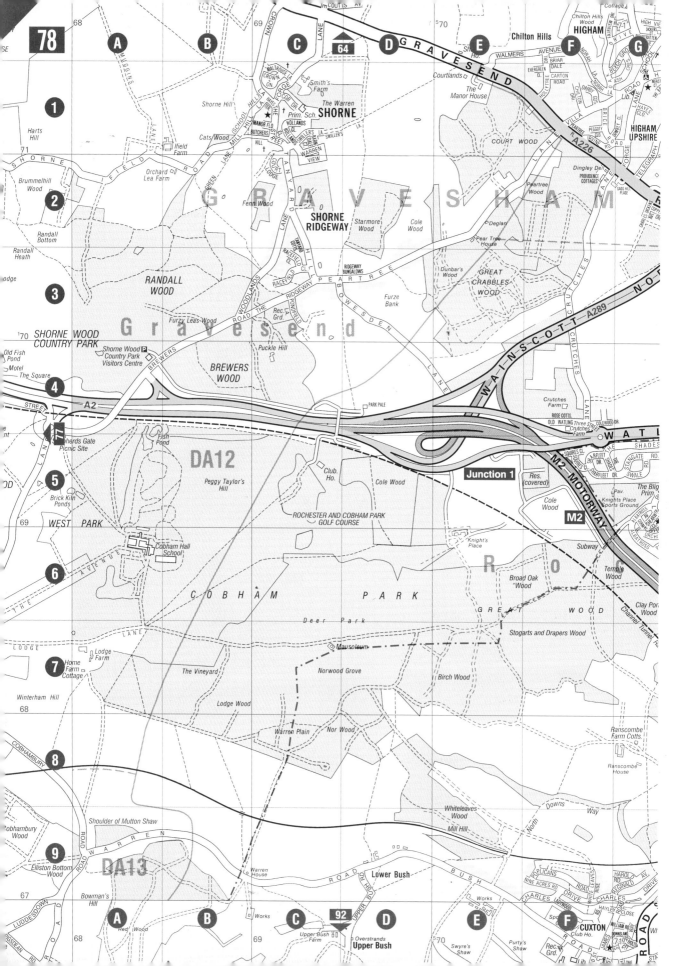

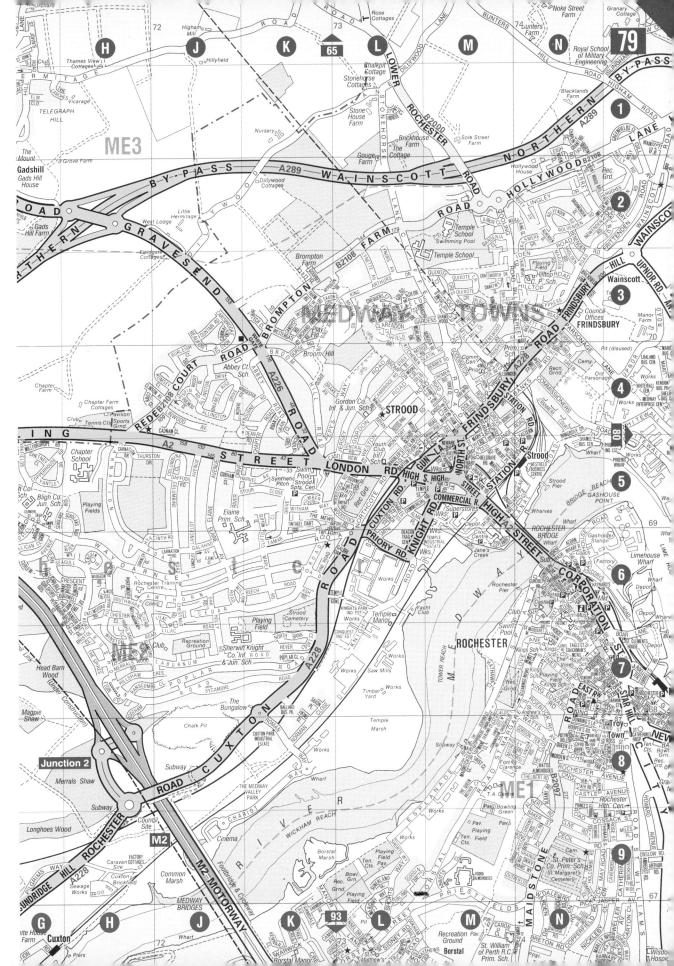

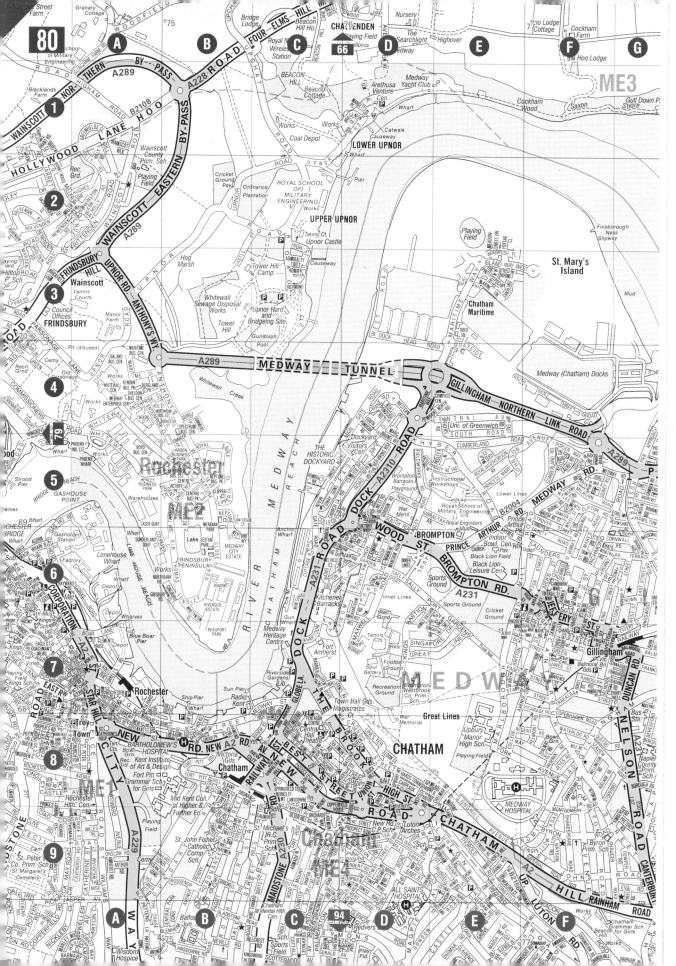

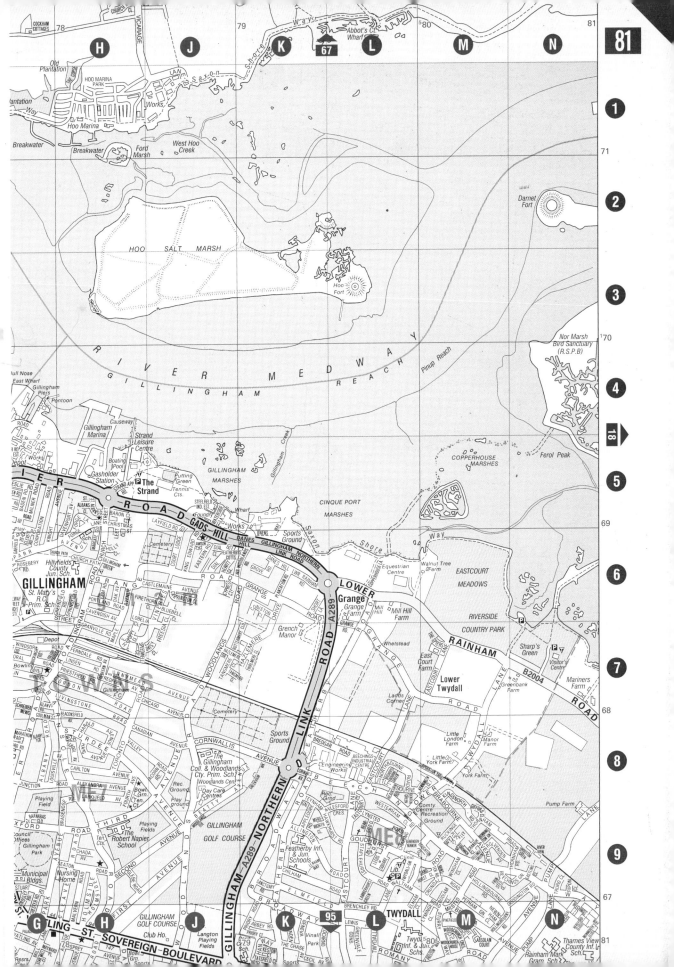

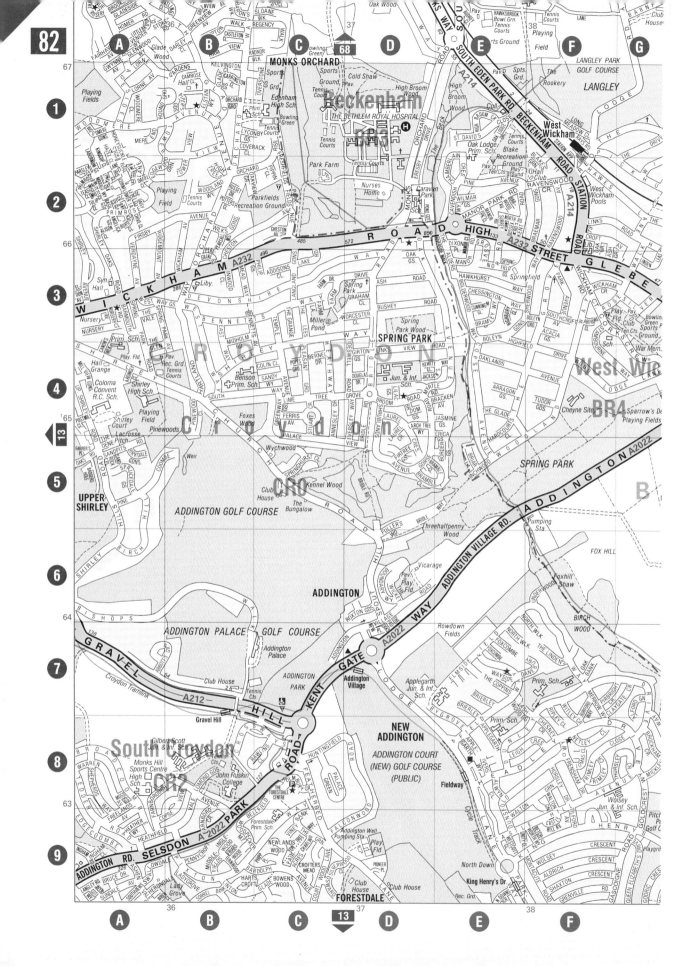

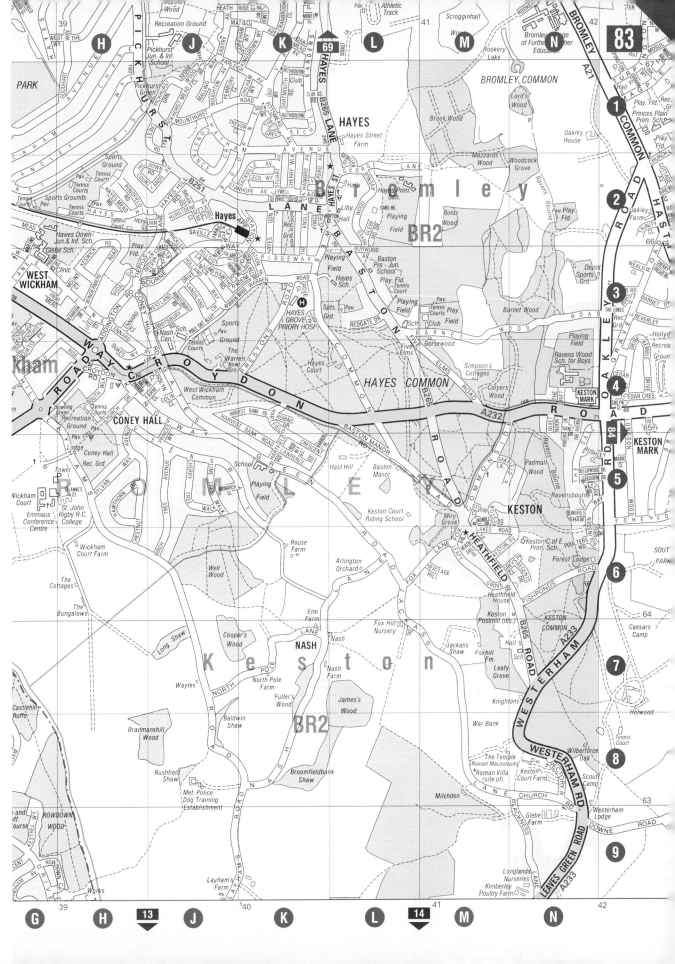

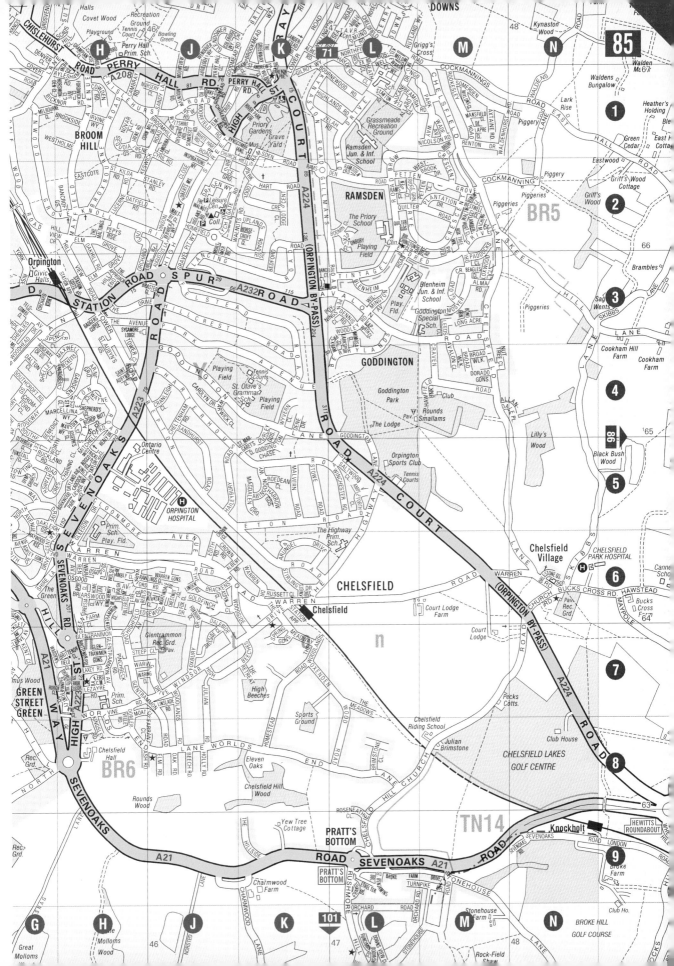

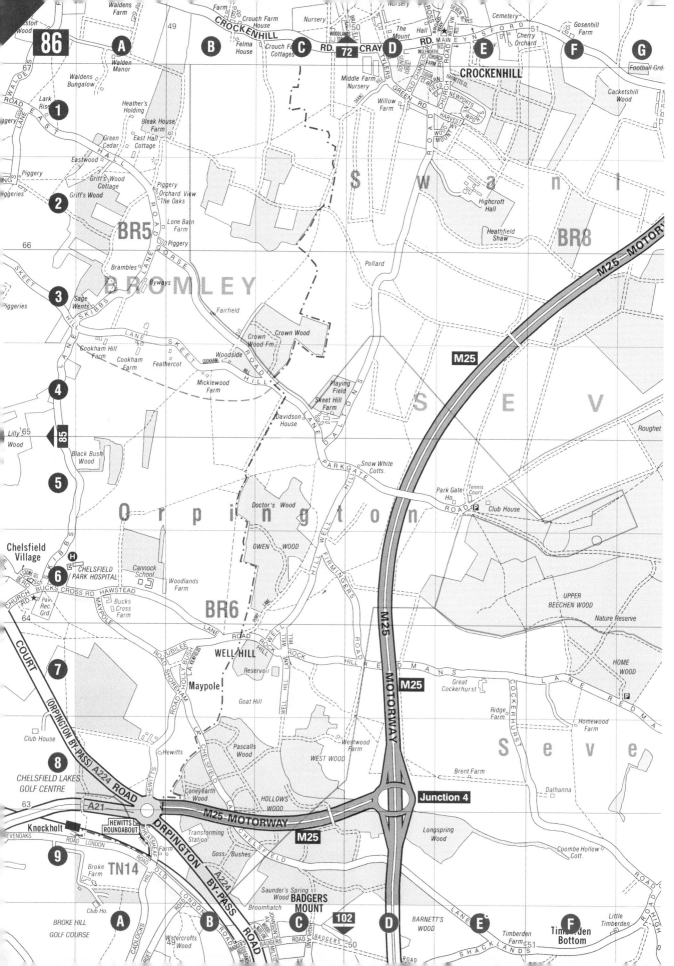

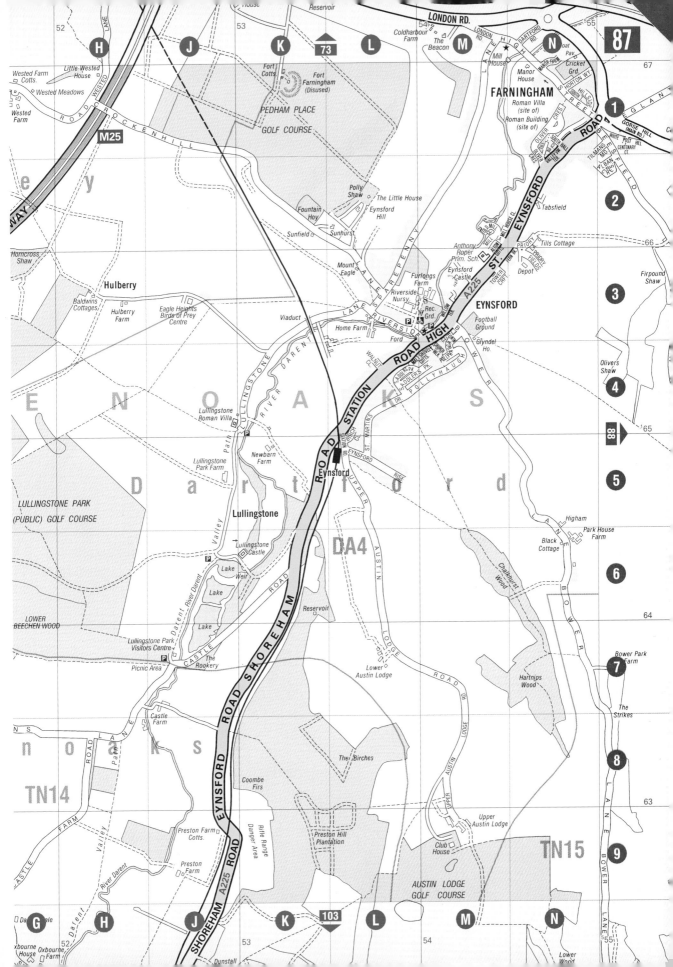

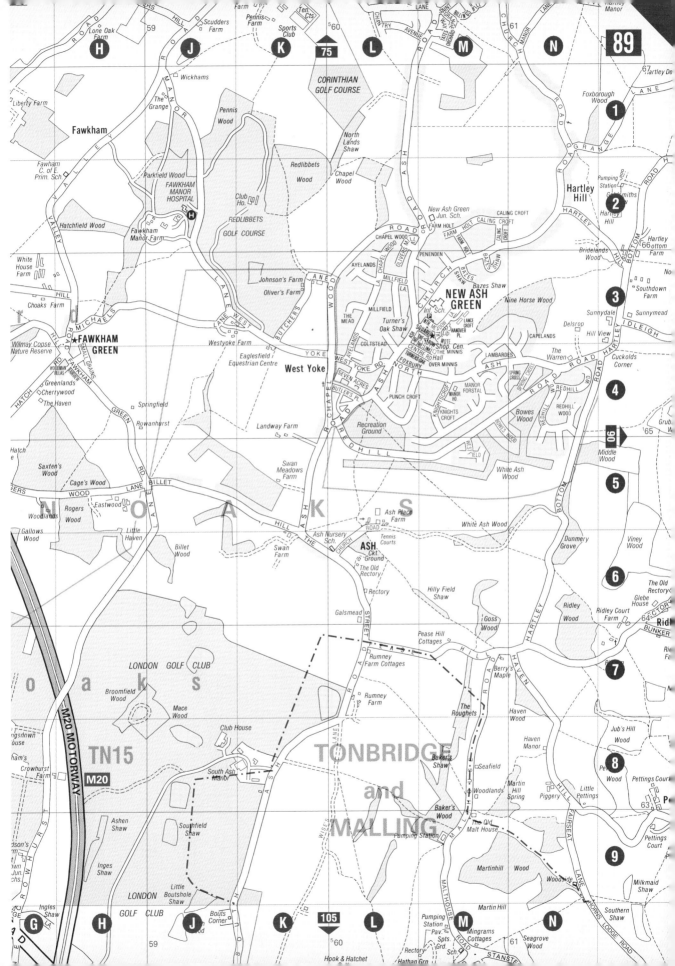

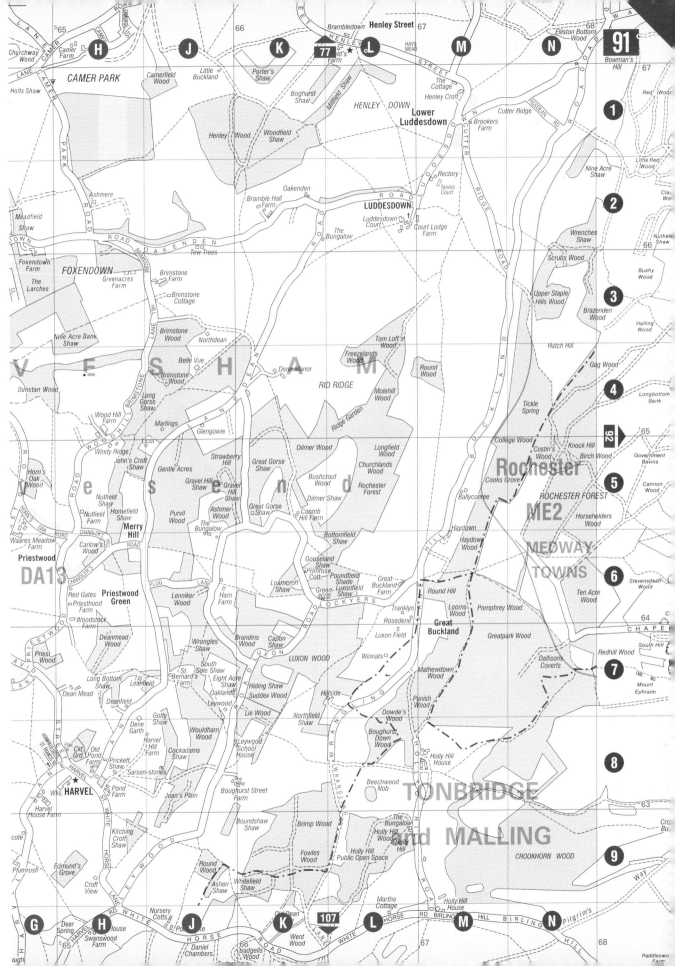

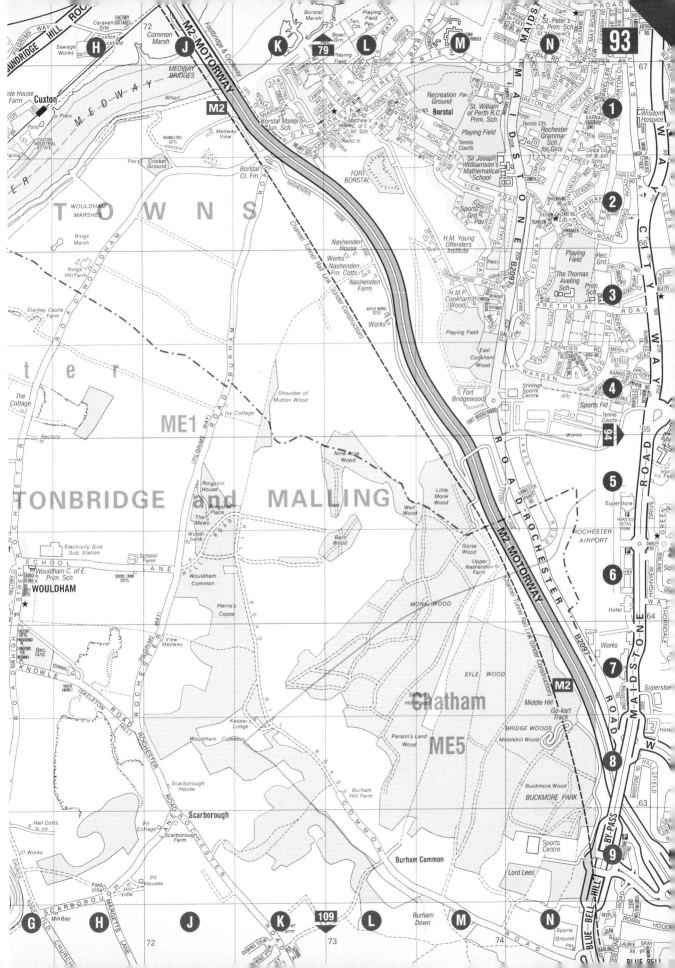

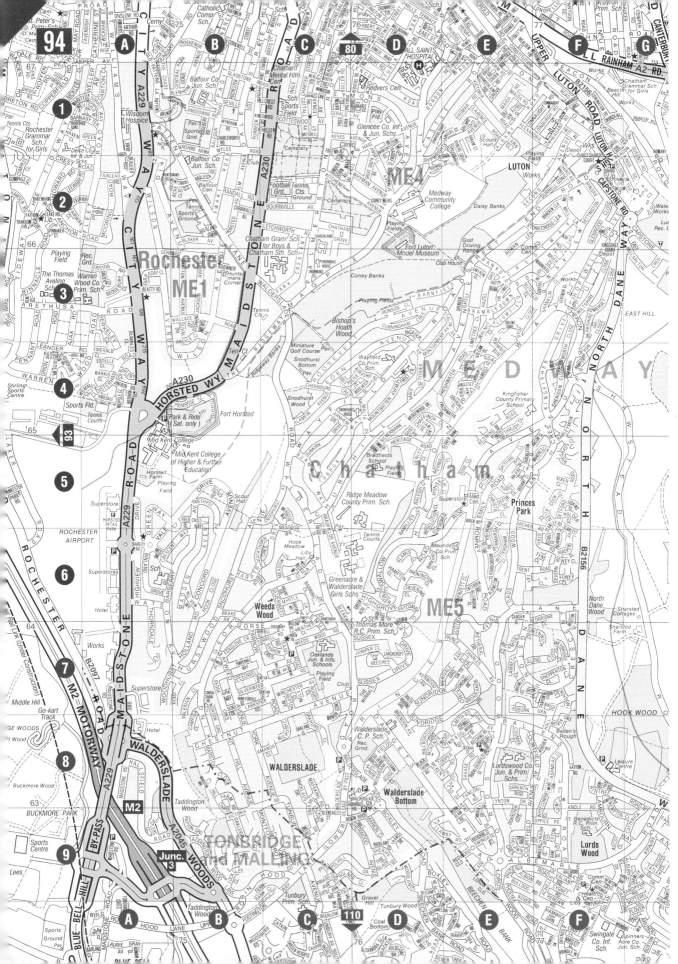

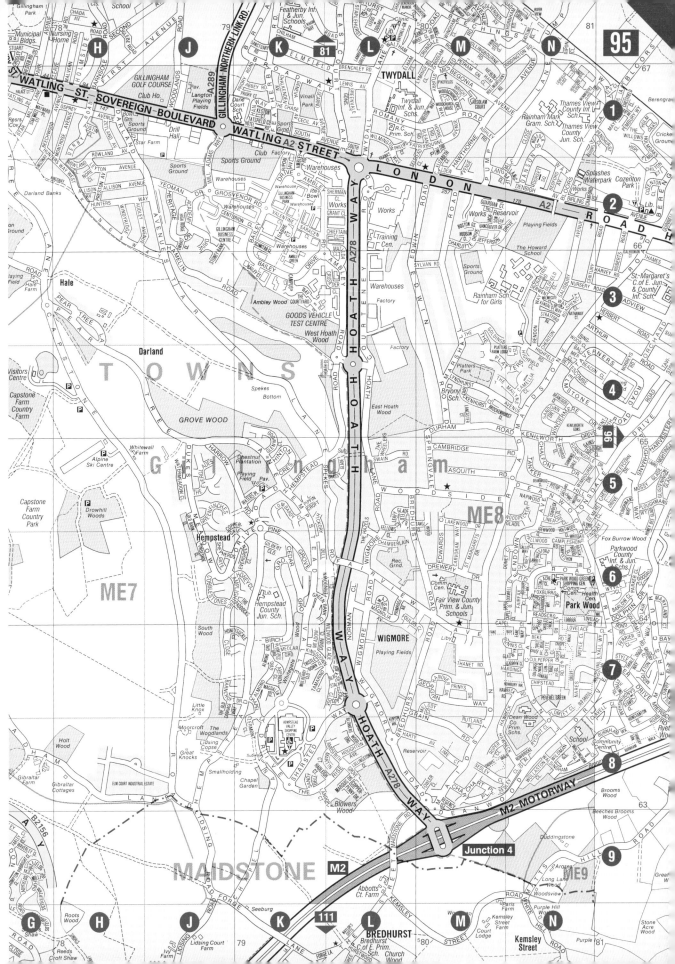

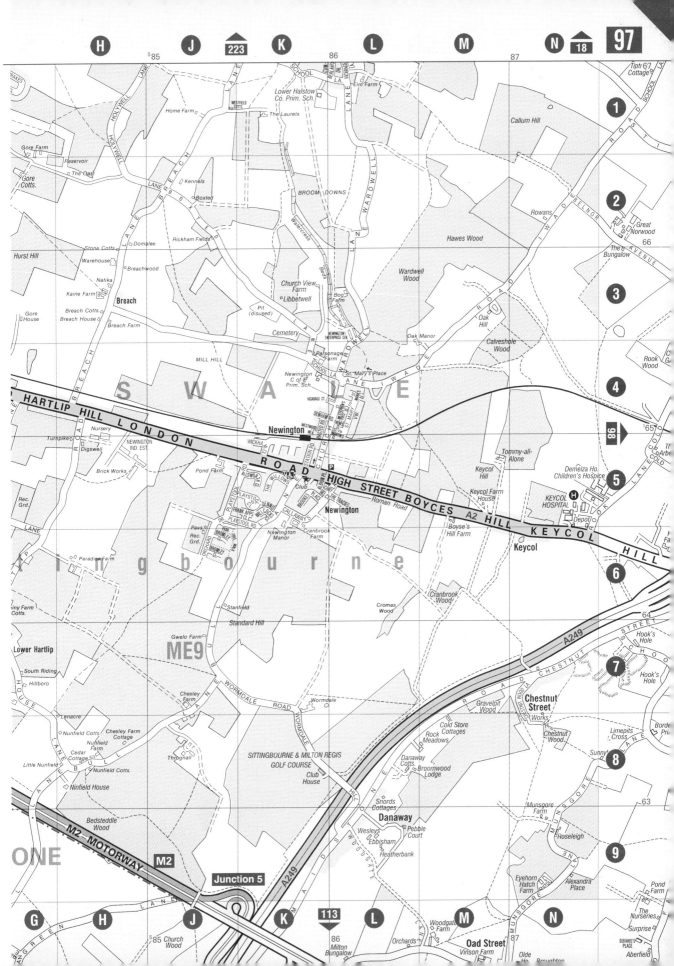

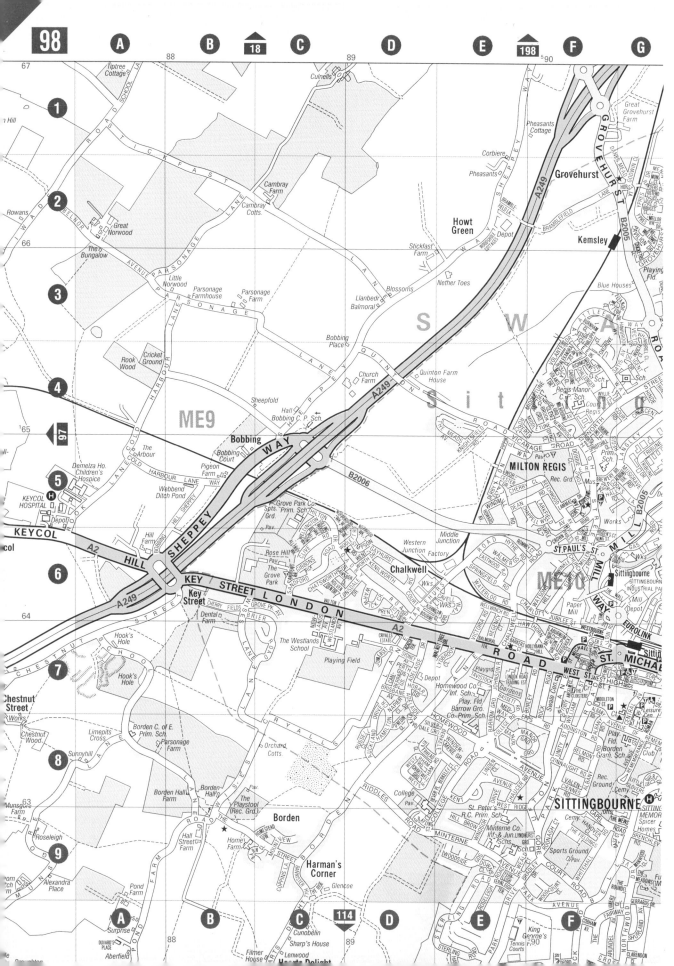

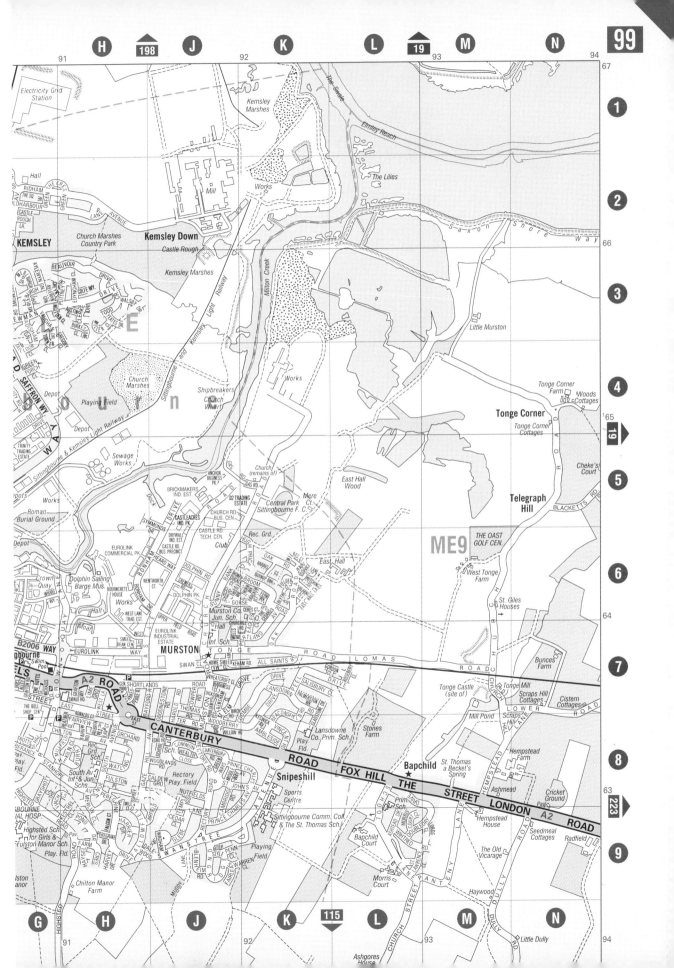

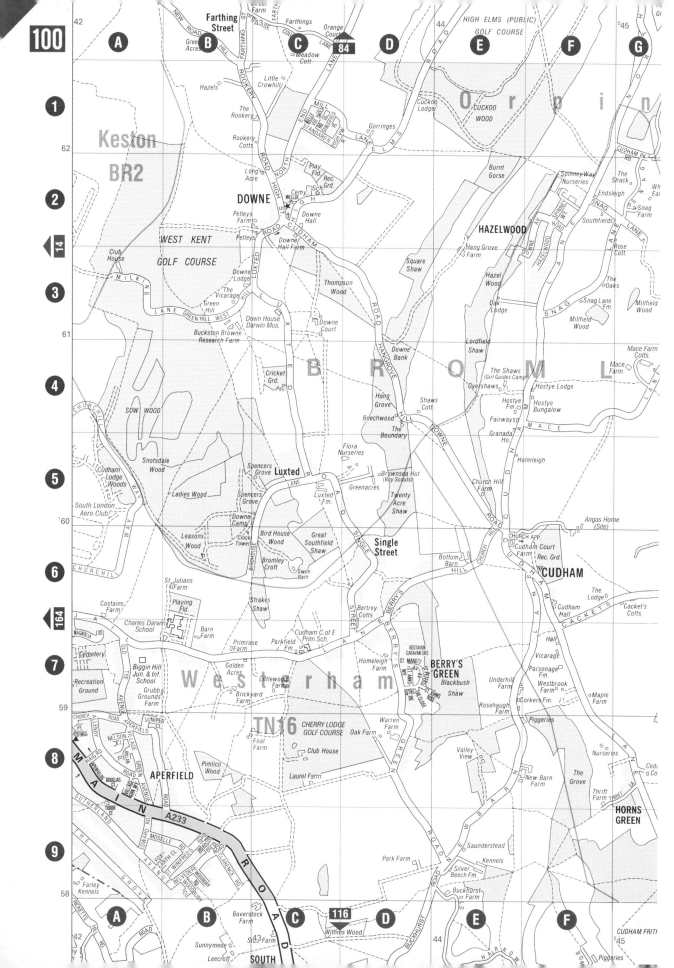

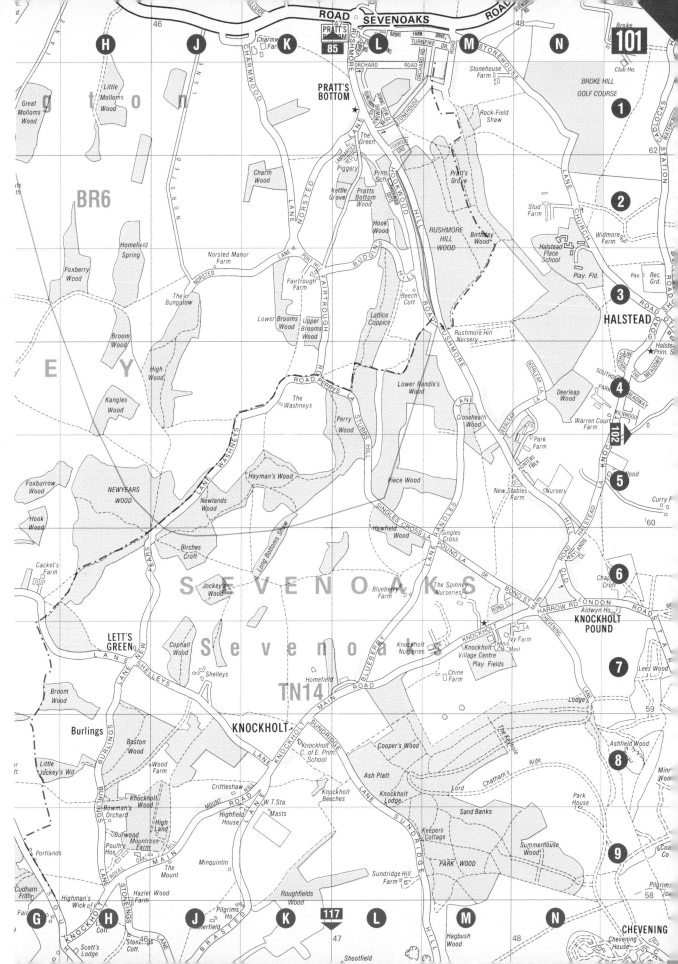

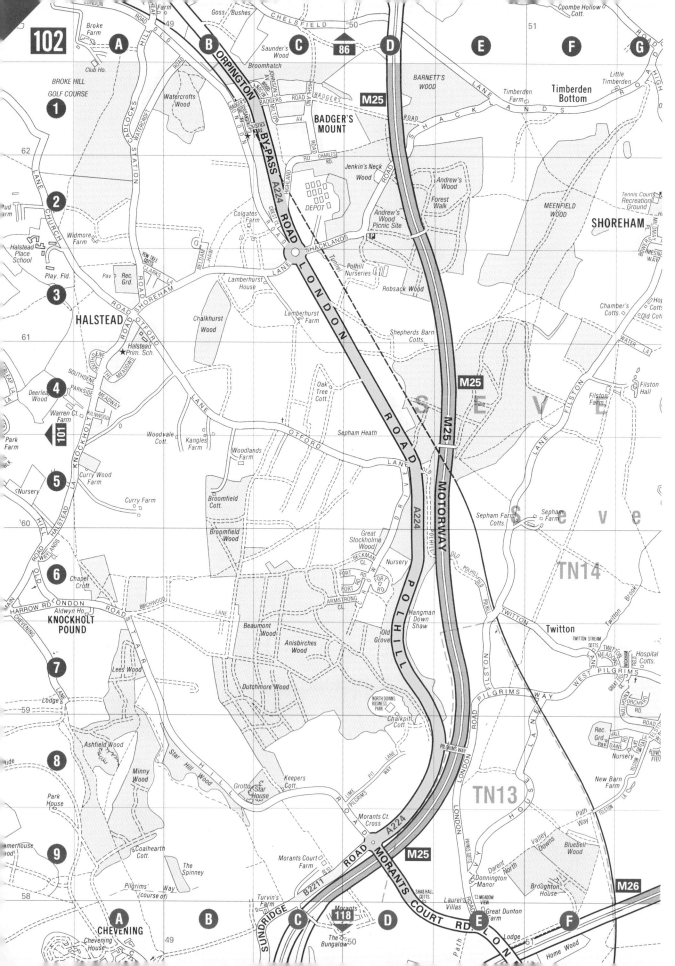

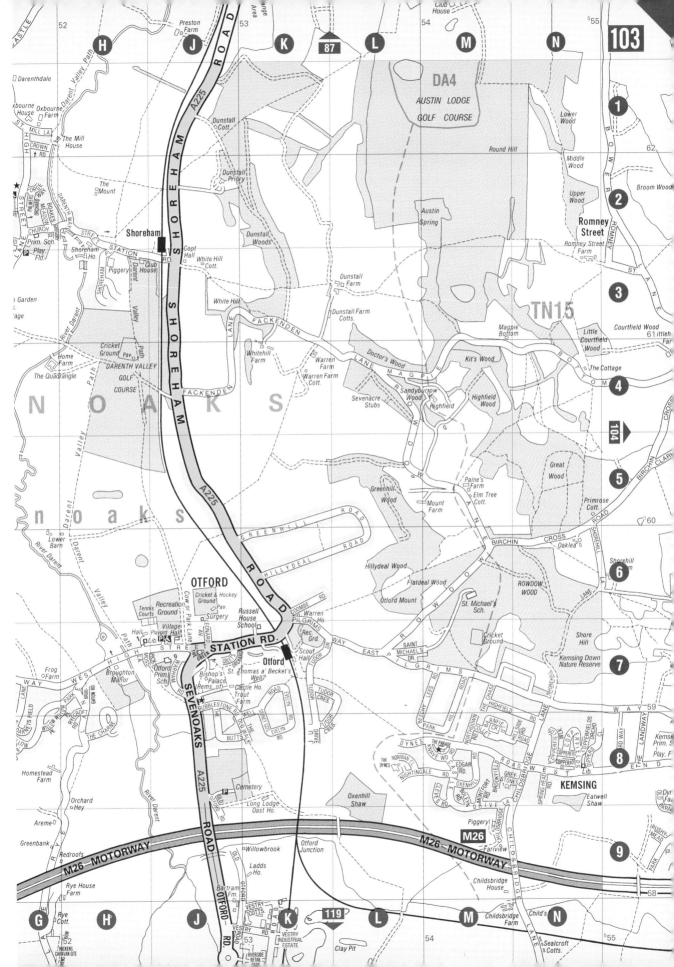

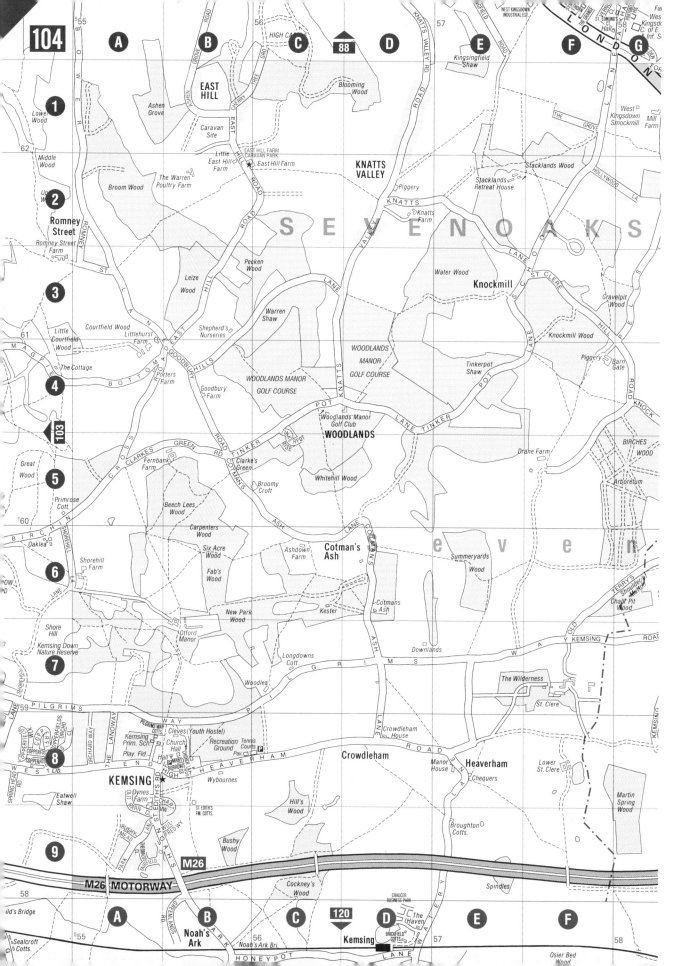

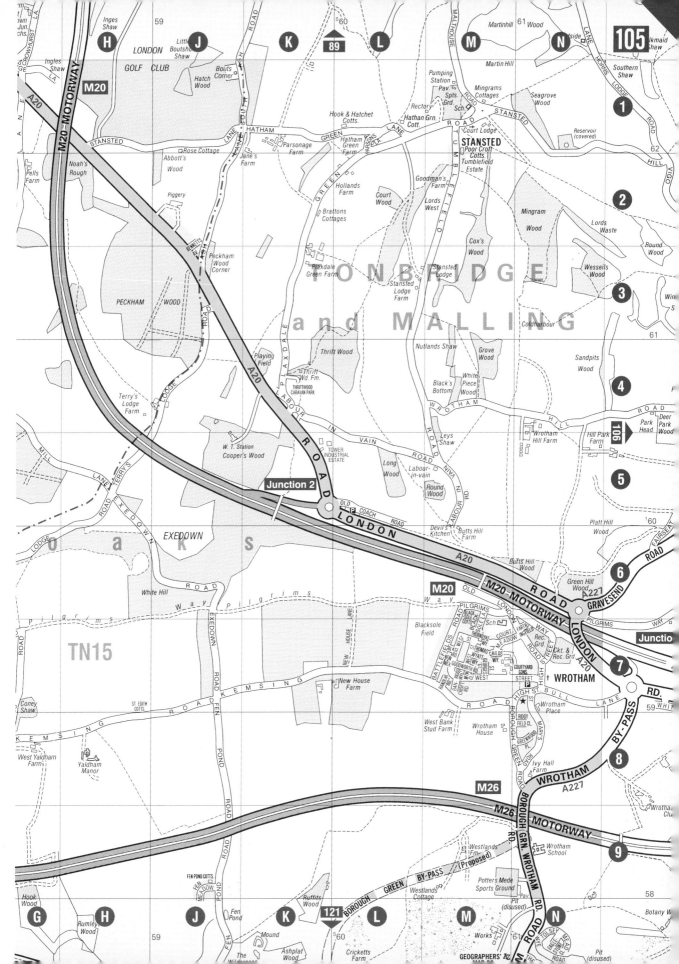

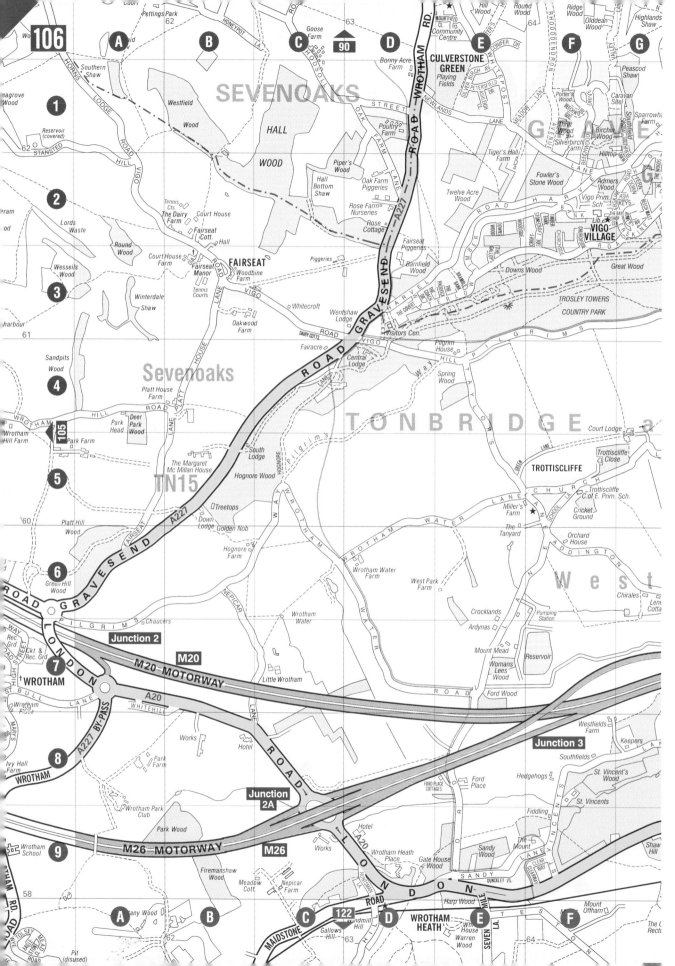

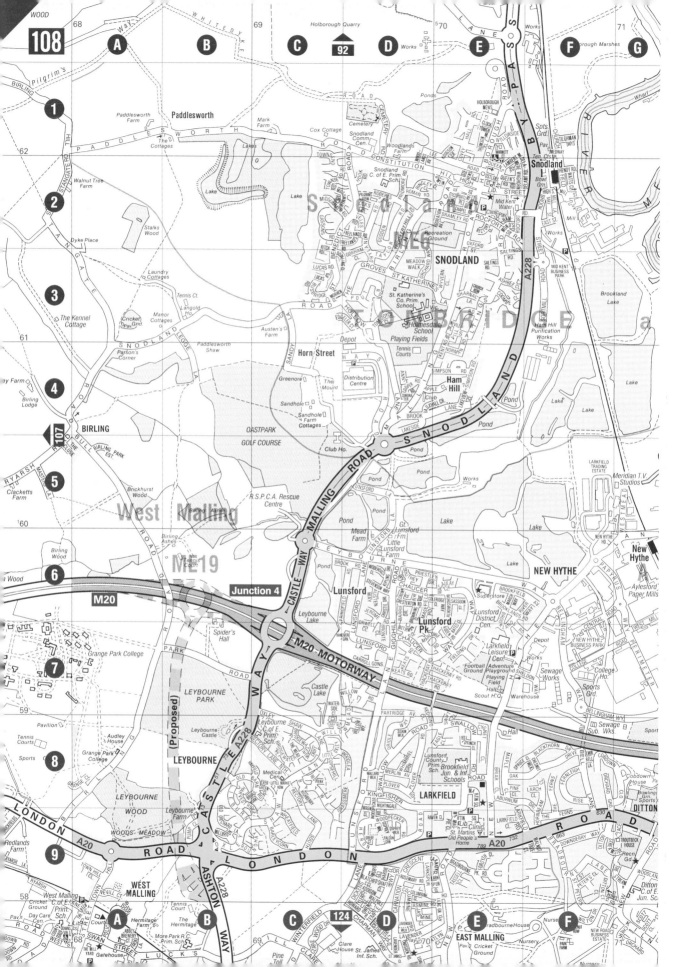

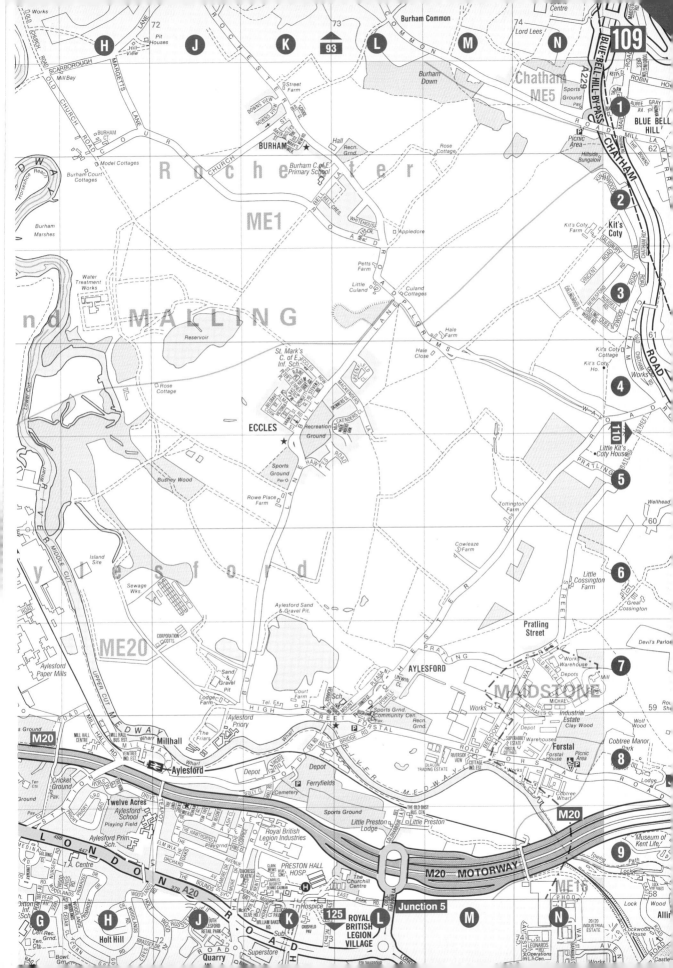

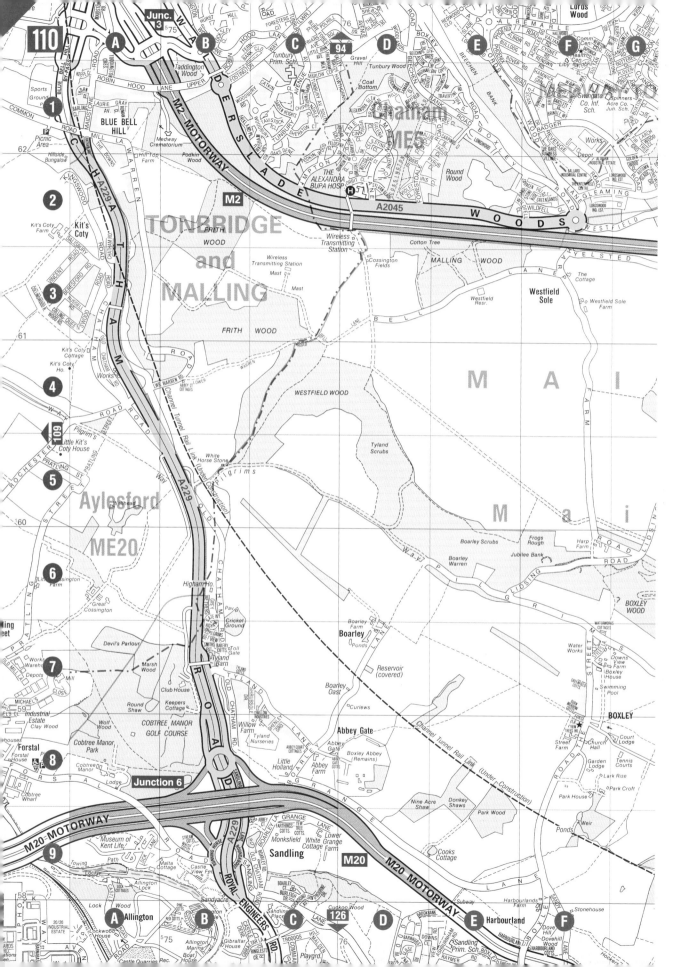

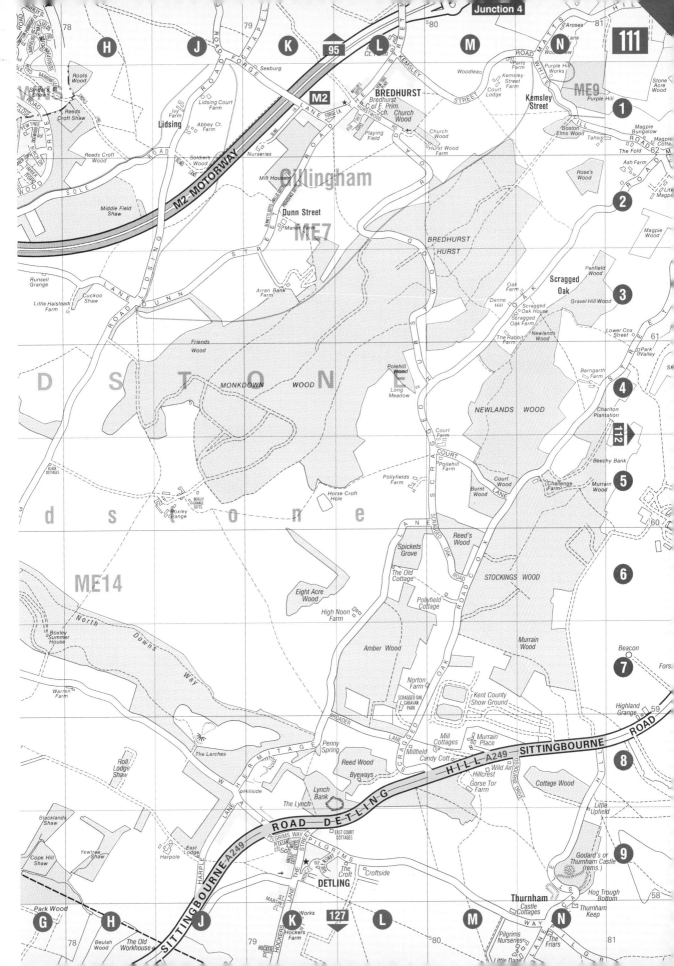

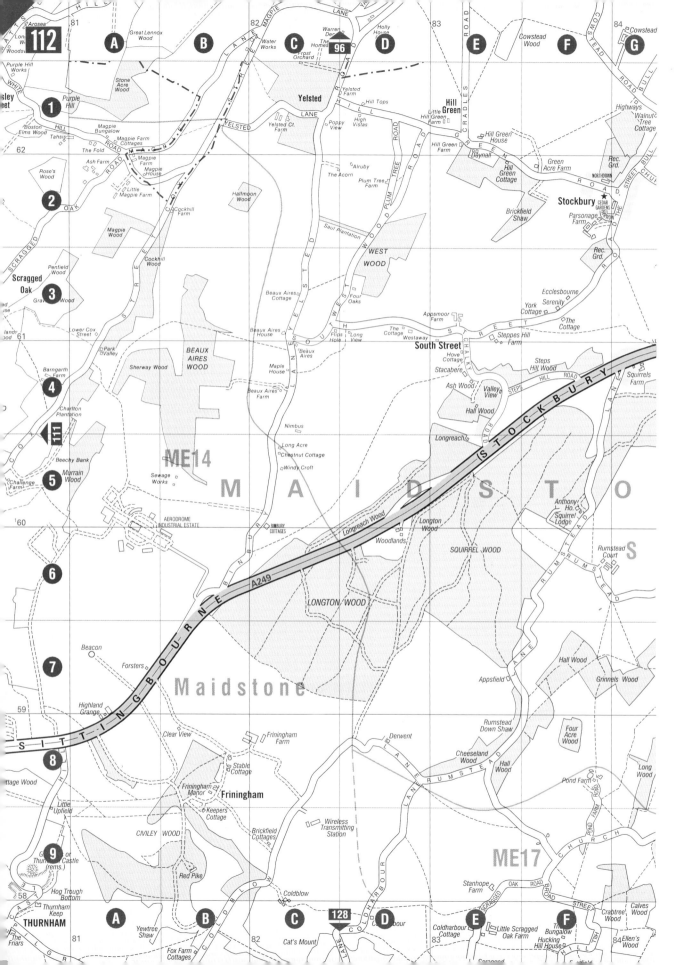

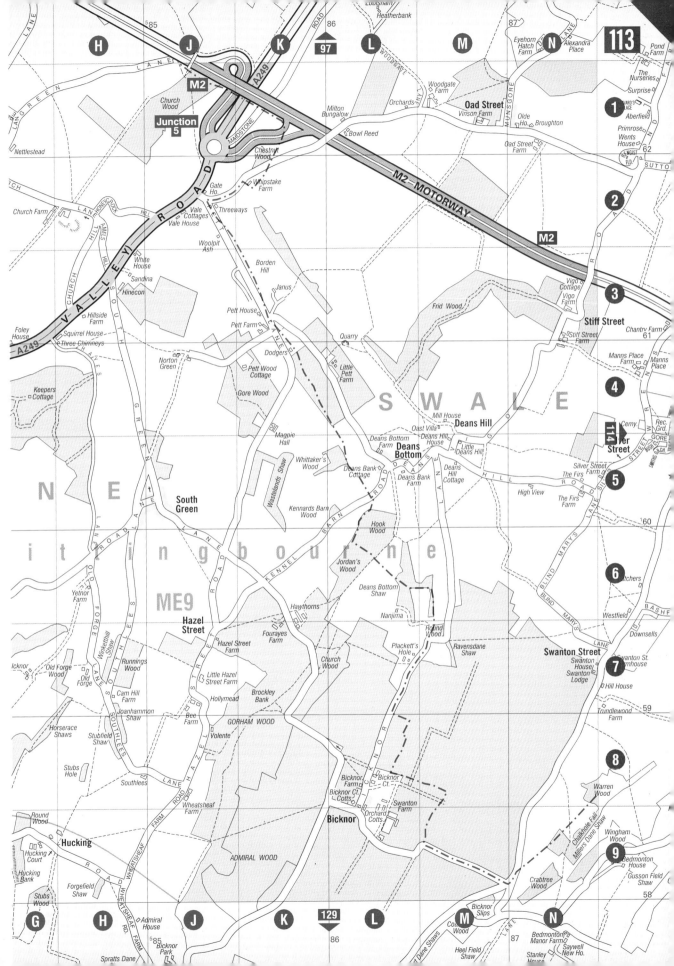

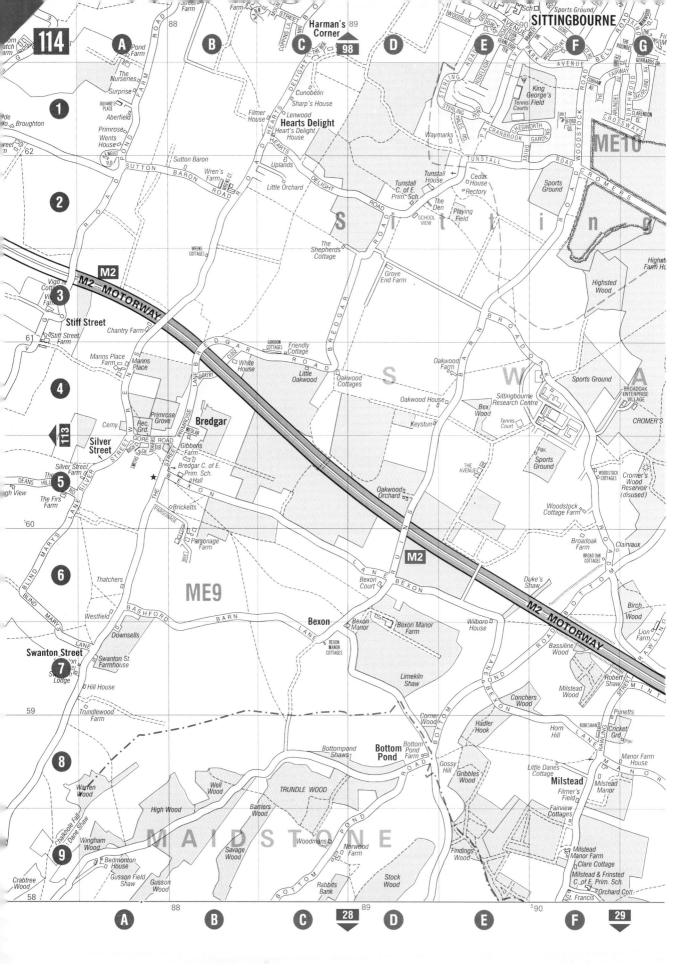

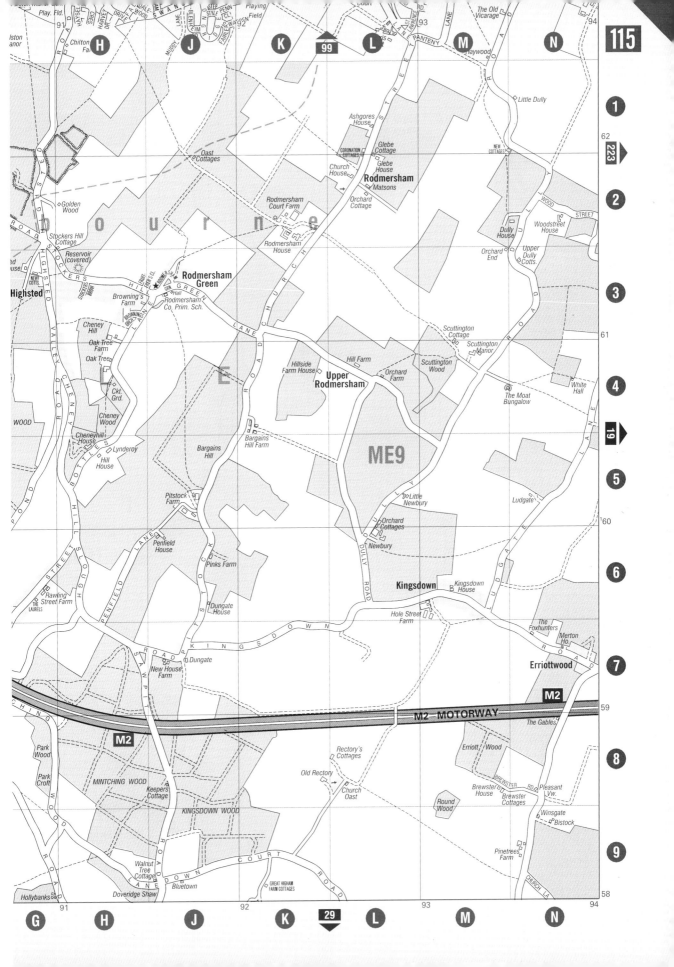

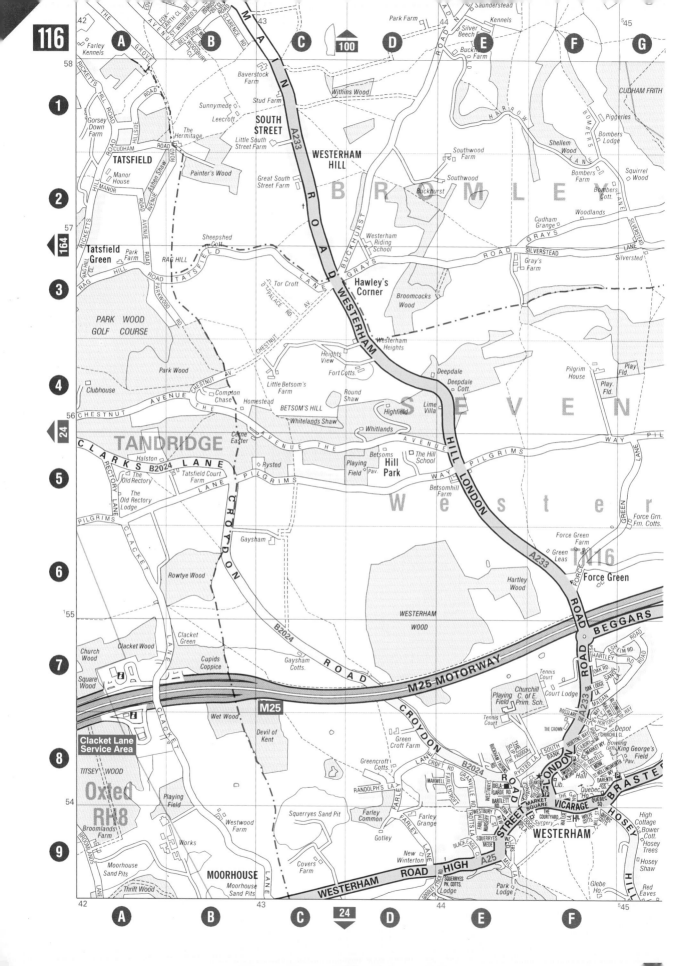

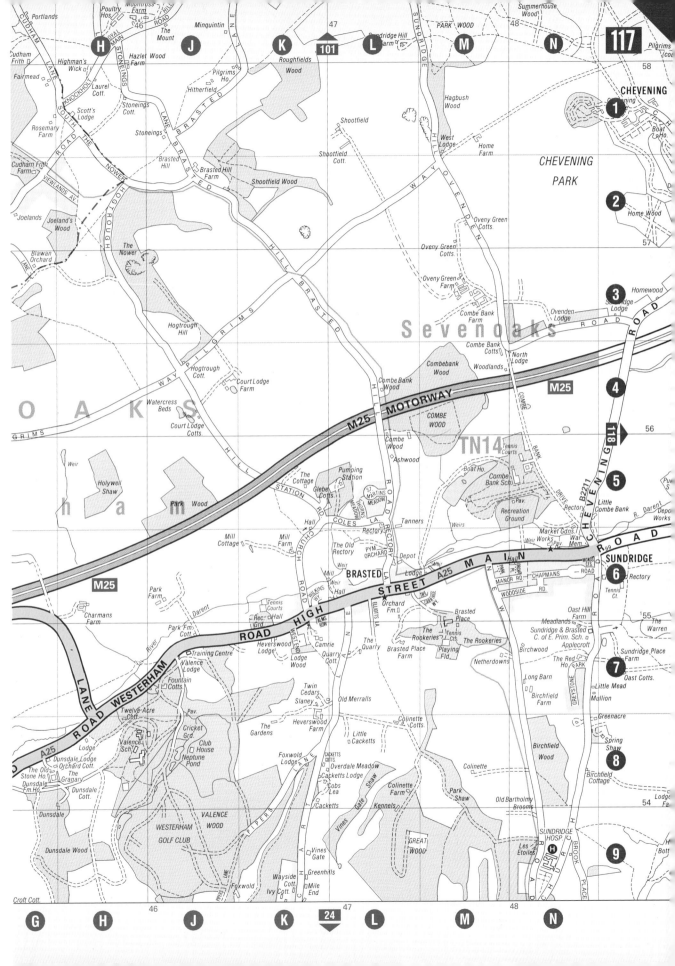

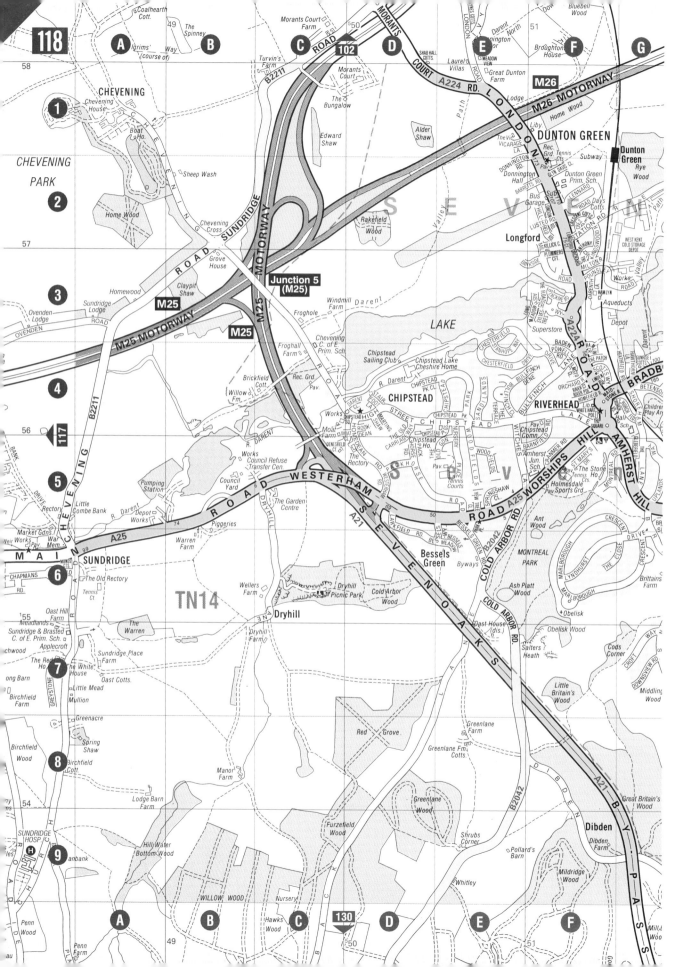

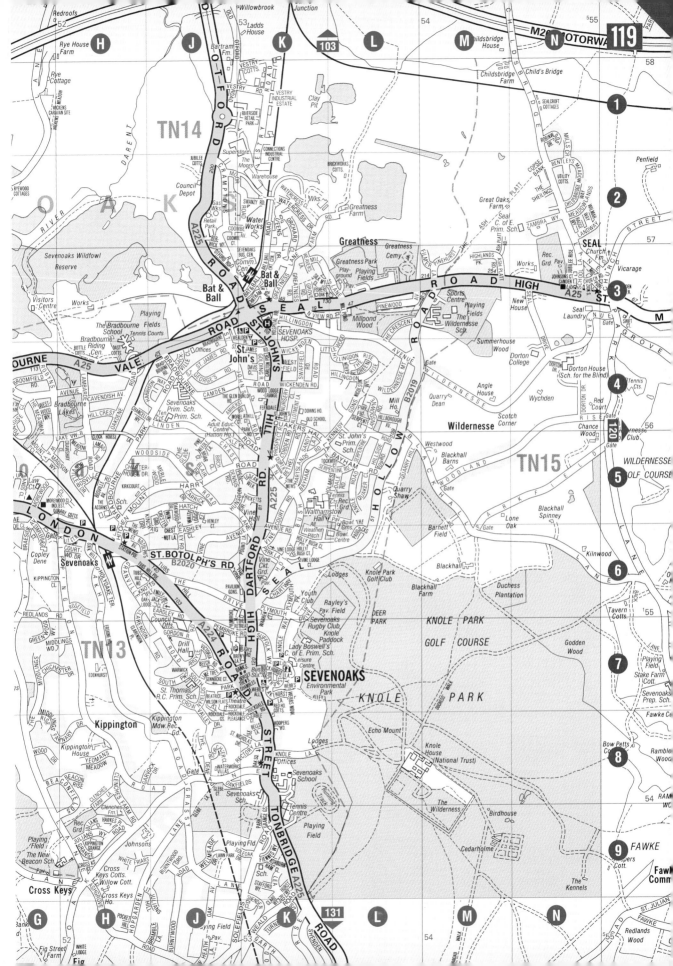

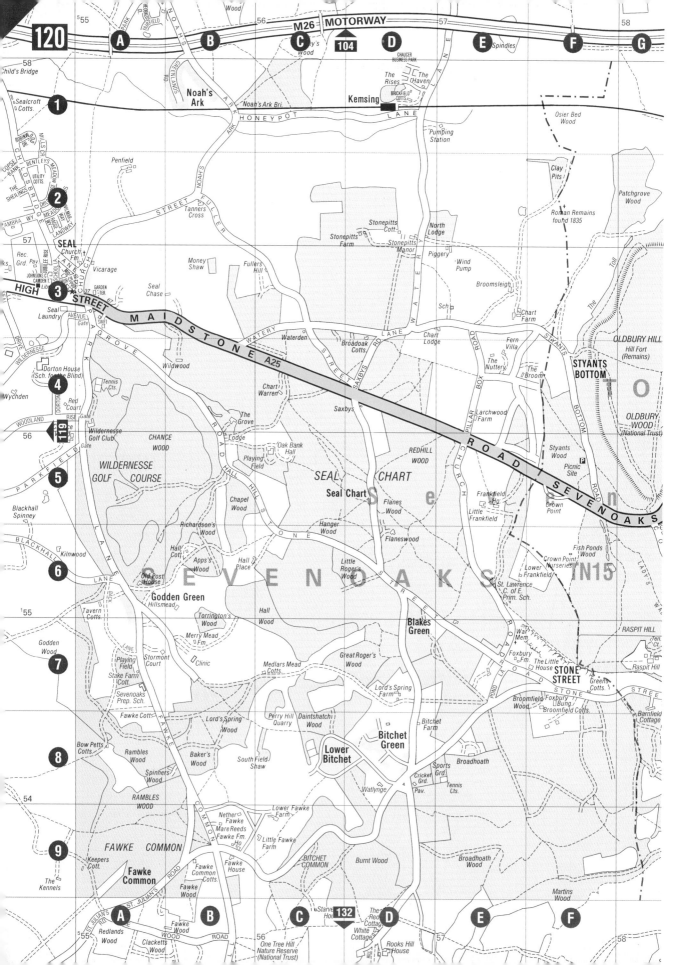

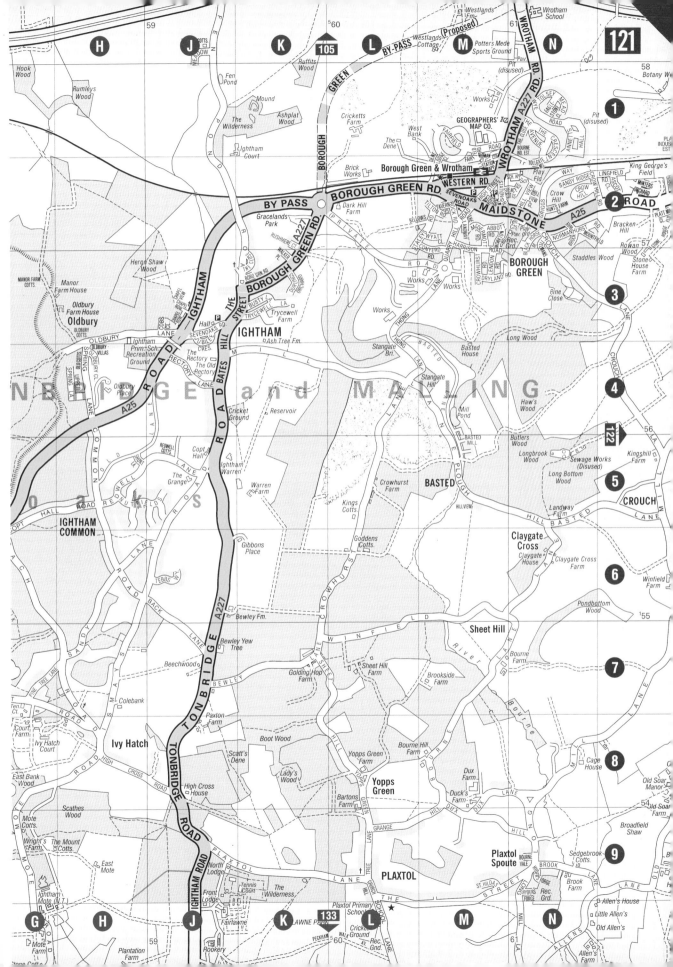

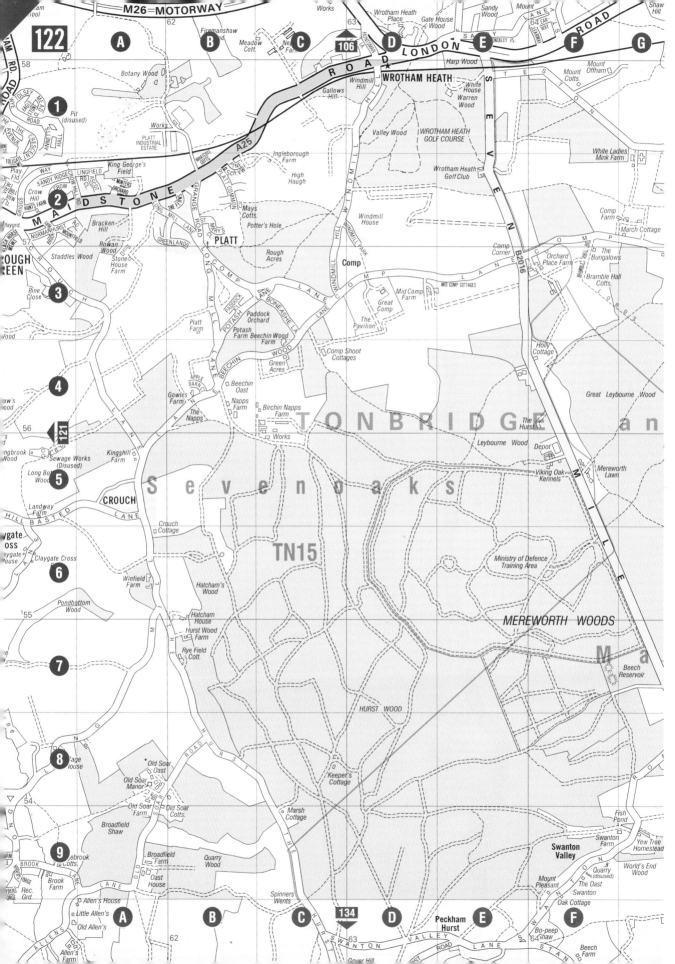

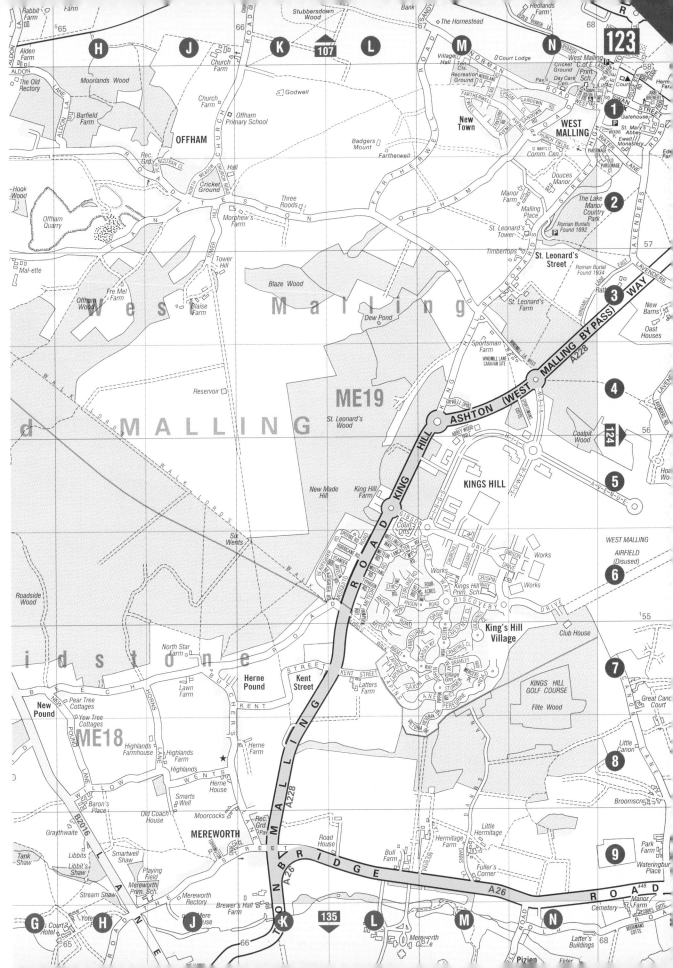

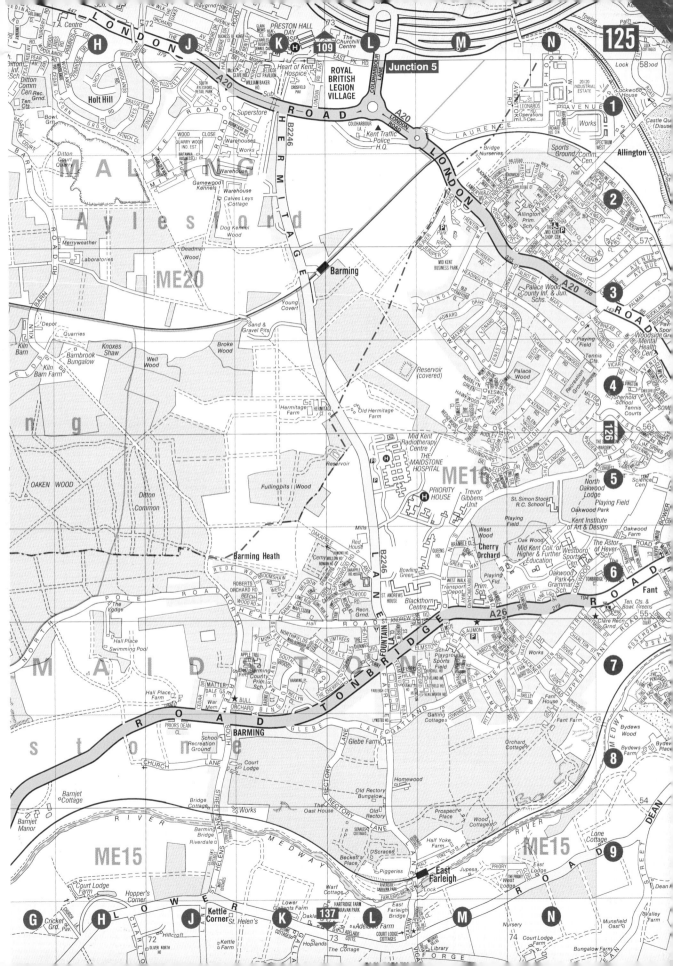

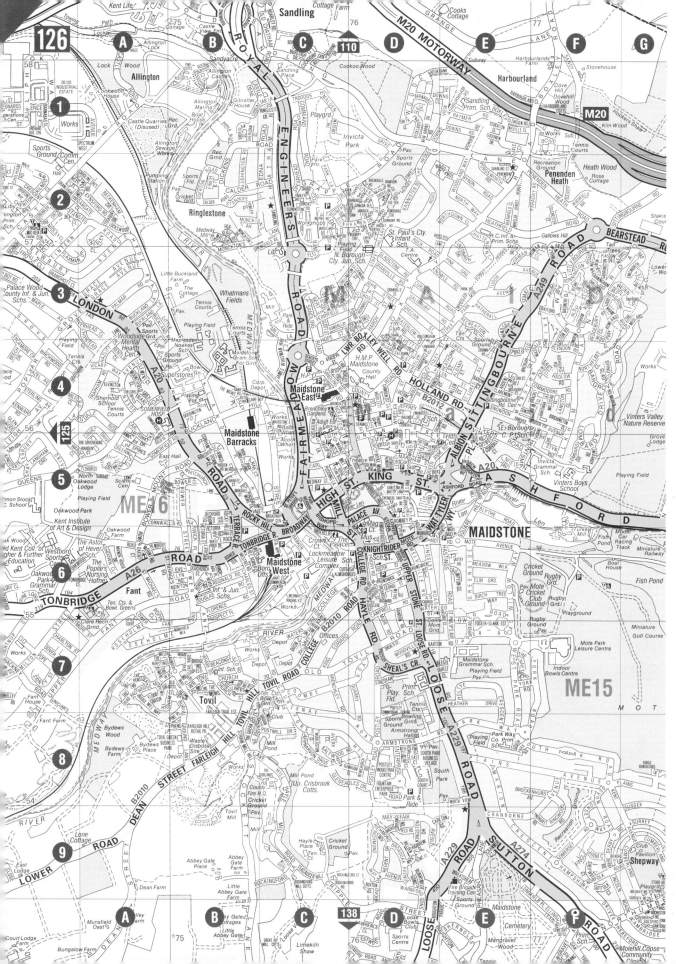

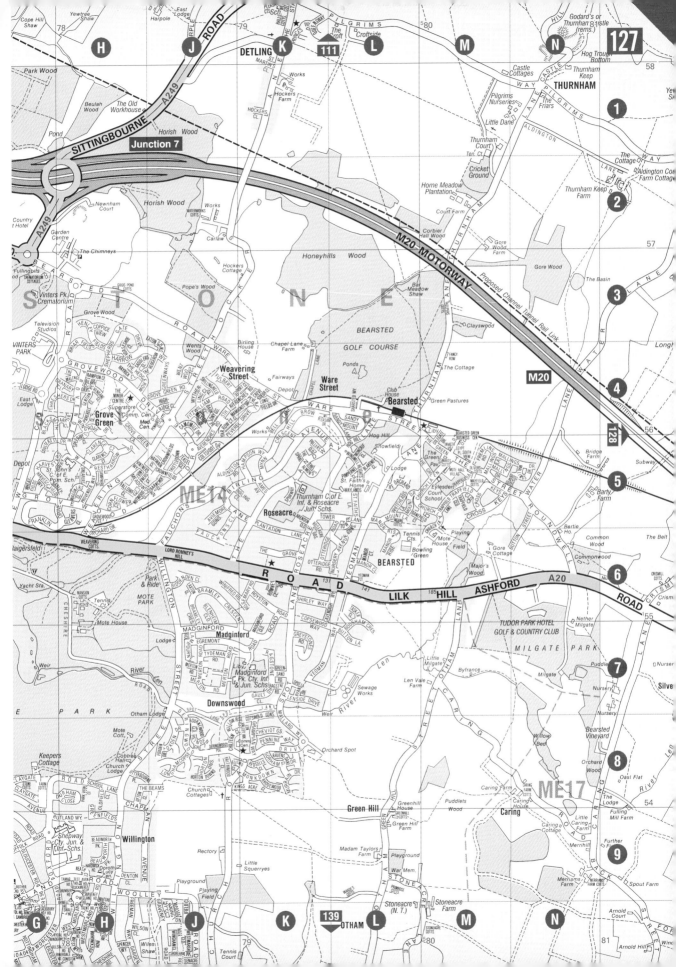

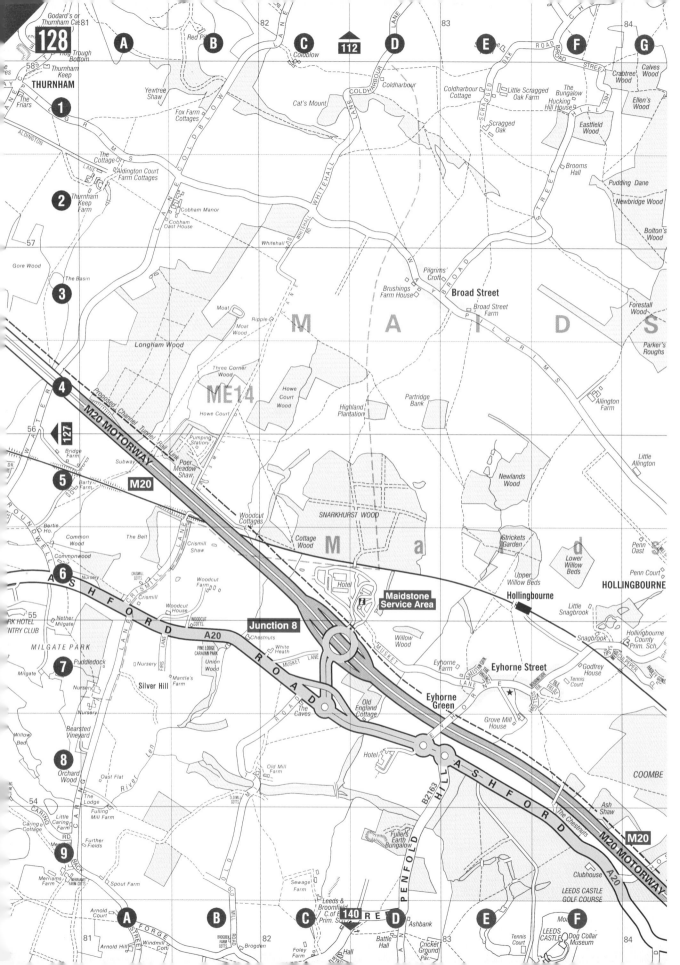

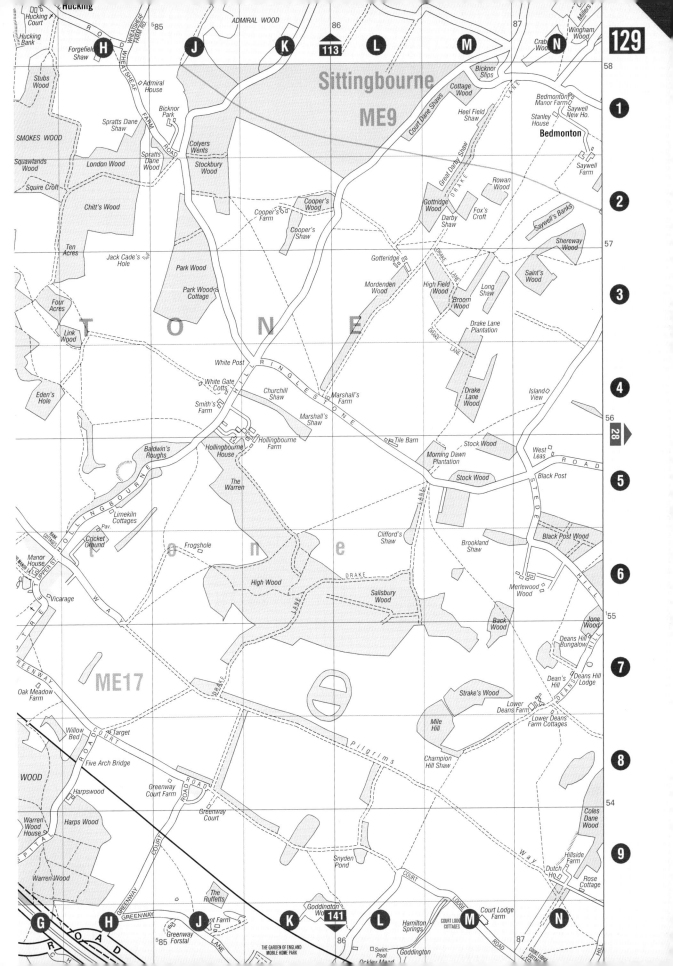

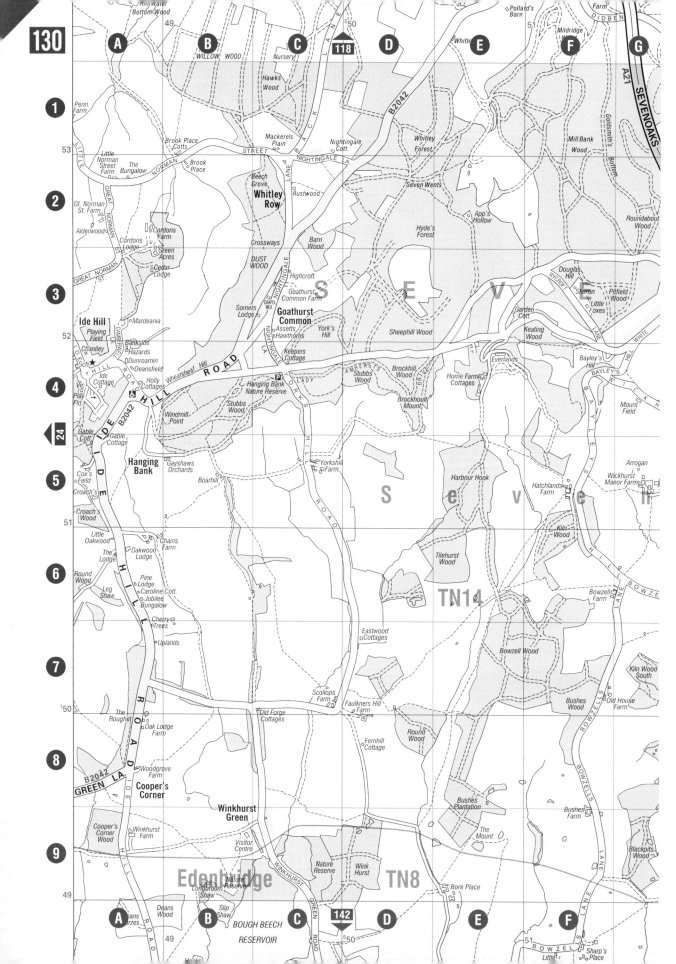

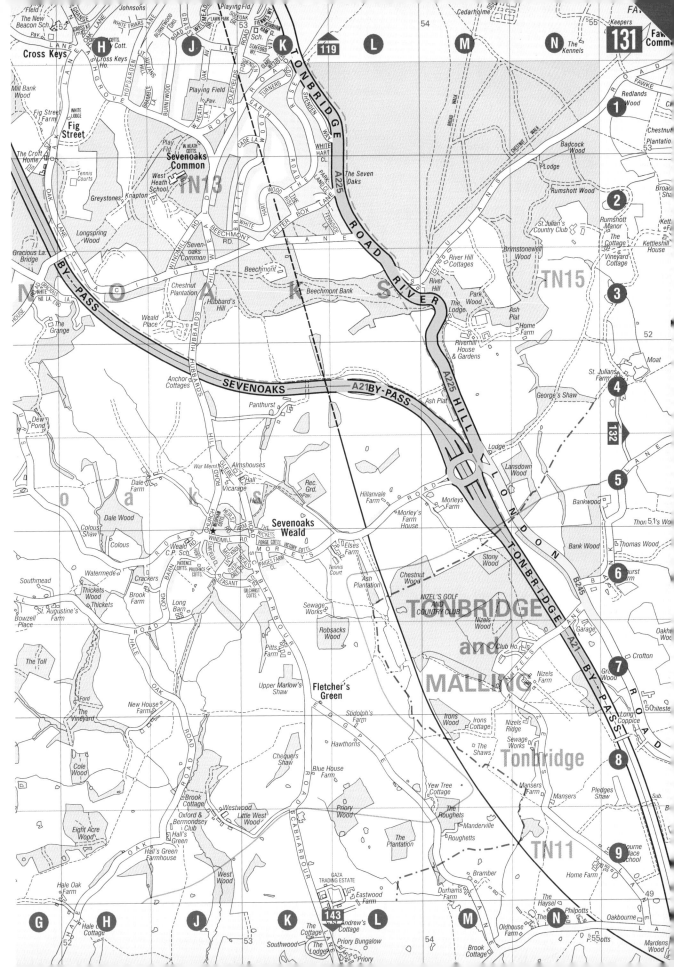

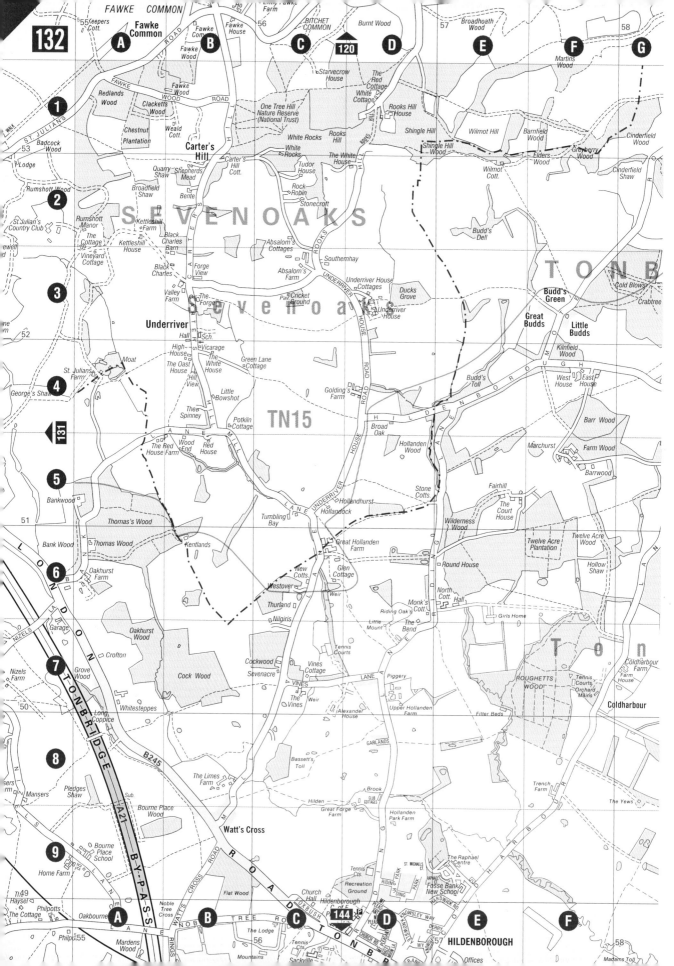

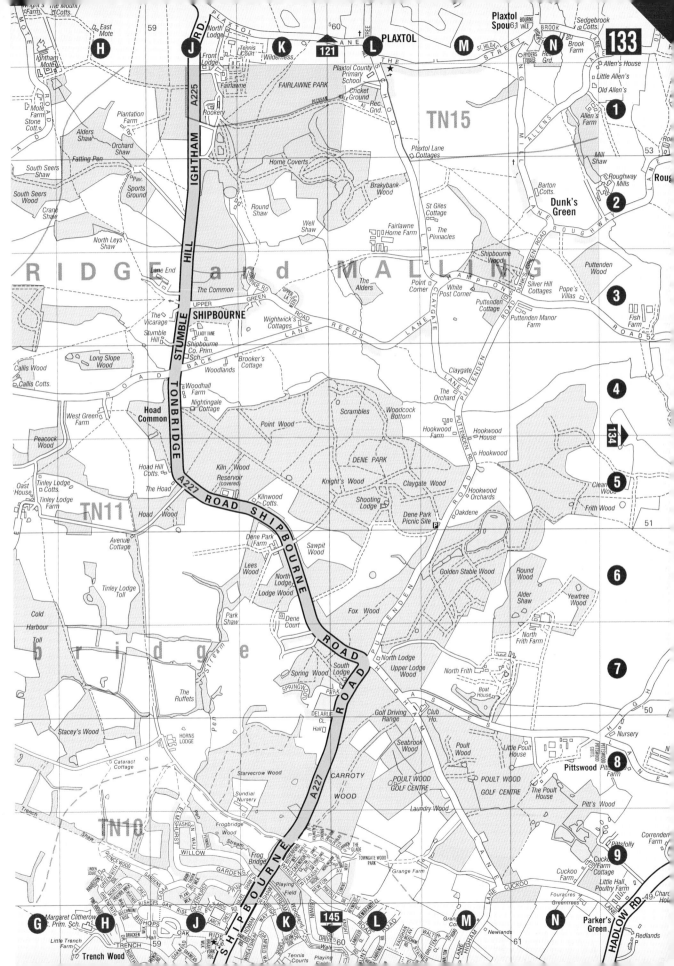

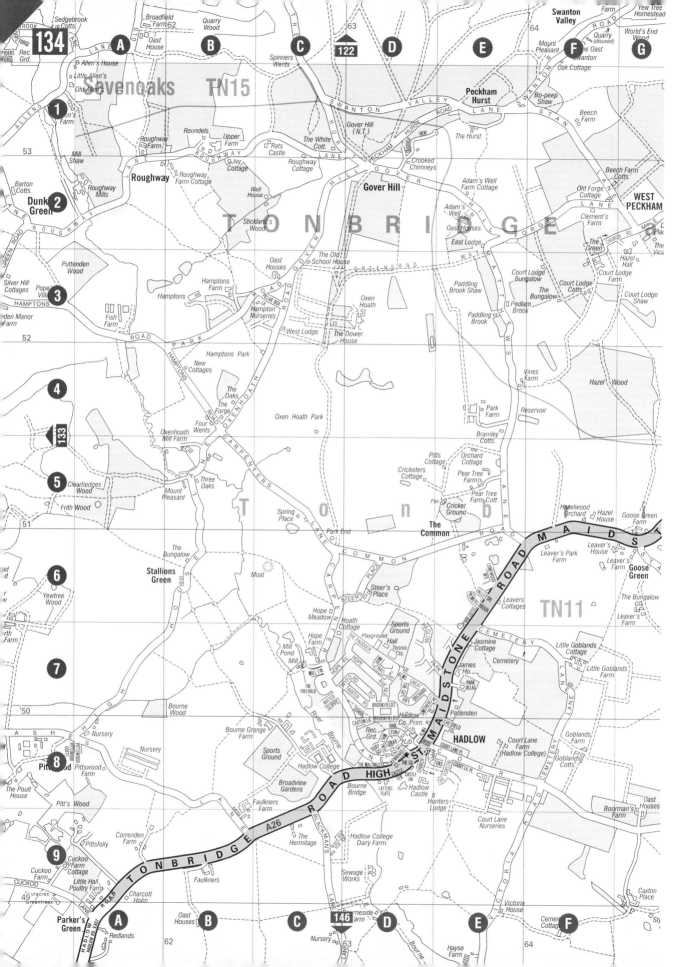

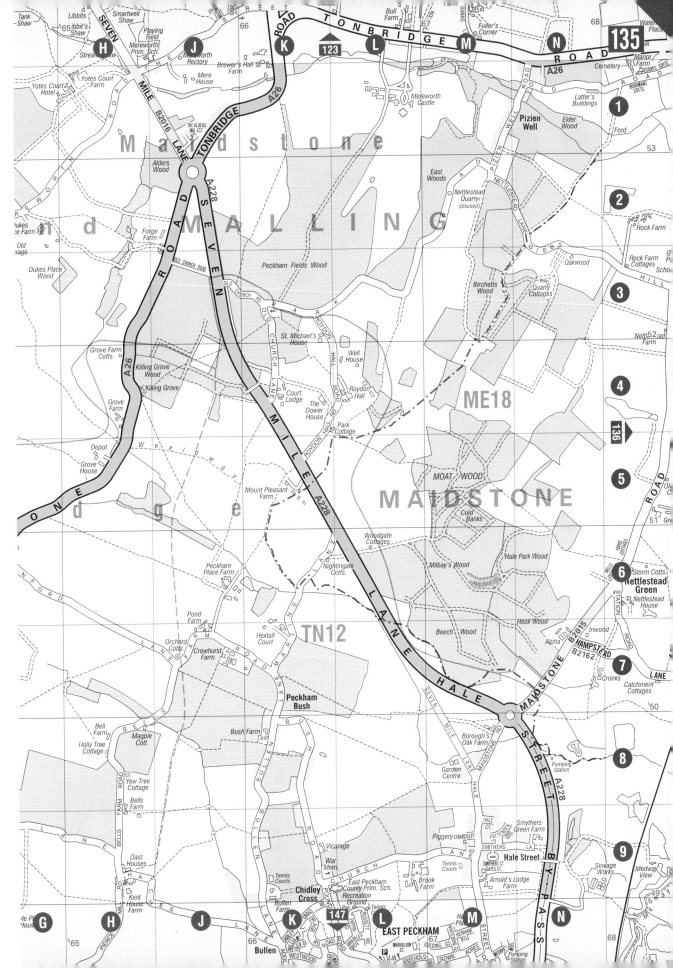

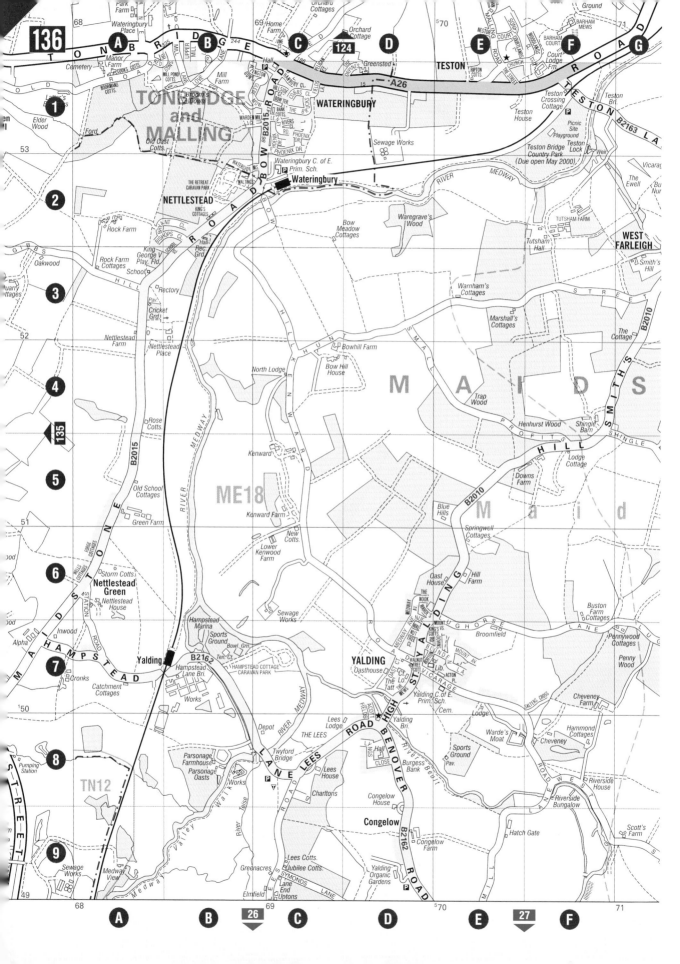

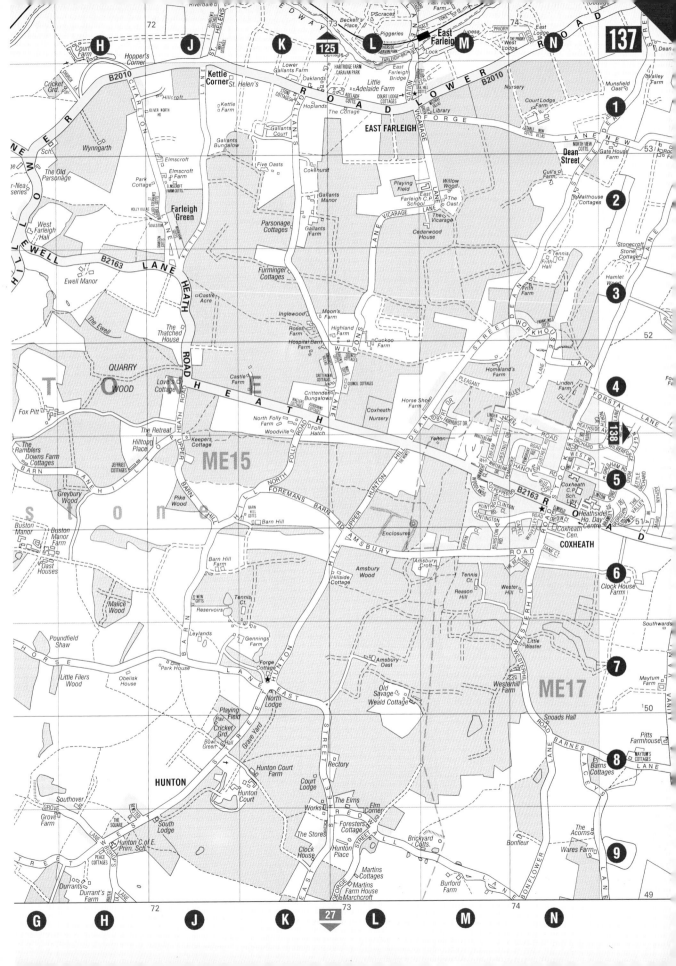

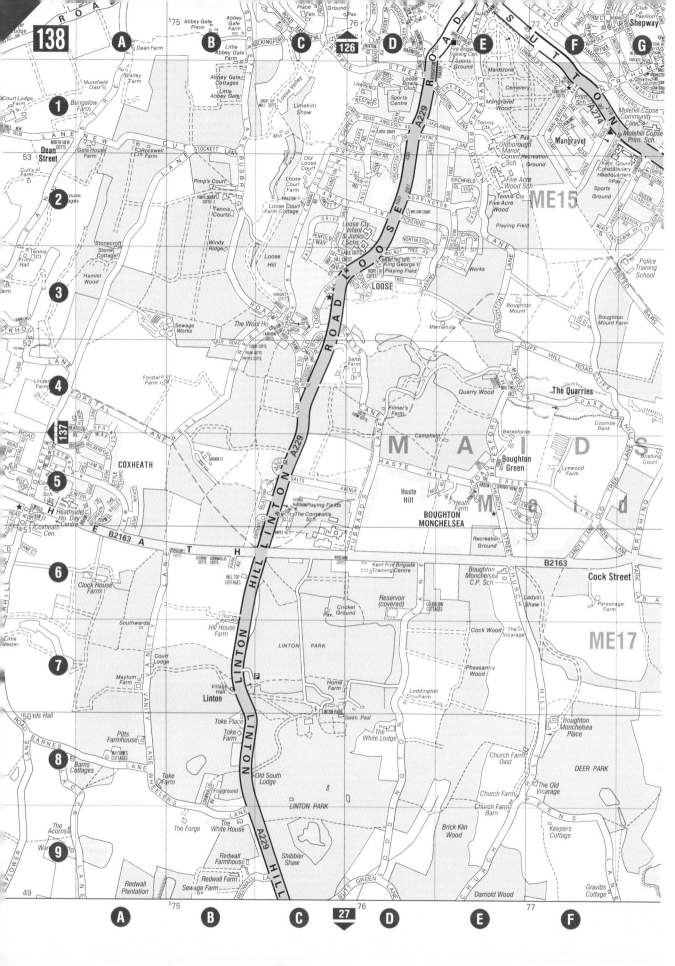

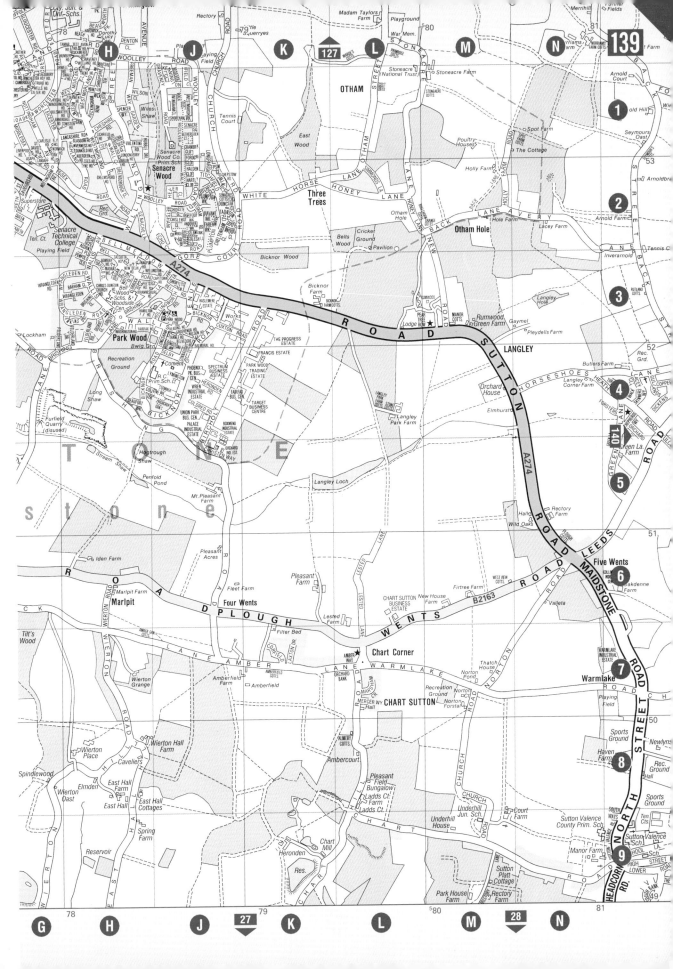

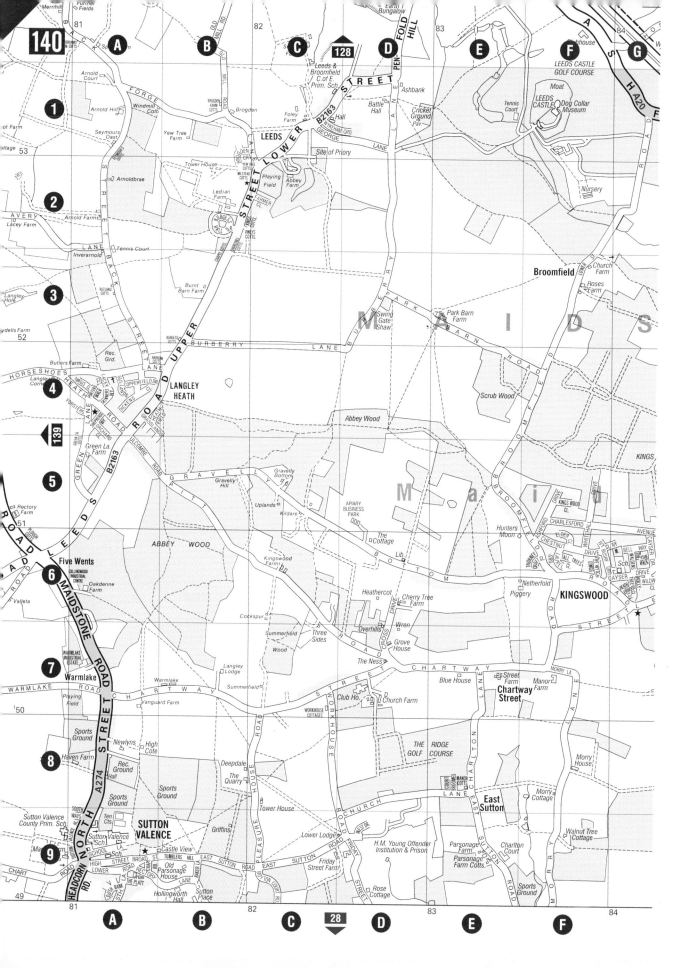

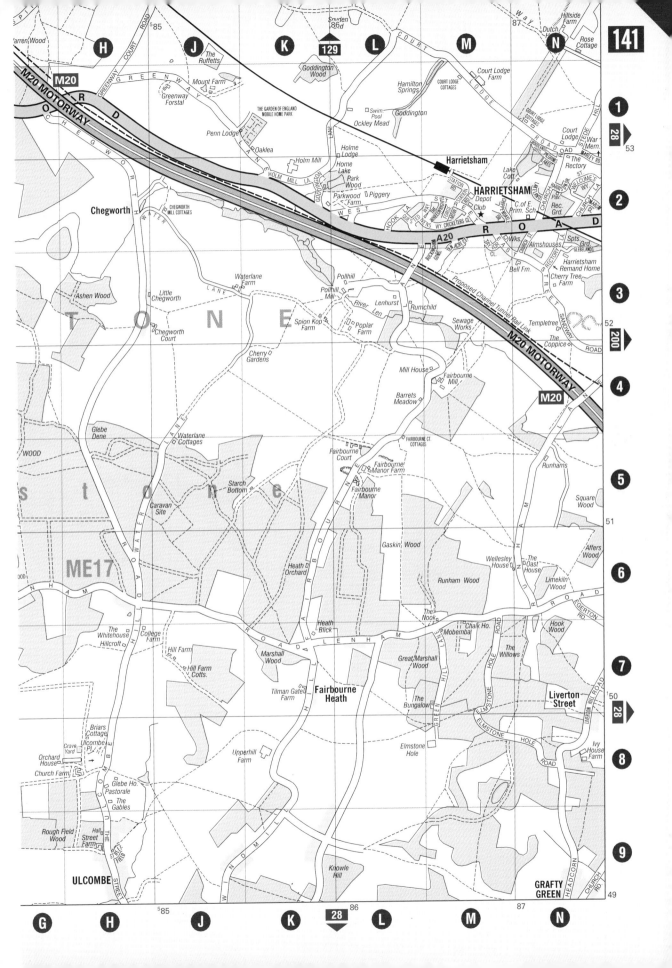

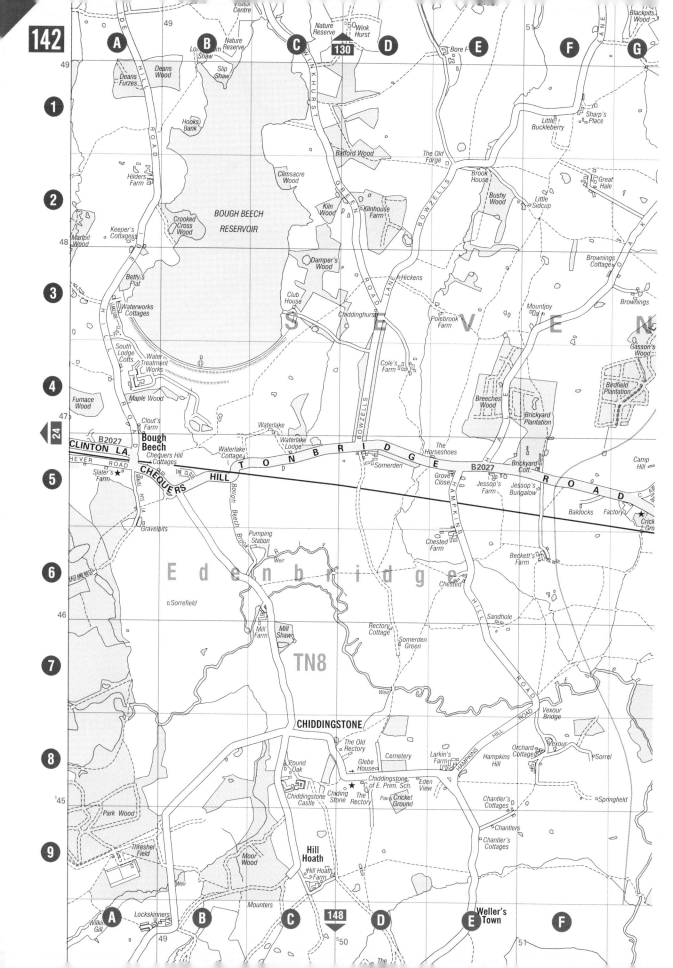

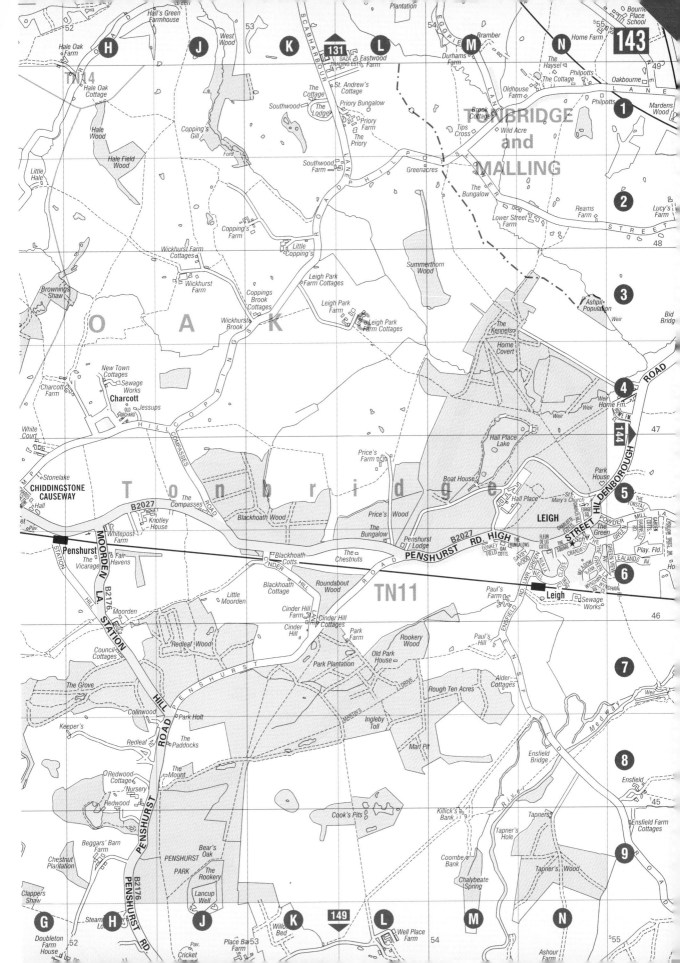

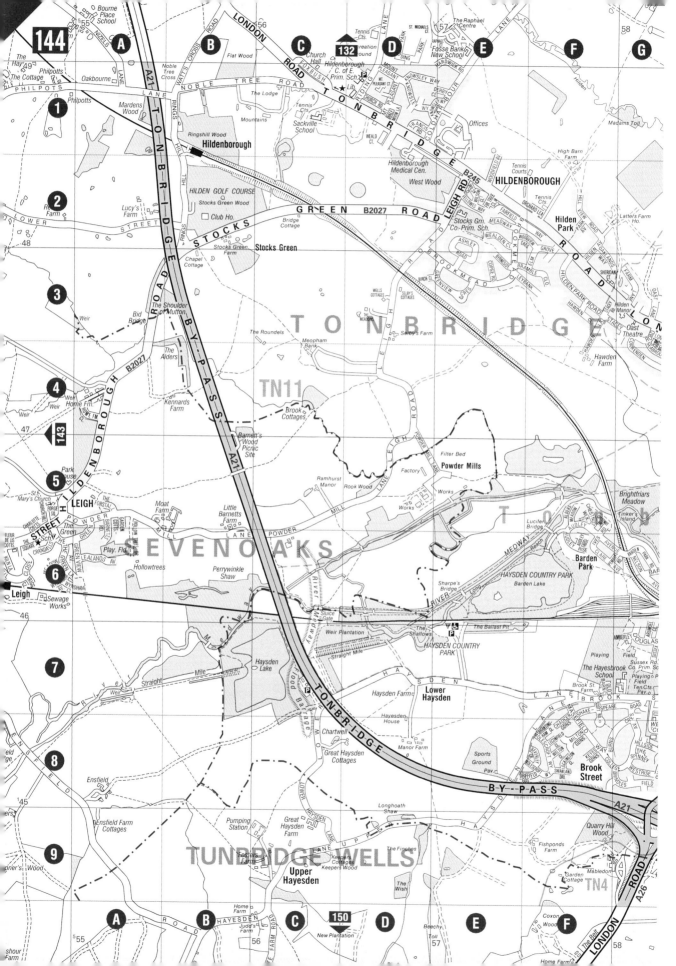

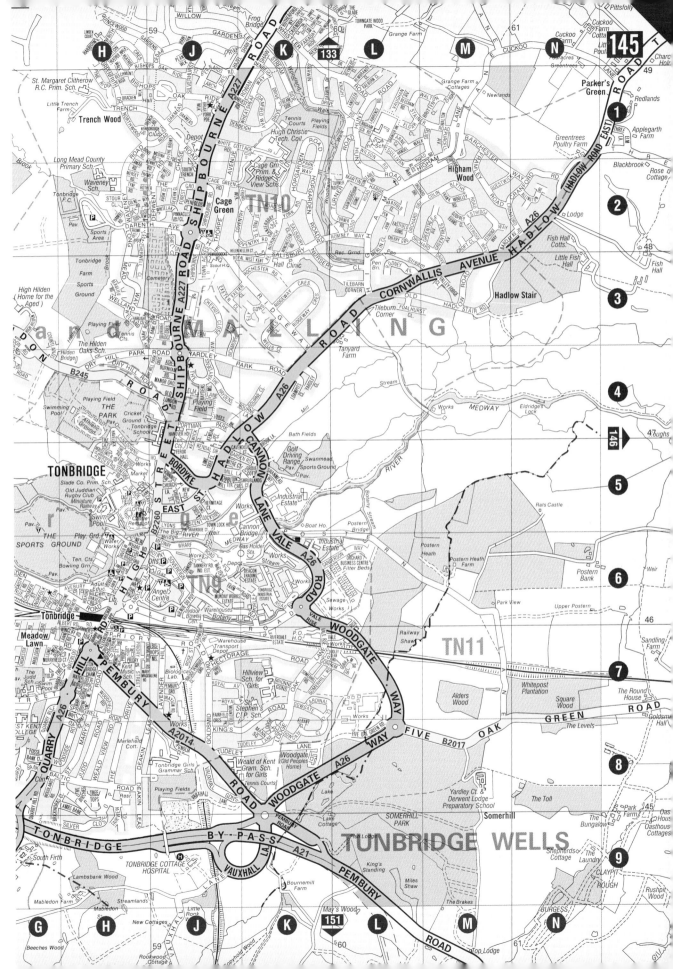

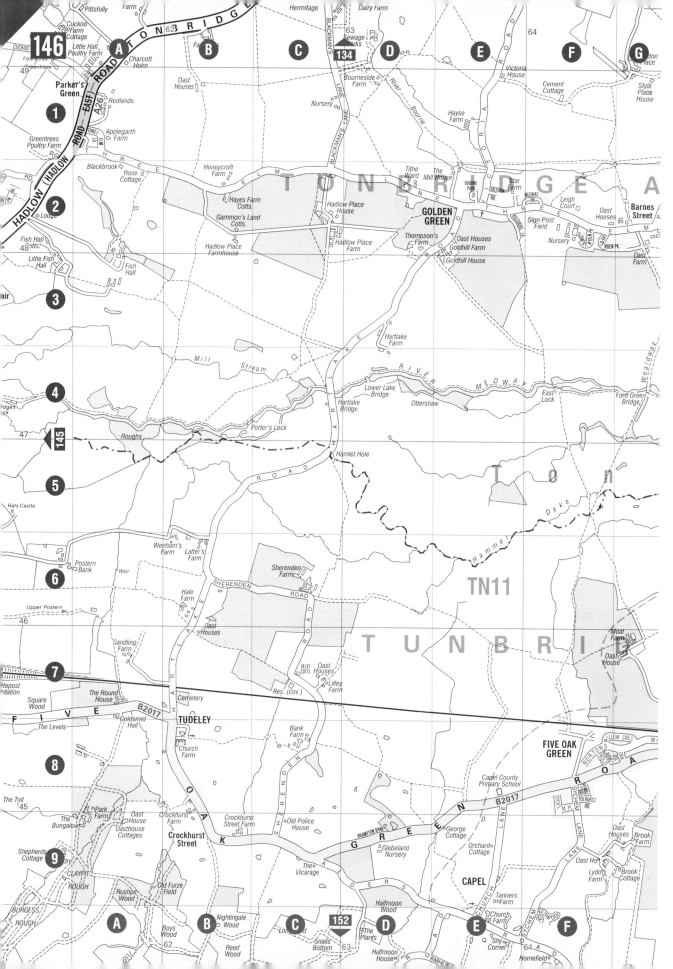

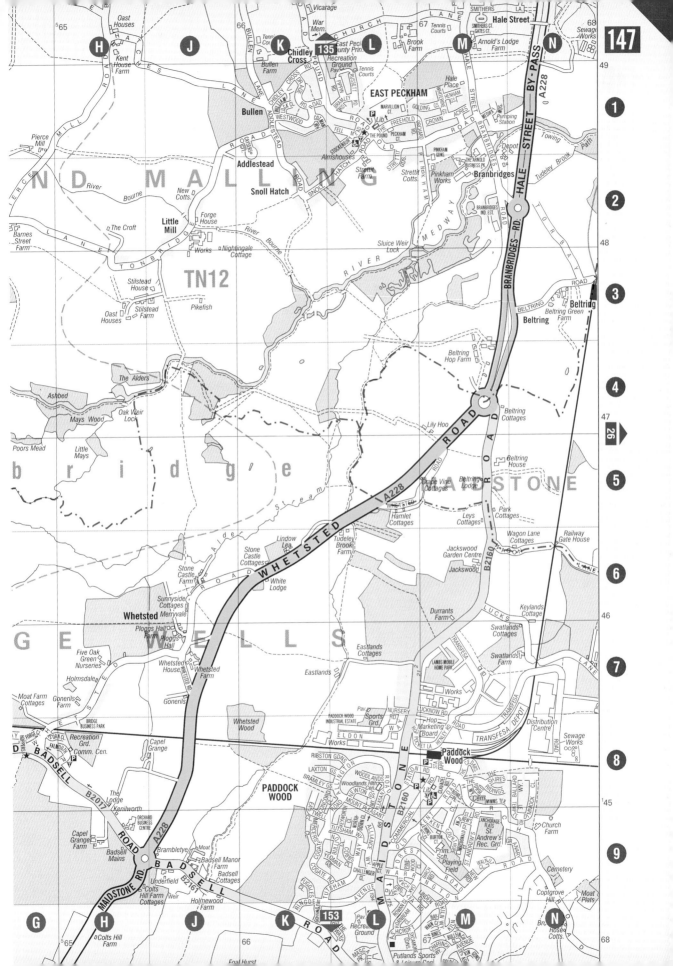

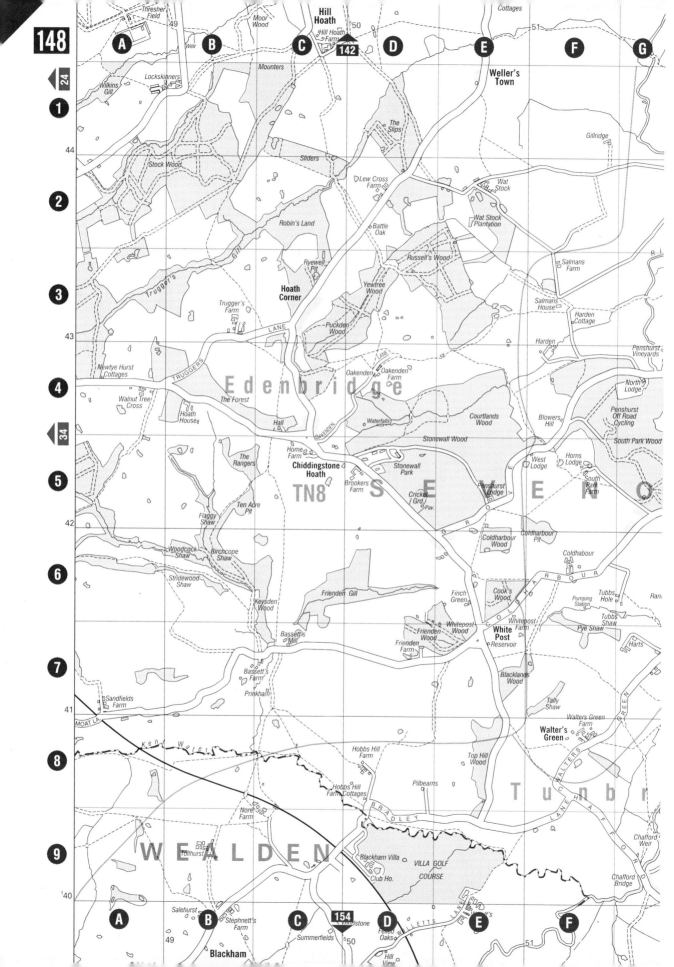

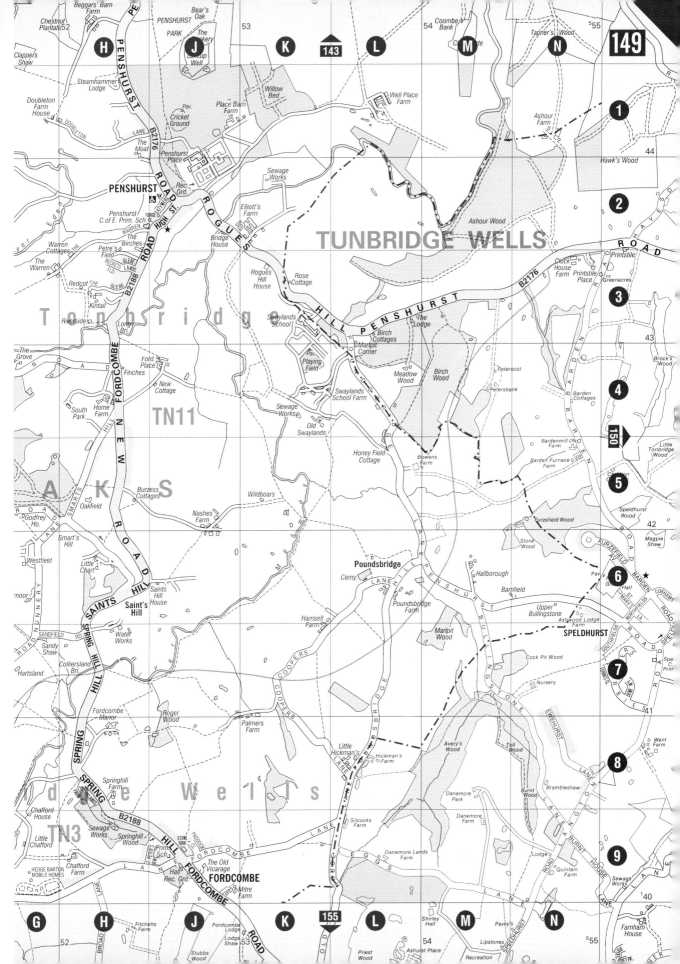

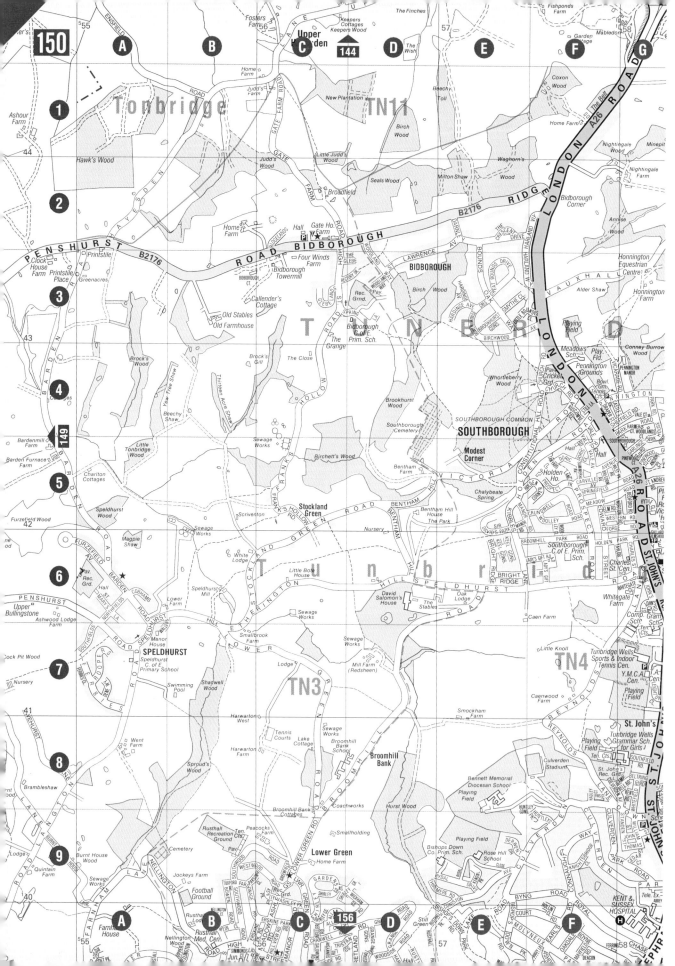

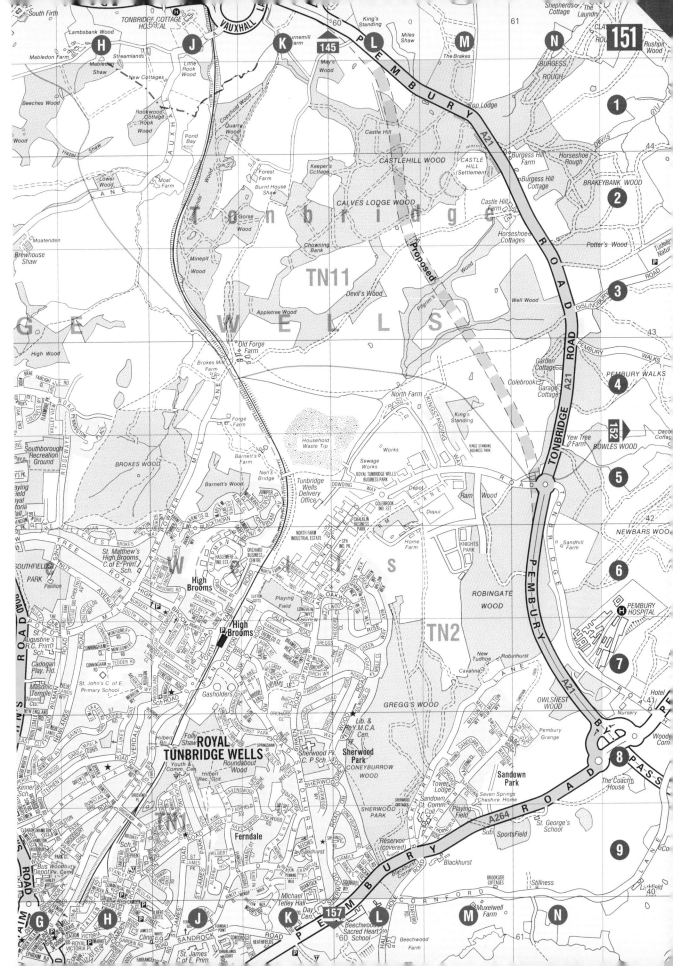

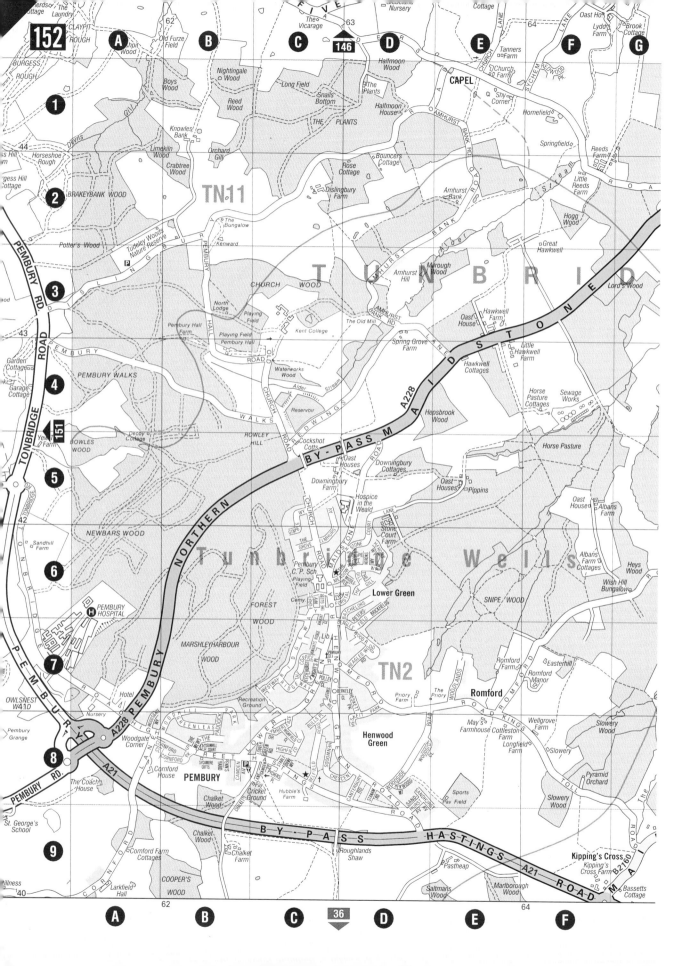

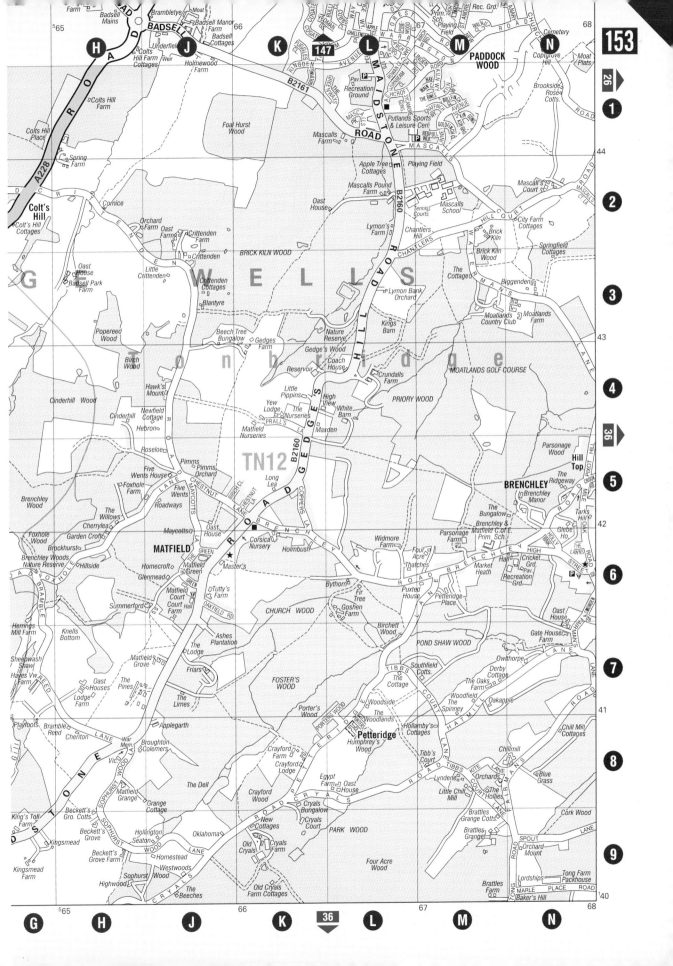

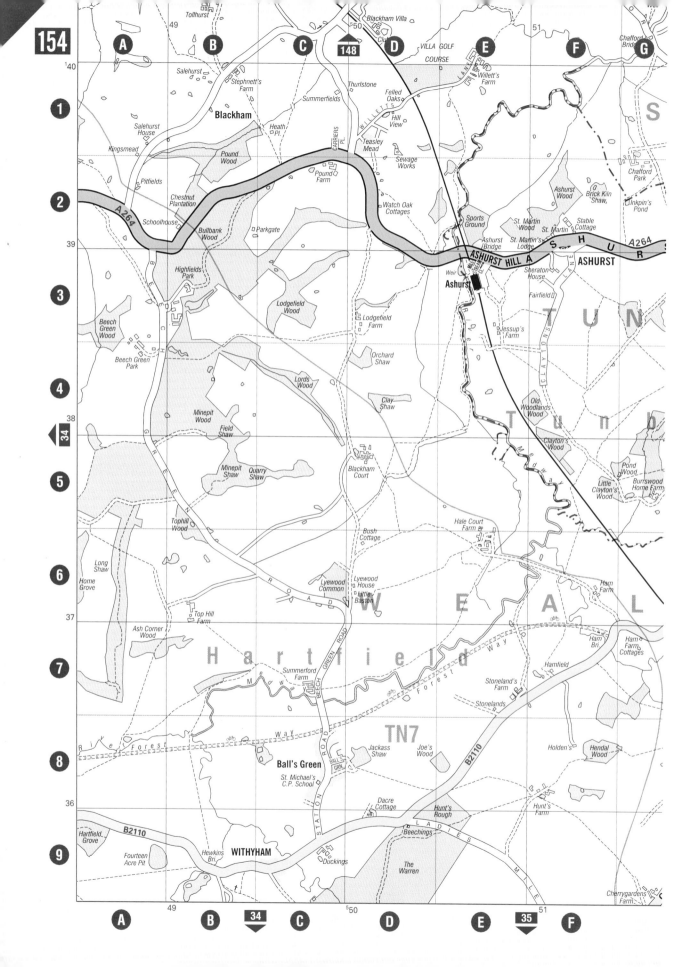

A B C 148 D E F G

1

Tollhurst
Blackham Villa
Club
VILLA GOLF
COURSE
Salehurst
Stephnett's Farm
Thurlstone
Felled Oaks
Willett's Farm
Blackham
Heath Pl.
Summerfields
Hill View
Salehurst House
Teasley Mead
Kingsmead
Pound Wood
Sewage Works
Pitfields
Pound Farm
Watch Oak Cottages
Chestnut Plantation
Ashurst Wood
Brick Kiln Shaw
Chafford Bridge
Chafford Park
Inkpin's Pond

2

A 264
Schoolhouse
Bullbank Wood
Parkgate
Sports Ground
St. Martin Wood
St. Martin
St. Martin
Stable Cottage
A 264

39

Highfields Park
Ashurst Bridge
ASHURST HILL A
ASHURST
Lodgefield Wood
St. Martin's Lodge
Sheraton House
Weir
Fairfield

3

Ashurst
Beech Green Wood
Lodgefield Farm
Jessup's Farm
TUN

Beech Green Park
Orchard Shaw
Old Woodlands Wood

4

38

Lords Wood
Clay Shaw
Tunb

34
Minepit Wood
Field Shaw
Clayton's Wood

5

Minepit Shaw
Quarry Shaw
Blackham Court
Pond Wood
Little Clayton's Wood
Burrswood Home Farm

Tophill Wood

6

Long Shaw
Home Grove
Bush Cottage
Hale Court Farm
Ham Farm

37

Lyewood Common
Lyewood House
Little Baston
W E A L
Ham Bri.
Ham Farm Cottages

Top Hill Farm

7

Ash Corner Wood
Summerford Farm
Hamfield
Stoneland's Farm
Hendal Wood
Stonelands
H a r t f i e l d
Forest Way

8

Ball's Green
Jackass Shaw
Joe's Wood
Holden's
TN7
B2110
River Forest
St. Michael's C.P. School

36

Dacre Cottage
Hunt's Rough
Hunt's Farm

9

Hartfield Grove
B2110
Fourteen Acre Pit
Hewkins Bri.
WITHYHAM
Duckings
Beechings
The Warren
Cherrygardens Farm

A 49 B 34 C 50 D E 35 F 51

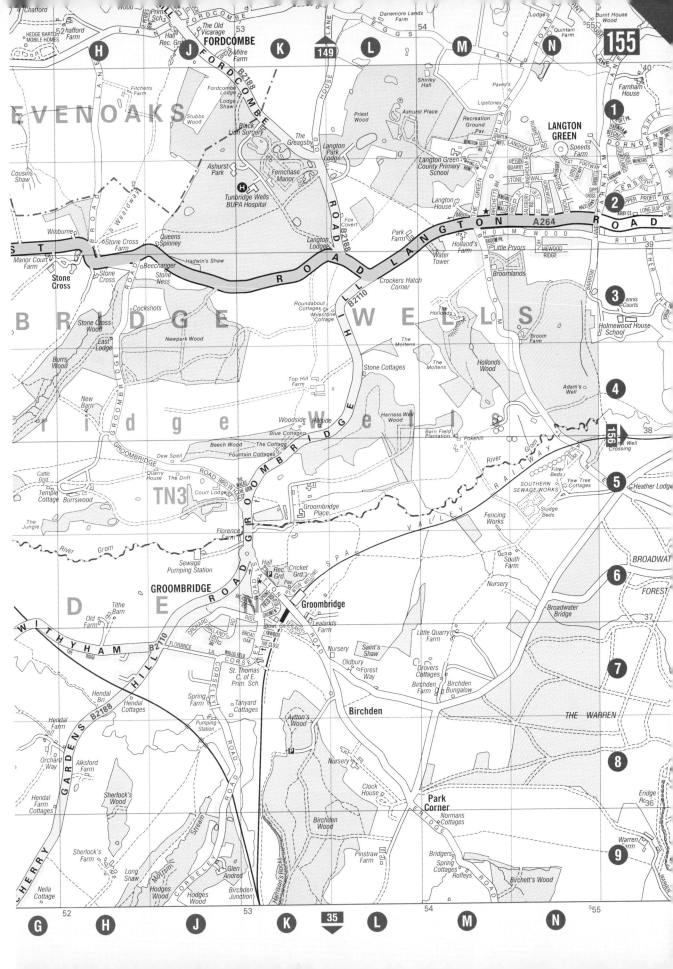

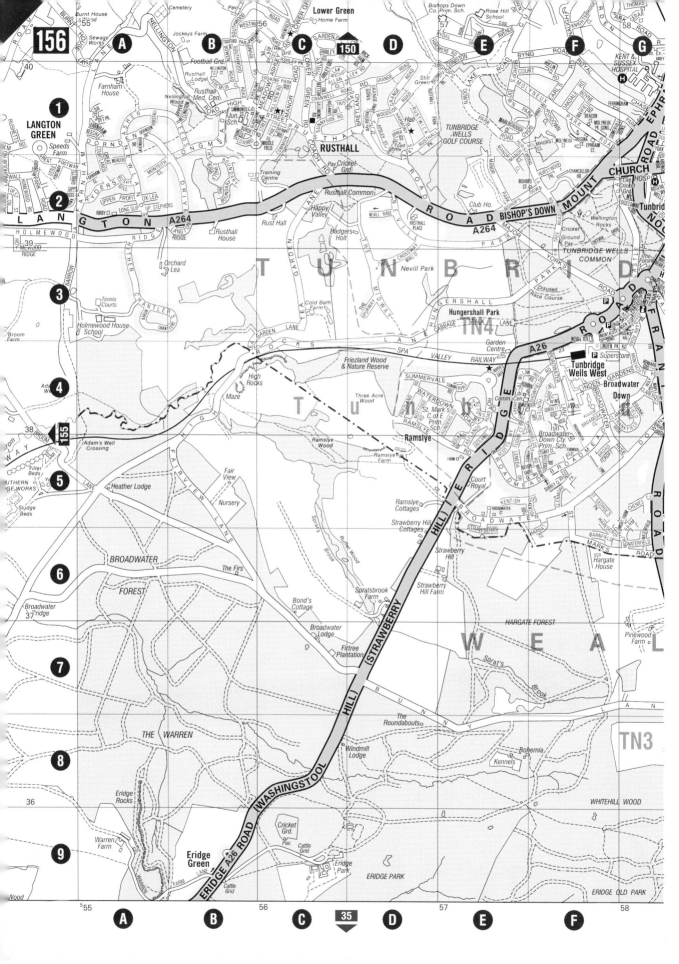

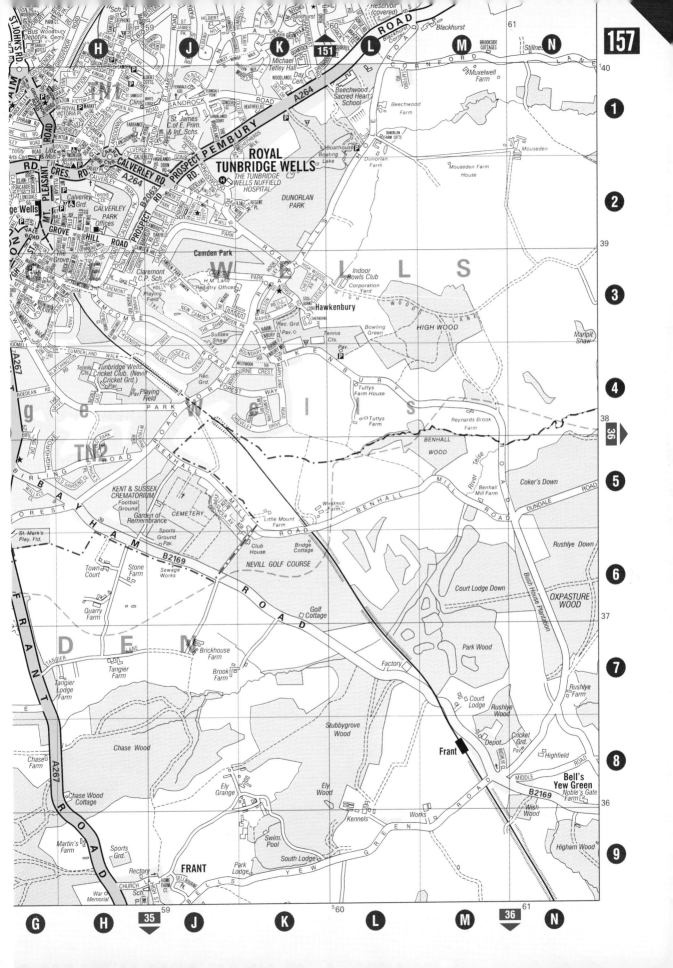

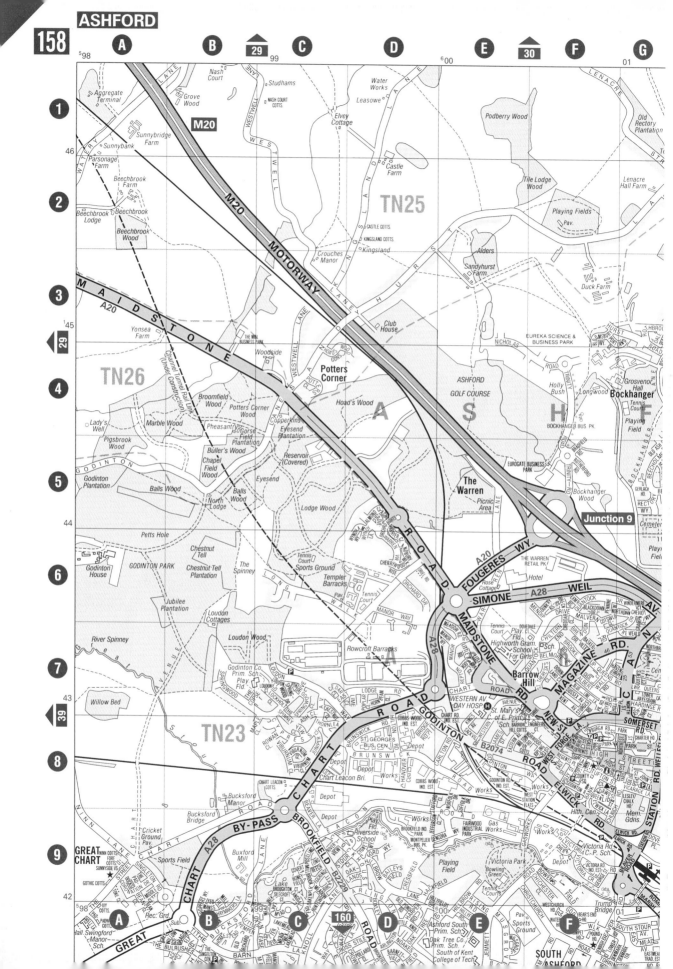

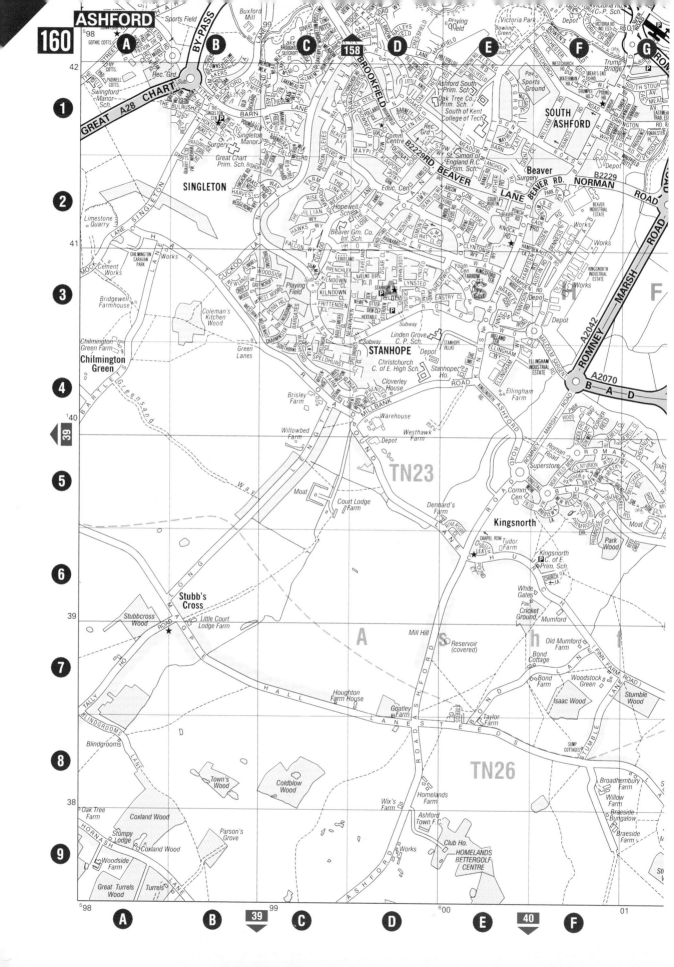

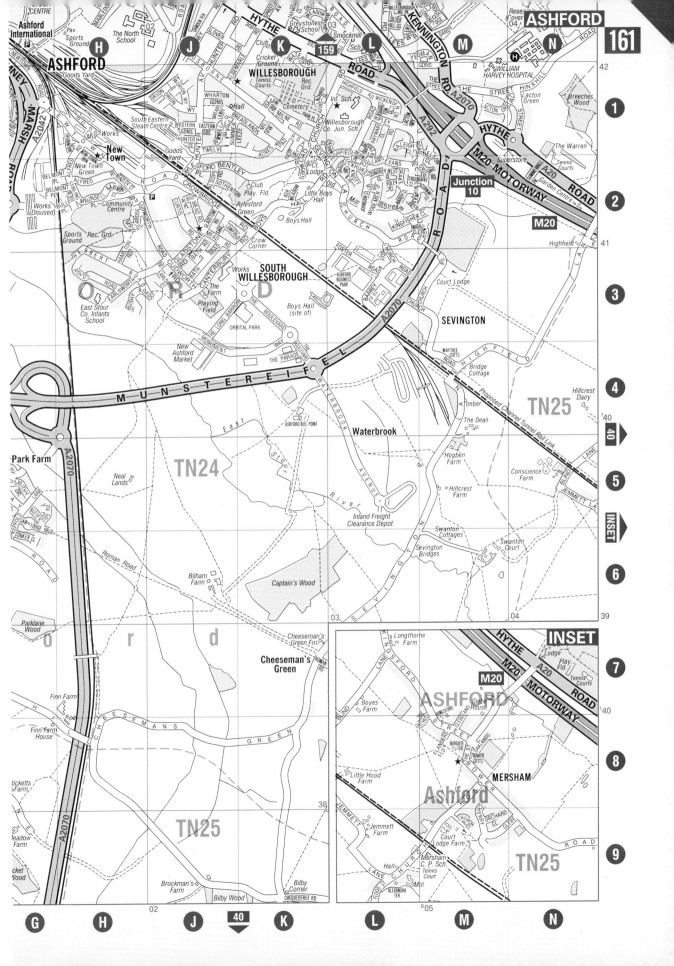

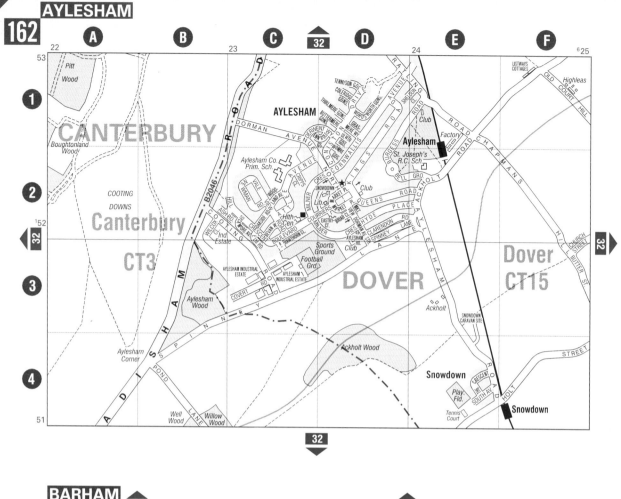

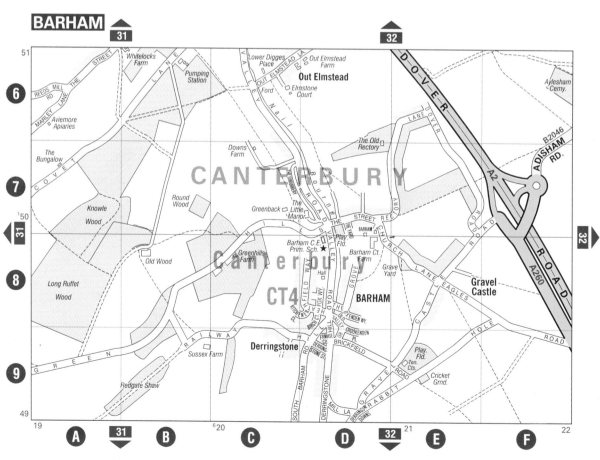

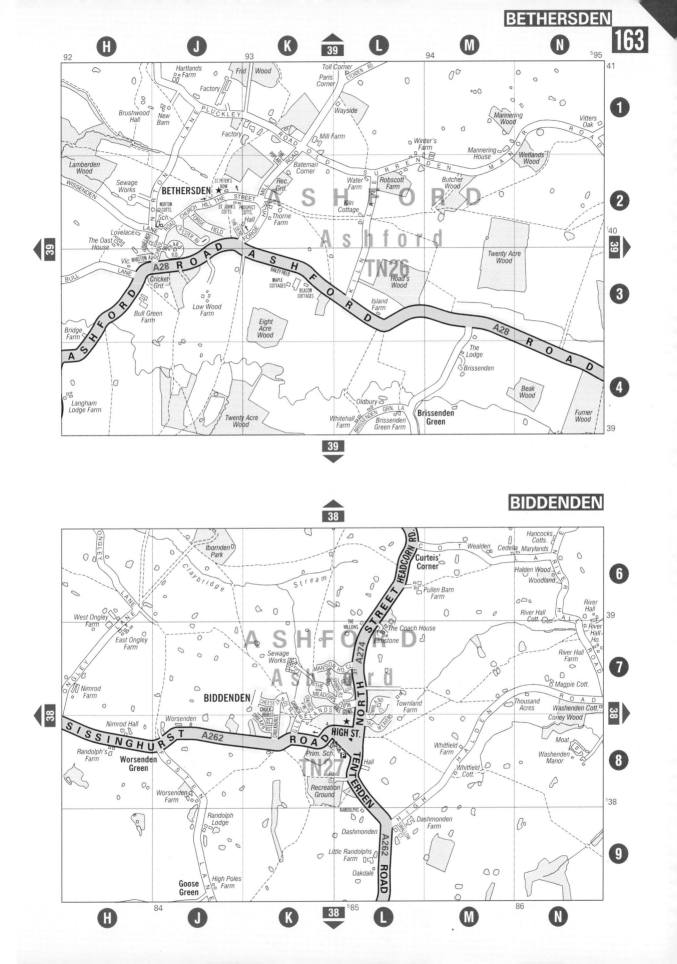

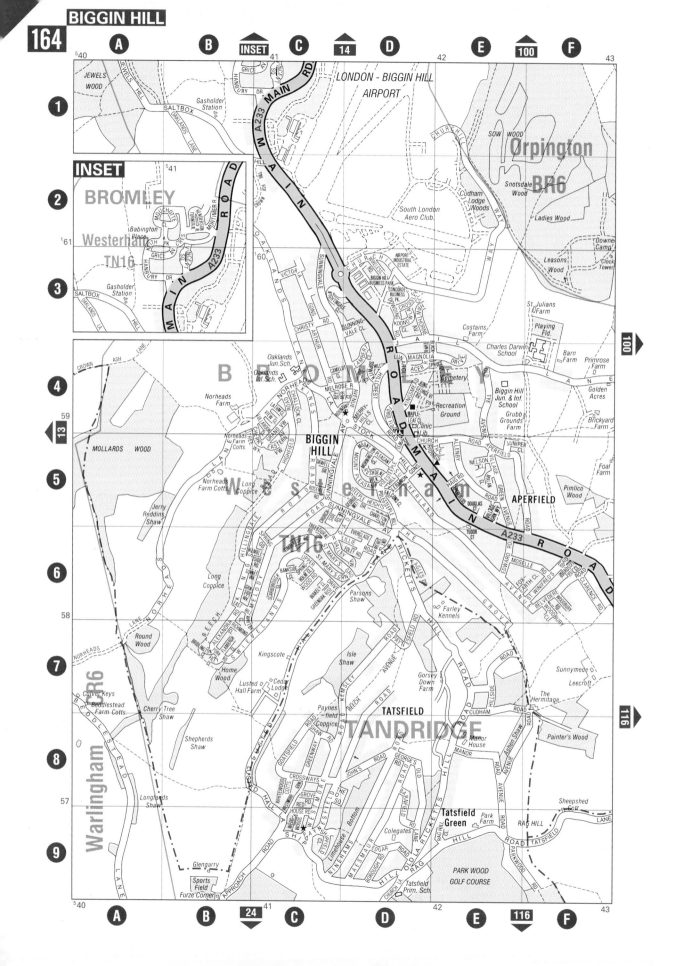

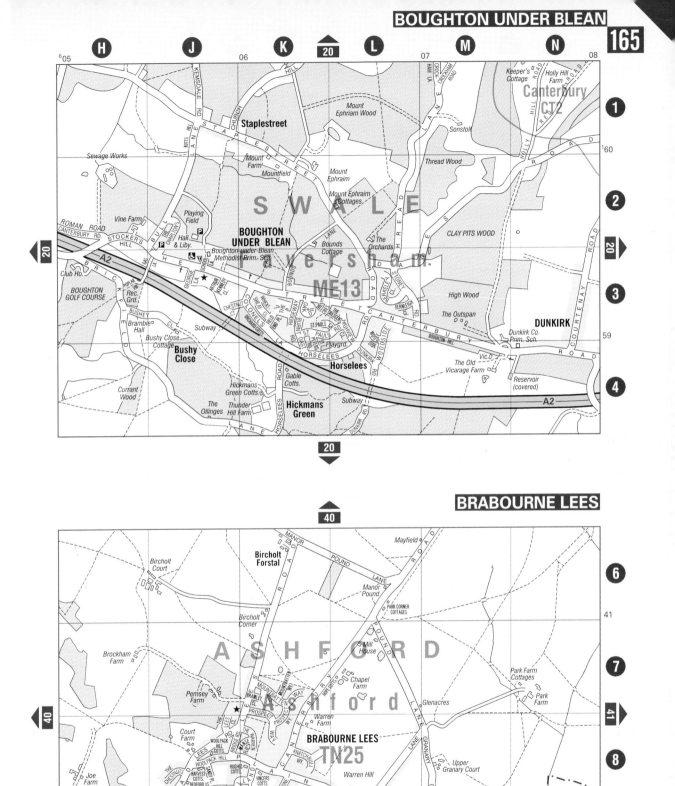

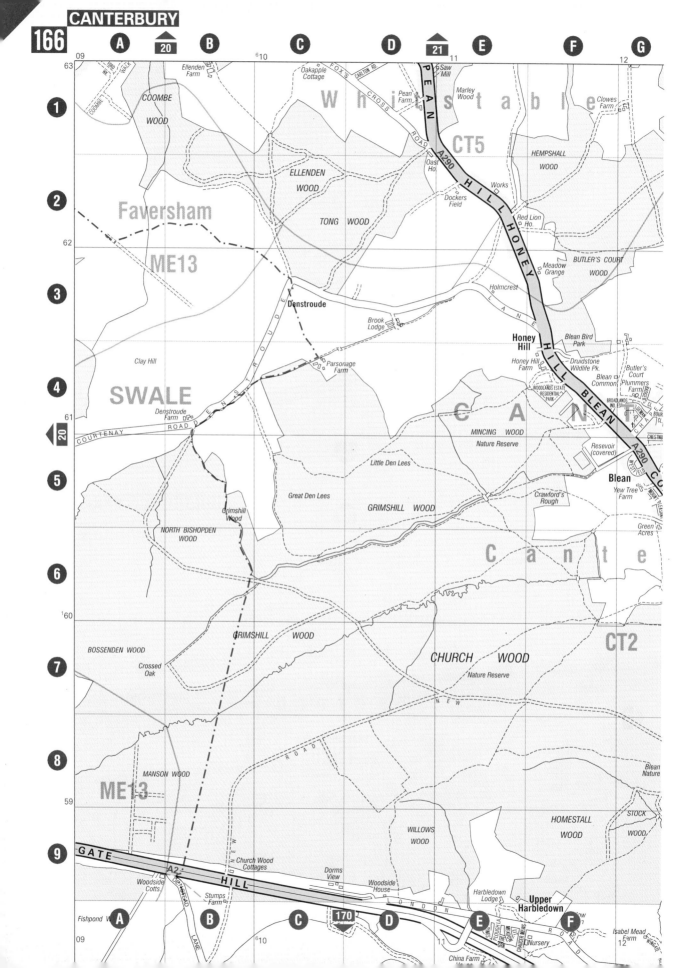

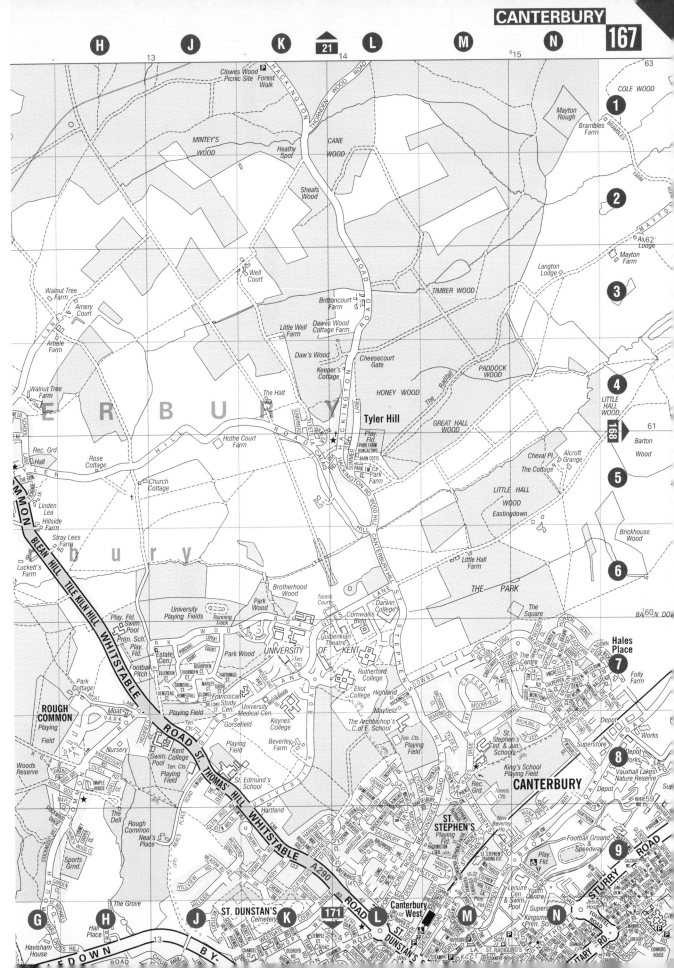

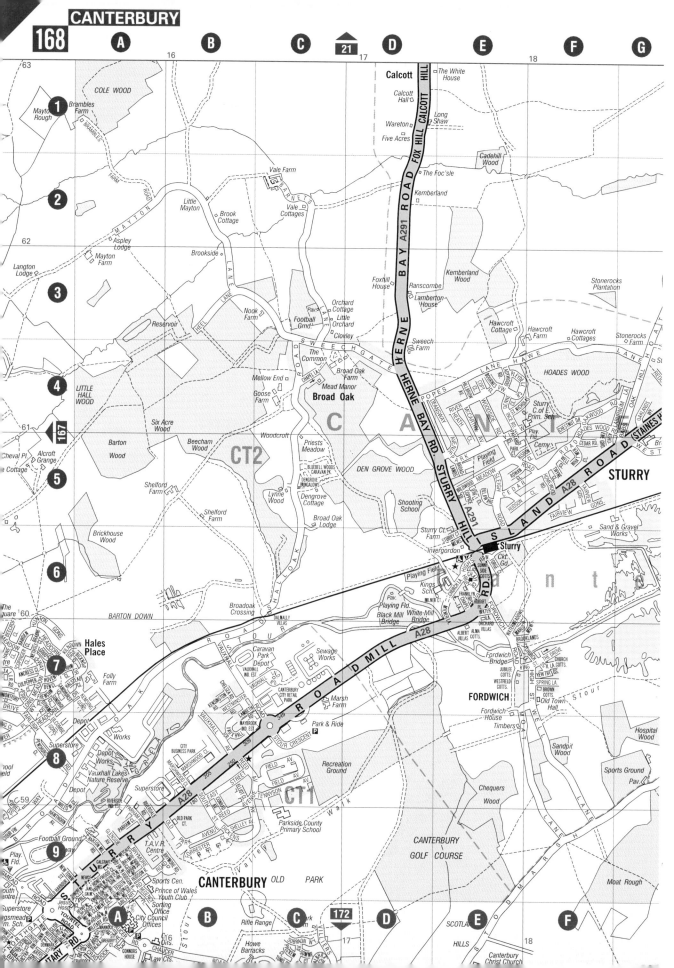

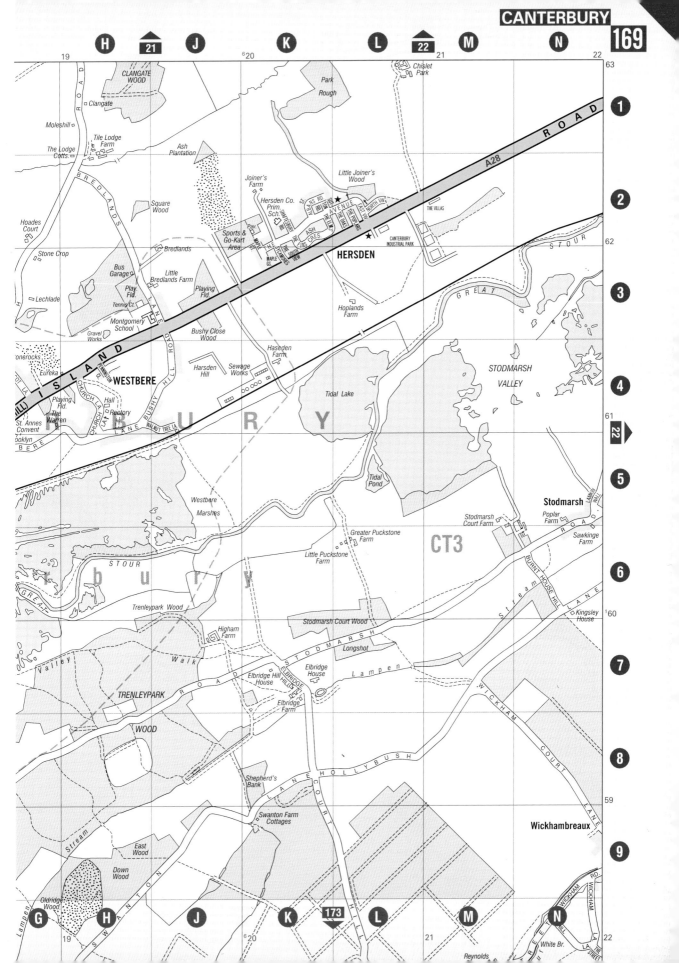

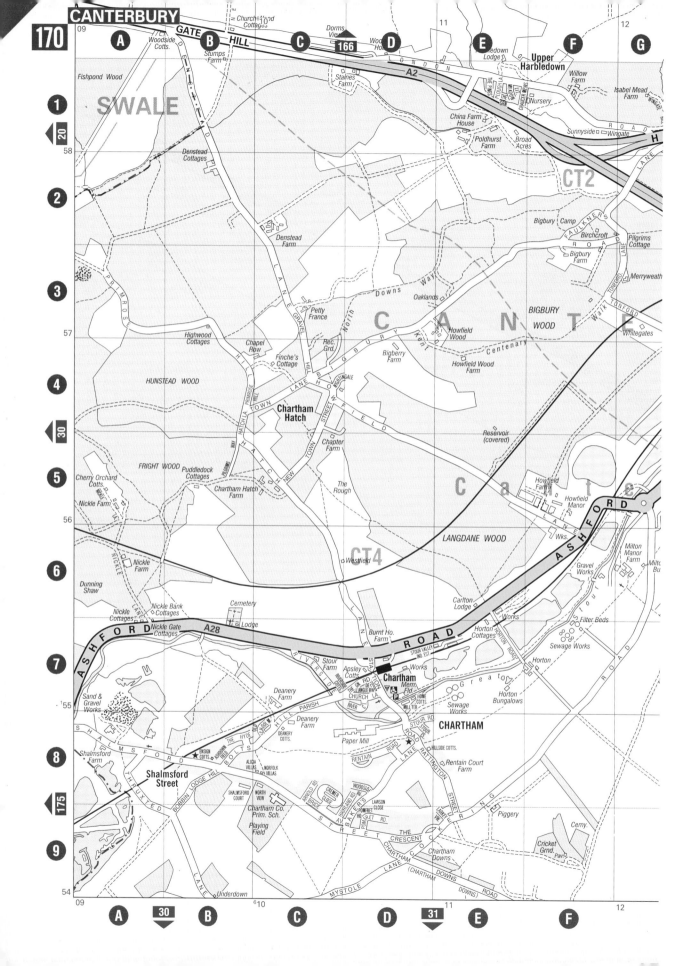

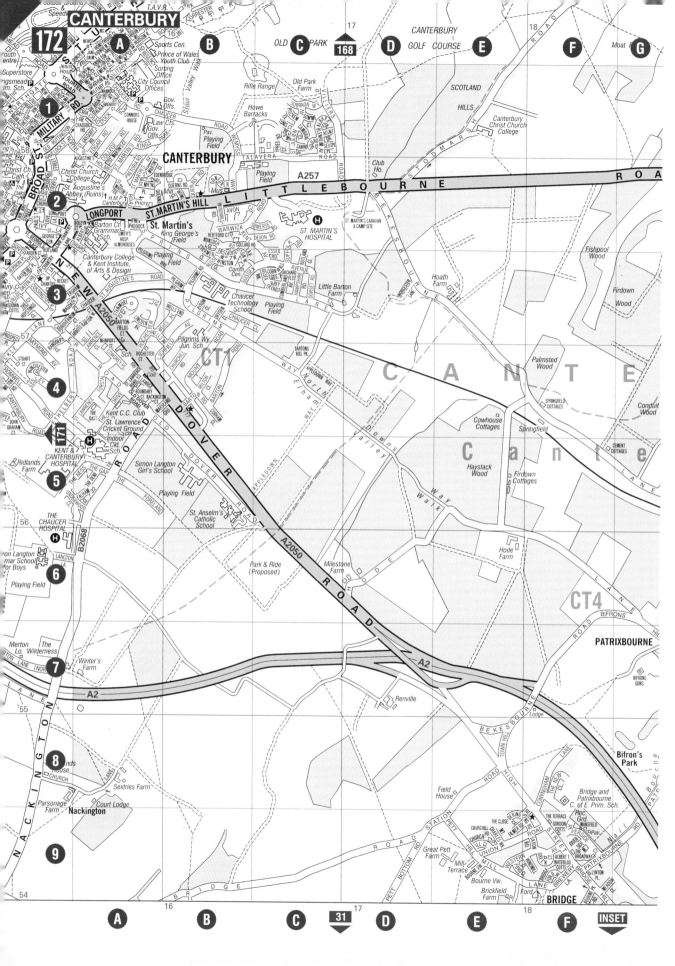

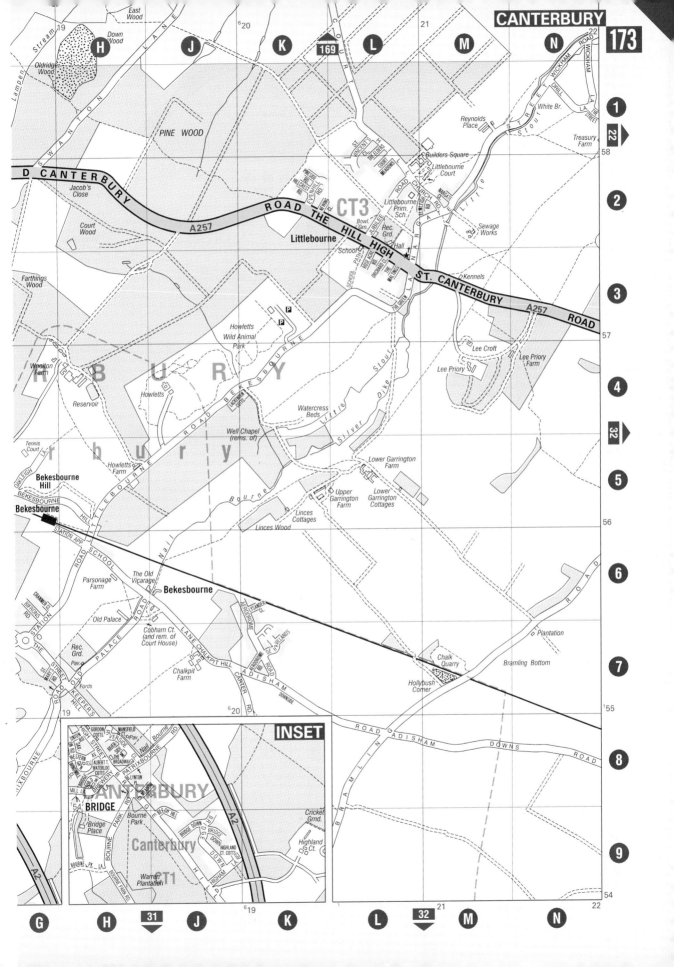

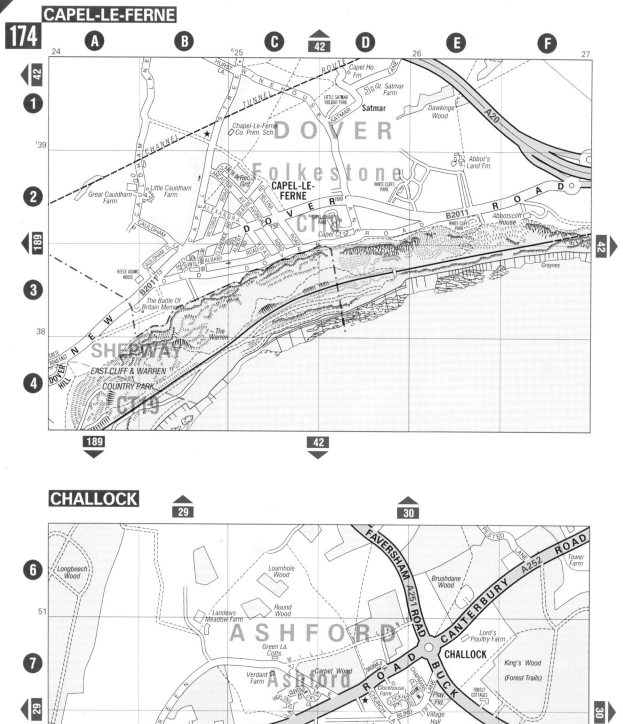

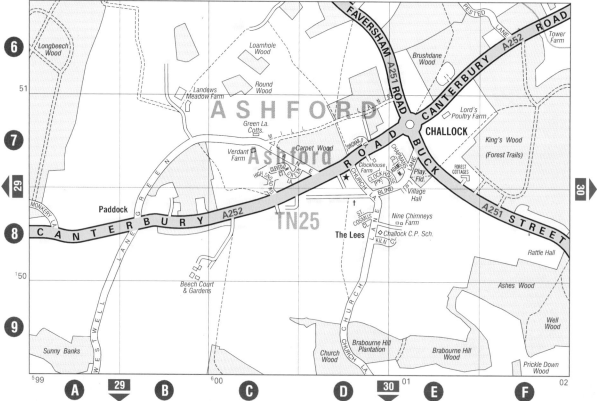

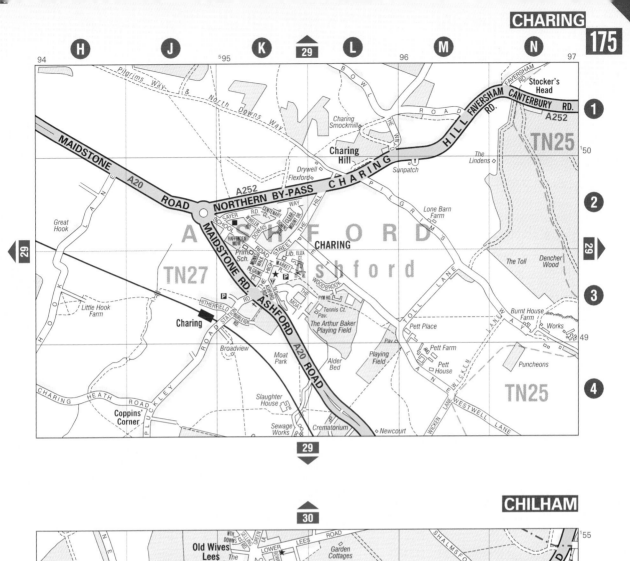

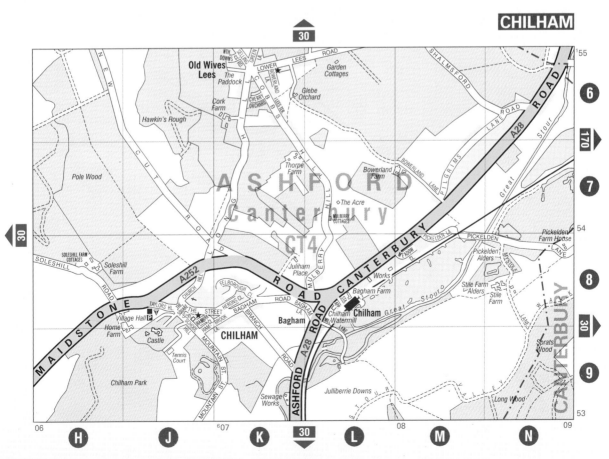

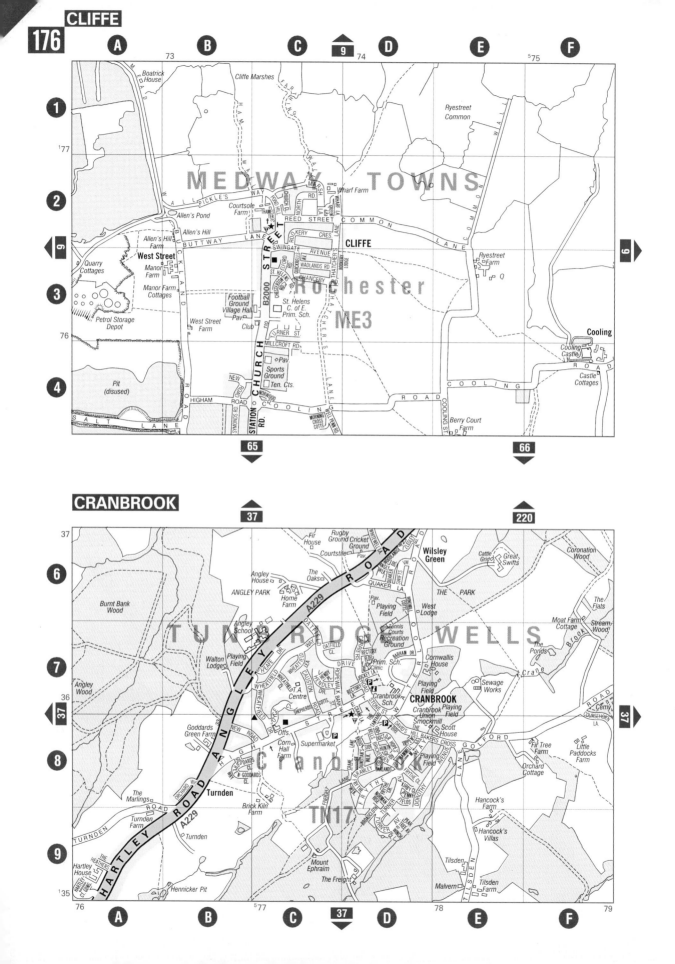

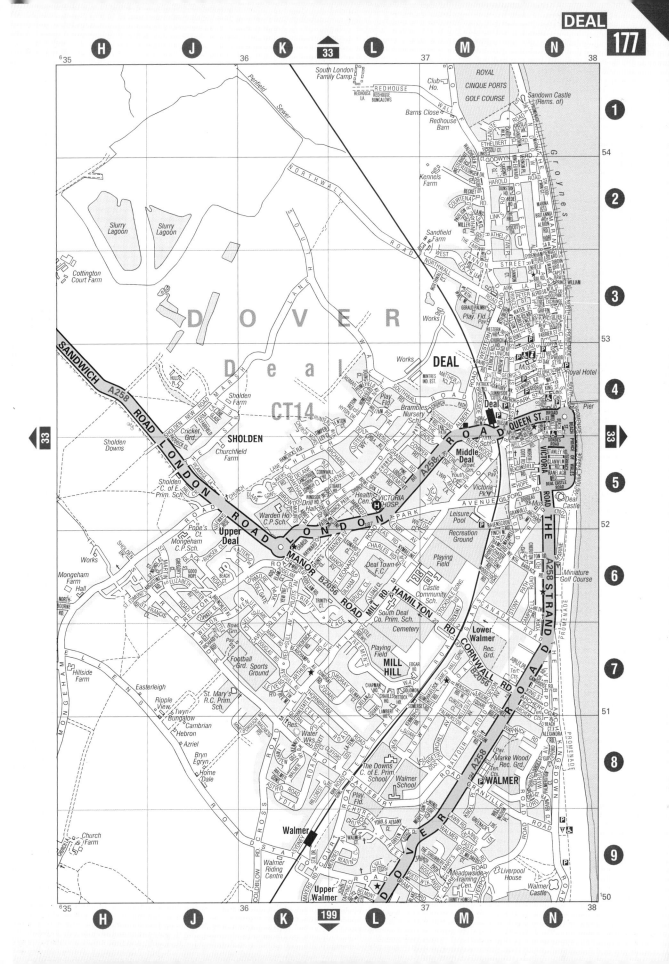

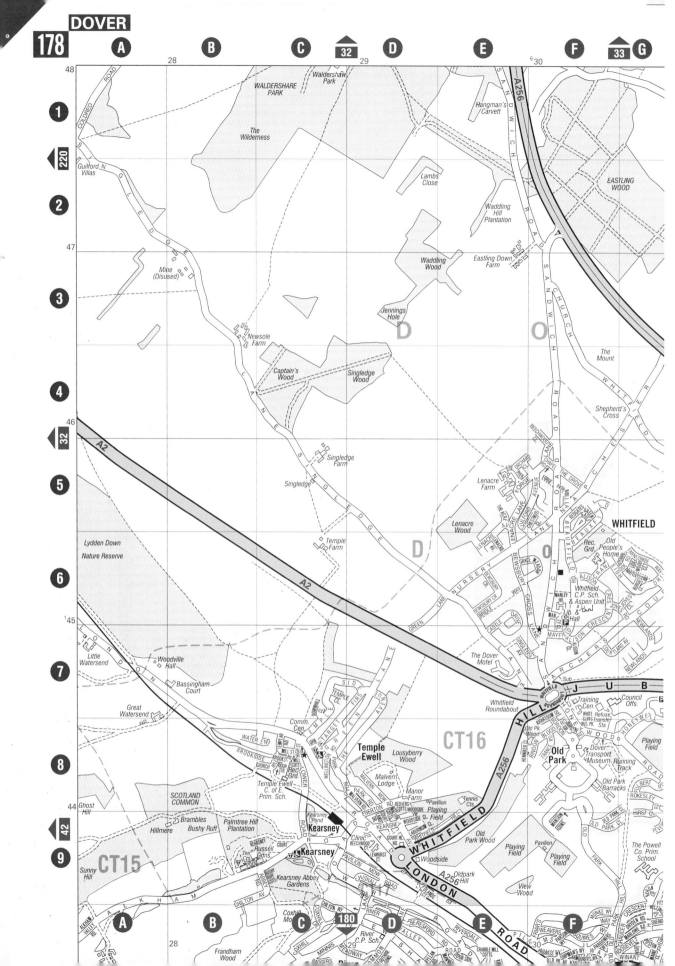

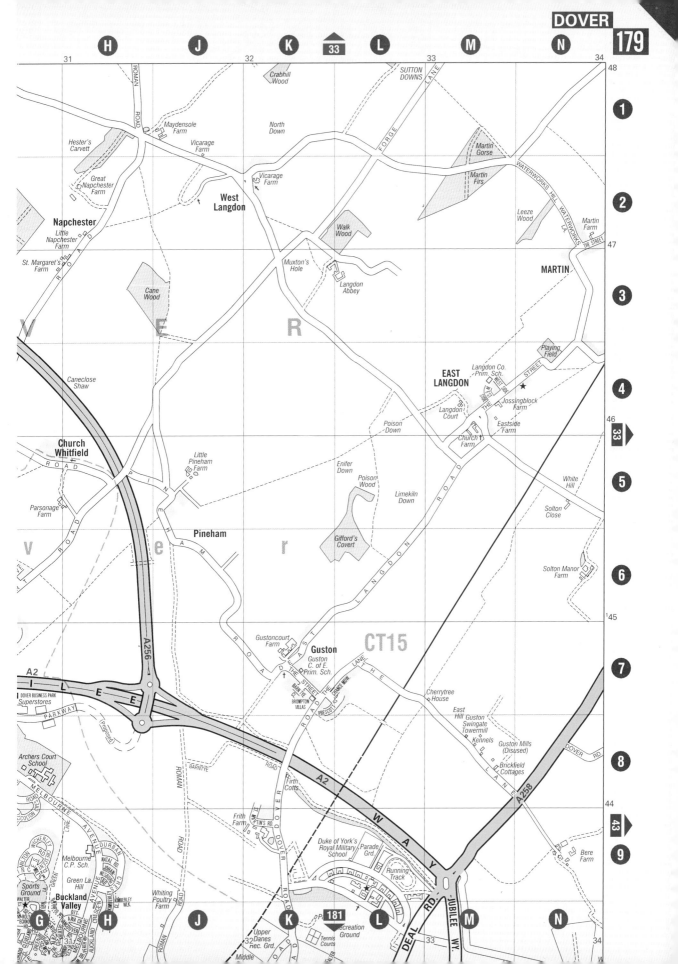

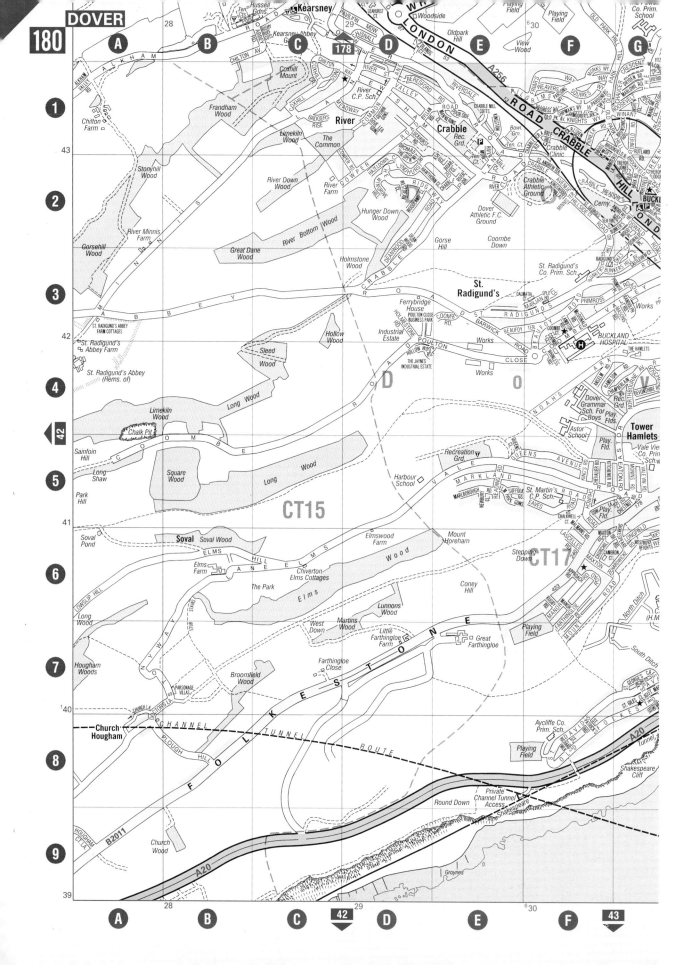

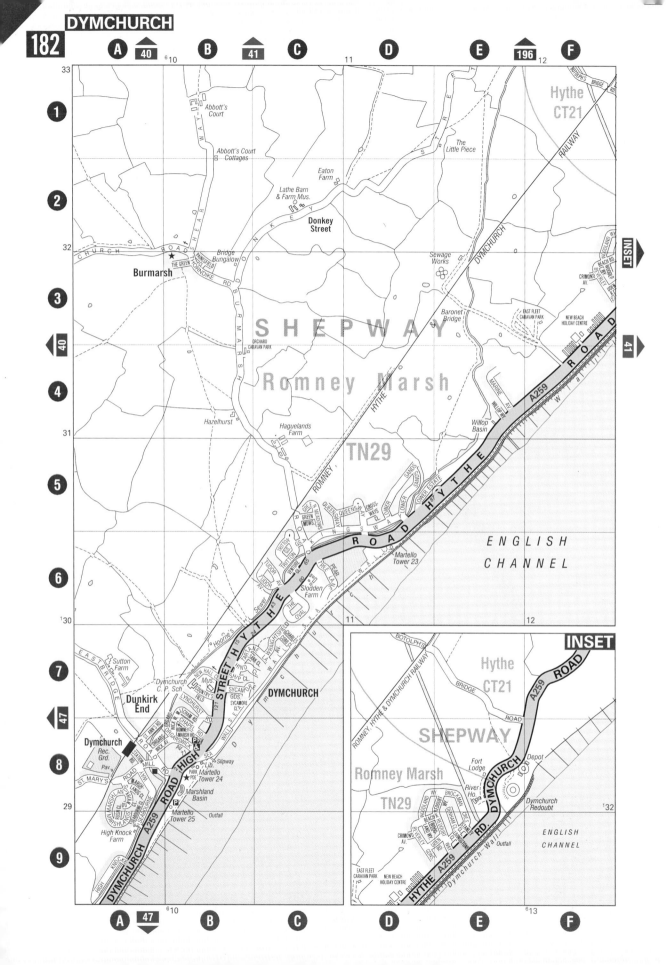

Hythe CT21

Abbott's Court

Abbott's Court Cottages

The Little Piece

Eaton Farm

Lathe Barn & Farm Mus.

Donkey Street

Bridge Bungalow

Burmarsh

THE GREEN

Sewage Works

Baronet Bridge

EAST FLEET CARAVAN PARK

NEW BEACH HOLIDAY CENTRE

CRIMOND AV.

BEACH RD.

INSET

SHEPWAY

Romney Marsh

ORCHARD CARAVAN PARK

Hazelhurst

Haguelands Farm

TN29

ROMNEY

WILLOP BASIN

Willop Basin

MARINE AV.

A259

ROAD

ROAD HYTHE

ENGLISH CHANNEL

GREEN MEADOWS

QUEENSWAY

TOWER ESTATE

Martello Tower 23

Slodden Farm

STREET HYTHE

DYMCHURCH

Dunkirk End

Dymchurch C.P. Sch

Sutton Farm

EASTBRIDGE

Dymchurch Rec. Grd.

St Mary's

High Knock Farm

DYMCHURCH A259

Martello Tower 24

Marshland Basin

Outfall

Martello Tower 25

HIGH ROAD

Lib.

PARK

Slipway

INSET

Hythe CT21

BOTOLPH'S

BRIDGE

ROAD

A259 ROAD

ROMNEY, HYTHE & DYMCHURCH RAILWAY

SHEPWAY

Romney Marsh

TN29

Fort Lodge

River Ho.

DYMCHURCH

Depot

Dymchurch Redoubt

ENGLISH CHANNEL

WOODLAND

BEACH RD.

CRIMOND AV.

REDOUBT

EAST FLEET CARAVAN PARK

NEW BEACH HOLIDAY CENTRE

HYTHE A259 RD.

Dymchurch Wall

Outfall

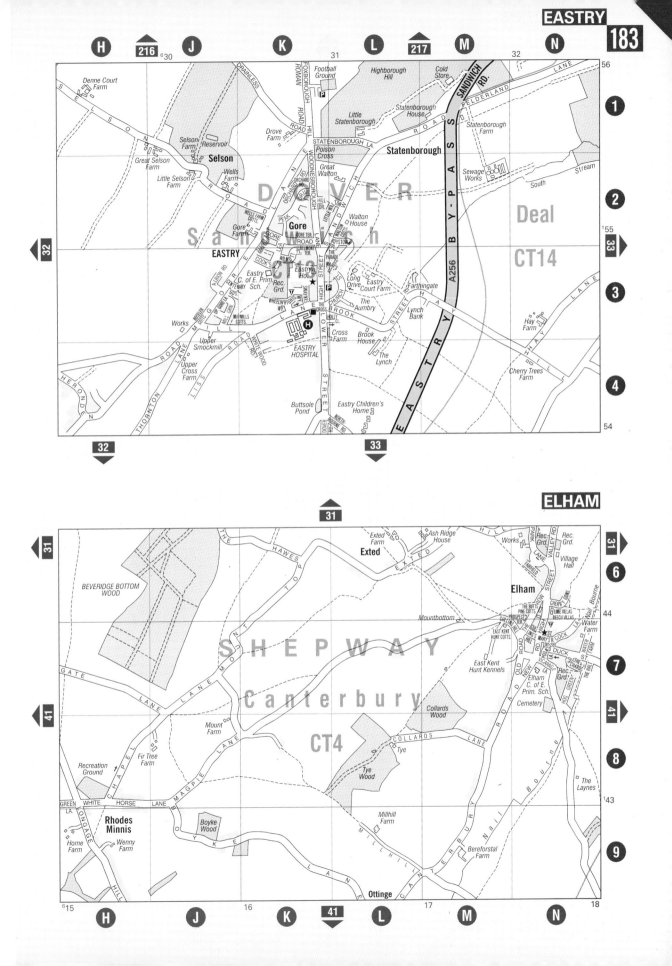

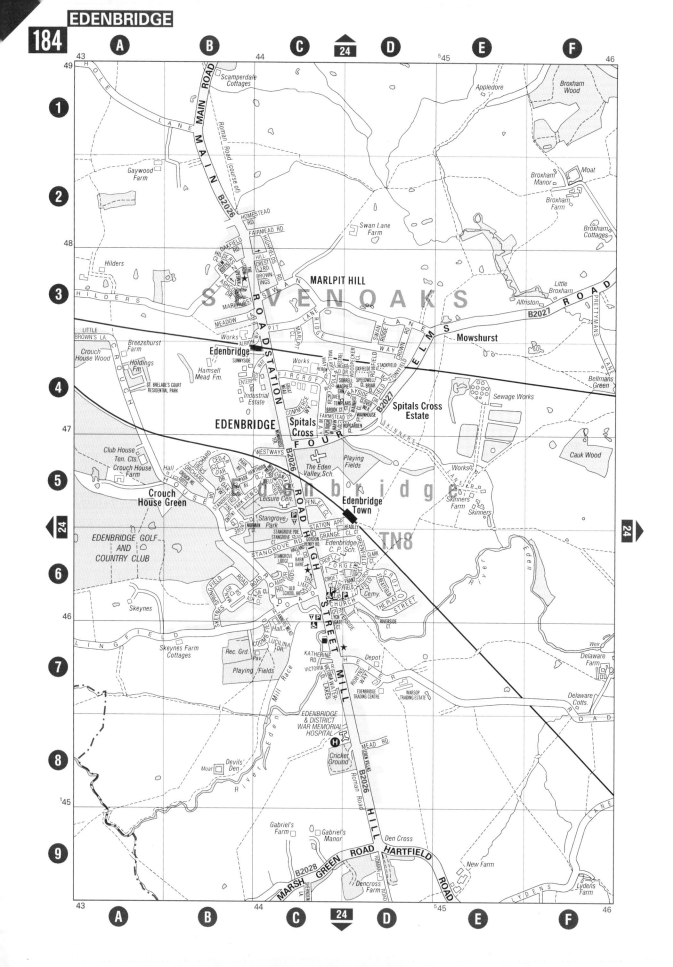

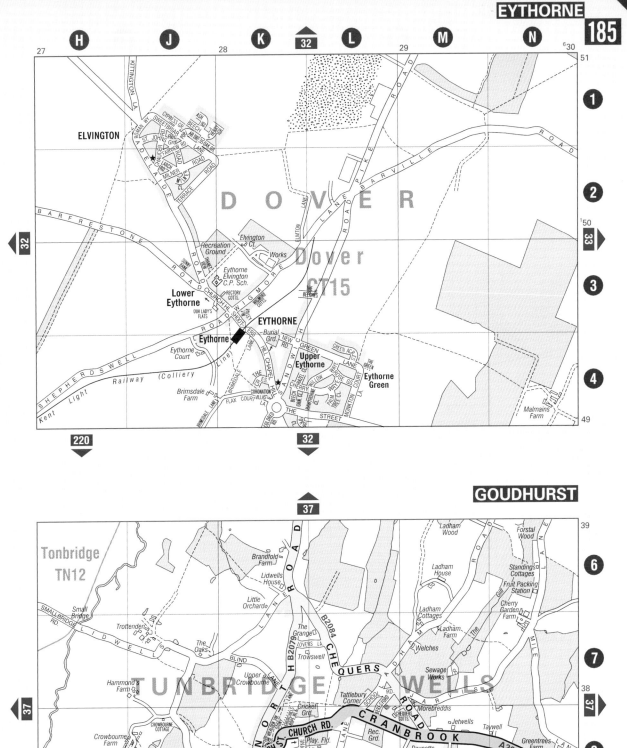

GOUDHURST

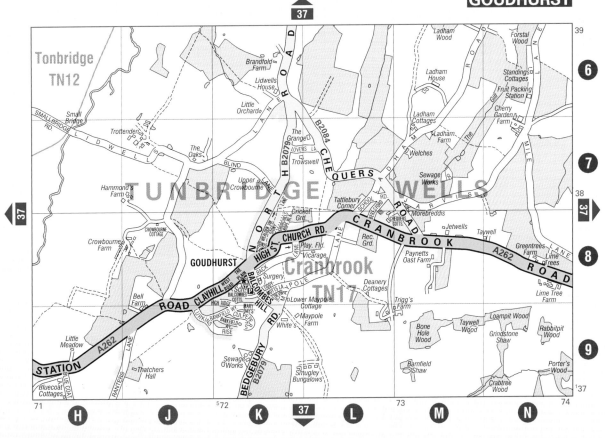

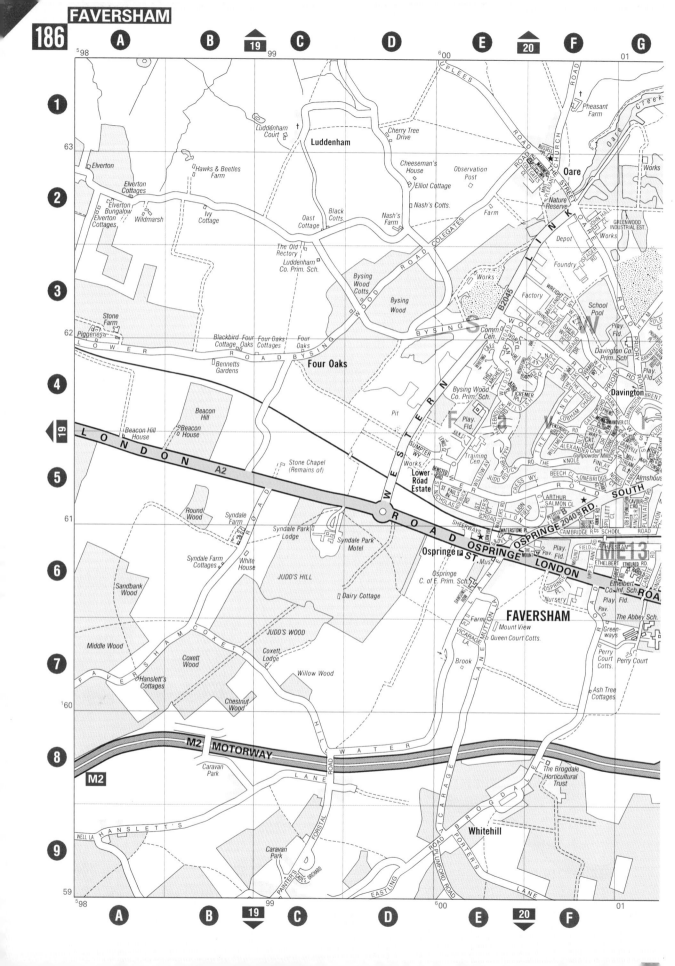

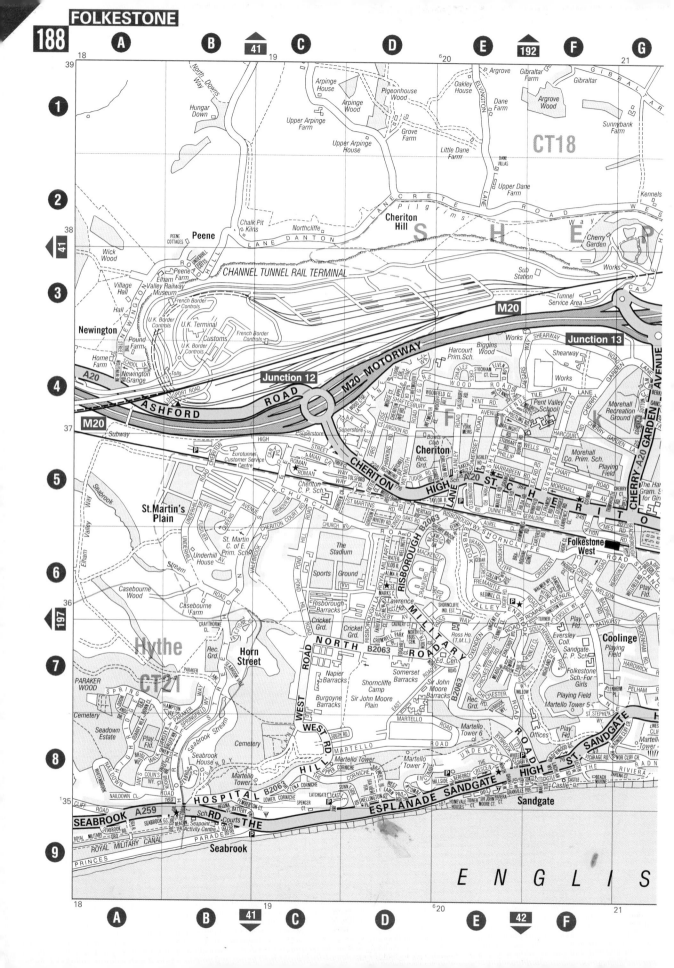

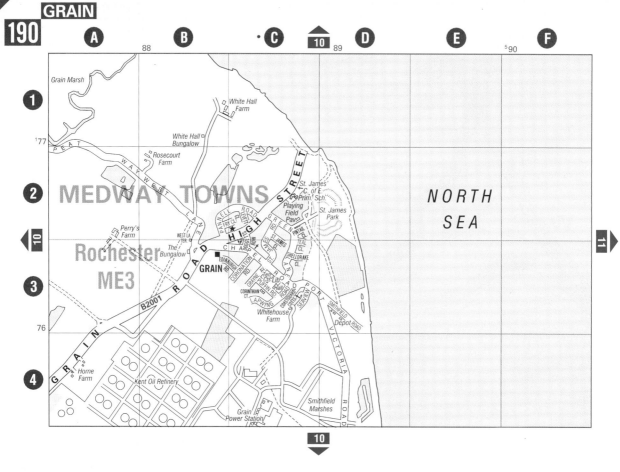

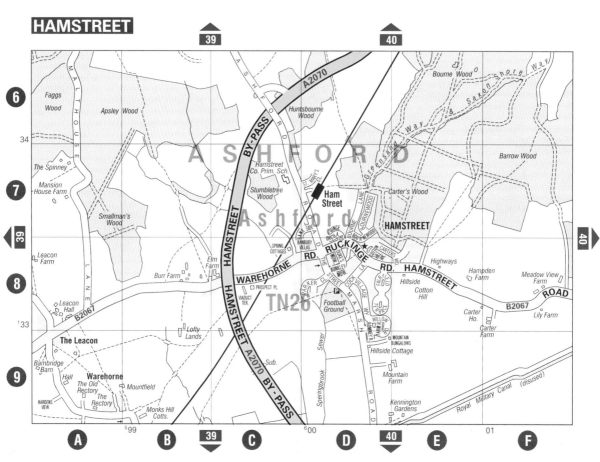

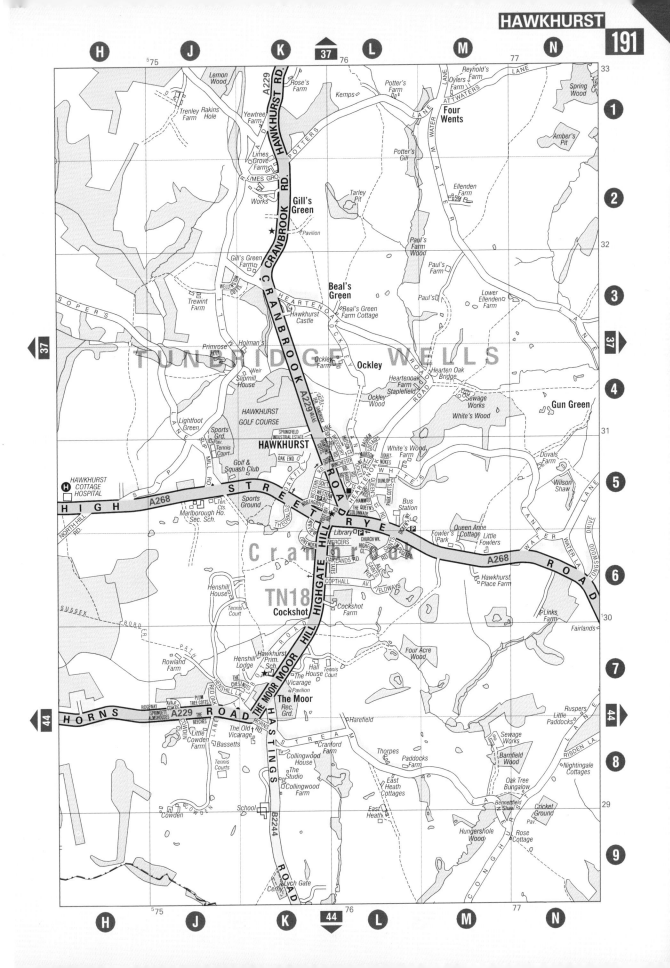

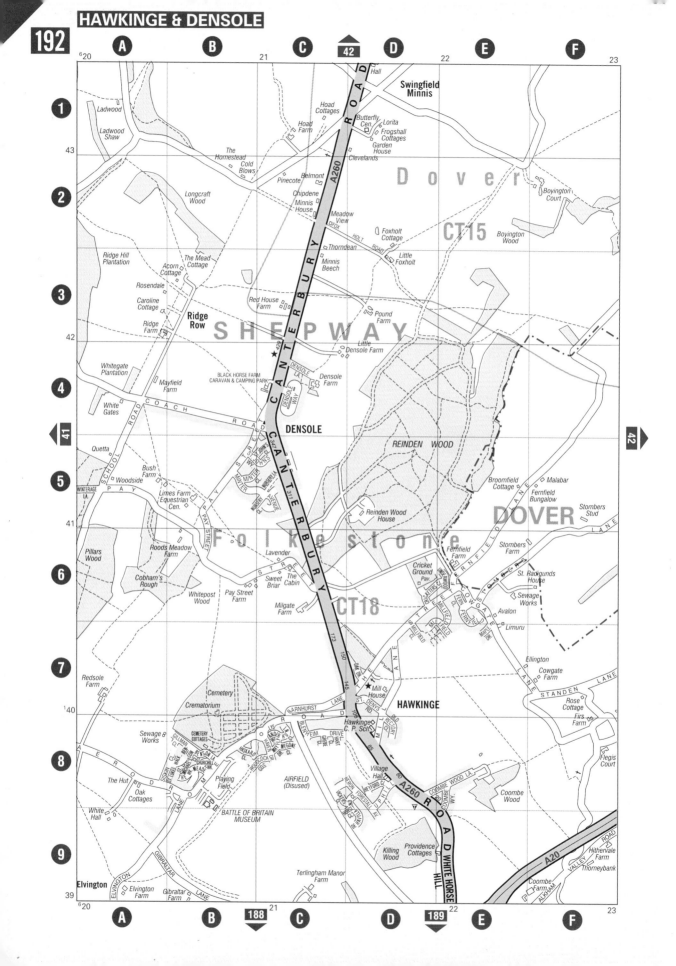

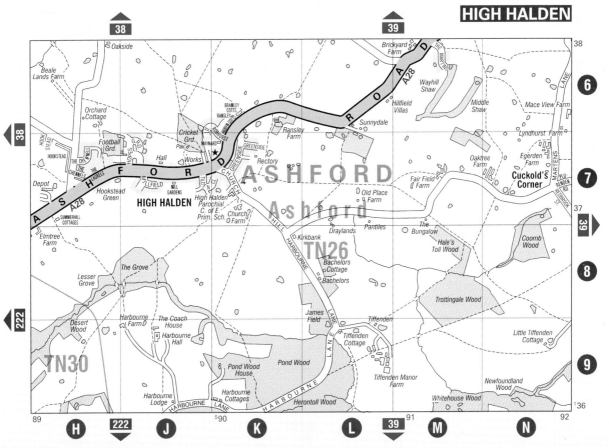

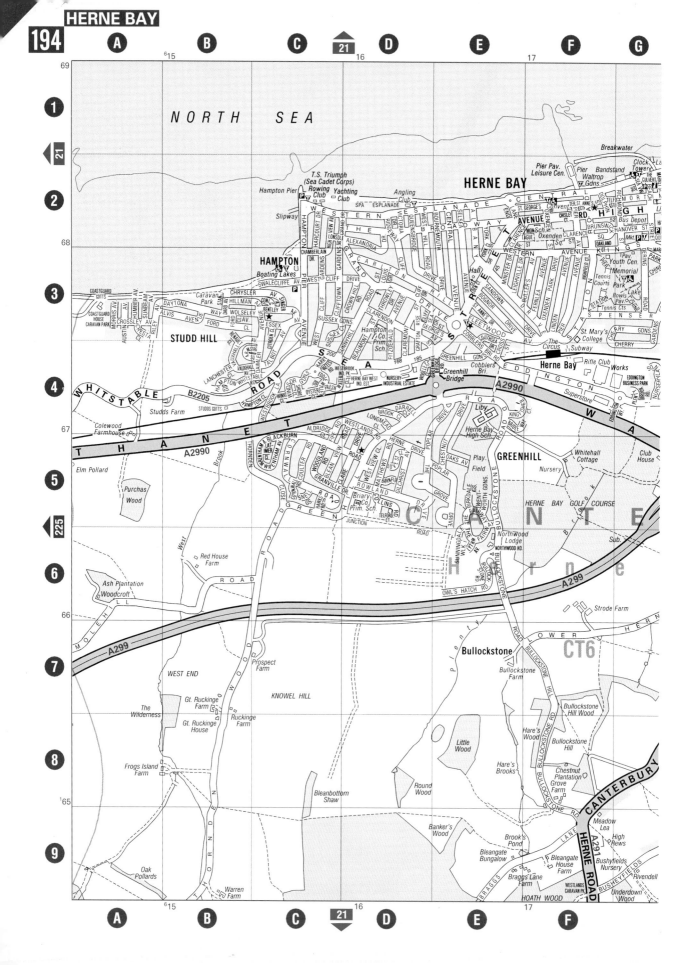

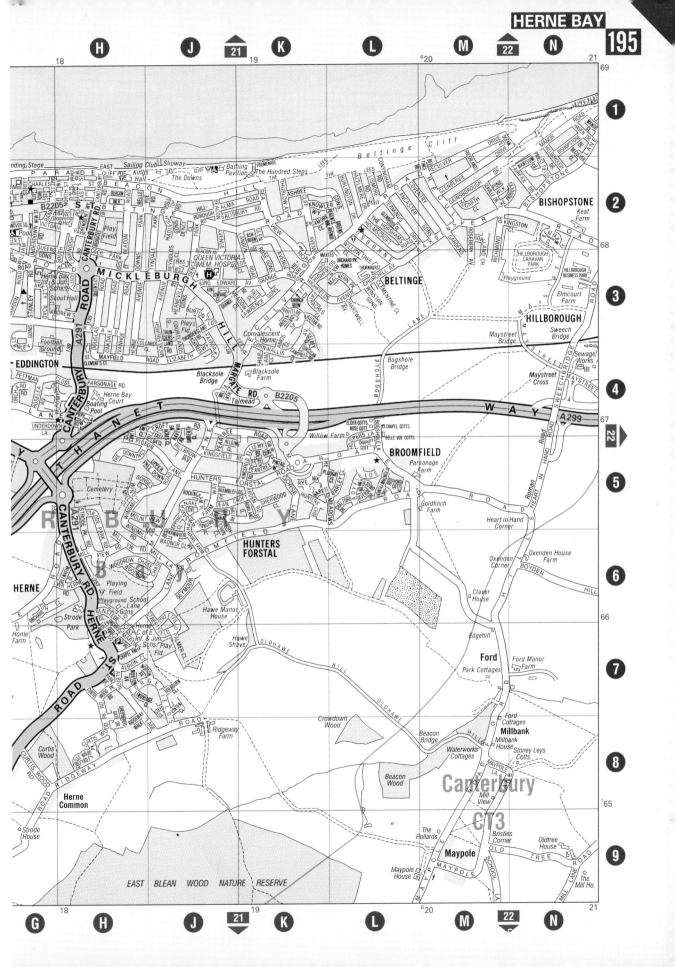

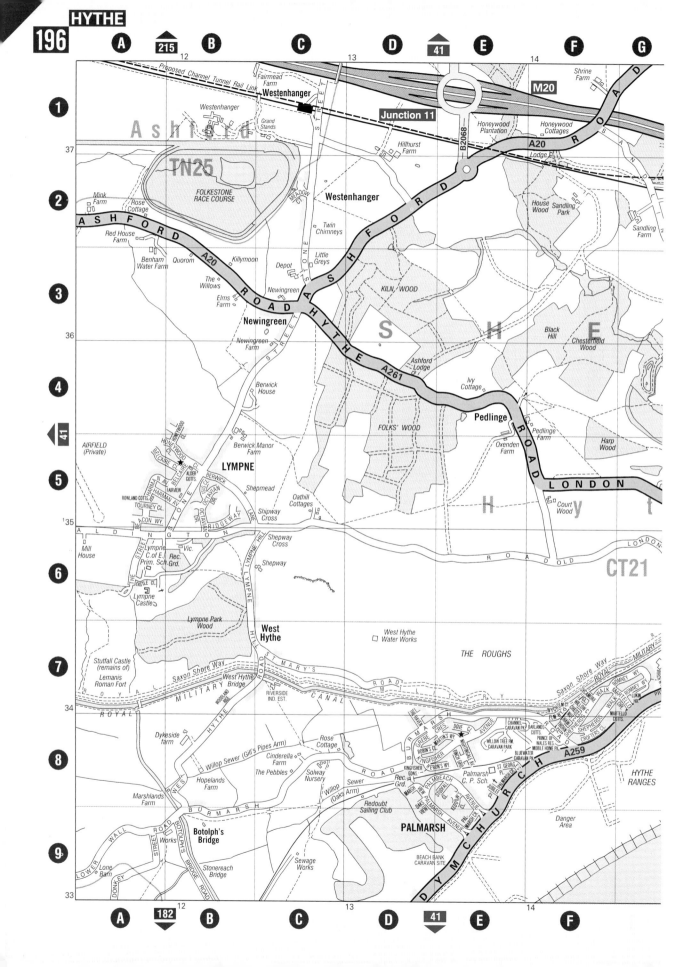

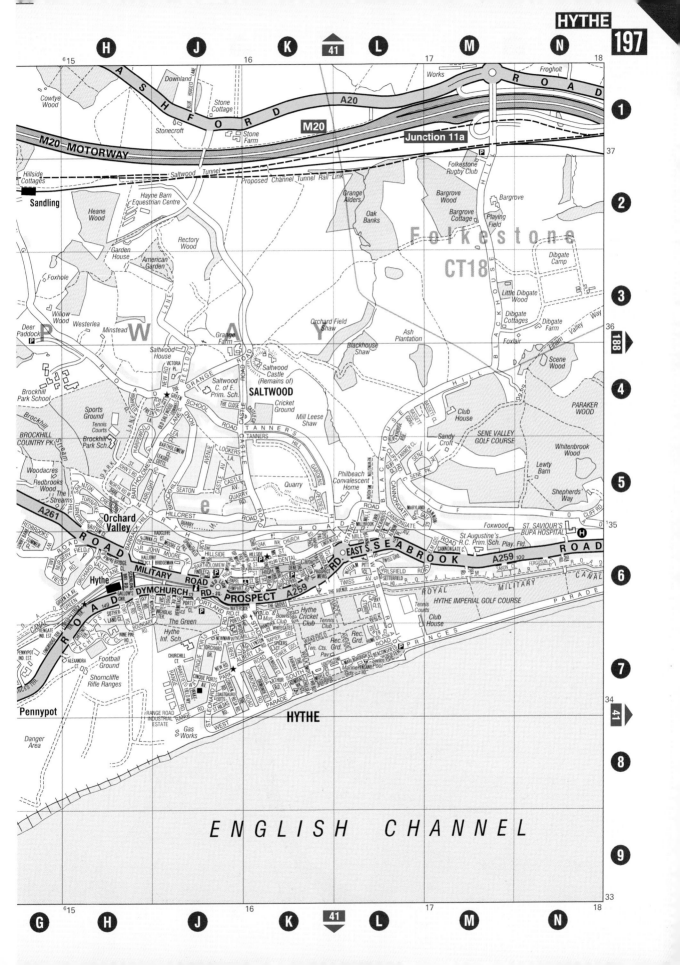

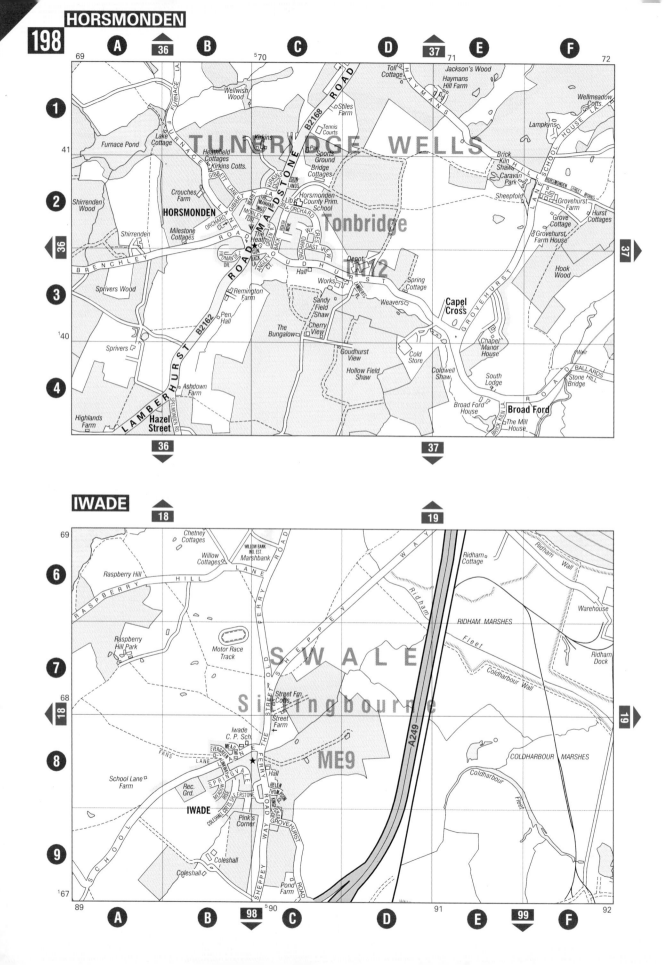

HORSMONDEN map

A | 36 | B | 5 70 | C | D | 37 71 | E | F | 72
69

TUNBRIDGE WELLS

Tonbridge

TN12

HORSMONDEN

Furnace Pond
Lake Cottage
Furnace La
Wellwish Wood
Heathfield Cottages
Kirkins Cotts.
Kirkins
Crouches Farm
Shirrenden Wood
Milestone Cottages
Shirrenden
The Heath
Sprivers Wood
Remington Farm
Pen Hall
The Bungalow
Cherry View
Sandy Field Shaw
Goudhurst View
Hollow Field Shaw
Sprivers
Ashdown Farm
Highlands Farm
Hazel Street
Spelmonden Rd
LAMBERHURST B2162
BRENCHLEY

Stiles Farm
Tennis Courts
Sports Ground
Park
Bridge Cottages
Horsmonden County Prim. School
Lib
Hall
Works
Depot
Weavers
Cold Store
Coldwell Shaw
Spring Cottage
Capel Cross
Broad Ford House
Broad Ford
The Mill House

Toll Cottage
Jackson's Wood
Haymans Hill Farm
Wellmeadow Cotts
Lampkyns
Brick Kiln Shaws
Caravan Park
Sheepfold
Grovehurst Farm
Grove Cottage
Grovehurst Farm House
Hurst Cottages
Hook Wood
Chapel Manor House
South Lodge
Weir
Stone Hill Bridge
BALLARDS
Horsmonden Street Works
SCHOOL HOUSE LA
HAYMANS
B2168
MAIDSTONE ROAD
GROVEHURST ROAD
BRICK KILN LA

36 | 37

IWADE map

18 | 19

A | B | 98 5 90 | C | D | 91 | E | 99 | F | 92
69

SWALE

Sittingbourne

ME9

Chetney Cottages
Willow Cottages
WILLOW BANK IND. EST. Marshbank
Raspberry Hill
Raspberry Hill Park
Motor Race Track
Street Fm Cotts
Street Farm
Iwade C.P. Sch.
Evergreen
School Lane Farm
Rec. Grd.
IWADE
Pink's Corner
Coleshall
Coleshall
Pond Farm
Hall
Ridham Cottage
RIDHAM MARSHES
Fleet
Warehouse
Ridham Dock
Ridham Wall
COLDHARBOUR MARSHES
Coldharbour Wall
Coldharbour
Fleet
A249
FERRY ROAD
SHEPPEY WAY
OLD FERRY ROAD
RASPBERRY HILL
RIDHAM
SCHOOL
GROVEHURST ROAD
SHEPPEY WAY
SPRINGVALE

18 | 19

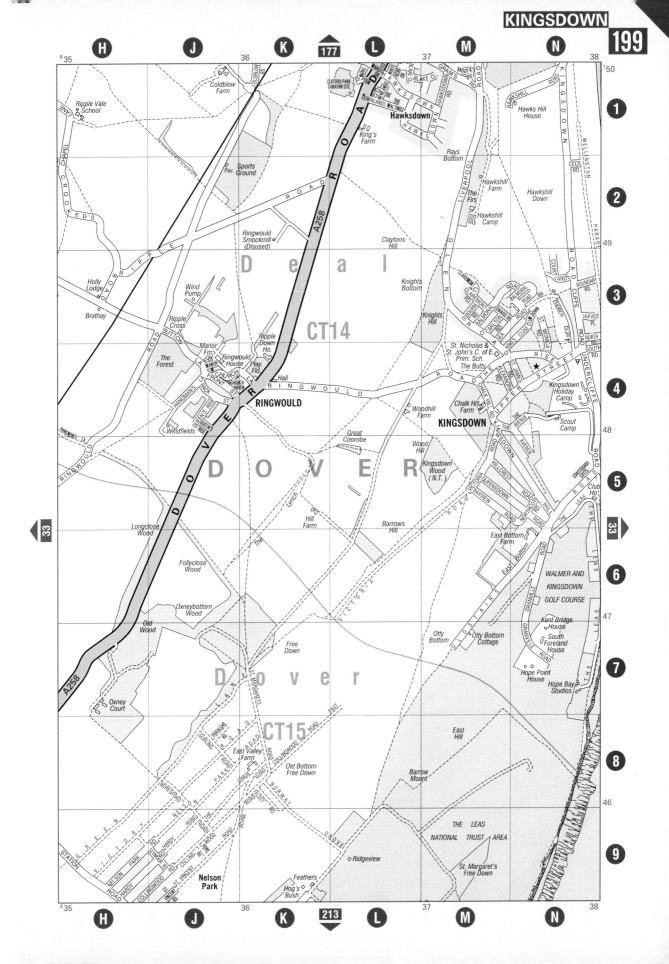

1
2
3
4
5
6
7
8
9

33

33

Hawksdown

Ripple Vale School

Coldblow Farm

CLIFFORD PARK CARAVAN SITE

DOWNLANDS MALTINGS

King's Farm

Hawks Hill House

Rays Bottom

Hawkshill Farm

The Firs

Hawkshill Down

Hawkshill Camp

Sports Ground

Pav.

Ringwould Smockmill (Disused)

Deal

Claytons Hill

Knights Bottom

Holly Lodge

Brathay

Wind Pump

Ripple Cross

Ripple Down Ho.

CT14

Knights Hill

St. Nicholas & St. John's C. of E. Prim. Sch.

The Butts

Kingsdown Holiday Camp

Manor Fm.

The Forest

Ringwould House

Play. Fld.

Hall

Woodhill Farm

Chalk Hill Farm

KINGSDOWN

Scout Camp

RINGWOULD

Westfields

Great Coombe

Wood Hill

Kingsdown Wood (N.T.)

DOVER

Longclose Wood

Lynch Hill Farm

Barrows Hill

East Bottom Farm

Club Ho.

Follyclose Wood

WALMER AND KINGSDOWN GOLF COURSE

Oxneybottom Wood

Old Wood

Free Down

Otty Bottom

Otty Bottom Cottage

Kent Bridge House

South Foreland House

Dover

Hope Point House

Hope Bay Studios

Oxney Court

CT15

East Valley Farm

Old Bottom Free Down

East Hill

Barrow Mount

THE LEAS

NATIONAL TRUST AREA

Nelson Park

Ridgeview

Feathers

Hog's Bush

St. Margaret's Free Down

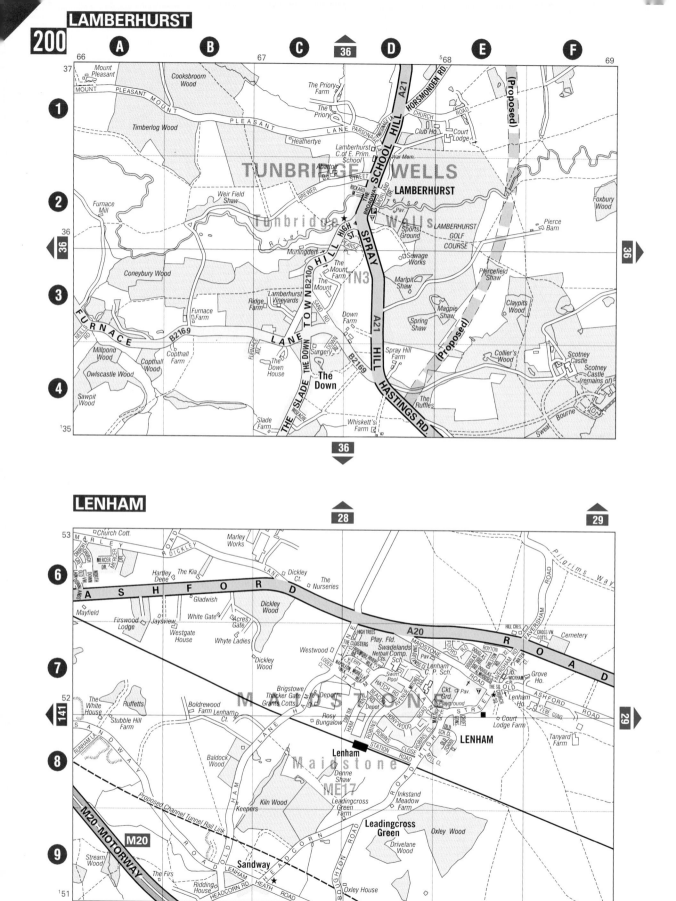

LAMBERHURST (map)

Mount Pleasant · Cooksbroom Wood · The Priory Farm · The Priory · Heatherfye · Lamberhurst C. of E. Prim. School · Club Ho. · Court Lodge · CHURCH ROAD · (Proposed)

MOUNT PLEASANT · Timberlog Wood · PLEASANT · Parsonage

TUNBRIDGE WELLS · LAMBERHURST

Furnace Mill · Weir Field Shaw · Tunbridge Wells · War Mem. · Pav. · Sports Ground · LAMBERHURST GOLF COURSE · Pierce Barn · Foxbury Wood

River · Murlingden · Pearse Pl · High St. · The Mount Farm · The Mount · TN3 · Sewage Works · Marlpit Shaw · Piercefield Shaw · Claypits Wood

Coneybury Wood · Lamberhurst Vineyards · Ridge Farm · Furnace Farm · Down Farm · Magpie Shaw · Spring Shaw

FURNACE · B2169 · Neil's Rd · THE DOWN · B2100 · LANE · TOWN · SPRAY HILL · A21 · Collier's Wood · Scotney Castle

Millpond Wood · Copthall Wood · Copthall Farm · FURNACE AV. · The Down House · Surgery · B2169 · Spray Hill Farm · Scotney Castle (remains of)

Owlscastle Wood · THE SLADE · WISEACRE · The Down · A21 HASTINGS RD · The Ruffles

Sawpit Wood · Slade Farm · Whiskett's Farm · Bourne · Sweat

LENHAM (map)

Church Cott. · MARLEY · Marley Works · ROAD · DICKLEY LANE · Dickley Ct. · The Nurseries

MERCER DR. · Hartley Dene · The Kia · Gladwish · Dickley Wood

Mayfield · Firswood Lodge · Jaysview · White Gate · Acres Gate · Whyte Ladies · Dickley Wood · Westwood · HIGH TREES · Play. Fld. · Swadelands Sch. · Netball Comp. Cts. · Lenham C. P. Sch. · HILL CRES. · CROSS VW. COTTS. · Cemetery

ASHFORD · A20 · Swim Pool · Pav. · Grove Ho. · Lib. · ASHFORD ROAD

The White House · Ruffetts · Boldrewood Farm · Lenham Ct. · Brigstowe · Thacker Gate · Grants Cotts · Depot · Rosy Bungalow · Depot · Ckt. Grd. · Pav. · Playground · Lenham Ho. · Court Lodge Farm · Tanyard Farm

Stubble Hill Farm · Baldock Wood · Lenham · LENHAM

MAIDSTONE · ME17 · Denne Shaw · Leadingcross Green Farm · Inkstand Meadow Farm

Kiln Wood · Keepers · Leadingcross Green · Oxley Wood · Drivelane Wood

M20 MOTORWAY · M20 · Proposed Channel Tunnel Rail Link · RUNHAM LANE · LENHAM HEATH ROAD · BOUGHTON ROAD · HEADCORN ROAD

Stream Wood · The Firs · Ridding House · Sandway · Oxley House

36 · 28 · 29 · 141

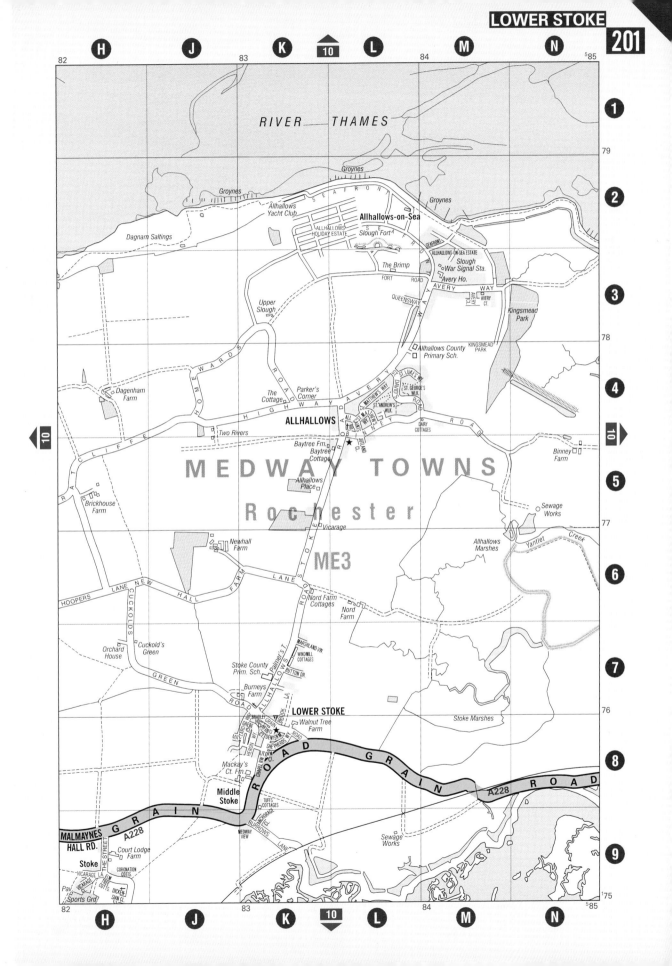

RIVER — THAMES

Groynes

Groynes

Groynes

Allhallows
Yacht Club

Dagnam Saltings

Allhallows
HOLIDAY ESTATE

Allhallows-on-Sea

Slough Fort

The Brimp

ALLHALLOWS-ON-SEA ESTATE

Slough
War Signal Sta.
Avery Ho.

FORT ROAD

QUEENSWAY

AVERY WAY

AVERY CT.

Kingsmead
Park

Upper
Slough

Allhallows County
Primary Sch.

KINGSMEAD
PARK

Dagenham
Farm

Parker's
Corner

The
Cottage

St. Luke's Wk.

St. David's

Matthew's Way

St. George's

St. Andrew's Wk.

Two Rivers

HIGH WAY

HOMEWARDS ROAD

RATCLIFFE

ALLHALLOWS

ALL SAINTS RD.

PINNEY

JUTLAND

Dairy
Cottages

Baytree Fm.
Baytree
Cottage

M E D W A Y   T O W N S

Binney
Farm

Brickhouse
Farm

Allhallows
Place

R o c h e s t e r

Vicarage

Sewage
Works

Newhall
Farm

STOKE ROAD

LANE

FARM

ME3

Allhallows
Marshes

Yantlet
Creek

HOOPERS   LANE

NEW HALL

CUCKOLDS

Orchard
House

Cuckold's
Green

GREEN

ROAD

Nord Farm
Cottages

Nord
Farm

MARSHLAND VW.

WINDMILL
COTTAGES

BUTTON DR.

Stoke County
Prim. Sch

Palmer's St.

ALLHALLOWS

Burneys
Farm

LOWER STOKE

BRADLEY GRAIN

GREEN CL.

DENISON

MRS.

HEDDON WY.

CHAPEL RW.

BRENDON LA.

SHE PHERDS

JUTTON
CT.

Walnut Tree
Farm

Stoke Marshes

Mackay's
Ct. Fm.

**Middle
Stoke**

TUFFS
COTTAGES

BURROWS' LANE

MEDWAY
VIEW

GRAIN   ROAD

ROAD

A228   ROAD

D

Sewage
Works

MALMAYNES
HALL RD.

THE STREET

A228

GRAIN

Stoke

Court Lodge
Farm

VICARAGE LA.

ELM
COTTS.

CLIFFE
COTTS.

DICKEN-
SIAN CL.

CORONATION
COTTS.

Pav.
Sports Grd.

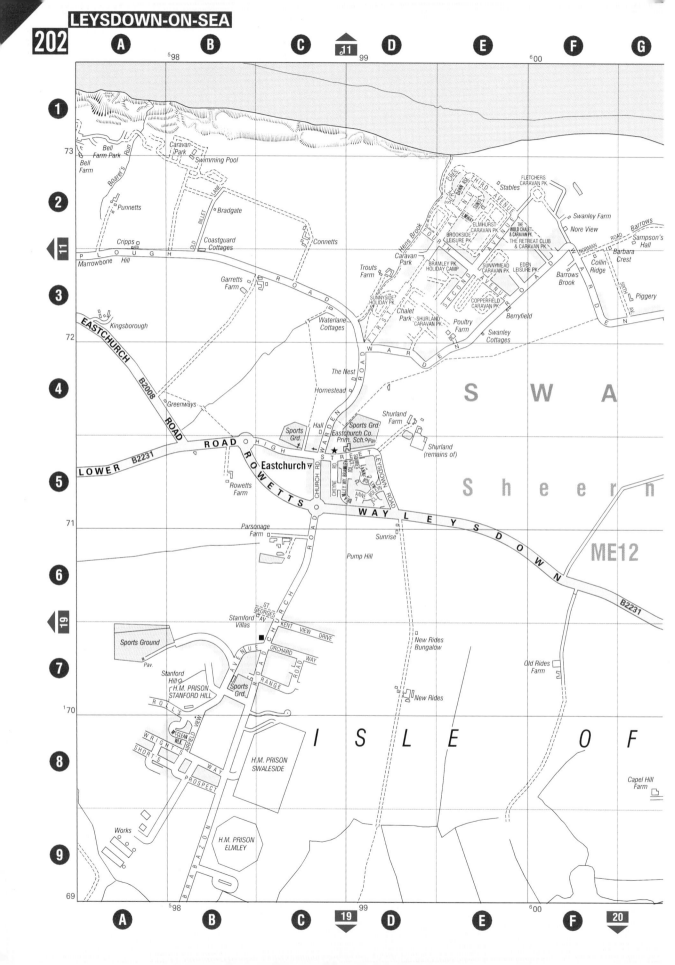

NORTH SEA

THE BAY

WARDEN

LEYSDOWN-ON-SEA

St. James Church
(site of)

Warden Point

Coastguard
Lookout

Coastgaurd Station

Cartts
Farm

Whispering
Sisters

Brook

Warden Way

Barnland
Cotts.

Barnland

THORN HILL

WARDEN SPRING
CARAVAN PARK

Furze
Hill

CLIFF

CONSTABLE
LA.

PRESTON HALL

SEA

ST. JAMES
CL.

APPROACH

DRIVE

KNOLL

IMPERIAL

EMPRESS
GDS.

WINDSOR

CLARENCE
GDS.

LEICESTER
GDS.

WATERSIDE

EMERALD

MELVIL

BEACH

SEA

APPROACH

GARDENS

Boating Pool

Rayham
Court

Rayham

Mustards

SEAVIEW
HOLIDAY CAMP

WARDEN BAY
CARAVAN PARK

WARDEN BAY
HOLIDAY CAMP

Happy
Valley

SHEPPEY
HOLIDAY
CAMP

LOVES
HOLIDAY
CAMP

LITTLE GROVES
HOLIDAY
CAMP

CENTRAL
BEACH CAMP

GROVE AV.

THE MANOR

SHEPPEY BEACH
VILLAS

EASTERN
HOLIDAY
CAMP

EASTERN
RD.

NUTTS
CARAVAN
SITE

NUTTS

SHELLNESS

MUSTARDS
RD.

MUSTARDS

Holiday
Camp

OCEAN
TER.

CORONATION

ST.
CLEMENTS
DR.

BAY

DRIVE

DANES

Rides

Rides Farm

WARDEN VIEW
GDS.

CLIFF
VIEW

Church Cotts.

Hall

Paradise

B2231

VANITY

VANITY
HOLIDAY
CAMP

VANITY FARM
HOLIDAY CAMP

HARTS
HOLIDAY
CAMP

HOLIDAY CAMPS

PARK

PRIORY HILL
HOLIDAY
CAMP

PARK
AVENUE
HOLIDAY
VILLAGE

Leysdown
Coastal Park

SHURLAND AV.

TYLER

WING

Priory
Hill

ROAD

L E Y S D O W N R O A D

FERRY

HARTY

ROAD

Capel

Fleet

S H E P P E Y

Newhouse

LEYSDOWN MARSHES

Leysdown Coastal Park

GROVENEY

WARDEN BAY ROAD

Groynes

Groynes

Groynes

JETTY

THORN

ROAD

MANOR
RD.

MANOR WAY

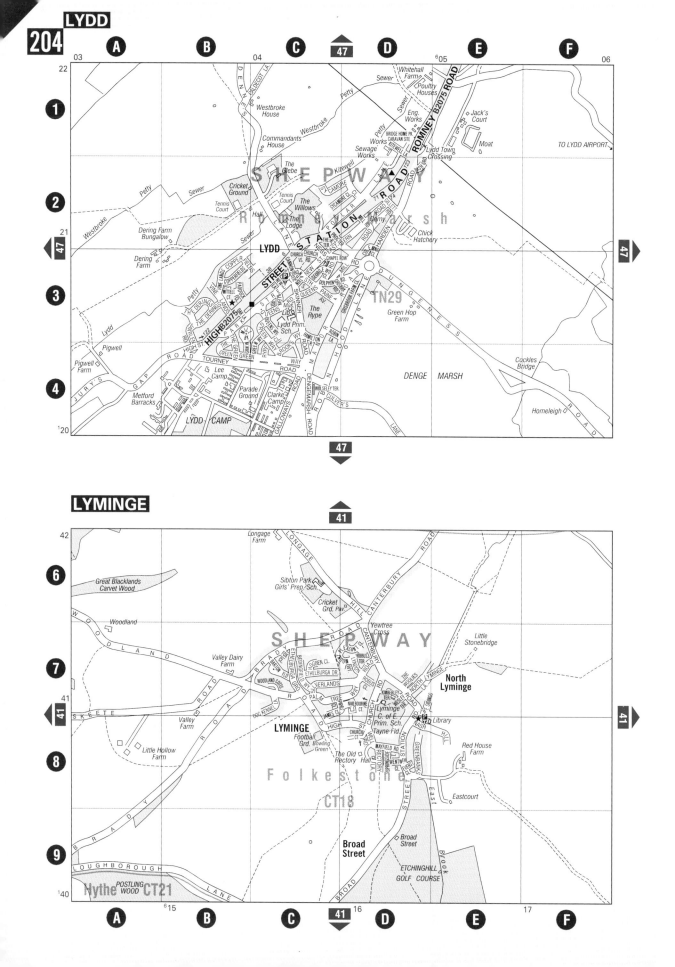

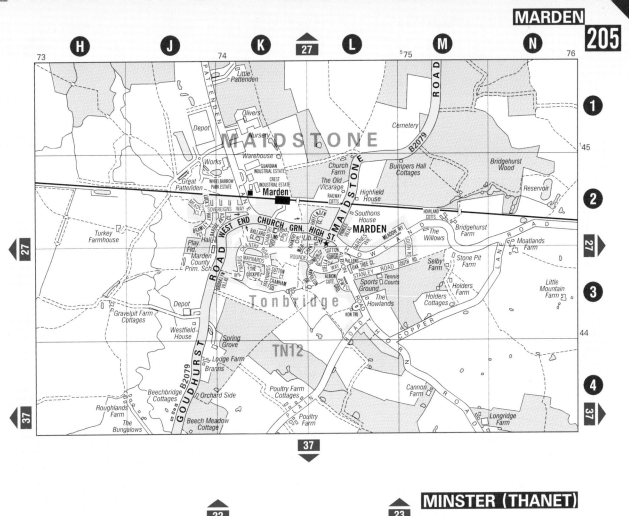

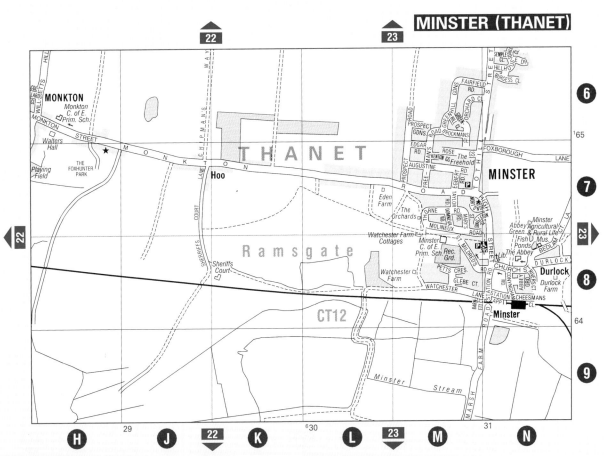

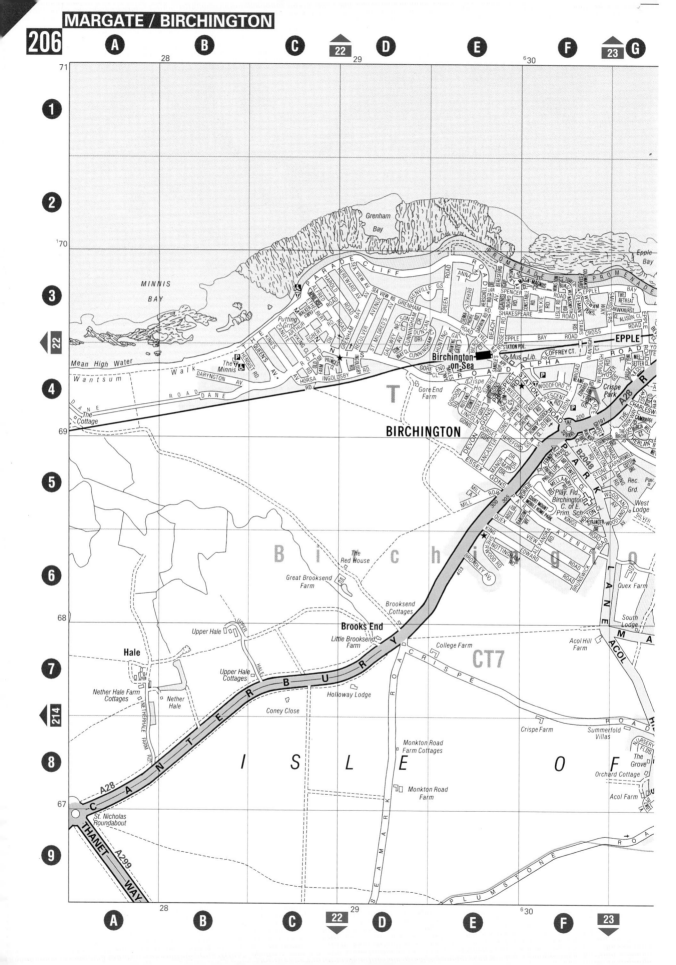

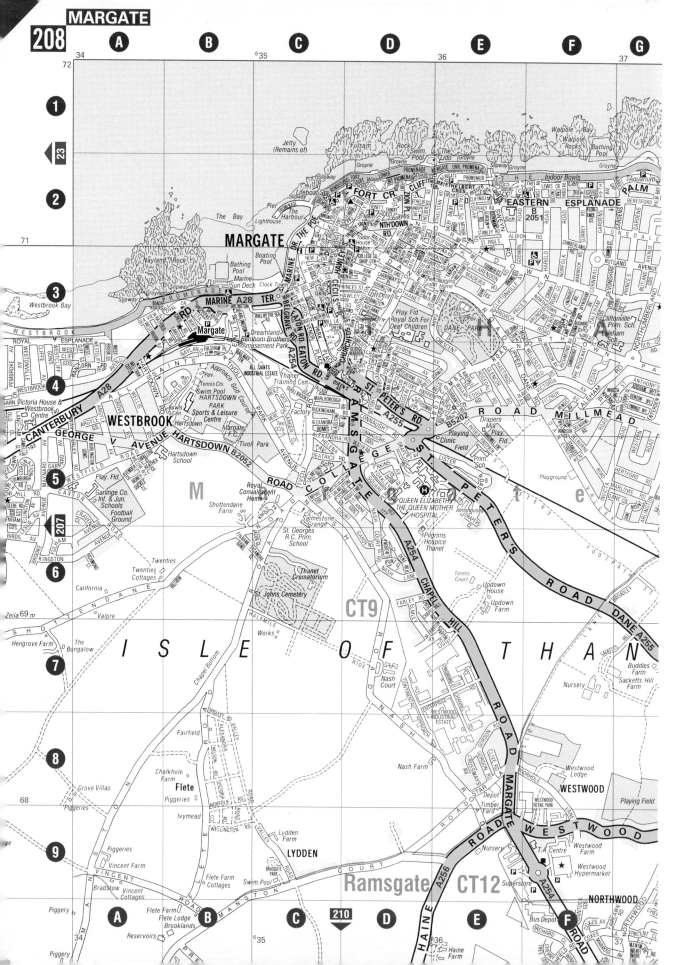

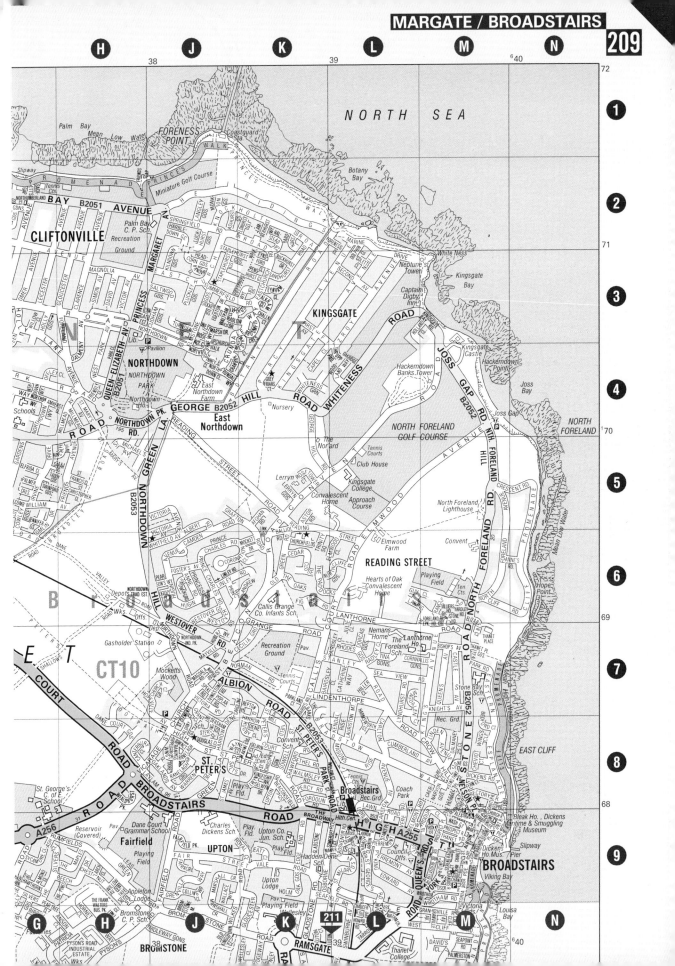

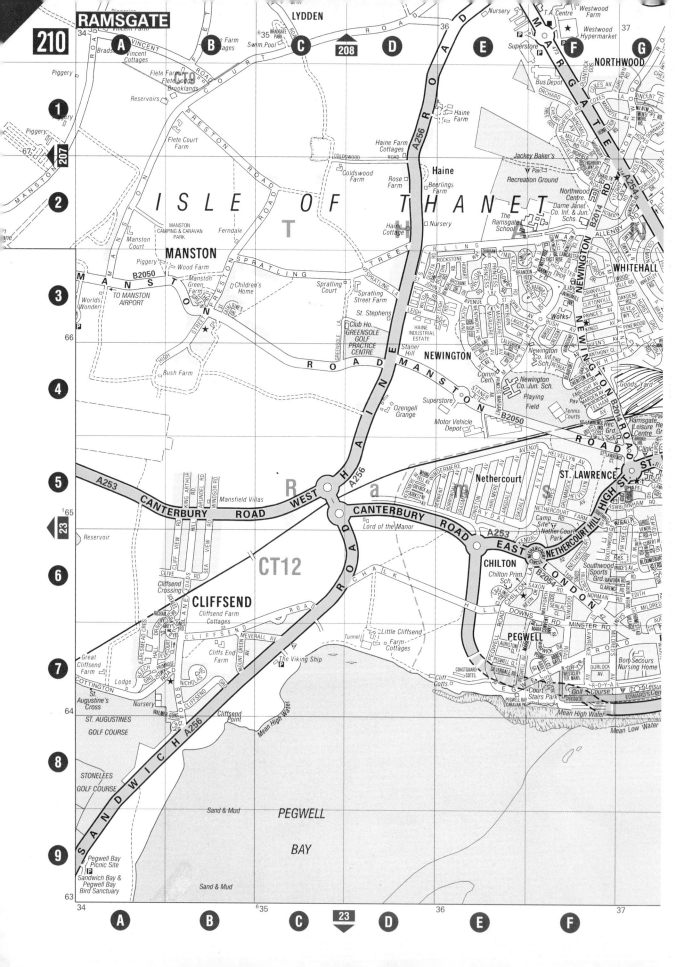

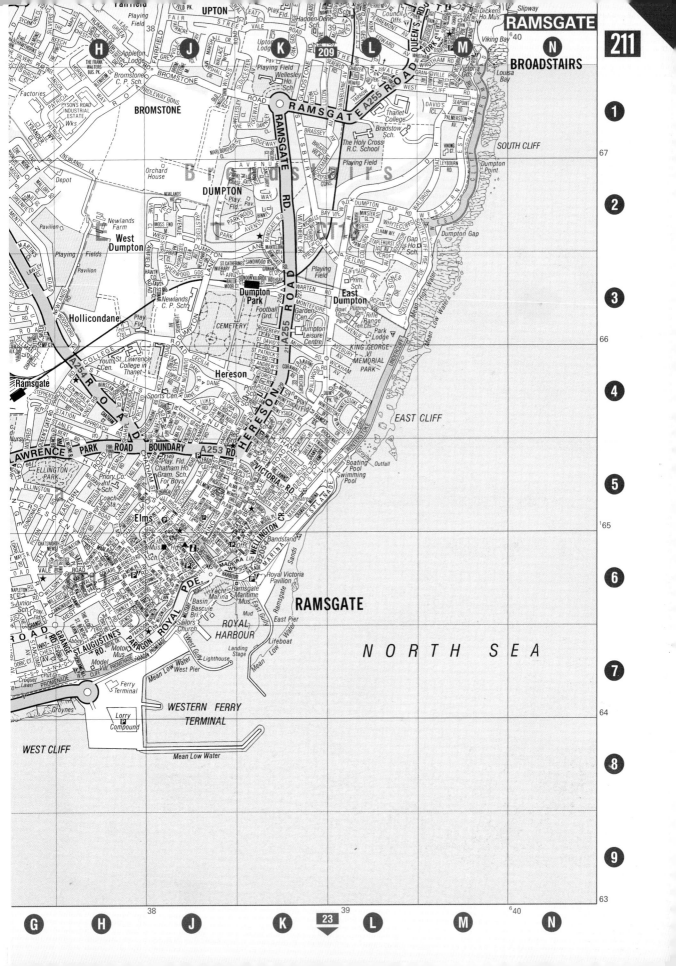

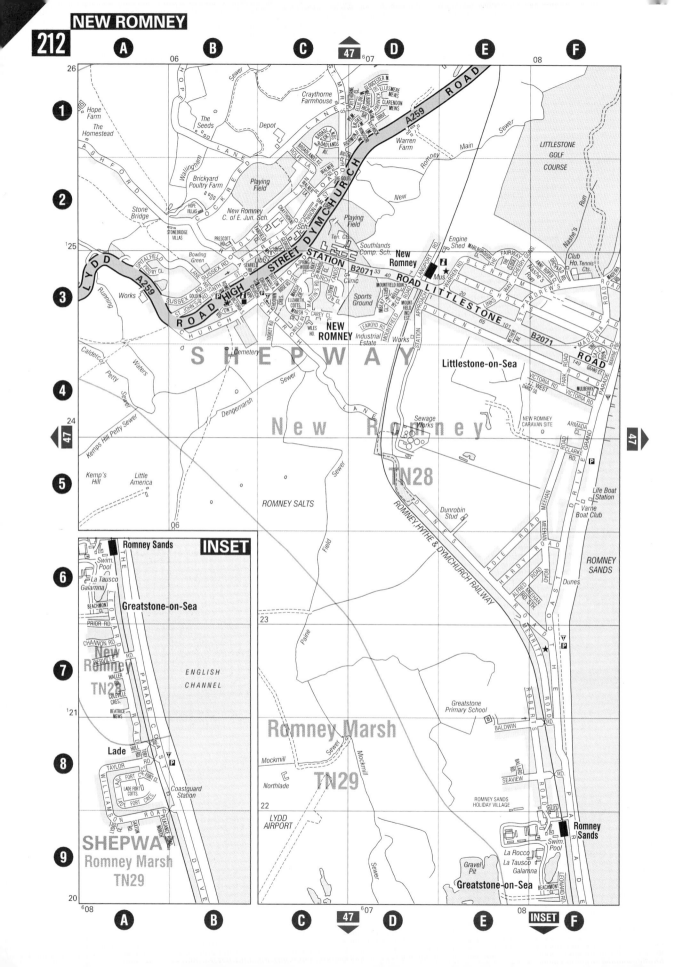

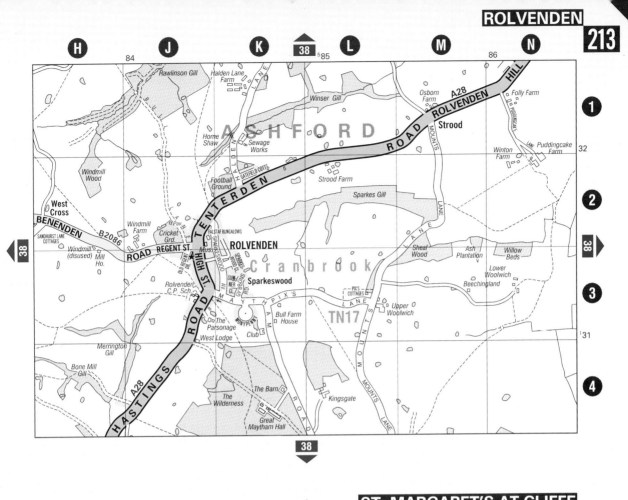

38

ST. MARGARET'S AT CLIFFE

199

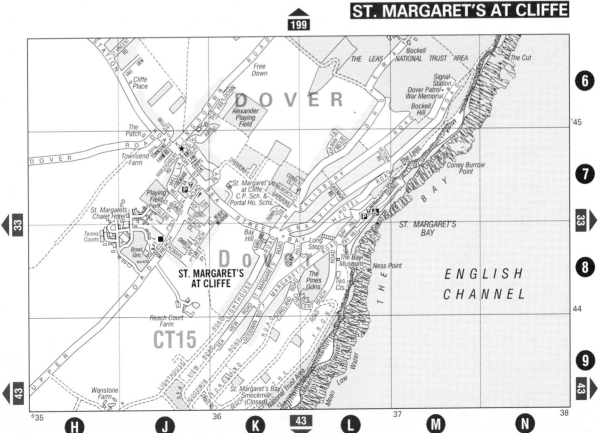

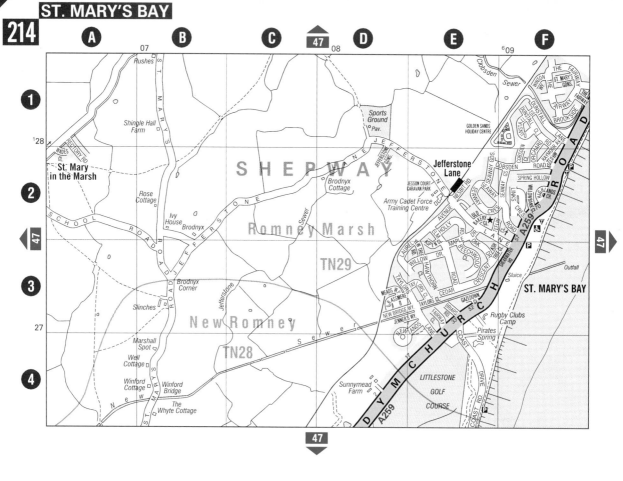

ST. NICHOLAS AT WADE

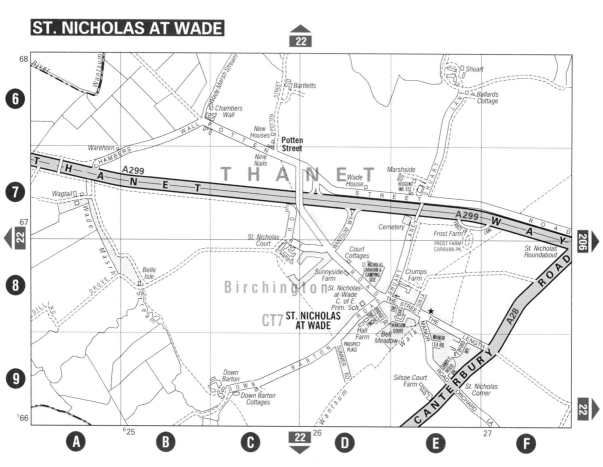

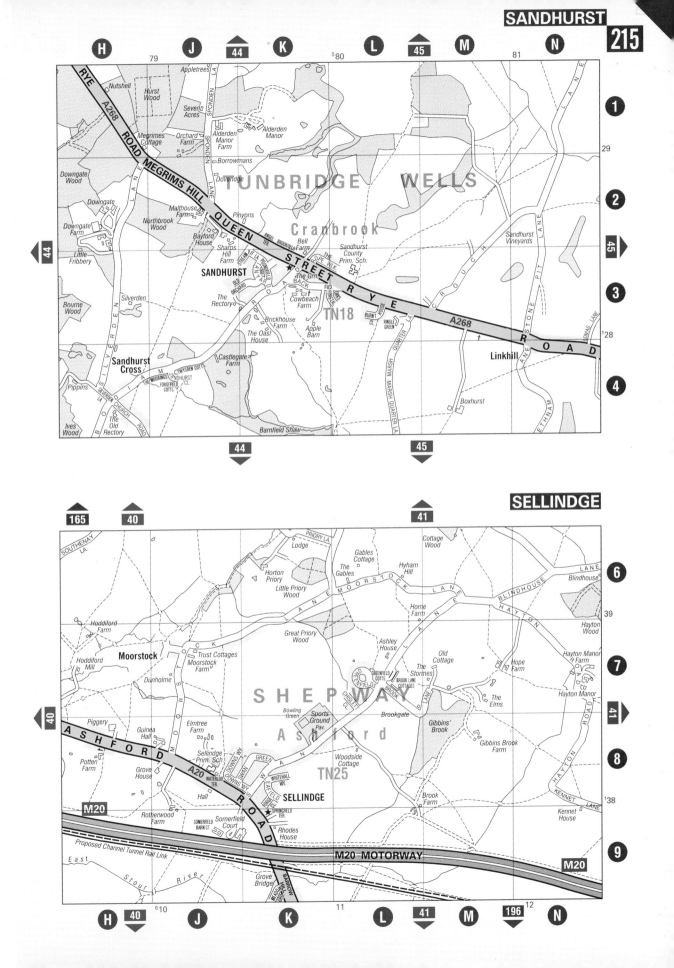

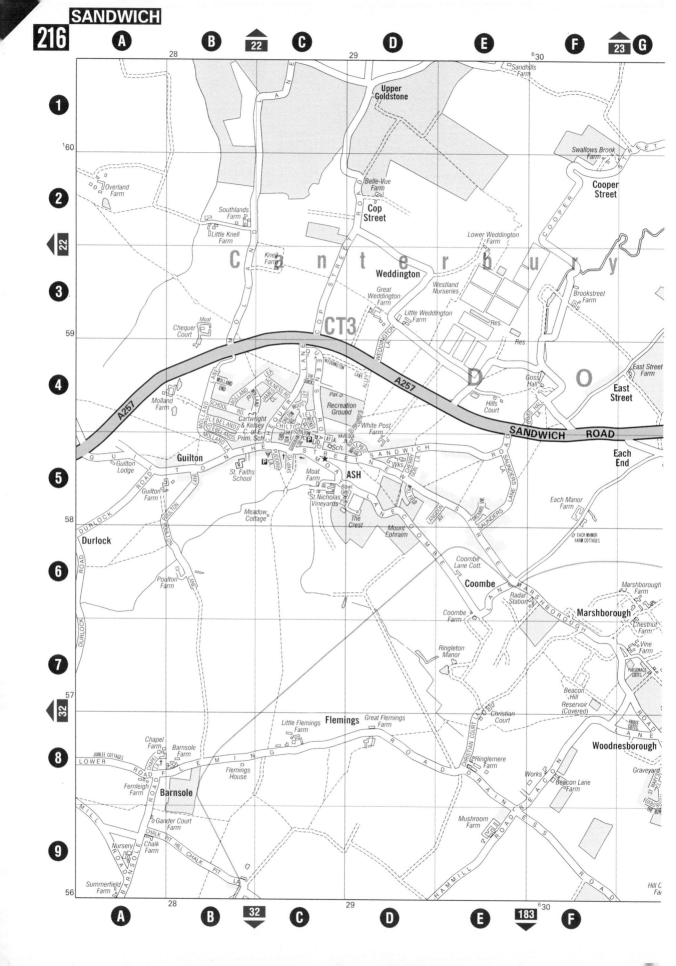

Upper Goldstone

Sandhills Farm

Swallows Brook Farm

Cooper Street

Overland Farm

Belle-Vue Farm

Southlands Farm

Little Knell Farm

Cop Street

Lower Weddington Farm

Canterbury

Knell Farm

Weddington

Westland Nurseries

Brookstreet Farm

Great Weddington Farm

Little Weddington Farm

Res.

Chequer Court

Moat

CT3

Res.

East Street Farm

Molland End

Molland Farm

Recreation Ground

Goss Hall

East Street

Molland School

Cartwright & Kelsey C. of E. Prim. Sch.

Pav.

White Post Farm

Hills Court

Glebelands

Sch.

SANDWICH ROAD

Each End

Guilton

St. Faiths School

Moat Farm

ASH

Wks

Each Manor Farm

Guilton Lodge

Guilton Farm

Meadow Cottage

St. Nicholas Vineyards

The Crest

Mount Ephraim

Each Manor Farm Cottages

Durlock

Poulton Farm

Coombe Lane Cott.

Coombe

Marshborough Farm

Radar Station

Marshborough

Chestnut Farm

Coombe Farm

Vine Farm

Ringleton Manor

Parsonage Cotts.

Beacon Hill Reservoir (Covered)

Flemings

Little Flemings Farm

Great Flemings Farm

Christian Court

Woodnesborough

Chapel Farm

Barnsole Farm

Jubilee Cottages

Ringlemere Farm

Works

Graveyard

Flemings House

Fernleigh Farm

Barnsole

Beacon Lane Farm

Gander Court Farm

Mushroom Farm

Nursery

Chalk Farm

Summerfield Farm

Hill Cₒ Fa

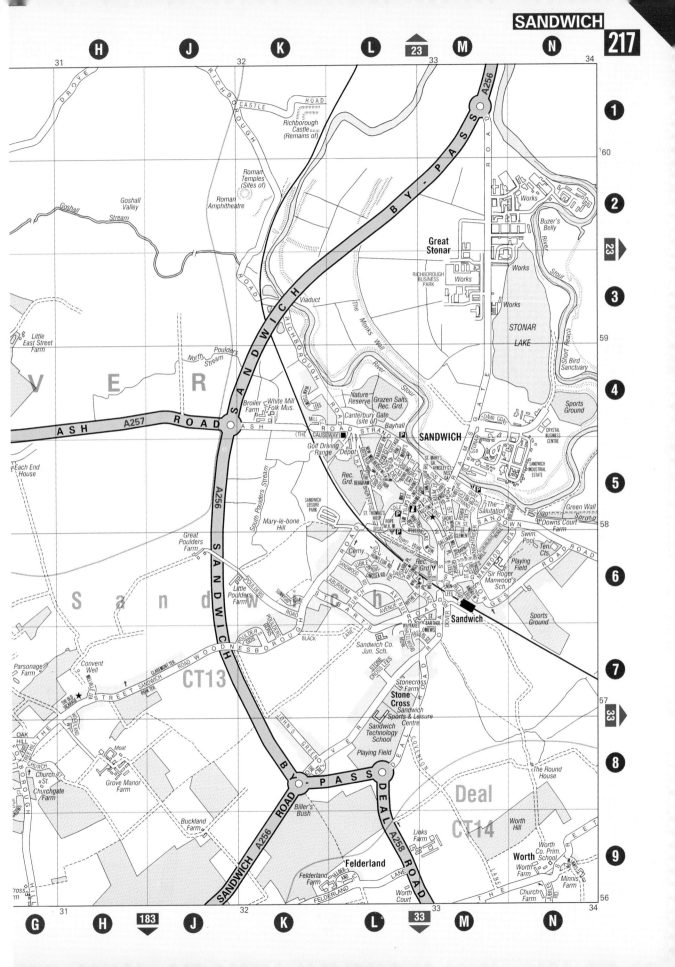

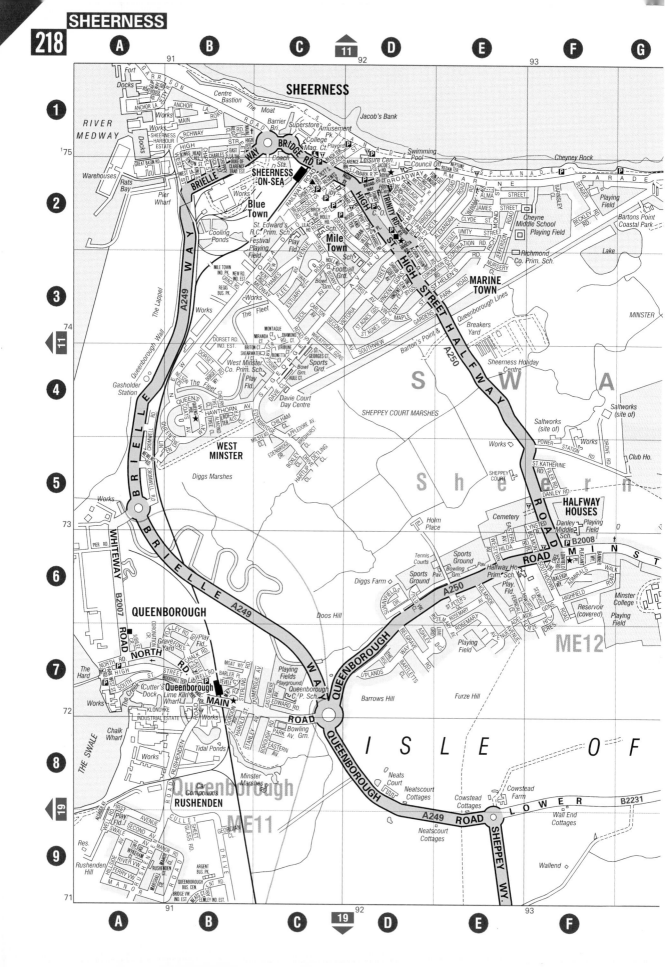

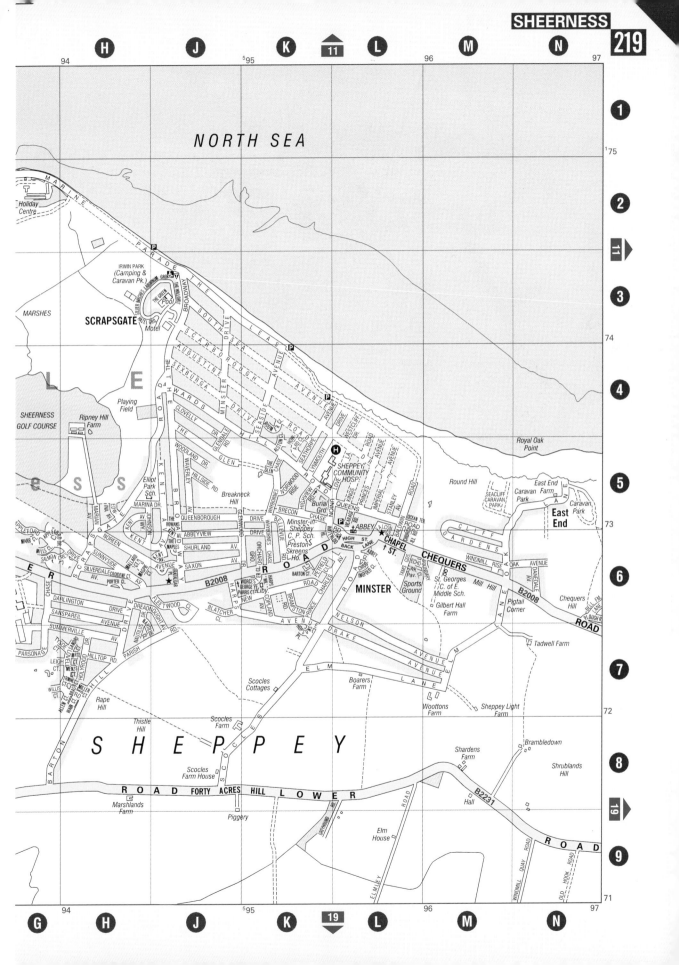

NORTH SEA

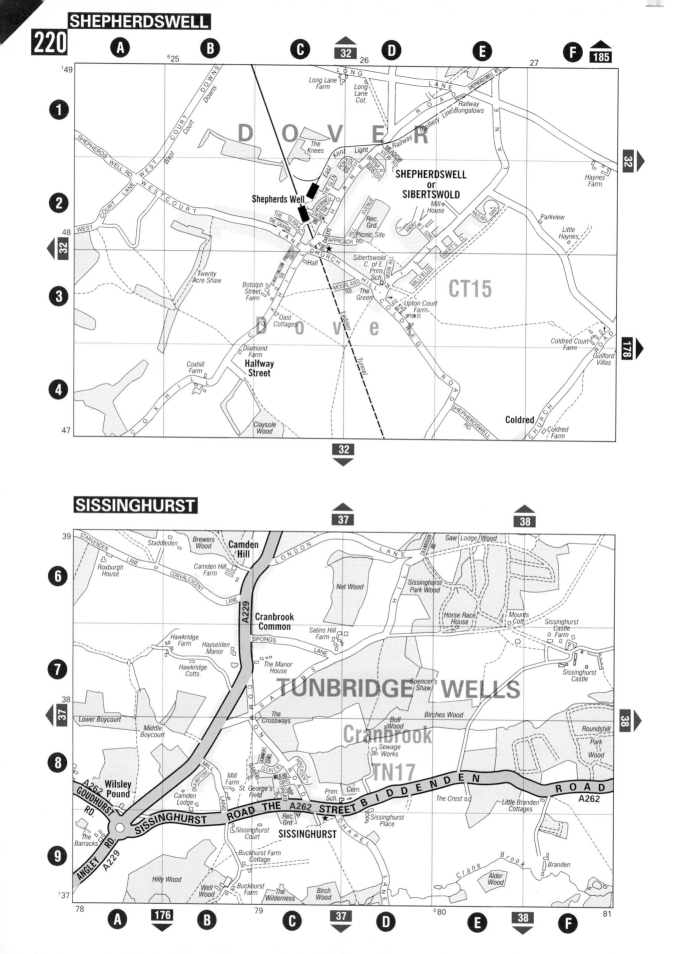

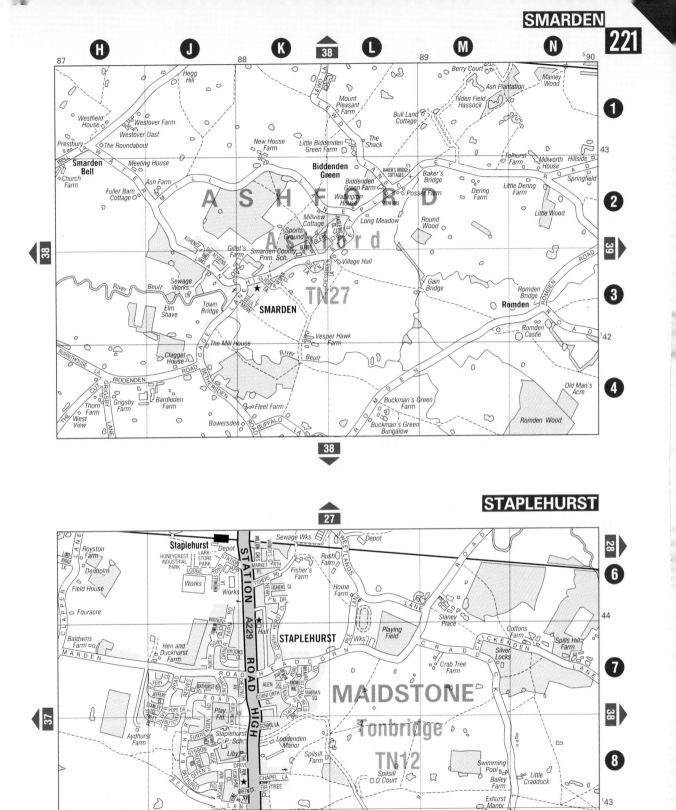

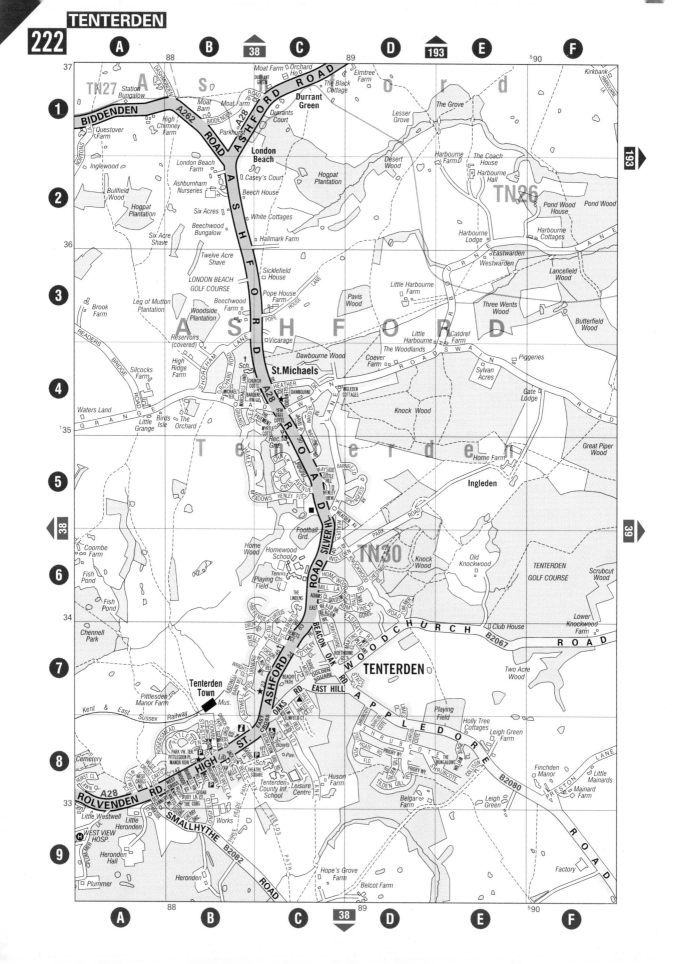

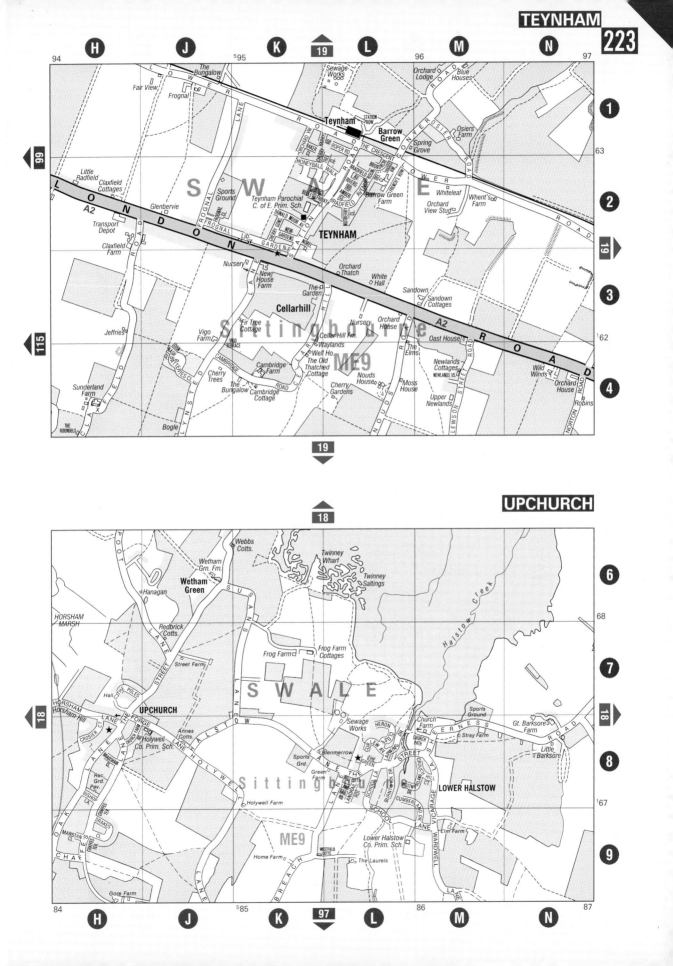

TEYNHAM map

Fair View · Frognal · The Bungalow · Sewage Works · Orchard Lodge · Blue Houses

Little Radfield · Claxfield Cottages · Glenbervie · Transport Depot · Claxfield Farm

S W A L E

Sports Ground · Teynham Parochial C. of E. Prim. Sch. · Teynham · Barrow Green · Spring Grove · Osiers Farm · Whiteleaf · Whent's · Orchard View Stud · Barrow Green Farm

TEYNHAM

LONDON A2

Nursery · New House Farm · Orchard Thatch · White Hall · Sandown · Sandown Cottages

The Garden · **Cellarhill** · Fir Tree Cottage · Jeffries · Vigo Farm · Nursery · Cellar Hill Fm. · Orchard House · Oast House · A2 · Newlands Cottages · Newlands Vs. · Wild Winds · Orchard House · Robins

Sitting bourne ME9

Waylands · Well Ho. · The Old Thatched Cottage · Cambridge Farm · Cherry Trees · Cambridge Cottage · The Bungalow · Cambridge Gardens · Nouds House · Moss House · Cherry Gardens · Upper Newlands · The Elms

Sunderland Farm · THE ROUNDELS · Bogle

19

18

UPCHURCH map

Webbs Cotts. · Wetham Grn. Fm. · Twinney Wharf · Twinney Saltings

HORSHAM MARSH · Hanagan · **Wetham Green** · Redbrick Cotts. · Street Farm · Frog Farm · Frog Farm Cottages · Halstow Creek

S W A L E

Hall · The Poles · **UPCHURCH** · Annes Cotts. · Sewage Works · Heron · Church Farm · Sports Ground · Gt. Barksore Farm · Stray Farm · Little Barksore

Horsham Hill · Forge · Holywell Co. Prim. Sch. · Blenmerrow · Church Farm · Church Path

Sitting bourne · Rec. Grd. Pav. · Bishop La. · Sports Grd. · Green Farm · Lane Green · **LOWER HALSTOW**

Marstan Cl. · Drakes · Holywell Farm · School La. · Lower Halstow Co. Prim. Sch. · Elm Farm

ME9 · Home Farm · Westfield Cotts. · The Laurels · Gore Farm · Breach Lane

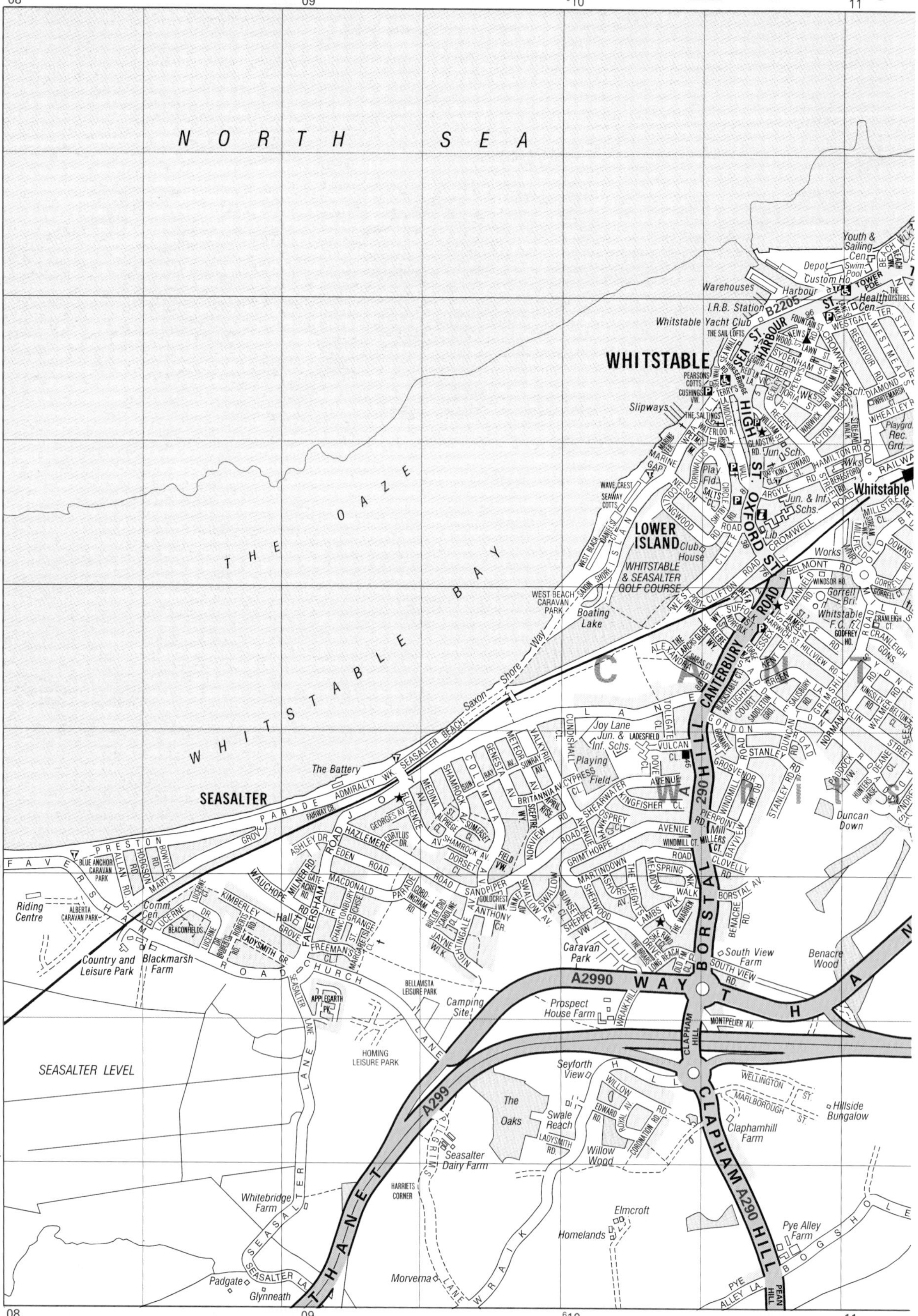
A
B
20
C
D
E
21
F
G
1
2
3
4
5
6
7
8
9
NORTH SEA
THE OAZE
WHITSTABLE BAY
WHITSTABLE
LOWER ISLAND
SEASALTER
SEASALTER LEVEL
Whitstable
Youth & Sailing Cen.
Depot
Custom Ho.
Warehouses
Harbour
I.R.B. Station
Whitstable Yacht Club
Slipways
WHITSTABLE & SEASALTER GOLF COURSE
Club House
WEST BEACH CARAVAN PARK
Boating Lake
Saxon Shore Way
The Battery
Joy Lane Jun. & Inf. Schs.
Playing Field
Riding Centre
Comm. Cen.
Country and Leisure Park
Blackmarsh Farm
Hall
Caravan Park
Prospect House Farm
Camping Site
HOMING LEISURE PARK
BELLAVISTA LEISURE PARK
APPLEGARTH PK.
Seyforth View
The Oaks
Swale Reach
Willow Wood
Seasalter Dairy Farm
HARRIETS CORNER
Whitebridge Farm
Padgate
Glynneath
Morverna
Homelands
Elmcroft
Pye Alley Farm
Claphamhill Farm
Hillside Bungalow
South View Farm
Benacre Wood
Duncan Down
Whitstable F.C.
Gorrell Bri.
Works
Jun. & Inf. Schs.
Jun. Sch.
Rec. Grd.
A2990
A299
A290
B2205
THANET WAY
BORSTAL HILL
CLAPHAM HILL
HIGH ST.
OXFORD ST.
CANTERBURY ROAD
SEASALTER BEACH
FAVERSHAM ROAD
CHURCH LANE
SEASALTER LANE
PRESTON PARADE
GROVE PARADE
ADMIRALTY WK.
WRAIK HILL
PYE ALLEY LA.
BOGSHOLE LA.
08
09
10
11
68
67
66
65
64

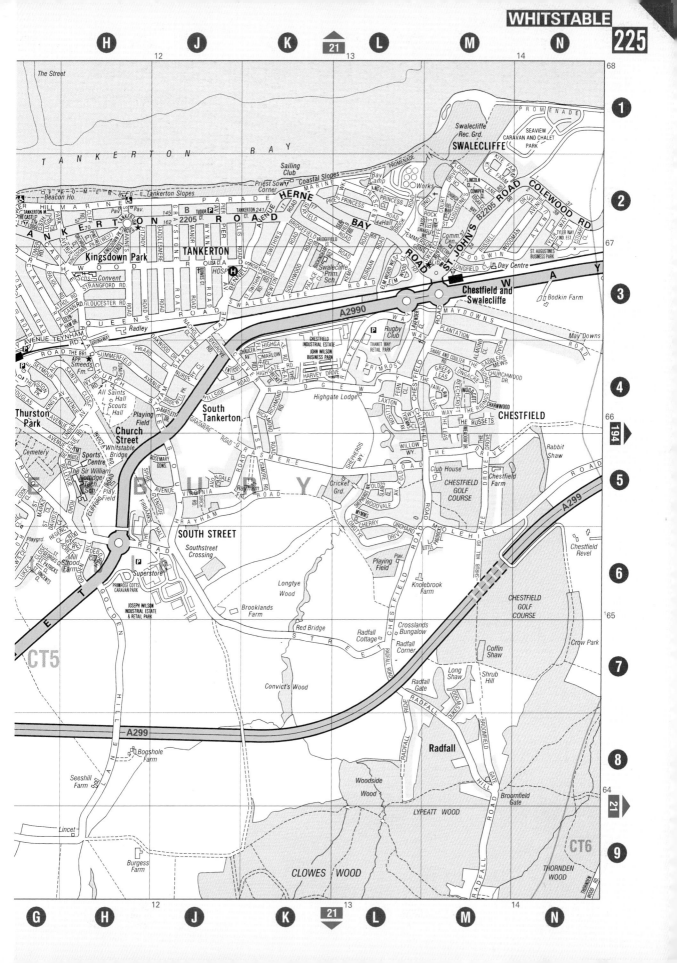

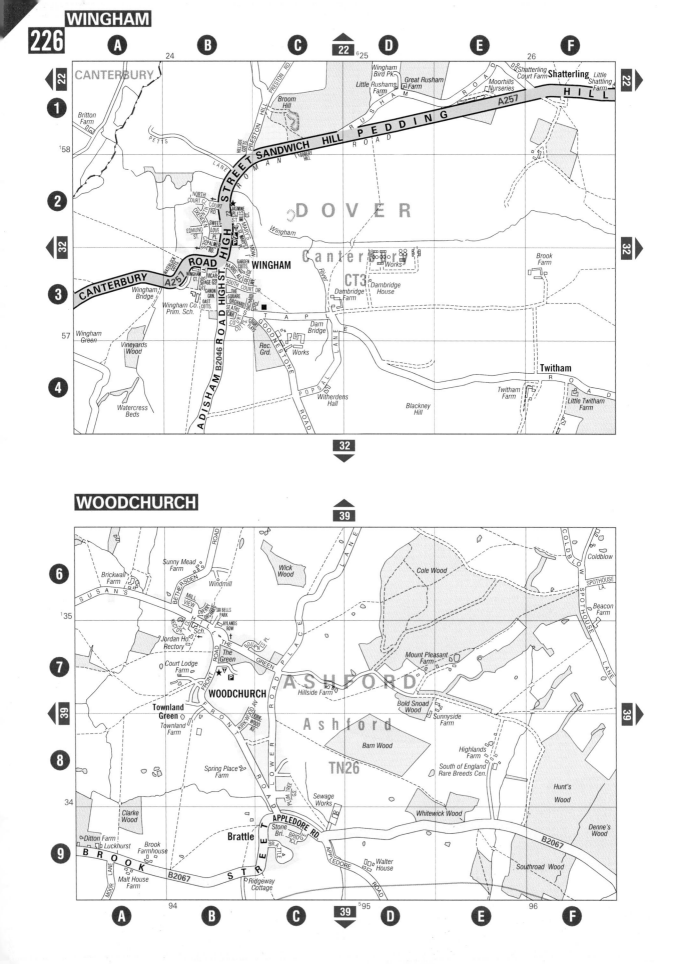

INDEX

Including Streets, Places & Areas, Industrial Estates, Selected Junction Names,
Selected Subsidiary Addresses and Selected Tourist Information.

HOW TO USE THIS INDEX

1. Each street name is followed by its Postal District (or, if outside the London Postal District, by its Posttown or Postal Locality), and then by its map reference; e.g. Abbeville Rd. *SW4* —4C **4** is in the South West 4 Postal District and is to be found in square 4C on page **4**. The page number being shown in bold type.
   A strict alphabetical order is followed in which Av., Rd., St., etc. (though abbreviated) are read in full and as part of the street name; e.g. Abbeyview Dri. appears after Abbey Trad. Est. but before Abbey Way.
2. Streets and a selection of Subsidiary names not shown on the Maps, appear in the index in *Italics* with the thoroughfare to which it is connected shown in brackets; e.g. *Acacia Ho. S'ness —2C **218** (off Pepys Av.)*
3. Places and areas are shown in the index in **bold type**, the map reference referring to the actual map square in which the town or area is located and not to the place name; eg. **Abbey Gate. —8C 110**
4. Streets that appear on the 3 Inches to 1 Mile Street Mapping (red pages) and 1 Inch to 1 Mile Street Mapping (blue pages) are given two references; e.g. Abbey Rd. *SE2 & Belv* —4M **51** (3B **6**) is to be found in square 4M on page **51** on the 3 Inches to 1 Mile Street Mapping and in square 3B on page **6** on the 1 Inch to 1 Mile Street Mapping.
5. With the now general usage of Postcodes for addressing mail, it is not recommended that this index is used for such a purpose.

GENERAL ABBREVIATIONS

All : Alley
App : Approach
Arc : Arcade
Av : Avenue
Bk : Back
Boulevd : Boulevard
Bri : Bridge
B'way : Broadway
Bldgs : Buildings
Bus : Business
Cvn : Caravan
Cen : Centre
Chu : Church
Chyd : Churchyard
Circ : Circle
Cir : Circus
Clo : Close
Comn : Common
Cotts : Cottages
Ct : Court
Cres : Crescent
Dri : Drive
E : East
Embkmt : Embankment
Est : Estate
Gdns : Gardens
Ga : Gate
Gt : Great
Grn : Green
Gro : Grove
Ho : House
Ind : Industrial
Junct : Junction
La : Lane
Lit : Little
Lwr : Lower
Mnr : Manor
Mans : Mansions
Mkt : Market
M : Mews
Mt : Mount
N : North
Pal : Palace
Pde : Parade
Pk : Park
Pas : Passage
Pl : Place
Quad : Quadrant
Rd : Road
Shop : Shopping
S : South
Sq : Square
Sta : Station
St : Street
Ter : Terrace
Trad : Trading
Up : Upper
Vs : Villas
Wlk : Walk
W : West
Yd : Yard

POSTTOWN AND POSTAL LOCALITY ABBREVIATIONS

Acol : Acol
Acr : Acrise
Adtn : Addington
Adm : Adisham
Adgtn : Aldington
Alk : Alkham
Allh : Allhallows
All : Allington
App : Appledore
Ash : Ash (Aldershot)
Ah : Ash (Canterbury)
As : Ash (Sevenoaks)
Afrd : Ashford
Ash B : Ashford Business Park
Ashl : Ashley
Asht : Ashtead
A'st : Ashurst
Ash W : Ashurst Wood
Ave : Aveley
Ayle : Aylesford
Aysm : Aylesham
Badg D : Badgers Dene
Badg M : Badgers Mount
Bad : Badlesmere
Bans : Banstead
Bap : Bapchild
B'hm : Barham
Bark : Barking
Barm : Barming
B'hurst : Barnehurst
B'le : Barnsole
Bas : Basildon
Batt : Battle
Bean : Bean
Bear : Bearsted
Beck : Beckenham
Beckl : Beckley
Bedd : Beddington
Bek : Bekesbourne
Bells Y : Bells Yew Green
Belv : Belvedere
Bene : Benenden
Ben : Benfleet
Berr G : Berrys Green
Beth : Bethersden
Bett : Betteshanger
Bex : Bexley
Bexh : Bexleyheath
Bic : Bicknor
Bidb : Bidborough
Bidd : Biddenden
Big H : Biggin Hill
Big A : Biggin Hill Airport
Bils : Bilsington
Bilt : Bilting
Birch G : Birchetts Green
Birch : Birchington
Birl : Birling
Bis : Bishopsbourne
Blac : Blackham
Blad : Bladbean
Blean : Blean
Blue B : Blue Bell Hill
Blue T : Blue Town
Bob : Bobbing
Bdm : Bodiam
Bod : Bodsham
Bon : Bonnington
B'den : Borden
Bor G : Borough Green
Bos : Bossingham
Bough B : Bough Beech
Bou L : Boughton Lees
Bou M : Boughton Monchelsea
Bou B : Boughton-under-Blean
Boxl : Boxley
Bchly : Brenchley
B'ling : Brightling
B Oak : Broad Oak
B'lnd : Brookland
B End : Brooks End
Bra L : Brabourne Lees
Bram : Bramling
Bram : Bramshott
Bras : Brasted
Brede : Brede
Bre : Bredgar
Bred : Bredhurst
Bren : Brentford
Bztt : Brenzett
Bri : Bridge
Broad : Broadstairs
Brom : Bromley
Bromp : Brompton
Brook : Brook
Broom : Broomfield
Bkld : Buckland
Bulp : Bulphan
Bur : Burcott
B Hts : Burgoyne Heights
Burh : Burham
Burm : Burmarsh
Cmbr : Camber
Cant : Canterbury
Can I : Canvey Island
Cap F : Capel-le-Ferne
Cars : Carshalton
Cat : Caterham
Chaf H : Chafford Hundred
C'lck : Challock
Charc : Charcott
Char : Charing
Char H : Charing Heath
Cha : Chartham
Cha H : Chartham Hatch
Cha S : Chart Sutton
Chat : Chatham
Chatt : Chattenden
Cheam : Cheam
Chels : Chelsfield
Chel G : Chelwood Gate
Chess : Chessington
Ches : Chestfield
Chev : Chevening
Chid : Chiddingstone
Chid C : Chiddingstone Causeway
Chid H : Chiddingstone Hoath
Chi : Chilham
Chill : Chillenden
Chip : Chipstead
Chst : Chislehurst
C'let : Chislet
Chu H : Church Hougham
Cli : Cliffe
C'snd : Cliffsend
Clif : Clifton
Clift : Cliftonville
Cob : Cobham
Col : Coldred
Cole H : Colemans Hatch
Coll S : Collier Street
Con : Conyer
C'ing : Cooling
Corr : Corringham
Coul : Coulsdon
Cous W : Cousley Wood
Cowd : Cowden
Cox : Coxheath
C'brk : Cranbrook
Cray : Crayford
Crock : Crockenhill
Crook C : Crookham Common
Crock H : Crockham Hill
Crou : Crouch
Crowb : Crowborough
Crow : Crowhurst
Croy : Croydon
Crun : Crundale
Cud : Cudham
Culv : Culverstone
Cux : Cuxton
Dag : Dagenham
Dar : Dargate
Dart : Dartford
Deal : Deal
Dens : Densole
Denst : Denstroude
Dent : Denton
Det : Detling
Dit : Ditton
Dod : Doddington
D'land : Dormansland
Dor P : Dormans Park
Dover : Dover
Dow : Downe
Down : Downswood
Drel : Drellingore
Dunk : Dunkirk
D Grn : Dunks Green
Dun G : Dunton Green
Dur : Durgates
Dym : Dymchurch
E Bra : East Brabourne
E'chu : Eastchurch
E End : East End
E Far : East Farleigh
E Grn : Eridge Green
E Grin : East Grinstead
E Gul : East Guldeford
E Lan : East Langdon
E'lng : Eastling
E Mal : East Malling
E Peck : East Peckham
E'try : Eastry
E Stu : East Studdal
E Sut : East Sutton
E Til : East Tilbury
Eccl : Eccles
Edd B : Eddington Bus. Pk.
Eden : Edenbridge
Eger : Egerton
Elham : Elham
Evtn : Elvington
Eps : Epsom
Eri : Erith
E'ham : Etchingham
Etch : Etchinghill
Ewe : Ewell
Ewe M : Ewell Minnis
Ewh G : Ewhurst Green
Eyns : Eynsford
Eyt : Eythorne
Fair : Fairseat
Farn : Farnborough
F'ham : Farningham
Fav : Faversham
Fawk : Fawkham
Fin : Finglesham
Five G : Five Oak Green
Flete : Flete
Flim : Flimwell
Fob : Fobbing
Folk : Folkestone
Ford : Fordcombe
F'wch : Fordwich
F Row : Forest Row
Four E : Four Elms
Frant : Frant
Free H : Free Heath
Frin : Frinsted
Frit : Frittenden
F'hm : Frogham
Gar : Garlinge
Gill : Gillingham
Gill B : Gillingham Bus. Pk.
God G : Godden Green
Godm : Godmersham
Gold G : Golden Green
Good : Goodnestone
Goud : Goudhurst
Graf G : Grafty Green
G'ney : Graveney
Grav : Gravesend
Grays : Grays
Gt Cha : Great Chart
Gt Mon : Great Mongeham
G'stne : Greatstone
Grnh : Greenhithe
Grn St : Green Street Green
Groom : Groombridge
Guest : Guestling
Gus : Guston
Hackl : Hacklinge
Hdlw : Hadlow
Hall : Halling
Hals : Halstead
Ha : Ham (Kent)
Ham : Ham (Surrey)
Hamm : Hammerwood
Hams : Hamstreet
Harb : Harbledown
H'shm : Harrietsham
Hartf : Hartfield
Hart : Hartley
H'lip : Hartlip
H'lgh : Hastingleigh
H'bury : Hawkenbury
Hawkh : Hawkhurst
H'nge : Hawkinge
Hawl : Hawley
Haw : Hawthorn
Hay : Hayes (Kent)
Hayes : Hayes (Middx)
H'crn : Headcorn
H'ley : Headley
Hem : Hempstead
Hen I : Henwood Ind. Est.
H Bay : Herne Bay
Hern : Hernhill
Her : Hersden
Hever : Hever
Hex : Hextable
High : Higham
H Hal : High Halden
H Hals : High Halstow
Hild : Hildenborough
Hin : Hinxhill
Hoath : Hoath
Hock : Hockley
Hods : Hodsoll Street
Holl : Hollingbourne
Hoo : Hoo
Horn : Hornchurch
Horn H : Horndon-on-the-Hill
Hors : Horsell
Horsm : Horsmonden
Hor K : Horsted Keynes
Hort K : Horton Kirby
Hoth : Hothfield
Hou : Hougham
Huc : Hucking
Hunt : Hunton
Hrst G : Hurst Green
Hythe : Hythe
I'hm : Ickham
I'ham : Icklesham
Ide H : Ide Hill
Iden : Iden
I Grn : Iden Green
Igh : Ightham
Ilf : Ilford
Isle G : Isle of Grain
Ivy : Ivychurch
Ivy H : Ivy Hatch
Iwade : Iwade
Jur G : Jurys Gap
Kear : Kearsney
Kems : Kemsing
Kem : Kemsley
Ken : Kenardington
Kenl : Kenley
Kenn : Kennington
Kes : Keston
Kiln : Kilndown
Kgdn : Kingsdown
King H : Kings Hill
Kgnt : Kingsnorth
Kgtn : Kingston
King T : Kingston upon Thames
Kgswd : Kingswood
Knat : Knatts Valley
Knock : Knockholt
Ladd : Laddingford
Lam : Lamberhurst
Lang H : Langdon Hills
Langl : Langley
L'tn G : Langton Green
Lark : Larkfield
L'lnd : Leaveland
Leeds : Leeds
Leigh : Leigh
Lgh S : Leigh-on-Sea
Len : Lenham
Len H : Lenham Heath
Leyb : Leybourne
Ley S : Leysdown-on-Sea
Limp : Limpsfield
Linf : Linford
Ling : Lingfield
Lin : Linton
L'brne : Littlebourne
L Char : Little Chart
L'stne : Littlestone
Long : Longfield
Loose : Loose
Lwr Hal : Lower Halstow
Lwr Har : Lower Hardres
Lwr Sto : Lower Stoke
Lwr U : Lower Upnor
Ludd : Luddesdown
Lydd : Lydd
Lyd : Lydden
Lydd S : Lydd on Sea
Lym : Lyminge
Lymp : Lympne
Lyn : Lynsted
Maid : Maidstone
Mans : Manston
Mard : Marden
Mgte : Margate
Mark B : Mark Beech
Mark X : Mark Cross
M'boro : Marshborough
M Grn : Marsh Green
M'sde : Marshside
Mart : Martin
Mart M : Martin Mill
Matf : Matfield
Meop : Meopham
Mere : Mereworth
Mer : Mersham
Mid S : Middle Stoke
Mils : Milstead
Mil R : Milton Regis
Min : Minster
Min S : Minster on Sea
Mitc : Mitcham
Mol : Molash
M Hor : Monks Horton
Monk : Monkton
Mord : Morden
M'fld : Mountfield
Murs : Murston
Mys : Mystole
Nack : Nackington
Neth : Netherfield
Nett : Nettlestead
New Ad : New Addington
New Ash : New Ash Green
Newch : Newchurch
Newe : Newenden
N'grn : Newingreen
N'tn : Newington
N Mald : New Malden
Newn : Newnham
New R : New Romney
Non : Nonington
N'fleet : Northfleet
N'iam : Northiam
N Stif : North Stifford
N Hth : Northumberland Heath
Nor : Norton
Oare : Oare
Off : Offham
Old R : Old Romney
Old L : Old Wives Lees
Orp : Orpington
Ors : Orsett
Osp : Ospringe
Otf : Otford
Otham : Otham
O'den : Otterden
O'nge : Ottinge
Oxt : Oxted
Pad W : Paddock Wood
P For : Painters Forstal
Pat : Patrixbourne
P'den : Playden
Peas : Peasmarsh (Guildford)
P'mrsh : Peasmarsh (Rye)
Peene : Peene
Pem : Pembury
P'hst : Penhurst
Pens : Penshurst
P'hm : Petham
Pett : Pett
Pet W : Petts Wood
Pits : Pitsea
Platt : Platt
P Hth : Platts Heath
Plax : Plaxtol
P'ley : Pluckley
Post : Postling
Prat B : Pratts Bottom
Pres : Preston
Purf : Purfleet
Purl : Purley
Pys R : Pysons Road Ind. Est.
Quar W : Quarry Wood
Queen : Queenborough
Rain : Rainham
Ram : Ramsgate
R Min : Rhodes Minnis
R'boro : Richborough
Rich : Richmond
R'wld : Ringwould
Ripp : Ripple
River : River
Riv : Riverhead
Rob : Robertsbridge
Roch : Rochester
Rod : Rodmersham
Rol : Rolvenden
Romf : Romford
Roth : Rotherfield
R Comn : Rough Common
Rough : Roughway
Roy B : Royal British Legion Village
Ruck : Ruckinge
R'den : Rushenden
Rust : Rusthall
Rya : Ryarsh
Rye : Rye
Rye F : Rye Foreign
St D : St Dunstans
St Jhn : St Johns
St Law : St Lawrence
St Mc : St Margarets-at-Cliffe
St Mb : St Margarets Bay
St M : St Mary Cray
St Mh : St Mary Hoo
St Mm : St Mary in the Marsh
St Mar : St Marys Bay
St Mi : St Marys Island
St Mic : St Michaels
St Mil : St Mildreds
St N : St Nicholas at Wade
St P : St Pauls Cray
St Pet : St Peters
Salt : Saltwood
S'gte : Sandgate
Sand : Sandhurst
S'lng : Sandling
S'wy : Sandway
S'wch : Sandwich
S'wch B : Sandwich Bay
Sarre : Sarre
Seal : Seal
Sea : Seasalter
Sed : Sedlescombe
S'ndge : Sellindge
Sell : Selling
Sels : Selsted
Sev : Sevenoaks
Svgtn : Sevington
Shad : Shadoxhurst
Sharp : Sharpthorne
Shtng : Shatterling
S'ness : Sheerness
Shel : Sheldwich
Shel L : Sheldwich Lees
S'wll : Shepherdswell
S'brne : Shipbourne
Shoe : Shoeburyness
Shol : Sholden
Shor : Shoreham
Shorne : Shorne
Short : Shortlands
Shott : Shottenden
Shov G : Shovers Green
Sidc : Sidcup
Siss : Sissinghurst
Sit : Sittingbourne
Smar : Smarden
Sme : Smeeth
Snar : Snargate
Snave : Snave
Snod : Snodland
Snow : Snowdown
Sole S : Sole Street
S'boro : Southborough
S Croy : South Croydon
S Dar : South Darenth
Sth S : Southend-on-Sea
S'fleet : Southfleet
S Grn : South Green
S Ock : South Ockendon
S Stif : South Stifford
S St : South Street
Spar G : Sparrows Green
Speld : Speldhurst
Stal : Stalisfield
Stanf : Stanford
Stan H : Stanford-le-Hope
Stans : Stansted
S'le : Staple
Stapl : Staplecross
S'hrst : Staplehurst
S Min : Stelling Minnis
S'bry : Stockbury
Stod : Stodmarsh
Stone : Stone (Dartford)
Stne : Stone (Tenterden)
Stour : Stourmouth
Stow : Stowting
Stow C : Stowting Common
Str E : Street End
Strood : Strood
Stu X : Stubbs Cross
Sturry : Sturry
Sund : Sundridge
Surb : Surbiton
Sutt : Sutton
S at H : Sutton at Hone
Sut V : Sutton Valence
Swan : Swanley
Swans : Swanscombe
S'fld : Swingfield
Tad : Tadworth
Tats : Tatsfield
Temp E : Temple Ewell
Tent : Tenterden
Tstn : Teston
Tey : Teynham
T Oaks : Three Oaks
T Hth : Thornton Heath
Throw : Throwley
T'hm : Thurnham
Tic : Ticehurst
Til : Tilbury
Tilm : Tilmanstone
T'sey : Titsey
Tonb : Tonbridge
Tonge : Tonge
Ton : Tonwell
Tovil : Tovil
Toys : Toys Hill
Tros : Trottiscliffe
Tud : Tudeley
Tun W : Tunbridge Wells
Tun : Tunstall
T Hill : Tyler Hill
Udi : Udimore
Ulc : Ulcombe
Under : Underriver
Upc : Upchurch
Upm : Upminster
Upnor : Upnor
Up H'lng : Upper Halling
Up Harb : Upper Harbledown
Up Hard : Upper Hardres
Up Har : Upper Hartfield
Up Stok : Upper Stoke
Ups : Upstreet
Van : Vange
Wadh : Wadhurst
Wain : Wainscott
Wald : Waldershare
W'slde : Walderslade
Wallc : Wallcrouch
Wall : Wallington
Walm : Walmer
Walt : Waltham
Ward : Warden
Ware : Ware
W'hrne : Warehorne
Warl : Warlingham
War S : Warren Street
W'bury : Wateringbury
Weald : Weald
Weav : Weavering
Well : Welling
Wemb : Wembley
Wen : Wennington
W Bra : West Brabourne
W'bre : Westbere
Wclf S : Westcliff-on-Sea
Wnhgr : Westenhanger
W'ham : Westerham
W Far : West Farleigh
Westf : Westfield
Wgte S : Westgate-on-Sea
W Hou : West Hougham
W Hyt : West Hythe
W King : West Kingsdown

A-Z Kent Atlas 227

POSTTOWN AND POSTAL LOCALITY ABBREVIATIONS

W Mal : West Malling
W Peck : West Peckham
W Sto : West Stourmouth
W Thur : West Thurrock
W Til : West Tilbury
Westw : Westwell
W'wd : Westwood
W Wick : West Wickham
What : Whatlington
Whitf : Whitfield
Whits : Whitstable
Whyt : Whyteleafe
Wich : Wichling
Wickh : Wickhambreaux
W'boro : Willesborough
Wilm : Wilmington
Win : Wincheap
Win I : Wincheap Ind. Est.
W'sea : Winchelsea
W'sea B : Winchelsea Beach
W'hm : Wingham
W'hm W : Wingham Well
W'mre : Wingmore
Wint : Winterbourne
With : Withyham
Wit : Wittersham
Wold : Woldingham
Wom : Womenswold
Wdchu : Woodchurch
Wdboro : Woodnesborough
W Grn : Woolage Green
W Vil : Woolage Village
Woot : Wootton
Wor Pk : Worcester Park
W'hll : Wormshill
Worth : Worth
Woul : Wouldham
Wro : Wrotham
Wro H : Wrotham Heath
Wych X : Wych Cross
Wye : Wye
Yald : Yalding
Yel : Yelsted
York : Yorkletts

INDEX

Abbeville Ho. Roch —8N 79
Abbeville Rd. SW4 —4C 4
Abbey Brewery Ct. W Mal —1A 124
Abbey Clo. Deal —5K 177
Abbey Clo. Min S —6L 219
Abbey Cotts. S'lng —9C 110
Abbey Ct. Tun W —9G 150
Abbey Ct. Cotts. Chat —4B 110
Abbey Ct. Cotts. S'lng —8C 110
Abbey Cres. Belv —4B 52
Abbey Fields Fav —5J 187
(in two parts)
Abbey Fields Ct. Fav —5J 187
Abbey Gdns. Cant —9N 167
Abbey Gate. —8C 110
Abbey Ga. Ram —7F 210
Abbey Ga. Cotts. S'lng —8C 110
Abbey Gro. SE2 —4K 51
Abbey Gro. Min —8N 205
Abbey Gro. Ram —7F 210
Abbey Hill Rd. Sidc —7L 57
Abbey La. E15 —2E 5
Abbey La. Beck —3D 68
Abbey Mt. Belv —5A 52
Abbey Pk. Beck —3D 68
Abbey Pl. Dart —3L 59
Abbey Pl. Fav —4H 187
Abbey Rd. E15 —2E 5
Abbey Rd. NW6 & NW8 —2B 4
Abbey Rd. NW10 —2A 4
Abbey Rd. SE2 & Belv —4M 51 (3B 6)
Abbey Rd. Alk —3A 180 (1B 42)
Abbey Rd. Bark —1A 6
Abbey Rd. Bexh —2N 57
Abbey Rd. Fav —4H 187
Abbey Rd. Gill —1K 95
Abbey Rd. Grav —6K 63 (4B 8)
Abbey Rd. Grnh —3J 61
Abbey Rd. Roch —4K 79
Abbey Rd. Temp E —9C 178
Abbey St. SE1 —3D 5
Abbey St. Fav —4H 187
Abbey Ter. SE2 —4L 51
Abbey Trad. Est. SE26 —1C 68
Abbeyview Dri. Min S —6J 219
Abbey Way. W'boro —8L 159
Abbey Wood. —4L 51 (3B 6)
Abbey Wood Camping & Cvn. Site. SE2 —5L 51
Abbey Wood Rd. SE2 —4K 51
Abbey Wood Rd. King H —4M 123
Abbots Barton Wlk. Cant —3A 172
Abbotsbury Rd. Brom —3J 83
Abbotsbury Rd. Mord —2B 12
Abbots Clo. Orp —2E 84
Abbots Ct. Rd. Hoo —8J 67
Abbots Field. Grav —2H 77
Abbots Field. Maid —7M 125
Abbotshall Rd. SE6 —6G 54
Abbot's Hill. Ram —6J 211
Abbots Pl. Cant —1M 171 (4D 21)
Abbots Rd. Fav —5J 187
Abbots, The. Dover —4H 181
Abbots Wlk. Wye —2M 159
Abbots Way. Beck —8B 68
Abbotswell Rd. SE4 —3C 54
Abbots Wood. Bos —3E 31
Abbotswood Clo. Belv —3N 51
Abbott Rd. E14 —2E 5
Abbott Rd. Bor G —2M 121
Abbott Rd. Folk —5L 189
Abbotts Clo. Roch —9M 79
Abbotts Clo. Swan —7H 73
Abbotts Dri. Stan H —2C 8
Abbott's Grn. Croy —7A 82
Abbotts Rd. Sutt —2B 12
Abbott's Wlk. Bexh —7M 51
Abbs Cross La. Horn —1D 7
Aberconway Rd. Mord —1B 12
Abercorn Pl. NW8 —2B 4
Aberdare Clo. W Wick —3F 82
Aberdeen Clo. Ups —3A 22
Aberdeen Ho. Maid —1H 139
Aberdeen Rd. NW10 —1A 4
Aberdeen Rd. Croy —2D 13
Aberford Gdns. SE18 —8A 50
Abergeldie Rd. SE12 —4L 55
Abernethy Rd. SE13 —2H 55
Abery St. SE18 —4G 50
Abigail Cres. W'slde —1C 110
Abingdon Gro. Ups —3A 22
Abingdon Rd. Maid —8K 125
Abingdon Way. Orp —5K 85
Abinger Clo. Brom —6A 70
Abinger Dri. Chat —9G 94
Aboyne Rd. SW17 —4B 4
Absolam Ct. Gill —1M 95
Acacia Clo. Orp —8F 70
Acacia Ct. Grav —5F 62
Acacia Dri. Sth S —1C 11
Acacia Gdns. W Wick —3F 82
Acacia Ho. S'ness —2C 218
(off Pepys Av.)
Acacia Rd. Beck —6C 68
Acacia Rd. Dart —6L 59
Acacia Rd. Grnh —4E 60
Acacia Ter. Sit —7D 98
Acacia Wlk. Swan —5E 72
Acacia Way. Sidc —6H 57
Acadamy Dri. Gill —2J 95
Academy Pl. SE18 —8B 50
Academy Rd. SE18 —8B 50 (3A 6)
Acer Av. Tun W —5J 157
Acer Rd. Big H —4D 164
Achilles Rd. Chat —9F 94
Ackerley Ct. Afrd —3D 160
(off Luddenham Clo.)
Ackholt Rd. Aysm —2E 162 (2B 32)
Ackroyd Rd. SE23 —5A 54
Acland Clo. SE18 —7F 50
Acol. —8G 207 (2C 23)
Acol Hill. Acol —7G 206 (2C 23)
Acorn Clo. Chst —1E 70
Acorn Clo. Five G —8G 147
Acorn Gro. Dit —1H 125
Acorn Ind. Pk. Dart —3G 59
Acorn Pl. Maid —2H 139
Acorn Rd. Dart —3G 59
Acorn Rd. Gill —8J 81
Acorns, The. Sev —5H 119
Acorns, The. Smar —3J 221
Acorn St. S'ness —3D 218
Acorn Way. SE23 —8A 54
Acorn Way. Orp —5D 84
Acorn Wharf Rd. Roch —6N 79
Acre Clo. Chat —2B 94
Acre Gro. Hall —7E 92
Acre La. SW2 —4C 5
Acre La. Cars & Wall —2C 12
Acre, The. Whitf —5E 178
Acrise. —1E 41
Acton. —2A 4
(nr. Ealing)
Acton. —1A 46
(nr. Wittersham)
Acton Green. —3A 4
Acton La. NW10 —2A 4
Acton La. W4 —3A 4
(in two parts)
Acton La. Wit —2A 46
Acton Pl. Yald —7E 136
Acton Rd. Whits —4F 224
Acworth Pl. Dart —4K 59
Adam Clo. SE6 —9D 54
Adam Clo. Cox —5A 138
Adams Clo. Tent —6C 222
Adams Clo. Tonb —7J 145
Adams La. N'iam —3C 45
Adamsrill Rd. SE26 —9A 54
Adams Rd. Beck —8B 68
Adams Sq. Bexh —1N 57
Ada Rd. Cant —4K 171
A Day At The Wells. —3G 156
(off Linden Pk. Rd.)
Adbert Dri. E Far —4M 137
Adcock Wlk. Orp —5H 85
Addelam Clo. Deal —6K 177
Addelam Rd. Deal —6K 177
Adderley Gdns. SE9 —9C 56
Addington. —6D 82 (2E 13)
(nr. Croydon)
Addington. —8J 107 (4B 16)
(nr. Wrotham)
Addington Gro. SE26 —9B 54
Addington La. Tros —6F 106 (4B 16)
Addington Pl. Ram —6J 211
Addington Rd. Croy —2E 13
Addington Rd. Mgte —3D 208
Addington Rd. Sit —8F 98
Addington Rd. S Croy —9A 82 (3D 13)
Addington Rd. W Wick —5F 82
Addington Sq. Mgte —3D 208
Addington St. W1 —2B 4
Addington St. Mgte —3D 208
Addington St. Ram —6H 211
Addington Village Rd. Croy —7C 82 (2E 13)
(in two parts)
Addiscombe. —2D 13
Addiscombe Gdns. Mgte —4D 208
Addiscombe Rd. Croy —2D 13
Addiscombe Rd. Mgte —4E 208 (1E 23)
Addison Clo. E Mal —9D 108
Addison Clo. Orp —9E 70
Addison Cres. W14 —3B 4
Addison Dri. SE12 —3L 55
Addison Rd. W14 —3B 4
Addison Rd. Brom —8N 69
Addisons Clo. Croy —3C 82
Addlestead. —1K 147 (3B 26)
Addlestead Rd. E Peck —1K 147 (3B 26)
Adelaide Av. SE4 —2C 54 (4E 5)
Adelaide Cotts. Maid —1L 137
Adelaide Ct. Beck —3C 68
Adelaide Dri. Sit —7D 98
Adelaide Gdns. Min S —7E 218
Adelaide Gdns. Ram —6J 211
Adelaide Pl. Cant —2M 171 (1D 31)
Adelaide Rd. NW3 —1B 4
Adelaide Rd. Chst —1D 70
Adelaide Rd. Evtn & Eyt —3B 32
Adelaide Rd. Gill —8F 80
Adelaide, The. High —7G 65
Adenmore Rd. SE6 —5D 54
Aden Ter. Maid —2D 126
Adie Rd. G'stne —6E 212
Adisham. —2A 32
Adisham Downs Rd. Adm —2A 32
Adisham Downs Rd. Bek —8L 173
Adisham Dri. Maid —2M 125
Adisham Grn. Kem —3G 99
Adisham Rd. B'hm —7F 162 (3A 32)
Adisham Rd. Bek —7K 173 (2A 32)
Adisham Rd. W'hm —4B 226 (2A 32)
Adisham Way. Mgte —4G 208
Admaston Rd. SE18 —7E 50
Admers Wood Meop —2G 106
Admiral Clo. Orp —7M 71
Admiral Moore Dri. Roy B —9K 109
Admiral Seymour Rd. SE9 —2B 56
Admirals Wlk. Bene —3A 38
Admirals Wlk. Chat —8E 94
(Lords Wood La.)
Admiral's Wlk. Chat —5C 80
(Main Ga. Rd.)
Admirals Wlk. Grnh —3H 61
Admirals Wlk. Hythe —7K 197
Admirals Wlk. Min S —6F 218
Admirals Wlk. Tent —6D 222
Admiralty Rd. Upnor —3C 80
Admiralty Ter. Gill —5D 80
Admiralty Ter. Upnor —3C 80
Admiralty Wlk. Whits —6C 224
Adolf St. SE6 —9E 54
Adrian M. Wgte S —2L 207
Adrian Sq. Wgte S —2L 207
Adrian St. Dover —5J 181
Aerodrome Ind. Est. Det —5B 112
Aerodrome Rd. Bek —6K 173
Aerodrome Rd. H'nge —8A 192 (2A 42)
Afghan Rd. Broad —5K 209
Afghan Rd. Chat —8B 80
Agar Gro. NW1 —1C 4
Agaton Rd. SE9 —7E 56
Agester La. Dent —4A 32
Agincourt Rd. NW3 —1B 4
Agnew Rd. SE23 —5A 54
Agricultural & Rural Life Museum. —8N 205 (2C 23)
Ainsdale Clo. Folk —4H 189
Ainsdale Clo. Orp —2F 84
Aintree Clo. Grav —8G 63
Aintree Ho. Maid —2J 139
(off Epsom Clo.)
Aintree Rd. Chat —8F 94
Airedale Clo. Dart —6C 60
Airedale Clo. Mgte —4E 208
Airfield Way. Horn —1D 7
Airport Ind. Est. Big H —3D 164
Aisher Way. Riv —3F 118
Aislibie Rd. SE12 —2H 55
Aisne Dri. Cant —1C 172
Aitken Rd. SE6 —7E 54
Ajax Rd. Roch —4N 93
Akehurst La. Sev —7K 119
Akerman Rd. SW9 —3C 5
Alabama St. SE18 —7F 50
Alamein Av. Chat —4C 94
Alamein Clo. B Hts —2L 181
Alamein Gdns. Dart —5D 60
Alamein Rd. Swans —4K 61
Alanbrooke. Grav —5H 63
Alan Clo. Dart —2K 59
Alanthus Clo. SE12 —4K 55
Albacore Cres. SE13 —4E 54
Alban Cres. F'ham —2A 88
Albany Clo. Bex —5L 57
Albany Clo. Tonb —8K 145
Albany Dri. H Bay —2E 194
Albany Hill. Tun W —9J 151
Albany Ho. Dover —5J 181
(off Albany Pl.)
Albany M. Brom —2K 69
Albany Pl. Dover —5J 181
Albany Rd. SE5 —3D 5
Albany Rd. Belv —6A 52
Albany Rd. Bex —5L 57
Albany Rd. Cap F —3B 174
Albany Rd. Chat —1E 94
Albany Rd. Chst —1D 70 (1A 14)
Albany Rd. Gill —8G 81
Albany Rd. Roch —8N 79
Albany Rd. Sit —8F 98 (3C 19)
Albany St. NW1 —2C 4
Albany St. Maid —4E 126
Albany Ter. Chat —8B 80 (2D 17)
Albany Ter. Gill —8G 81
Albatross Av. Roch —5G 78
Albatross Lodge. Dover —2G 181
Albatross St. SE18 —7G 50
Albemarle Pk. Beck —4E 68
Albemarle Rd. Beck —4E 68 (1E 13)
Albemarle Rd. Chat —9E 94
Albemarle Rd. W'slde —3E 17
Albemarle Rd. W'boro —1J 161
Alberta Cvn. Pk. Sea —7A 224
Alberta Clo. Dover —1G 181
Alberta Rd. Eri —8D 52
Albert Bri. SW3 & SW11 —3B 4
Albert Bri. Rd. SW11 —3B 4
Albert Costain Ct. Folk —6K 189
(off Foord Rd.)
Albert Cotts. Tun W —1J 157
Albert Ct. Whits —3F 224
Albert Embkmt. SE1 —3C 5
Albert La. Hythe —7J 197
Albert Mnr. Gill —7E 80
Albert M. SE4 —2B 54
Albert Murray Clo. Grav —5H 63
Albert Pl. Maid —2E 27
Albert Pl. Roch —5M 79
Albert Rd. E16 —1A 50 (2A 6)
Albert Rd. SE9 —8A 56
Albert Rd. SE20 —2A 68
Albert Rd. Afrd —7F 158
Albert Rd. Belv —5A 52 (3C 6)
Albert Rd. Bex —4B 58
Albert Rd. Broad —6J 209
Albert Rd. Brom —8N 69
Albert Rd. Cant —2A 172
Albert Rd. Chat —9D 80
Albert Rd. Chels —6J 85
Albert Rd. Dart —8K 59
Albert Rd. Deal —4M 177 (2E 33)
Albert Rd. Dover —3J 181
Albert Rd. Folk —5K 189
Albert Rd. Gill —8F 80
Albert Rd. Hythe —7J 197
Albert Rd. Mgte —3B 208
Albert Rd. Ram —5K 211
Albert Rd. Roch —8N 79
Albert Rd. St M —9K 71
Albert Rd. Swans —4M 61
Albert Rd. Tonb —6H 145
Albert Rd. Est. Belv —5A 52
Albert St. Maid —3C 126
Albert St. Ram —6H 211
Albert St. Tun W —1H 157
Albert St. Whits —3F 224
Albert Ter. NW1 —2B 4
Albert Ter. Bri —8H 173
Albert Ter. Mgte —3C 208
Albert Vs. Sturry —7E 168
Albert Wlk. E16 —2C 50
Albhuera Sq. Cant —1C 172
Albion Clo. H Bay —7H 195
Albion Cottage. Mard —3L 205
Albion Dri. E8 —2D 5
Albion Hill. Ram —6J 211
Albion Ho. E16 —1D 50
(off Church St.)
Albion La. H Bay —7H 195 (2E 21)
Albion M. Ram —6J 211
Albion M. Rd. Folk —7K 189
Albion Pde. Grav —4J 63
Albion Pl. Cant —1N 171 (4D 21)
Albion Pl. Fav —5G 187
Albion Pl. Lwr U —1D 80
Albion Pl. Maid —5D 126
Albion Pl. Mgte —2D 208
Albion Pl. N'tn —5K 97
Albion Pl. Ram —6J 211
Albion Pl. S'ness —2D 218
Albion Pl. W'boro —2J 161
Albion Rd. N16 —1D 5
Albion Rd. Bexh —2A 58 (4C 6)
Albion Rd. Birch —4F 206
Albion Rd. Broad —7J 209 (1E 23)
Albion Rd. Chat —9E 94
Albion Rd. Clift —2E 208
Albion Rd. Deal —2N 177
Albion Rd. E'try —3J 183
Albion Rd. Folk —5K 189
Albion Rd. Grav —5H 63
Albion Rd. Hythe —6L 197
Albion Rd. Mard —3L 205 (4D 27)
Albion Rd. Ram —5K 211
Albion Rd. Tun W —9H 151
Albion St. Broad —9M 209 (2E 23)
Albion Ter. Grav —4H 63
Albion Ter. Sit —5G 98
Albion Vs. Folk —7K 189
Albion Way. SE13 —2F 54
Albion Way. Eden —4B 184
Albury Av. Bexh —9N 51
Albury Clo. Chat —9G 94
Albyfield. Brom —7B 70
Alchins Cotts. Langl —6B 138
Alconbury. Bexh —3C 58
Alder Clo. S'ness —4B 218
Alder Clo. Tun W —5J 151
Alder Cotts. Lymp —5B 196
Alder Ho. SE4 —1D 54
Alder La. Rol —4A 38
Aldermary Rd. Brom —4K 69
Aldermoor Rd. SE6 —8C 54
Alderney Gdns. Broad —8J 209
Alderney Rd. Eri —7H 53
Alder Rd. Folk —5J 189
Alder Rd. Sidc —8H 57
Aldersbrook. —1A 6
Aldersbrook Rd. E11 & E12 —1A 6
Aldersford Clo. SE4 —3A 54
Aldersgate St. EC1 —2D 5
Aldersgrove Av. SE9 —8N 55
Aldershot Rd. Chat —4D 94
Alders Ind. Est., The. Mere —1J 135
Aldersmead Av. Croy —9A 68
Alders Meadow. Tonb —5F 144
Aldersmead Rd. Beck —3B 68
Alders Rd. Tud —9C 146 (4A 26)
Alders, The. W Wick —3E 82
Alder Way. Swan —5E 72
Alderwood Rd. SE9 —4F 56
Aldgate. (Junct.) —2D 5
Aldington. —2B 40
Aldington Clo. Chat —6E 94
Aldington Frith. —2B 40
Aldington La. T'hm —1N 127
Aldington Rd. Bear —5J 127
Aldington Rd. Lymp —6A 196 (3C 40)
Aldon. —1B 26
Aldon Clo. Maid —3F 126
Aldon Ct. Maid —3F 126
Aldon La. Off —1G 123
Aldon La. W Mal —4B 16
Aldred Rd. Fav —6G 187
Aldrich Cres. New Ad —9F 82
Aldridge Clo. H Bay —4C 194
Aldrington Rd. SW16 —1C 12
Aldwick Clo. SE9 —8F 56
Aldworth Gro. SE13 —4F 54
Aldwych. WC2 —2C 5
Aldwych Clo. Tonb —9K 133
Alen Sq. S'hrst —7K 221
Alers Rd. Bexh —3M 57
Alexander Cen., The. Fav —5H 187
Alexander Clo. Brom —2K 83
Alexander Clo. Fav —4F 186
Alexander Clo. Sidc —4G 57
Alexander Cotts. High —7G 65
Alexander Ct. Beck —4G 69
Alexander Ct. Roch —4M 79
Alexander Dri. Fav —5F 186
Alexander Evans M. SE23 —7A 54
Alexander Rd. Bexh —9M 51
Alexander Rd. Chst —2D 70
Alexander Rd. Grnh —3J 61
Alexandra Av. W4 —3A 4
Alexandra Av. Gill —8H 81
Alexandra Clo. Sit —4F 98
Alexandra Clo. Swan —5F 72
Alexandra Ct. Hythe —7H 197
Alexandra Cres. Brom —2J 69
Alexandra Dri. H Bay —2D 194
Alexandra Dri. Surb —2A 12
Alexandra Gdns. Folk —7K 189
Alexandra Glen. W'slde —1D 110
Alexandra Homes. Mgte —4C 208
Alexandra Pl. Dover —3H 181
Alexandra Rd. SE26 —2A 68
Alexandra Rd. SW19 —1B 12
Alexandra Rd. Big H —7B 164
Alexandra Rd. Birch —6F 206
Alexandra Rd. Broad —9M 209
Alexandra Rd. Cap F —2B 174
Alexandra Rd. Chat —1E 94
Alexandra Rd. Eps —3A 12
Alexandra Rd. Eri —6G 52
Alexandra Rd. Flete —8B 208
Alexandra Rd. Grav —5K 63
Alexandra Rd. Kgdn —4M 199
Alexandra Rd. Mgte —5C 208
Alexandra Rd. Ram —4H 211
Alexandra Rd. S'ness —2E 218
Alexandra Rd. Tonb —7H 145
Alexandra Rd. Walm —8N 177
Alexandra Rd. Whits —5E 224
Alexandra St. Folk —4L 189 (2A 42)
Alexandra St. Maid —3C 126
Alexandra St. Sth S —1C 10
Alexandra Ter. Mgte —4C 208
Alexandra Ter. Mer —9L 161
Alfan La. Dart —1E 72
Alford Grn. New Ad —7G 82
Alford Rd. Eri —5D 52
Alfred Clo. Cant —4J 171
Alfred Clo. Chat —1E 94
Alfred Cotts. Ram —5J 211
Alfred Ho. Grav —6E 62
Alfred Pl. N'fleet —6E 62
Alfred Rd. Afrd —2H 161
Alfred Rd. Belv —5A 52
Alfred Rd. Birch —3C 206
Alfred Rd. Cant —4J 171
Alfred Rd. Dart —9M 59
(in two parts)
Alfred Rd. Dover —2G 181
Alfred Rd. Grav —7G 62
Alfred Rd. G'stne —6E 212
Alfred Rd. Mgte —4F 208
Alfred Row. Deal —3N 177
Alfred Sq. Deal —3N 177
Alfreds Way. Bark —2B 6
Algernon Rd. SE13 —2E 54
Algiers Rd. SE13 —2D 54

Alice Bright La.—Ashen Tree La.

Alice Bright La. *Crowb* —4C **35**
Alice Thompson Clo. *SE12* —7M **55**
Alicia Av. *Mgte* —3M **207**
Alicia Ho. *Well* —8K **51**
Alicia Vs. *Cha* —8C **170**
Alington Ho. *Mgte* —3B **208**
Alison Clo. *Birch* —3G **206**
Alison Clo. *Croy* —2A **82**
Alison Clo. *Whitf* —7F **178**
Alison Cres. *Whitf* —7F **178**
Alkali Row. Mgte —2C **208**
(off King St.)
Alkerden La. *Grnh & Swans* —4J **61** (4E **7**)
Alkham. —**1B 42**
Alkham Clo. *Clift* —3K **209**
Alkham Rd. *Alk* —1A **180** (1B **42**)
Alkham Rd. *Maid* —5F **126**
Alkham Valley Rd. *Alk* —1A **180**
Alkham Valley Rd. *Folk* —1J **189** (2A **42**)
(in two parts)
Allan Clo. *Tun W* —1C **156**
Allandale Pl. *Orp* —4M **85**
Allandale Rd. *Tun W* —8K **151**
Alland Grange La. *Mans* —9K **207** (2D **23**)
Allan Rd. *Sea* —6A **224**
Allard Clo. *Orp* —1L **85**
Allen Av. *Wgte S* —4J **207**
Allenby Av. *Deal* —5L **177**
Allenby Rd. *SE23* —8B **54**
Allenby Rd. *Big H* —5E **164**
Allenby Rd. *Ram* —2F **210** (2E **23**)
Allenby Wlk. *Sit* —6C **98**
Allen Clo. *Chat* —5F **94**
Allen Ct. *Min S* —7H **219**
Allendale Clo. *SE26* —1A **68**
Allendale Clo. *Dart* —6D **60**
Allendale St. *Folk* —5K **189**
Allen Field. *Afrd* —1D **160**
Allen Rd. *Beck* —5A **68**
Allen Rd. *S'gte* —8D **188**
Allens. *Mard* —3L **205**
Allens La. *Plax* —1N **133** (2A **26**)
Allen St. *Maid* —4D **126**
Allenswood Rd. *SE9* —1A **56**
Allerford Rd. *SE6* —8E **54**
Alleyn Pk. *SE21* —4D **5**
Allhallows. —**5L 201 (3A 10)**
Allhallows Holiday Est. *Allh* —2K **201**
Allhallows-on-Sea. —**3M 201 (3A 10)**
Allhallows-on-Sea Est. *Allh* —3M **201**
Allhallows Rd. *Lwr Sto* —7K **201** (3A **10**)
Alliance Rd. *SE18* —6J **51**
Alliance Rd. *Ram* —6K **211**
Alliance Way. *Pad W* —9L **147**
Allington. —**1A 126 (1D 27)**
Allington Clo. *Grav* —6L **63**
Allington Dri. *Roch* —4J **79**
Allington Dri. *Tonb* —2N **145**
Allington Gdns. *W'bury* —1B **136**
Allington Rd. *Gill* —9K **81**
Allington Rd. *Orp* —3F **84**
Allington Rd. *Pad W* —8L **147**
Allington Way. *Maid* —3M **125**
Allison Av. *Gill* —2H **95**
Allnutt Mill Clo. *Tovil* —7B **126**
Allotment La. *Sev* —4K **119**
All Saints' Av. *Mgte* —4A **208** (1D **23**)
All Saints Clo. *Swans* —3M **61**
All Saints Clo. *Whits* —4G **225**
All Saints Ct. Cant —2M **171** *(1D* **31***)*
(off All Saints La.)
All Saints Ind. Est. *Mgte* —4B **208**
All Saints La. *Cant* —2M **171** (1D **31**)
All Saints Rise. *Tun W* —8G **151**
All Saints Rd. *Allh* —4L **201**
All Saints Rd. *Hawkh* —6L **191**
All Saints Rd. *N'fleet* —6E **62**
All Saints Rd. *Sit* —7K **99**
All Saints Rd. *Sutt* —2B **12**
All Saints Rd. *Tun W* —8G **151**
Allsop Pl. *NW1* —2B **4**
All Souls Av. *NW10* —2A **4**
Allsworth Clo. *N'tn* —5K **97**
Allwood Clo. *SE26* —9A **54**
Alma Cotts. *Sturry* —7E **168**
Alma Pl. *Cant* —1N **171**
Alma Pl. *Hdlw* —8D **134**
Alma Pl. *Ram* —5J **211**
Alma Pl. *Roch* —5L **79**
Alma Rd. *Cars* —2B **12**
Alma Rd. *Eccl* —4K **109**
Alma Rd. *Folk* —6D **188**
Alma Rd. *H Bay* —2J **195**
Alma Rd. *Mgte* —4D **208**
Alma Rd. *Orp* —3M **85**
Alma Rd. *Ram* —4J **211**
Alma Rd. *S'ness* —2D **218**
Alma Rd. *Sidc* —8J **57** (4B **6**)
Alma Rd. *Swans* —3M **61**
Alma Rd. *W Mal* —1M **123**
Alma St. *Cant* —1N **171**
Alma St. *S'ness* —2E **218**
Alma St. Pas. S'ness —2E **218**
(off Telescope All.)
Alma, The. *Grav* —9L **63**
Almery Cotts. *Cha S* —8L **139**
Almond Clo. *Afrd* —5D **158**
Almond Clo. *Broad* —9G **209**
Almond Clo. *Brom* —1C **84**
Almond Clo. *Ches* —4M **225**
Almond Dri. *Swan* —5E **72**
Almond Gro. *Hem* —7K **95**
Almond Ho. *Maid* —6L **125**
Almond Rd. *Dart* —5C **60**
Almonds, The. *Bear* —5K **127**
Almond Tree Clo. *S'ness* —4B **218**
Almond Way. *Brom* —1C **84**
Almon Pl. *Roch* —7A **80**
Almshouse Rd. *Stal* —2E **29**
Alms Row. *Bras* —6K **117**
Alnwick Ct. Dart —4B **60**
(off Osbourne Rd.)
Alnwick Rd. *SE12* —5L **55**
Alpha Clo. *Hoo* —6N **67**
Alpha Rd. *Birch* —4F **206** (1C **23**)
Alpha Rd. *Ram* —6H **211**
Alpine Copse. *Brom* —5C **70**
Alsager Av. *Queen* —9A **218**
Alsike Rd. *Eri* —3M **51**
Alsops Rd. *W'boro* —2J **161**
Alston Clo. *Min S* —5K **219**
Altash Way. *SE9* —7B **56**
Altbarn Ind. Est. *Chat* —2F **110**
Alton Av. *Gill* —1K **95**
Alton Clo. *Bex* —6N **57**
Alton Cotts. *F'ham* —2M **87**
Alton Gdns. *Beck* —3D **68**
Alton M. *Gill* —8F **80**
Altyre Clo. *Beck* —8C **68**
Altyre Way. *Beck* —8C **68**
Alverstone Gdns. *SE9* —6E **56**
Alvis Av. *H Bay* —3B **194**
Alwold Cres. *SE12* —4L **55**
Alwyn Clo. *New Ad* —8E **82**
Amage Rd. *Wye* —4B **30**
Amanda Clo. *Chat* —8C **94**
Amar Ct. *SE18* —4H **51**
Amar Deep Ct. *SE18* —5H **51**
Amber Clo. *Tey* —2L **223**
Amberfield Cotts. *Cha S* —7K **139**
Amber Grn. Cotts. *Cha S* —7H **139**
Amber La. *Cha S* —7J **139** (3E **27**)
Amberleaze Dri. *Pem* —8C **152**
Amberley Clo. *Orp* —6H **85**
Amberley Clo. *Tonb* —7G **144**
Amberley Ct. *Beck* —3C **68**
Amberley Ct. *Sidc* —1L **71**
Amberley Rd. *SE2* —6M **51**
Amber Way. *Cha S* —7L **139**
Amberwood Rise. *N Mald* —2A **12**
Amblecote Clo. *SE12* —8L **55**
Amblecote Meadows. *SE12* —8L **55**
Amblecote Rd. *SE12* —8L **55**
Ambleside. *Brom* —2G **69**
Ambleside. *Fav* —6J **187**
Ambleside. *Sit* —8K **99**
Ambleside Av. *SW16* —1C **12**
Ambleside Av. *Beck* —8B **68** (2E **13**)
Ambleside Rd. *Bexh* —9B **52**
Ambley Grn. *Gill B* —3K **95**
Ambley Rd. *Gill B* —2K **95**
Ambrooke Rd. *Belv* —3B **52**
Ambrose Clo. *Cray* —2G **59**
Ambrose Clo. *Orp* —4H **85**
Ambrose Hill. *Chat* —1F **94**
Amels Hill. *S'bry* —2H **113**
Ames Av. *Bear* —5K **127**
Amesbury Rd. *Brom* —6N **69**
Ames Rd. *Swans* —4L **61**
Amethyst Av. *Chat* —5B **94**
Amherst Clo. *Maid* —5A **126**
Amherst Clo. *Mgte* —4G **209**
Amherst Clo. *Orp* —7K **71**
Amherst Dri. *Orp* —7H **71**
Amherst Hill. *Gill* —6D **80**
Amherst Hill. *Sev* —5G **118** (2C **25**)
Amherst Redoubt. *Gill* —7D **80**
Amherst Rd. *Roch* —9A **80**
Amherst Rd. *Sev* —4J **119**
Amherst Rd. *Tun W* —9G **151**
Amhurst Bank Rd. *Pem* —3D **152** (1A **36**)
Amhurst Rd. *N16 & E8* —1D **5**
Amhurst Vs. *Maid* —4K **137**
Amhurst Wlk. *SE28* —1J **51**
Amies Ho. *Maid* —6C **138**
Amos Clo. *Shel L* —1A **30**
Ampleforth Clo. *Orp* —5L **85**
Ampleforth Rd. *SE2* —2K **51**
Amsbury Rd. *Hunt* —6L **137** (3D **27**)
Amwell St. *EC1* —2C **5**
Amy Clo. *SE3* —2M **55**
Amyruth Rd. *SE4* —3D **54**
Ancaster M. *Beck* —6A **68**
Ancaster Rd. *Beck* —6A **68**
Ancaster St. *SE18* —7G **50**
Anchorage Clo. *Mid S* —9K **201**
Anchorage Flats. *Pad W* —9M **147**
Anchor Bay Ind. Est. *Eri* —6H **53**
Anchor Boulevd. *Dart* —2C **60**
Anchor Bus. Pk. *Sit* —5J **99**
Anchor Ct. *Eri* —7G **53**
Anchor Hill. *Mgte* —3D **208**
Anchor La. *Deal* —4M **177**
Anchor La. *S'ness* —1A **218**
(in two parts)
Anchor Rd. *Roch* —2N **93**
Ancona Rd. *SE18* —5F **50**
Ancress Clo. *Cant* —7N **167**
Andace Pk. Gdns. *Brom* —5M **69**
Anderson Way. *Belv* —2C **52**
Andorra Ct. *Brom* —4M **69**
Andover Rd. *Orp* —3G **84**
Andover Wlk. *Maid* —2J **139**
Andreck Ct. *Beck* —5E **68**
Andrew Broughton Way. *Maid* —5E **126**
Andrew Clo. *Dart* —3E **58**
Andrew Ct. *SE23* —7A **54**
Andrew Mnr. *Gill* —6E **80**
Andrew Rd. *Tun W* —6J **151**
Andrew's Clo. *Orp* —5M **71**
Andrews Clo. *Tun W* —9K **151**
Andrews Pl. *SE9* —4D **56**
Andrews Wlk. *Sit* —6C **98**
Andwell Clo. *SE2* —2K **51**
Anerley. —**1D 13**
Anerley Clo. *Maid* —2A **126**
Anerley Hill. *SE19* —1D **13**
Anerley Rd. *SE20 & SE19* —1D **13**
Angel. (Junct.) —2C **5**
Angel Hill. *Sutt* —2B **12**
Angelica Gdns. *Croy* —2A **82**
Angel La. *E15* —1E **5**
Angel La. *Tonb* —6H **145**
Angel Ter. *Sand* —2K **215**
Angel Wlk. *Tonb* —6H **145**
Anglesea Av. *SE18* —4D **50**
Anglesea Cen. *Grav* —4G **62**
Anglesea Rd. *SE18* —4D **50**
Anglesea Rd. *Orp* —9L **71**
Anglesey Av. *Maid* —2D **138**
Anglesey Clo. *Chat* —4E **94**
Angley Ct. *Horsm* —3C **198**
Angley Rd. *C'brk* —8B **176** (2E **37**)
Angley Wlk. *C'brk* —6D **176**
Ankerdine Cres. *SE18* —7D **50**
Annandale Rd. *Sidc* —5G **57**
Anna Pk. *Birch* —3E **206**
Anne Boleyn Clo. *E'chu* —5D **202**
Anne Boleyn Ct. *SE9* —4F **56**
Anne Clo. *Birch* —4G **206**
Anne Figg Ct. *Roch* —8N **79**
Anne Grn. Wlk. *Cant* —9A **168**
Anne of Cleeves Ct. *SE9* —4F **56**
Anne of Cleves Rd. *Dart* —3L **59**
Anne Roper Clo. *New R* —3F **212**
Annesley Dri. *Croy* —4C **82**
Anne's Rd. *Broad* —6M **209**
Anne Sutherland Ho. *Beck* —3B **68**
Annetts Hall. *Bor G* —1N **121**
Annie Rd. *Snod* —4D **108**
Ann's Rd. *Ram* —4J **211**
Ann St. *SE18* —5E **50**
(in two parts)
Annvera Ho. *Gill* —5F **80**
Ansdore. —**3C 31**
Ansell Av. *Chat* —1D **94**
Anselm Clo. *Sit* —7F **98**
Anselm Rd. *Dover* —4F **180**
Ansford Rd. *Brom* —1F **68**
Anson Clo. *Chat* —5F **94**
Anson Clo. *Pys R* —1H **211**
Anson Rd. *NW2* —1A **4**
Anson Rd. *W Mal* —6L **123**
Anstee Rd. *Dover* —3H **181**
Anstridge Path. *SE9* —4F **56**
Anstridge Rd. *SE9* —4F **56**
Antelope Rd. *SE18* —3B **50**
Anthony Clo. *Dun G* —2F **118**
Anthony Clo. *Ram* —4F **210**
Anthony Cres. *Whits* —7D **224**
Anthony La. *Swan* —4H **73**
Anthony Rd. *Well* —8J **51**
Anthony's Way. *Roch* —3A **80** (1D **17**)
(in two parts)
Anvil Clo. *Birch* —5F **206**
Anvil Green. —**3C 31**
Anvil Grn. Farm Rd. *Walt* —3C **31**
Anvil Grn. Rd. *Walt* —3C **31**
Anzio Cres. *B Hts* —2K **181**
Aperfield. —**5E 164 (4A 14)**
Aperfield Rd. *Big H* —5E **164**
Aperfield Rd. *Eri* —6G **53**
Aperfields. *W'ham* —5E **164**
Apex Clo. *Beck* —4E **68**
Apiary Bus. Pk. *Kgswd* —5D **140**
Apollo Av. *Brom* —4L **69**
Apollo Way. *SE28* —3F **50**
Apple Barn Ct. *Crou* —4B **122**
Appleby Clo. *Roch* —4A **94**
Apple Clo. *Snod* —4D **108**
Apple Ct. *Pad W* —9L **147**
Appledore. —**1B 46**
Appledore Av. *Bexh* —8D **52**
Appledore Av. *S'ness* —4C **218**
Appledore Clo. *Brom* —8K **69**
Appledore Clo. *Mgte* —4G **208**
Appledore Ct. *Maid* —2N **125**
Appledore Cres. *Folk* —4D **188**
Appledore Cres. *Sidc* —8G **57**
Appledore Heath. —**4D 39**
Appledore Rd. *Gill* —9K **81**
Appledore Rd. *Stne & Apul* —1B **46**
Appledore Rd. *Tent* —7D **222** (3C **38**)
Appledore Rd. *Wdchu* —9C **226** (3D **39**)
Appledown Way. *Cant* —5C **172**
Appleford Dri. *Min S* —5G **219**
Applegarth. *New Ad* —8E **82**
(in two parts)
Applegarth Dri. *Dart* —7M **59**
Applegarth Ho. *Eri* —9G **52**
Applegarth Pk. *Sea* —7C **224**
Applegarth Rd. *SE28* —1K **51**
Apple Orchard. *Swan* —7E **72**
Appleshaw Clo. *Grav* —1F **76**
Appleton Dri. *Dart* —8J **59**
Appleton Rd. *SE9* —1A **56**
Appletons. *Hdlw* —8D **134**
Apple Tree Clo. *Barm* —7K **125**
Apple Tree La. *Tun W* —6K **151**
Appola Rd. *H Bay* —3K **195**
Appold St. *Eri* —6G **53**
Approach Rd. *SW20* —1A **12**
Approach Rd. *Broad* —1L **211**
Approach Rd. *Dover* —6F **180**
Approach Rd. *Mgte* —3E **208** (1E **23**)
Approach Rd. *S'wll* —2C **220**
Approach Rd. *Tats* —9B **164**
Approach Rd. *W'ham* —2A **24**
Approach, The. *Orp* —3H **85**
April Clo. *Orp* —6H **85**
April Glen. *SE23* —8A **54**
April Rise. *Birch* —3C **206**
April Rise. *Whits* —6D **224**
Apsledene. *Grav* —2J **77**
Apsley St. *Afrd* —8F **158**
Arabin Rd. *SE4* —2B **54**
Aragon Clo. *Afrd* —2C **160**
Aragon Clo. *Brom* —2B **84**
Arbor Clo. *Beck* —5E **68**
Arbroath Rd. *SE9* —1A **56**
Arbrook Clo. *Orp* —6J **71**
Arbuthnot La. *Bex* —4N **57** (4C **6**)
Arcadian Av. *Bex* —4N **57**
Arcadian Clo. *Bex* —4N **57**
Arcadian Flats. Mgte —2C **208**
(off Fort Hill)
Arcadian Rd. *Bex* —4N **57**
Arcadia Rd. *Grav* —4E **76** (1A **16**)
Archbishop's Palace. —6C **126**
Archcliffe Rd. *Dover* —7H **181** (1C **43**)
Archer Rd. *Chat* —5E **94**
Archer Rd. *Folk* —5K **189**
Archer Rd. *Orp* —8J **71**
Archers Ct. *Brom* —7L **69**
Archer's Ct. Rd. *Whitf* —7F **178** (4C **33**)
Archer Way. *Swan* —5G **73**
Archery Clo. *Cli* —6M **65**
Archery Rd. *SE9* —3B **56**
Archery Sq. *Walm* —7N **177** (3E **33**)
Archibald Ho. *Maid* —2D **126**
Archway Rd. *Ram* —6J **211**
Archway Rd. *S'ness* —1B **218**
Arcon Clo. *Afrd* —2E **160**
Arcon Rd. *Afrd* —2E **160**
Arcus Rd. *Brom* —2H **69**
Arden Bus. Pk. *Roch* —5B **80**
Arden Ct. *Cant* —3N **171** (1D **31**)
Arden Dri. *Afrd* —7G **159**
Arden Gro. *Orp* —5D **84**
Ardenlee Dri. *Maid* —4E **126**
Arden Rd. *Fav* —5J **187**
Arden Rd. *H Bay* —5J **195**
Arden St. *Gill* —6F **80**
Ardfillan Rd. *SE6* —6G **55**
Ardgowan Rd. *SE6* —5H **55**
(in two parts)
Ardingly Clo. *Croy* —4A **82**
Ardley Clo. *SE6* —8B **54**
Ardmere Rd. *SE13* —4G **55**
Ardoch Rd. *SE6* —7G **54**
Arethusa Rd. *Roch* —3N **93** (2D **17**)
Argali Ho. Eri —3N **51**
(off Kale Rd.)
Argent Bus. Pk. *Queen* —9B **218**
Argent Rd. *Queen* —9B **218**
Argent St. *Grays* —3A **8**
Argent Ter. *Chat* —6C **94**
Argles Clo. *Grnh* —3G **60**
Argyle Av. *Mgte* —4A **208**
Argyle Cen, The. Ram —6J **211**
(off York St.)
Argyle Clo. *Roch* —3B **94**
Argyle Gdns. *Mgte* —4A **208**
Argyle Rd. *Sev* —7J **119**
Argyle Rd. *Tun W* —4G **151**
Argyle Rd. *Whits* —4F **224**
Argyll Dri. *Ram* —3J **211**
Arica Rd. *SE4* —2B **54**
Ariel Clo. *Grav* —9L **63**
Arisdale Av. *S Ock* —2E **7**
Arkindale Rd. *SE6* —8F **54**
Ark La. *Deal* —3M **177**
Arkley Rd. *H Bay* —3G **195**
Arklow Sq. *Ram* —5K **211**
Arkwright Rd. *NW3* —1B **4**
Arkwright Rd. *S Croy* —3D **13**
Arlington. *Afrd* —9D **158**
Arlington Clo. *Sidc* —5G **56**
Arlington Gdns. *Mgte* —5G **208**
Arlington Ho. Mgte —3B **208**
(off All Saints' Av.)
Arlington Sq. *Mgte* —3B **208**
Arlott Clo. *Maid* —3C **126**
Armada Clo. *L'stne* —4F **212**
Armada Way. *Chat* —9C **80**
Armourer's Wlk. *Dover* —1F **180**
Armoury Dri. *Grav* —5H **63**
Armoury Way. *SW18* —4B **4**
Armstrong Aq. *H Bay* —4B **194**
Armstrong Clo. *Brom* —6A **70**
Armstrong Clo. *Hals* —6C **102**
Armstrong Rd. *Maid* —8D **126**
Armytage Clo. *Hoo* —9H **67**
Arne Clo. *Tonb* —1L **145**
Arne Gro. *Orp* —4H **85**
Arne Wlk. *SE3* —2J **55**
Arngask Rd. *SE6* —5G **54**
Arnhem Dri. *Chat* —4C **94**
Arnhem Dri. *New Ad* —3E **13**
Arnold Av. *Meop* —3G **90**
Arnold Bus. Pk., The. *E Peck* —2M **147**
Arnolde Clo. *Roch* —5B **80**
Arnold Rd. *Cha* —8C **170**
Arnold Rd. *Grav* —7J **63**
Arnold Rd. *Mgte* —4D **208**
Arnold's La. *S at H* —2N **73** (1D **15**)
Arnott Clo. *SE28* —1L **51**
Arnsberg Way. *Bexh* —2B **58** (4C **6**)
Arnside Rd. *Bexh* —8B **52**
Arnulf St. *SE6* —9E **54**
Arpinge. —**2E 41**
Arragon Gdns. *W Wick* —4E **82**
Arran Clo. *Eri* —6E **52**
Arran M. *Cant* —9A **168**
Arran Rd. *SE6* —7E **54**
Arran Rd. *Maid* —2D **138**
Arrowhead La. *App* —1C **46**
Arsenal F.C. —1D **5**
Arsenal Rd. *SE9* —9B **50**
Artemis Clo. *Grav* —5K **63**
Arterial Rd. *Grays & N Stif* —3E **7**
Arterial Rd. *Purf* —3D **7**
Arterial Rd. *Stan H* —2C **8**
Arthurdon Rd. *SE4* —3D **54**
Arthur Gro. *SE18* —4E **50**
Arthur Kennedy Clo. *Bou B* —3J **165**
Arthur Rd. *SW19* —1B **12**
Arthur Rd. *Big H* —3C **164**
Arthur Rd. *Birch* —3C **206**
Arthur Rd. *Deal* —7K **177**
Arthur Rd. *Gill* —3N **95**
Arthur Rd. *Hythe* —7K **197**
Arthur Rd. *Mgte* —2E **208**
Arthur Rd. *Roch* —9A **80**
Arthur Salmon Clo. *Fav* —5F **186**
Arthur St. *Eri* —7G **52**
Arthur St. *Folk* —5L **189**
Arthur St. *Grav* —5F **62**
Arthur St. *Sit* —7F **98**
Arthur St. W. *Grav* —5F **62**
Artillery Gdns. *Cant* —1N **171** (4D **21**)
Artillery Ho. SE18 —5C **50**
(off Connaught M.)
Artillery Ho. Cant —1N **171** *(4D* **21***)*
(off Victoria Row)
Artillery Pl. *SE18* —4C **50** (3A **6**)
Artillery Rd. *Ram* —5K **211**
Artillery Row. *Grav* —6H **63**
Artillery St. *Cant* —1N **171** (4D **21**)
Artington Clo. *Orp* —5E **84**
Arundel Av. *Sit* —1F **114**
Arundel Clo. *Bex* —4A **58**
Arundel Clo. *Chat* —1G **110**
Arundel Clo. *Tonb* —7G **144**
Arundel Ct. *Short* —5H **69**
Arundel Dri. *Orp* —6K **85**
Arundel Rd. *C'snd* —5B **210**
Arundel Rd. *Dart* —2K **59**
Arundel Rd. *Mgte* —3F **208**
Arundel St. *Maid* —3C **126**
Ascot Clo. *Bor G* —2A **122**
Ascot Clo. *Chat* —9F **94**
Ascot Ct. *Bex* —5A **58**
Ascot Gdns. *Wgte S* —4K **207**
Ascot Ho. Maid —2J **139**
(off Epsom Clo.)
Ascot Rd. *Grav* —8G **63**
Ascot Rd. *Orp* —7H **71**
Ascott Fields. *Yald* —7D **136**
Ash. —**6K 89 (2E 15)**
(nr. Fawkham Green)
Ash. —**5C 216 (4C 22)**
(nr. Sandwich)
Ashbee Clo. *Snod* —3E **108**
Ashbee Gdns. *H Bay* —2K **195**
Ashborne Clo. *Kenn* —4H **159**
Ashbourne Av. *Bexh* —7N **51**
Ashbourne Rise. *Orp* —5G **84**
Ashburn Gdns. *H Bay* —2K **195**
Ashburnham Clo. *Sev* —9K **119**
Ashburnham Ct. *Beck* —5F **68**
Ashburnham Rd. *SW10* —3B **4**
Ashburnham Rd. *Belv* —4D **52**
Ashburnham Rd. *Maid* —1E **126**
Ashburnham Rd. *Ram* —5F **210**
Ashburnham Rd. *Tonb* —4J **145**
Ashburton Clo. *W'boro* —8J **159**
Ashburton Rd. *Croy* —2D **13**
Ashby Clo. *Hall* —7E **92**
Ash By-Pass. *Ah* —4B **22**
Ash Clo. *Afrd* —7C **158**
Ash Clo. *Ayle* —9J **109**
Ash Clo. *Broad* —9G **209**
Ash Clo. *Chat* —2F **94**
Ash Clo. *Dover* —2E **180**
Ash Clo. *Eden* —6B **184**
Ash Clo. *Gill* —9L **81**
Ash Clo. *H Bay* —6G **195**
Ash Clo. *Orp* —8F **70**
Ash Clo. *Sidc* —8K **57**
Ash Clo. *Swan* —5D **72**
Ash Clo. *Tun W* —5K **157**
Ashcombe Dri. *Eden* —3B **184**
Ash Ct. *C'snd* —8B **210**
Ash Cres. *Her* —2K **169**
Ash Cres. *High* —1G **78**
Ashcroft Av. *Sidc* —4J **57**
Ashcroft Ct. *Dart* —5A **60**
Ashcroft Cres. *Sidc* —4J **57**
Ashcroft Rd. *Pad W* —1L **153**
Ashdale Rd. *SE12* —6L **55**
Ashdene Gro. *Sturry* —5F **168**
Ashden Wlk. *Tonb* —9J **133**
Ashdown Clo. *Beck* —5E **68**
Ashdown Clo. *Bex* —5D **58**
Ashdown Clo. *H Bay* —5J **195**
Ashdown Clo. *Maid* —6A **126**
Ashdown Clo. *Tun W* —1F **156**
Ashdown Ct. *Afrd* —7G **158**
Ashdown Cres. *New R* —3C **212**
Ashdown Field. *Cha* —8B **170**
Ashdown Forest Centre. —3A **34**
Ashdown Llama Farm. —4A **34**
Ashdown Rd. *Len & Wich* —2C **29**
Ashdowns Cotts. *Maid* —4K **137**
Ashenden. *Smar* —2J **221**
Ashenden Clo. *Cant* —5J **171**
Ashenden Clo. *Wain* —2N **79**
Ashenden Wlk. *Tun W* —6L **151**
Ashen Dri. *Dart* —5H **59**
Ashenfield Rd. *H'lgh* —4C **30**
Ashen Gro. Rd. *Knat* —1B **104**
Ashentree La. *B'lnd* —2C **47**
Ashen Tree La. *Dover* —4K **181**

Ashen Vale—Banstead Rd.

Ashen Vale. S Croy —9A 82
Asher Reeds. L'tn G —1A 156
Ashes La. Hdlw —7L 133 (3A 26)
Ashfield Clo. Beck —3D 68
Ashfield La. Chst —2D 70 (1B 14)
(in three parts)
Ashford. —8F 158
Ashford Borough Museum. —8F 158
(off Churchyard)
Ashford Bus. Pk. Ash B —3L 161
Ashford Bus. Point. W'boro —4K 161
Ashford Dri. Kgswd —5F 140
Ashford Rd. Beth —4H 163 (2D 39)
Ashford Rd. Char —3K 175 (3D 29)
Ashford Rd. Cha & Cant
—7A 170 (2C 30)
Ashford Rd. Fav —8G 187 (4A 20)
Ashford Rd. Godm & Chi
—9K 175 (3B 30)
Ashford Rd. Gt Cha —1E 39
Ashford Rd. Hams —6C 190 (3E 39)
Ashford Rd. H Hal —7H 193
Ashford Rd. L'Ind & Shel —2A 30
Ashford Rd. Maid & Holl
—5E 126 (2E 27)
Ashford Rd. N'grn —2A 196 (2D 41)
Ashford Rd. N'tn —4A 188
Ashford Rd. New R & Snave —2A 212
Ashford Rd. S'ndge —8H 215 (2C 40)
Ashford Rd. Shad & Kgnt
—9D 160 (2E 39)
Ashford Rd. Snave & New R —1C 47
Ashford Rd. St Mic & Tent
—2B 222 (2C 38)
Ash Gro. SE12 —6K 55
Ashgrove. Afrd —5D 158
Ash Gro. Evtn —1J 185
Ash Gro. Lydd —2D 204
Ash Gro. Maid —3N 125
Ash Gro. W Wick —3F 82
Ashgrove Rd. Brom —2G 69 (1E 13)
Ashgrove Rd. Sev —9H 119 (2D 25)
Ash Hill. Ruck —3A 40
Ash Ho. New Ash —3L 89
Ashington Clo. Sit —6D 98
Ash Keys. Meop —2G 106
Ash La. As —3E 15
Ash La. W King —3J 105
Ashlar Pl. SE18 —4D 50
Ashleigh Clo. Meop —1E 106
Ashleigh Gdns. H'crn —2L 193
Ashleigh Point. SE23 —8A 54
Ashley. —3C 33
Ashley Av. Eps —3A 12
Ashley Av. Folk —5E 188 (2A 42)
Ashley Clo. Min S —7D 218
Ashley Clo. Ram —2F 210
Ashley Clo. Sev —6J 119
Ashley Dri. Sea —6C 224
Ashley Gdns. Orp —6G 85
Ashley Gdns. Tun W —1C 156 (1E 35)
Ashley Ho. Folk —5E 188
Ashley Mill Cotts. Folk —4F 188
(off Ashley Av.)
Ashley Pk. Tun W —9C 150
Ashley Pk. Clo. Tun W —9C 150
Ashley Rd. Eps —3A 12
Ashley Rd. Gill —1M 95
Ashley Rd. Hild —2E 144
Ashley Rd. Sev —6J 119
Ashmead Clo. Chat —8F 94
Ashmead Ga. Brom —4M 69
Ash Meadow. W'boro —2K 161
Ashmere Av. Beck —5G 68
Ashmore Gro. Well —1F 56
Ashmore La. Kes —1B 164 (3A 14)
Ash Pl. Folk —3L 189
Ash Platt Rd. Seal —3M 119
Ash Platt, The. Seal —2M 119
Ashridge Cres. SE18 —7E 50
Ash Rd. Ah & S'wch —4H 217 (4C 23)
Ash Rd. As & New Ash —5K 89
Ash Rd. Aysm —2B 162
Ash Rd. Croy —3D 82
Ash Rd. Dart —6L 59
Ash Rd. Grav —9H 63
Ash Rd. Hart —6L 75 (1A 16)
Ash Rd. Hawl —9N 59
Ash Rd. Orp —8H 85
Ash Rd. Roch —6K 79
Ash Rd. W'ham —7F 116
Ash Row. Brom —1C 84
Ashtead. —4A 12
Ashtead Dri. Bap —9L 99
Ashtead Park. —4A 12
Ashton Clo. Gt Mon —3D 33
Ashton Way. King N —4M 123
Ashton Way. W Mal —1B 26
Ash Tree Clo. Croy —9B 68
Ashtree Clo. Orp —5D 84
Ash Tree Clo. St Mar —3E 214
Ash Tree Clo. W King —9F 88
Ash Tree Dri. W King —9F 88
Ashtree Ho. Sit —8J 99
(off Woodberry Dri.)
Ash Tree La. Chat —1G 94 (2E 17)
Ash Tree Rd. Folk —5L 189
Ash Tree Way. Croy —8A 68
Ashurst. —3E 154 (2C 35)
Ashurst Av. Whits —7E 224
Ashurst Clo. Dart —1G 58
Ashurst Gdns. Clift —2J 209
Ashurst Hill. A'st —3E 154 (2C 35)
Ashurst Rd. A'st —2F 154 (2C 35)
Ashurst Rd. Maid —4F 126
Ashurstwood. —2A 34
Ashwater Rd. SE12 —6K 55
Ashwood Clo. Cli —6N 65
Ashwood Gdns. New Ad —7E 82
Ashwood Pl. Bean —8H 61
Askern Clo. Bexh —2M 57
Askes Ct. Afrd —1B 160
Askew Rd. W12 —3A 4
Aspdin Rd. N'fleet —8C 62
Aspen Clo. Orp —6J 85
Aspen Clo. St Mar —3E 214
Aspen Clo. Swan —4E 72
Aspen Copse. Brom —5B 70
Aspen Ct. Dart —4A 60
(off Norfolk Clo.)
Aspen Grn. Eri —3A 52
Aspen Ho. Folk —7K 189
Aspen Ho. Sidc —8J 57
Aspen Way. E14 —2E 5
Aspen Way. Chat —7B 94
Aspen Way. Tun W —5J 151
Aspian Dri. Cox —5A 138
Aspinall Rd. SE4 —1A 54
Aspley St. Tun W —1D 156
Asquith Rd. Gill —5M 95
Association Wlk. Roch —4N 93
Astey Ho. Maid —6E 126
Astley Av. Dover —2H 181
Astley Ct. Dover —2H 181
Astley St. Maid —5D 126
Aston Clo. Chat —9D 94
Aston Clo. Sidc —8J 57
Astor Av. Dover —5G 180 (1C 43)
Astor Dri. Deal —5M 177
Astor Rd. Broad —5K 209
Astor Rd. W King —7E 88
Astra Dri. Grav —1K 77
Astrid Rd. Walm —8K 177
Athelney St. SE6 —7D 54
Athelstan Grn. Holl —7E 128
Athelstan Pl. Deal —2M 177
Athelstan Rd. Cant —5J 171
Athelstan Rd. Chat —1C 94
Athelstan Rd. Fav —6F 186
Athelstan Rd. Folk —4K 189
Athelstan Rd. Mgte —2E 208
Athelstan Way. Orp —4J 71
Athenlay Rd. SE15 —3A 54
Athill Ct. Sev —4K 119
Athol Pl. Fav —4E 186
Athol Rd. Afrd —2D 160
Athol Rd. Eri —5D 52
Athol Rd. Whits —3H 225
Athol Ter. Dover —4L 181
Atkins Dri. W Wick —3G 83
Atkinson Clo. Orp —6J 85
Atkinson Wlk. Kenn —5K 159
Atkins Rd. SW12 —4C 4
Atlanta Ct. Chat —9A 80
Atlas Rd. Dart —1N 59
Atterbury Clo. W'ham —8F 116
Attlee Av. Aysm —2C 162
Attlee Cotts. Hall —5E 92
Attlee Dri. Dart —3A 60
Attlee Way. Sit —3F 98
Attwaters La. Hawkh —1M 191 (3E 37)
Atwater Ct. Len —7E 200
Aubretia Wlk. Sit —8H 99
Auckland Av. Ram —3E 210
Auckland Cres. Dover —1H 181
Auckland Dri. Sit —8D 98
Auckland Rd. SE19 —1D 13
Auckland Rd. Tun W —8J 151
Auden Rd. Lark —7E 108
Audley Av. Gill —2H 95
Audley Av. Mgte —2M 207
Audley Av. Tonb —5F 144
Audley Clo. Maid —5M 125
Audley Rise. Tonb —6F 144
Audley Rd. Folk —6F 188
Audley Wlk. Orp —9L 71
Audrey Clo. Beck —9E 68
Augusta Clo. Gill —5F 80
Augusta Gdns. Folk —7J 189
Augusta Pl. Ram —5K 211
Augusta Rd. Ram —5K 211
Augustine Rd. Grav —5H 63
(in two parts)
Augustine Rd. Min —7M 205
Augustine Rd. Min S —4J 219
Augustine Rd. Orp —6M 71
Augustus La. Orp —3J 85
Augustus Rd. SW19 —4B 4
Aultmore Ct. Tun W —2J 157
Austell Mnr. Gill —6F 80
(off Skinner St.)
Austen Clo. SE28 —1K 51
Austen Clo. Grnh —4J 61
Austen Gdns. Dart —2N 59
Austen Rd. Eri —7C 52
Austens Orchard. Tent —9B 222
Austen Way. Lark —6D 108
Austin Av. Brom —8A 70
Austin Av. H Bay —3A 194
Austin Clo. SE23 —5C 54
Austin Clo. Kem —3H 99
Austin Rd. Afrd —3F 160
Austin Rd. N'fleet —6E 62
Austin Rd. Orp —9J 71
Austins La. S'wch —5M 217
Austral Clo. Sidc —8H 57
Autumn Glade. Chat —2G 110
Avalon Clo. Orp —4M 85
Avalon Rd. Orp —3L 85
Avard Gdns. Orp —5E 84
Avards Clo. Hawkh —7J 191
Avebury Av. Ram —4L 211
Avebury Av. Tonb —6H 145
Avebury Rd. Orp —4F 84
Aveley. —2D 7
Aveley By-Pass. S Ock —2E 7
Aveley Clo. Eri —6G 53
Aveley Rd. Upm —1D 7
Aveling Clo. Hoo —7G 66
Aveling Ct. Roch —5M 79
Avenue Du Puy. Tonb —6J 145
Avenue Gdns. Clift —3G 208
Avenue of Rememberance. Sit
—8F 98 (3C 19)
Avenue Rd. NW3 & NW8 —2B 4
Avenue Rd. SE20 —4A 68
Avenue Rd. Belv —4C 52
Avenue Rd. Bexh —1N 57 (4C 6)
Avenue Rd. Dover —3H 181
Avenue Rd. Eps —3A 12
Avenue Rd. Eri —7D 52
(in three parts)
Avenue Rd. H Bay —2F 194 (1E 21)
Avenue Rd. Ram —5K 211
Avenue Rd. Sev —6K 119
Avenue Rd. Sutt —3B 12
Avenue Rd. Tats —8E 164
Avenue, The. NW6 —2A 4
Avenue, The. SE9 —4B 56
Avenue, The. SW4 —4C 4
Avenue, The. W4 —3A 4
Avenue, The. Ayle —9J 109
Avenue, The. Beck —4E 68
Avenue, The. Bex —5M 57
Avenue, The. Bor G —1N 121
Avenue, The. Brom —6N 69
Avenue, The. Cob —6A 78
Avenue, The. Deal —3M 177
Avenue, The. Grav —5F 62
Avenue, The. Grnh —3H 61 (4E 7)
Avenue, The. Her —3K 169
Avenue, The. Hythe —6K 197
Avenue, The. Kes —4N 83
Avenue, The. Kgdn —4M 199
Avenue, The. Mgte —4E 208
Avenue, The. Orp —3H 85
Avenue, The. Sit —5E 114
Avenue, The. St Mc —7J 213
Avenue, The. St P —4K 71
Avenue, The. Temp E —8C 178
Avenue, The. Wemb —1A 4
Avenue, The. W'ham —4B 116
Avenue, The. W Wick —1H 83 (2E 13)
Avenue, The. Wor Pk —2A 12
Averang Gdns. Folk —5H 189
Averenches Rd. Bear —4J 127
Averenches Rd. S. Bear —5J 127
Avereng Rd. Folk —5H 189
Avery Clo. Allh —3M 201
Avery Clo. Maid —8C 126
Avery Ct. Allh —3M 201
Avery Hill. —4F 56 (4B 6)
Avery Hill Rd. SE9 —4F 56 (4B 6)
Avery La. Otham —2N 139 (2A 28)
Avery Way. Allh —4L 201 (3A 10)
Aviemore Clo. Beck —8C 68
Aviemore Gdns. Bear —5J 127
Aviemore Way. Beck —8B 68
Avignon Rd. SE4 —1A 54 (4D 5)
Avington Clo. Maid —8C 126
Avocet M. SE28 —3F 50
Avocet Wlk. Chat —9F 94
Avon Clo. Cant —2B 172
Avon Clo. Grav —7J 63
Avon Clo. Tonb —2J 145
Avondale Clo. Whits —5J 225
Avondale Pl. Mgte —2C 208
(off Market St.)
Avondale Rd. SE9 —7A 56
Avondale Rd. Brom —2J 69
Avondale Rd. Cap F —2C 174
Avondale Rd. Gill —7G 80
Avondale Rd. Well —9L 51
Avon Ho. Maid —9H 127
Avonmouth Rd. Dart —3L 59
Avon Rd. SE4 —1D 54
Avonstowe Clo. Orp —4E 84
Avon St. Tun W —9J 151
Avontar Rd. S Ock —2E 7
Awliscombe Rd. Well —9H 51
Axminster Cres. Well —8L 51
Axtaine Rd. Orp —1M 85
Axtane. S'fleet —3M 75
Axtane Clo. S at H —4C 74
Aycliff. —7G 180 (1C 43)
Aycliffe Clo. Brom —7B 70
Ayelands. New Ash —3L 89
Ayelands La. New Ash —4L 89
Aylesbury Rd. Brom —6K 69
Aylesford. —7L 109 (4D 17)
Aylesford Av. Beck —8B 68
Aylesford Cres. Gill —9L 81
Aylesford Pl. W'boro —2J 161 (1A 40)
Aylesham. —2D 162 (2A 32)
Aylesham Ho. Aysm —2D 162
Aylesham Ind. Est. Aysm —3C 162
Aylesham Rd. Aysm —2E 162
Aylesham Rd. Orp —1H 85
Aylesham Rd. Snow —2B 32
Ayleswade La. H'crn —1B 38
Aylewyn Gn. Kem —3G 99
Aylward Rd. SE23 —7A 54
Aynscombe Angle. Orp —1J 85
Aynsley Ct. S'wch —5M 217
Ayton Rd. Ram —6G 211
Azalea Dri. Swan —7E 72

Babbacombe Rd. Brom —4K 69
Babb's La. Bene —3E 37
Babs Oak Hill. Sturry —4G 168 (3E 21)
Babylon La. Cha S —4E 27
Backfields. Roch —8M 79
Bk. Forge La. Leeds —2A 28
Back La. Bex —5B 58
Back La. Bou M —3E 27
Back La. Cha S —6G 138
Back La. Fav —5H 187
Back La. God G —6A 120
Back La. Horsm —2C 198
Back La. Ide H & Sev —1C 130 (2C 24)
Back La. Igh —6J 121
Back La. Maid —2M 139
Back La. Min S —6L 219 (4D 11)
Back La. Sev —6E 118 (2E 25)
Back La. S'brne —4J 133 (2E 25)
Back Rd. Sand —3K 215
Back Rd. Sidc —9J 57
Back Rd. W. Dover —4L 181
Back St. Leeds —9N 127
Back St. R'wld —4J 199
Baddlesmere Rd. Whits —2J 225
Baden. Belv —3B 52
Baden Powell Rd. Sev —4F 118
Baden Rd. Gill —5G 81
Bader Cres. Chat —4D 94
Bader Wlk. N'fleet —8E 62
Badger Rd. Chat —1F 110
Badgers Bri. Etch —2E 41
Badgers Clo. Blean —4G 166
Badgers Copse. Orp —3H 85
Badgers Croft. SE9 —8C 56
Badgers Hole. Croy —5A 82
Badger's Mount. —1B 102 (3C 14)
Badgers Oak. Afrd —1B 160
Badger's Rise. Badg M —1B 102
Badgers Rise. Dover —1C 180
Badgers Rise. Walm —1M 199
Badgers Rd. Badg M —1C 102
Badlesmere. —2A 30
Badlesmere Clo. Afrd —3C 160
Badlow Clo. Eri —7F 52
Bad Munstereifel Rd. Afrd & Svgtn
—4F 160 (1A 40)
Badsell Park Farm. —3H 153 (1B 36)
Badsell Rd. Five G —8G 147 (4B 26)
Baffin Clo. Chat —1C 94
Bagham. —8L 175 (2C 30)
Bagham La. Chi —8K 175 (2B 30)
Bagham Rd. Chi —8K 175 (2B 30)
Bagshill Rd. L'Ind —2E 29
Bagshot Ct. SE18 —8C 50
Bailey Bri. Rd. Ayle —8K 109
Bailey Ct. Gill —3K 95
Bailey Dri. Gill B —2K 95
Bailey Field. Beth —3K 163
Bailey Pl. SE26 —2A 68
Baileys Field. Afrd —9D 158
Baird's Hill. Broad —7K 209 (1E 23)
Bairdsley Clo. Broad —7K 209
(in two parts)
Bakenham Ho. Roch —2N 93
Baker Beal Ct. Bexh —1C 58
Baker Clo. Tey —1K 223
Bakerhill Clo. N'fleet —9E 62
Baker La. H'crn —1N 193 (4B 28)
Baker La. Sut V —9B 140 (3A 28)
Baker Rd. SE18 —7A 50
Baker Rd. Folk —5E 188
Bakers Av. W King —8E 88
Baker's Bri. Cotts. Smar —2L 221
Bakers Clo. Cant —3J 171
Baker's Cross. —3E 37
Bakers Cross. C'brk —8D 176 (3E 37)
Baker's La. Cha —9D 170 (2C 31)
Bakers La. Ling —1A 34
Bakers M. Grn St —7H 85
Bakers Pas. Dover —4H 181
Baker Street. —2A 8
Baker St. NW1 & W1 —2B 4
Baker Street. (Junct.) —2B 4
Baker St. Burh —1K 109
Baker St. Ors —2A 8
Baker St. Roch —9N 79
Bakers Wlk. Roch —6N 79
Bakery Cotts. S'lng —7B 110
Balaam St. E13 —2A 6
Balaclava La. Spar G —3A 36
Balcaskie Rd. SE9 —3B 56
Balcomb Cres. Mgte —5G 209
Balcombe Clo. Bexh —2M 57
Balcombe La. Sharp & Chel G —4A 34
Balcombes Cotts. Goud —8K 185
Balcombes Hill. Goud —8K 185 (2D 37)
Balder Rise. SE12 —7L 55
Baldric Rd. Folk —6F 188
Baldwin Rd. G'stne —8E 212
Baldwin Rd. Min S —6L 219
Baldwins La. Tun W —6J 151
Baldwin Ter. Folk —5K 189
Baldwyn's Pk. Bex —7E 58 (4C 7)
Baldwyn's Rd. Bex —7E 58
Balfour Ct. Folk —8G 189
Balfour Rd. Brom —8N 69
Balfour Rd. Chat —1B 94
Balfour Rd. Dover —3H 181
Balfour Rd. Walm —8M 177
Balgowan Rd. Beck —5B 68
Balgowan St. SE18 —4H 51
Balham. —4C 4
Balham High Rd. SW17 & SW12 —4C 4
Balham Hill. SW12 —4C 4
Baliol Rd. Whits —3G 225
Ballamore Rd. Brom —8K 55
Ballard Bus. Pk. Roch —7K 79
Ballard Clo. Mard —2K 205
Ballard Ind. Est. Chat —2F 110
Ballard Rd. G'stne —8E 212
Ballards Hill. Goud —4F 198 (2C 37)
Ballards Rd. Dag —2C 6
Ballards Way. S Croy & Croy —3D 13
Ballard Way. Pad W —8N 147
Ballens Rd. Chat —8E 94
Balliemoor Ct. Ram —3J 211
Ballina St. SE23 —5A 54
Balliol Rd. Broad —6K 209 (1E 23)
Balliol Rd. Well —9K 51
Ball La. Kenn —3J 159 (4A 30)
Balloch Rd. SE6 —6G 54
Balls Ct. Chatt —9C 66
Ball's Grn. With —8C 154
Ball's Green. —8C 154 (2C 35)
Balls Pond Rd. N1 —1D 5
Balmer Clo. Gill —4N 95
Balmoral Av. Beck —7B 68
Balmoral Ct. SE12 —9L 55
Balmoral Ct. Beck —4F 68
Balmoral Gdns. Bex —5A 58
Balmoral Ho. Maid —3J 139
Balmoral Pl. Ram —5K 211
Balmoral Rd. E7 —1A 6
Balmoral Rd. Gill —7F 80 (1E 17)
Balmoral Rd. Kgdn —3M 199
Balmoral Rd. Mgte —3N 207
Balmoral Rd. S at H —3B 74
Balmoral Ter. Sit —7E 98
Balstonia. —2C 8
Baltic Ho. Tun W —1H 157
(off Goods Sta. Rd.)
Baltic Rd. Tonb —8G 145
Baltimore Pl. Well —9H 51
Bamford Rd. Brom —1F 68
Bamford Way. Deal —6M 177
Bampton Rd. SE23 —8A 54
Banavie Gdns. Beck —4F 68
Banbury Vs. Hams —8D 190
Banbury Vs. S'fleet —2M 75
Banckside. Hart —7L 75
Bancroft Gdns. Orp —2H 85
Bancroft Rd. Wro —7M 105
Bangor Rd. Roch —6H 79
Bank Cotts. Holl —6G 129
Bank Ct. Dart —4M 59
Bankfields. H'crn —3K 193
Bankfields Clo. Gill —2D 96
Bankfield Way. Goud —9K 185
Bankfoot Rd. Brom —9H 55
Bankhurst Rd. SE6 —5C 54
Bank La. Hild —6N 131
Bank La. Sev —3D 25
Bank Rd. Adgtn —2B 40
Banks Cotts. W'bury —1C 136
Bankside. Chat —3E 94
Bankside. Dun G —3E 118
Bank Side. Hams —8D 190
Bankside. N'fleet —4B 62
Bankside Clo. Bex —9E 58
Bankside Clo. Big H —6C 164
Banks La. Bexh —2A 58
Banks Rd. Afrd —2E 160
Banks Rd. Roch —4N 79 (1D 17)
Banks, The. Broad —7K 209
Bank St. Afrd —8F 158
Bank St. Chat —9E 80
Bank St. C'brk —7C 176
Bank St. Fav —5G 187
Bank St. Grav —4G 63
Bank St. H Bay —2G 195
Bank St. Hythe —6K 197
Bank St. Maid —5C 126
Bank St. Sev —7J 119
Bank St. Tonb —5H 145
Bankwell Rd. SE13 —2H 55
Banky Meadow. Maid —6K 125
Banner Farm Rd. Tun W —3H 157
Banner Way. Min S —6F 218
Banning St. Roch —4M 79
Bannister Gdns. Orp —6L 71
Bannister Hill. B'den —9C 98 (3C 18)
Bannister Rd. Maid —2D 126
Bannockburn Rd. SE18 —4G 51
Banstead. —4B 12
Banstead Rd. Cars —3B 12
Banstead Rd. Eps & Bans —3A 12
Banstead Rd. Purl —3C 13

Banstead Rd. S.—Beckford Dri.

Banstead Rd. S. *Sutt* —3B **12**
Banwell Rd. *Bex* —4M **57**
Bapchild. —8L 99 (3D 19)
Bapchild Pl. *Orp* —7L **71**
Barbados Ter. *Maid* —2D **126**
Barberry Av. *Chat* —6A **94**
*Barbers Almshouses. Ram —6H **211***
(off Elms Av.)
Barcham Ct. *Maid* —3C **138**
Barchester Way. *Tonb* —1M **145**
Barclay Av. *Tonb* —2M **145**
Barclay Rd. *Croy* —2D **13**
Barcombe Clo. *Orp* —6J **71**
Bardell Ter. *Roch* —7A **80**
Barden Ct. *Maid* —4E **126**
Barden Park. —6F 144 (4E 25)
Barden Pk. Rd. *Tonb* —6G **144**
Barden Rd. *Speld* —4N **149** (1D **35**)
Barden Rd. *Tonb* —6G **144**
Bardens Row. *St Mic* —4B **222**
Barden St. *SE18* —7G **50**
Bardolph Av. *Croy* —9B **82**
Bardown. —4B 36
Bardown Rd. *Shov G* —4B **36**
Bardsley Clo. *E Peck* —9M **135**
Barfield. *S at H* —4B **74**
Barfield Rd. *Brom* —6C **70**
*Barfleur Mnr. Gill —6D **80***
(off Middle St.)
Barfreston Clo. *Maid* —7C **126**
Barfrestone. —3B 32
Barfrestone Rd. *Eyt* —2H **185** (3B **32**)
Bargate Clo. *SE18* —5H **51**
Bargates. *Afrd* —3C **160**
Barge Ho. Rd. *E16* —2D **50**
Bargery Rd. *SE6* —6E **54**
Bargrove Cres. *SE6* —7C **54**
Bargrove Rd. *Maid* —4F **126**
Barham. —8D 162 (3A 32)
Barham Clo. *Brom* —2A **84**
Barham Clo. *Chst* —1D **70**
Barham Clo. *Maid* —3H **139**
Barham Ct. *B'hm* —7D **162**
Barham Ct. *Tstn* —9F **124**
Barham Dri. *C'brk* —7D **176**
Barham M. *Tstn* —9F **124**
Barham Rd. *Chst* —1D **70**
Barham Rd. *Dart* —5A **60**
Barham's Mill Rd. *Eger* —4B **28**
Baring Clo. *SE12* —7K **55**
Baring Rd. *SE12* —5K **55** (4A **6**)
Barker Rd. *Maid* —6C **126**
Barkers Ct. *Sit* —7E **98**
Bark Hart Rd. *Orp* —2K **85**
Barking. —1B 6
Barking Northern Relief Rd. *Bark* —1A **6**
Barking Rd. *E13 & E6* —2E **5**
Barkis Clo. *Roch* —4A **94**
Barlby Rd. *W10* —2A **4**
Barler Pl. *Queen* —7B **218**
Barley Clo. *Mart H* —4D **33**
Barleycorn. *Leyb* —9C **108**
Barleycorn Dri. *Gill* —5A **96**
Barley Ct. *H Bay* —5L **195**
Barleyfields. *Weav* —5G **127**
Barleymow Clo. *Chat* —5F **94**
Barling Clo. *Chat* —1A **110**
*Barlings Ho. SE4 —2A **54***
(off Frendsbury Rd.)
Barlow Clo. *Gill* —6A **96**
Barmeston Rd. *SE6* —7E **54**
Barming. —7K 125 (2D 27)
Barming Heath. —6K 125 (2D 27)
Barming Pl. *Maid* —7K **125**
Barming Rd. *W'bury* —7D **124**
Barmouth Rd. *Croy* —3A **82**
Barnaby Ter. *Roch* —1N **93**
Barnard Clo. *SE18* —3C **50**
Barnard Clo. *Chst* —4F **70**
Barnard Ct. *Chat* —1D **94**
*Barnard Ct. Dart —4B **60***
(off Clifton Wlk.)
Barnberry Clo. *Afrd* —1C **160**
Barn Clo. *B'den* —9B **98**
Barn Clo. *Hoath* —2A **22**
Barn Clo. *York* —3C **20**
Barn Cotts. *T Hill* —5L **167**
Barn Cres. *Mgte* —2N **207**
Barncroft Clo. *Weav* —5J **127**
Barncroft Dri. *Hem* —7J **95**
Barndale Ct. *Shorne* —1C **78**
Barned Ct. *Maid* —7K **125**
Barnehurst. —1D 58 (4C 7)
Barnehurst Av. *Eri & Bexh* —8D **52**
Barnehurst Clo. *Eri* —8D **52**
Barnehurst Rd. *Bexh* —9D **52** (3C 7)
Barn End Dri. *Dart* —9K **59**
Barn End La. *Dart* —9K **59** (1D **15**)
Barnes. —3A 4
Barnes Av. *Mgte* —2N **207**
Barnes Ct. *Cant* —4K **171**
Barnes Cray. —2H 59 (4D 7)
Barnes Cray Rd. *Dart* —2H **59**
Barnesdale Cres. *Orp* —9J **71**
Barnesende Ct. *S'wch* —6M **217**
Barnes High St. *SW13* —3A **4**
Barnes La. *SW20* —1A **12**
Barnes La. *Lin* —8N **137** (3D **27**)
Barnes Street. —2G 146 (3B 26)
Barnes Wlk. *Mard* —3L **205**
Barnet Dri. *Brom* —3A **84**
Barnet's La. *B Oak* —2C **168**
Barnett Clo. *Eri* —9G **52**
Barnett Ct. *Min* —8M **205**
Barnett Ct. *Ram* —3F **210**
Barnettfield. *Afrd* —1D **160**
Barnetts Clo. *Tun W* —5J **151**
Barnetts Rd. *Leigh* —5A **144**
Barnetts Way. *Tun W* —5J **151**
Barnet Wood Rd. *Brom* —3M **83**
Barnfield. *Chat* —3D **94**
Barnfield. *Grav* —7F **62**
Barnfield. *H Bay* —5D **194**
Barnfield. *St Mic* —5C **222**
Barnfield. *Tun W* —6F **156**
Barnfield Clo. *Grnh* —4F **60**
Barnfield Clo. *Long* —6C **76**
Barnfield Clo. *Swan* —1D **86**
Barnfield Cres. *Kems* —8M **103**
Barnfield Gdns. *SE18* —6D **50**
Barnfield Pk. La. *Eger* —4D **29**
Barnfield Rd. *SE18* —6D **50**
(in two parts)
Barnfield Rd. *Belv* —6A **52**
Barnfield Rd. *Fav* —4G **186**
Barnfield Rd. *Folk* —4J **189**
Barnfield Rd. *Orp* —6M **71**
Barnfield Rd. *Sev* —5F **118**
Barnfield Rd. *Tats* —8D **164**
Barnfield Wood Clo. *Beck* —9G **69**
Barnfield Wood Rd. *Beck* —9G **68**
Barnham Clo. *Grav* —6L **63**
Barn Hawe. *Eden* —6C **184**
Barn Hill. *Hunt* —7J **137** (3D **27**)
Barnhill Av. *Brom* —8J **69**
Barn Hill Cotts. *Maid* —5K **137**
Barnhouse La. *B'Ind* —2C **47**
Barnhurst La. *H'nge* —7C **192** (1A **42**)
Barnhurst Rd. *Maid* —1D **126**
Barn Meadow. *Up H'lng* —7C **92**
Barnmead Rd. *Beck* —4A **68**
Barn Platt. *Afrd* —1E **160**
Barnsbury. —1C 5
Barnsbury Rd. *N1* —2C **5**
Barns Clo. *Fav* —4F **186**
Barnsley Clo. *S'ness* —2F **218**
Barnsole. —8B 216 (1C 32)
Barnsole Rd. *Gill* —7G **81** (2E **17**)
Barnsole Rd. *S'le* —9A **216** (1B **32**)
*Barnstable Ho. SE12 —3J **55***
(off Taunton Rd.)
Barnstable La. *SE13* —2F **54**
Barn Tye Clo. *Gus* —7K **179**
Barntye Rd. *Gus* —8J **179**
Barnwell Rd. *Dart* —1N **59**
Baron Clo. *Roch* —3M **93**
Baron Clo. *Bear* —4J **127**
Baron Clo. *Gill* —5H **81**
Barons Ct. *Tun W* —9G **151**
Baron's Wlk. *Croy* —9B **68**
Barrack Hill. *Hythe* —6H **197** (3D **41**)
Barrack Row. *Grav* —4G **62**
Barr Bank Ter. *Wilm* —9K **59**
Barrell Arch Clo. *Mard* —2K **205**
Barretts Rd. *Dun G* —2E **118**
Barretts Rd. *Hawkh* —5L **191**
Barrey Rd. *Ash B* —3L **161**
Barrie Dri. *Lark* —6D **108**
Barrier R. *Chat* —7C **80**
Barrington Clo. *Chat* —6C **94**
Barrington Cres. *Birch* —4G **207**
Barrington Rd. *Bexh* —9M **51**
Barrington Vs. *SE18* —8C **50**
Barrowfields. *Chat* —1G **111**
Barrow Green. —1L 223 (3D 19)
Barrow Grn. Rd. *Oxt* —2A **24**
Barrow Gro. *Sit* —8E **98**
Barrow Hill. —7F 158 (2C 41)
Barrow Hill. *S'ndge* —9K **215** (2C **41**)
Barrow Hill Cotts. *Afrd* —8E **158**
Barrow Hill Pl. *Afrd* —7F **158**
Barrow Hill Rise. *S'ndge* —2C **41**
*Barrow Hill Ter. Afrd —7F **158***
(off Barrow Hill Pl.)
Barrow La. *L'tn G* —3N **155**
Barrows Clo. *Birch* —5F **206**
Barr Rd. *Grav* —7L **63**
Barry Av. *Bexh* —7N **51**
Barry Clo. *Orp* —4G **84**
Barry Rd. *SE22* —4D **5**
Bartholomew Clo. *Hythe* —5J **197**
Bartholomew La. *Hythe*
—5H **197** (3D **41**)
Bartholomew St. *Dover* —3H **181**
Bartholomew St. *Hythe* —6J **197**
Bartholomew Way. *Swan*
—6F **72** (1C **15**)
Barth Rd. *SE18* —4G **51**
Bartlets La. *Afrd* —4A **160** (2E **39**)
Bartlett Clo. *Chat* —1F **110**
Bartlett Dri. *Whits* —4J **225**
Bartlett Rd. *Grav* —6F **62**
Bartlett Rd. *W'ham* —8E **116**
Bartletts Clo. *Min S* —7D **218**
Bartlett Ter. *Croy* —3B **82**
Bartley Mill. —3A **36**
Bartley Mill Rd. *Lam* —3A **36**
Barton Clo. *Bexh* —3N **57**
Barton Ct. *Min S* —6K **219**
Barton Field. *Lym* —7C **204**
Bartonfields Ct. *Cant* —3A **172**
Barton Hill Dri. *Min S* —8G **219** (1D **19**)
Barton Mill Rd. *Cant* —9A **168**
Barton Path. *Dover* —3H **181**
Barton Rd. *Cant* —4B **172**
Barton Rd. *Dover* —2H **181** (1C **43**)
Barton Rd. *Maid* —7D **126** (2E **27**)
Barton Rd. *Roch* —5L **79**
Barton Rd. *Sidc* —2N **71**
Barton Rd. *S at H* —4B **74**
Bartons Bus. Pk. *Cant* —4C **172**
Barton's Point Coastal Park.
—2G **218** (4D **11**)
Barton View Ter. *Dover* —3H **181**
Bartram Rd. *SE4* —3B **54**
Barts Clo. *Beck* —8D **68**
Barville Clo. *SE4* —2B **54**
Barville Rd. *Wald* —2L **185** (3C **32**)
Barwick Rd. *Dover* —3E **180** (1C **42**)
Barwood Av. *W Wick* —2E **82**
Basden Cotts. *Hawkh* —5L **191**
Bashford Barn La. *Bre* —6A **114** (4B **18**)
Basi Clo. *Roch* —3N **79**
Basildon Rd. *SE2* —5J **51** (3B **6**)
Basildon Zoo. —3C **9**
Basil Gdns. *Croy* —2A **82**
Basilon Rd. *Bexh* —9N **51**
Basing Clo. *Maid* —6E **126**
Basing Dri. *Bex* —4A **58**
Baskerville. *Afrd* —7F **158**
Basket Gdns. *SE9* —3A **56**
Basmere Clo. *Maid* —3F **126**
Bassant Rd. *SE18* —6H **51**
Bassett Clo. *Hythe* —4M **197**
Bassett Gdns. *Hythe* —4L **197**
Bassett Rd. *Sit* —7E **98**
Bassett's Clo. *Orp* —5D **84**
Bassett's Way. *Orp* —5D **84**
Basted. —5M 121 (2A 26)
Basted La. *Crou* —4M **121** (1A **26**)
(in two parts)
Bastion Rd. *SE2* —5J **51**
Baston Mnr. Rd. *Brom* —4L **83**
Baston Rd. *Brom* —3L **83** (2A **14**)
Baston Rd. *Dover* —5H **181**
Bat & Ball. —3K 119 (1D 25)
Bat & Ball Rd. *Sev* —3K **119**
Batchelors. *Pem* —6D **152**
Batchelor St. *Chat* —8D **80**
Batchwood Grn. *Orp* —6J **71**
Bates Clo. *Lark* —7E **108**
Bates Clo. *S'le* —1B **32**
Bates Hill. *Igh* —4J **121** (1E **25**)
Bateson St. *SE18* —4G **50**
Bath Ct. *Folk* —8H **189**
Bath Hard. *Roch* —7A **80**
Bathhurst Clo. *S'hrst* —7J **221**
Bath Pl. *Mgte* —2D **208**
Bath Rd. *W4* —3A **4**
Bath Rd. *Dart* —5J **59**
Bath Rd. *Mgte* —3D **208** (1D **23**)
Bath Rd. *W'boro* —3J **161**
Baths Rd. *Brom* —7N **69**
Bath St. *EC1* —2D **5**
Bath St. *Grav* —4G **62** (4B **8**)
Bathurst Clo. *Ram* —3F **210**
Bathurst Rd. *Folk* —6F **188**
Bathurst Rd. *S'hrst* —8J **221**
Bathway. *SE18* —4C **50**
Batteries Clo. *Lyn* —4J **223**
Battersby Rd. *SE6* —7G **55**
Battersea. —3B 4
Battersea Bri. *SW3 & SW11* —3B **4**
Battersea Bri. Rd. *SW11* —3B **4**
Battersea Pk. Rd. *SW11 & SW8* —3B **4**
Battersea Rise. *SW11* —4B **4**
Battery Point. *S'gte* —9B **188**
Battery Rd. *SE28* —2G **50**
Battery Rd. *Lydd S* —4E **47**
Batteson St. *SE18* —4G **50**
Battle. —4B 44
Battle Abbey. —4B **44**
Battlefields Rd. *Wro* —7M **105** (4A **16**)
Battle Hill. *Batt* —4B **44**
Battle La. *Mard* —4D **27**
*Battle of Britain Homes. Dover —5J **181***
(off Chapel Pl.)
Battle of Britian Memorial.
—3B **174** (2B **42**)
Battle of Britian Museum.
—9B **192** (2A **42**)
Battle Rd. *Belv & Eri* —4D **52** (3C **7**)
Battle Rd. *Stapl* —3B **44**
Battlesmere Rd. *Cli* —5M **65**
Battle Street. —6L 77
Battle St. *Cob* —6L **77**
Batt's Cotts. *Shorne* —8L **77**
Batt's Rd. *Cob* —2B **16**
Batt's Rd. *Ludd* —8M **77**
Baudwin Rd. *SE6* —7H **55**
Baugh Rd. *Sidc* —1L **71**
Bawden Clo. *Cant* —7N **167**
Baxendale Ct. *Afrd* —2H **161**
Bayard Ct. *Bexh* —2C **58**
Bay Cotts. *St Mc* —7L **213**
Baydon Ct. *Short* —6J **69**
Baye La. *I'hm* —4A **22**
Bayfield. *P For* —4E **19**
*Bayfield Ho. SE4 —2A **54***
(off Coston Wlk.)
Bayfield Rd. *SE9* —2N **55**
Bayford. —1B 18
Bayford Rd. *Sit* —7H **99**
Bayhall Rd. *Tun W* —2J **157** (2E **35**)
Bayham Abbey. —2B **36**
Bayham Rd. *Sev* —5K **119** (2D **25**)
Bayham Rd. *Tun W* —5H **157** (2E **35**)
Bayham St. *NW1* —2C **4**
Bay Hill. *St Mb* —8K **213** (4E **33**)
Bay Hill Clo. *St Mc* —8K **213**
Bayle Ct. *Folk* —7L **189**
Bayle St. *Folk* —6L **189**
Bayle, The. *Folk* —7L **189**
Bayley's Hill. —3C 25
Bayley's Hill. *Sev* —3C **25**
Bayley's Hill. *Weald* —4F **130**
Bayley's Hill Rd. *Chid C & Weald* —3C **25**
Bayley Wlk. *SE2* —5N **51**
Bayly Rd. *Dart* —4A **60**
Bay Museum, The. —8L **213** (4E **33**)
Baynham Clo. *Bex* —4A **58**
Bay Shop. Cen., The. *Meop* —2F **106**
Bayswater. —2B 4
Bayswater Dri. *Deal* —2N **177**
Bayswater Dri. *Gill* —7A **96**
Bayswater Rd. *W2* —2B **4**
Baythorne St. *E3* —9C **54**
Bay Tree Clo. *Brom* —4N **69**
Baytree Clo. *Sidc* —6H **57**
Bay View. —1A 20
Bay View Gdns. *Ley S* —6J **203**
*Bay View Heights. Birch —3C **206***
(off Ethelbert Rd.)
Bay View Rd. *Broad* —2L **211**
Bayview Rd. *Kgdn* —5M **199**
Bayview Rd. *Whits* —6F **224**
Baywell. *Leyb* —8C **108**
Bazes Shaw. *New Ash* —3M **89**
(in two parts)
*Beach All. Whits —3F **224***
(off Island Wall)
Beach App. *Ward* —5K **203**
Beach Av. *Birch* —3E **206** (1C **22**)
Beach Bank Cvn. Site. *Hythe* —9D **196**
Beachborough Rd. *Brom* —9F **54**
Beachborough Rd. *Folk*
—5G **188** (2A **42**)
Beach Ct. *Bene* —3A **38**
Beach Ct. *Deal* —6J **177**
Beach Ct. *Walm* —8N **177**
Beach Houses. *Mgte* —3A **208**
Beach Marine. *S'gte* —8F **188**
Beachmont Clo. *G'stne* —6A **212**
Beach Ride. *Wgte S* —2L **207**
Beach Rd. *Dym* —9D **182**
Beach Rd. *St Mb* —9K **123**
Beach Rd. *Wgte S* —2L **207**
Beach St. *Deal* —3N **177** (2E **33**)
Beach St. *Folk* —6L **189**
Beach St. *H Bay* —2G **194**
Beach St. *S'ness* —2C **218**
Beach Ter. *S'ness* —2C **218**
Beach, The. *Walm* —7N **177** (3E **33**)
Beach Wlk. *Whits* —2G **224**
Beachy Path. *Tent* —7C **222**
Beacon Av. *H Bay* —2J **195**
Beacon Clo. *Gill* —4N **95**
Beacon Cotts. *Beth* —3K **163**
Beacon Dri. *Bean* —8H **61**
Beaconfields. *Sea* —7B **224**
Beaconfields. *Sev* —8G **119**
Beacon Hill. —3A 38
Beacon Hill. *Chat* —2F **94**
Beacon Hill. *H Bay* —2H **195** (1E **21**)
Beacon Hill La. *Chatt* —9C **66**
Beacon La. *Stapl* —3C **44**
Beacon La. *Wdboro* —8F **216** (1C **33**)
Beacon Oak Rd. *Tent* —7C **222** (3C **38**)
Beacon Rise. *Sev* —8H **119**
Beacon Rd. *SE13* —4G **54**
Beacon Rd. *Broad* —7J **209** (1E **23**)
Beacon Rd. *Chat* —1F **94**
Beacon Rd. *Crowb* —4C **35**
Beacon Rd. *Eri* —7J **53**
Beacon Rd. *H Bay* —3H **195**
Beacon Rd. *Len* —7D **200**
Beaconsfield Av. *Dover* —3H **181**
Beaconsfield Av. *Gill* —7H **81**
Beaconsfield Gdns. *Broad* —8K **209**
Beaconsfield Pde. *SE9* —9A **56**
Beaconsfield Rd. *SE9* —7A **56**
Beaconsfield Rd. *W4* —3A **4**
Beaconsfield Rd. *Bex* —7F **58**
Beaconsfield Rd. *Brom* —6N **69**
Beaconsfield Rd. *Cant* —9L **167** (4D **21**)
Beaconsfield Rd. *Chat* —1C **94**
Beaconsfield Rd. *Chel G* —4A **34**
Beaconsfield Rd. *Deal* —5N **177**
Beaconsfield Rd. *Dover* —3H **181**
Beaconsfield Rd. *Maid* —7B **126**
Beaconsfield Rd. *Sit* —8K **99**
Beaconsfield Ter. *Hythe* —7L **197**
Beacons, The. *Cox* —6N **137**
Beacon Ter. *Hythe* —9B **188**
Beacontree Heath. —1C 6
Beacon Wlk. *H Bay* —2H **195**
Beacon Wlk. *Tent* —6C **222**
Beacon Way. *Lymp* —5A **196**
Beacon Wood Country Park. —9H **61**
Beadnell Rd. *SE23* —6A **54**
Beadon Rd. *W6* —3A **4**
Beadon Rd. *Brom* —7K **69**
Beagles Clo. *Orp* —3M **85**
Beagles Wood Rd. *Pem* —7D **152**
Beagrams, The. *S'wch* —5L **217**
Beal Clo. *Well* —8J **51**
Beales La. *N'iam* —2D **45**
Beal's Green. —3K 191 (4E 37)
Beamish Rd. *Orp* —1L **85**
Beamont Clo. *Mans* —9L **207**
Beams, The. *Maid* —8H **127**
Bean. —8H 61 (4E 7)
Bean Clo. *Gt Cha* —9A **158**
(in two parts)
Beaney's La. *Shott* —2A **30**
Bean Hill Cotts. *Grn St* —9J **61**
(in two parts)
Bean La. *Bean* —7H **61** (4E **7**)
Bean Rd. *Bexh* —2M **57**
Bean Rd. *Grnh* —6G **61** (4E **7**)
Beanshaw. *SE9* —9C **56**
Bear's End Ho. *Afrd* —1F **160**
Bear's La. *Afrd* —1E **39**
Bearstead Rd. *Maid* —2F **126**
Bearsted. —5M 127 (2A 28)
Bearsted Clo. *Gill* —9L **81**
Bearsted Grn. Bus. Cen. *Bear* —5M **127**
Bearsted Rise. *SE4* —3C **54**
Bearsted Rd. *W'ing* —1E **27**
Bearsted Ter. *Beck* —4D **68**
Bearsted Vineyard. —8N **127** (2A **28**)
Beatrice Gdns. *N'fleet* —7D **62**
Beatrice M. *G'stne* —7A **212**
Beatrice Rd. *Cap F* —2C **174**
Beatrice Rd. *Mgte* —5C **208** (1D **23**)
*Beatrice Wilson Flats. Sev —7J **119***
(off Rockdale Rd.)
Beatty Av. *Gill* —9J **81**
Beatty Clo. *Folk* —3L **189**
Beatty Rd. *Folk* —4K **189**
Beatty Rd. *Roch* —3A **94**
Beauchamp Av. *Deal* —7K **177**
Beauchamp Clo. *Kenn* —5J **159**
Beauchamp Pl. *SW3* —3B **4**
Beauchamps La. *Non* —2B **32**
Beaufighter Rd. *W Mal* —6K **123**
Beaufort Av. *Ram* —4F **210**
Beaufort Ct. *Roch* —6B **80**
Beaufort Pk. *Roch* —7B **80**
Beaufort Rd. *Roch* —3J **79**
Beaufort St. *SW3* —3B **4**
Beaufort Wlk. *Maid* —4H **139**
Beaufoy Rd. *Dover* —3F **180**
Beaufoy Ter. *Dover* —3E **180**
Beaulieu Rise. *Roch* —2A **94**
Beaulieu Rd. *Tonb* —3H **145**
Beaulieu Wlk. *Maid* —2N **125**
Beaumanor. *H Bay* —4H **195**
Beaumanor Gdns. *SE9* —9C **56**
Beaumont Davy Clo. *Fav* —7G **187**
Beaumont Dri. *N'fleet* —5D **62**
Beaumont Rd. *SW19* —4B **4**
Beaumont Rd. *Maid* —7M **125**
Beaumont Rd. *Orp* —9F **70**
Beaumont St. *H Bay* —4D **194**
Beaumont Ter. *Fav* —6H **187**
Beauvoir Dri. *Kem* —3H **99**
Beauworth Pk. *Maid* —9H **127**
Beauxfield. *Whitf* —6F **178**
Beaver. —2E 160
Beaverbank Rd. *SE9* —6F **56**
Beavercote Wlk. *Belv* —5A **52**
Beaver Ct. *Afrd* —2E **160**
Beaver Ct. *Beck* —3E **68**
Beaver Ind. Est. *Afrd* —2F **160**
Beaver La. *Afrd* —1C **160** (1E **39**)
(Brookfield Rd.)
Beaver La. *Afrd* —8C **158**
(Leacon Rd.)
Beaver Rd. *Afrd* —2F **160** (1A **40**)
(in three parts)
Beaver Rd. *Maid* —2M **125**
Beavers Lodge. *Sidc* —9H **57**
Beaverwood Rd. *Chst* —1G **71**
Beazley Ct. *Afrd* —2H **161**
Bebbington Rd. *SE18* —4G **50**
Beblets Clo. *Orp* —6H **85**
Beck Ct. *Beck* —6A **68**
Beckenham. —4D 68 (1E 13)
Beckenham Bus. Cen. *Beck* —2B **68**
Beckenham Dri. *Maid* —2A **126**
Beckenham Gro. *Brom* —5G **69**
Beckenham Hill Est. *Beck* —1E **68**
Beckenham Hill Rd. *Beck & SE6*
—2E **68** (1E **13**)
Beckenham La. *Brom* —5H **69** (1E **13**)
Beckenham Pk. *Gill* —2A **18**
Beckenham Pl. Pk. *Beck* —3E **68**
Beckenham Rd. *Beck* —4A **68** (1D **13**)
Beckenham Rd. *W Wick* —1F **82** (2E **13**)
Becket Av. *Cant* —1K **171**
Becket Clo. *Ah* —4C **216**
Becket Clo. *Deal* —2M **177**
Becket Clo. *Whits* —4K **225**
Becket Ho. *Cant* —3N **171** (1D **31**)
Becket M. *Cant* —1M **171** (4D **21**)
Beckets Field. *Pens* —3H **149**
Beckets Wood. *Ups* —3A **22**
Beckett Clo. *Belv* —3A **52**
Beckett Ct. *H'crn* —3L **193**
Becketts Clo. *H'lgh* —4C **30**
Becketts Clo. *Orp* —4H **85**
Beckett St. *Fav* —5G **186**
Beckett Wlk. *Beck* —2B **68**
Beckford Dri. *Orp* —1F **84**

Bexley Rd.—Bonetta Ct.

Bexley Rd. Eri —7D 52 (3C 7)
(in two parts)
Bexley St. Whits —3F 224
Bexon. —7C 114 (4C 18)
Bexon La. Bre —5B 114 (3C 18)
Bexon Mnr. Cotts. Bre —7C 114
Beynon Rd. Cars —2B 12
Bhutan Rd. H Bay —3K 195
Bickley. —6A 70 (1A 14)
Bickley Cres. Brom —7A 70
Bickley Pk. Rd. Brom —6A 70 (1A 14)
Bickley Rd. Brom —5N 69 (1A 14)
Bickley Rd. Tonb —7H 145
Bickmore Way. Tonb —4J 145
Bicknor. —8L 113 (4B 18)
Bicknor Clo. Cant —7A 168
Bicknor Farm Cotts. Langl —3K 139
Bicknor La. Bic —8L 113 (4B 18)
Bicknor Rd. Maid —3J 139
Bicknor Rd. Orp —1G 85
Bidborough. —3C 150 (1E 35)
Bidborough Clo. Brom —8J 69
Bidborough Ct. Bidb —3B 150
Bidborough Ridge. Bidb —2C 150 (1E 35)
Biddenden. —8L 163 (2B 38)
Biddenden Clo. Bear —6J 127
Biddenden Clo. Mgte —4G 208
(off Denton Way.)
Biddenden Green. —2L 221 (1C 38)
Biddenden Rd. Frit —1A 38
Biddenden Rd. H'crn —4M 193 (1B 38)
Biddenden Rd. Siss —8D 220 (2E 37)
Biddenden Rd. Smar —4H 221 (1B 38)
Biddenden Rd. St Mic & H Hal —1A 222 (2B 38)
Biddenden Vineyards. —2B 38
Biddenden Way. SE9 —9C 56
Biddenden Way. Grav —3D 76
Biddulph Ho. SE18 —4B 50
Bideford Rd. Brom —8J 55
Bideford Rd. Well —7K 51
Bierce Ct. Birch —4E 206
Bifrons Gdns. Pat —7G 172
Bifrons Hill. Pat —6F 172 (2E 31)
Bifron's Park. —8G 172
Bifrons Rd. Bek —6G 173
Bigbury Rd. Cha H —4C 170 (1C 31)
Biggin Hill. —5D 164 (4A 14)
Biggin Hill Airport. —2D 164
Biggin Hill Airport. —3A 14
Biggin Hill Bus. Pk. Big H —3D 164
Biggin St. Dover —4J 181
Biggins Wood Rd. Folk —4D 188
Biggleswade Pas. Cant —3L 171
Bignell Rd. SE18 —5D 50
Big Pett. Stow C —1C 41
Bilberry Clo. Weav —4H 127
Billet Hill. As —5J 89 (2E 15)
Billet La. Stan H —2C 8
Bill Hamling Clo. SE9 —7B 56
Billingford Clo. SE4 —2A 54
Billingsgate Fish Market. —2E 5
Billings Hill Shaw. Hart —9M 75
Billington Gdns. Kenn —4J 159
Bills Hill. Blad —4E 31
Bill St. Rd. Roch —3N 79 (1D 17)
Bilsby Gro. SE9 —9N 55
Bilsington. —3B 40
Bilsington Clo. Chat —6E 94
Bilsington Rd. Ruck —3A 40
Bilting. —3B 30
Bilting La. Bilt —3B 30
Bilton Rd. Eri —7H 53
Bilton Sq. Mgte —3C 208
Binbury Cotts. Det —6C 112
Binbury La. Det —6B 112 (4A 18)
Bindon Blood Rd. Whitf —8F 178
Bines, The. Pad W —1M 153
Bingham Rd. Croy —2D 13
Bingham Rd. Roch —3N 79
Bingley Rd. Snod —2D 108
Binland Gro. Chat —6A 94
Binnacle Rd. Roch —3N 93
Binney Rd. Allh —4L 201
Binnie Clo. Broad —2K 211
Binsey Wlk. SE2 —2L 51
Birbetts Rd. SE9 —7B 56
Bircham Path. SE4 —2A 54
(off Aldersford Clo.)
Birchanger Rd. SE25 —2D 13
Birch Clo. Broad —1G 211
Birch Clo. Eyns —5L 87
Birch Clo. Hild —3D 144
Birch Clo. Long —5B 76
Birch Clo. Matf —5J 153
Birch Clo. Sev —5J 119
Birch Clo. Tun W —7K 151
Birch Clo. W'boro —8J 159
Birch Ct. B'hm —8D 162
Birch Cres. Ayle —1H 125
Birchden. —7L 155 (2D 35)
Birchdene Dri. SE28 —1J 51
Birch Dri. Chat —1G 111
Birches, The. Birch —4G 206
Birches, The. Orp —5C 84
Birches, The. Swan —5F 72
Birches, The. Tonb —8H 145
Birchett. Afrd —9C 158
Birchetts Av. L'tn G —2M 155
Birchett's Green. —4B 36
Birchetts Grn. La. Birch G & Tic —4B 36
Birchfield Clo. Maid —2E 138
Birchfields. Chat —8D 94
Birch Gro. SE12 —5J 55
Birch Gro. Hem —7K 95
Birch Gro. Well —2J 57
Birchgrove. —4A 34
Birchgrove La. Chel G —4A 34
Birchgrove Rd. Hor K —4A 34
Birch Hill. Croy —6A 82
Birch Hill Ct. Birch —4G 206
Birch Ho. Barm —6L 125
(off Springwood Rd.)
Birch Ho. S'ness —2C 218
Birch Ho. Sit —7J 99
Birchin Cross Rd. Knat —6M 103 (4D 15)
Birchington. —4F 206 (1C 22)
Birchington Clo. Bexh —8C 52
Birchington Clo. Maid —4F 126
Birchington Clo. Orp —2L 85
Birchmead. Orp —3C 84
Bircholt Forstal. —6K 165 (1C 40)
Bircholt Rd. Maid —4J 139
Birch Pl. Grnh —4E 60
Birch Rd. Pad W —9M 147
Birch Rd. Whits —5J 225
Birch Row. Brom —1C 84
Birch Tree Av. W Wick —6J 83
Birch Tree Way. Maid —6E 126
Birch Wlk. Eri —6D 52
Birch Way. Hythe —7G 196
Birch Way. Tun W —7K 151
Birchway. W King —9F 88
Birchwood Av. Beck —7C 68
Birchwood Av. Sidc —8K 57
Birchwood Dri. Dart —9F 58
Birchwood La. Knock —6A 102
Birchwood Pde. Wilm —9F 58
Birchwood Pk. Av. Swan —6F 72
Birchwood Rise. Dover —5H 181
Birchwood Rd. Maid —4N 125
Birchwood Rd. Orp —7F 70
Birchwood Rd. Swan & Dart —4D 72 (1C 15)
Birchwood Wlk. Cant —9L 167
Birdbrook Rd. SE3 —1M 55
Birdcage Wlk. Tun W —2H 157
Birdham Clo. Brom —8A 70
Birdhouse La. Orp —3F 164
Bird in Hand La. Brom —5N 69
Bird in Hand St. Groom —5J 155 (2D 35)
Birds Av. Mgte —4N 207
Birdwood Av. Deal —5K 177
Birkbeck Rd. W3 —2A 4
Birkbeck Rd. Beck —5A 68
Birkbeck Rd. Sidc —8J 57
Birkdale. Tun W —8H 151
Birkdale Clo. Orp —1F 84
Birkdale Ct. Maid —5B 126
Birkdale Dri. Folk —4G 189
Birkdale Gdns. Croy —5A 82
Birkdale Gdns. H Bay —5E 194
Birkdale Rd. SE2 —4J 51
Birken Rd. Tun W —8K 151 (1E 35)
Birkhall Clo. Chat —6D 94
Birkhall Rd. SE6 —6G 55
Birling. —5N 107 (3C 16)
Birling Av. Bear —5J 127
Birling Av. Rain —2N 95 (2A 18)
Birling Clo. Maid —5J 127
Birling Dri. Tun W —4G 157
Birling Hill. Meop —1M 107
Birling Hill. Snod —3B 16
Birling Pk. Av. Tun W —5H 157
Birling Pk. Est. Birl —5A 108
Birling Rd. Afrd —8H 159
Birling Rd. Eri —7E 52
Birling Rd. Rya —6M 107 (4B 16)
Birling Rd. Snod —3D 108 (3C 16)
Birling Rd. Tun W —5G 157 (2E 35)
Birling Rd. W Mal —9N 107 (4C 16)
Birnam Sq. Maid —5B 126
Birtrick Dri. Meop —8E 76
Biscoe Way. SE13 —1G 55
Bishop Butt Clo. Orp —4H 85
Bishop Ct. Mil R —6F 98
(off St Paul's St.)
Bishopden Ct. Cant —7J 167
Bishop La. Upc —8H 223
Bishop's Av. Broad —7M 209
Bishops Av. Brom —5M 69
Bishopsbourne. —2E 31
Bishopsbourne Grn. Gill —8L 81
Bishop's Bri. W2 —2B 4
Bishops Clo. SE9 —7E 56
Bishops Clo. Nett —2A 136
Bishops Ct. Grnh —3F 60
Bishop's Ct. Tun W —2E 156
Bishop's Down. Tun W —2E 156 (2E 35)
Bishop's Down Pk. Rd. Tun W —1E 156
Bishop's Down Rd. Tun W —2E 156
Bishopsford Rd. Mord —2B 12
Bishopsgate. EC2 —2D 5
Bishops Grn. Afrd —2C 160
Bishops Grn. Brom —4M 69
(off Up. Park Rd.)
Bishop's La. Hunt —9H 137 (3C 27)
Bishop's La. Rob —3A 44
Bishops M. Tonb —7J 145
Bishops Oak Ride. Tonb —1H 145
Bishopsthorpe Rd. SE26 —9A 54
Bishopstone. —2N 195 (1A 22)
Bishopstone Dri. H Bay —1N 195
Bishopstone La. H Bay —2N 195 (1A 22)
Bishops Wlk. Chst —4E 70
Bishops Wlk. Croy —6A 82
Bishops Wlk. Roch —7A 80
Bishop's Way. E2 —2D 5
Bishops Way. Cant —1K 171
Bishopsway. Maid —5C 126
Bitchet Green. —8D 120 (2E 25)
Bixley La. Beckl —3D 45
(in two parts)
Blackberry Field. Orp —4J 71
Blackberry La. Ling —1A 34
Blackberry Rd. Ling —1A 34
Blackbird Hill. NW9 —1A 4
Blackbrook La. Brom —8C 70 (2A 14)
Black Bull Rd. Folk —5K 189 (2A 42)
Blackburn Rd. H Bay —5C 194
Black Bush La. Horn H —2B 8
Black Charles. —3B 132
Black Cotts. Boxl —5G 111
Blackdon Hill. E Grn —3D 35
Blackdown Dri. Afrd —6F 158
Black Eagle Clo. W'ham —9E 116
Blacketts Rd. Tonge —5N 99 (2D 19)
Blackfen. —4J 57 (4B 6)
Blackfen Pde. Sidc —4J 57
Blackfen Rd. Sidc —3G 57 (4B 6)
Blackfriars Bri. SE1 —2C 5
Blackfriars Rd. SE1 —2C 5
Blackfriars St. Cant —1M 171 (4D 21)
(in two parts)
Black Griffin La. Cant —2M 171 (1D 31)
(in two parts)
Blackhall La. Sev —5L 119 (2D 25)
Blackham. —1B 154 (2C 34)
Blackheath. — 1J 55 (4E 5)
Black Heath. —3E 5
Blackheath Hill. SE10 —3E 5
Blackheath Park. —2K 55 (4A 6)
Blackheath Pk. SE3 —1J 55
Blackheath Rd. SE10 —3E 5
Blackheath Village. SE3 —1J 55 (3E 5)
Black Hill. Crowb —4B 34
Black Horse Farm Cvn. & Camping Pk. Dens —4B 192
Black Horse La. Croy —2D 13
Black Horse M. Bor G —2N 121
Blackhorse Rd. Sidc —9J 57
Blackhouse Hill. Hythe —5L 197 (3E 41)
Blackhouse Rise. Hythe —5L 197
Blackhurst. —1A 36
Blackhurst La. Tun W —9L 151
Blacklands E Mal —2D 124
(in two parts)
Blacklands Dri. E Mal —1D 124
Blacklands Rd. SE6 —9F 54
Black La. S'wch —7K 217
Blackman Clo. Hoo —6G 66
Blackmans Clo. Dart —6K 59
Blackman's La. Hdlw —9C 134 (3A 26)
Blackman's La. Warl —3E 13
Blackmanstone Way. Maid —2M 125
Blackmead. Riv —3F 118
Black Mill La. H'crn —3J 193
Blackness La. Kes —8N 83 (3A 14)
Blackness Rd. Crowb —4C 35
Black Prince Interchange. (Junct.) —4C 58 (4C 6)
Black Robin La. Kgtn —3A 32
Black Rock Gdns. Hem —7L 95
Blackshaw Rd. SW17 —1B 12
Blackshots La. Grays —2A 8
Blacksmith Dri. Weav —4G 127
Blacksmith La. Wadh —4B 36
Blacksmith's La. Orp —8L 71 (2B 14)
Blacksole Cotts. Wro —6M 105
Blacksole La. Wro —7M 105
Blacksole Rd. Wro —7M 105
Blackstable Ct. Whits —5F 224
Blackstock Rd. N4 & N5 —1C 5
Blackthorn Av. Chat —8D 94
Blackthorn Av. Tun W —5J 151
Blackthorn Clo. W King —9F 88
Blackthorn Dri. Lark —8F 108
Blackthorne Rd. Gill —3D 96
Blackthorn Gro. Bexh —1N 57
Blackthorn Rd. Big H —4D 164
Blackwall Rd. N. W'boro —8L 159
Blackwall La. SE10 —3E 5
(in two parts)
Blackwall Rd. Hin —1A 40
Blackwall Rd. W'boro —8M 159
Blackwall Rd. N. W'boro —1A 40
Blackwall Rd. S. W'boro —8L 159 (1A 40)
Blackwall Tunnel Northen App. E3 & E14 —2E 5
Blackwall Tunnel Southern App. SE10 —3E 5
Blackwell Hollow. E Grin —2A 34
Blackwell Rd. E Grin —2A 34
Bladbean. —4E 31
Bladford Gdns. Sit —1F 114
Bladindon Dri. Bex —5L 57
Blagdon Rd. SE13 —4E 54
Blair Clo. Sidc —3G 56
Blair Ct. Beck —4E 68
Blair Dri. Sev —5J 119
Blake Clo. Walm —1L 199
Blake Clo. Well —8G 51
Blake Ct. W'boro —1K 161
Blake Dri. Lark —6D 108
Blake Gdns. Dart —2N 59
Blakemore Way. Belv —3N 51
Blakeney Av. Beck —4C 68
Blakeney Clo. Bear —5L 127
Blakeney Rd. Beck —3C 68 (1E 13)
Blaker Av. Roch —2B 94
Blakes Green. —7D 120
Blake's Grn. W Wick —2F 82
Blakeway. Tun W —7K 151
Blanchard Clo. SE9 —8A 56
Blandford Av. Beck —5B 68
Blandford Rd. Beck —5A 68
Bland St. SE9 —2N 55
Blanmerle Rd. SE9 —6D 56
Blann Clo. SE9 —4N 55
Blashford St. SE13 —5G 55
Blatcher Clo. Min S —6J 219
Blatchford Clo. E Mal —9D 108
Blatchington Rd. Tun W —4H 157
Blaxland Clo. Fav —4F 186
Bleak Hill La. SE18 —6H 51
Bleak House. —9M 209 (1E 23)
Bleak Rd. Lydd —3C 204
Bleakwood Rd. Chat —6C 94
Blean. —5G 167 (3D 21)
Blean Bird Park. —4F 166 (3C 21)
Blean Comn. Blean —4F 166 (3C 21)
Blean Hill. Blean —6G 167 (3D 21)
Blean Rd. Gill —1M 95
Blean Sq. Maid —3F 126
Blean View Rd. H Bay —5C 194
Bleddyn Clo. Sidc —4L 57
Blendon. —4M 57
Blendon Dri. Bex —4M 57
Blendon Path. Brom —3J 69
Blendon Rd. Bex —4M 57 (4B 6)
Blendon Rd. Maid —4F 126
Blendon Ter. SE18 —5E 50
Blenheim Av. Cant —1C 172
Blenheim Av. Chat —1B 94
Blenheim Av. Fav —7J 187
Blenheim Clo. Bear —6J 127
Blenheim Clo. Dart —4K 59
Blenheim Clo. H Bay —6H 195
Blenheim Clo. Meop —3F 90
Blenheim Clo. Pys R —1H 211
Blenheim Ct. Brom —7J 69
Blenheim Ct. Sidc —8F 56
Blenheim Dri. Dover —1H 181
Blenheim Dri. H'nge —8C 192
Blenheim Dri. Well —8H 51
Blenheim Gro. Grav —5H 63
Blenheim Pl. Folk —7F 188
Blenheim Rd. Brom —7A 70
Blenheim Rd. Dart —4K 59
Blenheim Rd. Deal —5N 177
Blenheim Rd. L'stne —3E 212
Blenheim Rd. Orp —3L 85
Blenheim Rd. Sidc —6L 57
Blenheim Rd. Sit —9J 99
Blenheim Rd. W Mal —6L 123
Bleriot Memorial. —3L 181
Blessington Clo. SE13 —1G 55
Blessington Rd. SE13 —2G 55
Bletchenden Rd. H'crn —1A 38
Bletchinglye La. Mark X —4E 35
Blewbury Ho. SE2 —2M 51
Bliby. —2A 40
Bligh Rd. Grav —4F 62
Bligh's Rd. Sev —7K 119
Bligh Way. Roch —5G 78 (1C 17)
Blindgrooms La. Shad —8A 160
Blindhouse La. M Hor —6N 215 (2D 41)
Blind La. Bred —1K 111
Blind La. C'ck —8D 174 (3A 30)
Blind La. Det —2J 111
Blind La. Goud —7K 185 (2D 37)
Blind La. Mer —5N 161 (2B 40)
Blind Mary's La. Bre —6N 113 (4B 18)
Bliss Way. Tonb —2L 145
Blithdale Rd. SE2 —4J 51
Blockmakers Ct. Chat —1E 94
Bloemfontein Rd. W12 —2A 4
Bloodden. —2A 32
Bloomfield Rd. SE18 —5D 50
Bloomfield Rd. Brom —8N 69
Bloomfield Ter. W'ham —7G 116
Bloomsbury Rd. Ram —6G 210
Bloomsbury St. WC1 —2C 4
Bloomsbury Wlk. Maid —5D 126
(off Wyatt St.)
Bloomsbury Way. Kenn —3F 158
Bloors La. Rain —2N 95 (2A 18)
(in two parts)
Bloors Wharf Rd. Gill —2A 18
Blowers Hill. Cowd —1B 34
Blowers Wood Gro. Hem —8L 95
Bloxam Gdns. SE9 —3A 56
Blue Anchor Cvn. Pk. Sea —6A 224
Blue Anchor La. W Til —3B 8
Bluebell Clo. Gill —6J 81
Bluebell Clo. Kgnt —5F 160
Bluebell Clo. Orp —3E 84
Blue Bell Hill. —1A 110 (3D 17)
Blue Bell Hill By-Pass. Chat —1N 109
Blue Bell Hill By-Pass. W'slde —3D 17
Bluebell Railway. —7J 87
Bluebell Rd. Kgnt —5F 160 (2A 40)
Bluebell Woods Cvn. Pk. B Oak —5C 168
Blueberry La. Knock —7L 101 (4B 14)
Blue Boar La. Roch —7N 79
Blue Chalet Ind. Pk. W King —7D 88
Blue Circle Heritage Centre. —4A 8
Blue Coat La. Goud —9H 185 (2C 37)
Bluehouse La. Oxt —2A 24
Blue Ho. La. Salt —1J 197
Blue Line La. Afrd —7F 158
Bluemans La. Sed —4C 44
Bluetown. —1C 29
(nr. Doddington)
Blue Town. —2C 218 (4C 11)
(nr. Minster)
Bluett St. Maid —3D 126
Blue Water. —4E 7
Bluewater Cvn. Pk. Hythe —8E 196
Blue Water Retail Pk. Grnh —5F 60
Blunden La. Yald —7E 136
Blunts Rd. SE9 —3C 56
Blythe Clo. SE6 —5C 54
Blythe Clo. Sit —6K 99
Blythe Ct. Hythe —6L 197
(off Prospect Rd.)
Blythe Hill. —5C 54
Blythe Hill. SE6 —5C 54
Blythe Hill. Orp —4H 71
Blythe Hill La. SE6 —5C 54
Blythe Rd. Maid —5E 126
Blythe Vale. SE6 —6C 54
Blyth Rd. Brom —4J 69
Blyth Wood Pk. Brom —4J 69
Boakes Meadow. Shor —2G 103
Boarders La. E'ham —2A 44
Boarders La. Tic —4B 36
Boarley. —7D 110 (4E 17)
Boarley Ct. S'lng —9C 110
Boarley La. S'lng —9C 110 (4E 17)
(in two parts)
Boarley Rd. S'lng —9C 110
Boarman's La. B'lnd —2C 46
Boarshead. —3D 35
Boathouse Rd. S'ness —1A 218
Boat La. Adgtn —3B 40
Bobbing. —5B 98 (2C 18)
Bobbing Hill. Bob —6A 98 (2B 18)
Bobbin Lodge Hill. Cha —9B 170 (2C 30)
Bockham La. W Bra —1B 40
Bockhanger. —4G 158 (4A 30)
Bockhanger Bus. Pk. Kenn —4F 158
Bockhanger Ct. Kenn —5H 159
Bockhanger La. Kenn —5G 158
(in two parts)
Bockingford Ct. Maid —9C 126
Bockingford Ho. Maid —9C 126
Bockingford La. Maid —9C 126 (2D 27)
Bockingford Mill Cotts. Maid —9C 126
Bodenham Rd. Folk —7G 188
Bodiam. —2B 44
Bodiam Castle. —2C 44
Bodiam Clo. Gill —9M 81
Bodiam Rd. Sand —4H 215 (2C 44)
Bodle Av. Swans —5L 61
Bodmin Clo. Orp —2L 85
Bodsham. —4C 31
Bodsham Cres. Bear —7L 127
Boevey Path. Belv —5A 52
Bogey La. Orp —8C 84
Bogey La. Tun W —1F 156
Bogle La. Lyn —3D 19
Bognor Dri. H Bay —3E 194
Bognor Rd. Well —8M 51
Bogshole La. H Bay —4L 195
(in two parts)
Bogshole La. Whits —9F 224 (3C 21)
Bolderwood Way. W Wick —3E 82
Boley Hill. Roch —6N 79 (1D 17)
Boleyn Av. Mgte —2M 207
Boleyn Ct. Cant —2A 172
Boleyn Gdns. W Wick —3E 82
Boleyn Gro. W Wick —3F 82
Boleyn Rd. N16 —1D 5
Boleyn Rd. Kems —8M 103
Boleyn Way. Swans —5L 61
Bolingbroke Gro. SW11 —4B 4
Bollo La. W3 & W4 —3A 4
Bolner Clo. Chat —9C 94
Bolters La. Bans —3B 12
Bolton Gdns. Brom —2J 69
Bolton Rd. Folk —5K 189
Bolton St. W1 —2C 4
Bolton St. Ram —4H 211
Bolts Hill. Cha —8B 170 (2C 30)
Bombay Ho. Maid —3H 139
Bombers La. W'ham —1F 116
Bonar Pl. Chst —3A 70
Bonaventure Ct. Grav —9L 63
Bonchester Clo. Chst —3C 70
Bond Clo. Knock —6M 101
Bondfield Clo. S'boro —5G 151
Bondfield Rd. E Mal —1D 124
Bondfield Wlk. Dart —1N 59
Bond La. Kgnt —8E 160 (2A 40)
Bond Rd. Afrd —1E 160
Bond Rd. Gill —7A 96
Bond St. Knock —6N 101
Bond Way. SW8 —3C 5
Boneashe La. Platt —3C 122
Boneta Rd. SE18 —3B 50
Bonetta Ct. S'ness —4C 218

Bonfield Rd.—Brent La.

Bonfield Rd. SE13 —2F 54
Bonflower La. Lin —9N 137 (3D 27)
Bonham Dri. Sit —6H 99
Bonner Rd. E2 —2D 5
Bonners All. Whits —3F 224
(off Middle Wall)
Bonney Way. Swan —5F 72
Bonnington. —3B 40
Bonnington Grn. Gill —9M 81
Bonnington Rd. Bils —3B 40
Bonnington Rd. Maid —3F 126
Bonny Bush Hill. Kgtn —2E 31
Bonsor Rd. Folk —5K 189
Bonville Rd. Brom —1J 69
Boones Rd. SE13 —2H 55
Boone St. SE13 —2H 55
Boormans Cotts. W'bury —1A 136
Bootham Clo. Roch —8H 79
Booth Clo. SE28 —1K 51
Booth Pl. Mgte —2D 208
Booth Rd. Chat —1C 94
Borden. —9B 98 (3C 18)
Borden La. B'den —9C 98 (3C 18)
Border Gdns. Croy —5E 82
Bordyke. Tonb —4E 25
Boresisle. St Mic —5C 222
Borgard Rd. SE18 —4B 50
Borkwood Pk. Orp —5H 85
Borkwood Way. Orp —5G 84
Borland Clo. Grnh —3G 61
Borland Rd. SE15 —2A 54
Bornefields. Afrd —2E 160
Borough Green. —2M 121 (1A 26)
Borough Grn. Rd. Bor G —3K 121
(in two parts)
Borough Grn. Rd. Igh —1E 25
Borough Grn. Rd. Wro —4A 16
Borough High St. SE1 —3D 5
Borough Museum. —5M 59
Borough Rd. SE1 —3C 5
Borough Rd. Gill —8G 80
Borough Rd. Queen —8C 218
Borough Rd. Tats —9D 164
Borough, The. —3D 5
Borough, The. Cant —1N 171 (4D 21)
Borrowdale Av. Ram —5E 210
Borstal. —1L 93 (2D 17)
Borstal Av. Whits —7F 224
Borstal Hill. Whits —7F 224 (2C 21)
Borstal M. Roch —1L 93
Borstal Rd. Roch —9L 79 (2D 17)
Borstal St. Roch —1L 93 (2D 17)
Borton Clo. Yald —7D 136
Bosbury Rd. SE6 —8F 54
Bosco Clo. Orp —5H 85
Boscombe Rd. Folk —5J 189
Bosney Banks. Lyd —4B 32
Bossingham. —3D 31
Bossingham Rd. S Min —3D 31
Bossington. —2A 32
Bossington Rd. Adm —2A 32
Bostall Hill. SE2 —5J 51 (3B 6)
Bostall La. SE2 —5K 51
Bostall Mnr. Way. SE2 —4K 51
Bostall Pk. Av. Bexh —7N 51
Bostall Rd. Orp —3K 71
Bostal Row. Bexh —1A 58
Boston Clo. Dover —1G 180
Boston Gdns. Gill —2M 95
Boston Rd. Chat —9F 94
Bosville Av. Sev —5H 119
Bosville Dri. Sev —5H 119
Bosville Rd. Sev —5H 119
Boswell Clo. Orp —9L 71
Bosworth Ho. Eri —5F 52
(off Saltford Clo.)
Botany. Tonb —6J 145
Botany Bay La. Chst —5E 70
Botany Clo. S'ness —3C 218
Botany Rd. Broad —4K 209 (1E 23)
Boteler Cotts. E'try —3J 183
Botolph's Bridge. —8B 196 (3D 41)
Botolph's Bri. Rd. W Hyt —9B 196 (3D 41)
Botsom La. W King —7C 88 (3E 15)
Bottle Cotts. Sev —4H 119
Bottlescrew Hill. Bou M —4E 138 (3E 27)
Bottles La. Rod —5H 115 (3C 19)
Bottom Pond. —8D 114 (4C 18)
Bottom Pond Rd. W'hll —9C 114 (1C 28)
Bott Rd. Dart —9N 59
Boucher Dri. N'fleet —8E 62
Bough Beech. —5A 142 (4C 24)
Bough Beech Rd. Four E —3B 24
Boughton Aluph. —3A 30
Boughton Av. Broad —2L 211
Boughton Av. Brom —1J 83
Boughton Clo. Gill —9M 81
Boughton Corner. —4B 30
Boughton Green. —5E 138 (3E 27)
Boughton Hill. Dunk —3M 165 (4B 20)
Boughton La. Maid —1E 138 (2E 27)
Boughton Lees. —4A 30
Boughton Malherbe. —3C 28
Boughton Monchelsea. —5E 138 (3E 27)
Boughton Monchelsea Place. —3E 27
Boughton Pde. Maid —1D 138
Boughton Rd. SE28 —3G 51
Boughton Rd. S'wy —9C 200 (3C 28)
Boughton Under Blean. —3J 165 (4B 20)
Boulevard Courriers. Aysm —2C 162
Boulevard, The. W'boro —3K 161 (1A 40)
Boundary Clo. Min S —6M 219
Boundary Ct. Cant —4A 172
Boundary Houses. Grav —6E 62
(off Victoria Rd.)
Boundary Rd. E13 —2A 6
Boundary Rd. NW8 —2B 4
Boundary Rd. Cant —4K 171
Boundary Rd. Cars —3C 12
Boundary Rd. Chat —9A 80
Boundary Rd. Kgdn —3N 199
Boundary Rd. Ram —5J 211 (2E 23)
Boundary Rd. Sidc —3G 56
Boundary Rd. Tun W —4K 157
Boundary St. Eri —7G 52
Boundary Ter. Hythe —7H 197
Boundary, The. L'tn G —2B 156
Boundary Way. Croy —6D 82
Boundfield Rd. SE6 —8H 55
Bounds La. Bou B —3K 165
Bounds Oak Way. Tun W —3E 150
Bounds, The. Ayle —9J 109
Bourbon Ho. SE6 —1F 68
Bourchier Clo. Sev —8J 119
Bourg-de-Peage Av. E Grin —2A 34
Bournbrook Rd. SE3 —1N 55
Bourncrete Ho. Sit —6H 99
Bourne Clo. Tonb —4K 145
Bourne Gro. Sit —6D 98
Bourne Ind. Est. Bor G —1N 121
Bourne Ind. Pk., The. Dart —3F 58
Bourne La. Hams —7D 190
Bourne La. Plax —8M 121
Bourne La. Rob —2B 44
Bourne La. Sev —2A 26
Bourne Lodge Clo. Blean —4G 166
Bourne Mead. Bex —3E 58
Bournemouth Dri. H Bay —2E 194
Bournemouth Gdns. Folk —5J 189
Bournemouth Pk. Rd. Sth S —1C 10
Bournemouth Rd. Folk —5J 189
Bourne Pde. Bex —5C 58
Bourne Pk. Gold G —2E 146
Bourne Pk. Rd. Bri —9H 173 (2E 31)
Bourne Rd. Bex & Dart —5C 58 (4C 6)
Bourne Rd. Bon —2B 40
Bourne Rd. Brom —7N 69
Bourne Rd. Grav —7L 63
Bournes Clo. Sturry —4E 168
Bournes Green. —1C 11
Bournes Grn. Chase. Sth S —1C 11
Bournes Hill. Blad —4E 31
Bourneside Gdns. SE6 —1F 68
Bourneside Ter. Holl —7F 128
Bournes Pl. Wdchu —7B 226
Bourne Vale. Brom —2J 83
Bourne Vale. Plax —9N 121
Bourne View. Bri —9E 172
Bourne Way. Brom —3J 83 (2E 13)
Bourne Way. Swan —6D 72
Bournewood. Hams —7D 190
Bournewood Clo. Down —8J 127
Bournewood Rd. SE18 —7J 51
Bournewood Rd. Orp —1L 85
Bournville Av. Chat —2C 94
Bournville Rd. SE6 —5D 54
Bouverie Pl. Folk —7K 189
Bouverie Rd. W. Folk —7G 189 (3A 42)
Bouverie Sq. Folk —7K 189
Boveney Rd. SE23 —5A 54
Bovill Rd. SE23 —5A 54
Bow. —2E 5
Bow Arrow La. Dart —4A 60
Bowater Rd. SE18 —3A 50
Bow Common. —2E 5
Bow Comn. La. E3 —2E 5
Bowdell La. B'lnd & Snar —2C 46
Bowden Cres. Folk —5C 188
Boweashe La. Sev —1A 26
Bowen Rd. Folk —5E 188
Bowen Rd. Tun W —9B 150
Bowen's Field. Afrd —9F 158
Bowens Wood. Croy —9C 82
Bower Clo. Maid —5B 126
Bower Cotts. Mer —8M 161
Bower Grn. Chat —1F 110
Bowerland La. Chi —7M 175
Bowerland La. Ling —4A 24
Bowerland La. Old L —6K 175
Bower La. Eyns & Knat —4M 87 (2D 15)
Bower La. Maid —6B 126
Bower Mt. Rd. Maid —6A 126 (2D 27)
Bower Pl. Maid —6B 126
Bower Rd. Mer —8M 161 (2B 40)
Bower Rd. Swan —3H 73
Bowers Av. N'fleet —9E 62
Bowers Rd. Shor —2G 102
Bower St. Maid —5B 126
Bower Ter. Maid —6B 126
Bower Wlk. S'hrst —8J 221
Bowes Av. Mgte —2M 207
Bowes Clo. Sidc —4K 57
Bowes Ct. Dart —4B 60
(off Osbourne Rd.)
Bowes Ct. Whits —3J 225
Bowesden La. Shorne —3C 78
Bowes La. H Bay —4H 195
Bowes Rd. Roch —4M 79
Bowes Wood. New Ash —4M 89
Bowford Av. Bexh —8N 51
Bow Hill. Bos —3D 31
Bow Hill. Up Hard —3D 31
Bow Hill. W'bury & Yald —2C 136
Bow Interchange. (Junct.) —2E 5
Bowland Clo. H Bay —5K 195
Bowler's Town. —3A 46
Bowleswell Gdns. Folk —4M 189
Bowley La. S'wy —3C 28
Bowl Field. H'lgh —4C 30
Bowl Grn. La. Deal —5L 177
Bowling Grn. Row. SE18 —3B 50
Bowling Grn. Ter. Dover —5J 181
Bowling St. S'wch —5L 217
Bowl Rd. Char —1L 175 (3D 29)
Bowls Pl. Pad W —8M 147
Bowman Clo. Chat —6F 94
Bowmans. —5G 59
Bowman's Rd. Dart —5G 58
Bowmead. SE9 —7B 56
Bowness Rd. SE6 —5E 54
Bowness Rd. Bexh —9C 52
Bow Rd. E3 —2E 5
Bow Rd. W'bury —2C 136 (2C 26)
Bowser Clo. Deal —6J 177
Bow St. WC2 —2C 5
Bow Ter. W'bury —1C 136
Bowyer Rd. Sea —6B 224
Bowzell Rd. Weald —6G 130 (3C 25)
Bowzells La. Bough B —5D 142
Bowzell's La. Chid C —4C 25
Boxgrove Rd. SE2 —3L 51
Box La. Osp —4E 19
Boxley. —8F 110 (1E 27)
Boxley. Afrd —1D 160
Boxley Clo. Maid —1E 126
Boxley Clo. S'ness —5C 218
Boxley Grange Cotts. Boxl —5J 111
Boxley Rd. Boxl —1E 27
Boxley Rd. Chat —3E 17
Boxley Rd. Maid —3D 126
Boxley Rd. W'slde —9D 94 (3E 17)
Boxmend Ind. Est. Maid —4J 139
Boxted La. N'tn —2J 97 (2B 18)
Box Tree Wlk. Orp —2M 85
Boyard Rd. SE18 —5D 50
Boyces Hill. N'tn —5L 97 (2B 18)
Boy Ct. Rd. H'crn —4B 28
Boyd Bus. Cen. Roch —5A 80
Boyden Gate. —2A 22
Boyden Ga. Hill. Hoath —2A 22
Boyden Hill. Hoath —6N 195 (2A 22)
Boyes La. Good —2B 32
Boyke La. R Min —9J 183 (1D 41)
Boyland Rd. Brom —1J 69
Boyne Pk. Tun W —1F 156
Boyne Rd. SE13 —1F 54
Boyne Rd. St Mc —9K 199
Boys Hall Rd. W'boro —2K 161 (1A 40)
Boystown Pl. E'try —2L 183
Boyton Ct. Rd. Sut V —9C 140 (3A 28)
Brabazon Rd. E'chu —9B 202
Brabner Clo. Folk —3L 189
Brabourne. —1C 41
Brabourne Clo. Cant —7N 167
Brabourne Cres. Bexh —6A 52
Brabourne Gdns. Folk —6E 188
Brabourne La. Stow C —1C 41
Brabourne Lees. —8J 165 (1B 40)
Brabourne Rise. Beck —8F 68
Brabourne Rd. Brook —4B 30
Bracken Av. Croy —4E 82
Bracken Clo. Kenn —4G 159
Bracken Clo. Tun W —9L 151
Bracken Ct. Broad —8J 209
Bracken Ct. Sit —6K 99
Brackendene. Dart —9F 58
Bracken Hill. Chat —1D 110
Bracken Hill Clo. Brom —4J 69
Bracken Hill La. Brom —4J 69
Bracken Lea. Chat —2F 94
Bracken Rd. Tun W —9L 151
Brackens. Beck —3D 68
Brackens, The. Orp —6J 85
Bracken Wlk. Tonb —1H 145
Brack La. B'lnd —2B 46
Brackley Clo. Maid —4F 126
Brackley Rd. Beck —3C 68
Bracondale Av. Grav —4E 76
Bracondale Rd. SE2 —4J 51
Bradbourne Av. Gill —8M 81
Bradbourne Ct. Sev —3J 119
Bradbourne La. Dit —9F 108
Bradbourne Pk. Rd. E Mal —9E 108
Bradbourne Pk. Rd. Sev —5H 119 (2D 25)
Bradbourne Rd. Bex —5B 58
Bradbourne Rd. Sev —4J 119 (1D 25)
Bradbourne Vale Rd. Sev —4G 118 (1C 25)
Bradbridge Grn. Afrd —1B 160
Bradbury Ct. Grav —6E 62
Braddick Clo. Maid —2E 138
Bradenham Av. Well —2J 57
Bradfield Av. Tey —2L 223
Bradfields Av. Chat —5C 94
Bradfields Av. W. Chat —5C 94
Bradfiled Rd. Kenn —5F 158
Bradfoord Ct. Folk —6K 189
(off Foord Rd.)
Bradford Clo. Brom —2B 84
Bradford St. Tonb —6H 145
Bradgate Pk. Mgte —9C 208
Bradgate Rd. SE6 —4E 54
Bradley Dri. Sit —9F 98 (3C 19)
Bradley Ho. Lwr Sto —8K 201
Bradley La. Blac —9D 148 (1C 35)
Bradley Rd. Folk —5M 189
Bradley Rd. Ram —3G 210
Bradley Rd. Up H'lng —6C 92
Bradshaw Clo. Upc —8H 223
Bradstone Av. Folk —5K 189
Bradstone New Rd. Folk —6K 189
Bradstone Rd. Folk —6K 189
Bradstone St. Folk —2A 42
Bradstow Way. Broad —8K 209
Brady Rd. Lym —9A 204 (1D 41)
Braemar Av. Bexh —2D 58
Braemar Gdns. Sidc —8F 56
Braemar Gdns. W Wick —2F 82
Braeside. Beck —1D 68
Braeside Av. Sev —6G 119
Braeside Clo. Sev —5G 118
Braeside Cres. Bexh —2D 58
Braes, The. High —1G 78
Braesyde Clo. Belv —4A 52
Braggs La. H Bay —9E 194
Braham St. E1 —2D 5
Braidwood Rd. SE6 —6G 54
Brake Av. Chat —6B 94
Brakefield Rd. S'fleet —2A 76
Brake Pl. W King —7E 88
Bramber Ct. Dart —4B 60
(off Bow Arrow La.)
Bramble Av. Bean —8J 61
Bramble Bank. Meop —3E 106
Bramblebury Rd. SE18 —5E 50
Bramble Clo. Croy —5D 82
Bramble Clo. Hild —3E 144
Bramble Clo. Maid —6M 125
Bramble Croft. Eri —4D 52
Brambledown. Chat —3E 94
Brambledown. Folk —5K 189
Brambledown. Hart —7M 75
Brambledown Clo. W Wick —8H 69
Bramblefield Clo. Long —6L 75
Bramblefield La. Iwade —2E 98
(in two parts)
Bramblefields Clo. H Bay —5J 195
Bramble Hall Rd. Off —3F 122
Bramblehill Rd. Fav —4G 187
Bramble La. Sev —1J 131
Bramble La. Upm —2E 7
Bramble La. Wye —1L 159 (4B 30)
Bramble Reed La. Matf —6G 153 (1B 36)
Brambles Clo. Wye —1L 159
Brambles Farm Rd. B Oak —1A 168
Brambles Wildlife Park. —3E 21
Brambletree Cotts. Roch —1J 93
Brambletree Cres. Roch —1K 93
Bramble Wlk. Tun W —7K 151
Brambley Cres. Folk —6E 188
Bramcote Wlk. Ram —5G 211
Bramdean Cres. SE12 —6K 55
Bramdean Gdns. SE12 —6K 55
Bramerton Rd. Beck —6C 68
Bramley Av. Cant —4J 171
Bramley Av. Fav —6J 187
Bramley Bank Nature Reserve. —3D 13
Bramley Clo. Bra L —7K 165
Bramley Clo. E'chu —5C 202
Bramley Clo. Gill —3D 96
Bramley Clo. Grav —3E 76
Bramley Clo. Orp —2D 84
Bramley Clo. Swan —7F 72
Bramley Ct. Mard —2J 205
Bramley Ct. Well —8K 51
Bramley Cres. Bear —6J 127
Bramley Dri. C'brk —8D 176
Bramley Gdns. Afrd —3E 160
Bramley Gdns. Cox —5A 138
Bramley Gdns. Pad W —8K 147
Bramley Hill. S Croy —2C 13
Bramley Pk. Holiday Camp. E'chu —3D 202
Bramley Pl. Dart —2H 59
Bramley Rise. Roch —4J 79
Bramley Rd. E Peck —1L 147
Bramley Rd. Snod —2E 108
Bramleys. H'crn —3M 193
Bramley Way. E'chu —5C 202
Bramley Way. King H —7M 123
Bramley Way. W Wick —3E 82
Bramling. —1A 32
Bramling Rd. Bek —9L 173 (2A 32)
Brampton Bank. Tud —9D 146
Brampton Rd. Bexh & SE2 —1M 57 (3B 6)
Bramshaw Rd. Cant —9L 167
Bramshott Clo. Maid —3N 125
Bramston Rd. Min S —6K 219
Branbridges. —2M 147 (3B 26)
Branbridges Ind. Est. E Peck —2M 147
Branbridges Rd. E Peck (in two parts) —1M 147 (3B 26)
Branbrook Rd. Goud —8L 185
Brancaster La. Purl —3D 13
Branch Hill. NW3 —1B 4
Branch Rd. Chi —8K 175 (2B 30)
Branch St. Dover —3H 181
Brandfold. —2D 37
Brandon Ho. Beck —1E 68
(off Beckenham Hill Rd.)
Brandon Rd. Dart —5A 60
Brandon Rd. Ram —3E 210
Brandon St. Grav —5G 62
Brandon Way. Birch —5G 206
Brandram Rd. SE13 —1H 55
Brands Hatch Motor Racing Circuit. —6F 88 (2E 15)
Brands Hatch Pk. Fawk —4F 88
Brands Hatch Rd. Fawk —5G 88 (2E 15)
Brangbourne Rd. Brom —1F 68
Branksome Av. Stan H —2C 8
Branscombe Ct. Brom —8J 69
Branscombe St. SE13 —1E 54
Bransell Clo. Swan —9D 72
Bransgore Clo. Gill —4N 95
Branston Cres. Orp —2F 84
Brantingham Clo. Tonb —8F 144
Branton Rd. Grnh —4F 60
Brantwood Av. Eri —7D 52
Brantwood Rd. Bexh —9C 52
Brantwood Way. Orp —6L 71
Brasenose Rd. Gill —9H 81
Brasier Ct. Min S —7H 219
Brassey Av. Broad —1K 211
Brassey Dri. Ayle —1H 125
Brasted. —6L 117 (2B 24)
Brasted Chart. —2B 24
Brasted Clo. Bexh —3M 57
Brasted Clo. Orp —3J 85
Brasted Ct. Roch —3L 79
Brasted Hill. Knock —2J 117 (1B 24)
Brasted Hill Rd. Bras —3K 117 (1B 24)
Brasted La. Knock —1J 117 (1B 24)
Brasted Lodge. SE20 —3D 68
Brasted Rd. Eri —7F 52
Brasted Rd. W'ham —8G 116 (2B 24)
Brattle. —9C 226 (3D 39)
Brattle. Wdchu —9C 226
Brattle Farm Museum. —1E 37
Brattle Wood. Sev —2J 131
Braundton Av. Sidc —6H 57
Braxfield Rd. SE4 —2B 54
Bray Gdns. Maid —3C 138
Braywood Rd. SE9 —2F 56
Breach. —3H 97 (2B 18)
Breach La. Lwr Hal —4H 97 (2B 18)
Breadlands Clo. W'boro —1J 161
Breadlands Rd. W'boro —1K 161
Breakneck Hill. Grnh —3H 61
Breakspears Dri. Orp —4J 71
Breakspears Rd. SE4 —2C 54
Brecknock Rd. N19 & N7 —1C 4
Breckonmead. Brom —5M 69
Brecon Chase. Min S —5K 219
Brecon Rise. Afrd —6F 158
Brecon Sq. Ram —3E 210
Brede. —4D 45
Brede Hill. Brede —4D 45
Brede La. Sed —4C 44
Brede Rd. Westf —4D 45
Brede Waterworks. —4C 45
Bredgar. —5A 114 (3C 18)
Bredgar Clo. Afrd —3D 160
Bredgar Clo. Maid —4E 126
Bredgar Rd. Gill —8K 81
Bredgar Rd. Tun —4B 114 (3C 18)
Bredhurst. —1L 111 (3E 17)
Bredhurst Clo. S'ness —5C 218
Bredhurst Rd. Gill —5L 95
Bredlands La. Hoath —2H 169 (3E 21)
Breedon Av. Tun W —5F 150
Bremner Clo. Swan —7H 73
Brenchley. —6N 153 (1B 36)
Brenchley Av. Deal —6J 177
Brenchley Av. Grav —1G 77
Brenchley Clo. Afrd —3C 160
Brenchley Clo. Brom —9J 69
Brenchley Clo. Chst —4C 70
Brenchley Clo. Roch —1A 94
Brenchley Gdns. SE23 —3A 54 (4D 5)
Brenchley Ho. Maid —4C 126
Brenchley Rd. Gill —1L 95
Brenchley Rd. Horsm —3A 198 (1C 36)
Brenchley Rd. Maid —7C 126
Brenchley Rd. Matf —5K 153 (1B 36)
Brenchley Rd. Orp —5H 71
Brenchley Rd. Sit —9G 98
Brenda Ter. Swans —5L 61
Brendon Av. Chat —8D 94
Brendon Clo. Eri —8F 52
Brendon Clo. Tun W —9K 151
Brendon Dri. Afrd —7F 158
Brendon Rd. SE9 —7F 56
Brenley Gdns. SE9 —2N 55
Brenley La. Bou B —9L 187 (4A 20)
Brenley Rd. Bou B —8N 187 (4B 20)
Brennan Rd. Til —3B 8
Brent Clo. Bex —6N 57
Brent Clo. Chat —6B 94
Brent Clo. Dart —4B 60
Brentfield. NW10 —1A 4
Brentfield Rd. NW10 —1A 4
Brentfield Rd. Dart —4A 60
Brent Hill. Fav —4G 186 (3A 20)
Brentlands Dri. Dart —6A 60
Brent La. Dart —5N 59

Brent Rd.—Broomfield

Brent Rd. SE18 —7D 50
Brent Rd. Fav —4G 187 (3A 20)
Brents Ind. Est. Fav —3H 187
Brents, The. —3H 187 (3A 20)
Brent, The. Dart —5A 60 (4D 7)
Brent, The. Tonb —1J 145
Brent Way. Dart —4B 60
Brentwood. Afrd —4D 160
Brentwood Clo. SE9 —6E 56
Brentwood Rd. Bulp & Grays —1B 8
Brentwood Rd. Grays —3B 8
Brenzett. —2C 46
Brenzett Aeronautical Museum. —2C 47
Brenzett Clo. Chat —6E 94
Brenzett Green. —1C 47
Bretland Rd. Tun W —1D 156
Breton Rd. Roch —1N 93
Brett Wlk. Gill —7N 95
Brewer Rd. Cli —6M 65
Brewer's Field. Dart —9K 59
Brewer's Hill. S'gte —8D 188
Brewers Rd. Shorne —4A 78 (1C 16)
Brewer St. Deal —4N 177
Brewer St. Lam —2C 200
Brewer St. Maid —4D 126
Brewery La. Bri —8H 173 (2E 31)
Brewery La. Sev —7J 119
Brewery Rd. N7 —1C 5
Brewery Rd. SE18 —5F 50 (3B 6)
Brewery Rd. Brom —2A 84
Brewery Rd. Sit —5F 98
Brewery Sq. W Sto —3B 22
Brewhouse Rd. SE18 —4B 50
Brewhouse Yd. Grav —4G 63
Brewster Rd. Kgdn —8M 115
Brian Cres. Tun W —6H 151
Brian Roberts Ho. H Bay —2G 194
(off Beach St.)
Briar Clo. Aysm —2D 162
Briar Clo. Dover —2E 180
Briar Clo. Eden —4D 184
Briar Clo. Kenn —4G 159
Briar Clo. Lark —8E 108
Briar Clo. Bus. Pk. Wye —1L 159
Briar Dale. High —9F 64
Briar Fields. Weav —4H 127
Briar Gdns. Brom —2J 83
Briar La. Croy —5E 82
Briar Rd. Bex —8E 58
Briars Rd. St Mar —3E 214
Briars, The. W King —7D 88
Briars, The. Whits —7E 224
Briars Wlk. Broad —1K 211
Briars Way. Hart —8N 75
Briarswood Way. Orp —6H 85
Briar Wlk. Tonb —1J 145
Briary Clo. Mgte —3L 207
Briary Ct. Sidc —1K 71
Briary Gdns. Brom —1L 69
Briary Lodge. Beck —4F 68
Brice Av. Cha —8C 170
Brice Rd. High —1F 78
Brickenden Rd. C'brk —8D 176
Brickfield Cotts. SE18 —6H 51
Brickfield Cotts. Kems —1D 120
Brickfield Farm Gdns. Orp —5E 84
Brickfield La. Bou B —3H 165 (4B 20)
Brickfield Rd. B'hm —9D 162 (3A 32)
Brickfields. Pem —6D 152
Brickfields. W Mal —9N 107
Brickfield View. Roch —3N 79
Brick Kiln La. E Sut —3A 28
Brick Kiln La. Horsm —4E 198 (2C 37)
Brick Kiln La. Oxt —2A 24
Brick La. E1 —2D 5
Bricklayer's Arms. (Junct.) —3D 5
Brickmakers Ind. Est. Sit —5J 99
Brickwall House. —3D 45
Brickworks Clo. Tonb —9G 145
Brickworks Cotts. Sev —2L 119
Brickworks La. Brook —4B 30
Brickyard La. Mark X —4E 35
Bridewell La. Tent —8B 222
Bridewell Pk. Whits —4J 225
Bridge. —8H 173 (2E 31)
Bridge App., The. Whits —4H 225
Bridge Bus. Pk. Five G —8H 147
Bridge Clo. Hythe —6H 197
Bridge Clo. Tonb —7J 145
Bridge Clo. Wdchu —9C 226
Bridge Cotts. E Far —9J 125
(St Helens La.)
Bridge Cotts. E Far —1M 137
(Station Hill)
Bridge Down. Bri —9J 173
Bridgefield Ct. Whits —2K 225
Bridgefield Rd. Whits —2K 225
Bridgeford Way. Bri —8H 173
Bridge Hill. Ayle —9J 109
Bridge Hill. Bri —8H 173 (2E 31)
Bridge Hill. Hackl —2D 33
Bridge Home Pk. Cvn. Site. Lydd —1D 204
Bridge Ho. SE4 —2C 54
Bridge Ho. Dart —5M 59
Bridge Ho. Ram —5G 210
Bridge Ho. Tonb —6J 145
(off High St. Tonbridge,)
Bridge Ind. Est. Tovil —7B 126
Bridgeman Ct. Hythe —6J 197
Bridge Mill Way. Tovil —7A 126
Bridgen. —5N 57
Bridgen Rd. Bex —5N 57 (4C 6)
Bridge Rd. E15 —2E 5
Bridge Rd. Afrd —8D 158
Bridge Rd. Beck —3C 68 (1E 13)
Bridge Rd. Bexh —9N 51
Bridge Rd. Bra L —8J 165 (1B 40)
Bridge Rd. Deal —3N 177
Bridge Rd. Eps —3A 12
Bridge Rd. Eri —9G 52 (3C 7)
Bridge Rd. Fav —4G 187
Bridge Rd. Gill —5F 80
Bridge Rd. Grays —3A 8
Bridge Rd. Mgte —3M 207 (1D 23)
Bridge Rd. Nack —9B 172 (2D 31)
Bridge Rd. Orp —9K 71
Bridge Rd. Rain —2C 7
Bridge Rd. Roch —1N 93
Bridge Rd. S'ness —1C 218 (4C 11)
Bridges Clo. St N —8D 214
Bridges Dri. Dart —3B 60
Bridgeside. Deal —4M 177
Bridge St. Dover —3H 181 (1C 43)
Bridge St. Folk —5L 189
Bridge St. Loose —3C 138
Bridge St. Wye —2L 159 (4B 30)
Bridge View Ind. Est. Queen —9B 218
Bridgewater Clo. Chst —6G 71
Bridgewater Pl. Leyb —8C 108
Bridgewater Rd. S'ness —4C 218
Bridgeway. Whits —3H 225
Bridle Rd. Croy —4D 82 (2E 13)
(in two parts)
Bridle Rd., The. Purl —3C 13
Bridle Way. Croy —5D 82
Bridle Way. H Bay —4E 194
Bridle Way. Hythe —8A 188
Bridle Way. Orp —5E 84
Bridle Way. Whitf —6E 178
Bridleway Gdns. Broad —1J 211
Bridleway La. Kgnt —5F 160
Bridlington Clo. Big H —7B 164
Brielle Way. S'ness —5A 218 (4C 11)
Brier Clo. Chat —3F 94
Brierley. New Ad —7E 82
(in two parts)
Brier Rd. Sit —6B 98
Bright Clo. Belv —4M 51
Brightfield Rd. SE12 —3H 55
Brightlands. N'fleet —9D 62
Brightling Rd. SE4 —4C 54
Brightling Rd. Rob —3A 44
Brightlingsea Rd. S'wch —6L 217
Brighton Rd. Bans —4B 12
Brighton Rd. Hool & Coul —4C 12
Brighton Rd. Purl & S Croy —3C 13
Bright Ridge. Tun W —6E 150
Bright Rd. Chat —1E 94
Brightside Rd. SE13 —4G 55
Bright's Pl. Ram —5K 211
Brigstock Rd. Belv —4C 52
Brigstock Rd. T Hth —2C 13
Brimpsfield Clo. SE2 —3K 51
Brimsdale La. Eyt —4K 185
Brimstone Clo. Orp —8L 85
Brimstone Hill. Meop —3H 91 (2B 16)
Brimstone La. Meop —4H 91 (2B 16)
Brindle Ga. Sidc —6G 56
Brindles Field. Tonb —8G 144
Brindle Way. Chat —1F 110
Brindley Clo. Bexh —1C 58
Brindley Way. Brom —1K 69
Brinkburn Clo. SE2 —4J 51
Brinker's La. Wadh —4A 36
Brinklow Cres. SE18 —7D 50
Brionne Gdns. Tonb —7K 145
Brisbane Av. Sit —7D 98
Brisbane Dri. Ram —3E 210
Brisbane Rd. Chat —9D 80
Briset Rd. SE9 —1N 55
Brishing Clo. Maid —3H 139
Brishing La. Bou M —6G 138 (3E 27)
Brishing La. Maid —3H 139
Brishing Rd. Cha S —3E 27
Brishing Rd. Maid & Cha S —4H 139
Brisley La. Ruck —3A 40
Brisley's Row. Burh —1K 109
Brissenden Clo. New R —1C 212
Brissenden Clo. Upnor —1D 80
Brissenden Green. —4L 163 (2D 39)
Brissenden Grn. La. Beth —4L 163 (2D 39)
Bristol Clo. Roch —7H 79
Bristol Ho. Maid —1G 138
Bristol Pl. Ram —5H 211
Bristol Rd. Cant —4M 171
Bristol Rd. Grav —8J 63
Bristow Rd. Bexh —8N 51
Britannia Av. Whits —6D 224
Britannia Bus. Pk. Quar W —2J 125
Britannia Clo. Hall —7E 92
Britannia Clo. Sit —4F 98
Britannia Dri. Grav —1L 77
Britannia Rd. Deal —2N 177
Britannia Rd. High H —4E 9
Britannia Rd. H Hals —1H 67
Briton Ct. S'ness —4B 218
Briton Rd. Fav —5G 186
Brittain Ho. SE9 —6A 56
Brittains La. Sev —6G 119 (2C 25)
Brittania Junction. (Junct.) —1C 4
Britten Clo. Hythe —5H 197
Britten Clo. Tonb —1M 145
Brittenden Clo. Orp —7H 85
Brittenden Pde. Grn St —7H 85
Britton Clo. SE6 —5G 54
Britton Farm Rd. Gill —6F 80
Britton Farm Rd. Wickh —4A 22
Britton St. Gill —7E 80
(in two parts)
Brixham Rd. Well —8M 51
Brixham St. E16 —1C 50
Brixton. —4C 5
Brixton Hill. SW2 —4C 5
Brixton Rd. SW9 —4C 5
Brixton Water La. SW2 —4C 5
Broadacre. Lyd —4B 32
Broadacre. Tey —2L 223
Broadcloth. C'brk —9D 176
Broadcoombe. S Croy —8A 82
Broadcroft. Tun W —5F 156
Broadcroft Rd. Orp —1F 84
Broad Ditch Rd. Meop —1A 16
Broad Ditch Rd. S'fleet —3B 76
Broader La. Det —8L 111 (4E 17)
Broadfield Cres. Folk —6G 188
Broadfield Rd. SE6 —5H 55
Broadfield Rd. Folk —6G 189
Broadfield Rd. Maid —9D 126
Broad Ford. —4E 198 (2C 37)
Broad Green. —2D 13
Broadgrove. Tun W —4G 156
Broadham Grn. Rd. Oxt —3A 24
Broadheath Dri. Chst —1B 70
Broadhurst Dri. Kenn —3H 159
Broadhurst Gdns. NW6 —1B 4
Broadland Row. —4D 45
Broadlands. Sturry —5E 168
Broadlands Av. New R —1C 212
Broadlands Cres. New R —1C 212
Broadlands Dri. Chat —7E 94
Broadlands Ind. Est. Blean —4F 166
Broadlands Rd. Brom —9L 55
Broad La. Bett —2D 33
Broad La. Dart —9H 59 (1D 15)
Broad La. Ford —2H 155 (2D 35)
Broad Lawn. SE9 —7C 56
Broadley Av. Birch —6E 206
Broadley Rd. Broad —6G 208
Broadmead. SE6 —8D 54
Broadmead. Afrd —3C 160
Broadmead. Tun W —5E 156
Broadmead Av. Tun W —5F 156
Broadmeadow. Folk —4H 189
Broadmead Rd. Folk —6J 189
Broadmead Village. —5G 189
Broad Oak. —4C 168 (3E 21)
Broad Oak. Bchly —1C 36
Broad Oak. Groom —7K 155
Broadoak. Leyb —8B 108
Broadoak Av. Maid —1D 138
Broad Oak Clo. Bchly —1C 36
Broad Oak Clo. Bor G —5J 71
Broadoak Clo. S at H —2A 74
Broadoak Clo. Tun W —4F 156
Broad Oak Cotts. Mils —6F 114
Broadoak Enterprise Village. Rod —4G 114
Broad Oak Rd. Cant —9N 167 (4D 21)
Broadoak Rd. Eri —7E 52
Broadoak Rd. Tun —3E 114 (3C 18)
Broadoaks Way. Brom —8J 69
Broad Rd. Swans —4L 61
Broad Sanctuary. SW1 —3C 4
Broadsole La. W Hou —1B 42
Broadstairs. —9M 209 (2E 23)
Broadstairs North Foreland Lighthouse. —5M 209 (1E 23)
Broadstairs Rd. Broad —8H 209 (1E 23)
Broadstone. —4B 28
Broad Street. —8E 66 (1E 17)
(nr. Chattenden)
Broad Street. —3E 128 (1A 28)
(nr. Hollingbourne)
Broad Street. —9D 204 (1E 41)
(nr. Lyminge)
Broad St. Cant —1N 171 (4D 21)
(in two parts)
Broad St. Dag —1C 6
Broad St. Deal —4N 177 (2E 33)
Broad St. I'ham —4E 45
Broad St. Lym —9D 204 (1E 41)
Broad St. Mgte —2C 208
Broad St. Ram —5J 211 (2E 23)
Broad St. S'ness —2C 218
Broad St. Sut V —9A 140 (3A 28)
Broad St. Hill. Huc —3E 128 (1A 28)
Broad Tenterden. —3C 38
Broadview. Folk —5C 188
Broadview Av. Gill —3A 96
Broadview Gardens. —8C 134 (3A 26)
Broadviews. Hythe —7L 197
(off South Rd.)
Broad Wlk. SE3 —9A 50 (3A 6)
Broad Wlk. Orp —4M 85
Broad Wlk. Sev —1M 131
Broadwater Ct. Tun W —5E 156
Broadwater Down. —4F 156 (2E 35)
Broadwater Down. Tun W —2E 35
Broadwater Gdns. Orp —5D 84
Broadwater La. Tun W —4F 156
Broadwater Rise. Tun W —4F 156
Broadwater Rd. SE28 —3F 50
Broadwater Rd. W Mal —4B 124 (1C 26)
Broadway. E15 —1E 5
Broadway. Bexh —2N 57 (4C 6)
Broadway. Gill —9K 81
Broadway. Lgh S —1B 10
Broadway. Maid —6C 126 (2D 27)
Broadway. P'hm —3D 31
Broadway. Rain —2C 7
Broadway. S'ness —2D 218 (4D 11)
Broadway. Swan —9E 72 (2C 15)
Broadway Ct. Beck —6F 68
Broadway Ho. Brom —1G 69
(off Bromley Rd.)
Broadway Mkt. E8 —2D 5
Broadway Shop. Cen. Bexh —2B 58
Broadway Shop. Cen. Maid —5C 126
Broadway, The. SW19 —1B 12
Broadway, The. Broad —9K 209 (2E 23)
Broadway, The. Cheam —3B 12
Broadway, The. Crowb —4C 35
Broadway, The. H Bay —2D 194 (1E 21)
Broadway, The. Horn —1D 7
Broadway, The. Lam —2D 200 (2B 36)
Broadway, The. Min S —4J 219 (4D 11)
Broadway, The. P'hm —8H 173
Broadway, The. Ram —6H 211
Broadway, The. Sth S —1C 11
Broadway W. Lgh S —1A 10
Broadwood. Grav —1G 77
Broadwood Rd. Chatt —9D 66
Brockdene Dri. Kes —5N 83
Brockenhurst Av. Maid —8E 126
Brockenhurst Clo. Cant —9L 167
Brockenhurst Clo. Gill —4M 95
Brockenhurst Rd. Ram —4K 211
Brockham Cres. New Ad —8G 82
Brockhill Country Park. —4G 197
Brockhill Rd. Hythe —5J 197 (3D 41)
Brockill Cres. SE4 —2B 54
Brocklebank Ho. E16 —1C 50
(off Glenister St.)
Brockley. —2C 54 (4D 5)
Brockley Cross. SE4 —1B 54
Brockley Cross Bus. Cen. SE4 —1B 54
Brockley Footpath. SE4 —3B 54
(in two parts)
Brockley Gro. SE4 —3C 54 (4E 5)
Brockley Hall Rd. SE4 —3B 54
Brockley M. SE4 —3B 54
Brockley M. SE22 —3B 54
Brockley Pk. SE23 —5B 54
Brockley Rise. SE23 —6B 54 (4E 5)
Brockley Rd. SE4 —1C 54 (4E 5)
Brockley Rd. Mgte —3D 208
Brockley View. SE23 —5B 54
Brockley Way. SE4 —3A 54
Brockman Cres. Dym —8E 182
Brockman Rise. Brom —9G 54
Brockman Rd. Folk —6J 189
Brockmans Clo. Min —6M 205
Brockway. Bor G —2N 121
Brockwell Clo. Orp —8H 71
Brodrick Gro. SE2 —4K 51
Brogdale Horticultural Trust. —8F 186 (4A 20)
Brogdale Rd. Osp —9E 186 (4A 20)
Brogden Cres. Leeds —2B 140
Brogden Farm Cotts. Leeds —1B 140
Brograve Gdns. Beck —5E 68
Broke Farm Dri. Orp —9L 85
Brokes Way. Tun W —6H 151
Brome Rd. SE9 —1B 56
Bromhedge. SE9 —8B 56
Bromholm Rd. SE2 —3K 51
Bromley. —5K 69 (1E 13)
Bromley Av. Brom —3H 69
Bromley Clo. Chat —7E 94
(in two parts)
Bromley Clo. N'tn —6J 97
(in two parts)
Bromley Common. —2A 84 (2A 14)
Bromley Comn. Brom —7M 69 (1A 14)
Bromley Cres. Brom —6J 69
Bromley Gdns. Brom —6J 69
Bromley Green. —2E 39
Bromley Grn. Rd. Ruck —2E 39
Bromley Gro. Brom —5G 69
Bromley Hill. Brom —2H 69 (1E 13)
Bromley Ind. Cen. Brom —6N 69
Bromley La. Chst —3E 70 (1B 14)
Bromley Museum. —1K 85 (2B 14)
Bromley Park. —4H 69
Bromley Pk. Brom —4J 69
Bromley Rd. SE6 & Brom —6E 54 (4E 5)
Bromley Rd. Beck & Short —4E 68 (1E 13)
Bromley Rd. Chst —4D 70 (1A 14)
Brompton. —6D 80 (1E 17)
Brompton Clo. Chat —6C 80
Brompton Dri. Eri —7J 53
Brompton Farm Rd. Roch —3K 79 (1D 17)
Brompton Hill. Chat —6C 80
Brompton La. Roch —4L 79
Brompton Rd. SW3 —3B 4
Brompton Rd. Gill —6E 80 (1E 17)
Brompton Ter. SE18 —8B 50
Brompton Vs. Gus —7K 179
Bromstone. —1J 211 (2E 23)
Bromstone M. Broad —1J 211
Bromstone Rd. Broad —1J 211 (2E 23)
Brondesbury. —1B 4
Brondesbury Park. —1A 4
Brondesbury Pk. NW2 & NW6 —1A 4
Brondesbury Rd. NW6 —2B 4
Bronington Clo. Chat —6D 94
Bronte Clo. Eri —7C 52
Bronte Clo. Lark —7D 108
Bronte Gro. Dart —2N 59
Bronte View. Grav —6H 63
Bronze Age Way. Belv —2C 52
Bronze Age Way. Eri —3C 7
Brook. —4B 30
Brookbank. Maid —1D 126
Brookbank Rd. SE13 —1D 54
Brook Clo. H Bay —4D 194
Brook Clo. Hythe —8B 188
Brook Ct. Eden —4C 184
Brookdale Rd. SE6 —5E 54
Brookdale Rd. Bex —4N 57
Brookdene Rd. SE18 —4H 51
Brooke Av. Mgte —4N 207
Brooke Dri. Grav —6N 63
Brookehowse Rd. SE6 —7D 54
Brookend Rd. Sidc —6G 56
Brooke Rd. Afrd —7F 158
Brooker's Pl. High —7G 65
Brookes Pl. N'tn —5K 97
Brookfield. Four E —3B 24
Brookfield. Kems —8M 103
Brookfield. Sand —2K 215
Brookfield Av. Dover —2G 180 (1C 43)
Brookfield Av. Lark —6E 108
Brookfield Ct. Afrd —1D 160
Brookfield Ind. Est. Afrd —9D 158
Brookfield Pl. Dover —2G 180
Brookfield Rd. Afrd —9C 158 (1E 39)
Brookfield Rd. Dover —1F 180
Brookfields. Hdlw —7D 134
Brook Green. —3A 4
Brook Hill Clo. SE18 —5D 50
Brookhill Rd. SE18 —5D 50
Brookhurst Gdns. Tun W —3E 150
Brookland. —2C 46
Brooklands. Dart —6M 59
Brooklands. H'crn —2K 193
Brooklands. Tun W —7K 151
Brooklands Av. Sidc —7F 56
Brooklands Clo. F'wch —7E 168
Brooklands Farm Clo. Ford —8H 149
Brooklands Pk. SE3 —1K 55
Brooklands Rd. Lark —6E 108
Brooklands Way. E Grin —2A 34
Brook La. Bex —4M 57
Brook La. Brom —2K 69
Brook La. H Bay —1A 22
Brook La. Lwr Sto —8K 201
Brook La. Plax —9N 121 (2A 26)
Brook La. S'ndge —7L 215
Brook La. Snod —4D 108
Brook La. Tonb —5K 145
Brook La. Cotts. S'ndge —7L 215
Brooklyn Paddock. Gill —6G 80
Brooklyn Rd. Brom —8N 69
Brooklyn Vs. Mard —3K 205
Brookmead. Hild —3E 144
Brookmead Av. Brom —8B 70
Brookmead Clo. Orp —9K 71
Brookmead Rd. Cli —6M 65
Brookmead Way. Orp —9K 71
Brookmill Rd. SE8 —3E 5
Brook Pl. Ide H —9N 117 (2C 24)
Brook Pumping Station Museum. —8C 80
Brook Rd. Fav —4G 187
Brook Rd. Lark —6C 108
Brook Rd. N'fleet —6D 62
Brook Rd. Swan —6E 72
Brook Rd. Tun W —7J 151
Brook Rd. Whits —2L 225
Brooksby's Wlk. E9 —1D 5
Brooks Clo. SE9 —7C 56
Brooks Clo. S'hrst —7J 221
Brooks Clo. Tonb —9K 133
Brooks End. —7D 206 (2C 22)
Brookside. C'brk —8D 176
Brookside. Hoo —8H 67
Brookside. Orp —1H 85
Brookside. Temp E —8B 178
Brookside Cotts. Tun W —9M 151
Brookside Leisure Pk. E'chu —2E 202
Brookside Rd. Grav —3E 76
Brookside Way. Croy —9A 68
Brooks Pl. Maid —5D 126
Brook Street. —8F 144 (4E 25)
Brook St. Belv & Eri —5C 52 (3C 6)
Brook St. E'try —3L 183 (2C 33)
Brook St. Snod —2F 108 (3C 17)
Brook St. Tonb —4E 25
Brook St. Wdchu —9A 226 (3C 39)
Brooks Way. Lydd —4C 204
Brooks Way. St P —5L 71
Brook, The. Chat —7C 80 (1D 17)
Brook Vale. Eri —8C 52
Brookway. SE3 —1K 55
Brookwood Clo. Brom —7J 69
Broom Av. Orp —5K 71
Broom Clo. Brom —9A 70
Broomcroft Rd. Gill —1B 96
Broomfield. —5L 195 (2A 22)
(nr. Herne Bay)

Broomfield—Calgary Cres.

Broomfield. —3F 140 (2A 28)
(nr. Kingswood)
Broomfield Cres. Clift —3K 209
Broomfield Ga. Whits —8M 225
Broomfield La. H Bay —5L 195
Broomfield Rd. Beck —6C 68
Broomfield Rd. Bexh —3B 58
Broomfield Rd. Fav —3G 187
Broomfield Rd. Folk —5E 188
Broomfield Rd. H Bay —6J 195 (2E 21)
Broomfield Rd. Kgswd —5E 140 (3A 28)
Broomfield Rd. Sev —4G 119
Broomfield Rd. Swans —3L 61
Broomfields. Hart —8L 75
Broom Gdns. Croy —4D 82
Broom Hill. —1H 85
Broom Hill. Flim —4C 37
Broomhill Bank. —8D 150
Broomhill Pk. Rd. Tun W —6E 150
Broom Hill Rise. Bexh —3B 58
Broomhill Rd. Dart —4J 59
Broomhill Rd. Orp —1J 85
Broom Hill Rd. Roch —4K 79
Broomhill Rd. Tun W —8C 150 (1E 35)
Broomhills. S'fleet —9L 61
Broomlands La. Oxt —9A 116
Broom La. L'tn G —2M 155 (2D 35)
Broom Mead. Bexh —3B 58
Broom Pk. L'tn G —2M 155
Broom Rd. Croy —4D 82
Broom Rd. Sit —6K 99
Broomshaw Rd. Maid —6K 125
Broomsleigh Bus. Pk. SE26 —1C 68
(off Worsley Bri. Rd.)
Broom Street. —3B 20
Broomwood Clo. Bex —6E 58
Broomwood Clo. Croy —8A 68
Broomwood Rd. SW11 —4B 4
Broomwood Rd. Orp —5K 71
Broseley Gro. SE26 —1B 68
Brotherhood Clo. Cant —7K 167
Brougham Ct. Dart —4B 60
(off Hardwick Cres.)
Broughton Ct. Afrd —9C 158
Broughton Monchelsea Place. —8F 138
Broughton Rd. Orp —3F 84
Broughton Rd. Otf —7H 103
Brow Clo. Orp —1M 85
Brow Cres. Orp —2L 85
Brown Cotts. F'wch —7F 168
Browndens Rd. Up H'lng —7C 92
Brownelow Copse. W'slde —1D 110
Brownhill Clo. Chat —7D 94
Brownhill Rd. SE6 —5E 54 (4E 5)
Browning Clo. Lark —6D 108
Browning Clo. Well —8G 51
Browning Pl. Folk —4L 189
Browning Rd. E12 —1A 6
Browning Rd. Dart —2N 59
Brownings. Eden —3C 184
Brownings Orchard. Rod —3H 115
Brown Rd. Grav —6K 63
Browns La. Eden —4A 24
Brownspring Dri. SE9 —9D 56
Brown St. Rain —2A 96
Brownswood Rd. N4 —1C 5
Broxbourne Rd. Orp —2H 85
Broxhall Rd. Up Hard —3D 31
Broxted Rd. SE6 —7C 54
Bruce Clo. Deal —6L 177
Bruce Clo. Well —8K 51
Bruce Ct. Sidc —9H 57
Bruce Dri. S Croy —9A 82
Bruce Gro. Orp —2J 85
Brucks, The. W'bury —1C 136
Bruges Ct. Kem —2G 98
Brummel Clo. Bexh —1D 58
Brunel Clo. Til —1G 62
Brunel Rd. SE16 —3D 5
Brunger's Wlk. Tonb —2H 145
Brunner Ho. SE6 —9F 54
Brunswick Clo. Bexh —2M 57
Brunswick Ct. Ram —5J 211
(off Hardres St.)
Brunswick Field. Con —2E 19
Brunswick Gdns. Dover —1G 180
Brunswick Rd. Afrd —8D 158
Brunswick Rd. Bexh —2M 57
Brunswick Rd. Birch —6F 206
Brunswick Sq. H Bay —2F 194
Brunswick St. Maid —6D 126
Brunswick St. Ram —5J 211
Brunswick St. E. Maid —6D 126
Brunswick Wlk. Grav —5J 63
Bruswick Ter. Tun W —3G 157
Bruton Clo. Chst —3B 70
Bruton St. W1 —2C 4
Bryant Clo. Nett —2A 136
Bryant Rd. Roch —4L 79
Bryant St. Chat —9D 80
Bryden Clo. SE26 —1B 68
Brymore Clo. Cant —9A 168
Brymore Rd. Cant —9A 168
Bubblestone Rd. Otf —7J 103
Bubhurst La. Frit —1A 38
Buckden Clo. SE12 —4J 55
Buckham Thorns Rd. W'ham —8E 116
Buckhold Rd. SW18 —4B 4
Buckhole Farm Rd. H Hals —1F 66
Buckhurst. —1A 38
Buckhurst Av. Sev —7K 119
Buckhurst Dri. Clift —3K 209
Buckhurst La. Sev —7K 119
Buckhurst La. Wadh —4A 36
Buckhurst Rd. W'ham —3C 116 (1A 24)
Buckingham Av. Well —2G 57
Buckingham Clo. Orp —1G 84
Buckingham Dri. Chst —1E 70
Buckingham Gdns. H'shm —3M 141
Buckingham Hill Rd. Stan H —2E 9
Buckingham La. SE23 —5B 54
Buckingham Palace. —3C 4
Buckingham Pal. Rd. SW1 —3C 4
Buckingham Rd. Broad —9M 209
Buckingham Rd. Gill —7G 81
Buckingham Rd. Mgte —4C 208
Buckingham Rd. N'fleet —5C 62
Buckingham Rd. Tun W —3H 157
Buckingham Rd. Whits —3K 225
Buckingham Row. Maid —1H 139
Buckland. —2G 180 (1C 43)
Buckland Av. Dover —2G 180 (1C 43)
Buckland Clo. Chat —9D 94
Buckland Cres. NW3 —1B 4
Buckland Hill. Maid —4B 126 (1D 27)
Buckland La. Maid —3A 126
(in two parts)
Buckland La. S'le —2B 32
Buckland Pl. Maid —5B 126
Buckland Rd. Cli —3B 176
Buckland Rd. High —4D 9
Buckland Rd. Ludd —5M 91 (2B 16)
Buckland Rd. Maid —4B 126
Buckland Rd. Orp —5G 85
Buckland Ter. Dover —3H 181
Buckland Valley. —1G 181 (1C 43)
Buckler Gdns. SE9 —8B 56
Bucklers Clo. Tun W —2J 157
Bucklers Clo. Ward —4K 203
Buckles Ct. Belv —4M 51
Buckley Clo. Dart —9G 53
Buckmans Grn. La. Smar —1C 38
Bucks Cross Rd. N'fleet —8E 62
Bucks Cross Rd. Orp —6N 85 (2C 14)
Bucksford La. Afrd —1B 160 (1E 39)
Buck St. C'lck —7E 174 (3A 30)
Buckthorn Clo. Deal —3M 177
Buckthorne Rd. SE4 —3B 54
Buckthorn Ho. Sidc —8H 57
(off Longlands Rd.)
Buckwheat Ct. Eri —3M 51
Budds. —2E 25
Budd's Green. —3F 132
Budd's La. Wit —2A 46
Budgin's Hill. Prat B —3L 101 (3B 14)
Budleigh Cres. Well —8L 51
Buenos Aryes. Mgte —3B 208
Buffalo La. Smar —4K 221 (1C 38)
Buffs Av. Folk —5B 188
Buffs Regimental Museum. —2M 171
Bugglesden Rd. St Mic —2B 38
Bug Hill. Wold & Warl —4D 13
Buglehorn Cotts. Maid —2L 139
Bugsby's Way. SE10 & SE7 —3E 5
Bullace La. Dart —4M 59
Bull All. Well —1K 57
Bullbanks Rd. Belv —4D 52
Bulldog Rd. Chat —9E 94
Bulleid Pl. Afrd —2H 161
Bullen. —1K 147
Bullen La. E Peck —8K 135 (3B 26)
Buller Gro. Sea —7D 224
Buller Rd. Chat —1C 94
Buller's Av. H Bay —3F 194
Bullers Clo. Sidc —1N 71
Bullers Wood Dri. Chst —3B 70
Bullfields. Snod —2E 108
Bullfinch Clo. Pad W —1M 153
Bullfinch Clo. Sev —4E 118
Bullfinch Dene. Sev —4E 118
Bullfinch La. Sev —4E 118 (1C 25)
Bull Hill. Hort K —7C 74
Bull Hill. Len H —3C 29
Bullingstone La. Speld —6M 149 (1D 35)
Bullion Clo. Pad W —9L 147
Bullivant Clo. Grnh —3G 60
Bull La. Beth —3H 163 (2C 39)
Bull La. Bou B —2J 165 (4B 20)
Bull La. Chst —3F 70
Bull La. Eccl —7K 109 (4D 17)
Bull La. High —6H 65 (4C 9)
Bull La. Roch —6N 79
Bull La. Rol —1J 213
Bull La. S'bry —1G 112 (3B 18)
Bull La. Wro —7N 105 (4A 16)
Bullockstone. —7E 194
Bullockstone Hill. H Bay —7F 194
Bullockstone Rd. H Bay —8F 194
(Canterbury Rd.)
Bullockstone Rd. H Bay —6E 194 (2E 21)
(Greenhill Rd.)
Bull Orchard. Maid —7K 125
Bull Rd. Birl —5A 108 (3C 16)
Bulls Cotts. Hythe —7J 197
(off St Leonard's Rd.)
Bulls Farm Rd. Tonb —3B 26
Bulls Head Yd. Dart —4M 59
(off High St. Dartford,)
Bulls Pas. Hythe —6K 197
(off Dental St.)
Bulls Pl. Pem —8C 152
Bulltown La. W Bra —1B 40
Bullwark Rd. Deal —3N 177
Bullwark St. Dover —7J 181
Bull Yd. Grav —4G 63
Bulphan. —1A 8
Bulphan By-Pass. Upm —1B 8
Bulrush Clo. Chat —8C 94
Bulrushes, The. Afrd —1A 160
Bulwark, The. S'wch —5N 217
Bumbles Clo. Roch —3A 94
Bunce Ct. Rd. War S & Stal —2D 29
Bungalows, The. Hoo —8G 67
Bungalows, The. Leigh —6M 143
Bungalows, The. Tent —8E 222
Bungalows, The. Wdboro —9G 216
Bunhill Row. EC1 —2D 5
Bunkers Hill. Belv —4B 52
Bunker's Hill. Dover —2F 180
Bunker's Hill. Hods —7A 90
Bunkers Hill. Sev —2A 16
Bunkers Hill. Sidc —8A 58 (4C 6)
Bunkers Hill. W'mre —4E 31
Bunkers Hill Av. Dover —3F 180
Bunkers Hill Rd. Dover —3F 180
Bunkley Meadow. Hams —8D 190
Bunny La. Tun W —7D 156 (2E 35)
Bunters Hill Rd. Cli —8L 65 (4D 9)
Bunton St. SE18 —3C 50
Burberry La. Leeds —4B 140 (2A 28)
Burcharbro Rd. SE2 —6M 51
Burch Av. S'wch —6L 217
Burch Rd. N'fleet —4E 62
Burdett Av. Shorne —9C 64
Burdett Clo. Sidc —1N 71
Burdett Rd. E3 & E14 —2E 5
Burdett Rd. Tun W —1B 156
Burdock Clo. Croy —2A 82
Burdon La. Sutt —3B 12
Burford Rd. SE6 —7C 54
Burford Rd. Brom —7A 70
Burford's All. Ah —4D 216
Burford Way. New Ad —7F 82
Burgate. Cant —2N 171 (1D 31)
Burgate Clo. Dart —1G 58
Burgate La. Cant —2N 171 (1D 31)
Burgate Ter. Mer —8M 161
Burgess Clo. Min —6N 205
Burgess Clo. Whitf —6G 178
Burgess Cotts. Leeds —3B 140
Burgess Grn. Hackl —2D 33
Burgess Hall Dri. Leeds —2B 140
Burgess Rd. Aysm —2D 162
Burgess Rd. Roch —5M 79
Burgess Row. Tent —8B 222
Burghclere Dri. Maid —7M 125
Burghfield Rd. Grav —3E 76
Burgh Heath. —4A 12
Burgh Heath Rd. Eps —3A 12
Burgh Hill. —2A 44
Burgh Hill. E'ham —2A 44
Burghill Rd. SE26 —9B 54
Burghley Rd. SW19 —1B 12
Burgoyne Ct. Maid —2C 126
Burgoyne Gro. Whitf —8F 178
Burgoyne Heights. Gus —2K 181
Burham. —1K 109 (3D 17)
Burham Common. —9L 93 (3D 17)
Burham Court. —3C 17
Burham Rd. Roch —4J 93
Burham St. Burh —1H 109
Burial Ground La. Maid —7B 126
Burial Ground La. Tovil —2D 27
Burkestone Clo. Kem —3H 99
Burleigh Av. Sidc —3H 57
Burleigh Clo. Roch —4J 79
Burleigh Dri. Maid —9C 110
Burleigh Rd. Char —3K 175
Burleigh Wlk. SE6 —6F 54
Burley Rd. Sit —7F 98
Burlings. —8H 101
Burlings La. Knock —8H 101 (4B 14)
Burlington Clo. Orp —3D 84
Burlington Dri. H Bay —2L 195
Burlington Gdns. Gill —7A 96
Burlington Gdns. Mgte —5A 208
Burlington La. W4 —3A 4
Burlington Rd. N Mald —1A 12
Burlington Rd. W. N Mald —1A 12
Burma Cres. Cant —1C 172
Burman Clo. Dart —5C 60
Burmarsh. —3B 182 (3C 40)
Burmarsh Rd. Dym —3B 182
Burmarsh Rd. Hythe —9B 196 (3D 41)
Burma Way. Chat —5C 94
Burnaby Rd. N'fleet —5D 62
Burnan Rd. Whits —3L 225
Burnell Av. Well —9J 51
Burnett Rd. Eri —6L 53
Burnham Clo. Mil R —3F 98
Burnham Cres. Dart —2K 59
Burnham Rd. Dart —2K 59 (4D 7)
Burnham Rd. Sidc —7N 57
Burnham Rd. Woul —2D 17
Burnham Ter. Dart —3L 59
Burnham Trad. Est. Dart —2L 59
Burnham Wlk. Gill —8A 96
(in two parts)
Burnham Way. SE26 —1C 68
Burnhill Rd. Beck —5D 68
Burnings La. Knock —8H 101
Burn Meadow Cotts. Boxl —7F 110
Burns Av. Sidc —4K 57
Burns Clo. Eri —8G 52
Burns Clo. Well —8H 51
Burns Cres. Tonb —8F 144
Burns Rd. Gill —5F 80
Burns Rd. Maid —7N 125
Burnt Ash Hill. SE12 —4J 55 (4E 5)
(in two parts)
Burnt Ash La. Brom —3K 69 (1A 14)
Burnt Ash Rd. SE12 —3J 55 (4E 5)
Burntash Rd. Quar W —1J 125
Burnt Ho. Clo. Sand —3L 215
Burnt Ho. Clo. Wain —2N 79
Burnt Ho. Hill Stod —6N 169 (3A 22)
Burnt Ho. La. Dart —9M 59
(in two parts)
Burnt Ho. La. L'tn G —9N 149 (1D 35)
Burnthouse La. Smar —4H 221 (1B 38)
Burnt Lodge La. Wallc —4B 36
Burnt Mill Rd. Eger —3C 29
Burnt Oak La. Sidc —4J 57
Burnt Oak Ter. Gill —6F 80
Burnt Oast Rd. Bou B —3K 165
Burntwick Dri. Lwr Hal —8L 223
Burntwood Gro. Sev —9J 119
Burntwood La. SW17 —4B 4
Burntwood Rd. Sev —1J 131
Burnup Bank. Sit —6K 99
Burrage Gro. SE18 —4E 50
Burrage Pl. SE18 —5D 50
Burrage Rd. SE18 —5E 50 (3A 6)
Burr Bank Ter. Dart —9K 59
Burr Clo. Bexh —1A 58
Burrell Clo. Croy —9B 68
Burrell Row. Beck —5D 68
Burrfield Dri. Orp —8M 71
Burritt M. Roch —9N 79
Burrow Rd. Folk —5L 189
Burrows La. Mid S —9K 201
Burrs Hill. —1C 36
Burrs, The. Sit —8H 99
Burrstock Way. Rain —2D 96
Burrswood. —2C 35
Bursdon Clo. Sidc —7H 57
Bursill Cres. Ram —3F 210
Burslem Rd. Tun W —8K 151
Bursted Hill. Up Hard —3D 31
Burston Rd. Cox —6M 137
Burton Clo. Folk —4G 189
Burton Clo. Wain —1N 79
Burton Ct. Pad W —9M 147
Burton Fields. H Bay —3J 195
Burton Rd. Kenn —4J 159
Burtons La. Mard —4C 27
Burwash Ct. St M —8L 71
Burwash Rd. SE18 —5F 50
Burwood Av. Brom —3L 83
Busbridge Rd. Loose —2B 138 (2D 27)
Busbridge Rd. Snod —3C 108
Bush Av. Ram —3F 210
Bush Clo. Bre —5A 114
Bushell Way. Chst —1C 70
Bushey Av. Orp —1F 84
Bushey Clo. Bou B —3H 165
Busheyfields Rd. H Bay —9F 194 (2E 21)
Bushey Mead. —1A 12
Bushey Rd. SW20 —1A 12
Bushey Rd. Croy —3D 82
Bushey Way. Beck —9G 68
Bushfield Wlk. Swans —4L 61
Bushmeadow Rd. Gill —1B 96
Bushmoor Cres. SE18 —7D 50
Bush Rd. SE8 —3D 5
Bush Rd. Cux —9E 78 (2C 16)
Bush Rd. E Peck —8K 135 (3B 26)
Bush Row. Ayle —7L 109
Bushy Close. —3J 165
Bushy Gill. L'tn G —2A 156
Bushy Gro. Kgswd —6F 140
Bushy Hill Rd. W'bre —4H 169 (3E 21)
Bushy Lees. Sidc —4H 57
Bushy Royds. W'boro —3H 161
Bushy Ruff Cotts. Temp E —9C 178
Buss's Green. —3B 36
Busty La. Igh —3K 121
Butcherfield La. Hartf —2B 34
Butcher Row. E1 —2D 5
Butchers Hill. Shorne —1C 78
Butcher's La. Mere —7J 123 (2B 26)
Butcher's La. New Ash —3K 89 (2E 15)
Butchers La. Non —3B 32
Butcher's La. T Oaks —4D 45
Butcher Wlk. Swans —5L 61
Butchery La. Cant —2M 171 (1D 31)
Butchery, The. S'wch —5M 217
Butler's Hill. Dar —3B 20
Butler's Pl. As —4L 89
Butterfly Centre, The. —1D 192 (1A 42)
Butterfly La. SE9 —4D 56
Butterly Av. Dart —7N 59
Buttermere. Fav —6J 187
Buttermere Clo. Folk —5H 189
Buttermere Clo. Gill —7J 81
Buttermere Gdns. Aysm —1D 162
Buttermere Rd. Orp —7M 71
Butterside Rd. Kgnt —5G 161
Butter St. Non —3F 162 (3B 32)
Butt Field Rd. Afrd —1C 160
Butt Grn. La. Lin —9D 138 (3D 27)
Butt Law Clo. Hoo —8H 67
Buttmarsh Clo. SE18 —5D 50
Button Cotts. Lwr Sto —7K 201
Button Dri. Lwr Sto —7K 201
Button Ho. Chatt —7B 66
Button La. Bear —7L 127
Button St. Swan —5K 73 (1D 15)
Butts Hill. Bou B —1J 165 (3B 20)
Butts Ho. Cant —1N 171 (4D 21)
(off Artillery Rd.)
Butts La. Stan H —2C 8
Buttsole. —2C 33
Butts Rd. Brom —1H 69
Butts, The. Elham —6N 183
Butts, The. Otf —8J 103
Butts, The. S'wch —5L 217
Butts, The. Sit —7G 99
Buttway La. Cli —2B 176 (3D 9)
Buxton Clo. Chat —1G 110
Buxton Clo. Maid —9D 126
Buxton La. Cat —4D 13
Buxton Rd. Eri —7E 52
Buxton Rd. Ram —2F 210
Bybrook. —5H 159 (4A 30)
Bybrook Ct. Kenn —6G 159
Bybrook Field. S'gte —8E 188
Bybrook Rd. Kenn —6H 159 (4A 30)
Bybrook Way. S'gte —7E 188
Bychurch Pl. Maid —6D 126
Bycliffe M. Grav —5E 62
Bycliffe Ter. Grav —5E 62
Bycroft St. SE20 —3A 68
Bygrove. New Ad —7D 82
Bylands Clo. SE2 —3K 51
Byllan Rd. Dover —1D 180
Byng Rd. Tun W —9E 150
Bynon Av. Bexh —1A 58
Byrneside. Hild —3E 144
Byron Av. Mgte —4D 208
Byron Clo. SE26 —1B 68
Byron Clo. SE28 —1L 51
Byron Clo. Cant —3B 172
Byron Cres. Dover —9G 178
Byron Dri. Eri —7C 52
Byron Ho. Dart —3F 58
Byron Rd. Dart —2B 60
Byron Rd. Gill —9F 80
Byron Rd. Maid —2E 126
Bysing Wood Rd. Fav —4C 186 (3E 19)
(in three parts)
Bythorne Ct. Rain —2D 96
Bywood Av. Croy —9A 68

Cabbage Stalk La. Tun W —3E 156
Cables Clo. Belv —3D 52
Cable St. E1 —2D 5
Cacket's La. Cud —6F 100 (4B 14)
Cacketts Cotts. Bras —8L 117
Cackle Street. —4D 45
(nr. Broad Oak)
Cackle Street. —4A 44
(nr. Netherfield)
Cackle St. Brede —4D 45
Cade La. Sev —1K 131
Cade Rd. Afrd —2F 160
Cades Orchard. P For —9C 186
Cades Rd. Hoth —4E 29
Cadlocks Hill. Hals —1A 102 (3C 14)
Cadnam Clo. Cant —8L 167
Cadnam Clo. Roch —4J 79
Cadogan Av. Dart —5D 60
Cadogan Clo. Beck —4G 69
Cadogan Gdns. Tun W —1H 157
Cadogan Ter. E9 —1E 5
Cadwallon Rd. SE9 —7D 56
Caerleon Clo. Sidc —1L 71
Caerleon Ter. SE2 —4K 51
Caernarvon Dri. Maid —8C 126
Caernarvon Gdns. Broad —8M 209
Caesars Way. Folk —4E 188
Cage Green. —2J 145 (3E 25)
Cage Grn. Rd. Tonb —2J 145
Cage La. Smar —4J 221 (1B 38)
Cairndale Clo. Brom —3J 69
Cairns Clo. Dart —3L 59
Caister Rd. Tonb —6G 145
Caithness Gdns. Sidc —4H 57
Calais Cotts. Fawk —3G 88
Calais Hill. T Hill —5K 167 (3D 21)
Calcott. —1D 168 (3E 21)
Calcott Hill. Sturry —1D 168 (3E 21)
Calcott Wlk. SE9 —9A 56
Calcraft M. Cant —9A 168
Calcutta Ho. Maid —3H 139
Calcutta Rd. Til —3A 8
Caldbec Hill. Batt —4B 44
Caldecote Clo. Rain —2D 96
Caldecot La. Lydd —1C 204 (3D 47)
Calder Rd. Maid —2B 126
Calderwood. Grav —2K 77
Calderwood St. SE18 —4C 50
Caldew Av. Gill —2M 95
Caldew Gro. Sit —8J 99
Caldy Rd. Belv —3C 52
Caledonian Ct. Gill —3A 96
Caledonian Rd. N1 & N7 —2C 5
Caledon Ter. Cant —3N 171
Calehill Clo. Maid —3F 126
Calehill Rd. L Char —4D 29
Caley Rd. Tun W —6K 151
Calfstock La. F'ham —7N 73
Calgary Cres. Folk —3L 189

Calgary Ter.—Catford Gyratory. (Junct.)

Calgary Ter. Dover —1G 181
Caling Croft. New Ash —2M 89
Caliph Clo. Grav —8L 63
Callaghan Clo. SE13 —2H 55
Callams Clo. Gill —5N 95
Calland. Sme —8J 165
Callander Rd. SE6 —7E 54
Callaways La. N'tn —5K 97
Callenders Cotts. Belv —2E 52
Calleywell La. Adgtn —2B 40
Callis Ct. Rd. Broad —7K 209 (1E 23)
Callis Way. Gill —6N 95
Calmont Rd. Brom —2G 69 (1E 13)
Calonne Rd. SW19 —1A 12
Calshot Ct. Dart —4B 60
(off Osbourne Rd.)
Calthorpe St. WC1 —2C 5
Calton Av. SE21 —4D 5
Calverden Rd. Ram —3E 210
Calverley Clo. Beck —2E 68
Calverley Ct. Tun W —1H 157
Calverley Pk. Tun W —2H 157
Calverley Pk. Cres. Tun W —2H 157
Calverley Pk. Gdns. Tun W —1H 157 (2E 35)
Calverley Rd. Tun W —1H 157 (2E 35)
Calverley Row. Tun W —1H 157
Calverley St. Tun W —1H 157
Calvert Clo. Belv —4B 52
Calvert Clo. Sidc —2N 71
Calvin Clo. Orp —6M 71
Camber. —4B 46
Camber Castle. —4A 46
Camber Rd. E Gul —3A 46
Cambert Way. SE3 —2L 55
Camberwell. —3D 5
Camberwell Chu. St. SE5 —3D 5
Camberwell Grn. SE5 —3D 5
Camberwell Green. (Junct.) —3D 5
Camberwell La. Ide H —3A 130
Camberwell New Rd. SE5 —3C 5
Camberwell Rd. SE5 —3D 5
Camborne Mnr. Gill —6F 80
Camborne Rd. Sidc —8L 57
Camborne Rd. Well —9H 51
Cambourne Av. Wgte S —3J 207
Cambrai Ct. Cant —1C 172
Cambray Rd. Orp —1H 85
Cambria Av. Roch —1K 93
Cambria Clo. Sidc —6F 56
Cambria Cres. Grav —9K 63
Cambria Ho. Eri —7F 52
(off Larner Rd.)
Cambrian Cotts. Ram —6H 211
Cambrian Gro. Grav —5F 62
Cambrian Rd. Tun W —7J 151
Cambridge Av. S'wch B —1E 33
Cambridge Av. Well —2H 57
Cambridge Barracks Rd. SE18 —4B 50
Cambridge Clo. Birch —4G 206
Cambridge Cres. Maid —1G 138
Cambridge Dri. SE12 —3K 55
Cambridge Gdns. W10 —2A 4
Cambridge Gdns. Folk —6K 189
Cambridge Gdns. Tun W —3H 157
Cambridge Grn. SE9 —6D 56
Cambridge Heath Rd. E1 & E2 —2D 5
Cambridge Ho. Maid —1G 139
Cambridge La. Lyn —3D 19
Cambridge Rd. SE20 —1D 13
Cambridge Rd. SW11 —3B 4
Cambridge Rd. Brom —3K 69
Cambridge Rd. Cant —3M 171
Cambridge Rd. Dover —6J 181
Cambridge Rd. Fav —6F 186
Cambridge Rd. Gill —5M 95
Cambridge Rd. King T —1A 12
Cambridge Rd. Roch —4L 79
Cambridge Rd. Sidc —9G 57
Cambridge Rd. Sit —9J 99
Cambridge Rd. Tey —4J 223
Cambridge Rd. Walm —7N 177
Cambridge Rd. Wclf S —1B 10
Cambridge Row. SE18 —5D 50
Cambridge St. Tun W —2J 157
Cambridge Ter. Chat —8C 80
Cambridge Ter. Dover —5K 181
Cambridge Ter. Folk —6L 189
Cambridge Ter. Mgte —4F 208
Cambridge Way. Cant —4M 171
Camdale Rd. SE18 —7H 51
Camden Av. Pem —8B 152
Camden Clo. Chat —6E 94
Camden Clo. Chst —4E 70
Camden Clo. Grav —6B 62
Camden Cotts. Ram —6J 211
(off Camden Rd.)
Camden Ct. Belv —5B 52
Camden Ct. Pem —8C 152
Camden Ct. Tun W —1H 157
Camden Cres. Dover —5K 181
Camden Gro. Chst —2D 70
Camden High St. NW1 —2C 4
Camden Hill. —6C 220 (2E 37)
Camden Hill. Tun W —2H 157
Camden Park. —3J 157 (2E 35)
Camden Pk. Tun W —3J 157
(in three parts)
Camden Pk. Rd. NW1 —1C 4
Camden Pk. Rd. Chst —3B 70
Camden Rd. NW1 & N7 —1C 4
Camden Rd. Bex —6A 58
Camden Rd. Broad —6J 209
Camden Rd. Gill —5G 80
Camden Rd. Ram —6J 211
Camden Rd. Sev —4J 119
Camden Rd. Tun W —1H 157 (2E 35)
Camden Sq. Ram —5J 211
Camden St. NW1 —2C 4
Camden St. Maid —4D 126
Camden Ter. Seal —3N 119
Camden Ter. W'boro —9J 159
Camden Town. —2C 4
Camden Way. Chst —3B 70
Camellia Clo. Gill —4N 95
Camellia Clo. Mgte —3N 207
Camelot Clo. SE28 —2F 50
Camelot Clo. Big H —4C 164
Camel Rd. E16 —1A 50
Camer. —2B 16
Camer Gdns. Meop —9H 77
Cameron Clo. Bex —8F 58
Cameron Clo. Chat —3E 94
Cameron Ct. Dover —6F 180
Cameron Rd. SE6 —7C 54
Cameron Rd. Brom —8K 69
Cameron Ter. SE12 —8L 55
Camer Park Country Park. —1H 91
Camer Pk. Rd. Meop —1G 91 (2B 16)
Camer Rd. Meop —9G 77 (2B 16)
Camer St. Meop —9H 77
Camlan Rd. Brom —9J 55
Camomile Dri. Weav —4J 127
Campbell Clo. SE18 —8C 50
Campbell Clo. H Bay —4K 195
Campbell Rd. E3 —2E 5
Campbell Rd. Grav —6E 62
Campbell Rd. Maid —6D 126
Campbell Rd. Tun W —8G 150
Campbell Rd. Walm —7N 177
Campden Hill Rd. W8 —2B 4
Camperdown Mnr. Gill —6D 80
(off River St.)
Campfield Rd. SE9 —5N 55
Campfield Rd. Shoe —1D 11
Camp Hill. Chid C —5G 142 (4D 25)
Campion Clo. Chat —8B 94
Campion Clo. N'fleet —9D 62
Campion Cres. C'brk —3D 37
Campion Pl. SE28 —1J 51
Campleshon Rd. Gill —6N 95
Campshill Pl. SE13 —3F 54
Campshill Rd. SE13 —3F 54
Campus Way. Gill B —3K 95
Camp Way. Maid —1F 138
Camrose Av. Eri —6C 52
Camrose Clo. Croy —1B 82
Camrose St. SE2 —5J 51
Canada Clo. Folk —5C 188
Canada Farm Rd. S Dar & Dart —7G 75 (1E 15)
Canada Gdns. SE13 —3F 54
Canada Rd. Eri —7J 53
Canada Rd. Walm —6M 177
Canada Ter. Maid —2D 126
Canadia. —4B 44
Canadian Av. SE6 —5E 54 (4E 5)
Canadian Av. Gill —8H 81 (2E 17)
Canal Basin. Grav —4J 63
Canal Bridge. (Junct.) —3D 5
Canal Ind. Pk. Grav —4J 63
Canal Rd. Grav —4H 63
Canal Rd. High —5E 64 (4C 9)
Canal Rd. Strood —5N 79
Canary Wharf Tower. —2E 5
Canberra Gdns. Sit —7D 98
Canberra Rd. SE7 —6A 50 (3A 6)
Canberra Rd. Bexh —6M 51
Canbury Path. Orp —7J 71
Canfield Gdns. NW6 —1B 4
Canham Rd. SE25 —1D 13
Cann Hall. —1E 5
Cann Hall Rd. E11 —1E 5
Canning St. Maid —3D 126
Canning Town. —2A 6
Canning Town. (Junct.) —2E 5
Cannizaro Rd. SW19 —1A 12
Cannonbury Rd. Ram —6H 211
Cannongate Av. Hythe —5L 197
Cannongate Clo. Hythe —6M 197
Cannongate Gdns. Hythe —5M 197
Cannongate Rd. Hythe —5L 197 (3E 41)
Cannon Gro. S'ness —2F 218
Cannon La. Tonb —5K 145 (4E 25)
Cannon La. W'bury —2C 26
Cannon Pl. SE7 —5A 50
Cannon Rd. Bexh —8N 51
Cannon Rd. Ram —5H 211
Cannon St. EC4 —2D 5
Cannon St. Deal —3M 177
Cannon St. Dover —4J 181
Cannon St. Lydd —3C 204 (3D 47)
Cannon St. New R —2C 212
Cannon St. Rd. E1 —2D 5
Canon Appleton Ct. Cant —3L 171
Canonbury. —1C 5
Canonbury Pk. N. N1 —1D 5
Canonbury Rd. N1 —1C 5
Canon Clo. Roch —1M 93
Canon Grn. W'hm —3B 226
Canon La. W'bury —7A 124
Canon Rd. Brom —6M 69
Canons Ga. Rd. Dover —4K 181
Canon's Wlk. Croy —4A 82
Canon Woods Way. Kenn —4K 159
Cansiron La. Ash W & Eden —2A 34
Cansiron La. Cowd —2B 34
Canterbury. —2M 171 (1D 31)
Canterbury Av. Sidc —7K 57
Canterbury Bus. Cen., The. Cant —2M 171 (1D 31)
Canterbury Cathedral. —2N 171 (1D 31)
Canterbury City Retail Pk. Cant —7C 168
Canterbury Clo. Beck —4E 68
Canterbury Clo. Broad —8H 209
Canterbury Clo. Dart —5A 60
Canterbury Ct. SE12 —8L 55
Canterbury Ct. Afrd —8H 159
Canterbury Cres. Tonb —2K 145
Canterbury Hill. T Hill —6L 167 (3D 21)
Canterbury Ho. Eri —7G 52
Canterbury Ho. Maid —1G 138
Canterbury Ind. Pk. Her —2L 169
Canterbury La. Cant —2N 171 (1D 31)
Canterbury La. Gill —1D 96 (2A 18)
Canterbury La. H'lgh —4C 30
Canterbury Rd. Afrd —7G 158 (1A 40)
(in two parts)
Canterbury Rd. B'hm —3A 32
Canterbury Rd. Bou B —3L 165 (4B 20)
Canterbury Rd. Bra L —8K 165 (1C 40)
Canterbury Rd. B End & Birch —8A 206
Canterbury Rd. C'lck —8A 174
Canterbury Rd. Char —1N 175 (3E 29)
Canterbury Rd. Chi —8L 175 (2B 30)
Canterbury Rd. Croy —2C 13
Canterbury Rd. Dens & H'nge —4C 192 (2A 42)
Canterbury Rd. E Bra —1C 41
Canterbury Rd. Elham —9L 183
Canterbury Rd. Etch —2E 41
Canterbury Rd. Fav —7H 187 (3A 20)
(in two parts)
Canterbury Rd. Folk —2J 189 (2A 42)
Canterbury Rd. Grav —7H 63
Canterbury Rd. H Bay —8F 194 (2E 21)
(Herne Rd.)
Canterbury Rd. H Bay —4H 195 (2E 21)
(Thanet Way, in two parts)
Canterbury Rd. L'brne —3M 173 (1E 31)
Canterbury Rd. Lyd —4B 32
Canterbury Rd. Lym —7D 204 (1E 41)
Canterbury Rd. Pem —8D 152
Canterbury Rd. Sarre & Wgte S, —9E 214 (2B 22)
Canterbury Rd. Sit —8J 99 (3C 19)
(in two parts)
Canterbury Rd. Wgte S & Mgte —3J 207
Canterbury Rd. Whits —5F 224 (2C 21)
Canterbury Rd. W'boro —3J 161 (1A 40)
Canterbury Rd. W'hm —3A 226 (1A 32)
Canterbury Rd. E. Ram —5D 210 (2D 23)
Canterbury Rd. W. C'snd —5A 210 (2D 23)
Canterbury St. Gill —7F 80 (1E 17)
Canterbury Tales, The. —2M 171
Cantwell Rd. SE18 —7D 50
Canute Rd. Birch —3C 206
Canute Rd. Deal —1M 177
Canute Rd. Fav —6G 186
Canute Wlk. Deal —1M 177
Canvey Island. —2E 9
Canvey Rd. Can I —2E 9
Canvey Village. —2E 9
Canvey Way. Pits & Can I —1E 9
Cape Cotts. Maid —3C 138
Capel. —9E 146 (4A 26)
Capelands. New Ash —3N 89
Capel Clo. Broad —4K 209
Capel Clo. Brom —2A 84
Capel Clo. Gill —7M 95
Capel Ct. Pk. Cap F —2D 174
Capel Cross. —3E 198 (1C 37)
Capell Clo. Cox —5N 137
Capel-Le-Ferne. —2C 174 (2B 42)
Capel Pl. Dart —9K 59
Capel Rd. E7 —1A 6
Capel Rd. Fav —5F 186
Capel Rd. Hams —3E 39
Capel Rd. P'hm —3C 31
Capel Rd. Sit —9F 98
Capel St. Cap F —2B 174 (2B 42)
(in two parts)
Capel Ter. Sth S —1C 10
Capetown Ho. Maid —3J 139
Capstan Ct. Dart —2C 60
Capstan Row. Deal —3N 177
Capstone. —2E 17
Capstone Farm Country Park. —5G 95
Capstone Rd. Brom —9J 55
Capstone Rd. Chat —2F 94 (2E 17)
Captain's Clo. Sut V —3A 28
Captian Webb Memorial. —5K 181
(off Marine Pde.)
Carage Clo. Eri —6D 52
Cardens Rd. Cli —5M 65
Cardiff St. SE18 —7G 50
Cardinal Clo. Chst —4G 70
Cardinal Clo. Tonb —7K 145
Cardine Clo. Sit —4F 98
Cardwell Rd. SE18 —4C 50
Carey Clo. New R —3C 212
Carey Ct. Bexh —3C 58
Carey Ho. Cant —3M 171 (1D 31)
(off Station Rd. E.)
Carholme Rd. SE23 —6C 54
Caring. —8N 127 (2A 28)
Caring Farm Cotts. Leeds —8N 127
Caring La. Leeds —9N 127 (2A 28)
Caring Rd. Otham & Leeds —7M 127 (2A 28)
Carisbrooke Av. Bex —6M 57
Carisbrooke Ct. Dart —4B 60
(off Osbourne Rd.)
Carisbrooke Dri. Maid —4A 126
Carisbrooke Rd. Brom —7M 69
Carisbrooke Rd. Roch —3J 79
Carl Ekman Ho. Grav —5C 62
Carleton Pl. Hort K —7C 74
Carleton Rd. Dart —5A 60
Carlisle Clo. Roch —6G 79
Carlisle Ho. Maid —1G 139
Carlisle Rd. Dart —4A 60
Carlsden Clo. Dover —1F 180
Carlton Av. Broad —8L 209
Carlton Av. Gill —8H 81
Carlton Av. Grnh —4E 60
Carlton Av. Ram —6H 211
Carlton Av. S'ness —3C 218
Carlton Clo. Tonb —9K 133
Carlton Cres. Chat —3G 94
Carlton Cres. Tun W —1J 157
Carlton Gdns. Maid —9D 126
Carlton Hill. H Bay —3D 194
Carlton Leas. Folk —7J 189
Carlton Mans. Mgte —2E 208
Carlton Pde. Orp —1K 85
Carlton Pde. Sev —4K 119
Carlton Rise. Wgte S —3H 207
Carlton Rd. Afrd —8E 158
Carlton Rd. Eri —6C 52 (3C 6)
Carlton Rd. Kgdn —3M 199
Carlton Rd. Sidc —1H 71
Carlton Rd. S Croy —3D 13
Carlton Rd. Tun W —1J 157
Carlton Rd. Well —1K 57
Carlton Rd. Whits —1D 166
Carlton Rd. E. Wgte S —3J 207
Carlton Rd. W. Wgte S —3H 207
Carlton Vale. NW6 —2B 4
Carlyle Av. Brom —6N 69
Carlyle Rd. SE28 —1L 51 (2B 6)
Carlys Clo. SE20 —5A 68
Carman's Clo. Loose —6C 138
Carmelite Way. Hart —8M 75
Carmichael Rd. SE25 —2D 13
Carnatation Clo. E Mal —9E 108
Carnation Cres. E Mal —1D 124
Carnation Dri. Roch —5H 79
Carnation Rd. Roch —5H 79
Carnation St. SE2 —5K 51
Carn Brea. Mgte —3D 208
Carnbrook Rd. SE3 —1N 55
Carnecke Gdns. SE9 —3A 56
Caroland Clo. Sme —8J 165
Caroland Vs. Bra L —9J 165
Caroline Clo. Whits —7D 224
Caroline Ct. Brom —9G 54
Caroline Cres. Broad —7J 209
Caroline Cres. Maid —2A 126
Caroline Sq. Mgte —2D 208
Carolyn Dri. Orp —4J 85
Carpeaux Clo. Chat —8D 80
Carpenters Clo. Roch —1B 94
Carpenters La. Hdlw —5B 134 (3A 26)
Carpenter's Rd. E15 —1E 5
Carpinus Clo. Chat —1E 110
Carrack Ho. Eri —5F 52
(off Saltford Clo.)
Carr Gro. SE18 —4A 50
Carr Ho. Dart —3F 58
Carriage M. Cant —1M 171
Carriage Way, The. Bras —6M 117
Carrick Clo. Tonb —9L 133
Carrick Dri. Sev —5J 119
Carriers Pl. Blac —1C 154
Carriers Rd. C'brk —7D 176
Carrill Way. Belv —3M 51
Carrington Clo. Croy —1B 82
Carrington Clo. Gill —6J 81
Carrington Rd. Dart —4N 59
Carroll Gdns. Lark —7D 108
Carronade Pl. SE28 —3E 50
Carroway's Pl. Mgte —3D 208
Carrs Corner. Tun W —1H 157
Carshalton. —2B 12
Carshalton Beeches. —3B 12
Carshalton on the Hill. —3B 12
Carshalton Pk. Rd. Cars —3B 12
Carshalton Rd. Bans —3B 12
Carshalton Rd. Mitc —2C 12
Carshalton Rd. Sutt & Cars —2B 12
Carsington Gdns. Dart —7L 59
Carstairs Rd. SE6 —8F 54
Carston Clo. SE12 —3J 55
Carswell Rd. SE6 —5F 54
Carter La. B'lnd —2C 46
Carter Rd. Bek —7K 173 (2A 32)
Carter's Hill. —2B 132 (2D 25)
Carter's Hill. Under —3B 132 (3D 25)
Carters Hill Clo. SE9 —6M 55
Carter's Hill La. Meop —9E 90
Carters La. SE23 —7B 54
Carters Rd. Folk —6F 188
Carters Row. N'fleet —6E 62
Carters Wood. Hams —8D 190
Cartmel Rd. Bexh —8B 52
Carton Clo. Roch —1A 94
Carton Rd. High —1F 78
Carville Av. Tun W —5F 150
Carvoran Way. Gill —6M 95
Cascade Clo. Orp —6L 71
Casino Sq. Gus —2K 181
Caslocke St. Fav —5G 186
Cassilda Rd. SE2 —4J 51
Cassland Rd. E9 —1D 5
Casslee Rd. SE6 —5C 54
Casstine Clo. Swan —3G 73
Castalia Cotts. Walm —7N 177
(off Cambridge Rd.)
Castalia Ct. Dart —1N 59
Castelnau. —3A 4
Castelnau. SW13 —3A 4
Casterbridge Rd. SE3 —1K 55
Castile Rd. SE18 —4C 50
Castillon Rd. SE6 —7H 55
Castlands Rd. SE6 —7C 54
Castleacres Ind. Est. Sit —5J 99
Castle Av. Broad —7M 209
Castle Av. Dover —3J 181
Castle Av. Hythe —5J 197
Castle Av. Roch —8N 79
Castle Bay. S'gte —8C 188
Castle Clo. Brom —6H 69
Castle Clo. Lymp —6A 196
Castle Clo. S'gte —8F 188
Castlecombe Rd. SE9 —9A 56
Castle Cotts. Westw —2D 158
Castle Ct. SE26 —9B 54
Castle Cres. Salt —4K 197
Castle Dean. Maid —1B 126
Castle Dri. Kems —8M 103
Castle Dri. Whitf —7E 178
Castle Farm Rd. Sev —3C 15
Castle Farm Rd. Shor —9G 87
Castlefields. Grav —4E 76
Castlefields. Hartf —3C 34
Castlefields. Tonb —5H 145
Castleford Av. SE9 —6D 56
Castle Hill. —1C 36
Castle Hill. Det —1N 127 (4A 18)
Castle Hill. Folk —3G 188
Castle Hill. Hart —8K 75 (2E 15)
Castle Hill. Roch —6N 79
Castle Hill Av. Folk —6J 189 (2A 42)
Castle Hill Av. New Ad —9E 82
Castle Hill Pas. Folk —6J 189
Castle Hill Rd. Dover —3K 181 (1D 43)
Castle La. Grav —7N 63 (4B 8)
Castlemaine Av. Gill —6J 81
Castle Mkt. S'wch —5L 217
Castle Mayne Av. Wdchu —8L 207
Castlemere Av. Queen —7C 218
Castle M. Deal —7L 177
Castlemount Ct. Dover —4K 181
Castlemount Rd. Dover —3J 181
Castle Point Transport Museum. —2A 10
Castle Rd. All —3N 125
Castle Rd. Chat —1D 94 (2E 17)
Castle Rd. Eyns —7J 87
Castle Rd. Maid —1D 27
Castle Rd. R'boro —1K 217
Castle Rd. Salt —4J 197 (3D 41)
Castle Rd. S'gte —8F 188
Castle Rd. Sev & Dart —3D 15
Castle Rd. Sit —7H 99 (2C 19)
Castle Rd. Swans —4M 61
Castle Rd. Tun W —3G 156
Castle Rd. Whits —3G 225 (2C 21)
Castle Rd. Bus. Precinct. Sit —6J 99
Castle Rd. Technical Cen. Sit —6J 99
Castle Rough La. Kem —2G 99
Castle Row. Cant —3M 171 (1D 31)
Castle St. Afrd —8F 158
Castle St. Cant —3M 171 (1D 31)
Castle St. Dover —5J 181
Castle St. Grnh —3G 61
Castle St. Queen —7B 218
Castle St. S'boro —4F 150
Castle St. Swans —4M 61
Castle St. Tonb —5H 145
Castle St. Tun W —3G 157
Castle St. Upnor —3B 80
Castle St. Woul —7G 92
Castle Ter. Hdlw —8D 134
Castle Ter. Hawkh —4K 191
Castle, The. Whits —2G 225
Castleton Av. Bexh —8E 52
Castleton Clo. Croy —9B 68
Castleton Rd. SE9 —9N 55
Castle View. Hdlw —8D 134
Castleview Ct. Dover —3G 180
Castle View Rd. Roch —5K 79
Castle Wlk. Deal —1N 177
Castle Way. Leyb —9B 108 (4C 16)
Castlewood Dri. SE9 —9B 50
Caterfield La. Crow & Oxt —4A 24
Caterham Rd. SE13 —1F 54
Catford. —5E 54 (4E 5)
Catford B'way. SE6 —5E 54
Catford Greyhound Stadium. —4D 54 (4E 5)
Catford Gyratory. (Junct.) —5E 54 (4E 5)

Catford Hill—Chart View

Catford Hill. SE6 —7C 54 (4E 5)
Catford M. SE6 —5E 54
Catford Rd. SE6 —5D 54 (4E 5)
Catford Trad. Est. SE6 —7E 54
Cathall Rd. E11 —1E 5
Cathcart Dri. Orp —3G 84
Catherine Clo. Barm —6L 125
Catherine Howard Ct. SE9 —4F 56
Catherine of Aragon. SE9 —4F 56
Catherine Parr Ct. SE9 —4F 56
Catherine Pl. Tun W —1H 157
Catherine St. Roch —9A 80 (2D 17)
Catherine Way. Broad —7L 209
Catkin Clo. Chat —1C 110
Catling Clo. SE23 —8A 54
Catlyn Clo. E Mal —1E 124
Cator La. Beck —4C 68
Cator Rd. SE26 —2A 68
Catsfield Rd. Batt —4A 44
Catsole Hill. Good —2B 32
Cat St. Up Har —3B 34
Catterick Rd. Chat —9G 94
Cattistock Rd. SE9 —1B 70
Cattistock Rd. SE12 —1A 70
Catt's Hill. Mark X —4E 35
Catt's Hill. Stne —2A 46
Catt's Wood Rd. Up Hard —3D 31
Cauldham Clo. Cap F —3B 174
Cauldham La. Cap F —2A 174 (2B 42)
Caulfield Rd. Shoe —1D 11
Causeway, The. Cant —1M 171 (4D 21)
Causeway, The. S'wch —4K 217
Causton Rd. C'brk —7C 176
Cavalry Clo. Tonb —9L 133
Cave Hill. Maid —8B 126 (2D 27)
Cave La. W'hm —2B 32
Cavell Cres. Dart —2A 60
Cavell Sq. Deal —7K 177
Cavell Way. Sit —6E 98
Cavenagh Rd. St Mc —7L 213
Cavendish Av. Eri —6D 52
Cavendish Av. Gill —6H 81
Cavendish Av. Sev —4H 119
Cavendish Av. Sidc —5J 57
Cavendish Av. Well —1H 57
Cavendish Clo. Tonb —9K 133
Cavendish Ct. H Bay —2H 195
(off Cavendish Rd.)
Cavendish Ct. Tonb —5J 145
Cavendish Dri. Tun W —3H 157
Cavendish Gdns. Wclf S —1B 10
Cavendish Pl. Ram —6J 211
Cavendish Rd. NW6 —1B 4
Cavendish Rd. SW12 —4C 4
Cavendish Rd. H Bay —3H 195
Cavendish Sq. W1 —2C 4
Cavendish Sq. Long —6L 75
Cavendish St. Ram —5J 211
Cavendish St. Roch —9A 80
Cavendish Way. Bear —6K 127
Cavendish Way. W Wick —2E 82
Caversham Clo. Rain —2B 96
Caveside Clo. Chst —4C 70
Cavour Rd. Fav —5G 186
Cavour Rd. S'ness —2D 218
Caxton Clo. Hart —7M 75
Caxton Clo. Tent —8A 222
Caxton Ho. Afrd —7G 158
Caxton La. Hdlw —8D 134
Caxton Rd. Mgte —3N 207
Caygill Clo. Brom —7J 69
Cayser Dri. Kgswd —6G 140
Caysers Croft. E Peck —1K 147
Cazeneuve St. Roch —7N 79
Cazenove Rd. N16 —1D 5
Cecil Av. Gill —1K 95
Cecil Av. Roch —4M 79
Cecil Av. S'ness —3C 218
Cecil Burns Lodge. Tun W —3K 157
Cecil Ct. Afrd —7F 158
Cecil Ct. H Bay —3H 195
Cecilia Gro. Broad —7K 209
Cecilia Rd. Ram —4J 211
Cecil Pk. H Bay —3H 195
Cecil Rd. Grav —6E 62
Cecil Rd. Roch —9N 79 (2D 17)
Cecil Rd. Walm —2N 199
Cecil Sq. Mgte —3C 208
Cecil St. Mgte —3C 208 (1D 23)
Cecil Way. Brom —2K 83
Cedar Av. Grav —9H 63
Cedar Av. Sidc —5J 57
Cedar Clo. Afrd —7C 158
Cedar Clo. Broad —6K 209
Cedar Clo. Brom —4A 84
Cedar Clo. Dit —1H 125
Cedar Clo. Mgte —4F 208
Cedar Clo. Meop —9F 76
Cedar Clo. Sit —9J 99
Cedar Clo. Swan —5D 72
Cedar Copse. Brom —5B 70
Cedar Ct. Folk —6E 188
Cedar Ct. Maid —4E 126
Cedar Ct. Tent —8B 222
Cedar Ct. Tun W —9G 150
Cedar Cres. Brom —4A 84
Cedar Cres. St Mar —3E 214
Cedar Cres. Tonb —9J 133
Cedar Dri. Barm —7J 125
Cedar Dri. Eden —5B 184
Cedar Dri. S at H —5B 74
Cedar Gdns. S'bry —2F 112
Cedar Gro. Bex —4M 57
Cedar Gro. Hem —6K 95
Cedar Ho. S'ness —2C 218
(off Russell St.)
Cedarhurst. Brom —3H 69
Cedarhurst Cotts. Bex —6B 58
Cedarhurst Dri. SE9 —3M 55
Cedar Mt. SE9 —6N 55
Cedar Ridge. Tun W —8K 151
Cedar Rd. Brom —5M 69
Cedar Rd. Dart —6L 59
Cedar Rd. Eri —8H 53
Cedar Rd. Roch —6J 79
Cedar Rd. Sturry —5E 168
Cedar Rd. Sutt —3B 12
Cedars Av. Mitc —1C 12
Cedars Rd. SW4 —4C 4
Cedars Rd. W4 —3A 4
Cedars Rd. Beck —5B 68
Cedars, The. Pad W —8M 147
Cedars, The. Sit —6K 99
Cedar Ter. Dover —1G 181
(off Selkirk Rd.)
Cedar Ter. Rd. Sev —5K 119
Cedarview. Cant —1J 171
Cedric Rd. SE9 —8E 56
Cedric Rd. Wgte S —2K 207
Celandine Dri. SE28 —1K 51
Celestial Gdns. SE13 —2G 55
Celestine Clo. Chat —1D 110
Cellarhill. —3K 223 (3D 19)
Cellar Hill. Lyn —4K 223 (3D 19)
Celtic Av. Brom —6H 69
Celtic Rd. Deal —7K 177
Cement Cotts. Bek —5F 172
Cemetery Cotts. H'nge —8B 192
Cemetery Cotts. Maid —1F 138
Cemetery La. SE7 —6A 50
Cemetery La. Hdlw —7E 134 (3A 26)
Cemetery La. Kenn —6G 159
Cemetery Rd. SE2 —7K 51
Cemetery Rd. Hall —6E 92
Cemetery Rd. Snod —1D 108
Centenary Clo. Char —2K 175
Centenary Ct. F'ham —1A 88
Centenary Gdns. E'try —3J 183
Central Av. Chat —4E 80
Central Av. Grav —7G 63
Central Av. H Bay —2E 194 (2E 21)
Central Av. Sit —8G 98
Central Av. Sth S —1C 10
Central Av. Well —9H 51 (3B 6)
Central Beach Camp. Ley S —6M 203
Central Bus. Pk. Roch —5B 80
Central Hill. SE19 —1D 13
Central Pde. SE20 —3A 68
(off High St. Penge,)
Central Pde. H Bay —1E 21
Central Pde. New Ad —3E 13
Central Pde. Roch —1A 94
Central Pk. Gdns. Chat —1B 94
Central Pk. Rd. E6 —2A 6
Central Rd. Dart —3M 59
Central Rd. Lark —7F 108
Central Rd. Mord —2B 12
Central Rd. Ram —4H 211
Central Rd. Roch —5L 79
Central Rd. Wor Pk —2A 12
Central St. EC1 —2C 5
Central Ter. Beck —6A 68
Central Ter. Chatt —7C 66
Central Wall Rd. Can I —1E 9
Central Way. SE28 —1J 51 (2B 6)
Centre 2000. Sit —7H 99
Centre Comn. Rd. Chst —2E 70 (1B 14)
Centre Ct. Roch —5B 80
Centre Rd. E11 & E7 —1A 6
Centre Rd. Dover —6H 181 (1C 43)
Centre Rd. New Ash —4L 89
Centre, The. Mgte —3C 208
Centre, The. Ram —3E 210
Centurion Clo. Gill B —2J 95
Centurion Wlk. Kgnt —5F 160
Centurion Way. Eri —3A 52
Centurion Way. Purf —4N 53
(in two parts)
Centuryan Pl. Dart —2J 59
Century Building. Roch —7N 79
Century Rd. Fav —5J 187
Century Rd. Gill —3N 95
Century Wlk. Deal —4M 177
Ceres Ct. Sit —6K 99
Ceres Rd. SE18 —4H 51
Cerne Rd. Grav —9K 63
Cervia Way. Grav —8L 63
Chada Av. Gill —9H 81
Chadd Dri. Brom —6A 70
Chadwell By-Pass. Grays —3A 8
Chadwell Rd. Grays —3A 8
Chadwell St Mary. —3B 8
Chadwick Clo. N'fleet —8D 62
Chaffe's La. Upc —9H 223 (2B 18)
Chaffes Ter. Upc —9H 223
(in two Parts)
Chaffinch Av. Croy —9A 68
Chaffinch Bus. Pk. Beck —7A 68
Chaffinch Clo. Chat —4D 94
Chaffinch Clo. Croy —8A 68
Chaffinch Lodge. Dover —2G 181
Chaffinch Rd. Beck —4B 68
Chaffinch Way. Pad W —1M 153
Chafford Hundred. —3A 8
Chafford La. Ford —8F 148 (1C 35)
Chafy Cres. Sturry —6E 168
Chainhurst. —4D 27
Chain, The. S'wch —6M 217
Chalcombe Rd. SE2 —3K 51
Chalcroft Rd. SE13 —3H 55
Chalcroft Rd. S'gte —7E 188
Chaldon Way. Coul —4C 13
Chalet Clo. Bex —9E 58
Chalfont Dri. Gill —5N 95
Chalford Dri. H Bay —5L 195
Chalgrove M. Hall —6E 92
Chalice Way. Grnh —3E 60
Chalk. —6M 63 (4B 8)
Chalk Av. St Mic —5C 222
Chalk Clo. Folk —4G 189
Chalkenden Av. Gill —1K 95
Chalker's Corner. (Junct.) —3A 4
Chalket La. Pem —9B 152
Chalk Farm. —1C 4
Chalk Farm Rd. NW1 —1C 4
Chalk Hill. C'snd —6D 210
Chalk Hill Rd. Kgdn —4M 199 (3E 33)
Chalk La. C'brk —2D 37
Chalklin Bus. Pk. Tun W —5L 151
Chalk Pit Av. Orp —6L 71
Chalk Pit Cvn. Site. Sidc —3A 72
Chalk Pit Hill. B'le —9A 216 (1B 32)
Chalkpit Hill. Bek —7J 173 (2E 31)
Chalk Pit Hill. Chat —9D 80
Chalk Pit La. B'le —9B 216 (1C 32)
Chalk Pit Rd. Eps —4A 12
Chalk Pit Way. Sutt —3B 12
Chalk Rd. Grav —6M 63 (4B 8)
Chalk Rd. High —7G 64 (4C 9)
Chalk Rd. Queen —7B 218
Chalksole. —1B 42
Chalksole Grn. La. Alk —1B 42
Chalkstone Clo. Well —8J 51
Chalkwell. —6D 98 (2C 18)
Chalkwell Av. Wclf S —1B 10
Chalkwell Ct. Dover —5F 180
Chalkwell Esplanade. Wclf S —1B 10
Chalkwell Rd. Sit —7E 98 (2C 18)
Chalky Bank. Grav —9F 62
Chalky Bank Rd. Gill —1B 96
Chalky Rd. S'bry —4E 112 (3A 18)
Challenge Clo. Grav —9L 63
Challenger Clo. Pad W —9L 147
Challenger Clo. Sit —4F 98
Challock. —7D 174 (3A 30)
Challock Clo. Big H —4C 164
Challock Ct. Clift —3K 209
Challock Wlk. Maid —3F 126
Chalsey Rd. SE4 —2C 54
Chamberlain Av. Maid —7M 125
Chamberlain Clo. SE28 —3F 50
Chamberlain Ct. Gill —6L 95
Chamberlain Cres. W Wick —2E 82
Chamberlain Dri. H Bay —3C 194
Chamberlain Rd. Chat —1E 94
Chamberlain Rd. Dover —4F 180
Chamberlayne Rd. NW6 —2A 4
Chambers Clo. Grnh —3G 60
Chamber's Green. —1D 39
Chambers Grn. Rd. P'ley —4C 29
Chambers La. NW10 —1A 4
Chambers Wall. St N —7A 214 (2B 22)
Champion Cres. SE26 —9B 54
Champion Pk. SE5 —4D 5
Champion Rd. SE26 —9B 54
Chancel Clo. W King —8E 88
Chancel Ct. Cant —1K 171
Chancellor Ho. Tun W —2F 156
Chancellor Rd. Sth S —1C 10
Chancellor Way. Sev —4H 119
Chancelot Rd. SE2 —4K 51
Chance Meadow. Gus —7L 179
Chancery Ct. Dart —5A 60
Chancery La. WC2 —2C 5
Chancery La. Beck —5E 68
Chancery La. Maid —6D 126
Chancery Rd. Cli —3C 176
Chanctonbury Chase. Sea —7C 224
Chanctonbury Clo. SE9 —8D 56
Chandlers Corner. (Junct.) —2D 7
Chandlers Dri. Eri —4E 52
Chandler's Hill. Meop —5H 91
Chandler's Rd. Meop —6H 91 (2B 16)
Chandos Rd. Broad —9M 209
Chandos Rd. Tun W —9J 151
Chandos Sq. Broad —9M 209
Channel Cvn. Pk. Hythe —8E 196
Channel Clo. Folk —4H 189
Channel Lea. Walm —9M 177
Channel Rd. Mgte —7E 208
Channel Tunnel. —2E 41
Channel View. Folk —6L 189
(off North St.)
Channel View Ct. Ram —5K 211
(off Granville Marina)
Channel View Rd. Dover —6H 181
Channon Rd. G'stne —7A 212
Chantlers Hill. Pad W —3L 153 (1B 36)
Chantlers Mead. Cowd —1B 34
Chantry Av. Hart —9L 75
Chantry Clo. Sidc —1N 71
Chantry Ct. Cant —1M 171 (4D 21)
Chantry Ct. Grav —4H 63
Chantry La. Brom —8N 69
Chantry Pl. Mard —2K 205
Chantry Rd. Mard —2K 205
Chapel Clo. Dart —3F 58
Chapel Clo. Rya —5L 107
Chapel Cottage. H Bay —5L 195
Chapel Cotts. H Bay —4L 195
Chapel Cotts. Leeds —3B 140
Chapel Ct. Swans —4L 61
Chapel Farm Rd. SE9 —8B 56
Chapel Hill. Dart —3F 58
Chapel Hill. Eyt —4K 185 (3C 32)
Chapel Hill. Mgte —6D 208
Chapel Hill. Sed —4C 44
Chapel Hill Clo. Mgte —6D 208
Chapel La. Bear —4K 127
Chapel La. Blean —4G 166
Chapel La. Bred —9K 95
Chapel La. B Oak —4C 168
Chapel La. Burm —4B 40
Chapel La. Dover —5J 181
(off York St.)
Chapel La. Eger —4C 28
Chapel La. Hall —3C 16
Chapel La. Hem —7K 95 (3E 17)
Chapel La. I Grn —4A 38
Chapel La. R Min —8H 183 (1D 41)
Chapel La. Ripp —3D 33
Chapel La. Siss —9D 220 (2E 37)
Chapel La. S'hrst —8K 221
Chapel La. St Mc —7J 213
Chapel La. Sturry —6E 168
Chapel La. Tilm —3C 33
Chapel La. Up H'lng —7A 92
Chapel M. Afrd —8G 158
(off North St.)
Chapel Pl. Birch —4F 206
Chapel Pl. Dover —5J 181
Chapel Pl. Ram —6H 211
Chapel Pl. Tun W —3G 156
Chapel Pl. La. Ram —5H 211
Chapel Rd. SE27 —1C 13
Chapel Rd. Bexh —2B 58
Chapel Rd. Dym —8B 182
Chapel Rd. Hoth —4E 29
Chapel Rd. Ilf —1A 6
Chapel Rd. Isle G —3C 190 (3C 10)
Chapel Rd. Oxt —2A 24
Chapel Rd. Ram —5G 210
Chapel Rd. Snod —2E 108
Chapel Rd. Sut V —9A 140
Chapel Rd. Tilm —3C 33
Chapel Rd. Whitf —5F 178 (4C 33)
Chapel Row. Afrd —6E 160
Chapel Row. H Bay —7H 195
Chapel Row. Igh —3J 121
Chapel Row. Lwr Sto —4A 10
Chapel Row. Lydd —3C 204
Chapel Row. Mid S —8K 201
Chapel St. NW1 —2B 4
Chapel St. Deal —4N 177
Chapel St. E Mal —3E 124 (1C 27)
Chapel St. Fav —6H 187
Chapel St. H Bay —3H 195
Chapel St. Hythe —6J 197
Chapel St. Min S —6L 219 (4D 11)
Chapel St. Rya —5L 107 (3B 16)
Chapel St. S'ness —1B 218
Chapel St. W Mal —3B 16
Chapel View. Igh —3J 121
Chapel Wlk. Dover —4J 181
(off Priory Rd.)
Chapel Wlk. Ide H —3C 130
Chapel Wood. New Ash —2L 89
Chapel Wood Rd. As & Hart —4L 89 (2E 15)
Chapel Woods. Char —3E 29
Chaplin Clo. Wain —1N 79
Chaplin Dri. H'crn —3L 193
Chapman Av. Maid —8H 127
Chapman Ho. Deal —7L 177
Chapman Rd. E9 —1E 5
Chapman Rd. Belv —5C 52
Chapmans Clo. C'ick —7E 174
Chapmans Hill. Aysm —1E 162 (2B 32)
Chapman's Hill. Meop —7D 90 (3A 16)
Chapman's La. SE2 & Belv —4M 51
Chapman's La. Orp —5M 71
Chapmans Rd. Sund —6N 117
Chapman Way. E Mal —1D 124 (1C 26)
Chapman Way. Tun W —6J 151
Chappell Way. Sit —5F 98
Chapter Rd. NW2 —1A 4
Chapter Rd. Roch —5K 79
Charcoal La. Blad —4E 31
Charcott. —4H 143 (4D 25)
Chard Ct. Gill —7F 80
Chard Ho. Maid —2C 126
Charing. —3K 175 (3D 29)
Charing Clo. Orp —5H 85
Charing Clo. Ram —4G 211
Charing Ct. Short —5H 69
Charing Cres. Wgte S —4J 207
Charing Cross Rd. WC2 —2C 4
Charing Heath. —3D 29
Charing Heath Rd. Char —4H 175 (3D 29)
Charing Hill. —1L 175 (3D 29)
Charing Hill. Char —2L 175 (3D 29)
Charing Rd. Gill —9L 81
Chariot Way. Roch —9J 79
Charlbury Clo. Maid —6N 125
Charldane Rd. SE9 —8D 56
Charlecote Ct. Gill —3N 95
(off Derwent Way)
Charles Busby Ct. Roy B —9K 109
Charles Clo. Sidc —9K 57
Charles Clo. Snod —2E 108
Charles Cobb Clo. Dym —7C 182
Charles Ct. Eri —6F 52
Charles Cres. Folk —4E 188
Charles Dickens Av. High —2G 78
Charles Dri. Cux —9F 78
Charlesfield. SE9 —8M 55
Charlesford Av. Kgswd —5F 140
Charles Grinling Wlk. SE18 —4C 50
Charles Ho. Deal —7L 177
Charles Lister Ct. Dover —3G 181
Charles Rd. Badg M —1C 102
Charles Rd. Deal —6L 177
Charles Rd. Ram —4J 211
Charles St. Chat —9B 80
Charles St. Grnh —3F 60
Charles St. H Bay —2G 195
Charles St. Maid —6B 126
Charles St. Roch —5L 79
Charles St. S'ness —2B 218
Charles St. Tun W —6G 150
Charleston Ct. Broad —1M 211
(off W. Cliff Rd.)
Charlesworth Dri. Birch —4G 206
Charleworth Ho. Chat —1B 94
Charlieville Rd. Eri —7D 52
Charlotte Clo. Bexh —3N 57
Charlotte Clo. Chat —5E 94
Charlotte Cotts. Leigh —5N 143
Charlotte Ct. Ram —6J 211
Charlotte Dri. Gill —2M 95
Charlotte Pk. Av. Brom —6A 70
Charlotte Pl. Mgte —3D 208
Charlotte St. Broad —9M 209
Charlotte St. Folk —6L 189
Charlotte St. Sit —6F 98
Charlton. —3A 6
Charlton Arc. Dover —4H 181
(off High St. Dover,)
Charlton Athletic F.C. —3A 6
Charlton Av. Dover —3H 181
Charlton Chu. La. SE7 —3A 6
Charlton Clo. Ram —2F 210
Charlton Clo. W'boro —1L 161
Charlton Dri. Big H —5D 164
Charlton Grn. Dover —3H 181 (1C 43)
Charlton House (Library). —3A 6
Charlton La. E Sut —8E 140 (3A 28)
Charlton La. W Far —1H 137 (2C 27)
Charlton Mnr. Gill —7F 80
Charlton Pk. La. SE7 —3A 6
Charlton Pk. Rd. SE7 —6A 50 (3A 6)
Charlton Rd. SE3 & SE7 —3A 6
Charltons, The. Bou B —2J 165
Charlton St. Maid —7N 125
Charlton's Way. Tun W —4E 156
Charlton Ter. Tonb —5J 145
Charlton Way. SE3 —3E 5
Charlwood. Croy —9C 82
Charminster. Afrd —3C 160
Charminster Rd. SE9 —9N 55
Charmouth Rd. Well —8L 51
Charmwood La. Orp —9K 85 (3B 14)
Charne, The. Otf —8H 103
Charnock. Swan —7F 72
Charnwood Ches —4M 225
Charnwood Rd. H Bay —6J 195
Charsley Rd. SE6 —7E 54
Chart Av. Afrd —9A 158
Chart Clo. Brom —4H 69
Chart Clo. Fav —5F 186
Chart Corner. —7L 139 (3E 27)
Charter Dri. Bex —5N 57
Charter Ho. Afrd —8G 158
Charterhouse Dri. Sev —5H 119
Charterhouse Rd. Orp —4J 85
Charterhouse St. EC1 —2C 5
Charter St. Chat —1C 94
Charter St. Gill —5F 80
Chart Gunpowder Mills. —5F 186 (3A 20)
Chartham. —7D 170 (2C 31)
Chartham Downs. Cha —9D 170
Chartham Downs Rd. Cha —9D 170 (2C 31)
Chartham Hatch. —4C 170 (1C 31)
Chartham Hatch Rd. Harb —1G 171 (1D 31)
Chartham Ter. Ram —7H 211
(off St Augustines Rd.)
Chart Hill. —3E 27
Chart Hill Rd. Cha S —9K 139 (4E 27)
Chart La. Bras —9K 117
Chart La. W'ham —3B 24
Chart Leacon Cotts. Afrd —8C 158
Charton Clo. Belv —6B 52
Chart Pl. Gill —8M 95
Chart Rd. Afrd —2A 160 (1E 39)
Chart Rd. Cha S —9L 139 (3E 27)
Chart Rd. Folk —5F 188
Chart Rd. Gt Cha & Afrd —9A 158 (1E 39)
Chart Rd. Ind. Est. Afrd —8E 158
Chart Sutton. —7L 139 (3E 27)
Chart Sutton Bus. Est. Cha S —6L 139
Chart View. Kems —8B 104

Churchdown—Claydown M.

Churchdown. Brom —9H 55
Church Dri. W Wick —4H 83
Church Elm La. Dag —1C 6
Church End. —1A 4
Church Farm Clo. Hoo —9H 67
Church Farm Clo. Swan —9D 72
Church Farm Rd. Upc —8H 223
Churchfield. Adtn —8H 107
Church Field. Dart —7L 59
Churchfield. Eden —6D 184
Church Field. Snod —1F 108
Church Field. Stanf —2D 41
Churchfield Pl. Mgte —3C 208
Churchfield Rd. W3 —2A 4
Churchfield Rd. Well —1J 57
Churchfields. Broad —6K 209
Churchfields. Mgte —4D 208 (1D 23)
Church Fields. Sev —4G 118
Church Fields. W Mal —1N 123
Churchfields Rd. Beck —5A 68
Churchfields Ter. Roch —8M 79
Churchfield Way. Wye —2L 159 (4B 30)
Church Grn. Mard —2K 205 (4D 27)
Church Grn. Roch —4N 79
Church Grn. S'hrst —9J 221
Church Grn. Cotts. Bra L —9H 165
Church Gro. SE13 —3E 54
Church Haven. R'wld —4J 199
Church Hill. SE18 —3B 50
Church Hill. Bap —7M 99
Church Hill. Beth —2J 163 (1D 39)
Church Hill. Bou M —6E 138
Church Hill. Char H —3D 29
Church Hill. Chat —1F 94
Church Hill. Chi —8J 175 (2B 30)
Church Hill. Cray —2F 58
Church Hill. Crowb —3C 34
Church Hill. Cud —6E 100 (4B 14)
Church Hill. Dart —7L 59 (4D 7)
Church Hill. Dod —1D 29
Church Hill. E'ham —2A 44
Church Hill. Eyt —3J 185 (3B 32)
Church Hill. Grnh —3E 60
Church Hill. Harb —1J 171 (4D 21)
Church Hill. H'shm —3E 27
Church Hill. Hern —1J 165 (3B 20)
Church Hill. H Hal —7K 193 (2C 39)
Church Hill. Hythe —6K 197
Church Hill. Kgnt —6E 160 (2A 40)
Church Hill. Leigh —5N 143
Church Hill. Orp —1J 85
Church Hill. Plax —9L 121 (2A 26)
Church Hill. Ram —5J 211
Church Hill. Sed —4B 44
Church Hill. S'wll —3C 220 (4B 32)
Church Hill. Stan H —2C 8
Church Hill. Stne —2A 46
Church Hill. S'bry —3H 113 (3B 18)
Church Hill. Sutt —3D 33
Church Hill. Tats —1A 24
Church Hill. Temp E —8C 178
Church Hill Rd. Sutt —2A 12
Church Hill Wood. Orp —8H 71
Church Hougham. —8A 180 (1C 42)
Church Ho. Deal —3M 177
Church Hyde. SE18 —6G 50
Churchill Av. Chat —5C 94
Churchill Av. Folk —2A 42
Churchill Av. H Bay —3L 195
Churchill Av. Walm —8M 177
Churchill Clo. Bri —9E 172
Churchill Clo. Dart —6B 60
Churchill Clo. Folk —3K 189
Churchill Clo. St Mc —8J 213
Churchill Clo. W'ham —8F 116
Churchill Cotts. Leeds —3B 140
Churchill Ct. Farn —6E 84
Churchill Ct. Hythe —7J 197
Churchill Ho. Bri —9E 172
Churchill Ho. Dover —1G 181
(off Hudson Clo.)
Churchill Ho. Folk —6F 188
(off Coolinge La.)
Churchill Ho. Maid —7M 125
Churchill Ho. Sit —6J 99
Churchill Pk. Dart —3A 60
(off Attlee Dri.)
Churchill Rd. Cant —4B 172
Churchill Rd. Dover —6F 180
Churchill Rd. Grav —6E 62
Churchill Rd. Hort K —7C 74
Churchill Rd. Min S —6L 219
Churchill Sq. King H —6M 123
Churchills Rope Wlk. Goud —8K 185
Churchill St. Dover —3H 181
Churchill Wlk. H'nge —8B 192
Churchill Way. Big A —3D 164
Churchill Way. Brom —6K 69
Churchill Way. Fav —3F 186
Churchlands. Chat —2C 94
Churchlands, The. New R —3C 212
Church La. SW17 —1B 12
Church La. Adm —2A 32
Church La. Adgtn —2B 40
Church La. B'hm —7D 162 (3A 32)
Church La. Barm —8J 125 (2D 27)
Church La. Bear —5M 127
Church La. Beckl —3D 45
Church La. Bos —3D 31
Church La. Bztt —1C 47
Church La. Brom —2A 84
Church La. Cant —1N 171 (4D 21)
(St Radigund's St.)
Church La. Cant —2M 171 (1D 31)
(Stour St.)
Church La. C'lck —9D 174 (3A 30)
Church La. Cha —7D 170 (2C 31)
Church La. Chat —6C 80
Church La. Chst —4E 70
Church La. C'let —2A 22
Church La. Chu H —7A 180
Church La. Crun —3C 30
Church La. Deal —3D 33
Church La. Dod —9N 115 (1D 29)
Church La. E Peck —9K 135 (3B 26)
Church La. E Sut —8D 140 (3A 28)
Church La. E'ham —2A 44
Church La. Five G —1E 152 (4A 26)
Church La. F'wch —7F 168
Church La. Frant —9H 157 (3E 35)
Church La. Grav —7A 64 (4C 8)
Church La. H'shm —2N 141 (2B 28)
Church La. Hoth —4E 29
Church La. Iden —3A 46
Church La. Kems —8B 104
Church La. Kgnt —6F 160
Church La. Kgtn —3E 31
Church La. Lwr Har —2D 31
Church La. Lyd —4B 32
Church La. Nack —8N 171
Church La. N'tn —5K 97 (2B 18)
Church La. New R —3C 212 (2E 47)
Church La. N'iam —2D 45
Church La. Oxt —2A 24
Church La. P'mrsh —3E 45
Church La. R'wld —4J 199 (3D 33)
Church La. Ripp —9H 177
Church La. Sea —7C 224 (2C 20)
Church La. S'ndge —1C 41
Church La. Sell —1A 30
Church La. Shad —2E 39
Church La. Shol & Deal —5J 177
(in two parts)
Church La. S Min —3D 31
Church La. S'bry —2G 112 (3B 18)
Church La. Sturry —6E 168
Church La. Tats —9D 164
Church La. Tonb —5J 145
Church La. Tros —5F 106 (3A 16)
Church La. Upm —1A 8
Church La. Walt —3C 31
Church La. Warl —4E 13
Church La. W'bre —4H 169 (3E 21)
Church La. W'ham —1A 24
Church La. W Far —1H 137
Church La. Westf —4C 45
Church La. Westw —4A 30
Church La. Wom —3A 32
Church Manorway. SE2 —4J 51
Church Manorway. Eri —4E 52
Church Meadows. Deal —4K 177
Church M. Rain —3B 96
Church Path. Deal —6K 177
(in three parts)
Church Path. Gill —6G 81
(Parr Av.)
Church Path. Gill —6E 80
(Prince Arthur Rd.)
Church Path. Grnh —3F 60
Church Path. Lwr Hal —8M 223
Church Path. N'fleet —4B 62
Church Path. Strood —5M 79
Church Path. Swan —4J 73
Church Path. Tent —8B 222
Church Path. Walm —9M 177
Church Pl. Dover —4J 181
Church Pl. Woul —6G 93
Church Rise. SE23 —7A 54
Church Rd. E10 —1E 5
Church Rd. E12 —1A 6
Church Rd. NW10 —1A 4
Church Rd. SE19 —1D 13
Church Rd. SW13 —3A 4
Church Rd. SW19 & Mitc —1B 12
(Merton)
Church Rd. SW19 —1B 12
(Wimbledon)
Church Rd. As —6L 89 (2A 16)
Church Rd. Afrd —9F 158
Church Rd. Bexh —9A 52 (4C 6)
Church Rd. Big H —5D 164
Church Rd. Bra L —9H 165 (2B 40)
Church Rd. Bras —6K 117
Church Rd. Broad —9M 209
Church Rd. Brom —5K 69
Church Rd. Bulp —1A 8
Church Rd. Burm —3A 182
Church Rd. Char —3D 29
Church Rd. Cha S —8M 139 (3A 28)
Church Rd. Chels —8L 85 (3B 14)
Church Rd. Cob —5H 77 (1B 16)
Church Rd. Col —4F 220 (4B 32)
Church Rd. Corr —2C 9
Church Rd. Crowb —4C 35
Church Rd. Dover —5F 180
Church Rd. E'chu —1E 19
Church Rd. Eps —3A 12
Church Rd. Eri —5E 52
Church Rd. Farn —6E 84 (2B 14)
Church Rd. Fav —4H 187
(Bramblehill Rd.)
Church Rd. Fav —5H 187
(East St.)
Church Rd. Folk —5C 188 (2E 41)
Church Rd. Goud —8K 185 (2D 37)
Church Rd. Graf G —9N 141 (3B 28)
Church Rd. Grnh —3F 60
Church Rd. Hals —2N 101 (3C 14)
Church Rd. H'shm —2N 141
Church Rd. Hart —8M 75 (2A 16)
Church Rd. H'lgh —4C 30
Church Rd. Hoath —2A 22
Church Rd. H'sham —2B 28
Church Rd. Huc —9F 112 (4A 18)
Church Rd. Hythe —6K 197
Church Rd. Igh —2E 25
Church Rd. Ken —3E 39
Church Rd. Kenn —4J 159 (4A 30)
Church Rd. Kes —8N 83 (3A 14)
Church Rd. Kiln —3C 36
Church Rd. Lam —1D 200
Church Rd. Ling —1A 34
Church Rd. L'brne —2M 173 (1A 32)
Church Rd. Lydd —3C 204
Church Rd. Lym —7D 204 (1E 41)
Church Rd. Mgte —4D 208
Church Rd. Mer —9L 161 (2B 40)
Church Rd. Mol —2A 30
Church Rd. M'fld —3A 44
Church Rd. Murs —7J 99 (2C 19)
Church Rd. New Ash —3M 89
Church Rd. New R —3B 212 (2E 47)
Church Rd. Oare —2F 186 (3A 20)
Church Rd. Off —2J 123
Church Rd. Otham —2E 27
Church Rd. Pad W —8M 147 (4B 26)
Church Rd. Pem —5C 152
Church Rd. Ram —5J 211
Church Rd. Rob —2B 44
Church Rd. Roth —4D 35
Church Rd. Rya —7L 107
Church Rd. Sand —4H 215 (2C 44)
Church Rd. Seal —3N 119
Church Rd. Sev —5E 120 (3D 25)
Church Rd. Svgtn —3L 161 (1A 40)
Church Rd. Short —6H 69 (1E 13)
Church Rd. Sidc —9J 57
Church Rd. Sole S —2H 77
Church Rd. S'boro —4F 150 (1E 35)
Church Rd. Stal —3E 29
Church Rd. Sund —9N 117 (2C 24)
Church Rd. S at H —3M 73 (1D 15)
Church Rd. Swan —1E 86 (2C 15)
(Crockenhill)
Church Rd. Swan —4L 73 (1D 15)
(Swanley Village)
Church Rd. Swans —4M 61
Church Rd. Tent —8B 222
Church Rd. Til —3B 8
Church Rd. Tonge —7M 99 (2D 19)
Church Rd. Tovil —7B 126 (2D 27)
Church Rd. Tun W —2F 156 (2E 35)
Church Rd. Weald —5J 131
Church Rd. Well —9K 51
Church Rd. W'ham —2B 24
Church Rd. W King —8E 88
Church Rd. W Mal —1B 26
Church Rd. W Peck —2F 134 (2B 26)
Church Rd. W'boro —1K 161 (1A 40)
(in two parts)
Church Rd. Wor Pk —2A 12
Church Rd. Bus. Cen. Sit —5J 99
Church Rd. Cotts. Off —9K 107
Church Row. Chst —4E 70
Church Row. Snod —3E 108
Church Row M. Chst —3E 70
Churchsettle La. Shov G —4B 36
Churchside. Meop —2F 106
(in two parts)
Churchside Clo. Big H —5C 164
Church Sq. Broad —9M 209
Church Sq. Len —7E 200
Church Street. —4H 65 (4C 9)
(nr. Higham)
Church Street. —4H 225
(nr. Whitstable)
Church St. E16 —1D 50
Church St. Bou M —5E 138 (3E 27)
Church St. Broad —7J 209 (1E 23)
Church St. Bur —3D 17
Church St. Burh —2J 109
Church St. Chat —8D 80
(in two parts)
Church St. Cli —4C 176
Church St. Clif —4D 9
Church St. Cowd —1B 34
Church St. Croy —2D 13
Church St. Dover —5J 181
Church St. E'try —3L 183
Church St. Eden —6C 184
Church St. Eps —3A 12
Church St. Fav —4H 187
Church St. Folk —7K 189
Church St. Gill —6H 81 (1E 17)
Church St. Grav —4G 62
Church St. Hdlw —8D 134
Church St. H'shm —3N 141 (2B 28)
Church St. High —7G 65 (4C 9)
Church St. Hoo —9H 67 (4E 9)
Church St. Loose —3C 138 (2D 27)
Church St. Maid —5D 126
Church St. Mgte —4D 208
Church St. Mil R —6F 98
Church St. Min —8N 205 (2C 23)
Church St. Non —3F 162 (2B 32)
Church St. Roch —8A 80
Church St. Rod —3K 115 (3D 19)
Church St. S'wch —5M 217
Church St. Seal —3A 120 (1D 25)
Church St. Shor —2G 103 (3C 15)
Church St. Sit —7F 98
Church St. S'fleet —1N 75
Church St. St D —1L 171 (4D 21)
Church St. Tstn —1E 136
Church St. Tic —4C 36
Church St. Tonb —5J 145
Church St. Tovil —7B 126
Church St. Walm —9L 177
Church St. Whits —4H 225 (2C 21)
Church St. Wdboro —8G 217
Church St. Wye —2M 159 (4B 30)
Church St. St Mary's. S'wch —5L 217
Church St. St Paul's. Cant —2N 171 (1D 31)
Church Ter. SE13 —1H 55
Church Ter. Chat —1F 94
Church Ter. Maid —6E 126
Church Trad. Est., The. Eri —7G 53
Church Vale. SE23 —7A 54
Church View. Adgtn —2B 40
Church View. Bidd —7K 163
Church View. H Bay —3K 195
Church View. Newch —4B 40
Church View. Swan —6E 72
Church Vs. Lydd —3C 204
Church Vs. Sev —4F 118
Church Wlk. Ayle —7K 109
Church Wlk. Dart —8L 59
Church Wlk. E Mal —2E 124
Church Wlk. Elham —7N 183
(off Pound La.)
Church Wlk. Eyns —4M 87
Church Wlk. Grav —6J 63
Church Wlk. Hawkh —6L 191
Church Wlk. H'crn —3K 193
Church Way. S Croy —3D 13
Church Way. Whits —2M 225
Church Whitfield. —5G 179 (4C 33)
Church Whitfield Rd. Wald —3F 178
Church Whitfield Rd. Whitf —4C 33
Church Wood Clo. R Comn —9H 167
Churchwood Dri. Ches —4M 225
Church Yd. Afrd —8F 158
Churn La. Horsm —1C 36
Chute Clo. Gill —7N 95
Chyngton Clo. Sidc —8H 57
Cibber Rd. SE23 —7A 54
Cimba Wood. Grav —9K 63
Cinderford Way. Brom —9H 55
Cinder Hill. —4D 25
Cinder Hill La. Leigh —6K 143 (4D 25)
Cinder Path. Broad —9L 209
Cinnabar Clo. Chat —1D 110
Cinque Ports Av. Hythe —7J 197
Cinque Ports St. Rye —3A 46
Circular Rd. Bett —2D 33
Circular Rd. Dover —3N 181
Circular Way. SE18 —6B 50
Circus Rd. NW8 —2B 4
Cirrus Cres. Grav —1K 77
Citadel Cres. Dover —6G 181
Citadel Heights. Dover —6G 181
Citadel Rd. Dover —6G 181
Citroen Clo. H Bay —3C 194
City. —2D 5
City Bus. Pk. Cant —8B 168
City Rd. EC1 —2C 5
City View. Cant —2J 171
City Way. Roch —8A 80 (2D 17)
Clacket La. W'ham —6A 116 (2A 24)
Clackhams La. Crowb —4D 35
Clacton Rd. E6 —2A 6
Claire Ct. Broad —8M 209
Claire Ho. Maid —4B 126
Clairville Point. SE23 —8A 54
(off Dacres Rd.)
Clandon Rd. Chat —9G 94 (3E 17)
Clanricarde Gdns. Tun W —2G 157
Clanricarde Rd. Tun W —2G 157
Clanwilliam Rd. Deal —5N 177
Clapham. —4C 4
Clapham Common. (Junct.) —4C 4
Clapham Comn. N. Side. SW4 —4C 4
Clapham Comn. S. Side. SW4 —4C 4
Clapham Comn. W. Side. SW4 —4B 4
Clapham High St. SW4 —4C 4
Clapham Hill. Whits —8E 224 (2C 21)
Clapham Junction. —4B 4
Clapham Park. —4C 4
Clapham Pk. Rd. SW4 —4C 4
Clapham Rd. SW9 —4C 5
Claphatch La. Birch G —3B 36
Clap Hill. —2B 40
Clapper Hill. —2B 38
Clapper Hill. S Min —4D 31
Clapper La. S'hrst —7H 221 (4E 27)
Clappers, The. Rob —3A 44
Clapton Park. —1D 5
Clara Pl. SE18 —4C 50
Clare Av. Tonb —6F 144
Clare Corner. SE9 —5D 56
Clare Dri. H Bay —5D 194
Clare La. E Mal —1C 124 (1C 26)
Claremont Av. N Mald —2A 12
Claremont Clo. E16 —1C 50
Claremont Clo. Kgdn —3M 199
Claremont Clo. Orp —5C 84
Claremont Cres. Dart —2F 58
Claremont Gdns. Ram —5G 210
Claremont Gdns. Tun W —3H 157
Claremont Pl. Cant —3M 171
Claremont Pl. Chat —9D 80
Claremont Pl. Grav —5G 62
Claremont Pl. Ram —4J 211
Claremont Rd. NW2 —1A 4
Claremont Rd. Brom —7A 70
Claremont Rd. Deal —5L 177
Claremont Rd. Folk —6J 189
Claremont Rd. Kgdn —3M 199
Claremont Rd. Maid —4E 126
Claremont Rd. Swan —3F 72
Claremont Rd. Tun W —3H 157
Claremont St. E16 —2C 50
Claremont St. H Bay —4D 194
Claremont Ter. Wdboro —7J 217
Claremont Way. Chat —9C 80
Clarence Av. Brom —7A 70
Clarence Av. Clift —3H 209
Clarence Av. N Mald —1A 12
Clarence Av. Roch —8N 79
Clarence Ct. Weav —5H 127
Clarence Cres. Sidc —8K 57
Clarence Gdns. Ward —5J 203
Clarence La. SW15 —4A 4
Clarence Pl. Deal —3N 177
Clarence Pl. Dover —7J 181
Clarence Pl. Grav —5G 62
Clarence Rd. SE9 —7A 56
Clarence Rd. Bexh —2N 57
Clarence Rd. Big H —6F 164
Clarence Rd. Brom —6N 69
Clarence Rd. Cap F —3B 174
Clarence Rd. Chat —1E 94
Clarence Rd. Grays —3A 8
Clarence Rd. H Bay —2E 194
Clarence Rd. Ram —6F 210
Clarence Rd. Sidc —8K 57
Clarence Rd. Tun W —2G 157
Clarence Rd. Walm —7N 177 (3E 33)
Clarence Row. Grav —5G 63
Clarence Row. S'ness —2D 218
Clarence Row. Tun W —2G 156
Clarence St. Folk —6K 189
Clarence St. H Bay —2F 194
Clarenden Pl. Wilm —1F 72
Clarendon. —5G 181
Clarendon Clo. Bear —5K 127
Clarendon Clo. Sit —1G 114
Clarendon Clo. St P —6J 71
Clarendon Ct. Beck —4E 68
(off Albemarle Rd.)
Clarendon Gdns. Dart —5D 60
Clarendon Gdns. Ram —6H 211
Clarendon Gdns. Roch —3L 79
Clarendon Gdns. Tun W —4G 156
Clarendon Grn. Orp —7J 71
Clarendon Gro. St P —7J 71
Clarendon M. Bex —6C 58
Clarendon M. Broad —9L 209
Clarendon M. New R —1D 212
Clarendon Path. St P —7J 71
(in two parts)
Clarendon Pl. Dover —5H 181
Clarendon Pl. Maid —5D 126
(off King St.)
Clarendon Pl. Sev —7H 119
Clarendon Rise. SE13 —2F 54
Clarendon Rd. W11 —2B 4
Clarendon Rd. Aysm —2D 162
Clarendon Rd. Broad —9L 209
Clarendon Rd. Dover —5H 181
Clarendon Rd. Grav —4H 63
Clarendon Rd. Mgte —3E 208
Clarendon Rd. Sev —6H 119
Clarendon St. Dover —5G 181
Clarendon St. H Bay —3D 194
Clarendon Way. Chst & St M —6H 71
Clarendon Way. Tun W —4F 156
Clarens St. SE6 —7C 54
Clare Rd. Whits —3G 225
Clareville Rd. Orp —3E 84
Clare Way. Bexh —8N 51
Clare Way. Sev —1K 131
Clare Wood Dri. E Mal —1C 124
Clark Clo. Eri —8H 53
Clarke Cres. Kenn —5J 159
Clarke Rd. G'stne —5F 212
Clarkes Clo. Deal —6J 177
Clarke's Grn. Rd. Sev —5A 104 (3D 15)
Clark M. Roy B —9K 109
Clarks La. Hals —3A 102
Clarks La. Warl & Tats —5A 116 (2A 24)
Claston Clo. Dart —2F 58
Clavadel Rd. Pad W —8M 147
Clavell Clo. Gill —8A 96
Clavering Ho. SE13 —2G 55
(off Blessington Rd.)
Claverton St. SW1 —3C 4
Claxfield Rd. Lyn —4H 223 (3D 19)
Claxton Path. SE4 —2A 54
(off Coston Wlk.)
Claybank Gro. SE13 —1E 54
Claybridge Rd. SE12 —9M 55
Claydown M. SE18 —5C 50

Combe Bank Dri.—Court Lodge

Combe Bank Dri. Sund —4N 117
Combeside. SE18 —7H 51
Combwell Cres. SE2 —3J 51
Combwell Priory. —3C 37
Comerford Rd. SE4 —2B 54
Command Rd. Maid —1C 126
Commerce Way. Eden —4C 184
Commercial Pl. Grav —4H 63
Commercial Rd. E1 & E14 —2D 5
Commercial Rd. Pad W —9L 147 (4B 26)
Commercial Rd. Roch —5L 79 (1D 17)
(in two parts)
Commercial Rd. Tonb —7H 145
Commercial Rd. Tun W —9H 151
Commercial St. E1 —2D 5
Commercial Way. SE15 —3D 5
Commissioners Rd. Strood —4N 79
Commodore Rd. Maid —4F 126
Common La. C'den —4D 9
Common La. Cli —2D 176
Common La. Clif —3D 9
Common La. Dart —7H 59 (4D 7)
Common La. Dover —1D 180 (1C 42)
Common Rd. Chat —8L 93 (3D 17)
Common Rd. Cli —8M 65
Common Rd. Hdlw —6D 134 (3A 26)
Common Rd. Igh —5H 121 (2E 25)
Common Rd. Rust —1C 156
Common Rd. Siss —7B 220 (2E 37)
Commonside. Kes —5M 83 (2A 14)
Commonside E. Mitc —1C 12
Commonside W. Mitc —1B 12
Common, The. —6E 134
Common, The. Roch —6N 79
Common Wall. Cli —2E 176
Common Way. Hoth —4E 29
(off School Rd.)
Commonwealth Clo. Sit —8J 99
Commonwealth Way. SE2 —5K 51
Commority Rd. Meop —1G 107 (3B 16)
Como Rd. SE23 —7B 54
Comp. —3D 122 (1A 26)
Compass Cen. Chat —4E 80
Compass Clo. Roch —2N 93
Compasses La. Stapl —3B 44
Compasses Rd. Charc —4J 143
Compasses Rd. Leigh —4D 25
Comp La. Platt —3B 122 (1A 26)
Comp Rd. Wro H —3D 122
Compton Clo. Chat —9G 95
Compton Pl. Eri —6G 52
Concord Av. Chat —6B 94
Concord Clo. Pad W —9K 147
Concord Clo. Tun W —1J 157
Concorde Bus. Pk. Big H —3D 164
Condover Cres. SE18 —7D 50
Conduit Rd. SE18 —5D 50
Conduit St. W1 —2C 4
Conduit St. Fav —4H 187
Coneyburrow Rd. Tun W —9L 151
Coney Hall. —4H 83 (2E 13)
Coney Hall Pde. W Wick —4H 83
Coney Hill Rd. W Wick —3H 83 (2E 13)
Coney M. Chat —2D 94
Conference Rd. SE2 —4L 51
Conference Wlk. Cant —2B 172
(off Russett Rd.)
Congelow. —9D 136 (3C 26)
Conghurst La. Hawkh —9M 191 (1B 44)
Congleton Gro. SE18 —5E 50
Congo Rd. SE18 —5F 50
Congress Rd. SE2 —4L 51
Congreve Rd. SE9 —1B 56
Conifer Av. Hart —9L 75
Conifer Clo. Orp —5F 84
Conifer Ct. Wgte S —2L 207
Conifer Dri. Chat —1G 110
Conifer Dri. Meop —9E 90
Conifer Ho. SE4 —2C 54
(off Brockley Rd.)
Conifer Way. Swan —4D 72
Coniffe Ct. SE9 —3D 56
Conisborough Ct. Dart —4B 60
(off Osbourne Rd.)
Conisborough Cres. SE6 —8F 54
Coniscliffe Clo. Chst —4C 70
Coniston Av. Ram —5E 210
Coniston Av. Tun W —1E 156
Coniston Av. Well —1G 56
Coniston Clo. Bexh —8D 52
Coniston Clo. Dart —6J 59
Coniston Clo. Eri —7F 52
Coniston Clo. Gill —6K 81
Coniston Dri. Aysm —2D 162
Coniston Ho. Maid —1H 139
Coniston Rd. Bexh —8D 52
Coniston Rd. Brom —2H 69
Coniston Rd. Folk —5H 189
Conker Clo. Afrd —6G 161
Connaught Bri. E16 —2A 6
Connaught Clo. Maid —4J 139
Connaught Gdns. Mgte —4D 208
Connaught M. SE18 —5C 50
Connaught M. Chat —1F 94
Connaught Rd. SE18 —5C 50
Connaught Rd. Chat —1E 94
Connaught Rd. Dover —3J 181 (1C 43)
Connaught Rd. Folk —6K 189
Connaught Rd. Gill —7G 80
Connaught Rd. Mgte —4D 208
Connaught Rd. Sit —8F 98
Connaught St. W2 —2B 4
Connaught Way. Tun W —9F 150
Connections Ind. Cen. Sev —1K 119
Connors Ho. Cant —1A 172
Conquest Ind. Est. Roch —7L 79
Conrad Av. Cant —8B 168
Conrad Clo. Gill —7N 95
(in two parts)
Consort Clo. Maid —4E 126
Constable Rd. Birch —3F 206
Constable Rd. N'fleet —8D 62
Constable Rd. Tonb —2L 145
Constables Rd. Dover —3K 181
Constable View. Walm —7M 177
Constance Cres. Brom —1J 83
Constance St. E16 —1A 50
Constitutional Hill Rd. Tun W
—5E 150 (1E 35)
Constitution Cres. Grav —6H 63
(off Constitution Hill)
Constitution Hill. Chat —9E 80
Constitution Hill. Grav —6H 63
Constitution Hill. Snod —2D 108 (3C 16)
Constitution Rise. SE18 —8C 50
Constitution Rd. Chat —9E 80
Consul Clo. H Bay —3C 194
Consul Gdns. Swan —3H 73
Contessa Clo. Orp —6G 84
Continental App. Mgte —7D 208
Convalescent La. Siss —6B 220
Convent Clo. Beck —3F 68
Convent Clo. St Mc —7K 213
Convent Rd. Broad —5K 209 (1E 23)
Convent Wlk. Ram —7F 210
Conway Clo. Birch —4D 206
Conway Clo. Roch —3J 79
Conway Clo. Salt —4J 197
Conway Rd. SE18 —4F 50
Conway Rd. Maid —3N 125
Conways Rd. Ors —2B 8
Conyer. —2E 19
Conyerd Rd. Bor G —2M 121
Conyer Rd. Con —2E 19
Conyer Rd. Tey —2L 223 (3E 19)
Conyers Wlk. Gill —7N 95
Conyngham Clo. Ram —2F 210
Conyngham La. Bri —8F 172
Conyngham Rd. H Bay —2L 195
Conyngham Rd. Min —8N 205
Cooden Clo. Brom —3L 69
Cooden Clo. Gill —1C 96
Cook Clo. Chat —5F 94
Cook Ct. Eri —7G 53
Cook Gro. Eden —6C 184
Cookham Dene Clo. Chst —4F 70
Cookham Hill. Orp —4B 86
Cookham Hill. Roch —1L 93
Cookham Rd. Swan —4B 72 (1C 14)
Cookham Wood Pl. Bear —6K 127
Cookham Wood Rd. Roch —3M 93
Cookhill Rd. SE2 —2K 51
Cook La. Afrd —2F 160
Cooks Cotts. W'bury —1A 136
Cook's La. Sit —5F 98
Cook's Lea. E'try —3K 183
Cookson Gro. Eri —7C 52
Cook Sq. Eri —7G 53
Cooling. —4F 176 (4D 9)
Cooling Clo. Maid —3F 126
Cooling Comn. Cli —5N 65 (4D 9)
Coolinge. —6F 188 (2A 42)
Coolinge La. Folk —6F 188 (2A 42)
Coolinge Rd. Folk —6J 189
Cooling Rd. Cli —4C 176
(in two parts)
Cooling Rd. Clif —4D 9
Cooling Rd. C'ing —1E 66
Cooling Rd. H Hals —1F 66
Cooling Rd. Roch —2M 79 (1D 17)
Cooling Street. —3A 66 (4D 9)
Cooling St. Cli —4E 176 (4D 9)
Coombe. —6E 216 (1C 32)
Coombe Av. Sev —2J 119
Coombe Clo. Chat —8E 94
Coombe Clo. Dover —3F 180
Coombe Clo. Snod —3E 108
Coombe Ct. Dover —3F 180
Coombe Ct. Sev —2J 119
Coombe Dri. Sit —7K 99
Coombe Farm La. St Mh —3A 10
Coombe Gro. Hoth —4E 29
Coombelands. Wit —2E 45
Coombe La. SW20 —1A 12
Coombe Lane. (Junct.) —1A 12
Coombe La. Ah —6D 216 (1C 32)
Coombe La. Croy —2D 13
Coombe La. Tent —8B 222
Coombe La. Flyover. King T & SW20
—1A 12
Coombe La. W. King T —1A 12
Coombe Lea. Brom —6A 70
Coombe Rd. Croy —2D 13
Coombe Rd. Dover —5A 180 (1B 42)
(in two parts)
Coombe Rd. Folk —5F 188
Coombe Rd. Grav —7H 63
Coombe Rd. Hoo —8H 67
Coombe Rd. King T —1A 12
Coombe Rd. Maid —7C 126
Coombe Rd. N Mald —1A 12
Coombe Rd. Otf —6K 103
Coombe Valley Rd. Dover
—4F 180 (1C 43)
Coombe Wlk. York —1A 166 (3C 20)
Coombe Way. H'nge —8E 192
Coombe Wood La. H'nge —8E 192
Coombfield. Eden —7C 184
Coombfield Dri. Dart —9D 60
Coomb Hill. —2B 16
Cooper Clo. Grnh —3F 60
Cooper Rd. Chat —8D 94
Cooper Rd. Snod —4D 108
Coopers Clo. S Dar —4D 74
Cooper's Corner. —8A 130 (3C 24)
Coopers Hill. H Bay —2G 195
Cooper's La. SE12 —7L 55
Coopers La. Cant —3L 171
Coopers La. Ford —7K 149 (1D 35)
Cooper's La. S'ndge —2C 40
Cooper's La. W Til —3B 8
Coopers Rd. N'fleet —6E 62
Coopers Rd. Swans —4M 61
Cooper Street. —2F 216 (4C 23)
Cooper St. Drove. Ah —2F 216 (4C 23)
Coote Rd. Bexh —8A 52
Cooting La. Adm —2A 32
Cooting Rd. Aysm —2B 162 (2A 32)
Copenhagen Rd. Gill —7F 80
Copenhagen St. N1 —2C 5
Copers Cope Rd. Beck —3C 68
Copinger Clo. Cant —7N 167
Copland Av. Min S —6K 219
Copley Dene. Brom —4N 69
Coppards La. N'iam —2D 45
Coppelia Rd. SE3 —2J 55
Copper Beech Clo. Grav —5J 63
Copper Beech Clo. Orp —8L 71
Copperfield Cvn. Pk. E'chu —3E 202
Copperfield Clo. Grav —6M 63
Copperfield Clo. Kenn —4G 159
Copperfield Ct. Broad —8M 209
Copperfield Cres. High —2G 78
Copperfield Dri. Langl —4A 140
Copperfield Ho. Chat —8C 80
Copperfield Rd. Roch —1N 93
Copperfields. Beck —4F 68
Copperfields. Dart —4M 59
(off Spital St.)
Copperfields. Kems —8N 103
Copperfields. Lydd —3B 204
Copperfields Clo. Kems —8N 103
Copperfields Orchard. Kems —8N 103
Copperfields, The. Roch —8M 79
Copperfields Wlk. Kems —8N 103
Copperfield Way. Chst —2E 70
Coppergate. Cant —9M 167
Coppergate. Hem —6J 95
Coppergate Clo. Brom —4L 69
Copperhouse La. Gill —6L 81
Copperhouse Rd. Roch —5G 79
Copperhurst Wlk. Clift —3J 209
Copper La. Mard —3M 205 (4D 27)
Copperpenny Dri. Hem —8L 95
Coppers La. Matf —5K 153 (1B 36)
Copper Tree Ct. Maid —3D 138
Coppertree Wlk. Chat —1F 110
Copperwood. Afrd —6G 159
Coppice Ct. Hem —7L 95
Coppice Rd. Chat —9F 94
Coppice, The. Ayle —9J 109
Coppice, The. Meop —2G 106
Coppice, The. Pem —7C 152
Coppice, The. Sturry —5E 168
Coppice View. Weav —3H 127
Coppings Rd. Charc —4J 143
Copping's Rd. Leigh —4D 25
Coppins' Corner. —4J 175 (3D 29)
Coppins La. B'den —9C 98
Coppins, The. New Ad —7E 82
Coppin St. Deal —4N 177
Copse Av. W Wick —4E 82
Copse Bank. Seal —2N 119
Copse Hill. —1A 12
Copse Hill. SW20 —1A 12
Copsehill. Leyb —8C 108
Copse Rd. Hild —3E 144
Copse Side. Hart —6L 75
Copse, The. Afrd —7B 158
Copse, The. Hoo —1H 81
Copse View. S Croy —9A 82
Copsewood Clo. Sidc —4G 56
Copsewood Way. Bear —6K 127
Cop Street. —2D 216 (4C 22)
Cop St. Rd. Ah —3C 216 (4C 22)
Copt Clo. Sturry —4E 168
Coptefield Dri. Belv —3M 51
Copthall Av. Hawkh —6L 191
Copthall Gdns. Folk —6K 189
Copt Hall Rd. Cob —7G 76 (1B 16)
Copt Hall Rd. Igh —5G 121 (2E 25)
Copthorne Av. Brom —3B 84
Copton. —9H 187 (4A 20)
Coralline Wlk. SE2 —2L 51
Corbets Tey. —1E 7
Corbets Tey Rd. Upm —1D 7
Corbett Ct. SE26 —9C 54
Corbylands Rd. Sidc —6G 56
Cordelia Cres. Roch —1K 93
Cordingham Rd. Sea —7C 224
Cordova Ct. Folk —7H 189
Cordwell Rd. SE13 —3H 55
Corelli Rd. SE3 —9A 50
Corhaven Ho. Eri —7F 52
Corinthian Ct. Isle G —3C 190
Corinthian Manorway. Eri —4E 52
Corinthian Rd. Eri —4E 52
Cork La. S'hrst —1E 37
Corkscrew Hill. W Wick —3F 82 (2E 13)
Cork St. Eccl —4K 109
Corkwell St. Chat —9B 80
Cormorant Clo. Roch —5G 78
Cornel Ho. Sidc —8J 57
Cornelia Pl. Eri —6F 52
Cornell Clo. Sidc —2N 71
Corner Farm Rd. S'hrst —7J 221
Corner Field. Kgnt —4F 160
Corner, The. —1C 37
Corn Exchange, The. Maid —5C 126
(off Market Bldgs.)
Cornfield Way. Tonb —1K 145
Cornflower Clo. Weav —5H 127
Cornflower La. Croy —2A 82
Cornford Clo. Brom —8K 69
Cornford Clo. Tun W —8B 152
Cornford La. Tun W —1L 157 (2A 36)
Cornford Pk. Pem —8B 152
Cornford Rd. Birch —5F 206
Cornforth Clo. S'hrst —7K 221
Cornhill. Ram —6J 211
Corniche, The. S'gte —8C 188
Corn Mill Dri. Orp —1J 85
Cornmill La. SE13 —1F 54
Cornwall Av. Ram —4K 211
Cornwall Av. Well —1G 57
Cornwall Clo. Maid —1H 139
Cornwall Cres. W11 —2B 4
Cornwall Cres. Woul —7H 93
Cornwall Dri. Orp —3L 71
Cornwall Gdns. Cant —3C 172
Cornwall Gdns. Clift —3F 208
Cornwall Ga. Purf —4D 52
Cornwall Ho. Deal —5K 177
Cornwall Ho. Dover —5J 181
(off Military Rd.)
Cornwallis Av. SE9 —7F 56
Cornwallis Av. Aysm —2D 162
Cornwallis Av. Chat —2B 94
Cornwallis Av. Folk —5H 189 (2A 42)
Cornwallis Av. Gill —8J 81 (2E 17)
(in two parts)
Cornwallis Av. H Bay —4K 195
Cornwallis Av. Lin —9B 138
Cornwallis Av. Tonb —3L 145 (4A 26)
Cornwallis Circ. Whits —4E 224
Cornwallis Clo. Eri —6G 53
Cornwallis Clo. Folk —5H 189
Cornwallis Clo. W'boro —2M 161
Cornwallis Cotts. Langl —6B 138
Cornwallis Gdns. Broad —7L 209
Cornwallis Ho. S'ness —2B 218
(off Sheppey St.)
Cornwallis Rd. Maid —5A 126
Cornwallis Wlk. SE9 —1B 56
Cornwall Rd. Dart —1N 59
Cornwall Rd. Gill —6G 80
Cornwall Rd. H Bay —5C 194
Cornwall Rd. Roch —9N 79
Cornwall Rd. Walm —7M 177 (3E 33)
Cornwell Av. Grav —8H 63
Corona Rd. SE12 —5K 55
Corona Ter. Snod —4D 108
Coronation Clo. Bex —4M 57
Coronation Clo. Broad —6J 209
Coronation Cotts. Folk —5D 188
(off Cheriton High St.)
Coronation Cotts. Rod —1L 115
Coronation Cotts. Up Stok —9H 201
Coronation Ct. Eri —7E 52
Coronation Cres. Mgte —3N 207
Coronation Cres. Queen —7A 218
Coronation Dri. Gt Cha —9A 158
Coronation Dri. Horn —1D 7
Coronation Dri. Ley S —6J 203
Coronation Flats. Chat —9C 80
Coronation Pde. Folk —6M 189
Coronation Rd. NW10 —2A 4
Coronation Rd. Chat —1F 94
Coronation Rd. Isle G —3C 190
Coronation Rd. Ram —6H 211
Coronation Rd. S'ness —3D 218
Coronation Rd. Whits —8E 224
Coronation Sq. Lydd —3C 204
Coronation Vs. Eyt —4K 185
Corone Clo. Folk —4G 188
Corporation Cotts. Ayle —7J 109
Corporation Rd. Gill —6G 81
Corporation St. Roch —6N 79 (1D 17)
Corporation Yd. Gill —8M 81
Corral Clo. Chat —1G 94
Corrall Almshouses. Maid —6D 126
Corrance Grn. Maid —9D 126
Correnden Rd. Tonb —3G 144
Corringham. —2C 9
Corringham Rd. Stan H —2C 8
Corseley Rd. Groom —7J 155 (3D 35)
Corsican Wlk. H Bay —4K 195
Cortland Clo. Sit —5F 98
Cortland M. Sit —5F 98
Corunna Clo. Hythe —6H 197
Corunna Pl. B Hts —1K 181
Corylus Dri. Whits —6C 224
Corys Rd. Roch —6N 79
Coryton. —2D 9
Cossack St. Roch —9N 79
Cossington Rd. Cant —3N 171 (1D 31)
Cossington Rd. Chat —2D 110
(in two parts)
Costells Meadow. W'ham —8F 116
Coston Wlk. SE4 —2A 54
Costume Museum. —5N 177
Cotchford Hill. Hartf —3B 34
Cot La. Bidd —6M 163 (2B 38)
Cotleigh Av. Bex —7M 57
Cotmandene Cres. Orp —5K 71
Cotman's Ash. —6D 104 (4D 15)
Cotman's Ash La. Kems
—5B 104 (3D 15)
Cotman Way. E Peck —1K 147
Coton Rd. Well —1J 57
Coton St. E14 —2E 5
Cotswold Clo. Afrd —6F 158
Cotswold Clo. Bexh —9F 52
Cotswold Gdns. Down —8K 127
Cotswold Rise. Orp —9H 71
Cotswold Rd. N'fleet —8D 62
Cotswold Rd. Sutt —3B 12
Cottage Av. Brom —2A 84
Cottage Field Clo. Sidc —6L 57
Cottage Ind. Est. Ayle —8M 109
Cottage La. Sed —4C 44
Cottage Rd. Chat —6C 80
Cottage Rd. Ram —6J 211
Cottage Row. S'wch —5L 217
Cottall Av. Chat —1C 94
Cottenham Clo. E Mal —2D 124
Cottenham Park. —1A 12
Cottenham Pk. Rd. SW20 —1A 12
Cottingham Rd. SE20 —3A 68
Cottington Rd. C'snd —7A 210 (2D 23)
Cottongrass Clo. Croy —2A 82
Cotton Hill. Brom —9F 54
Cotton Hill Houses. Hams —8D 190
(off Ruckinge Rd.)
Cotton Hill Wlk. Hams —8D 190
Cotton La. Dart & Grnh —4C 60 (4E 7)
Cotton Rd. Win I —3K 171
Couldridge La. Eri —3M 51
Coulgate St. SE4 —1B 54
Coulman St. Gill —8G 81
Coulsdon. —4C 12
Coulsdon La. Coul —4C 12
Coulsdon Rd. Coul & Cat —4C 13
Coulson Gro. N'brne —3D 33
Coulter Ho. Grnh —3J 61
Coulter Rd. H Bay —5C 194
Coulters Clo. Weav —5G 127
Coulton Av. N'fleet —5D 62
Council Av. N'fleet —4B 62
Council Cotts. Maid —4L 137
Countess Mountbatten Ct. Wgte S
—3K 207
Country's Field. Dym —7B 182
Country Way. Afrd —5F 160
(off Roman Way)
County Ga. SE9 —8E 56
County Gro. W Mal —1N 123
County Rd. Maid —4D 126
County Sq. Afrd —8F 158
Coupland Pl. SE18 —5E 50
Coursehorn La. C'brk —7F 176 (3E 37)
Course, The. SE9 —8C 56
Court App. Folk —7J 189
Court-at-Street. —3C 40
Courtauld Clo. SE28 —1J 51
Court Av. Belv —5A 52
Court Broomes. E Sut —8E 140
Court Cotts. W'hm —3B 226
Court Cres. Swan —7F 72
Court Downs Rd. Beck —5E 68
Court Dri. Maid —5A 126
Courtenay Dri. Beck —5G 68
Courtenay Rd. SE20 —2A 68
Courtenay Rd. Deal —2M 177
Courtenay Rd. Dunk —4N 165 (4B 20)
Courteney Rd. Gill —4L 95
Courtenwell. L'tn G —1M 155
Court Farm Rd. SE9 —7N 55
Courtfield Av. Chat —9E 94
Courtfield Rise. W Wick —4G 83
Court Flats. W'hm —3B 226
Court Hall. Queen —7A 218
(off North Rd.)
Court Hall Museum. —5F 98 (2C 19)
Court Hill. L'brne —8K 169 (4A 22)
Court Hill Ho. Temp E —9D 178
Courthill Rd. SE13 —2F 54 (4E 5)
Courthope. Pad W —9M 147
Courtland Av. Whitf —7F 178
Courtland Dri. Dover —9D 178
Courtlands. Tstn —9E 124
Courtlands. Tonb —3G 145
Courtlands. Walm —3N 199
Courtlands Av. SE12 —3L 55
Courtlands Av. Brom —2H 83
Courtlands Way. Wgte S —2L 207
Court La. SE21 —4D 5
Court La. Det —5M 111 (3A 18)
Court La. Hdlw —8E 134 (3A 26)
Court La. Pres —3B 22
Court La. Pl. Hdlw —8E 134
(in two parts)
Courtleet Dri. Eri —8C 52
Court Lodge. Belv —5B 52
Court Lodge. Shorne —2C 78

Court Lodge Cotts.—Crownfields

Court Lodge Cotts. H'shm —1M 141
(in two parts)
Court Lodge Cotts. Maid —1L 137
Court Lodge Rd. App —1B 46
Court Lodge Rd. Gill —6J 81
Court Lodge Rd. H'shm —9L 129
Court Meadow. Wro —7M 105
Court Meadows. L'brne —2L 173
Court Mt. Mobile Home Pk. Birch —5F 206
Courtnay Rd. Maid —7C 126
Court Pl. Folk —7J 189
(off Castle Hill Av.)
Courtrai Rd. SE23 —4B 54
Court Rd. SE9 —4B 56 (4A 6)
Court Rd. Bur —3C 17
Court Rd. Burh —1H 109
Court Rd. Dart —1E 74
Court Rd. Gill —3C 96
Court Rd. Orp —1K 85 (2B 14)
Court Rd. S'gte —9B 188
Court Rd. Sit —4G 98
Court Rd. St N —7C 214 (2B 22)
Court Rd. Tun W —1E 156
Court Rd. Walm —9K 177 (3E 33)
Courts, The. Mgte —2M 207
Court St. Brom —5K 69
Court St. Fav —5H 187
Courtwood Dri. Sev —6H 119
Court Wood La. Croy —9C 82
Court Wurtin. Afrd —2E 160
Court Yd. SE9 —4B 56
Courtyard, The. Gill B —3K 95
Courtyard, The. W'ham —9F 116
Cousley Wood. —3B 36
Cousley Wood Rd. Spar G & Cous W —3A 36
Coutts Av. Shorne —9C 64
Covell's Row. Mgte —3C 208
Coventina Ho. Ram —5H 211
(off High St. Ramsgate,)
Coventon La. S'wch & Worth —8L 217
Coventry Clo. Roch —6H 79
Coventry Gdns. H Bay —2L 195
Coventry Ho. Maid —1G 138
Coventry Rd. Tonb —2K 145
Coverack Clo. Croy —1B 82
Coverdale Av. Maid —2G 138
Coverdale Clo. Chat —4E 94
Covert La. W'wd —3E 31
Covert Rd. Aysm —3C 162
Covert, The. Chat —1D 110
Covert, The. Meop —3D 106
Covert, The. Orp —9G 70
Covet La. Kgtn —7A 162
Covet Wood Clo. Orp —9H 71
Covey Hall Rd. Snod —2E 108
Cowbeck Clo. Gill —5N 95
Cowden. —1B 34
Cowden Clo. Hawkh —8J 191
Cowden La. Hawkh —8J 191
Cowden M. Cowd —1B 34
Cowden Pound. —1B 34
Cowden Rd. Maid —4F 126
Cowden Rd. Orp —1H 85
Cowden St. SE6 —9D 54
Cowdray Rd. Deal —7K 177
Cowdray Sq. Deal —7L 177
Cowdrey Clo. Maid —8M 125
Cowdrey Clo. Roch —1M 93
Cowdrey Clo. W'boro —2L 161
Cowdrey Ct. Dart —5J 59
Cowdrey Pl. Cant —4A 172
Cowgate Hill. Dover —5J 181
Cowgate La. H'nge —6E 192 (1A 42)
Cow La. Dover —5F 180
Cow La. Mark B —1B 34
Cow La. Win I —3K 171
Cowley Av. Grnh —3F 60
Cowley Rise. Mgte —5G 209
Cowper Clo. Brom —7N 69
Cowper Clo. Well —3J 57
Cowper Clo. Whits —2M 225
Cowper Rd. Belv —4B 52
Cowper Rd. Brom —7N 69
Cowper Rd. Deal —5L 177
Cowper Rd. Dover —2D 180
Cowper Rd. Gill —9G 80
Cowper Rd. Mgte —4D 208
Cowper Rd. Sit —7J 99
Cowstead La. Gill —2A 18
Cowstead Rd. H'lip —8F 96 (3A 18)
Coxes Av. Ram —1F 210
Coxett Hill. Osp —7B 186 (3E 19)
Coxheath. —5N 137 (3D 27)
Coxhill. S'wll —4A 220 (4B 32)
Coxhill Cres. Dover —1C 180
Coxhill Gdns. Dover —1C 180
Coxland. App —1B 46
Cox La. Chess —2A 12
Cox's Clo. Snod —2D 108
Cox St. Det —6M 111
Coxwell Rd. SE18 —5F 50
Cozenton Clo. Gill —2A 96
Crabble. —1E 180 (1C 42)
Crabble Av. Dover —2F 180
Crabble Clo. Dover —2E 180
Crabble Corn Mill. —1E 180 (1C 42)
(off Lower Rd.)
Crabble Hill. Dover —1F 180 (1C 43)
Crabble La. Dover —3D 180 (1C 42)
Crabble Meadows. Dover —2F 180
Crabble Mill Cotts. Dover —1E 180
Crabble Rd. Dover —1F 180 (1C 42)
Crabbs Croft Clo. Orp —6E 84
Crab Hill. Beck —3G 68
Crabtree Clo. King H —7M 123
Crabtree La. Len H —3C 29
Crabtree Manorway N. Belv —2D 52
Crabtree Manorway S. Belv —3D 52
(in two parts)
Crabtree Rd. Gill —3N 95
Craddock Dri. Cant —1A 172
Craddock Ho. Cant —1A 172
Craddock Rd. Cant —1A 172
Craddocks Av. Asht —4A 12
Craddock Way. Gill —6N 95
Cradduck La. S'hrst —7M 221 (1E 37)
Cradle Bri. Dri. W'boro —8J 159
Cradles Rd. S'bry —1E 112 (3A 18)
Cradley Rd. SE9 —6F 56
Crafford St. Dover —4J 181
Cragie Wlk. Gill —7A 96
Craigholm. SE18 —9C 50
Craigton Rd. SE9 —2B 56
Crammavill St. Grays —2A 8
Cramonde Ct. Well —9J 51
Crampton Ct. Broad —9L 209
Cramptons. Siss —8B 220
Cramptons Rd. Sev —2J 119
Crampton Tower Museum. —9L 209 (2E 23)
Cranborne Av. Maid —9E 126
Cranborne Wlk. Cant —8L 167
Cranbourne Clo. Ram —4K 211
Cranbrook. —7D 176 (3E 37)
Cranbrook Clo. Brom —9K 69
Cranbrook Clo. Clift —4J 209
Cranbrook Clo. Gill —9M 81
Cranbrook Clo. Maid —1J 139
Cranbrook Common. —7C 220 (2E 37)
Cranbrook Dri. Sit —1E 114
Cranbrook Ho. Eri —7G 52
(off Boundary St.)
Cranbrook Rd. Bene —3E 37
Cranbrook Rd. Bexh —8A 52
Cranbrook Rd. Bidd —2A 38
Cranbrook Rd. Goud —8L 185 (2D 37)
Cranbrook Rd. Hawkh —3K 191 (3D 37)
Cranbrook Rd. Ilf —1A 6
Cranbrook Rd. Siss —6D 220 (2A 38)
Cranbrook Rd. S'hrst —1E 37
Cranbrook Rd. Tent —3B 38
Cranbrooks. Mer —5N 161
Cranbrook Windmill. —8D 176 (2E 37)
Crandalls. Leigh —6N 143
Crane La. C'brk —7D 176
Cranfield Rd. SE4 —1C 54
Cranford Clo. Gill —2N 95
Cranford Rd. Dart —6M 59
Cranford Rd. Tonb —2N 145
Cranham Sq. Mard —3K 205
Cranleigh Clo. Bex —4C 58
Cranleigh Clo. Orp —4J 85
Cranleigh Ct. Whits —5G 224
Cranleigh Dri. Lgh S —1B 10
Cranleigh Dri. Swan —7F 72
Cranleigh Dri. Whitf —6F 178
Cranleigh Gdns. Chat —9A 80
Cranleigh Gdns. Maid —2N 125
Cranleigh Gdns. Whits —5G 224
Cranley Pde. SE9 —9A 56
(off Beaconsfield Rd.)
Cranmer Clo. Bek —6G 173
Cranmer Ct. Maid —9E 126
Cranmere Ct. Strood —4N 79
Cranmer Ho. Cant —1K 171
Cranmer Rd. Mitc —1B 12
Cranmer Rd. Sev —5F 118
Cranmore Rd. Brom —8J 55
Cranmore Rd. Chst —1B 70
Cranston Rd. SE23 —6B 54 (4E 5)
Cranston Rd. E Grin —2A 34
Crantock Rd. SE6 —7E 54
Cranwell Rd. Tun W —1C 156
Crathie Rd. SE12 —4L 55
Craufurd Grn. Folk —6D 188
Craven Clo. Mgte —5A 208
Craven Hill. W2 —2B 4
Craven Pk. NW10 —2A 4
Craven Pk. Rd. NW10 —2A 4
Craven Rd. W2 —2B 4
Craven Rd. Orp —4M 85
Crawford Gdns. Mgte —3F 208
Crawford Rd. Broad —8K 209
Crawfords. Swan —3F 72
Crawley Ct. Grav —3G 62
Crawshay Clo. Sev —5H 119
Cray Av. Orp —9K 71 (2B 14)
Craybrooke Rd. Sidc —9K 57
Crayburne. S'fleet —1M 75
Craybury End. SE9 —7E 56
Cray Clo. Dart —2H 59
Craydene Rd. Eri —8G 53
Crayfield Ind. Pk. Orp —5L 71
Crayford. —3F 58 (4C 7)
Crayford Clo. Maid —3F 126
Crayford Greyhound Stadium. —4F 58
Crayford High St. Dart —3F 58
Crayford Ind. Est. Cray —3G 58
Crayford Rd. Dart —3G 58 (4C 7)
Crayford Way. Dart —3G 58 (4C 7)
Craylands. Orp —6L 71
Craylands La. Swans —3K 61 (4E 7)
Craylands Sq. Swans —3K 61
Craymill Sq. Dart —9G 53
Cray Rd. Belv —6B 52
Cray Rd. Sidc —2L 71 (1B 14)
Cray Rd. Swan —9D 72 (2C 15)
Crayside Ind. Est. Dart —2J 59
Crays Pde., The. St P —5L 71
Craythorne. Tent —7C 222
Craythorne Clo. Hythe —7B 188
Craythorne Clo. New R —1D 212
Craythorne La. New R —2C 212
Cray Valley Rd. Orp —8J 71
Crazy La. Sod —4C 44
Creat Viewpoint, The. —3E 106
Credenhall Dri. Brom —2B 84
Creek La. Up Stok —4A 10
Creekmouth. —2B 6
Creek Rd. SE8 & SE10 —3E 5
Creek, The. Grav —3A 62
Creeland Gro. SE6 —6C 54
Creffield Rd. W5 & W3 —2A 4
Creighton Flats. S'wch —5L 217
(off School Rd.)
Crematorium Cotts. Weav —3G 127
Cremer Clo. Cha —8C 170
Cremer Pl. Fav —4E 186
Cremers Rd. Sit —6J 99
Cremorne Rd. SW10 —3B 4
Cremorne Rd. N'fleet —5E 62
Crendon Pk. S'boro —5G 150
Crescent Cotts. Sev —2F 118
Crescent Dri. Orp —9D 70
Crescent Gdns. Swan —5D 72
Crescent Rd. SE18 —5D 50
Crescent Rd. Beck —5E 68
Crescent Rd. Birch —4F 206
Crescent Rd. Broad —5M 209
Crescent Rd. Brom —3K 69
Crescent Rd. Eri —6G 53
Crescent Rd. Fav —3A 20
Crescent Rd. Mgte —3B 208
Crescent Rd. Ram —5G 211 (2E 23)
Crescent Rd. Sev —2F 118
Crescent Rd. Sidc —8H 57
Crescent Rd. Tun W —2H 157 (2E 35)
Crescent St. Sit —7G 98
Crescent, The. Beck —4D 68
Crescent, The. Bex —5L 57
Crescent, The. Bor G —1N 121
Crescent, The. Bou B —3K 165
(in two parts)
Crescent, The. Cant —8M 167
(Manwood Av.)
Crescent, The. Cant —3M 171 (1D 31)
(off Castle Row)
Crescent, The. Cha —9D 170 (2C 31)
Crescent, The. Eyt —4K 185
Crescent, The. Grnh —3J 61
Crescent, The. Kem —2G 99
Crescent, The. Long —6L 75
Crescent, The. Maid —1C 126
Crescent, The. Min S —6F 218
Crescent, The. N'fleet —7E 62
Crescent, The. S'gte —8E 188
Crescent, The. S'wch —8K 217
Crescent, The. Sev —3L 119
Crescent, The. Sidc —9H 57
Crescent, The. Snow —4E 162
Crescent, The. St Mc —8K 213
Crescent, The. Tey —1L 223 (3D 19)
Crescent, The. Tonb —5H 145
Crescent, The. Tun W —2E 150
Crescent, The. W Wick —9H 69
Crescent Way. SE4 —1D 54
Crescent Way. Chat —6A 94
Crescent Way. Orp —6G 85
Cressey Ct. Chat —8B 80
Cressfel. Sidc —1K 71
Cressfield. Afrd —9D 158
Cressingham Rd. SE13 —1F 54
Cress Way. Fav —5E 186
Cresswell Pk. SE3 —1J 55
Cresta Clo. H Bay —3A 194
Crest Clo. Badg M —2C 102
Crest Ind. Est. Mard —2K 205
Crest Rd. Brom —1J 83
Crest Rd. Roch —2N 93
Crest View. Grnh —2H 61
Crest View Dri. Pet W —8D 70
Crestway. Chat —3E 94
Crete Hall Rd. Grav —4C 62
Crete Rd. E. Folk —2J 189 (2A 42)
Crete Rd. W. Folk —2D 188 (2A 42)
Creteway Clo. Folk —3K 189
Creton St. SE18 —3C 50
Creve Coeur Clo. Bear —4K 127
Crichton Ho. Sidc —2M 71
Cricketers Clo. Eri —5F 52
Cricketers Clo. H'shm —2M 141
Cricketers Clo. H'nge —6D 192
Cricketers Clo. Kem —2G 98
Cricketers Dri. Meop —4F 90
Cricketfield Rd. E5 —1D 5
Cricket Grn. Mitc —1B 12
Cricket Ground Rd. Chst —4D 70
Cricket La. Beck —2B 68
Cricklewood. —1A 4
Cricklewood B'way. NW2 —1A 4
Cricklewood La. NW2 —1A 4
Crimond Av. Dym —9D 182
Criol La. Shad —2E 39
Cripple Hill. H Hal —2C 38
Cripple St. Maid —9C 126 (2D 27)
Cripps Clo. Aysm —2C 162
Cripp's Corner. —3B 44
Cripps La. St Mc —7J 213
Crismill Cotts. Bear —6A 128
Crismill La. Bear & T'hm —6A 128
(in two parts)
Crispe Clo. Gill —7N 95
(in two parts)
Crispe Pk. Clo. Birch —4G 206
Crispe Rd. Acol —7D 206 (2C 22)
Crispin Clo. Fav —4H 187
Crispin Ct. Cox —5N 137
Crispin Dri. King H —6M 123
Crispin Rd. Roch —4J 79
Criterion Pas. S'ness —1B 218
(off High St. Sheerness,)
Crit Hill. —3E 37
Crittall's Corner. (Junct.) —3L 71 (1B 14)
Crittenden Cotts. Maid —4K 137
Crittenden Rd. Matf —2G 153 (1B 36)
Crockenhall Way. Grav —3D 76
Crockenhill. —9E 72 (2C 15)
Crockenhill La. Eyns —1H 87
Crockenhill La. Swan & Eyns —2D 15
Crockenhill Rd. Eger —4C 28
Crockenhill Rd. Orp & Swan —8M 71 (2B 14)
Crockenhill Rd. Swan —9C 72
Crockham Hill. —3A 24
Crockham La. Dunk —1M 165
Crockham La. Hern —3B 20
Crockham La. Stow C —4D 31
Crockham Rd. Dunk —1M 165
Crockham Rd. Hern —3B 20
Crockham Way. SE9 —9C 56
Crockhurst Street. —8B 146 (4A 26)
Crockshard La. W'hm W —2B 32
Crocus Clo. Croy —2A 82
Croft Av. W Wick —2F 82
Croft Clo. Belv —5A 52
Croft Clo. Chat —1F 110
Croft Clo. Chst —1B 70
Croft Clo. Tonb —3M 145
Croft Ct. SE13 —4F 54
Croft Ct. Eden —6C 184
Crofters Clo. Hythe —8F 196
Crofters Mead. Croy —9C 82
Crofters, The. Rain —4B 96
Croft Gdns. Len —8E 200
Croft La. Eden —6C 184
Croft La. Folk —6F 188
Crofton. —3F 84 (2B 14)
Crofton Av. Bex —5M 57
Crofton Av. Orp —3E 84
Crofton Clo. Kenn —4G 159
Croftongate Way. SE4 —3B 54
Crofton La. Orp —2F 84 (2B 14)
Crofton Park. —3C 54
Crofton Pk. Rd. SE4 —4C 54
Crofton Rd. Orp —4C 84 (2A 14)
Crofton Rd. Wgte S —4K 207
Crofton Roman Villa. —3G 85
(adjacent Orpington Station)
Croft Rd. Afrd —8H 159
Croft Rd. Brom —2K 69
Croft Rd. Crowb —4C 35
Croft Rd. W'ham —8K 116
Croftside. Meop —2F 106
Croft's Pl. Broad —9M 209
Croft, The. Leyb —8C 108
Croft, The. Swan —6D 72
Croft, The. Tent —8C 222
Croft Vs. Afrd —8H 159
(off Croft Rd.)
Croft Way. Sev —7G 118
Croft Way. Sidc —8G 56
Croftwood. Afrd —3B 160
Croham Rd. S Croy —2D 13
Croham Valley Rd. S Croy —3D 13
Croidene Ct. Min S —6H 219
Crombie Rd. Sidc —6F 56
Cromer Pl. Orp —2F 84
Cromer Rd. Roch —4M 79
Cromers Rd. Sit —2F 114 (3C 19)
Cromer St. Tonb —6G 145
Cromford Clo. Orp —4G 85
Cromlix Clo. Chst —5D 70
Crompton Gdns. Maid —6E 126
Crompton Pl. Eri —6G 52
Cromwell Av. Brom —7L 69
Cromwell Clo. Brom —7L 69
Cromwell Lodge. Bexh —3N 57
Cromwell Pk. Pl. Folk —7D 188
Cromwell Rd. SW5 & SW7 —3B 4
Cromwell Rd. Beck —5B 68
Cromwell Rd. Cant —4N 171
Cromwell Rd. Maid —4D 126
Cromwell Rd. S'ness —5A 218
Cromwell Rd. Tun W —2J 157
Cromwell Rd. Whits —3F 224 (2C 21)
Cromwell Ter. Chat —9D 80
Cronin Clo. Lark —6D 108
Crooked La. Grav —4G 63
Crooked's Rd. Deal —2H 199 (3D 33)
Crookenden Pl. B'hm —9D 162
Crook Log. Bexh —1M 57 (4B 6)
Crook Rd. Bchly —5N 153 (1C 36)
Crook's Ct. La. W Hou —2B 42
Crookston Rd. SE9 —1C 56
Croom's Hill. SE10 —3E 5
Crosfield Pavilion. Roy B —1K 125
Crosier Ct. Upc —8H 223
Crosley Rd. Gill —1G 95
Cross-at-Hand. —4E 27
Crossbrook Rd. SE3 —1A 56
Cross Dri. Kgswd —7D 140
Cross Keys. —9H 119 (2D 25)
Cross Keys. Bear —5M 127
Cross Keys Clo. Sev —9H 119
Cross Keys Cotts. Bear —5M 127
Cross Keys Cotts. Sev —9H 119
Cross La. Bex —5A 58
Cross La. Fav —5G 187 (2E 29)
Cross La. Sit —5F 98
(off Brewery Rd.)
Cross La. Tic —4C 36
Cross La. E. Grav —7G 63 (4B 8)
Cross La. W. Grav —7G 62 (4B 8)
Crossley Av. H Bay —3A 194
Crossley Clo. Big H —3D 164
Crossmead. SE9 —6B 56
Crossness Footpath. Eri —1A 52
Cross Rd. Birch —3F 206
Cross Rd. Brom —3A 84 (2A 14)
Cross Rd. Dart —4K 59
Cross Rd. Hawl —9N 59
Cross Rd. N'fleet —4E 62
Cross Rd. Orp —8K 71
Cross Rd. Sidc —9K 57
Cross Rd. St Mc —9J 213
Cross Rd. Walm —9K 177 (3E 33)
Cross Stile. Afrd —1D 160
Cross St. N1 —2C 5
Cross St. Cant —1L 171 (4D 21)
Cross St. Chat —8D 80
Cross St. Eri —6F 52
Cross St. Gill —6F 80
Cross St. Grav —4G 63
Cross St. H Bay —4E 194
Cross St. Maid —3D 126
Cross St. Roch —4M 79
Cross St. S'ness —2C 218
Cross, The. E'try —3K 183
Cross View Cotts. Len —7F 200
Crossway. SE28 —2B 6
Crossway. SW20 —1A 12
Crossway. Chat —5B 94
Crossway. Orp —7F 70
Cross Way. Roch —9N 79
Crossways. Cant —7M 167
Crossways. Sit —1F 114
Crossways. S Croy —8B 82
Crossways. Tats —8C 164
Crossways Av. Mgte —8E 208
Crossways Boulevd. Dart —2C 60 (4E 7)
Crossways Clo. Dym —5D 182
Crossways Rd. Beck —7D 68
Crossways 25 Bus. Pk. Dart —2C 60
Crossway, The. SE9 —7N 55
Crossway, The. Tun W —3D 156
Crothall Haven. Afrd —7F 158
(off Blue Line La.)
Crouch. —5A 122 (2A 26)
Crouch. Sidc —1K 71
Crouch Clo. Beck —2D 68
Crouch Croft. SE9 —8C 56
Crouch Hill Ct. Lwr Hal —8M 223
Crouch Ho. Cotts. Eden —5B 184
Crouch House Green. —5B 184
Crouch Ho. Rd. Eden —4A 184 (4A 24)
Crouch La. Bor G —2N 121 (1A 26)
Crouch La. Sand —3M 215 (1C 45)
Crouch La. Sell —1B 30
Crowborough. —4C 35
Crowborough Hill. Crowb —4D 35
Crowborough Warren. —4C 35
Crowbourne Cottage. Goud —8J 185
Crowbridge Rd. W'boro —2J 161 (1A 40)
Crowders La. Batt —4A 44
Crowdleham. —8D 104
Crow Dri. Hals —6D 102
Crow Hill. Bor G —2N 121
Crow Hill. Broad —8M 209 (1E 23)
Crow Hill Rd. Bor G —2N 121
Crow Hill Rd. Mgte —3N 207
Crowhurst. —4A 24
Crowhurst La. Bor G —6K 121
Crowhurst La. Igh —2E 25
Crowhurst La. W King —9G 89 (3E 15)
Crowhurst Rd. Bor G —3M 121
Crowhurst Rd. Crow —4A 24
Crowhurst Village Rd. Crow —4A 24
Crowhurst Way. Orp —8L 71
Crow La. Roch —7N 79
Crown Acres. E Peck —1M 147
Crown Ash La. Warl & Big H —4A 164
Crown Clo. Orp —5J 85
Crown Ct. SE12 —4L 55
Crown Ct. Deal —4N 177
(off Middle St.)
Crown Crest Ct. Sev —3K 119
(off Seal Rd.)
Crown Dale. SE19 —1C 13
Crowndale Rd. NW1 —2C 4
Crownfield. Afrd —1D 160
Crownfield Rd. E15 —1E 5
Crownfields. Sev —7J 119
Crownfields. Weav —5J 127

Deans Hill—Downderry Rd.

Deans Hill. H'shm —7N 129
Deans Hill Rd. Bre —5L 113 (3B 18)
Dean Street. —1N 137 (3D 27)
Dean St. W1 —2C 4
Dean St. E Far —5L 137 (3D 27)
Dean's Wlk. Afrd —2D 160
Deansway Av. Sturry —4E 168
Deanwood Clo. Gill —5N 95
Deanwood Dri. Gill —9M 95 (3A 18)
Deanwood Rd. Dover —3D 180
De Beauvoir Rd. N1 —2D 5
De Beauvoir Town. —2D 5
Deborah Clo. Whits —6H 225
Debrabant Clo. Eri —6E 52
De Burgh Hill. Dover —3H 181
De Burgh St. Dover —4H 181
Decoy Hill Rd. H Hals —3E 9
Deedes Clo. Hythe —5K 197
Deepdale Av. Brom —7J 69
Deepdene Point. SE23 —8A 54
Deepdene Rd. Well —1J 57
Deerhurst Clo. Long —6B 76
Deerhurst Gdns. Maid —5A 126
Deerleap La. Hals —4M 101
Deer Pk. Way. W Wick —3J 83
Deerson La. Pres —4B 22
Deerton Street. —3E 19
Defiance Wlk. SE18 —3B 50
Defiant Clo. Chat —5E 94
Defoe Clo. Chat —5E 94
Defoe Clo. Eri —8G 52
De Frene Rd. SE26 —9A 54
Degema Rd. Chst —1D 70
De Havilland Clo. H'nge —9D 192
De Havillands. Bek —7K 173
Deirdre Chapman Ho. Swans —4L 61
(off Craylands La.)
Delacourt Clo. C'snd —7A 210
Delagarde Rd. W'ham —8E 116
Delamark Rd. S'ness —2D 218
Delamere Gdns. Snod —2E 108
Delamere Rd. Snod —2F 108
Delancey St. NW1 —2C 4
Delane Rd. Deal —5K 177
De L'angle Row. Cha —7D 170
De Lapre Clo. Orp —1M 85
Delarue Clo. Tonb —7K 133
Delaware Clo. Sturry —5E 168
Delaware Rd. Shoe —1D 11
Delce Rd. Roch —2D 17
Delfside. S'wch —6M 217
Delf St. S'wch —5L 217 (4D 23)
Delice Rd. Roch —8A 80
Delius Dri. Tonb —1M 145
Dell Dri. Tun W —1K 157
Dellfield Clo. Beck —4F 68
Dell, The. SE2 —5J 51
Dell, The. Bex —6F 58
Delmar Clo. Whits —2M 225
Delmonden Rd. Hawkh —4D 37
Delting Clo. Gill —1M 95
De Luci Rd. Eri —5D 52
De Lucy St. SE2 —4K 51
Delvan Clo. SE18 —7C 50
Delves Av. Tun W —4J 157
De Mere Clo. Gill —5N 95
Demesne Rd. Wall —2C 12
Denbeigh Dri. Tonb —1J 145
Denberry Dri. Sidc —8K 57
Denbigh Av. Gill —2N 95
Denbigh Clo. Chst —2B 70
Denbigh Clo. Sit —4F 98
Denbigh Pl. Afrd —1F 160
Denbigh Rd. Ram —3E 210
Denbigh Rd. Tun W —7J 151
Denbridge Rd. Brom —5B 70
Dence Clo. H Bay —2J 195
Dence Pk. H Bay —3J 195
Den Clo. Beck —6G 69
Dencora Way. Afrd —9E 158
Dene Av. Sidc —5K 57
Dene Clo. SE4 —1B 54
Dene Clo. Brom —2J 83
Dene Clo. Dart —9F 58
Dene Dri. Long —5A 76
Dene Dri. Orp —4K 85
Dene Holm Rd. N'fleet —8C 62
Dene Lodge Clo. Bor G —2M 121
Dene Rd. Asht —4A 12
Dene Rd. Dart —5N 59
Denesfield Ct. Sev —5D 118
Denesway. Meop —9F 76
Dene, The. Beth —2J 163
Dene, The. Cant —5A 172
Dene, The. Croy —5A 82
Dene, The. Hythe —6K 197
Dene, The. Sev —8J 119
Dene Wlk. Long —6L 75
Dene Wlk. Mgte —6D 208
Dene Way. Speld —7A 150
Dengemarsh Rd. Lydd —4C 204 (3D 47)
Dengrove Bungalows. B Oak —5C 168
Denham Clo. Dym —9E 182
Denham Clo. Well —1L 57
Denham Rd. N'tn —4K 97
Denison M. Lwr Sto —8K 201
Deniston Av. Bex —6N 57
Den La. Ladd —4C 27
Denmark Hill. —4D 5
Denmark Hill. SE5 —3D 5
Denmark Pl. Cant —1N 171 (4D 21)
Denmark Rd. Brom —4L 69
Denmark Rd. Ram —5J 211
Denmark St. Folk —5L 189
Denmark Ter. Afrd —1G 160
Dennard Way. Farn —5C 84
Denne Clo. Sturry —4E 168
Denne Hill. —3A 32
Denne Mnr. La. Shott —2B 30
Denne's La. Lydd —1B 204 (3D 47)
Dennes Mill Clo. Wye —2L 159
Denness Rd. Afrd —2F 160
Dennett Rd. Croy —2C 13
Dennettsland Rd. Crock H —3B 24
Denning Av. Croy —2C 13
Dennis Cadman Ho. Roy B —9K 109
Dennises La. Upm —2E 7
Dennis Rd. Grav —8F 62
Dennis Rd. S Ock —2E 7
Dennis Way. Folk —4E 188
Dennis Willcocks Clo. N'tn —5K 97
Denny Bottom. —2E 35
Denny Ct. Dart —4B 60
(off Bow Arrow La.)
Den Rd. Brom —6G 69
Densham Rd. E15 —2E 5
Densole. —4C 192 (1A 42)
Densole Clo. Beck —4B 68
Densole La. Dens —4C 192
Densole Way. Dens —4C 192
Denstead Ct. Cant —7J 167
Denstead La. Cha H —1B 170
Denstead La. Dunk & Cha H —4C 20
Denstead Wlk. Maid —2J 139
Denstroude. —3C 166 (3C 21)
Denstroude La. Denst —4B 166 (3C 20)
Dental St. Hythe —6K 197
Dent-de-Lion. —3M 207
Dent-de-Lion Ct. Mgte —3M 207
Dent-de-Lion Rd. Mgte —3M 207
Dent-de-Lion Rd. Wgte S —2K 207
Denton. —5K 63 (4B 8)
Denton Cvn. Site. Grav —6L 63
Denton Clo. Maid —9H 127
Denton Ct. Rd. Grav —5K 63
Denton Grn. Gill —8L 81
Denton Rd. Bex —7F 58
Denton Rd. Dart —5F 58 (4C 7)
Denton Rd. Well —7L 51
Denton St. Grav —5K 63
Denton Ter. Bex —7F 58
Denton Way. Mgte —4G 208
Denver Clo. Orp —9G 71
Denver Rd. Dart —5H 59
Denwood. SE23 —8A 54
Denwood St. Wye & Crun —3B 30
Denzil Rd. NW10 —1A 4
Deptford. —3E 5
Deptford Bri. SE8 —3E 5
Deptford B'way. SE8 —3E 5
Deptford Chu. St. SE8 —3E 5
Deptford High St. SE8 —3E 5
Derby Clo. Hild —1E 144
Derby Clo. Sit —5E 98
Derby Rd. Croy —2C 13
Derby Rd. Grays —3A 8
Derby Rd. Maid —9F 126
Dereham Ho. SE4 —2A 54
(off Frendsbury Rd.)
Dering Clo. Bri —9E 172
Dering Clo. P'ley —1D 39
Dering Rd. Afrd —8H 159
Dering Rd. Bri —8H 173
Dering Rd. H Bay —3G 194
Derings, The. Lydd —3B 204
Dering Way. Grav —6L 63
Deringwood Dri. Down —8J 127
Deringwood Dri. D'wd —2E 27
Deringwood Pde. Down —8J 127
Dermody Gdns. SE13 —3G 54
Dermody Rd. SE13 —3G 54
Dernier Rd. Tonb —3J 145
Derrick Rd. Beck —6C 68
Derringstone. —9D 162 (3A 32)
Derringstone Downs. B'hm —9D 162 (3A 32)
Derringstone Hill. B'hm —9D 162 (3A 32)
Derringstone St. B'hm —9D 162 (3A 32)
Derry Downs. —9L 71 (2B 14)
Derry Downs. Orp —9L 71
Derville Rd. G'stne —7A 212
Derwent Av. Ram —5E 210
Derwent Clo. Dart —6J 59
Derwent Cres. Bexh —9B 52
Derwent Dri. Orp —1F 84
Derwent Dri. Tun W —9E 150
Derwent Ho. Maid —1H 139
Derwent Rd. Tonb —2J 145
Derwent Way. Aysm —1C 162
Derwent Way. Gill —3N 95
Desmond Cres. Fav —7L 187
D'este Rd. Ram —5K 211
Detillens La. Oxt —2A 24
Detling. —9K 111 (1E 27)
Detling Av. Broad —3L 211
Detling Clo. S'ness —5C 218
Detling Hill. Det —4E 17
Detling Rd. Brom —1K 69
Detling Rd. Eri —7E 52
Detling Rd. N'fleet —6C 62
Devas St. E3 —2E 5
Devenish Rd. SE2 —2J 51
Devil's Den. —4A 28
Devon Av. Walm —7M 177
Devon Clo. Chat —4F 94
Devon Clo. Gill —2B 96
Devon Ct. S at H —4J 73
Devon Gdns. Birch —5E 206 (1C 22)
Devon Rd. Cant —2C 172
Devon Rd. Folk —6K 189
Devon Rd. Maid —8F 126
Devon Rd. S Dar —4B 74 (1D 15)
Devonshire Av. Dart —4J 59
Devonshire Clo. Tun W —5E 156
Devonshire Gdns. Mgte —3F 208
Devonshire Ho. Bus. Cen. Brom —7L 69
Devonshire Rd. SE9 —7A 56
Devonshire Rd. SE23 —5A 54 (4D 5)
Devonshire Rd. Bexh —2N 57
Devonshire Rd. Dover —4G 180
Devonshire Rd. Gill —5G 80
Devonshire Rd. Grav —6G 63
Devonshire Rd. Orp —1J 85
Devonshire Road Nature Reserve. —5A 54
Devonshire Sq. Brom —7L 69
Devonshire Ter. Broad —8M 209
Devonshire Way. Croy —3B 82
Devons Rd. E3 —2E 5
Dewhurst La. Wadh —3A 36
Dewlands Av. Dart —5B 60
Dew La. P'mrsh —3E 45
Dexter Ho. Eri —3N 51
(off Kale Rd.)
Dhekelia Clo. Maid —2D 126
Dial Clo. Gill —6J 81
Dial Clo. Grnh —3K 61
Dial Rd. Gill —6J 81
Diameter Rd. Orp —9E 70
Diamond Ct. S'ness —3C 218
Diamond Rd. Whits —3G 224
Diana Ct. Eri —6F 52
Diana Gdns. Deal —5K 177
Dianthus Clo. SE2 —5K 51
Dibden. —9F 118 (2C 25)
Dibden La. Ide H & Sev —8F 118 (2C 25)
Dibdin Rd. Deal —3N 177
Dickens Av. Cant —9B 168
Dickens Av. Dart —2A 60
Dickens Centre. —7A 80 (1D 17)
Dickens Clo. Eri —7C 52
Dickens Clo. Hart —8M 75
Dickens Clo. Langl —4A 140
Dickens Ct. High —9G 64
Dickens Ct. Roch —4A 80
Dickens Dri. Chst —2E 70
Dickens Dri. E Mal —9D 108
Dickens House Museum. —9M 209 (2E 23)
Dickensian Clo. Up Stok —9H 201
Dickens Rd. Broad —8M 209
Dickens Rd. Grav —6K 63
Dickens Rd. Maid —2B 126
Dickens Rd. Roch —1N 93
Dickens Wlk. C'ing —1C 66
Dickens Way. Hawkh —5L 191
Dickerage La. N Mald —1A 12
Dickerage Rd. King T —1A 12
Dickley La. H'shm —6B 200 (2C 28)
Dickson Ct. Sit —7J 99
Dickson Rd. SE9 —1A 56
Dickson Rd. Dover —4H 181
Dickson's Bourne. Adgtn —2B 40
Dieu Stone La. Dover —4J 181
Digby Rd. Folk —6E 188
Digdog La. Frit —2A 38
Dignals Clo. Gill —1B 96
Dilhorne Clo. SE12 —8L 55
Diligent Dri. Sit —4G 98
Dillon Way. Tun W —8K 151
Dillwyn Clo. SE26 —9B 54
Dillywood La. Roch & High —2J 79 (1D 17)
Dilnot La. Acol —8G 206
Dimmock Clo. Pad W —9N 147
Dingleden. —4A 38
Dingley. Sidc —1K 71
Dippers Clo. Kems —8N 103
Discovery Dri. King H —6M 123
Discovery Wlk. Cant —3B 172
Dislingbury Rd. Tud —3N 151 (1A 36)
Disraeli Clo. SE28 —1L 51
Disraeli Clo. Maid —3H 139
Dittisham Rd. SE9 —9A 56
Ditton. —9G 108 (4C 17)
Ditton Ct. Clo. Dit —9F 108
Ditton Pl. Dit —9F 108
Ditton Rd. Bexh —3M 57
Dixon Clo. Maid —7C 126
Dixon Pl. W Wick —2E 82
Dixter La. N'iam —2D 45
Dixter Rd. N'iam —2D 45
Dixwell Clo. Gill —6N 95
Dixwell Rd. Folk —7G 189
Dobbie Clo. Sit —5F 98
Dobell Rd. SE9 —3B 56
Dobells. C'brk —8D 176
Dobson Rd. Grav —1K 77
Dock Exit Rd. Dover —4L 181
Dock Head Rd. Chat —3D 80
Docklands. —2A 6
Dockland St. E16 —1C 50
(in two parts)
Docklands Visitor Centre. —3E 5
Dock Rd. Chat —7C 80 (1D 17)
Dock Rd. Grays —3A 8
Dock Sq. Chat —3E 80
Dock St. E1 —2D 5
Doctor Hope's Rd. C'brk —8D 176
Doctor's La. Chu H —8A 180 (1B 42)
Doddington. —1D 29
Doddington Ct. Maid —4B 126
Doddington Place. —1D 29
Doddington Rd. Gill —1N 95
Dodd Rd. Tonb —2L 145
Dodds La. Dover —1F 180
Doebury Wlk. SE18 —7J 51
(off Prestwood Clo.)
Does All. Sit —7G 99
Doesgate La. Bulp —1B 8
Doggerel Acre. Whits —6H 225
Doggett Rd. SE6 —5D 54
Doggetts Row. Isle G —3C 190
Doggett's Sq. Roch —5M 79
Doghurst La. Coul —4B 12
Dog Kennel Hill. SE22 —4D 5
Dog Kennel La. Lym —7C 204
Dogs Hill Rd. W'sea B —4A 46
Dogwood Clo. Chat —1G 111
Dogwood Clo. N'fleet —9E 62
Dola Av. Deal —4L 177
Doleham Hill. Westf —4D 45
Doleham La. Westf —4D 45
Dollis Hill. —1A 4
Dollis Hill La. NW2 —1A 4
Dolphin Clo. Broad —3L 209
Dolphin Dri. Gill —6A 96 (2A 18)
Dolphin Ho. S'ness —2B 218
(off Sheppey St.)
Dolphin La. Dover —5K 181
Dolphin Pk. Sit —6J 99
Dolphin Pas. Dover —5K 181
Dolphin Pl. Dover —5K 181
Dolphin Rd. Lydd —3C 204
Dolphin Rd. Sit —6J 99 (2C 19)
Dolphin Sailing Barge Museum. —6H 99 (2C 19)
Dolphins Rd. Folk —4J 189
Dolphin St. Deal —3N 177
Dolphin St. H Bay —2F 194
Dombey Clo. High —1G 78
Domneva Rd. Min —7M 205
Domneva Rd. Wgte S —3J 207 (1C 23)
Domonic Dri. SE9 —9D 56
Donald Biggs Dri. Grav —5J 63
Donald Moor Av. Tey —2K 223
Donaldson Rd. SE18 —8C 50
Doncaster Clo. Maid —2J 139
Donegal Rd. Cant —2B 172
Donemowe Dri. Kem —3G 98
Donet Clo. Gill —6N 95
Dongola Rd. Roch —3M 79
Donkey Field. Leigh —6M 143
Donkey La. Adm —2A 32
Donkey La. F'ham —3B 88 (2D 15)
Donkey Street. —2C 182 (3C 41)
Donkey St. Burm —3B 182 (3C 41)
Donnahay Rd. Ram —1G 210
Donnington Ct. Dart —4B 60
(off Bow Arrow La.)
Donnington Rd. NW10 —2A 4
Donnington Rd. Dun G —2E 118
Donnithorne Ho. H Bay —2F 194
(off Brunswick Sq.)
Doon Brae. Tun W —4G 151
Dorado Gdns. Orp —4M 85
Doran Gro. SE18 —7G 50
Dorcas Gdns. Broad —7L 209
Dorchester Av. Bex —6M 57
Dorchester Clo. Cli —6M 65
Dorchester Clo. Dart —5N 59
Dorchester Clo. Orp —3K 71
Dorchester Gro. W4 —3A 4
Dorchester Rd. Grav —8J 63
Dorcis Av. Bexh —9N 51
Doria Dri. Grav —8K 63
Doric Av. Tun W —5F 150
Doric Clo. Tun W —5F 150
Doric Ct. Ram —7G 211
Doris Av. Eri —8D 52
Dorking Rd. Eps —4A 12
Dorking Rd. Tun W —8J 151
Dorman Av. N. Aysm —1C 162 (2A 32)
Dorman Av. S. Aysm —2D 162 (2A 32)
Dormansland. —1A 34
Dormans Park. —1A 34
Dormans Rd. D'land —1A 34
Dormers Dri. Meop —1G 90
Dornden Dri. L'tn G —1A 156
Dornden Gdns. Chat —9E 94
Dorney Rise. Orp —7H 71
Dorn Ho. Tun W —2J 157
Dorothy Av. C'brk —8D 176
Dorothy Dri. Ram —2G 210
Dorothy Evans Clo. Bexh —2C 58
Dorrit Way. Chst —2E 70
Dorrit Way. Roch —1A 94
Dorryn Ct. SE26 —1A 68
Dorset Av. Well —2H 57
Dorset Clo. Whits —6D 224
Dorset Ct. Walm —8N 177
Dorset Cres. Grav —9K 63
Dorset Gdns. Birch —4E 206
Dorset Gdns. Walm —8M 177
Dorset M. Deal —5M 177
Dorset Pl. Fav —5G 187
Dorset Rd. SE9 —7A 56
Dorset Rd. SW19 —1B 12
Dorset Rd. Beck —6A 68
Dorset Rd. Cant —3C 172
Dorset Rd. S'ness —4B 218
Dorset Rd. Tun W —3K 157
Dorset Rd. Ind. Est. S'ness —3B 218
Dorset Sq. Gill —2N 95
Dorset St. Sev —7K 119
Dorset Way. Maid —8F 126
Dorton Dri. Sev —4N 119
Dorville Rd. SE12 —3J 55
Dossett Ct. Deal —8K 177
Dothill Rd. SE18 —7E 50
Dotterel Clo. Chat —9G 94
Doubleday Dri. Bap —9L 99
Doubleton La. Pens —1H 149
Douglas Almshouses. Len —7E 200
Douglas Av. Hythe —6K 197
Douglas Av. Whits —4G 224
Douglas Clo. Broad —8J 209
Douglas Ct. Big H —5E 164
Douglas Dri. Croy —4D 82
Douglas Rd. Deal —7K 177
Douglas Rd. Dover —4G 181
Douglas Rd. H Bay —3H 195
Douglas Rd. Len —7E 200
Douglas Rd. Maid —6B 126 (2D 27)
Douglas Rd. Tonb —7G 144
Douglas Rd. Well —8K 51
Douglas Ter. Deal —5N 177
Douro Clo. Cant —1C 172
Douro Pl. Dover —5K 181
Dour Side. River —1E 180
Dour St. Dover —4J 181
Dour Ter. Temp E —8C 178
Doust Way. Roch —7A 80
Dove Clo. Chat —5E 94
Dove Clo. Hythe —8E 196
Dove Clo. Whits —6E 224
Dove Ct. Dover —2G 181
(off Mayfield Av.)
Dovedale. Birch —4G 207
Dovedale Clo. Well —9J 51
Dovedale Ct. Afrd —7F 158
Dove Dale Ct. Birch —4G 207
Dovedale Rd. Dart —6C 60
Dove Lea Gdns. Dover —1D 180
Doveney Clo. Orp —6L 71
Dover. —4J 181 (1C 43)
Dover (Admiralty Pier) Lighthouse. —8M 181
Dover Bus. Pk. Whitf —7G 179
Dover Castle. —4K 181 (1D 43)
Dover Hill. —2A 42
Dover Hill. Folk —3L 189 (2A 42)
Dover Ho. Rd. SW15 —4A 4
Dover Museum. —5J 181
Dove Rd. Tonb —1H 145
Dover Patrol Memorial. —6M 213
Dover Pl. Afrd —9G 158
Dover (Prince of Wales Pier) Lighthouse. —7L 181
Dover Rd. B'hm —6E 162 (3A 32)
(in two parts)
Dover Rd. Dent —4A 32
Dover Rd. E'try —4K 183 (2C 33)
Dover Rd. Folk —6K 189 (2A 42)
Dover Rd. Gus —9K 179 (1D 43)
Dover Rd. Mart M & R'wld —5J 199 (4D 33)
Dover Rd. N'fleet —5C 62 (4A 8)
Dover Rd. S'wch —8K 217 (1D 33)
Dover Rd. St Mc —8N 179 (4D 33)
(in two parts)
Dover Rd. Tilm —3C 33
Dover Rd. E. Grav —5D 62 (4A 8)
Dovers Corner. (Junct.) —2D 7
Dover Southern Breakwater E. Lighthouse. —6N 181
Dover Southern Breakwater W. Lighthouse. —7M 181
Dover St. Cant —2N 171 (1D 31)
Dover St. Maid —7N 125
Dover St. Sit —7F 98
Dover Transport Museum. —4C 33
Dover Western Heights Viewpoint. —5H 181
Doves Clo. Brom —3A 84
Dowanhill Rd. SE6 —6G 55
Dowding Rd. Big H —3D 164
Dowding Wlk. N'fleet —8D 62
Dowding Way. Tun W —5L 151
Dower Ho. Cres. Tun W —3E 150
Dowgate Clo. Tonb —7K 145
Dowle Clo. Old R —2D 47
Dowlerville Rd. Orp —7H 85
Dowle St. P'ley —1D 39
Dowling Clo. Snod —3C 108
Dowling Ho. Belv —3N 51
Downage, The. Grav —7F 62
Down Av. Lam —4C 200
Downbank Av. Bexh —8E 52
Down Barton Rd. St N —9C 214 (2B 22)
Down Ct. Afrd —4C 160
Down Ct. Rd. Dod —9J 115
Downderry Rd. Brom —8G 55

E. Northdown Clo.—Ely Gdns.

E. Northdown Clo. Clift —4J 209
East Northdown Farm. —4J 209
E. Park Rd. Roy B —9L 109
East Peckham. —1L 147 (3B 26)
East Rise. Ram —3F 210
East Rd. N1 —2D 5
East Rd. Folk —7D 188
East Rd. Well —9K 51
E. Rochester Way. Bex —4C 58
E. Rochester Way. Sidc —2G 56 (4B 6)
E. Roman Ditch. Dover —4L 181
East Row. Roch —7N 79 (1D 17)
Eastry. —3K 183 (2C 33)
Eastry Av. Brom —9J 69
Eastry By-Pass. E'try —4L 183 (2C 33)
Eastry Clo. Afrd —3E 160
Eastry Clo. Maid —2N 125
Eastry Ct. Aysm —2D 162
Eastry Rd. Eri —7B 52
East Sheen. —4A 4
E. Smithfield. E1 —2D 5
E. Stour Ct. Afrd —9H 159
East Stourmouth. —3B 22
East Street. —7K 107 (nr. Addington)
East Street. —4F 216 (4C 23) (nr. Sandwich)
East St. Adtn —8J 107 (in two parts)
East St. Afrd —8F 158
East St. Bexh —2B 58
East St. Brom —5K 69
East St. Cant —8B 168
East St. Chat —9D 80
East St. Dover —4H 181
East St. Eps —3A 12
East St. Fav —5H 187 (3A 20)
East St. Folk —6L 189
East St. Gill —6G 80
East St. H'shm —2M 141 (2B 28)
East St. H Bay —2H 195
East St. Hunt —9K 137 (3D 27)
East St. Hythe —6L 197 (3E 41)
East St. Sit —7H 99
East St. Snod —2F 108
East St. Sth S —1B 10
East St. Tonb —5J 145 (4E 25)
East Studdal. —3D 33
East Sutton. —8E 140 (3A 28)
E. Sutton Rd. E Sut —8E 140
E. Sutton Rd. H'crn —4A 28
E. Sutton Rd. Sut V —9B 140 (3A 28)
East Ter. Grav —4H 63
East Ter. Sidc —6G 57
E. Thurrock Rd. Grays —3A 8
East Tilbury. —3B 8
E. Tilbury Rd. Linf —3B 8
East View. Her —2L 169
Eastview Av. SE18 —7G 51
East Way. E15 —1E 5
East Way. Brom —1K 83
East Way. Croy —3B 82
E. Weald Dri. Tent —6C 222
Eastwell Barn M. Tent —7B 222
Eastwell Clo. Beck —3B 68
Eastwell Clo. Maid —4F 126
Eastwell Clo. Pad W —8K 147
Eastwell Clo. Shad —2E 39
Eastwell Meadows. Tent —8B 222
East Wickham. —8L 51 (3B 6)
Eastwood. —3B 28
Eastwood Rd. Lgh S —1A 10
Eastwood Rd. Sit —6E 98
E. Woodside. Bex —6N 57
Eatenden La. Batt —4A 44
Eaton Hill. Mgte —3C 208
Eaton Rd. Dover —5G 180 (1C 43)
Eaton Rd. Mgte —3C 208 (1D 23)
Eaton Rd. Sidc —7M 57
Eaton Sq. SW1 —3C 4
Eaton Sq. Long —6L 75
Eaves Rd. Dover —5F 180
Ebbsfleet Ind. Est. N'fleet —3N 61
Ebbsfleet La. Ram —2D 23
Ebbsfleet Wlk. N'fleet —4A 62
Ebdon Way. SE3 —1L 55
Ebony Wlk. Maid —6M 125
Ebsworth St. SE23 —5A 54
Ebury Bri. Rd. SW1 —3C 4
Ebury Clo. Kes —4A 84
Eccles. —4K 109 (3D 17)
Eccles Row. Eccl —4K 109
Eccleston Clo. Orp —2F 84
Eccleston Rd. Tovil —7C 126
Eccleston St. SW1 —3C 4
Echo Clo. Maid —2J 139
Echo Ct. Grav —7H 63
Echo Ho. Sit —8J 99
Echo Sq. Grav —7H 63
Echo Wlk. Min S —6L 219
Ector Rd. SE6 —7H 55
Edam Ct. Sidc —8J 57
Eddie Willet Rd. H Bay —4C 194
Eddington. —4G 194 (2E 21)
Eddington Bus. Pk. Edd B —4G 194
Eddington Clo. Maid —2E 138
Eddington La. H Bay —4F 194 (2E 21)
Eddington Way. Edd B —2E 21
Eddington Way. H Bay —4F 194
Eddystone Rd. SE4 —3B 54
Eden Av. Chat —4C 94
Edenbridge. —6C 184 (4B 24)
Edenbridge Clo. Orp —7M 71
Edenbridge Dri. S'ness —4C 218
Edenbridge Ho. Cant —2A 172
Edenbridge Rd. Hartf —2B 34
Edenbridge Trad. Cen. Eden —7D 184
Eden Clo. Bex —9E 58
Eden Ct. Hawkh —5L 191
Eden Ct. H Bay —3E 194
Edendale Rd. Bexh —8E 52
Edenfield. Birch —4G 206
Edenhurst. Sev —7H 119
Eden Leisure Pk. E'chu —3E 202
Eden Park. —8D 68 (2E 13)
Eden Pk. Av. Beck —7B 68 (1E 13) (in two parts)
Eden Pl. Grav —5G 63
Eden Rd. Beck —7B 68
Eden Rd. Bex —9D 58
Eden Rd. H Hals —1H 67
Eden Rd. Sea —6C 224
Eden Rd. Tun W —3G 157
Eden Wlk. Tun W —3G 157
Eden Way. Beck —8C 68
Edgar Clo. Swan —6G 72
Edgar Clo. Whits —2M 225
Edgar Ho. Deal —7L 177
Edgar Pl. Maid —5D 126
Edgar Rd. Cant —1A 172
Edgar Rd. Dover —3G 181
Edgar Rd. Kems —8M 103
Edgar Rd. Mgte —2E 208
Edgar Rd. Min —7M 205
Edgar Rd. Tats —9D 164
Edgeborough Way. Brom —3N 69
Edgebury. Chst —9D 56
Edgebury Wlk. Chst —9E 56
Edgecoombe. S Croy —9A 82
Edge End Rd. Broad —9K 209
Edgefield Clo. Dart —6B 60
Edge Hill. SE18 —6D 50
Edgehill Clo. Folk —7D 188
Edge Hill Ct. Sidc —9H 57
Edgehill Gdns. Grav —4E 76
Edgehill Rd. Chst —8E 56
Edgehill Rd. Purl —3C 13
Edgeler Ct. Snod —3C 108
Edgewood Dri. Orp —6J 85
Edgewood Grn. Croy —2A 82
Edgeworth Rd. SE9 —2M 55
Edgington Way. Sidc —3L 71 (1B 14)
Edgware Rd. NW2 —1A 4
Edgware Rd. W2 & W9 —2B 4
Edinburgh Ct. Eri —7E 52
Edinburgh Ho. Deal —5K 177
Edinburgh Ho. Dover —5J 181 (off Durham Hill)
Edinburgh Pl. Folk —8H 189 (off Earls Av.)
Edinburgh Rd. Afrd —8F 158
Edinburgh Rd. Chat —1F 94
Edinburgh Rd. Gill —7G 80
Edinburgh Rd. Isle G —3B 190
Edinburgh Rd. Mgte —3N 207
Edinburgh Sq. Maid —2F 138
Edinburgh Wlk. Mgte —3N 207 (off Edinburgh Rd.)
Edington Rd. SE2 —3K 51
Edisbury Wlk. Gill —6N 95
Edison Gro. SE18 —7H 51 (3B 6)
Edison Rd. SE18 & Well —3B 6
Edison Rd. Brom —5K 69
Edison Rd. Well —8H 51
Edith Gro. SW10 —3B 4
Edith Rd. Fav —6G 186
Edith Rd. Orp —6J 85
Edith Rd. Ram —6G 210
Edith Rd. Wgte S —2L 207
Ediva Rd. Meop —8F 76
Edmanson Av. Mgte —2M 207
Edmonton Ho. Dover —1G 181 (off Alberta Clo.)
Edmund Clo. Barm —6L 125
Edmund Clo. Meop —8F 76
Edmund Rd. Orp —9L 71
Edmund Rd. Well —1J 57
Edmunds Av. Orp —6M 71
Edmund St. W'hm —2B 226
Edna Rd. Maid —2C 126
Edred Rd. Dover —4G 181
Edward Ct. Chat —2F 94
Edward Dri. Birch —4G 207 (Canterbury Rd.)
Edward Dri. Birch —4F 206 (Neame Rd.)
Edward Rd. SE20 —2A 68
Edward Rd. Big H —6E 164
Edward Rd. Brom —3L 69
Edward Rd. Cant —2N 171 (1D 31)
Edward Rd. Chst —1D 70
Edward Rd. Folk —5K 189
Edward Rd. Kgdn —3M 199
Edward Rd. Queen —7C 218
Edward Rd. Whits —8E 224
Edwards Clo. Gill —6M 95
Edwards Gdns. Swan —7E 72
Edwards Pas. S'ness —1B 218 (off High St. Sheerness,)
Edwards Rd. Belv —4B 52
Edwards Rd. Dover —4J 181
Edward St. SE14 —3E 5
Edward St. Chat —9D 80
Edward St. Roch —5M 79
Edward St. Rust —1B 156
Edward St. S'boro —5F 150
Edward Ter. Folk —5L 189
Edward Tyler Rd. SE12 —7L 55
Edward Wlk. E Mal —1D 124
Edwina Av. Min S —5H 219
Edwin Arnold Ct. Sidc —9H 57
Edwin Clo. Bexh —6A 52
Edwin Petty Pl. Dart —5C 60
Edwin Rd. Dart —8J 59
Edwin Rd. Gill —3L 95 (2A 18)
Edwin St. Grav —5G 63
Edyngham Clo. Kem —3H 99
Effingham Cres. Dover —4J 181
Effingham Pas. Dover —5J 181
Effingham Rd. SE12 —3H 55
Effingham St. Dover —4J 181
Effingham St. Ram —6J 211
Effra Rd. SW2 —4C 5
Egbert Rd. Fav —6F 186
Egbert Rd. Min —7M 205
Egbert Rd. Wgte S —2K 207
Egdean Wlk. Sev —5K 119
Egdert Rd. Birch —3C 206
Egerton. —4C 29
Egerton Av. Swan —3G 72
Egerton Clo. Dart —6J 59
Egerton Dri. SE10 —3E 5
Egerton Dri. Clift —3J 209
Egerton Forstal. —4C 28
Egerton Ho. Rd. Eger —4C 28
Egerton La. Eger & P'ley —4C 29
Egerton Rd. Char H —3D 29
Egerton Rd. Dover —9D 178
Egerton Rd. Maid —2B 126
Egerton Rd. P Hth —6N 141 (3B 28)
Egerton Vs. Folk —4L 189
Eggarton La. Godm —3B 30
Eggpie La. Hild —7K 131
Eggpie La. Weald —3D 25
Eggringe. Afrd —9C 158
Eglantine La. F'ham —1A 88 (2D 15)
Eglinton Hill. SE18 —6D 50
Eglinton Rd. SE18 —6C 50
Eglinton Rd. Swans —4L 61
Egremont Rd. Bear —7J 127
Egypt Pl. Bear —5M 127
Eighteen Acre La. Old R —2C 47
Elaine Av. Roch —5J 79
Elaine Ct. Roch —6J 79
Elbridge Hill. Sturry —7K 169 (4A 22)
Elchin Hill. H'lgh —4C 31
Elder Clo. Kgswd —6F 140
Elder Clo. Sidc —6H 57
Elder Cotts. H Bay —4L 195
Elder Ct. Gill —5L 95
Elder Rd. SE27 —1D 13
Elderslie Clo. Beck —9E 68
Elderslie Rd. SE9 —3C 56
Elders, The. L'brne —1L 173
Elderton Rd. SE26 —9B 54
Eldertree Rd. Can I —2A 10
Eldon Av. Croy —3A 82
Eldon Pl. Broad —9M 209
Eldon St. Chat —8D 80
Eldon Way. Pad W —8L 147
Eldred Dri. Orp —3L 85
Eleanor Wlk. SE18 —4A 50
Elephant & Castle. (Junct.) —3C 5
Elford Clo. SE3 —2L 55
Elford Rd. Cli —3C 176
Elfrida Clo. Mgte —5G 209
Elfrida Cres. SE6 —9D 54
Elgal Clo. Orp —6D 84
Elgar Clo. Tonb —1L 145
Elgar Pl. Ram —4J 211
Elgin Av. W9 —2B 4
Elgin Cres. W11 —2B 4
Elgin Gdns. Roch —7H 79
Elham. —7N 183 (1E 41)
Elham Clo. Brom —3N 69
Elham Clo. Gill —1L 95
Elham Clo. Mgte —4G 208 (off Lyminge Way.)
Elham Pk. S Min —4E 31
Elham Rd. Cant —4L 171
Elham Valley Railway Museum. —3A 188
Elham Valley Rd. B'hm —4E 31
Elham Valley Vineyard. —4E 31
Elham Way. Broad —2L 211
Elibank Rd. SE9 —2B 56
Eling Ct. Maid —9D 126
Eliot Pk. SE13 —1F 54
Eliot Rd. Dart —3B 60
Elizabeth Carter Av. Deal —6J 177
Elizabeth Clo. Maid —5D 126
Elizabeth Cotts. New R —3C 212
Elizabeth Ct. Broad —6M 209
Elizabeth Ct. Eri —7E 52 (off Valence Rd.)
Elizabeth Ct. Gill —2M 95
Elizabeth Ct. Grav —4F 62
Elizabeth Ct. H Bay —2G 194 (off Queen St.)
Elizabeth Dri. Cap F —2B 174
Elizabeth Gdns. Hythe —7J 197
Elizabeth Garlick Ct. Tun W —9H 151
Elizabeth Garrett Anderson Ho. Belv (off Ambrooke Rd.) —3B 52
Elizabeth Ho. Maid —3D 126
Elizabeth Huggins Cotts. Grav —7G 62
Elizabeth Kemp Ct. Ram —3G 211
Elizabeth Rd. Dover —6J 181
Elizabeth Rd. Grays —3A 8
Elizabeth Rd. Ram —6K 211
Elizabeth Smith Ct. E Mal —2D 124
Elizabeth St. Grnh —3E 60
Elizabeth Ter. SE9 —4B 56
Elizabeth Way. H Bay —4J 195
Elizabeth Way. Orp —8L 71
Eliza Ct. Char —3K 175
Elkstone Rd. W10 —2B 4
Ellen Av. Ram —3J 211
Ellenborough Rd. Sidc —1M 71
Ellen Clo. Brom —6N 69
Ellenden Ct. Cant —7J 167
Ellens Rd. Deal —7H 177 (3D 33)
Ellenswood Clo. Down —8J 127
Ellenwhorne La. Stapl —3C 44
Ellerdale St. SE13 —2E 54
Ellerslie. Grav —5J 63
Ellesmere Av. Beck —5F 68
Ellesmere M. New R —1D 212
Ellesmere Rd. W4 —3A 4
Ellingham Ind. Est. Afrd —4F 160
Ellingham Leas. Maid —1F 138
Ellingham Way. Afrd —4E 160
Ellington Av. Mgte —3N 207
Ellington Pl. Ram —5G 210
Ellington Rd. Ram —5G 211
Elliot Clo. Cant —8B 168
Elliott Rd. Brom —7N 69
Elliotts La. Bras —6L 117
Elliotts Pl. Fav —5H 187
Elliott St. Grav —5J 63
Ellis Clo. SE9 —7E 56
Ellis Clo. Swan —7E 72
Ellis Dri. New R —1D 212
Ellison Clo. Ches —4L 225
Ellison Ct. Fav —6J 187
Ellison Rd. Sidc —6F 56
Ellisons Wlk. Cant —2B 172 (off Nonsuch Clo.)
Ellison Way. Gill —1C 96
Ellis Rd. Whits —2J 225
Ellis Way. Dart —7N 59
Ellis Way. H Bay —5K 195
Elm Av. Chat —2B 94
Elm Av. Chatt —9D 66 (in two parts)
Elm Bank Dri. Brom —5M 69
Elmbourne Dri. Belv —4C 52
Elmbourne Trad. Est. Belv —3C 52
Elmbridge Av. Surb —2A 12
Elmbrook Gdns. SE9 —2A 56
Elm Clo. Dart —6K 59
Elm Clo. Eger —4C 29
Elm Clo. High —1G 79
Elm Ct. SE13 —1G 55
Elm Ct. Hythe —7F 196
Elm Ct. Wgte S —3K 207
Elm Ct. Ind. Est. Hem —8H 95
Elm Cres. E Mal —1D 124
Elmcroft Av. Sidc —5H 57
Elmcroft Rd. Orp —1J 85
Elmdene Clo. Beck —9C 68
Elmdene Rd. SE18 —5D 50
Elm Dri. Swan —5E 72
Elmer Rd. SE6 —5F 54
Elmers End. —7B 68 (1E 13)
Elmers End Rd. SE20 & Beck —6A 68 (1D 13)
Elmerside Rd. Beck —7B 68
Elmfield. Gill —9K 81
Elmfield. Tent —7C 222
Elmfield Clo. Grav —6G 62
Elmfield Ct. Cox —5N 137
Elmfield Ct. Tent —8C 222
Elmfield Ct. Well —8K 51
Elmfield Pk. Brom —6K 69
Elmfield Rd. Brom —5K 69
Elm Fields. Old R —2D 47
Elm Gdns. Hythe —6M 197
Elm Gro. Cant —8J 167
Elm Gro. Eri —7E 52
Elm Gro. Hild —3F 144
Elm Gro. Maid —6E 126
Elm Gro. Orp —2H 85
Elm Gro. Sit —7J 99
Elm Gro. Wgte S —3J 207
Elmhurst. Belv —6N 51
Elmhurst. Grnh —4H 61
Elmhurst Av. Pem —6C 152
Elmhurst Cvn. Pk. E'chu —2E 202
Elmhurst Gdns. Chat —9A 80
Elmhurst Rd. SE9 —7A 56
Elmington Clo. Bex —4C 58
Elmira St. SE13 —1E 54
Elm La. SE6 —7C 54
Elm La. Min S —7K 219 (4D 11)
Elm La. Tonb —4J 145
Elmlee Clo. Chst —2B 70
Elmleigh Rd. L'brne —2M 173
Elmley Ind. Est. Queen —9B 218
Elmley Rd. Min S —9L 219
Elmley St. SE18 —5F 50
Elmley Way. Mgte —6D 208
Elm Pde. Sidc —9J 57
Elm Park. —1D 7
Elm Pk. Av. Horn —1C 7
Elm Pk. Gdns. Dover —5E 180
Elm Pas. Hythe —6J 197
Elm Pl. Afrd —2D 160
Elm Rd. Aysm —2C 162
Elm Rd. Beck —5C 68
Elm Rd. Dart —6J 59
Elm Rd. Eri —8H 53
Elm Rd. Folk —5L 189
Elm Rd. Gill —6H 81
Elm Rd. Grav —8H 63
Elm Rd. Grnh —4E 60
Elm Rd. Lgh S —1B 10
Elm Rd. Orp —8J 85
Elm Rd. Shoe —1D 11
Elm Rd. Sidc —9J 57 (1B 14)
Elm Rd. St Mar —2E 214
Elm Rd. Tun W —5F 150
Elm Rd. W'ham —7G 116
Elms. —5H 211
Elms Av. Ram —5H 211
Elmscott Rd. Brom —1H 69
Elmscroft Farm Cotts. Maid —2J 137
Elms Hill. Hou —6B 180 (1C 42)
Elmshurst Gdns. Tonb —9J 133
Elmside. New Ad —7E 82
Elmsleigh Dri. Lgh S —1B 10
Elmstead. —2B 70 (1A 14)
Elmstead Av. Chst —1B 70
Elmstead Clo. Sev —4F 118
Elmstead Glade. Chst —2B 70
Elmstead La. Chst —3A 70 (1A 14)
Elmstead Pl. Folk —6L 189
Elmstead Rd. Eri —8F 52
Elmsted. —4D 31
Elmsted Cres. Well —6L 51
Elms, The. Her —2K 169
Elmstone. —3B 22
Elmstone Clo. Maid —7M 125
Elmstone Gdns. Clift —4J 209
Elmstone Hole Rd. Graf G —8M 141 (3B 28)
Elmstone La. Maid —7M 125
Elmstone Rd. Gill —4N 95
Elmstone Rd. Ram —5H 211
Elmstone Ter. St M —7L 71
Elms Vale Rd. Dover —6C 180 (1C 42)
Elm Ter. SE9 —4C 56
Elmton La. Eyt —2K 185
Elm Tree Cotts. Up Stok —9H 201
Elm Tree Dri. Roch —1L 93
Elm Vs. Cant —9J 167
Elm Vs. Chatt —8C 66
Elm Wlk. Ayle —9J 109
Elm Wlk. Orp —4B 84
Elmway. E'chu —2E 202
Elmwood Av. Broad —6L 209 (1E 23)
Elmwood Clo. Broad —6L 209
Elm Wood Clo. Whits —3L 225
Elmwood Dri. Bex —5N 57 (4B 6)
Elmwood Rd. Chatt —7C 66
Elm Wood W. Whits —3L 225
Elphicks. —2C 37
Elphick's Pl. Tun W —5H 157
Elphinstone Ho. Maid —2C 126
Elrick Clo. Eri —6F 52
Elsa Ct. Beck —4C 68
Elsa Rd. Well —9K 51
Elsdale St. E9 —1D 5
Elsiemaud Rd. SE4 —3C 54
Elsinore Rd. SE23 —6B 54
Elspeth Rd. SW11 —4B 4
Elstan Way. Croy —1B 82
Elstow Clo. SE9 —3C 56 (in two parts)
Elstree Gdns. Belv —4N 51
Elstree Hill. Brom —3H 69
Elswick Rd. SE13 —1E 54
Eltham. —4B 56 (4A 6)
Eltham Grn. SE9 —3N 55
Eltham Grn. Rd. SE9 —2M 55
Eltham High St. SE9 —4B 56 (4A 6)
Eltham Hill. SE9 —3N 55 (4A 6)
Eltham Palace. —5A 56 (4A 6)
Eltham Pal. Rd. SE9 —4M 55
Eltham Park. —2C 56
Eltham Pk. Gdns. SE9 —2C 56
Eltham Place. —4A 6
Eltham Rd. SE12 & SE9 —3K 55 (4E 5)
Elthruda Rd. SE13 —4G 55
Elventon Clo. Folk —4E 188
Elverland La. P For —4E 19
Elvington. —2J 185 (3B 32) (nr. Eythorne)
Elvington. —9A 192 (nr. Hawkinge)
Elvington Clo. Maid —4A 126
Elvington Grn. Brom —8J 69
Elvington La. H'nge —9A 192 (2A 42)
Elvino Rd. SE26 —1B 68
Elwick Ct. Dart —2H 59
Elwick La. Afrd —8F 158
Elwick Rd. Afrd —8F 158 (1A 40)
Elwill Way. Beck —7F 68
Elwill Way. Grav —4E 76
Elwyn Gdns. SE12 —5K 55
Ely Clo. Eri —9G 52
Ely Clo. Gill —1A 96
Ely Ct. Tun W —1H 157
Ely Gdns. Tonb —3K 145

Ely Ho. Maid —1G 139
Ely La. Tun W —1H 157
Elysian Av. Orp —9H 71
Embassy Clo. Gill —2J 95
Embassy Ct. Sidc —8K 57
Embassy Ct. Well —1K 57
Embassy Gdns. Beck —4C 68
Ember Clo. Orp —1E 84
Embleton Rd. SE13 —2E 54
Emerald Clo. Roch —4A 94
Emerald View. Ward —4K 203
Emersons Av. Swan —3G 73
Emerton Clo. Bexh —2N 57
Emes Rd. Eri —7D 52
Emily Jackson Clo. Sev —6J 119
Emily Rd. Chat —5E 94
Emmanuel Rd. SW12 —4C 4
Emmerson Gdns. Whits —2L 225
Emmet Hill La. Ladd —4C 26
Emmetts. —2B 24
Emmetts La. W'ham —2B 24
Empire Ter. Mgte —5C 208
Empire Way. Wemb —1A 4
Empress Dri. Chst —2D 70
Empress Gdns. Ward —4J 203
Empress Rd. Grav —5K 63
Emsworth Gro. Maid —3G 126
Enbrook Rd. S'gte —6E 188 (2A 42)
Enbrook Valley. Folk —6E 188 (2A 42)
Encombe. S'gte —8D 188
Endell St. WC2 —2C 5
Endwell Rd. SE4 —1B 54 (3E 5)
Enfield Rd. Deal —3N 177
Engate St. SE13 —2F 54
Engineer Clo. SE18 —6C 50
Engineers Ct. Afrd —8F 158
Engineers Way. Wemb —1A 4
Englands La. NW3 —1B 4
Englefield Clo. Orp —7H 71
Englefield Cres. Cli —6M 65
Englefield Cres. Orp —7H 71
Englefield Path. Orp —7J 71
Englefield Rd. N1 —1D 5
Engleheart Rd. SE6 —5E 54
Ennerdale. Fav —6J 187
Ennerdale Gdns. Aysm —1D 162
Ennerdale Ho. Maid —1H 139
Ennerdale Rd. Bexh —8B 52
Ennersdale Rd. SE13 —3G 54
Ennis Rd. SE18 —6E 50
Ensfield Rd. Leigh —7M 143 (4D 25)
Ensign Cotts. Cha —8B 170
Enslin Rd. SE9 —5C 56
Enterprise Bus. Est. Roch —5B 80
Enterprise Cen., The. Beck —1B 68
Enterprise Cen., The. Chat —2F 110
Enterprise Clo. Roch —4A 80
Enterprise Ho. Tonb —6H 145
(off Avebury Av.)
Enterprise Rd. Maid —8D 126
Enterprise Rd. Mgte —7D 208
Enterprise Way. Eden —4B 184
Enticott Clo. Whits —4J 225
Epaul La. Roch —6N 79
Ephraim Ct. Tun W —1F 156
Epping Clo. H Bay —5J 195
Epple. —3G 206
Epple Bay Av. Birch —3F 206 (1C 23)
Epple Bay Rd. Birch —3E 206
Epple Cotts. Birch —3G 207
Epple Rd. Birch —3G 206 (1C 23)
Epps Rd. Sit —8F 98
Epsom. —3A 12
Epsom Clo. Bexh —1C 58
Epsom Clo. Maid —2J 139
Epsom Clo. W Mal —1M 123
Epsom Downs. —4A 12
Epsom La. N. Eps & Tad —4A 12
Epsom Racecourse. —4A 12
Epsom Rd. Asht —4A 12
Epsom Rd. Croy —2C 13
Epsom Rd. Eps —3A 12
Epsom Rd. Sutt & Mord —2B 12
Epstein Rd. SE28 —1J 51
Eresby Dri. Beck —2D 82
Erica Ct. Swan —7F 72
Erica Gdns. Croy —4E 82
Erica Ho. SE4 —1C 54
Eric Rd. Dover —2G 180
Ericson Ho. SE13 —2G 55
(off Blessington Rd.)
Eridge. —3D 35
Eridge Green. —9B 156 (3D 35)
Eridge Grn. Clo. Orp —2L 85
Eridge Rd. Crowb —4C 35
(in two parts)
Eridge Rd. E Grn —9B 156 (3D 35)
Eridge Rd. Groom —9L 155 (3D 35)
Eridge Rd. Tun W —5E 156
Erin Clo. Brom —3H 69
Erindale. SE18 —6F 50
Erindale Ter. SE18 —6F 50
Erith. —5F 52 (3C 7)
Erith Clo. Maid —1D 126
Erith High St. Eri —5F 52 (3C 7)
Erith Library & Museum. —5F 52
Erith Museum. —5F 52 (3C 7)
(off Walnut Tree Rd.)
Erith Rd. Belv & Eri —2C 58 (3C 6)
Erith Rd. Bexh & N Hth —2C 58 (4C 6)
Erith Small Bus. Cen. Eri —6G 52
Erith St. Dover —3G 181
Ermine Rd. SE13 —2E 54
Ermington Rd. SE9 —7E 56
Ernest Clo. Beck —8D 68
Ernest Gro. Beck —8C 68
Ernest Rd. Chat —9D 80
Ernwell Rd. Folk —5K 189
Erriff Dri. S Ock —2E 7
Erriottwood. —7N 115 (4D 19)
Ersham Rd. Cant —3N 171 (1D 31)
Erskine Ho. Sev —7H 119
Erskine Pk. Rd. Tun W —1B 156
Erskine Rd. Meop —2G 106 (3B 16)
Erwood Rd. SE7 —5A 50
Eschol Rd. Hoo —4A 10
Escott Gdns. SE9 —9A 56
Escreet Gro. SE18 —4C 50
Eshcol Rd. Hoo —7M 67
Esher Clo. Bex —6N 57
Eskdale Av. Ram —5E 210
Eskdale Clo. Dart —6C 60
Eskdale Rd. Bexh —9B 52
Esmonde Dri. Mans —9L 207
Esplanade. Roch —9L 79 (2D 17)
Esplanade. S'ness —1C 218
Esplanade. Strood —6M 79
Esplanade. Wgte S —2H 207
Esplanade, The. Dover —6J 181
Esplanade, The. S'gte —9C 188 (3E 41)
Essella Pk. Afrd —9J 159
Essella Rd. Afrd —9J 159
Essenden Rd. Belv —5B 52
Essetford Rd. Afrd —2D 160
Essex Av. H Bay —3C 194
Essex Clo. Tun W —5F 156
Essex Gdns. Birch —5E 206 (1C 22)
Essex Rd. N1 —2C 5
Essex Rd. Cant —3C 172
Essex Rd. Dart —4L 59
(in two parts)
Essex Rd. Grav —6F 62
Essex Rd. Hall —6E 92
Essex Rd. Long —5K 75
Essex Rd. Maid —2H 139
Essex Rd. Wgte S —3L 207
Essex St. Whits —5F 224
Essex Way. Ben —1E 9
Estcots Dri. E Grin —2A 34
Estelle Clo. Roch —4A 94
Esther Ct. Mil R —3F 98
Estridge Way. Tonb —2M 145
Estuary Clo. Whits —2N 225
Estuary Rd. S'ness —3C 218
Etchden Rd. Beth —1L 163 (1D 39)
Etchingham. —2A 44
Etchinghill. —2E 41
Etfield Gro. Sidc —1K 71
Ethelbert Clo. Brom —5K 69
Ethelbert Cres. Mgte —2E 208 (1E 23)
Ethelbert Gdns. Mgte —2D 208
Ethelbert Rd. Birch —3C 206
Ethelbert Rd. Brom —6K 69
Ethelbert Rd. Cant —4N 171 (1D 31)
Ethelbert Rd. Dart —9M 59
Ethelbert Rd. Deal —1M 177
Ethelbert Rd. Dover —4H 181
Ethelbert Rd. Eri —7D 52
Ethelbert Rd. Fav —6F 186
Ethelbert Rd. Folk —4K 189
Ethelbert Rd. Mgte —2D 208 (1D 23)
Ethelbert Rd. Orp —6M 71
Ethelbert Rd. Ram —6H 211
Ethelbert Rd. Roch —8N 79
Ethelbert Sq. Wgte S —2K 207
Ethelbert Ter. Mgte —2D 208 (1E 23)
Ethelburga Dri. Lym —7C 204
Ethelburga Gro. Lym —7C 204
Ethel-Maud Ct. Gill —5G 80
Ethelred Ct. Fav —6G 186
Ethelred Rd. Wgte S —2K 207
Ethel Rd. Broad —8K 209
Ethel Ter. Orp —9L 85
Etherington Hill. Speld —7B 150 (1E 35)
Ethnam La. Sand —4N 215 (2C 45)
Ethronvi Rd. Bexh —1N 57
Eton Clo. Chat —7C 94
Eton Gro. SE13 —1H 55
Eton Rd. Orp —5K 85
Eton Way. Dart —2K 59
Ettrick Ter. Hythe —6H 197
Eureka Science & Bus. Pk. Kenn —3F 158
Eurogate Bus. Pk. Kenn —5E 158
Eurolink Commercial Pk. Sit —6H 99
Eurolink Ind. Est. Sit —7J 99
Eurolink Way. Sit —7G 98 (2C 19)
Europa Trad. Est. Eri —5E 52
Europe Rd. SE18 —3B 50
Eustace Pl. SE18 —4B 50
Euston Rd. NW1 —2C 4
Euston Underpass. (Junct.) —2C 4
Evans Clo. Grnh —3G 60
Evans Rd. SE6 —7H 55
Evans Rd. W'boro —2L 161
Eva Rd. Gill —9G 80
Evegate Farm Museum. —2B 40
Evelina Rd. SE15 —4D 5
Evelings All. Whits —3F 224
(off Middle Wall)
Evelyn Ct. Hythe —6N 197
Evelyn Rd. Maid —6B 126
Evelyn Rd. Otf —7K 103
Evelyn St. SE8 —3D 5
Evenden Rd. Meop —1F 90
Evenhill Rd. L'brne —2K 173
Evening Hill. Beck —3F 68
Evenlode Ho. SE2 —2L 51
Everard Av. Brom —2K 83
Everard Way. Fav —4F 186
Everest Clo. N'fleet —8D 62
Everest Dri. Hoo —9H 67
Everest La. Roch —3M 79
Everest M. Hoo —9H 67
Everest Pl. Swan —7E 72
Everest Rd. SE9 —3B 56
Everett Wlk. Belv —5A 52
Everglade. Big H —6D 164
Everglade Clo. Hart —7M 75
Everglades, The. Hem —5J 95
Evergreen Clo. Hem —6K 95
Evergreen Clo. High —1F 78
Evergreen Clo. Iwade —8B 198
Evergreen Clo. Leyb —8C 108
Evering Rd. N16 & E5 —1D 5
Everist Clo. Lym —8D 204
Everist Ct. Lym —8D 204
(off Station Rd.)
Eversholt St. NW1 —2C 4
Eversley Av. Bexh —9E 52
Eversley Clo. Maid —3N 125
Eversley Cross. Bexh —9F 52
Eversley Rd. Hythe —8A 188
Eversley Way. Croy —4D 82
Eversley Way. Folk —6F 188
Evesham Rd. Grav —7J 63
Evington. —4C 31
Evington Pk. H'lgh —4C 30
Evison Clo. Dover —2G 181
Evry Rd. Sidc —2L 71
Ewart Rd. SE23 —5A 54
Ewart Rd. Chat —2B 94
Ewehurst La. Speld —8N 149
Ewell. —3A 12
Ewell Av. W Mal —1M 123
Ewell By-Pass. Eps —3A 12
Ewell La. W Far —3G 137 (2C 27)
Ewell Minnis. —1B 42
Ewell Rd. Surb —2A 12
Ewell Rd. Sutt —3A 12
Ewhurst Green. —2C 44
Ewhurst La. N'iam —3C 45
Ewhurst Rd. SE4 —4C 54
Ewins Clo. Pad W —9M 147
Exbury Rd. SE6 —7D 54
Exchange St. Deal —3N 177
Exedown Rd. Sev —5H 105 (3E 15)
Exeter Clo. Folk —5D 188
Exeter Clo. Tonb —3J 145
Exeter Ho. Maid —1G 139
Exeter Rd. Grav —8J 63
Exeter Rd. Well —9H 51
Exeter Wlk. Roch —4N 93
Exford Gdns. SE12 —6L 55
Exford Rd. SE12 —7L 55
Exhibition Rd. SW7 —3B 4
Exmoor Rise. Afrd —6F 158
Exmouth Rd. Gill —5F 80
Exmouth Rd. Well —8L 51
Exted. —6L 183 (4E 31)
Exted Hill. Elham —6L 183 (4E 31)
Exton Clo. Chat —9F 94
Exton Gdns. Weav —3J 127
Eyebright Clo. Croy —2A 82
Eyhorne Green. —7E 128
Eyhorne Street. —7E 128 (2A 28)
Eyhorne St. Holl —8D 128 (2A 28)
Eynesford Rd. Sev —3D 15
Eynsford. —3M 87 (2D 15)
Eynsford Castle. —3M 87 (2D 15)
Eynsford Clo. Clift —3K 209
Eynsford Clo. Orp —1E 84
Eynsford Cres. Bex —6L 57
Eynsford Rise. Eyns —5L 87
Eynsford Rd. F'ham —2N 87 (2D 15)
Eynsford Rd. Grnh —3J 61
Eynsford Rd. Maid —2A 126
Eynsford Rd. Shor & Eyns —8J 87
Eynsford Rd. Swan —9E 72 (2C 15)
Eynsham Dri. SE2 —4J 51 (3B 6)
Eynswood Dri. Sidc —1K 71
Eysdown Rd. SE9 —7A 56
Eythorne. —4K 185 (3C 32)
Eythorne Clo. Kenn —5H 159
Eythorne Green. —4L 185
Eythorne Rd. S'wll —2C 220 (3B 32)

Fackenden La. Shor —4J 103 (3D 15)
Factory Cotts. Cux —9H 79
Factory Cotts. Woul —7G 93
Factory Rd. E16 —3A 6
Factory Rd. N'fleet —4B 62
Fagus Clo. Chat —1E 110
Fairacre. Broad —9J 209
Fairacre Pl. Hart —6L 75
Fair Acres. Brom —8K 69
Fair Acres. Croy —9C 82
Fairacres Clo. H Bay —3K 195
Fairbank Av. Orp —3D 84
Fairbourne Ct. Cotts. H'shm —5L 141
Fairbourne Heath. —7K 141 (3B 28)
Fairbourne La. H'shm —6K 141 (3B 28)
Fairby Grange. Hart —8L 75
Fairby La. Hart —9L 75
Fairby Rd. SE12 —3L 55
Fairchildes Rd. Warl —3E 13
Fair Cross. —1B 6
Faircrouch La. Wadh —3A 36
Fairfax Bus. Cen. Maid —4J 139
Fairfax Clo. Folk —7D 188
Fairfax Clo. Gill —6N 95
Fairfax Dri. H Bay —2N 195
Fairfax Dri. Wclf S —1B 10
Fairfax Ho. Maid —3H 139
Fairfield. —9H 209 (2B 46)
Fairfield. Elham —6N 183
Fairfield. Shol —4J 177
Fairfield Av. Tun W —9J 151
Fairfield Clo. Kems —9A 104
Fairfield Clo. New R —2C 212
Fairfield Clo. Sidc —4H 57
Fairfield Cres. Tonb —7J 145
Fairfield Pk. Broad —9J 209
Fairfield Rd. E3 —2E 5
Fairfield Rd. Beck —5D 68
Fairfield Rd. Bexh —9A 52
Fairfield Rd. Bor G —1M 121
Fairfield Rd. Broad —9J 209 (2E 23)
Fairfield Rd. Brom —3K 69
Fairfield Rd. Croy —2D 13
Fairfield Rd. Min —6M 205
Fairfield Rd. New R —3B 212 (2E 47)
Fairfield Rd. Orp —9F 70
Fairfield Rd. Ram —2J 211
Fairfield St. SW18 —4B 4
Fairfield St. Whits —6E 224
Fairfield Ter. Hams —8D 190
Fairfield Way. Hild —2E 144
Fairford. SE6 —6D 54
Fairford Av. Bexh —8E 52
Fairford Av. Croy —8A 68
Fairford Clo. Croy —8B 68
Fairglen Rd. Wadh —4A 36
Fairhaven Av. Croy —9A 68
Fairhurst Dri. E Far —4M 137
Fairings, The. Tent —7C 222
(off Ashford Rd.)
Fairland Ho. Brom —7L 69
Fairlands Ct. SE9 —4C 56
Fair La. Rob —3B 44
Fairlawn. Ches —4M 225
Fairlawn Av. Bexh —9M 51
Fairlawn Clo. Tstn —9E 124
Fairlawn Pk. SE26 —1B 68
Fairlawn Rd. Ram —1F 210
Fairlead Rd. Roch —2A 94
Fairleas. Sit —9J 99
Fairlight Av. Ram —4F 210
Fairlight Clo. Tun W —4G 151
Fairlight Ct. Tonb —3H 145
Fairlight Cross. Long —6A 76
Fairlight Rd. Hythe —5H 197
Fairline Ct. Beck —5F 68
Fairman's La. Bchly —7N 153 (1B 36)
Fairman's Rd. Bchly —8N 153 (1B 36)
Fairmead. Brom —7B 70
Fairmead Clo. Brom —7B 70
Fairmeadow. Maid —5C 126 (1D 27)
Fairmead Rd. Eden —2C 184
Fairmile Rd. Tun W —9L 151
Fairmont Clo. Belv —5A 52
Fairoak Clo. Orp —1D 84
Fairoak Dri. SE9 —3F 56
Fairoaks. H Bay —3J 195
Fairseat. —3B 106 (3A 16)
Fairseat La. Fair —9N 89 (3A 16)
Fairseat La. Wro —6A 106 (3A 16)
Fairservice Clo. Sit —6K 99
Fair St. Broad —9J 209
Fairtrough Rd. Orp —3K 101 (3B 14)
Fairview. Eri —7G 52
Fairview. Fawk —4H 89
Fairview. Hawkh —5K 191
Fairview. Lymp —5B 196
Fairview Av. Gill —6L 95 (2E 17)
Fairview Clo. SE26 —1B 68
Fairview Clo. Mgte —3E 208
Fairview Clo. Tonb —9H 145
Fairview Cotts. Loose —3C 138
Fairview Cotts. W Far —2J 137
Fairview Dri. High —9F 64
Fairview Dri. Orp —5F 84
Fairview Gdns. Deal —8K 177
Fairview Gdns. Meop —8F 76
Fairview Gdns. Sturry —5F 168
Fairview La. Tun W —5B 156 (2D 35)
Fairview Rd. Evtn —2J 185
Fairview Rd. Grav —3C 76
Fairview Rd. Sit —8H 99
Fairwater Av. Well —2J 57
Fairway. Bexh —3N 57
Fairway. Grays —2A 8
Fairway. Orp —8F 70 (2B 14)
Fairway Av. Folk —4G 188
Fairway Clo. Croy —8B 68
Fairway Clo. Roch —2N 93
Fairway Clo. St Mar —3E 214
Fairway Cres. Sea —6C 224
Fairway Dri. Dart —5B 60
Fairway Gdns. Beck —9G 68
Fairways, The. Tun W —7G 151
Fairway, The. Brom —8B 70
Fairway, The. Deal —2M 177
Fairway, The. Grav —7G 62
Fairway, The. H Bay —5E 194
Fairway, The. Hythe —7K 197
Fairway, The. L'stne —3E 212
Fairway, The. Roch —2N 93
Fairway, The. Sit —1F 114
Fairwood Ind. Est. Afrd —9E 158
Fairwyn Rd. SE26 —9B 54
Falala Way. Cant —1A 172
Falcon Av. Brom —7A 70
Falcon Clo. Dart —3N 59
Falcon Ct. Sit —9H 99
Falcon Gdns. Min S —5L 219
Falcon Grn. Lark —9D 108
Falcon M. Grav —6D 62
Falcons Clo. Big H —5D 164
Falcon Way. Afrd —2C 160
Falconwood. —2H 57 (4B 6)
Falconwood. (Junct.) —2E 56 (4B 6)
Falconwood Av. Well —9F 50
Falconwood Pde. Well —2H 57
Falconwood Rd. Croy —9C 82
Falkland Ho. SE6 —9F 54
Falkland Pl. Chat —1B 110
Fallowfield. Chat —3E 94
Fallowfield. Sit —9H 99
Fallowfield Clo. Weav —5H 127
Falmouth Clo. SE12 —3J 55
Falmouth Pl. Five G —8H 147
Falstaf Bungalows. Rol —2J 213
Fambridge Clo. SE26 —9C 54
Fanconi Rd. Chat —8E 94
Fancy Row. Bear —4M 127
Fane Way. Gill —7M 95
(in two parts)
Fanshawe Av. Bark —1B 6
Fans La. Iwade —8B 198
Fant. —6A 126 (2D 27)
Fantail, The. (Junct.) —4B 84 (2A 14)
Fant La. Maid —7M 125 (2D 27)
Faraday Av. Sidc —7J 57 (4B 6)
Faraday Ride. Tonb —9K 133
Faraday Rd. Maid —2F 126
Faraday Rd. Well —1J 57
Faraday Way. Orp —7K 71
Fareham Wlk. Maid —2J 139
Faringdon Av. Brom —1C 84
Farleigh. —4E 13
Farleigh Av. Brom —1J 83
Farleigh Bri. E Far —9L 125
Farleigh Ct. Maid —7L 125
Farleigh Ct. Rd. Warl —3E 13
Farleigh Green. —2J 137 (2D 27)
Farleigh Hill. Tovil —8B 126 (2D 27)
Farleigh Hill Retail Pk. Tovil —8B 126
Farleigh La. Maid —7L 125 (2D 27)
Farleigh Rd. Cant —8N 167
Farleigh Rd. Warl —4D 13
Farleigh Trad. Est. Tovil —8B 126
Farley Clo. Chat —9G 94
Farley Clo. Shad —2E 39
Farleycroft. W'ham —8E 116
Farley La. W'ham —8D 116 (2A 24)
Farley Nursery. W'ham —9E 116
Farley Rd. SE6 —5E 54
Farley Rd. Grav —6L 63
Farley Rd. Mgte —6D 208
Farley Rd. S Croy —3D 13
Farlow Clo. N'fleet —8E 62
Farm Av. Swan —6D 72
Farm Clo. Afrd —2C 160
Farm Clo. W Wick —4J 83
Farmcombe Clo. Tun W —3H 157
Farmcombe La. Tun W —3H 157
Farmcombe Rd. Tun W —3H 157
Farmcote Rd. SE12 —6K 55
Farm Cotts. Maid —8G 127
Farm Ct. Non —2B 32
Farm Ct. Tun W —5E 156
Farm Cres. Sit —9H 99
Farmcroft. Grav —7F 62
Farmdale Av. Roch —1K 93
Farm Dri. Croy —3C 82
Farmer Clo. Hythe —5L 197
Farmer Clo. Leeds —2C 140
Farmfield Rd. Brom —1H 69
Farm Hill Av. Roch —3K 79
Farm Holt. New Ash —2M 89
Farmhouse Clo. B'hm —9D 162
Farm Ho. Clo. Whits —5H 225
Farming World. —4B 20
Farmland Wlk. Chst —1D 70
Farm La. Asht & Eps —4A 12
Farm La. Croy —3C 82
Farm La. Shol —4J 177
Farm La. Tonb —3G 144
Farm Pl. Dart —2H 59
Farm Rd. Chat —8B 94
Farm Rd. Hams —8D 190
Farm Rd. Mord —2B 12
Farm Rd. Sev —2K 119
Farmstead Dri. Eden —4C 184
Farmstead Rd. SE6 —9E 54
Farm Vale. Bex —4C 58
Farmworld. —2D 45
Farnaby Dri. Sev —8G 119
Farnaby Rd. SE9 —2M 55
Farnaby Rd. Brom —3G 69 (1E 13)
Farnborough. —6E 84 (2B 14)
Farnborough Av. S Croy —9A 82

Gainsborough Rd.—Goddington

Gainsborough Rd. Birch —3E 206
Gainsborough Sq. Bexh —1M 57
Gaitskell Rd. SE9 —6E 56
Galahad Av. Roch —6J 79
Galahad Rd. Brom —9K 55
Galbri Dri. Roch —6L 79
Galena Clo. Chat —1D 110
Gale St. Dag —1B 6
Gallants La. E Far —1K 137 (2D 27)
Gallards Almshouses. S'boro —5G 150
Galleon Boulevd. Dart —2D 60
Galleon Clo. Eri —4E 52
Galleon Clo. Roch —3N 93
Gallery Rd. SE21 —4D 5
Galley Hill Ind. Est. Swans —3L 61
Galley Hill Rd. Swans & N'fleet —3M 61 (4A 8)
Galliard St. S'wch —6M 217
Gallions Entrance. E16 —1E 50
Gallops, The. Meop —3E 106
Gallosson Rd. SE18 —4G 50
Galloways Rd. Lydd —4C 204 (4D 47)
Gallow's Corner. Hythe —6H 197
Gallows Wood. Fawk —5G 89
Gallus Sq. SE3 —1L 55
Gallwey Av. Birch —4D 206
Gallypot Hill. Hartf —3B 34
Gallypot Street. —3B 34
Galpins Rd. T Hth —1C 13
Galsworthy Clo. SE28 —1K 51
Galsworthy Rd. King T —1A 12
Galway Rd. S'ness —2D 218
Gamma Rd. Hoo —6N 67
Gammon's Farm La. Newch —4B 40
Gander Grn. La. Sutt —2B 12
Gandy's La. Bou M —6F 138 (3E 27)
Gann Rd. Whits —3H 225
Gaol La. Dover —5J 181
(off Queen St.)
Gapp Clo. W King —8E 88
Gap Rd. SW19 —1B 12
Gap, The. Blean —4G 166
Gap, The. Cant —5A 172
Garden Av. Bexh —1B 58
Garden Clo. SE12 —8L 55
Garden Clo. Maid —1H 139
Garden Clo. R Comn —9G 167
Garden Clo. Toy —3B 24
Garden Cotts. Leigh —5A 144
Garden Cotts. St P —5L 71
Garden Cotts. W'hm —3B 226
Gardeners Quay. S'wch —5M 217
(off Up. Strand St.)
Gardenia Clo. Roch —2M 79
Garden La. Brom —2L 69
Garden of England Mobile Home Pk., The. H'shm —1K 141
Garden Pl. Dart —8L 59
Garden Rd. Brom —3L 69
Garden Rd. Folk —5K 189
Garden Rd. Sev —4L 119
Garden Rd. Tonb —5J 145
Garden Rd. Tun W —1H 157
Garden Row. N'fleet —8E 62
Gardens, The. Beck —5G 68
Gardens, The. Cox —5N 137
(in two parts)
Gardens, The. Ivy —2D 47
Garden St. Gill —6D 80
Garden St. Tun W —1H 157
Garden Ter. Seal —3A 120
Garden Wlk. Beck —4C 68
Garden Wlk. Deal —3M 177
Garden Way. King H —7M 123
Gardiner Clo. Orp —5L 71
Gardiner St. Gill —6F 80
Gardner Ind. Est. Beck —1B 68
Gardner's Hill. Iden —2A 46
Gardyne M. Tonb —7H 145
Gareth Gro. Brom —9K 55
Garfield Pl. Fav —5H 187
Garfield Rd. Gill —6G 81
Garfield Rd. Mgte —3B 208
Garibaldi St. SE18 —4G 51
Garland Rd. SE18 —7F 50
Garlands. Hild —8D 132
Garlies Rd. SE23 —8B 54
Garlinge. —3N 207 (1D 23)
Garlinge Green. —2C 31
Garlinge Grn. Rd. P'hm —2C 31
Garlinge Rd. Tun W —5G 150
Garnet St. E1 —2D 5
Garnett Clo. SE9 —1B 56
Garrad's Rd. SW16 —4C 4
Garrard Av. Mgte —3N 207
Garrard Clo. Bexh —1B 58
Garrard Clo. Chst —1D 70
Garratt La. SW18 & SW17 —4B 4
Garratts La. Bans —4B 12
Garrick Dri. SE28 —3F 50
Garrick St. Grav —4G 62
Garrington Clo. Maid —3F 126
Garrison Clo. SE18 —7C 50
Garrison Rd. S'ness —1A 218
Garrolds Clo. Swan —5F 72
Garrow. Long —6A 76
Garside Clo. SE28 —3F 50
Garside Grn. SE9 —9B 50
Garsington M. SE4 —1C 54
Garthorne Rd. SE23 —5A 54
Garth Rd. Mord —2A 12
Garth Rd. Sev —1K 131
Garvock Dri. Sev —8H 119
Gascoigne Rd. Bark —2B 6
Gascoigne Rd. New Ad —9F 82 (3E 13)
Gascoyne Dri. Dart —1G 59
Gascoyne Rd. E9 —1D 5
Gas Ho. Rd. Roch —6N 79
Gas La. Bou B —3H 165
Gas Pas. Cant —3M 171 (1D 31)
Gas Rd. Murs —5J 99
Gas Rd. Sit —6G 98
Gasson Rd. Swans —4L 61
Gassons Rd. Snod —2C 108
Gas St. Cant —3M 171 (1D 31)
Gasworks La. Afrd —9F 158
Gatcombe Clo. Chat —6D 94
Gatcombe Clo. Maid —4M 125
Gatcombe Ct. Beck —3D 68
Gateacre Ct. Sidc —9K 57
Gateacre Rd. Sea —7C 224
Gate Farm Rd. Bidb —1C 150 (4E 25)
Gatefield Cotts. Rol —2K 213
Gatefield La. Fav —5H 187
(in two parts)
Gate Hill. Dunk —9A 166 (4C 20)
Gate La. R Min —7H 183 (1D 41)
Gateley Ho. SE4 —2A 54
(off Coston Wlk.)
Gates Ct. E Peck —9M 135
Gates Grn. Rd. W Wick —4J 83 (2E 13)
Gateway Ct. Ram —5K 211
(off Victoria Pde.)
Gateway Pde. Grav —9L 63
Gateway, The. Dover —5K 181
Gatland La. Maid —8L 125 (2D 27)
Gatling Rd. SE2 —5J 51
Gattons Way. Sidc —9A 58
Gatwick Rd. Grav —8G 63
Gault Clo. Bear —7K 127
Gaunt's Clo. Deal —6K 177
Gavestone Cres. SE12 —5L 55
Gavestone Rd. SE12 —5L 55
Gayhurst Clo. Gill —5N 95
Gayhurst Dri. Sit —6D 98
Gaynesford Rd. SE23 —7A 54
Gayton Rd. SE2 —3L 51
Gaza Trad. Est. Hild —9K 131
Gazedown Clo. St Mar —3E 214
Gaze Hill Av. Sit —8H 99
Gazelle Glade. Grav —1L 77
Gean Clo. Chat —1D 110
Geddes Pl. Bexh —2B 58
Geddinge La. Woot —4A 32
Gedge's Hill. Matf —5K 153 (1B 36)
Geffery's Ct. SE9 —8A 56
Gellatly Rd. SE14 —3D 5
General Gordon Pl. SE18 —4D 50
General Wolfe Rd. SE10 —3E 5
Genesta Av. Whits —6D 224
Genesta Clo. Sit —4F 98
Genesta Glade. Grav —1M 77
Genesta Rd. SE18 —6D 50
Genesta Rd. Wclf S —1B 10
Geneva Av. Gill —1K 95
Gentian Clo. Chat —7B 94
(in two parts)
Gentian Clo. Weav —4H 127
Geoffrey Ct. SE4 —1C 54
Geoffrey Ct. Birch —4F 206
Geoffrey Rd. SE4 —1C 54
George All. Deal —4N 177
George V Av. Mgte —3N 207 (1D 23)
George Gurr Cres. Folk —3K 189
George Hill. Rob —3A 44
George Hill Rd. Broad —4K 209 (1E 23)
George Hill Rd. Mgte —4J 209
George La. SE13 —4E 54
George La. Bou B —3J 165
George La. Brom —2L 83
George La. Folk —7K 189
George La. Leeds —1C 140 (2A 28)
George La. New R —2C 212
George La. Roch —6N 79
George Marsham Ho. Maid —5C 138
George Parris Ct. Min S —6K 219
George Roche Rd. Cant —4M 171
Georges Av. Whits —6C 224
Georges Clo. Orp —6L 71
George's Rd. Tats —8D 164
George St. W1 —2B 4
George St. Afrd —9F 158
George St. Bztt —2C 47
George St. Croy —2D 13
George St. Dover —3G 181
George St. Hunt —9L 137 (3D 27)
George St. Maid —6D 126
George St. Ram —5J 211
George St. Sit —8J 99
George St. S'hrst —4E 27
George St. Tonb —7H 145
George St. Tun W —2J 157
George Summers Clo. Roch —4B 80
George Warren Ct. Mgte —4D 208
George Wood Clo. Lydd —3C 204
Georgian Clo. Brom —2L 83
Georgian Clo. Queen —9B 218
Georgian Dri. Cox —5A 138
Georgian Way. Gill —7M 95
Geraint Rd. Brom —9K 55
Gerald Av. Chat —1C 94
Geraldine Rd. Folk —5F 188
Gerald Palmby Ct. Deal —3M 177
Gerald Rd. Grav —5K 63
Gerda Rd. SE9 —7E 56
Gerdview Dri. Dart —9K 59
Gerlach Ho. Kenn —5G 158
German St. W'sea —4A 46
Gerpins La. Upm —2D 7
Gerrard Av. Roch —3A 94
Gerrards Dri. Sit —9G 98
Gertrude Rd. Belv —4B 52
Ghent St. SE6 —7D 54
Gibbet La. Horsm —2B 198
Gibbett La. Horsm —2B 198 (1C 36)
Gibbetts. L'tn G —2N 155
Gibbon Rd. SE15 —3D 5
Gibbons Rd. Sit —6C 98
Gibbs Brook La. Oxt —3A 24
Gibbs Hill. H'crn —3M 193
Gibbs Hill. Nett —3N 135 (2B 26)
Gibney Ter. Brom —9J 55
Gibraltar. —2A 42
Gibraltar Av. Gill —5D 80
Gibraltar Hill. Chat —8C 80 (2D 17)
Gibraltar La. H'nge —9A 192 (2A 42)
Gibraltar La. Maid —1B 126
Gibralter Sq. Gus —1K 181
Gibson Clo. N'fleet —8E 62
Gibson Dri. King H —5L 123 (2B 26)
Gibson St. Sit —7F 98
Gidds Pond Cotts. Weav —3H 127
Giddyhorn La. Maid —5N 125
Gideon Clo. Belv —4C 52
Gifford Clo. Gill —9M 81
Giffords Cross Rd. Corr —2C 9
Gigger's Grn. Rd. Bon —3B 40
Gigghill Rd. Lark —7D 108
Gighill Rd. Leyb —4C 16
Giggs Hill. Orp —5J 71
Gilbert Clo. SE3 —8B 50
Gilbert Clo. Hem —6K 95
Gilbert Clo. Swans —4K 61
Gilbert Pl. S'gte —8E 188
Gilbert Rd. Afrd —8F 158
Gilbert Rd. Belv —3B 52 (3C 6)
Gilbert Rd. Brom —3K 69
Gilbert Rd. Ram —4H 211
Gilbert Ter. Maid —2D 126
Gilbourne Rd. SE18 —6H 51
Gilchrist Av. H Bay —5D 194
Gilchrist Cotts. Weald —6K 131
Gildenhill Rd. Swan —3K 73 (1D 15)
Gildersome St. SE18 —6C 50
Gildrage Hill. S Min —4D 31
Giles Gdns. Mgte —5D 208
Giles La. Cant —8J 167 (4D 21)
Giles Young Ct. Mil R —6F 98
(off St Paul's St.)
Gilford Rd. Deal —5M 177 (2E 33)
Gilham Gro. Deal —6L 177
Gillan Ct. SE12 —8L 55
Gill Av. Wain —1A 80
Gill Cres. N'fleet —8E 62
Gillespie Rd. N5 —1C 5
Gillett Rd. Lydd —2D 204
Gilletts La. E Mal —3E 124
Gillian St. SE13 —3E 54
Gillies Rd. W King —6E 88
Gillingham. —7F 80 (1E 17)
Gillingham Bus. Cen. Gill —2J 95
Gillingham Bus. Pk. Gill —2K 95
Gillingham Drove. Cant —8A 214
Gillingham F.C. —1E 17
Gillingham Ga. Rd. Gill —5F 80
Gillingham Grn. Gill —6H 81
Gillingham Northern Link Rd. Chat —4E 80
Gillingham Rd. Gill —8F 80 (1E 17)
Gill La. Mer —2A 40
Gill La. Ruck —3A 40
Gillman Clo. H'nge —8B 192
Gillmans Rd. Orp —2K 85
Gillon M. Cant —1A 172
Gill's Cotts. Roch —7B 80
Gills Ct. Roch —5B 80
Gill's Green. —2K 191 (3D 37)
Gills Rd. S Dar —4E 74 (1E 15)
Gill, The. Pem —6D 152
Gilmore Rd. SE13 —2G 54
Gilroy Way. Orp —1K 85
Gilton Rd. SE6 —8H 55
Giltspur St. EC1 —2C 5
Gimble Way. Pem —6C 152
Gingerbread La. Hawkh —4D 37
Ginsbury Clo. Roch —6B 80
Ginsbury Ho. Roch —6A 80
Gipps Cross La. L'tn G —2N 155
Gipsy Hill. SE19 —1D 13
Gipsy Rd. SE27 —1D 13
Gipsy Rd. Well —9M 51
Giraud Dri. Fav —4F 186
Girton Gdns. Croy —4D 82
Girton Rd. SE26 —1A 68
Gittens Clo. Brom —9J 55
Glack Rd. Deal —6J 177
Glade Gdns. Croy —1B 82
Gladeside. Croy —9A 68
Glades Pl. Brom —5K 69
Glades Shop. Cen., The. Brom —5K 69
Glades, The. Grav —2J 77
Gladeswood Rd. Belv —4C 52
Glade, The. Brom —5N 69
Glade, The. Chat —9D 94
Glade, The. Croy —1B 82 (2D 13)
Glade, The. Sev —5J 119
Glade, The. Shol —4J 177
Glade, The. Tonb —9L 133
Glade, The. W Wick —4E 82
Gladiator St. SE23 —5B 54
Gladstone Rd. Broad —1K 211 (2E 23)
Gladstone Rd. Chat —1B 94
Gladstone Rd. Dart —4N 59
Gladstone Rd. Folk —5L 189
Gladstone Rd. Maid —3D 126
Gladstone Rd. Mgte —4C 208
Gladstone Rd. Orp —6E 84
Gladstone Rd. Tonb —6H 145
Gladstone Rd. Tun W —1B 156
Gladstone Rd. Walm —7M 177
Gladstone Rd. Whits —3F 224
Gladstone Rd. W'boro —3J 161 (1A 40)
Gladwell Rd. Brom —2K 69
Gladwyn Clo. Gill —7N 95
(in two parts)
Glamford Rd. Roch —7H 79
Glamis Clo. Chat —6D 94
Glanfield Rd. Beck —7C 68
Glanville Rd. Brom —6L 69
Glanville Rd. Gill —7G 81
Glanville Rd. Roch —5L 79
Glasbrook Rd. SE9 —5N 55
Glasford St. SW17 —1B 12
Glasgow Ho. Maid —1H 139
Glassenbury. —2D 37
Glassenbury Rd. C'brk —2D 37
Glassmill La. Brom —5J 69 (1E 13)
(in two parts)
Glass Yd. SE18 —3C 50
Glastonbury Clo. Orp —2L 85
Glastonbury Ho. SE13 —3J 55
(off Wantage Rd.)
Gleaming Wood Dri. Chat —2F 110 (3E 17)
Gleaners Clo. Weav —5H 127
Gleanings M. Roch —7N 79
Glebe Clo. Smar —2K 221
Glebe Clo. St Mc —7J 213
Glebe Cotts. E'Lng —1E 29
Glebe Ct. SE3 —1H 55
Glebe Ct. Ram —8M 205
Glebe Ct. Sev —8J 119
Glebefield, The. Sev —5G 118
Glebe Gdns. Len —7F 200
Glebe Gdns. Mgte —3N 207
Glebe Ho. Dri. Brom —2L 83
Glebeland. Eger —4C 29
Glebeland. Mer —8M 161
Glebelands. Alk —1B 42
(in two parts)
Glebelands. Ah —4B 216
Glebelands. Bidb —3C 150
Glebelands. Bidd —8K 163
Glebelands. Dart —2G 58
Glebelands. H'shm —3N 141
Glebelands. Pens —3H 149
Glebe La. Maid —8K 125 (2D 27)
Glebe La. Sev —9J 119
Glebe La. Sit —9J 99
Glebe Meadow. W'bury —1C 136
Glebe Pl. Hort K —7C 74
Glebe Pl. Smar —3K 221
Glebe Rd. Brom —4K 69
Glebe Rd. Gill —9H 81
Glebe Rd. Grav —6E 62
Glebe Rd. Mgte —3N 207
Glebe Rd. Weald —5J 131 (3D 25)
Glebe, The. SE3 —1H 55
Glebe, The. Bidb —3C 150
Glebe, The. Chst —4E 70
Glebe, The. Cux —1G 92
Glebe, The. Pem —6C 152
Glebe, The. Pens —3H 149
Glebe Way. Eri —6F 52
Glebe Way. Kenn —3H 159
Glebe Way. W Wick —3F 82 (2E 13)
Glebe Way. Whits —5F 224
Gleeson Dri. Orp —5H 85
Glenalvon Way. SE18 —4A 50
Glen Av. H Bay —2K 195
Glenavon Ho. Broad —6M 209
(off Francis Rd.)
Glenavon Lodge. Beck —3D 68
Glenbarr Clo. SE9 —1D 56
Glenbervie Dri. H Bay —2M 195
Glenbow Rd. Brom —2H 69
Glenbrook Clo. H Bay —2L 195
Glenbrook Gro. Sit —4F 98
Glencoe Rd. Chat —1D 94
Glencoe Rd. Mgte —4E 208
Glen Ct. Sidc —9J 57
Glendale. Swan —8G 72
Glendale Clo. SE9 —1C 56
Glendale M. Beck —4E 68
Glendale Rd. Eri —4D 52
Glendale Rd. Min S —5J 219
Glendale Rd. N'fleet —9D 62
Glendower Cres. Orp —9J 71
Glendown Rd. SE2 —5J 51
Glen Dunlop Ho., The. Sev —4K 119
Gleneagles Clo. Orp —2F 84
Gleneagles Ct. Chat —9C 94
Gleneagles Dri. Maid —8C 126
Gleneagles Grn. Orp —2F 84
Glenesk Rd. SE9 —1C 56
Glenfarg Rd. SE6 —6F 54
Glenfield Rd. Dover —1G 180
Glengall Rd. Bexh —1N 57
Glen Gro. Dover —5G 181
Glenhead Clo. SE9 —1D 56
Glen Ho. E16 —1C 50
(off Storey St.)
Glenhouse Rd. SE9 —3C 56
Glenhurst. Beck —4F 68
Glenhurst Av. Bex —6A 58
Glen Iris Av. Cant —9J 167
Glen Iris Clo. Cant —9J 167
Glenister St. E16 —1C 50
Glenlea Rd. SE9 —3B 56
Glenlyon Rd. SE9 —3C 56
Glenmore Lodge. Beck —4E 68
Glenmore Pk. Tun W —5F 156
Glenmore Rd. Well —7H 51
Glenmount Path. SE18 —5E 50
Glen Rd. Kgdn —3M 199 (3E 33)
Glenrosa Gdns. Grav —1M 77
Glenrose Ct. Sidc —1K 71
Glensdale Rd. SE4 —1C 54
Glenshiel Rd. SE9 —3C 56
Glenside. Whits —5J 225
Glenside Av. Cant —9A 168
Glen, The. Brom —5H 69
Glen, The. Croy —4A 82
Glen, The. Min S —4J 219
(in two parts)
Glen, The. Orp —4C 84
Glen, The. S'wll —2C 220
Glen, The. Ups —3A 22
(off Nethergoing Hill)
Glenthorne Rd. W6 —3A 4
Glenton Rd. SE13 —2H 55
Glentrammon Av. Orp —7H 85
Glentrammon Clo. Orp —6H 85
Glentrammon Gdns. Orp —7H 85
Glentrammon Rd. Orp —7H 85
Glenure Rd. SE9 —3C 56
Glenview. SE2 —6M 51
Glen View. Grav —6H 63
Glenview Rd. Brom —5N 69
Glen Wlk. York —3C 20
Glenwood Clo. Chat —2F 94
Glenwood Clo. Hem —5K 95
Glenwood Clo. Maid —4N 125
Glenwood Clo. St Mic —4C 222
Glenwood Ct. Sidc —9J 57
Glenwood Dri. Min S —5J 219
Glenwood Rd. SE6 —6D 54
Glenwood Way. Croy —9A 68
Glimpsing Grn. Eri —3N 51
Glistening Glade. Gill —5A 96
Gload Cres. Orp —3M 85
Globe La. Chat —8C 80
(in two parts)
Globe Rd. E2 & E1 —2D 5
Globe Town. —2D 5
Glory La. H'lgh —4C 31
Gloster Ropewalk. Dover —7H 181
Gloster Way. Dover —7H 181
Gloucester Av. NW1 —2C 4
Gloucester Av. Broad —1K 211
Gloucester Av. Clift —3H 209
Gloucester Av. Sidc —7G 57
Gloucester Av. Well —2H 57
Gloucester Clo. Gill —3C 96
Gloucester M. New R —1D 212
Gloucester Pde. Sidc —3J 57
Gloucester Pl. NW1 & W1 —2B 4
Gloucester Pl. Folk —6K 189
Gloucester Rd. SW7 —3B 4
Gloucester Rd. Belv —5A 52
Gloucester Rd. Dart —5J 59
Gloucester Rd. Grav —9H 63
Gloucester Rd. King T —1A 12
Gloucester Rd. Maid —9G 127
Gloucester Rd. Whits —3H 225
Gloucester Ter. W2 —2B 4
Glover Clo. SE2 —4L 51
Glover Rd. W'boro —9J 159
Glovers Cres. Sit —8G 98
Glovers Mill. Roch —9A 80
Gloxinia Rd. S'fleet —2A 76
Glyn Davis Clo. Dun G —2F 118
Glyndebourne Pk. Orp —3D 84
Glynde Rd. Bexh —1M 57
Glynde St. SE4 —4C 54
Glyndon Rd. SE18 —4E 50
Glyn Dri. Sidc —9K 57
Glynne Clo. Gill —5N 95
Goatham Green. —4C 45
Goatham La. B Oak —3C 45
Goathurst Common. —3C 130 (2C 24)
Goat Lees. —2G 159
Goat Rd. Mitc —2B 12
Goatsfield Rd. Tats —8C 164
Gobery Hill. W'hm —1C 226
Goddard Rd. Beck —7A 68 (1D 13)
Goddards Clo. C'brk —8B 176
(in two parts)
Goddard's Green. —8B 176 (3E 37)
Goddard's Grn. Rd. Bene —3A 38
Godden Green. —6A 120 (2D 25)
Godden Rd. Cant —7N 167
Godden Rd. Snod —2D 108
Goddings Dri. Roch —9L 79
Goddington. —4L 85 (2B 14)

Goddington Chase—Greenbank

Goddington Chase. *Orp* —5K **85**
Goddington La. *H'shm* —2K **141** (2B **28**)
Goddington La. *Orp* —4L **85** (2B **14**)
Goddington Rd. *Roch* —4M **79**
Godfrey Clo. *Roch* —3K **79**
Godfrey Evans Clo. *Tonb* —2M **145**
Godfrey Hill. *SE18* —4A **50**
Godfrey Ho. *Whits* —5G **224**
Godfrey Rd. *SE18* —4B **50**
Godfrey Wlk. *Afrd* —1F **160**
Godington La. *Ashf* —5A **158**
Godington Rd. Ind. Est. *Afrd* —8E **158**
Godington Way. *Afrd* —8E **158**
Godinton House. —6A **158** (1E **39**)
Godinton La. *Gt Cha & Afrd* —1E **39**
Godinton Rd. *Afrd* —7D **158** (1A **40**)
(in two parts)
Godlands, The. *Tovil* —8C **126**
Godmersham. —3B 30
Godric Cres. *New Ad* —9G **82**
Godstone Rd. *Purl & Whyt* —3C **13**
Godstow Rd. *SE2* —2L **51**
Godwin Clo. *Kem* —2G **98**
Godwin Rd. *Brom* —6M **69**
Godwin Rd. *Cant* —4J **171**
Godwin Rd. *Clift* —3E **208**
Godwin Rd. *Dover* —4L **181**
Godwyn Ct. *Dover* —3J **181**
Godwyne Clo. *Dover* —4J **181**
Godwyne Path. *Dover* —3J **181**
Godwyne Rd. *Dover* —4J **181**
Godwyn Rd. *Deal* —2M **177** (2E **33**)
Godwyn Rd. *Folk* —6G **189**
Goffers Rd. *SE3* —3E **5**
Gogway. *Walt* —4D **31**
Goldcrest Wlk. *Whits* —7D **224**
Goldcrest Way. *New Ad* —9G **82** (3E **13**)
Golden Acre La. *Wgte S* —4J **207**
Golden Clo. *Wgte S* —4J **207**
Golden Green. —2E 146 (3A 26)
Golden Hill. *Elham* —4E **31**
Golden Hill. *Whits* —6H **225** (2C **21**)
(in two parts)
Golden La. *EC1* —2D **5**
Golden Sands Holiday Cen. *St Mar* —1E **214**
Golden Sq. *New R* —3B **212**
Golden Sq. *Tent* —7C **222**
Golden St. *Deal* —3N **177**
Golden Wood Clo. *Chat* —2G **110**
Goldfinch Clo. *Fav* —3G **186**
Goldfinch Clo. *H Bay* —5K **195**
Goldfinch Clo. *Lark* —8E **108**
Goldfinch Clo. *Orp* —6J **85**
Goldfinch Clo. *Pad W* —1M **153**
Goldfinch Rd. *SE28* —3F **50**
Goldhawk Rd. *W6 & W12* —3A **4**
Gold Hill. *Westw* —4E **29**
Golding Clo. *Dit* —9G **109**
Golding Gdns. *E Peck* —1M **147**
Golding Rd. *Sev* —4K **119**
Goldings. *Pad W* —1K **153**
Goldings Clo. *King H* —7M **123**
Goldings, The. *Gill* —3M **95**
Goldsel Rd. *Swan* —8E **72** (2C **15**)
Goldsmid Rd. *Tonb* —8J **145** (4E **25**)
Goldsmid St. *SE18* —5G **51**
Goldsmith Ct. *Tent* —6C **222**
Goldsmith Rd. *W3* —2A **4**
Goldsmith Rd. *Gill* —6A **96**
Goldsmith's Row. *E2* —2D **5**
Goldstone Drove. *Ah* —3C **22**
Goldstone Wlk. *Chat* —1D **110**
Gold Street. —8K 77
Gold St. *Sole S & Ludd* —8J **77** (2B **16**)
Goldsworth Dri. *Roch* —3L **79**
Goldthorne Clo. *Maid* —5F **126**
Goldups La. *Shott* —2B **30**
Goldwell Clo. *Adgtn* —2B **40**
Goldwell La. *Adgtn* —2B **40**
Goldwell La. *Gt Cha* —1E **39**
Golf Ct. *Deal* —1M **177**
Golf Ho. Rd. *Oxt* —2A **24**
Golf Links Av. *Grav* —1G **76**
Golford. —2E 37
Golford Rd. *C'brk* —8E **176** (3E **37**)
Golf Rd. *Brom* —6C **70**
Golf Rd. *Deal* —1M **177** (2E **33**)
Golfs, The. *New R* —2C **212**
Golgotha. —3B 32
Goodall Clo. *Gill* —6A **96**
Goodall Ho. *SE4* —2A **54**
Goodban Sq. *Ah* —5C **216**
Goodbury Rd. *Knat* —4B **104**
Goodcheap La. *Hin* —1B **40**
Goodfellow Way. *Dover* —4J **181**
Goodge St. *W1* —2C **4**
Goodhart Way. *W Wick* —1H **83**
Good Hope. *Deal* —6J **177**
Goodley Stock. —2A 24
Goodley Stock Rd. *Crock H & W'ham* —9D **116** (3A **24**)
Goodmayes. —1B 6
Goodmayes La. *Ilf* —1B **6**
Goodmead Rd. *Orp* —1J **85**
Goodnestone. —2B 32
(nr. Aylesham)
Goodnestone. —3B 20
(nr. Faversham)
Goodnestone Hill. *Good* —2B **32**
Goodnestone Park. —2B **32**
Goodnestone Rd. *Sit* —8J **99**
Goodnestone Rd. *W'hm* —3C **226** (1B **32**)
Goods Sta. Rd. *Tun W* —1G **157**
Goods Way. *NW1* —2C **5**
Goodwin Av. *Whits* —3M **225**
Goodwin Dri. *Maid* —1E **126**
Goodwin Dri. *Sidc* —8M **57**
Goodwin Rd. *Cli* —6M **65**
Goodwin Rd. *Ram* —6F **210**
Goodwin Rd. *St Mb* —9J **213**
Goodwins, The. *Tun W* —4F **156**
Goodwood Clo. *H Hals* —2H **67**
Goodwood Clo. *Maid* —2J **139**
Goodwood Cres. *Grav* —2H **77**
Goodwood Pde. *Beck* —7B **68**
Goodworth Rd. *Wro* —7M **105**
Goosander Way. *SE28* —3F **50**
Gooseberry Hall La. *Good* —2B **32**
Goose Clo. *Chat* —4D **94**
Goose Green. —9J 163 (2B 38)
(nr. Biddenden)
Goose Green. —6G 134 (3B 26)
(nr. Hadlow)
Goose Grn. Clo. *Orp* —5J **71**
Gooseneck La. *H'crn* —3K **193**
Gordon Av. *Queen* —8B **218**
Gordonbrock Rd. *SE4* —3D **54**
Gordon Clo. *Sit* —7K **99**
Gordon Cotts. *Bre* —4C **114**
Gordon Cotts. *Bri* —8H **173**
Gordon Ct. *Maid* —5B **138**
Gordon Gro. *Wgte S* —2K **207**
Gordon Henry Ho. *Eden* —6C **184**
Gordon Ho. Rd. *NW5* —1C **4**
Gordon Pl. *Grav* —4H **63**
Gordon Promenade. *Grav* —4H **63**
Gordon Promenade E. *Grav* —4J **63**
Gordon Rd. *Beck* —6C **68**
Gordon Rd. *Belv* —4D **52**
Gordon Rd. *Cant* —3M **171** (1D **31**)
Gordon Rd. *Cars* —3B **12**
Gordon Rd. *Chat* —1D **94**
(Magpie Hall Rd.)
Gordon Rd. *Chat* —5D **80**
(South Rd.)
Gordon Rd. *Corr* —2C **8**
Gordon Rd. *Dart* —5L **59**
Gordon Rd. *Fav* —4J **187**
Gordon Rd. *Folk* —5D **188**
Gordon Rd. *Gill* —7H **81**
Gordon Rd. *H Bay* —3G **195**
Gordon Rd. *Hoo* —8G **66**
Gordon Rd. *Mgte* —2E **208**
Gordon Rd. *N'fleet* —5D **62**
Gordon Rd. *Ram* —4H **211**
Gordon Rd. *Roch* —5L **79**
Gordon Rd. *Sev* —7J **119**
Gordon Rd. *Sidc* —3G **57**
Gordon Rd. *Tun W* —7J **151**
Gordon Rd. *W'wd* —8E **208**
Gordon Rd. *Whitf* —8F **178**
Gordon Rd. *Whits* —5F **224**
Gordon Sq. *WC1* —2C **4**
Gordon Sq. *Birch* —4E **206**
Gordon Sq. *Fav* —5J **187**
*Gordon Ter. Lydd —4C **204***
(off Rodin Hood La.)
Gordon Ter. *Roch* —8N **79**
Gordon Way. *Brom* —4K **69**
Gore. —2K 183 (2C 33)
Gore Clo. *E'try* —3K **183**
Gore Cotts. *Grn St* —8C **60**
Gore Ct. Rd. *Otham* —3J **139** (2E **27**)
Gore Ct. Rd. *Sit* —9F **98** (3C **19**)
Gore End Clo. *Birch* —4D **206**
Gore Green. —6H 65
Gore Grn. La. *High* —4C **9**
Gore Grn. Rd. *High* —7H **65**
Gore La. *E'try* —3J **183** (2C **33**)
Gore La. *Goud* —2D **37**
Gore M. *Cant* —9A **168**
Gore Rd. *Bre* —5A **114** (3B **18**)
Gore Rd. *Dart* —7C **60** (4E **7**)
Gore Rd. *E'try* —2K **183** (2C **33**)
Goresbrook Rd. *Dag* —2B **6**
Gore Street. —2B 22
Gore St. *Monk* —3B **22**
Gore Ter. *E'try* —2K **183**
Gorham Clo. *Snod* —3D **108**
Gorham Dri. *Down* —8K **127**
Gorham Dri. *Tonb* —7K **145**
Gorley Ho. *Dover* —5J **181**
Gorman Rd. *SE18* —4B **50**
Gorrell Ct. *Whits* —5G **224**
Gorrell Rd. *Whits* —4G **224**
Gorringe Av. *S Dar* —5D **74**
Gorse Av. *Chat* —7B **94**
Gorse Cres. *Dit* —1H **125**
Gorse Hill. *F'ham* —1A **88** (2D **15**)
Gorse La. *H Bay* —5K **195** (2E **21**)
Gorse Mead. *Afrd* —1D **160**
Gorse Rd. *Croy* —5D **82**
Gorse Rd. *Orp* —3B **86** (2C **14**)
Gorse Rd. *Roch* —4K **79**
(in two parts)
Gorse Rd. *Sit* —6J **99**
Gorse Rd. *Tun W* —9L **151**
Gorse Way. *Hart* —8M **75**
Gorsewood Rd. *Hart* —8M **75**
(in two parts)
Gorst St. *Gill* —7F **80**
Goschen Rd. *Dover* —4G **180**
Gosfield Rd. *H Bay* —3H **195**
Gosmere. —1A 30
Gospel Oak. —1C 4
Gossage Rd. *SE18* —5F **50**
Gosselin St. *Whits* —5F **224**
Gosset St. *E2* —2D **5**
Goss Hall La. *Ah* —4F **216**
Goss Hill. *Swan* —2K **73** (1D **15**)
Gosshill Rd. *Chst* —5C **70**
Gossington Clo. *Chst* —9D **56**
Goswell Rd. *EC1* —2C **5**
Goteley Mere. *Kenn* —3G **159**
Gothic Clo. *Dart* —8L **59**
Gothic Clo. *Walm* —9L **177**
Gothic Cotts. *Afrd* —9A **158**
Goudhurst. —8K 185 (2D 37)
Goudhurst Clo. *Cant* —7N **167**
Goudhurst Clo. *Maid* —5B **126**
Goudhurst Rd. *Brom* —1H **69**
Goudhurst Rd. *C'brk* —8A **220** (2D **37**)
Goudhurst Rd. *Gill* —9L **81**
Goudhurst Rd. *Horsm* —3C **198** (1C **37**)
Goudhurst Rd. *Lam* —2C **36**
Goudhurst Rd. *Mard* —4J **205** (1D **37**)
Goudhurst Rd. *S'hrst* —1E **37**
Gouge Av. *N'fleet* —6D **62**
Gough Rd. *S'gte* —8E **188**
Gould Rd. *Chat* —8E **94**
Goulston. *Maid* —2J **137**
Gourock Rd. *SE9* —3C **56**
Gover Hill. —2D 134 (2A 26)
Gover Hill. *Rough* —3C **134** (2A **26**)
Gover View. *Rough* —1D **134**
Gower St. *WC1* —2C **4**
Gowland Pl. *Beck* —5C **68**
Grace Av. *Bexh* —9A **52**
Grace Av. *Maid* —3A **126**
(in two parts)
Grace Clo. *SE9* —8N **55**
Grace Hill. *Folk* —6K **189** (2A **42**)
Grace Meadow. *Whitf* —6E **178**
Grace Rd. *S'ness* —3B **218**
Grace Wlk. *Deal* —5K **177**
Gracious La. *Sev* —3H **131** (2D **25**)
Gracious La. Bri. *Sev* —2H **131**
Gracious La. End. *Sev* —3G **131**
Grafton Av. *Roch* —3B **94**
Grafton Rise. *H Bay* —4D **194**
Grafton Rd. *Broad* —5J **209**
Grafton Rd. *Sit* —7G **99**
Grafton Rd. *Wor Pk* —2A **12**
Grafton Way. *Sit* —7H **99**
Grafty Green. —9N 141 (3B 28)
Graham Clo. *Croy* —3D **82**
Graham Clo. *Gill* —6C **80**
Graham Rd. *E8* —1D **5**
Graham Rd. *Bexh* —2A **58**
*Graham Ter. Sidc —4K **57***
(off Westerham Dri.)
Grain. —2C 190 (3C 10)
Grainey Field. *H'lip* —7G **96**
Grainger Wlk. *Tonb* —1L **145**
Grain Rd. *Gill* —7L **95**
Grain Rd. *Isle G* —4A **190** (4B **10**)
Grain Rd. *Mid S* —9H **201** (4A **10**)
Grampian Clo. *Orp* —9H **71**
Grampian Clo. *Tun W* —9K **151**
Grampian Way. *Down* —8K **127**
Grampion Clo. *Afrd* —7G **158**
Gram's Rd. *Walm* —9L **177** (3E **33**)
Granada St. *Maid* —5D **126**
Granary. *Pad W* —9N **147**
Granary Clo. *Gill* —2B **96**
Granary Clo. *Weav* —4H **127**
Granary Ct. Rd. *Sme* —9M **165** (1C **40**)
Granary Pl. *Whits* —6F **224**
Granby Rd. *SE9* —9B **50**
Granby Rd. *Grav* —4B **62**
Grand Acre. *Walt* —4C **31**
*Grand Ct. Folk —8H **189***
(off Earls Av.)
Grand Ct. *L'stne* —4F **212**
Grand Depot Rd. *SE18* —5C **50** (3A **6**)
Grand Dri. *SW20* —1A **12**
Grand Dri. *H Bay* —2C **194** (2E **21**)
Grand Dri. *Lgh S* —1B **10**
Grand Pde. *Lgh S* —1B **10**
Grand Pde. *L'stne* —5F **212** (2E **47**)
Grand Shaft. —6J **181**
Grandshore La. *Frit* —1E **37**
Grandsire Gdns. *Hoo* —7H **67**
Grandstand Rd. *Eps* —4A **12**
Grand View Av. *Big H* —5C **164**
Grange. —6L 81 (1E 17)
Grange Clo. *Eden* —6C **184**
Grange Clo. *Leyb* —8A **108**
Grange Clo. *Sidc* —8J **57**
Grange Clo. *W'ham* —8E **116**
Grange Cotts. *Maid* —2M **139**
*Grange Ct. Folk —7J **189***
(off Ingles Rd.)
Grange Ct. *Ram* —7G **211**
Grange Cres. *Dart* —4B **60**
Grange Cres. *St Mic* —4B **222**
Grange Dri. *Chst* —2A **70**
Grange Dri. *Orp* —9L **85**
Grange Gdns. *Tun W* —1D **156**
Grange Hill. *Chat* —9E **80**
Grange Hill. *Plax* —9L **121** (2A **26**)
Grangehill Pl. *SE9* —1B **56**
Grangehill Rd. *SE9* —2B **56**
Grange Ho. *Eri* —9H **53**
Grange Ho. *Grav* —5F **62**
Grange Ho. *Maid* —7L **125**
Grange La. *Hart* —1N **89** (2A **16**)
Grange La. *S'lng* —8C **110** (4E **17**)
(in two parts)
Grange M. *Fav* —5H **187**
Grangemill Rd. *SE6* —8D **54**
Grangemill Way. *SE6* —7D **54**
Grange Rd. *E13* —2E **5**
Grange Rd. *SE1* —3D **5**
Grange Rd. *Broad* —6K **209** (1E **23**)
Grange Rd. *Deal* —5L **177**
Grange Rd. *Folk* —5E **188**
Grange Rd. *Gill* —6H **81** (1E **17**)
Grange Rd. *Grav* —5F **62**
Grange Rd. *H Bay* —3J **195**
(in two parts)
Grange Rd. *Orp* —4F **84**
Grange Rd. *Platt* —2B **122** (1A **26**)
Grange Rd. *Ram* —5G **211** (2E **23**)
Grange Rd. *Roch* —5M **79**
Grange Rd. *Salt* —4J **197** (3D **41**)
Grange Rd. *Sev* —9H **119**
Grange Rd. *S'brne* —3K **133**
Grange Rd. *St Mic* —4A **222** (3B **38**)
Grange Rd. *T Hth & SE19* —1D **13**
Grange Rd. *Tun W* —1D **156**
Grange, The. *Croy* —3C **82**
Grange, The. *E Mal* —2E **124**
Grange, The. *Sea* —7C **224**
Grange, The. *S'wll* —2C **220**
Grange, The. *S Dar* —4D **74**
Grange, The. *W King* —9F **88**
Grange Way. *Broad* —2K **211**
Grange Way. *Eri* —7J **53**
Grange Way. *Hart* —9M **75**
Grange Way. *Roch* —9N **79**
Grangeways Clo. *N'fleet* —9E **62**
Grangewood. *Bex* —6A **58**
Grangewood La. *Beck* —2C **68**
Granite St. *SE18* —5H **51**
Grannies La. *Chill* —2B **32**
Granny's La. *Bos* —3D **31**
Grant Clo. *Broad* —7J **209**
Grant Clo. *Gill B* —2L **95**
Grantham Av. *Deal* —5K **177**
Grantley Clo. *Afrd* —2E **160**
Granton Rd. *Sidc* —2L **71**
Grant Rd. *Wain* —1N **79**
Grants La. *Oxt & Eden* —3A **24**
Granville Av. *Broad* —1M **211**
Granville Av. *Ram* —3F **210**
Granville Clo. *Fav* —5G **186**
Granville Ct. *Maid* —3D **126**
Granville Dri. *H Bay* —5C **194**
Granville Farm. *Ram* —5K **211**
Granville Gro. *SE13* —1F **54**
Granville Marina. *Ram* —5K **211**
*Granville Marina Ct. Ram —5K **211***
(off Granville Marina)
Granville M. *Sidc* —9J **57**
Granville Pde. *S'gte* —8E **188**
Granville Pk. *SE13* —1F **54**
Granville Pl. *S'ness* —2D **218**
Granville Rd. *Broad* —1M **211**
Granville Rd. *Gill* —7H **81**
Granville Rd. *Grav* —5E **62**
Granville Rd. *Kgdn* —6N **199**
Granville Rd. *Maid* —3D **126**
Granville Rd. *Sev* —6H **119**
Granville Rd. *S'ness* —2C **218** (4C **11**)
Granville Rd. *Sidc* —9J **57**
Granville Rd. *St Mb* —8K **213** (4E **33**)
Granville Rd. *Tun W* —9J **151**
Granville Rd. *Walm* —8M **177** (3E **33**)
Granville Rd. *Well* —1L **57**
Granville Rd. *W'ham* —8E **116**
Granville Rd. E. *S'gte* —8F **188**
Granville Rd. W. *S'gte* —8E **188**
Granville St. *Deal* —5N **177**
Granville St. *Dover* —3H **181**
Grapple Rd. *Maid* —2C **126**
Grasdene Rd. *SE18* —7J **51**
Grasmere Av. *Orp* —4D **84**
Grasmere Av. *Ram* —5E **210**
Grasmere Gdns. *Folk* —4H **189**
Grasmere Gdns. *Orp* —4D **84**
Grasmere Gro. *Roch* —3N **79**
Grasmere Rd. *Bexh* —9D **52**
Grasmere Rd. *Brom* —4J **69**
Grasmere Rd. *Kenn* —4G **159**
Grasmere Rd. *Orp* —3D **84**
Grasmere Rd. *Purl* —3C **13**
Grasmere Rd. *Whits* —4J **225**
(in two parts)
Grasmere Way. *Aysm* —1D **162**
Grassington Rd. *Sidc* —9J **57**
Grasslands. *Afrd* —2B **160**
Grasslands. *Langl* —4A **140**
Grassmere. *Leyb* —9D **108**
Grassmere. *St Mar* —3D **214**
Grass Rd. *Long* —8B **76**
Grassy Glade. *Hem* —5L **95**
Grassy La. *Sev* —8J **119**
Grave La. *Mard* —4E **27**
Gravel Castle. —8E 162 (3A 32)
Gravel Castle Rd. *B'hm* —9D **162** (3A **32**)
Gravel Hill. *Bexh* —3C **58** (4C **6**)
Gravel Hill. *Cha H* —3C **170**
Gravel Hill. *Croy* —7A **82** (3D **13**)
Gravel Hill Clo. *Bexh* —3C **58**
Gravel La. *Sev* —3E **130**
Gravel La. *W Hou* —2B **42**
Gravelly Bottom Rd. *Kgswd* —5B **140** (3A **28**)
Gravelly Ways. *Ladd* —4C **26**
Gravel Pit La. *SE9* —3D **56**
Gravel Pits La. *Bough B* —5A **142**
Gravel Pit Way. *Orp* —3J **85**
Gravel Rd. *Brom* —4A **84** (2A **14**)
Gravel Rd. *S at H* —3B **74**
Gravel Wlk. *Cant* —2M **171** (1D **31**)
Gravel Wlk. *Roch* —7A **80**
Gravelwood Clo. *Chst* —8E **56**
Graveney. —3B 20
Graveney Clo. *Cli* —6N **65**
Graveney Rd. *Fav* —5K **187** (3A **20**)
Graveney Rd. *Maid* —1J **139**
Gravesend. —4G 63 (4B 8)
Gravesend Rd. *High* —2H **79** (1C **17**)
Gravesend Rd. *Roch* —1D **17**
Gravesend Rd. *Shorne* —8B **64** (1C **16**)
Gravesend Rd. *Wro* —6N **105** (4A **16**)
Gravesham Ct. *Grav* —5G **63**
Gravesham Museum. —4G **63**
Grayland Clo. *Brom* —4N **69**
Grayne Av. *Isle G* —3C **190**
Grays. —3A 8
Grays Farm Rd. *Orp* —4K **71**
Grayshott Clo. *Sit* —8G **99**
Gray's Inn Rd. *WC1* —2C **5**
Grays Rd. *W'ham* —3D **116** (1A **24**)
Graystone Rd. *Whits* —2J **225**
Grays Way. *Cant* —4H **171**
Grazeley Clo. *Bexh* —3D **58**
Gt. Bounds Dri. *Tun W* —3E **150**
Gt. Brooms Rd. *Tun W* —6H **151**
Great Buckland. —7M 91 (3B 16)
Great Budds. —3F 132
Great Burgh. —4A 12
*Gt. Burton Houses. Kenn —5J **159***
(off Dudley Rd.)
Gt. Central Way. *NW10* —1A **4**
Great Chart. —9A 158 (1E 39)
Gt. Chart By-Pass. *Afrd* —1A **160** (1E **39**)
Gt. Chertsey Rd. *W4* —3A **4**
Great Comp Garden. —3D **122** (1A **26**)
Gt. Conduit St. *Hythe* —6K **197**
Gt. Courtlands. *L'tn G* —1A **156**
Great Dixter. —2C **45**
Gt. Dover St. *SE1* —3D **5**
Gt. Eastern Rd. *E15* —1E **5**
Gt. Eastern St. *EC2* —2D **5**
Great Elms. *Hdlw* —7D **134**
Gt. Elms Rd. *Brom* —7M **69**
Greatfield Clo. *SE13* —2D **54**
Gt. Footway. *L'tn G* —2N **155**
Gt. Hall Arc. *Tun W* —2H **157**
Gt. Harry Dri. *SE9* —8C **56**
Greathed Manor. —1A **34**
Gt. Higham Farm Cotts. *Dod* —9K **115**
Great Holt. *Bod* —4C **31**
Gt. Ivy Mill Cotts. *Maid* —1C **138**
Great Job's Cross. —1D 45
Great Lines. —8E 80
Great Lines. *Gill* —7D **80**
Gt. Marlborough St. *W1* —2C **4**
Great Maytham Hall. —4K **213** (4B **38**)
Gt. Mead. *Eden* —4C **184**
Great Mongeham. —3D 33
Greatness. —3L 119 (1D 25)
Greatness La. *Sev* —3K **119**
Greatness Rd. *Sev* —3K **119**
Gt. Norman St. *Ide H* —2A **130**
Gt. Norman St. *Sev* —2C **24**
Gt. Oak Row. *Afrd* —5F **160**
Gt. Portland St. *W1* —2C **4**
Gt. Queen St. *WC2* —2C **5**
Gt. Queen St. *Dart* —4N **59**
Gt. South Av. *Chat* —2D **94**
Great Stonar. —2M 217 (4D 23)
Greatstone-on-Sea. —6A 212 (3E 47)
Gt. Tattenhams. *Eps* —4A **12**
Gt. Thrift. *Orp* —7E **70**
Gt. Till Clo. *Otf* —7G **102**
Gt. Western Rd. *W9 & W11* —2B **4**
Gt. West Rd. *W4 & W6* —3A **4**
(Chiswick)
Gt. West Rd. *W4* —3A **4**
(Gunnersbury)
Greatwood. *Chst* —3C **70**
Grebe Clo. *H'nge* —8C **192**
Grebe Clo. *Lwr Sto* —8K **201**
Grebe Ct. *Lark* —9D **108**
Grebe Cres. *Hythe* —8D **196**
Grecian Rd. *Tun W* —3H **157**
Grecian St. *Maid* —3D **126**
Greenacre. *Dart* —7L **59**
Greenacre. *Kgtn* —3E **31**
Green Acre Clo. *Chat* —6D **94**
Greenacre Clo. *Swan* —7F **72**
Greenacre Dri. *Walm* —9M **177**
Greenacres. *SE9* —4C **56**
Green Acres. *Eyt* —4L **185**
Greenacres. *Sidc* —9J **57**
Green Acres Clo. *H Bay* —4J **195**
Greenacres Clo. *Orp* —5E **84**
Greenbank. *Chat* —3E **94**
Greenbank. *Kenn* —4H **159**

Green Bank Clo.—Hadlow Dri.

Green Bank Clo. Hem —6K 95
Greenbanks. Dart —7M 59
Greenbanks. Lym —8D 204
Greenborough Clo. Maid —2H 139
Green Clo. Brom —6H 69
Green Clo. Roch —1A 94
Green Cloth M. Cant —9A 168
(off Brymore Clo.)
Green Ct. Bri —8H 173
Green Ct. Folk —4L 189
Green Ct. S'hrst —8K 221
Greencourt Rd. Orp —8F 70
Green Ct. Rd. Swan —9E 72 (2C 15)
Greencroft. Afrd —3B 160
Greendale Wlk. N'fleet —9D 62
Green Dell. Cant —7N 167
Green Farm Clo. Orp —6H 85
Green Farm La. Shorne —7C 64 (4C 8)
Greenfield. Eden —6D 184
Greenfield Clo. Eccl —4L 109
Greenfield Clo. Tun W —9C 150
Greenfield Cotts. Boxl —7F 110
Greenfield Cotts. Cant —3M 171
Greenfield Cotts. S'ndge —7L 215
Greenfield Dri. Brom —5M 69
Greenfield Gdns. Orp —1F 84
Greenfield Rd. Dart —1E 72
Greenfield Rd. Folk —4L 189
Greenfield Rd. Gill —6H 81
Greenfield Rd. Ram —2G 211
Greenfields. Maid —9H 127
Greenfields. S'ndge —7L 215
Greenfields Clo. Wain —1A 80
Greenfinches. Hem —5J 95
Greenfinches. Long —6A 76
Greenfrith Dri. Tonb —9H 133
Green Gdns. Orp —6E 84
Greengates. Whitf —5F 178
Greenganate St. E13 —2A 6
Greenhill. —5E 194 (2E 21)
(nr. Herne Bay)
Green Hill. —9L 127 (2E 27)
(nr. Maidstone)
Green Hill. SE18 —5B 50
Green Hill. Orp —3B 100
Green Hill. Otham —9L 127
Greenhill Bri. Rd. H Bay —4E 194
Greenhill Clo. Min —6M 205
Greenhill Cotts. Maid —9L 127
Greenhill Gdns. H Bay —4E 194
Greenhill Gdns. Min —6M 205
Grn. Hill La. Eger —4C 29
Green Hill La. H'shm —8M 141
Greenhill Pk. NW10 —2A 4
Greenhill Rd. H Bay —5C 194 (2D 21)
Greenhill Rd. N'fleet —7E 62
Greenhill Rd. Otf —6K 103
Green Hills. B'hm —9A 162 (3E 31)
Greenhill Ter. SE18 —5B 50
Greenhithe. —2H 61 (4E 7)
Greenhithe. Maid —6C 126
Greenhithe Clo. Sidc —5G 56
Greenholm Rd. SE9 —3D 56
Greenhouse La. Cant —9L 167
Greenhurst La. Oxt —3A 24
Greening St. SE2 —4L 51
Greenlands. Platt —2A 122
Greenlands. Sole S —8J 77
Greenlands Rd. Kems —1B 120
Green La. SE9 & Chst —6D 56 (4A 6)
Green La. SE20 —3A 68 (1D 13)
Green La. SW16 & T Hth —1C 13
Green La. Afrd —4C 160
Green La. B'le —2B 32
Green La. Bene —3A 38
Green La. Bou M —5E 138 (3E 27)
Green La. Broad —8J 209 (1E 23)
Green La. Cap F —1D 41
Green La. C'lck —8B 174 (3E 29)
Green La. Cha S —3E 27
Green La. Cli —2C 176
Green La. Coll S —4C 27
Green La. Crowb —4D 35
Green La. Dover —2G 180 (1C 43)
Green La. E End —3A 38
Green La. Eyt —4L 185 (3C 32)
Green La. Folk —5L 189
Green La. Four E —8A 130 (3B 24)
Green La. Frit —1A 38
Green La. Hythe —6H 197
Green La. Ilf & Dag —1B 6
Green La. Isle G —2C 190
Green La. Lam —2B 36
Green La. Langl —5A 140 (3A 28)
Green La. Mgte —5H 209 (1E 23)
Green La. Meop —1G 90 (2B 16)
Green La. Mord —2B 12
Green La. Old L —6K 175
Green La. P Hth —3B 28
Green La. R Min —8H 183
Green La. Rod —3J 115 (3C 19)
Green La. Shorne —2B 78
Green La. Smar —3K 221
Green La. Stal —2D 29
Green La. St Mc —9H 199
Green La. S'bry —1G 113
Green La. Stod —4A 22
Green La. Temp E —8C 178
(in two parts)
Green La. Tros —5E 106
Green La. Walm —9L 177
Green La. W Bra —1B 40
Green La. Whits —5F 224
Green La. Av. Hythe —6H 197
Green La. Cotts. Langl —5A 140
Green Lanes. N4 & N16 —1D 5
Green La., The. Leigh —6N 143
Greenlaw St. SE18 —3C 50
Green Leas Ches —4M 225
Greenleas. Pem —8B 152
Greenleigh Av. St P —7K 71
Greenly Way. New R —3D 212
Green Mnr. Way. Grav —2M 61
Greenmead. Eri —3N 51
Green Meadows. Dym —5C 182
Greenoak Rise. Big H —6C 164
Green Pl. Dart —3F 58
Green Porch Clo. Sit —4G 99
Green Rd. Birch —3E 206
Green Rd. Dart —1E 15
Green Rd. Horsm —2C 198
Green Rd. S'brne —4A 26
Greensands. W'slde —2F 110
Greensand Way. Rough —3D 134
Green's Cotts. Maid —4L 137
Green's End. SE18 —4D 50
Greenside. Bex —6N 57
Greenside. H Hal —7K 193
Greenside. Maid —6E 126
Greenside. Swan —5E 72
Greenside Clo. SE6 —7G 54
Greenside Wlk. Big H —6B 164
Greensole La. Ram —4C 210
Green St. E7 & E13 —1A 6
Green St. Dart —4D 7
Green St. Gill —7F 80
Green Street Green. —2G 75 (1E 15)
(nr. Dartford)
Green Street Green. —7H 85 (3B 14)
(nr. Orpington)
Green St. Grn. Rd. Dart —6B 60
Green, The. Adtn —7J 107
Green, The. Bear —5M 127 (2A 28)
Green, The. Bene —3A 38
Green, The. Bexh —8B 52
Green, The. Blean —5G 167
Green, The. Bou M —5E 138 (3E 27)
Green, The. Brom —8K 55
(in two parts)
Green, The. Burm —3B 182
Green, The. Cha —7D 170 (2C 31)
Green, The. Col —4B 32
Green, The. Croy —9C 82
Green, The. E Far —1M 137
Green, The. Eyt —4L 185
Green, The. Groom —5K 155 (2D 35)
Green, The. Hay —1K 83
Green, The. L'tn G —2M 155 (2D 35)
Green, The. Leigh —6N 143
Green, The. L'brne —3L 173 (1A 32)
Green, The. Lwr Hal —8L 223
Green, The. Lydd —4B 204
Green, The. Mans —3B 210
Green, The. Matf —6J 153 (1B 36)
Green, The. Min S —3J 219
Green, The. Orp —6D 84 (2A 14)
Green, The. Otf —7J 103
Green, The. Salt —4J 197 (3D 41)
Green, The. Seal —3N 119
(off Church Rd.)
Green, The. Sev —4L 119
Green, The. Sidc —9J 57 (1B 14)
Green, The. St P —3K 71
Green, The. Til —3B 8
Green, The. Up Harb —1E 170
Green, The. Warl —4D 13
Green, The. Well —2G 56
Green, The. W'ham —8F 116
Green, The. W Mal —1A 124
Green, The. Wickh —4A 22
(off List, The)
Green, The. Wdchu —7B 226 (3D 39)
Green, The. W Grn —3A 32
(off Forstal Rd.)
Green, The. Wye —2M 159 (4A 30)
Green, The. Yald —7D 136
(off Vicarage Rd.)
Greentrees Av. Tonb —2M 145
Green Vale. Bexh —3M 57
Greenvale Gdns. Gill —1L 95
Greenvale Rd. SE9 —2B 56
Greenview Av. Beck —9B 68
Greenview Av. Croy —9B 68
Green View Av. Leigh —6A 144
Greenview Cres. Hild —3E 144
Greenview Wlk. Gill —8K 81
Green Wlk. Dart —3G 58
Green Way. SE9 —3N 55
Green Way. Brom —9A 70
Greenway. Chat —6A 94
Greenway. Chst —1C 70
Greenway. C'brk —8B 176
Greenway. Fav —4F 186
Green Way. Hart —8L 75
Green Way. Lydd —4B 204
Green Way. Maid —6M 125
Greenway. Tats —8C 164
Green Way. Tun W —6L 151
Greenway Ct. Rd. Holl —7G 128 (2B 28)
Greenway Gdns. Croy —4C 82
Greenway La. H'shm —1H 141 (2B 28)
Greenways. Beck —6D 68
Greenways. Long —6C 76
Greenways. Sit —8J 99
Greenways. Weav —4J 127
Greenways, The. Pad W —1L 153
Greenway, The. Orp —9K 71
Greenwich. —3E 5
Greenwich Borough Museum.
(off Speranza St.) —5H 51 (3B 6)
Greenwich Clo. Chat —7F 94
Greenwich Clo. Maid —5A 126
Greenwich High Rd. SE10 —3E 5
Greenwich La. Ewe M —1B 42
Greenwich Park. —3E 5
Greenwich S. St. SE10 —3E 5
Greenwood Clo. Orp —9G 70
Greenwood Clo. Sidc —7J 57
Greenwood Ho. SE4 —2A 54
Greenwood Ind. Est. Fav —2F 186
Greenwood Pl. Wro —8N 105
Greenwood Rd. Bex —9E 58
Greenwood Way. Sev —7G 119
Green Wrythe La. Cars —2B 12
Greggs Wood Rd. Tun W —8L 151
Gregory Clo. Brom —7J 69
Gregory Clo. Gill —7A 96
Gregory Clo. Kem —3H 99
Gregory Clo. Shor —2H 103
Gregory Ct. Wye —2M 159
Gregory Cres. SE9 —5N 55
Grenadier Clo. Rain —1D 96
Grenadier St. E16 —1C 50
Grenham Bay Av. Birch —3D 206
Grenham Rd. Birch —3D 206
Grenville Clo. Meop —3F 90
Grenville Gdns. Birch —3D 206
Grenville Rd. New Ad —9F 82
Grenville Way. Broad —9J 209
Gresham Av. Hart —8M 75
Gresham Av. Mgte —2M 207
Gresham Clo. Bex —4A 58
Gresham Clo. Rain —2B 96
Gresham Rd. Beck —5B 68
Gresham Rd. Cox —5A 138
Gresswell Clo. Sidc —8J 57
Greville Pl. NW6 —2B 4
Greybury La. M Grn —1A 34
Greycot Rd. Beck —1D 68
Greyfriars. Maid —4A 126
Greyfriars. —2M 171
Grey Friars Cotts. Cant —2M 171 (1D 31)
Grey Friars Ct. Broad —4K 209
Greyhound Commercial Cen., The. Dart —3F 58
Greyhound La. SW16 —1C 12
Greyhound Rd. Min S —9K 219
Greyhound Ter. SW16 —1C 12
Greyhound Way. Dart —3F 58
Greys Pk. Clo. Kes —6N 83
Greystone Pk. Sund —7N 117
Greystones Clo. Kems —8M 103
Greystones Rd. Bear —7K 127
Greystones Rd. C'snd —7B 210
Grey Wethers. S'lng —6B 110
Grey Willow Gdns. Afrd —1B 160
Gribble Bri. La. Bidd —2B 38
Grice Av. Big H —3A 164
Grierson Rd. SE23 —5A 54
Grieves Rd. N'fleet —8E 62
Griffin Mnr. Way. SE28 —3F 50
Griffin Rd. SE18 —5F 50 (3B 6)
Griffin St. Deal —3N 177
Griffin Wlk. Grnh —3F 60
Grigg. —4B 28
Grigg La. H'crn —3M 193 (4B 28)
Griggs App. Ilf —1B 6
Griggs Way. Bor G —2N 121
Grigsby La. Smar —4H 221 (1B 38)
Grimshill Ct. Cant —7J 167
Grimshill Rd. Whits —5F 224
Grimston Av. Folk —6H 189 (3A 42)
Grimston Gdns. Folk —7H 189
Grimthorpe Av. Whits —6E 224
Grinan Ct. Ram —3K 211
Grinsell Hill. Ram —2D 23
Grisbrook Farm Clo. Lydd —3D 204
Grisbrook Rd. Lydd —3C 204
Grizedale Clo. Roch —3A 94
Gromenfield. Groom —6K 155
Groombridge. —6K 155 (2D 35)
Groombridge Clo. Well —3J 57
Groombridge Hill. Groom —6K 155 (2D 35)
Groombridge La. E Grn —3D 35
Groombridge Place. —5K 155 (2D 35)
Groombridge Rd. Groom —4H 155 (2D 35)
Groombridge Sq. Maid —2J 139
Grosmont Rd. SE18 —6H 51
Grosvenor Av. N5 —1D 5
Grosvenor Av. Cars —3B 12
Grosvenor Av. Chat —9B 80
Grosvenor Bri. Tun W —9H 151 (1E 35)
Grosvenor Cres. Dart —3L 59
Grosvenor Gdns. SW1 —3C 4
Grosvenor Gdns. Mgte —4C 208 (1D 23)
Grosvenor Hill. Mgte —3C 208
Grosvenor Ho. Maid —3J 139
Grosvenor Pk. Tun W —1G 157
Grosvenor Pl. SW1 —3C 4
Grosvenor Pl. Mgte —3C 208
Grosvenor Pl. Tun W —8H 151
Grosvenor Rd. Belv —6B 52
Grosvenor Rd. Bexh —3M 57
Grosvenor Rd. Broad —9L 209
Grosvenor Rd. Gill B —2J 95
Grosvenor Rd. Kenn —3G 159
Grosvenor Rd. Orp —9G 71
Grosvenor Rd. Ram —5G 210
Grosvenor Rd. Tun W —1G 157 (2E 35)
Grosvenor Rd. Wall —3C 12
Grosvenor Rd. W Wick —2E 82
Grosvenor Rd. Whits —6F 224
Grosvenor Sq. Long —6L 75
Grosvenor St. W1 —2C 4
Grosvenor Ter. Folk —5L 189
(off Tram Rd., The)
Grosvenor Wlk. Tun W —1G 157
Grote Ct. Folk —6K 189
(off Dover Rd.)
Grotto Gdns. Mgte —3D 208
Grotto Hill. Mgte —3D 208
Grotto Rd. Mgte —3D 208
Grove. —3A 22
Grove Av. Ley S —6M 203
Grove Av. Tun W —3G 157
Grovebury Clo. Eri —6E 52
Grovebury Ct. Bexh —3C 58
Grovebury Rd. SE2 —2K 51
Grove Clo. SE23 —6B 54
Grove Clo. Brom —3K 83
Grove Clo. Fav —6E 186
Grove Cottage. Tonb —5K 145
Grove End. —3C 18
Grove End Rd. NW8 —2B 4
Gro. Ferry Hill. Ups —3A 22
Grove Gdns. Mgte —4A 208
Grove Green. —4H 127 (1E 27)
Grove Grn. La. Weav —4H 127
Grove Grn. Rd. E10 & E11 —1E 5
Grove Grn. Rd. Weav —4J 127
Groveherst Rd. Dart —1N 59
Grove Hill. —3A 22
Grovehill Ct. Brom —2J 69
Grove Hill Gdns. Tun W —3H 157
Grove Hill Rd. Tun W —2H 157 (2E 35)
Grovehurst. —2F 198 (1C 37)
(nr. Horsmonden)
Grovehurst. —2F 98
(nr. Kemsley)
Grovehurst Av. Kem —3G 98 (2C 19)
Grovehurst La. Horsm —3E 198 (1C 37)
Grovehurst Rd. Iwade —9C 198 (2C 19)
(in two parts)
Groveland Rd. Beck —6C 68
Grovelands Rd. Orp —3J 71
Grove La. SE5 —3D 5
Grove La. Bztt —2C 46
Grove La. Hunt —8G 137
Grove La. Iden —3A 46
Grove Mkt. Pl. SE9 —4B 56
Grove Park. —8L 55 (4A 6)
Grove Pk. Av. Sit —6C 98
Grove Pk. Rd. SE9 —8M 55 (4A 6)
Grove Pk. Rd. W4 —3A 4
Grove Rd. E3 —2D 5
Grove Rd. Belv —6A 52
Grove Rd. Bexh —2D 58
Grove Rd. Chat —1E 94
Grove Rd. Chid H —6E 148 (1C 35)
Grove Rd. Folk —6L 189
Grove Rd. Gill —6K 81
Grove Rd. Maid —2F 138
Grove Rd. Mitc —1C 12
Grove Rd. Monk —3B 22
Grove Rd. N'fleet —3A 62
Grove Rd. Ram —6H 211
Grove Rd. Roch —4M 79
Grove Rd. Seal —4A 120 (1D 25)
Grove Rd. Sell —2A 30
Grove Rd. Sev —3K 119
Grove Rd. S'le —1B 32
Grove Rd. Sutt —3B 12
Grove Rd. Tats —8C 164
Grove Rd. Up H'lng —6C 92
Grove Rd. Walm —7N 177
Grove Rd. Wickh —4A 22
Grover St. Tun W —1H 157
Groves, The. Snod —3D 108
Grove St. SE8 —3E 5
Grove Ter. Cant —3L 171
Grove Ter. Folk —5L 189
(off Dover Rd.)
Grove, The. E15 —1E 5
Grove, The. (Junct.) —4D 5
Grove, The. B'hm —8D 162
Grove, The. Bear —6K 127
Grove, The. Bexh —2M 57
Grove, The. Big H —6D 164
Grove, The. Deal —4M 177
Grove, The. Dover —3H 181
Grove, The. Grav —5G 63
Grove, The. H Bay —5D 194
Grove, The. Hythe —6K 197
Grove, The Kenn —4J 159
Grove, The. Pem —6C 152
Grove, The. Sidc —9N 57
Grove, The. Swan —6G 72
Grove, The. Swans —3M 61
Grove, The. Wgte S —3L 207
Grove, The. W King —1F 104
Grove, The. W Wick —3F 82
Grove Vale. SE22 —4D 5
Grove Vale. Chst —2C 70
Groveway. Ley S —6L 203
Grovewood Ct. Weav —5H 127
Grovewood Dri. Maid —1E 27
Grovewood Dri. Weav —5G 127
Grubb Street. —4H 75 (1E 15)
Grummock Av. Ram —5F 210
Grundy's Hill. Ram —6J 211
Guardian Ct. SE12 —3H 55
Guardian Ct. Gill —2M 95
Guardian Ind. Est. Mard —2K 205
Guestling Thorn. —4D 45
Guestwick. Tonb —2M 145
Guibal Rd. SE12 —5L 55
Guildables La. Eden —3A 24
Guildcount La. S'wch —5L 217
Guildersome St. SE18 —6C 50
Guildford Av. Wgte S —3J 207
Guildford Ct. Walm —8N 177
Guildford Gdns. Roch —6G 79
Guildford Ho. Maid —1G 138
Guildford Lawn. Ram —6H 211
Guildford Rd. Cant —4M 171
Guildford Rd. Tun W —2H 157
Guildhall St. Cant —2M 171 (1D 31)
Guildhall St. Folk —6K 189
Guildhall St. N. Folk —6K 189
Guild Rd. SE7 —6A 50
Guild Rd. Eri —7G 52
Guilford Av. Whitf —5E 178
Guilford Rd. S'wch B —1D 33
Guilford St. WC1 —2C 5
Guilton. —5B 216 (4B 22)
Guilton. Ah —5A 216 (4B 22)
Guldeford La. E Gul —3B 46
Guldeford Lane Corner. —3B 46
Guldeford Rd. E Gul —3A 46
Gullands. Langl —4A 140
Gulliver Rd. Sidc —7F 56
Gumping Rd. Orp —3E 84
Gun Back La. Horsm —3C 198
Gundulph Ho. Roch —6N 79
Gundulph Rd. Brom —6M 69
Gundulph Rd. Chat —8B 80
Gundulph Sq. Roch —6N 79
Gunfleet Clo. Grav —5K 63
Gun Green. —4N 191 (4E 37)
Gun Hill. W Til —3B 8
Gunlands. Horsm —2C 198
Gun La. Strood —5L 79 (1D 17)
Gunner La. SE18 —5C 50
Gunnersbury. —3A 4
Gunnersbury Av. W5 & W3 —3A 4
Gunnersbury La. W3 —3A 4
Gunning St. SE18 —4G 51
Gunnis Clo. Gill —7N 95
Gunn Rd. Swans —4L 61
Gunter Gro. SW10 —3B 4
Gurling Rd. St Mc —8J 199
Gushmere. —1A 30
Guston. —7K 179 (4D 33)
Guston Rd. Dover —3K 181 (1D 43)
Guston Rd. Maid —4F 126
Guthrie Gdns. Dover —1D 180
Guy Barnett Gro. SE3 —1K 55
Guy Clo. Broad —6L 209
Guyscliff Rd. SE13 —3F 54
Gwillim Clo. Sidc —3J 57
Gwydor Rd. Beck —6A 68
Gwydyr Rd. Brom —6J 69
Gwynne Av. Croy —1A 82
Gwynn Rd. N'fleet —7B 62
Gwyn Rd. Ram —2G 210
Gybbon Rise. S'hrst —8J 221
Gybbons Rd. Rol —3K 213
Gypsy Corner. (Junct.) —2A 4

Hackbridge. —2C 12
Hackbridge Rd. Wall —2C 12
Hacket Ho. Maid —2D 126
Hackfield. Afrd —9D 158
Hackington Clo. Cant —7L 167
Hackington Cres. Beck —2D 68
Hackington Pl. Cant —9M 167
Hackington Rd. T Hill —1K 167 (3D 21)
Hackington Ter. Cant —9M 167
Hacklinge. —2D 33
Hacklinge Hill. Hackl —2D 33
Hackney. —1D 5
Hackney Rd. E2 —2D 5
Hackney Rd. Maid —7N 125 (2D 27)
Hackney Wick. —1E 5
Hackney Wick. (Junct.) —1E 5
Hacton. —1D 7
Hacton La. Horn & Upm —1D 7
Hadden Rd. SE28 —3G 50
Haddington Rd. Brom —8G 55
Haddon Gro. Sidc —5H 57
Haddon Rd. Orp —8L 71
Hadleigh. —1A 10
Hadleigh Castle. —1A 10
Hadleigh Ct. Hem —8K 95
Hadleigh Gdns. H Bay —2J 195
Hadleigh Rd. Lgh S —1A 10
Hadley Clo. Meop —3G 90
Hadley Ct. Tun W —8F 150
Hadley Gdns. Holl —7G 128
Hadley Rd. Belv —4A 52
Hadlow. —8D 134 (3A 26)
Hadlow Dri. Clift —3J 209

Halsted Clo.—Herald Wlk.

Hasted Clo. Grnh —4J 61
Hasted Rd. N'tn —4K 97
Hasteds. Holl —7F 128
Haste Hill. —5D 138
Haste Hill Clo. Bou M —5D 138
Haste Hill Rd. Bou M —5D 138 (3E 27)
Hastingleigh. —4C 30
Hastings Av. Mgte —4E 208
Hastings Pl. S'wch —6L 217
Hastings Rd. Batt —4B 44
Hastings Rd. Brom —2A 84 (2A 14)
Hastings Rd. Flim —4C 37
Hastings Rd. Hawkh —8K 191 (1B 44)
Hastings Rd. I'ham —4E 45
Hastings Rd. Lam —4D 200 (3B 36)
Hastings Rd. Maid —6E 126 (2E 27)
Hastings Rd. Newe & Rol —4H 213 (1D 45)
Hastings Rd. N'iam —3D 45
Hastings Rd. Pem —8C 152 (1A 36)
Hatchard Gro. Swan —5G 73
Hatches La. E Peck —9H 135 (3B 26)
Hatch La. Cha H —4B 170 (1C 31)
Hatch Rd. Len —7D 200
Hatch St. Fav —5G 186
Hatcliffe Clo. SE3 —1J 55
Hatfield Rd. Mgte —3A 208
Hatfield Rd. Ram —5H 211
Hatfield Rd. Roch —4L 79
Hatham Grn. La. Stans —1K 105 (3E 15)
Hathaway Clo. Brom —2B 84
Hathaway Ct. Gill —3N 95
Hathaway Ct. Roch —7M 79
Hathaway Rd. Grays —3A 8
Hatherall Rd. Maid —3E 126
Hatherley Ct. Mgte —2E 208 (off Percy Rd.)
Hatherley Cres. Sidc —7J 57
Hatherley Gdns. E6 —2A 6
Hatherley Rd. Sidc —9J 57
Hathern Gdns. SE9 —9C 56
Hatmill La. Bchly —8M 153 (1B 36)
Hattersfield Clo. Belv —4A 52
Hatton Clo. SE18 —7F 50
Hatton Clo. N'fleet —8D 62
Hatton Garden. EC1 —2C 5
Hatton Rd. Chat —8F 94
Hault Farm. —3C 31
Havant Wlk. Maid —2J 139
Havelock Pl. Ah —5C 216
Havelock Rd. Belv —4A 52
Havelock Rd. Brom —7M 69
Havelock Rd. Dart —5J 59
Havelock Rd. Grav —5E 62
Havelock Rd. Tonb —4H 145
Havelock Rd. Walm —7M 177
Havelock St. Cant —2N 171 (1D 31)
Haven Clo. SE9 —8B 56
Haven Clo. Grav —4E 76
Haven Clo. Roch —1N 93
Haven Clo. Sidc —2L 71
Haven Clo. Swan —5G 72
Haven Ct. Beck —5F 68
Haven Dri. H'nge —8C 192
Haven Dri. H Bay —1N 195
Havengore Av. Grav —5K 63
Haven Hill. Hods —7N 89 (3A 16)
Haven Rd. Can I —2E 9
Haven St. Wain —7M 65 (4D 9)
Haven, The. Hythe —7D 196
Haven, The. Kgnt —4D 160
Haventhorpe. Afrd —7F 158
Haven Way. St Mi —3E 80
Havering Clo. Tun W —8M 151
Haverstock Ct. Orp —5K 71 (off Cotmandene Cres.)
Haverstock Hill. NW3 —1B 4
Haverthwaite Rd. Orp —3F 84
Haviker Street. —4D 27
Haviker St. Coll S —4C 27
Havisham Clo. Roch —1A 94
Havisham Rd. Grav —6M 63
Havock La. Maid —5C 126
Hawbeck Rd. Gill —8M 95
Hawden Clo. Hild —3F 144
Hawden La. Hild —3F 144
Hawden Rd. Tonb —5H 145
Hawe Clo. Cant —7N 167
Hawe Farm Way. H Bay —6J 195
Hawe La. Sturry —4F 168 (3E 21)
Hawes Av. Ram —5F 210
Hawes La. W Wick —2F 82
Hawes Rd. Brom —4L 69 (in two parts)
Hawes, The. Elham —6J 183
Hawes, The. S Min —4D 31
Hawfield Bank. Orp —4M 85
Hawk Clo. Whits —6E 224
Hawkenbury. —3K 157 (2E 35)
Hawkenbury Clo. Tun W —3K 157
Hawkenbury Mead. Tun W —4K 157
Hawkenbury Rd. H'bury —4A 28
Hawkenbury Rd. Tun W —3K 157 (2E 35)
Hawkesbury St. Dover —7J 181
Hawkesdown Rd. Walm —1M 199
Hawkesfield Rd. SE23 —7B 54
Hawkes Pl. Sev —9H 119
Hawkes Rd. Eccl —5K 109
Hawkhurst. —5L 191 (4D 37)
Hawkhurst Clo. Birch —3G 206
Hawkhurst Rd. Gill —9K 81
Hawkhurst Rd. Flim —4C 37
Hawkhurst Rd. Hawkh —1K 191 (3D 37)
Hawkhurst Way. Broad —2L 211
Hawkhurst Way. W Wick —3E 82
Hawkinge. —7D 192 (1A 42)
Hawkinge Wlk. Orp —6K 71
Hawkins Av. Grav —9H 63
Hawkins Clo. Chat —6C 80
Hawkins Clo. Mil R —4F 98
Hawkins Ct. SE18 —4A 50
Hawkins Rd. Folk —5D 188
Hawkins Way. SE6 —1D 68
Hawksbrook La. Beck —9E 68
Hawksdown. —1L 199
Hawksdown. Walm —1L 199
Hawkshead Clo. Brom —3H 69
Hawkshill Rd. Walm —1N 199
Hawkslade Rd. SE15 —3A 54
Hawk's La. Cant —2M 171 (1D 31)
Hawksmoor Clo. SE18 —5G 51
Hawks Rd. H Bay —5C 194
Hawks Rd. King T —1A 12
Hawkstone Rd. SE16 —3D 5
Hawks Way. Afrd —2C 160
Hawkwood. Maid —4M 125
Hawkwood Clo. Roch —8A 80
Hawkwood La. Chst —4E 70
Hawley. —9N 59 (1D 15)
Hawley Ct. Maid —5B 126
Hawley Rd. NW1 —1C 4
Hawley Rd. Dart —7M 59 (4D 7)
Hawley's Corner. —3D 116 (1A 24)
Hawley Sq. Mgte —3D 208
Hawley St. Mgte —3C 208 (1D 23)
Hawley Ter. Dart —1A 74
Hawley Vale. Dart —1A 74
Hawser Rd. Roch —2N 93
Hawstead La. Orp —6A 86 (2C 14)
Hawstead Rd. SE6 —4E 54
Hawthordene Rd. Beck —3J 83
Hawthorn. App —1B 46
Hawthorn Av. Big H —3D 164
Hawthorn Av. Cant —9N 167
Hawthorn Av. S'ness —4B 218 (4C 11)
Hawthorn Clo. Aysm —3C 162
Hawthorn Clo. Dover —2D 180
Hawthorn Clo. Eden —5C 184
Hawthorn Clo. Grav —9H 63
Hawthorn Clo. Hythe —8F 196
Hawthorn Clo. Orp —9F 70
Hawthorn Clo. Ram —3J 211
Hawthorn Clo. St Mar —3E 214
Hawthorn Corner. —2A 22
Hawthorn Cotts. Well —1J 57 (off Hook La.)
Hawthorndene Clo. Brom —3J 83
Hawthorndene Rd. Brom —3J 83
Hawthorn Dri. W Wick —5H 83
Hawthorne Av. Gill —2M 95
Hawthorne Clo. Brom —6B 70
Hawthorne Clo. Eyt —4L 185
Hawthorne Rd. Brom —6B 70
Hawthorn Ho. Barm —6L 125 (off Springwood Rd.)
Hawthorn Ho. Chat —6C 94
Hawthorn La. Sev —4G 118
Hawthorn Pl. Eri —5D 52
Hawthorn Rd. NW10 —1A 4
Hawthorn Rd. Bexh —2A 58
Hawthorn Rd. Dart —7L 59
Hawthorn Rd. Kgnt —5F 160
Hawthorn Rd. Roch —6H 79
Hawthorn Rd. Sit —7F 98
Hawthorns. Chat —1C 110
Hawthorns. Hart —7M 75
Hawthorns, The. Ayle —9J 109
Hawthorns, The. Broad —9G 209
Hawthorn Wlk. Tonb —9J 133
Hawthorn Wlk. Tun W —6L 151
Haxted. —4A 24
Haxted Mill. —4A 24
Haxted Mill & Museum. —4A 24
Haxted Rd. Brom —4L 69
Haxted Rd. Ling & Eden —4A 24
Haydens Clo. Orp —9L 71
Haydens M. Tonb —4J 145
Haydens, The. Tonb —4J 145
Haydons Rd. SW19 —1B 12
Hayes. —2L 83 (2A 14)
Hayes All. Whits —3F 224 (off Middle Wall)
Hayes Chase. W Wick —9G 69
Hayes Clo. Brom —3K 83
Hayes Clo. High —1G 78
Hayesden La. Tun W —2A 150 (1D 35)
Hayesford Pk. Dri. Brom —8J 69
Hayes Garden. Brom —2K 83
Hayes Hill. Brom —2H 83
Hayes Hill Rd. Brom —2J 83 (2E 13)
Hayes La. Beck —6F 68 (1E 13)
Hayes La. Brom —8K 69 (2A 14)
Hayes La. Kenl —4C 13 (in two parts)
Hayes La. Peas —3D 45
Hayes La. S'bry —4H 113
Hayes Mead Rd. Brom —2H 83
Hayes Rd. Brom —7K 69 (1A 14)
Hayes Rd. Grnh —5E 60
Hayes St. Brom —2L 83 (2A 14)
Hayes Ter. Shorne —1C 78
Hayes Way. Beck —7F 68
Hayes Wood Av. Brom —2L 83
Hayfield. Leyb —8C 108
Hayfield Rd. Orp —8J 71
Hayfields. Chat —9G 95
Hay Hill. E'try & Ha —3M 183 (2C 33)
Hay La. Ham —2D 33
Hay La. Ha —4N 183
Hayle Mill Cotts. Maid —9C 126
Hayle Mill Rd. Maid —8C 126
Hayle Rd. Maid —6D 126 (2E 27)
Hayles Clo. Tent —7C 222
Hayley Clo. Cux —1F 92
Haymakers La. Afrd —1B 160
Haymans Hill. Horsm —1D 198 (1C 37)
Hayman Wlk. Eccl —4K 109
Haymarket. SW1 —2C 4
Haymen St. Chat —9B 80
Hayne Rd. Beck —5C 68
Haynes Clo. SE3 —1H 55
Haynes Rd. N'fleet —8E 62
Hayrick Clo. Weav —4H 127
Haysden Country Park. —7E 144
Haysel. Sit —9H 99
Hays Mead. Ludd —9L 77
Hays Rd. Snod —4D 108
Hayton Rd. Stanf —8N 215 (2C 41)
Haywain Clo. Pad W —1M 153
Haywain Clo. Weav —5J 127
Hayward Av. Roch —4M 79
Hayward Clo. Dart —3E 58
Hayward Clo. Deal —6K 177
Hayward Clo. W'boro —1L 161
Hayward Dri. Dart —8N 59
Haywards Clo. New R —3C 212
Haywards Hill. Hock —2E 29
Hayward's Ho. Roch —6N 79
Haywards Yd. SE4 —3C 54 (off Lindal Rd.)
Haywood Rise. Orp —6G 85
Haywood Rd. Brom —7N 69
Hazebrouck Rd. Fav —5E 186
Hazel Av. Maid —4N 125
Hazelbank. L'tn G —2N 155
Hazelbank Rd. SE6 —7G 55 (4E 5)
Hazel Clo. Croy —1A 82
Hazel Clo. Eyt —4K 185
Hazelden Clo. W King —9G 88
Hazeldene Rd. Well —9L 51
Hazeldon Rd. SE4 —3B 54
Hazeldown Clo. River —2D 180
Hazel Dri. Eri —8J 53
Hazel End. Swan —8F 72
Hazel Gro. SE26 —9A 54
Hazel Gro. Chat —3E 94
Hazel Gro. Min S —3H 219
Hazel Gro. Orp —3D 84
Hazelhurst. Beck —4G 68
Hazelhurst Ct. SE6 —1F 68 (off Beckenham Hill Rd.)
Hazelmere Dri. H Bay —2L 195
Hazelmere Rd. Orp —7E 70
Hazelmere Way. Brom —9K 69
Hazel Rd. Dart —7L 59
Hazel Rd. Eri —8H 53
Hazel Shaw. Tonb —9J 133
Hazels, The. Gill —6L 95
Hazel Street. —7J 113 (4B 18) (nr. Bicknor)
Hazel Street. —4A 198 (2C 36) (nr. Horsmonden)
Hazel St. Rd. S'bry —8J 113 (4B 18)
Hazel Wlk. Broad —9G 209
Hazel Wlk. Brom —9C 70
Hazelwood. —2F 100 (3B 14)
Hazelwood Clo. Tun W —6K 151
Hazelwood Dri. Maid —4M 125
Hazelwood Houses. Short —6H 69
Hazelwood La. Coul —4B 12
Hazelwood Meadow. S'wch —7L 217
Hazelwood Rd. Cud —3F 100
Hazlemere Dri. Gill —7J 81
Hazlemere Rd. Sea —6C 224
Hazling Dane. S'wll —2E 220
Hazlitt Dri. Maid —4A 126
Headcorn. —3K 193 (4A 28)
Headcorn Dri. Cant —7N 167
Headcorn Flower Centre & Vineyard. —3M 193 (4B 28)
Headcorn Gdns. Clift —3J 209
Headcorn Rd. Bidd —6L 163 (1B 38)
Headcorn Rd. Brom —1J 69
Headcorn Rd. Frit —1A 38
Headcorn Rd. Gill —8L 81
Headcorn Rd. Graf G & Len —9N 141 (4B 28)
Headcorn Rd. S'wy & Len —9B 200
Headcorn Rd. Smar —1B 38
Headcorn Rd. S'hrst —7K 221 (1E 37)
Headcorn Rd. Sut V —9A 140 (3A 28)
Headcorn Rd. Ulc —4B 28
Head Hill Rd. Good —3B 20
Headingley Rd. Maid —3M 125
Headley Ct. Eden —5D 184
Headley Dri. New Ad —8E 82 (3E 13)
Headley Rd. Eps —4A 12
Head Race, The. Maid —7A 126
Heaf Gdns. Roy B —9K 109
Healy Dri. Orp —4H 85
Heard Way. Sit —6J 99
Hearnden Green. —4A 28
Hearne Clo. Sit —6K 99
Hearn's Rd. Orp —7L 71
Heartenoak Rd. Hawkh —5L 191 (4D 37)
Heart In Hand Rd. Haw —5N 195 (2A 22)
Hearts Delight. —1C 114 (3C 18)
Hearts Delight. B'den —1C 114 (3C 18)
Hearts Delight Rd. Tun —1C 114 (3C 18)
Heath Av. Bexh —6M 51
Heath Clo. Orp —1L 85
Heath Clo. Sturry —4E 168
Heathclose. Swan —5F 72
Heathclose Av. Dart —5J 59
Heathclose Rd. Dart —6H 59 (4D 7)
Heathdene Dri. Belv —4C 52
Heath End Rd. Bex —6F 58
Heatherbank. SE9 —9B 50
Heatherbank. Chst —5C 70
Heatherbank Clo. Dart —4F 58
Heather Clo. SE13 —5G 54
Heather Clo. Chat —7C 94
Heather Clo. Mgte —5A 208
Heather Clo. Sit —8H 99
Heather Ct. Sidc —2M 71
Heather Dri. Dart —5H 59
Heather Dri. Maid —7E 126
Heather Dri. St Mic —4C 222
Heather End. Swan —7E 72
Heather Rd. SE12 —6K 55
Heatherside Rd. Sidc —8M 57
Heathers, The. C'brk —9A 176
Heather Wlk. Tonb —9H 133 (in two parts)
Heather Way. S Croy —9A 82
Heatherwood Clo. Kgswd —6G 140
Heathfield. Chst —2E 70
Heathfield. Langl —4A 140
Heathfield Av. Dover —2G 181
Heathfield Av. Maid —2F 126
Heathfield Clo. Chat —4E 94
Heathfield Clo. Kes —6M 83
Heathfield Clo. Maid —2E 126
Heathfield Cotts. Swan —5E 72 (off London Rd.)
Heathfield Gdns. Rob —3A 44
Heathfield La. Chst —2D 70 (1A 14)
Heathfield Pde. Swan —5D 72
Heathfield Rd. Afrd —7G 158
Heathfield Rd. Bexh —2A 58
Heathfield Rd. Brom —3J 69
Heathfield Rd. Kes —6M 83 (2A 14)
Heathfield Rd. Maid —2E 126
Heathfield Rd. Sev —4G 118
Heathfields. Tun W —1K 157
Heathfield Ter. SE18 —6G 51
Heathfield Ter. W4 —3A 4
Heathfield Vale. S Croy —9A 82
Heathfield Way. B'hm —8D 162
Heath Gdns. Dart —6K 59
Heath Gro. Maid —7L 125
Heath Ho. Sidc —9H 57
Heathlands Rise. Dart —4J 59
Heath La. SE3 —1H 55
Heath La. Dart —4D 7
Heath La. (Lower) Dart —6K 59
Heath La. (Upper) Dart —7H 59
Heathlee Rd. SE3 —2J 55
Heathlee Rd. Dart —4F 58
Heathley End. Chst —2E 70
Heathorn St. Maid —4E 126
Heath Pk. Dri. Brom —6A 70
Heath Rise. Brom —9J 69
Heath Rd. App —4D 39
Heath Rd. Bex —6D 58
Heath Rd. Cox & Lin —5N 137
Heath Rd. Dart —4G 59
Heath Rd. Grays —2A 8
Heath Rd. Langl —4A 140 (3A 28)
Heath Rd. Maid —6K 125 (2D 27)
Heath Rd. W Far & E Far —3J 137 (3D 27)
Heath Side. —8G 58
Heathside. App —4D 39
Heathside. Orp —1F 84
Heathside Av. Bexh —9N 51
Heathside Av. Cox —4N 137
Heath St. NW3 —1B 4
Heath St. Dart —5L 59
Heath Ter. Horsm —2B 198
Heath, The. E Mal —4C 124 (1C 26)
Heath, The. Whits —4K 225
Heathview Av. Dart —4F 58
Heathview Cres. Dart —6J 59
Heathview Dri. SE2 —6M 51
Heath Vs. SE18 —5H 51
Heathway. (Junct.) —2C 6
Heathway. Croy —3C 82
Heathway. Dag —1C 6
Heath Way. Eri —8D 52
Heathwood Dri. Ram —3J 211
Heathwood Gdns. SE7 —4A 50
Heathwood Gdns. Swan —5D 72
Heathwood Point. SE23 —8A 54
Heathwood Wlk. Bex —6F 58
Heaton Rd. Cant —4L 171
Heaverham. —8E 104 (4E 15)
Heaverham Rd. Kems —8B 104 (4D 15)
Heavitree Clo. SE18 —5F 50
Heavitree Rd. SE18 —5F 50
Hectorage Rd. Tonb —7J 145 (4E 25)
Hector St. SE18 —4G 50
Hedge Barton Mobile Homes. Ford —9G 149
Hedgemans Rd. Dag —1B 6
Hedgend Ind. Est. St N —7E 214
Hedge Pl. Rd. Grnh —4F 60 (4E 7)
Hedgerows. Afrd —2B 160
Hedgerows, The. N'fleet —7D 62
Hedgerow, The. Weav —4H 127
Hedges, The. Maid —2D 126
Hedge Wlk. SE6 —1E 68
Hedgley M. SE12 —3J 55
Hedgley St. SE12 —3J 55
Hedley St. Maid —4D 126 (in two parts)
Heel La. B Oak —3B 168
Heel Rd. Stal —2E 29
Heights Ter. Dover —6H 181
Heights, The. Beck —3F 68 (in two parts)
Heights, The. Whits —6E 224
Helder Gro. SE12 —5J 55
Helding Clo. H Bay —5J 195
Helena Av. Mgte —5C 208 (1D 23)
Helena Corniche. S'gte —8C 188
Helena Rd. Cap F —2C 174
Helena Vs. S'gte —8B 188
Helen Clo. Dart —5J 59
Helen Keller Ct. Tonb —2J 145
Helen St. SE18 —4D 50
Helen Thompson Clo. Iwade —8C 198
Hellfire Corner & Underground Hospital. (off East Norman Rd.) —4L 181
Hellyer Ct. Roch —8N 79
Helmdon Clo. Ram —2G 210
Helvellyn Av. Ram —5F 210
Helvetia St. SE6 —7C 54
Hemmings Clo. Sidc —7K 57
Hempstead. —5K 95 (2E 17)
Hempstead La. Bap —8M 99 (3D 19)
Hempstead Rd. Hem —8J 95 (3E 17)
Hempstead St. Afrd —8F 158 (off Godinton Rd.)
Hempstead Valley Dri. Hem —5K 95 (2E 17)
Hempstead Valley Shop. Cen. Hem —8K 95
Hempton Hill. M Hor —2D 41
Hemsted. —1D 41
Hemsted Rd. Eri —7F 52
Henbane Clo. Weav —4H 127
Henbury La. W'mre —4E 31
Henderson Dri. Dart —2N 59 (4D 7)
Henderson Rd. Big H —2B 164
Hendley Dri. C'brk —7C 176
Hendon Way. NW4 & NW2 —1B 4
Hendry Ho. Chatt —7B 66
Hendy Clo. Whits —2L 225
Hendy Rd. Snod —2F 108
Henfield Clo. Bex —4B 58
Hengist Av. Mgte —4F 208
Hengist Ct. Maid —5D 126
Hengist Field. B'den —2A 114
Hengist Rd. SE12 —5L 55
Hengist Rd. Birch —4B 206
Hengist Rd. Deal —3N 177
Hengist Rd. Eri —7C 52
Hengist Rd. Wgte S —3J 207
Hengist Way. Brom —7H 69
Hengrave Rd. SE23 —5A 54
Hengrove Ct. Bex —6N 57
Henham Gdns. E Peck —1M 147
Henhurst. —4K 77 (1B 16)
Henhurst Rd. Cob —5K 77
Henhurst Rd. Sole S —1B 16
Heniker La. Sut V —3A 28
Henley Bus. Pk. Roch —5A 80
Henley Clo. Chat —5D 94
Henley Clo. Gill —3N 95
Henley Clo. Tun W —9J 151
Henley Ct. Sev —5J 119
Henley Deane. N'fleet —9D 62
Henley Fields. St Mic —5C 222
Henley Fields. Weav —3H 127
Henley Meadows. Tent —5B 222
Henley Rd. E16 —2B 50
Henley Street. —9L 77 (2B 16)
Henley St. Ludd —9L 77 (2B 16)
Henley View. St Mic —5C 222
Hennel Clo. SE23 —8A 54
Henniker Clo. Whitf —8E 178
Henniker Gdns. E6 —2A 6
Henry Cooper Way. SE9 —8N 55
Henry Ct. Cant —3M 171 (1D 31)
Henryson Rd. SE4 —3D 54
Henry St. Brom —4L 69
Henry St. Chat —9E 80
Henry St. Gill —2C 96
Henshill La. Hawkh —7J 191
Henson Clo. Orp —3D 84
Henville Rd. Brom —4L 69
Henwick Rd. SE9 —1N 55
Henwood. Hen I —8H 159
Henwood Green. —8D 152 (1A 36)
Henwood Grn. Rd. Pem —7C 152 (1A 36)
Henwood Ind. Est. Afrd —7J 159
Henwoods Cres. Pem —8C 152
Henwoods Mt. Pem —8D 152
Hepburn Gdns. Brom —2H 83
Hepplewhite M. Chat —1C 110
Herald Wlk. Dart —3N 59

Herbert Pl.—Hildenborough Gdns.

Herbert Pl. SE18 —6D 50
Herbert Rd. SE18 —7C 50 (3A 6)
Herbert Rd. Bexh —9N 51
Herbert Rd. Brom —8N 69
Herbert Rd. Chat —9D 80
Herbert Rd. Gill —3A 96
Herbert Rd. Ram —6G 210
Herbert Rd. Swan —2J 73
Herbert Rd. Swans —4M 61
Herbert Rd. W'boro —3H 161
Herberts Ct. Lwr Sto —8K 201
Herbert St. Dover —3G 181
Herbert Ter. SE18 —7D 50
Herdsdown. Hoo —8G 66
Herdson Rd. Folk —6G 188
Hereford Clo. Gill —1N 95
Hereford Gdns. SE13 —3H 55
Hereford Gdns. Birch —5E 206
Hereford Rd. Maid —1G 138
Hereson. —5J 211
Hereson Rd. Ram —4K 211 (2E 23)
Hereward Av. Birch —3D 206
Hereward Lincoln Ho. N'fleet —4C 62
Heritage Dri. Gill —2J 95
Heritage Hill. Kes —6M 83
Heritage Museum. —2M 171
Heritage Rd. Chat —5D 94
Heritage Rd. Folk —5D 188
Herman Ter. Chat —9D 80
Hermitage Clo. Hythe —6L 197
Hermitage Ct. Maid —4K 125
Hermitage Ct. Tonb —5J 145
Hermitage La. NW2 —1B 4
Hermitage La. SW16 —1C 13
Hermitage La. Ayle —1K 125 (1D 27)
Hermitage La. Bou M —3E 27
Hermitage La. Det —8K 111 (4E 17)
Hermitage Rd. SE19 —1D 13
Hermitage Rd. High —1G 78 (1C 17)
Hermit Rd. E16 —2E 5
Herne. —6H 195 (2E 21)
Herne Av. H Bay —4H 195
Herne Bay. —2F 194 (1E 21)
Herne Bay Rd. B Oak & Sturry —4D 168 (3E 21)
Herne Bay Rd. Whits —2K 225 (2D 21)
Herne Bay W. Ind. Est. H Bay —4D 194
Herne Common. —8G 195 (2E 21)
Herne Dri. H Bay —5D 194
Herne Hill. —4D 5
Herne Hill. SE24 —4D 5
Herne Hill Rd. SE5 —4D 5
Herne Pound. —8J 123 (2B 26)
Herne Rd. Gill —1M 95
Herne Rd. H Bay —9F 194 (2E 21)
Herne St. H Bay —6H 195 (2E 21)
Herneville Gdns. H Bay —3J 195
Herne Windmill. —5J 195 (2E 21)
Hernhill. —3B 20
Heron Clo. Eden —4C 184
Heron Clo. Lwr Hal —8L 223
Heron Ct. Brom —7M 69
Heron Cres. Sidc —8G 56
Herondale. S Croy —9A 82
Heronden. —2C 32
Heronden Rd. E'try —4H 183 (2C 32)
Heronden Rd. Maid —4J 139
Heron Forstall Av. H'nge —8D 192
Herongate Rd. Swan —2F 72
Heron Hill. Belv —5A 52 (3C 6)
Heron Hill La. Meop —7E 90
Heron Ho. Sidc —8K 57
Heron Lodge. Dover —2G 180
Heron Rd. Lark —9D 108
Herons Clo. Chi —8K 175
Heron's Way. Hythe —8D 196
Herons Way. Pem —6D 152
Herontye Dri. E Grin —2A 34
Heron Wlk. Afrd —1C 160
Heron Way. Chat —6D 94
Heron Way. Grays —3E 7
Heron Way. Lwr Sto —8K 201
Hero Wlk. Roch —4N 93
Heron Ct. Short —7J 69
Herschell Rd. SE23 —5B 54
Herschell Rd. Birch —3E 206
Herschell Rd. E. Walm —7M 177
Herschell Rd. W. Walm —7M 177
Herschell Sq. Walm —7M 177
Hersden. —2L 169 (3A 22)
Hertford Ct. Cant —2B 172
Hertford Ho. Ram —6J 211 (off Hertford Pl.)
Hertford Pl. Ram —6J 211
Hertford Rd. Mgte —5G 208
Hertford St. Ram —6H 211
Hertford Wlk. Belv —5B 52
Herts Cres. Loose —5C 138
Hertsfield Ho. Tonb —8G 144 (off Quarry Hill Rd.)
Herying Clo. Hall —7F 92
Hesiers Hill. Warl —4E 13
Hesiers Rd. Warl —4E 13
Hesketh Av. Dart —6B 60
Heskett Pk. Pem —7D 152
Hever. —4B 24
Hever Av. W King —8E 88
Hever Castle. —4B 24
Hever Clo. Maid —2J 139
Hever Cotts. Sole S —8K 77
Hever Ct. Rd. Grav —2H 77 (1B 16)
Hever Croft. SE9 —9C 56
Hever Croft. Roch —7K 79
Hever Gdns. Brom —5C 70
Heverham Rd. SE18 —4G 50
Hever Pl. Cant —8N 167
Hever Pl. Maid —6B 126
Hever Pl. Sit —8D 98
Hever Rd. Eden —7D 184 (4B 24)
Hever Rd. Hever & Bough B —5A 142 (4B 24)
Hever Rd. W King —7E 88
Heversham Rd. Bexh —9B 52
Hever Wood Rd. W King —8E 88
Hewett Pl. Swan —7E 72
Hewitt Clo. Croy —4D 82
Hewitt Clo. Gill —6J 81
Hewitt Rd. Dover —4J 181
Hewitts Pl. W'boro —9K 159
Hewitts Rd. Orp —8A 86 (3C 14)
Hewitts Roundabout. (Junct.) —8A 86 (3C 14)
Hexal Rd. SE6 —8H 55
Hextable. —3G 73 (1D 15)
Hextable Clo. Afrd —3D 160
Hextable Clo. Maid —2N 125
Heyford Clo. H'nge —8D 192
Heygate Av. Sth S —1C 10
Heywood M. Cant —1A 172
Hibbs Clo. Swan —5E 72
Hibernia Dri. Grav —8L 63
Hibernia Point. SE2 —2M 51 (off Wolvercote Rd.)
Hibernia St. Ram —6J 211
Hichisson Rd. SE15 —3A 54
Hickmans Green. —4K 165 (4B 20)
Hickory Dell. Hem —5K 95
Hick's Forstal. —3E 21
Hicks Forstal Rd. Hoath —3E 21
Higgins La. Chat —7C 80
Higham. —9G 64 (4C 9)
Higham Clo. Maid —7A 126
Higham Gdns. Tonb —2M 145
Higham La. Bri —9J 173
Higham La. Tonb —7L 133 (3A 26)
Higham Rd. Cli —4B 176
Higham Rd. Clif —4D 9
Higham Rd. Wain —1A 80 (1D 17)
Higham School Rd. Tonb —1L 145
Higham Upshire. —1G 78
Higham View. S'lng —7B 110
Higham Wood. —2M 145 (3A 26)
High Bank. Roch —1A 94
High Banks. Loose —3C 138 (2D 27)
Highbanks Clo. Well —7K 51
High Beeches. Orp —7J 85
High Beeches. Sidc —1N 71
High Beeches. Tun W —8K 151
Highberry. Leyb —8C 108
Highbrook Rd. SE3 —1N 55
High Broom Cres. W Wick —1E 82
High Broom Rd. Crowb —4C 35
High Brooms. —7J 151 (1E 35)
High Brooms Rd. Tun W —6H 151 (1E 35)
Highbury. —1C 5
Highbury Clo. W Wick —3E 82
Highbury Corner. (Junct.) —1C 5
Highbury Gdns. Ram —1F 210
Highbury Gro. N5 —1C 5
Highbury La. Tent —8B 222
Highbury Pk. N5 —1C 5
Highbury Wlk. Ram —2F 210
Highclere St. SE26 —9B 54
Highcombe Clo. SE9 —6N 55
High Croft Cotts. Swan —7H 73
Highcroft Grn. Maid —4J 139
Highcross Rd. Ivy H —8H 121 (2E 25)
Highcross Rd. S'fleet —1K 75 (1E 15)
High Dewar Rd. Gill —3C 96
High Elms. Gill —1A 96
High Elms Rd. Dow —2C 100 (3A 14)
Higher Dri. Purl —3C 13
Highfield Av. Eri —6C 52
Highfield Av. Orp —6H 85
Highfield Clo. SE13 —5G 55
Highfield Clo. Blean —8H 167
Highfield Clo. Gill —4N 95
Highfield Clo. Hawkh —6L 191
Highfield Clo. Pem —8C 152
Highfield Clo. Ram —1F 210
Highfield Clo. Salt —4H 197
Highfield Cotts. Dart —2J 73
Highfield Ct. H Bay —3F 194
Highfield Ct. Ram —2F 210
Highfield Dri. Brom —7H 69
Highfield Dri. W Wick —3E 82
Highfield Gdns. Mgte —4B 208
Highfield Ind. Est. Folk —5M 189
Highfield La. W'boro —4M 161 (1A 40)
Highfield Rd. Bexh —3A 58
Highfield Rd. Big H —5C 164
Highfield Rd. Brom —7B 70
Highfield Rd. Chst —6H 71
Highfield Rd. Dart —5L 59 (4D 7)
Highfield Rd. Gill —4N 95
Highfield Rd. Kems —7M 103
Highfield Rd. Min S —6F 218
Highfield Rd. Purl —3C 13
Highfield Rd. Ram —1F 210
Highfield Rd. Tun W —7J 151 (1E 35)
Highfield Rd. W'boro —2L 161
Highfield Rd. N. Dart —4L 59
Highfield Rd. S. Dart —5L 59
Highfields Av. H Bay —3K 195
Highfields Rd. Eden —2C 184
Highfields View. H Bay —3K 195
High Firs. Swan —7F 72
High Gables. Brom —5H 69
Highgate. —5L 191 (4E 37)
Highgate Hill. Hawkh —6K 191 (4D 37)
Highgate Rd. N6 & NW5 —1C 4
Highgate Rd. Ben —1E 9
Highgate Rd. Whits —4K 225
Highgate W. Hill. N6 —1C 4
High Gro. SE18 —7F 50
High Gro. Brom —4N 69
Highgrove. Tun W —5G 157
Highgrove Clo. Chst —4A 70
Highgrove Ct. Beck —3D 68
Highgrove Rd. Chat —6D 94
High Halden. —7K 193 (2C 38)
High Halden Rd. Bidd —9L 163 (2B 38)
High Halstow. —2H 67 (4E 9)
High Hilden Clo. Tonb —3G 145
High Holborn. WC1 —2C 5
High Ho. La. Hdlw —8A 134 (3A 26)
High Knocke. Dym —9A 182
Highland Clo. Folk —7F 188
Highland Ct. Cotts. Bri —9J 173
Highland Croft. Beck —1E 68
Highland Rd. Badg M —1C 102
Highland Rd. Bexh —3B 58
Highland Rd. Brom —4J 69
Highland Rd. Cha —9C 170
Highland Rd. Maid —1H 139
Highlands. Tun W —7K 151
Highlands Clo. Roch —7H 79
Highlands Cres. St Mar —2F 214
Highlands Hill. Swan —4H 73 (1D 15)
Highlands Ho. Tun W —2J 157
Highlands Pk. Seal —3M 119
Highlands Rd. Orp —1K 85
Highmead. SE18 —7G 51
High Mead. W Wick —3G 83
High Meadow. Dover —3H 181
High Minnis. S Min —4D 31
High Pk. N'iam —2D 45
High Point. SE9 —8D 56
High Ridge. Gill —2J 95
High Ridge. Goud —8K 185
Highridge. Hythe —8A 188
Highridge Clo. Weav —4J 127
High Rd. NW10 —1A 4
High Rd. Dart —8K 59 (4D 7)
High Rd. Horn H —1C 9
High Rd. Ilf & Romf —1B 6
High Rd. Lang H & Lain —1B 8
High Rd. N Stif —2E 7
High Rd. Ors —2A 8
High Rd. Reig & Coul —4B 12
High Rd. Stan H —2B 8
High Rd. Leytonstone. E11 —1E 5
High Rd. Wemb —1A 4
High Rocks. —2E 35
High Rocks. —4B 156 (2E 35)
High Rocks La. Tun W —4B 156 (2D 35)
High Snoad Wood. C'lck —7C 174
Highstead. —2A 22
Highstead Cres. Eri —8F 52
Highsted. —3G 115 (3C 19)
Highsted Rd. Sit —8G 99 (3C 19)
Highsted Valley Rod —3G 115 (3C 19)
High Street. —4D 37
(nr. Hawkhurst)
Highstreet. —3C 20
(nr. Yorkletts)
High St. Acton, W3 —2A 4
High St. Ashford, Afrd —8F 158 (in two parts)
High St. Aveley, S Ock —2E 7
High St. Aylesford, Ayle —7K 109 (4D 17)
High St. Banstead, Bans —4B 12
High St. Battle, Batt —4B 44
High St. Bean, Bean —8H 61 (4E 7)
High St. Beckenham, Beck —5D 68 (1E 13)
High St. Bidborough, Bidb —3C 150 (1E 35)
High St. Biddenden, Bidd —8L 163 (2B 38)
High St. Borough Green, Bor G —2M 121 (1A 26)
High St. Brasted, Bras —6K 117 (2B 24)
High St. Brenchley, Bchly —6N 153 (1B 36)
High St. Bridge, Bri —8E 172 (2E 31)
High St. Broadstairs, Broad —9L 209 (2E 23)
High St. Bromley, Brom —5K 69 (1A 14)
High St. Brompton, Bromp —6D 80
High St. Brookland, B'lnd —2C 46
High St. Canterbury, Cant —2M 171 (1D 31)
High St. Carshalton, Cars —2C 12
High St. Chatham, Chat —8C 80 (2E 17) (in two parts)
High St. Cheam, Sutt —3B 12
High St. Chipstead, Chip —4D 118 (1C 25)
High St. Chislehurst, Chst —2D 70 (1A 14)
High St. Colliers Wood. SW19 —1B 12
High St. Cowden, Cowd —1B 34
High St. Cranbrook, C'brk —8B 176 (3E 37)
High St. Crayford, Cray —4C 7
High St. Crowborough, Crowb —4C 35
High St. Croydon, Croy —2D 13
High St. Dartford, Dart —4M 59 (4D 7)
High St. Deal, Deal —3N 177 (2E 33)
High St. Dormansland, D'land —1A 34
High St. Dover, Dover —4H 181 (1C 43)
High St. Downe, Dow —2C 100 (3A 14)
High St. Dymchurch, Dym —8B 182 (1E 47)
High St. Eastchurch, E'chu —5C 202 (1E 19)
High St. East Malling, E Mal —2E 124 (1C 27)
High St. Eastry, E'try —3K 183 (2C 33)
High St. Edenbridge, Eden —5C 184 (4B 24)
High St. Elham, Elham —7N 183 (4E 31)
High St. Epsom, Eps —3A 12
High St. Etchingham, E'ham —2A 44
High St. Ewell, Ewe —3A 12
High St. Eynsford, Eyns —3M 87 (2D 15)
High St. Farnborough, Farn —6D 84 (2A 14)
High St. Farningham, F'ham —9N 73 (2D 15)
High St. Flimwell, Flim —4C 37
High St. Fordwich, F'wch —7F 168 (4E 21)
High St. Frant, Frant —9J 157 (3E 35)
High St. Garlinge, Gar —5N 207 (1D 23)
High St. Gillingham, Gill —6F 80 (1E 17) (in four parts)
High St. Goudhurst, Goud —8K 185 (2D 37)
High St. Grain, Isle G —2C 190 (3C 10)
High St. Gravesend, Grav —4G 62
High St. Greenhithe, Grnh —2H 61 (4E 7)
High St. Green Street Green, Grn St —8H 85 (3B 14)
High St. Hadlow, Hdlw —8D 134 (3A 26)
High St. Halling, Hall —6E 92 (2C 17)
High St. Harlesden. NW10 —2A 4
High St. Hartfield, Hartf —3B 34
High St. Hawkhurst, Hawkh —5H 191 (4D 37)
High St. Headcorn, H'crn —3K 193 (4A 28)
High St. Herne Bay, H Bay —2F 194 (1E 21)
High St. Hythe, Hythe —6J 197
High St. Kearsney, Kear —4C 32
High St. Kemsing, Kems —8B 104 (4D 15)
High St. Lamberhurst, Lam —2C 200 (2B 36)
High St. Leigh, Leigh —6M 143 (4D 25)
High St. Lenham, Len —8D 200 (3C 28)
High St. Limpsfield, Limp —2A 24
High St. Littlebourne, L'brne —3L 173 (1A 32)
High St. Lydd, Lydd —4B 204 (3D 47)
High St. Lyminge, Lym —8C 204 (1D 41)
High St. Maidstone, Maid —5C 126 (2D 27)
High St. Manston, Mans —4A 210 (2D 23)
High St. Marden, Mard —2L 205 (4D 27)
High St. Margate, Mgte —3C 208 (1D 23)
High St. Milton Regis, Mil R —5F 98 (2C 19)
High St. Minster, Min —7N 205 (2C 23) (nr. Ramsgate)
High St. Minster, Min S —6L 219 (4D 11) (nr. Sheerness)
High St. Newington, N'tn —5L 97 (2B 18)
High St. Newlands, Can I —2A 10
High St. New Malden, N Mald —1A 12
High St. New Romney, New R —3B 212 (2E 47)
High St. Northfleet, N'fleet —4A 62 (4A 8)
High St. Orpington, Orp —2J 85 (2B 14)
High St. Otford, Otf —7H 103 (4D 15)
High St. Pembury, Pem —8A 152 (1A 36)
High St. Penge, SE20 —1D 13
High St. Penshurst, Pens —2J 149 (1D 35)
High St. Queenborough, Queen —7A 218 (4C 11)
High St. Rainham, Rain —2A 96 (2A 18)
High St. Ramsgate, Ram —5H 211 (2E 23)
High St. Robertsbridge, Rob —3A 44
High St. Rochester, Roch (in two parts) —6N 79 (1D 17)
High St. Rolvenden, Rol —3J 213 (4B 38)
High St. Rotherfield, Roth —4D 35
High St. Rusthall, Rust —1B 156 (2D 35)
High St. St Gregory's. Cant —1N 171 (4D 21)
High St. St Lawrence. St Law —5F 210
High St. St Margaret's at Cliffe. St Mc —7J 213 (4D 33)
High St. St Mary Cray. St M —2B 14 (2B 14)
High St. St Peter's, St Pet —8J 209 (1E 23)
High St. Sandwich, S'wch —5M 217 (4D 23)
High St. Seal, Seal —3N 119 (1D 25)
High St. Sevenoaks, Sev —6K 119 (2D 25)
High St. Sheerness, S'ness (in two parts) —1B 218 (4D 11)
High St. Shoeburyness, Shoe —1D 11
High St. Shoreham, Shor —1G 102 (3C 15)
High St. Sidcup, Sidc —1B 14
High St. Sittingbourne, Sit —7F 98
High St. Smarden, Smar —3K 221 (1C 38)
High St. Snodland, Snod (in two parts) —2E 108 (3C 17)
High St. South Benfleet, Ben —1E 9
High St. Southend-on-Sea, Sth S —1C 10
High St. South Norwood, SE25 —1D 13
High St. Stanford-le-Hope, Stan H —2C 8
High St. Staplehurst, S'hrst —8K 221 (1E 37)
High St. Stratford, E15 —2E 5
High St. Strood, Strood —5L 79 (1D 17)
High St. Sturry, Sturry —6E 168
High St. Sutton, Sutt —2B 12
High St. Sutton Valence, Sut V —9A 140 (3A 28)
High St. Swanley, Swan —7G 72 (1C 15)
High St. Swanscombe, Swans —3M 61 (4A 8)
High St. Temple Ewell, Temp E —8C 178
High St. Tenterden, Tent —8B 222 (3C 38)
High St. Thornton Heath, T Hth —1D 13
High St. Ticehurst, Tic —4A 36
High St. Tonbridge, Tonb —6H 145 (4E 25)
High St. Tunbridge Wells, Tun W —3G 156 (2E 35)
High St. Upnor, Upnor —2C 80
High St. Upper Upnor, Upnor —1D 17
High St. Wadhurst, Wadh —3A 36
High St. Wallcrouch, Wallc —4B 36
High St. Westerham, W'ham —9E 116 (2A 24)
High St. West Ham, E13 —2A 6
High St. West Malling, W Mal —1N 123 (1B 26)
High St. West Wickham, W Wick —2E 82 (2E 13)
High St. Whitstable, Whits —3F 224 (2C 21)
High St. Wimbledon, SW19 —1A 12
High St. Winchelsea, W'sea —4A 46
High St. Wingham, W'hm —3B 226 (1B 32)
High St. Woolwich, SE18 —3A 6
High St. Wouldham, Woul —7G 93 (3C 17)
High St. Wrotham, Wro —7N 105 (4A 16)
High St. Wye, Wye —2M 159 (4B 30)
High St. Yalding, Yald —8D 136 (3C 26)
High St. N. E12 & E6 —1A 6
Highstreet Rd. Hern —3B 20
High St. S. E6 —2A 6
High St., The. Char —3K 175 (3D 29)
High Tor Clo. Brom —3L 69
High Trees. Croy —6E 82
High Trees. Len —7D 200
High Trees Clo. W'boro —9L 159
High View. High —9G 64
Highview. Meop —2G 106
High View Av. H Bay —3C 194
Highview Clo. Bou B —3L 165
Highview Clo. Maid —9D 126
Highview Dri. Chat —6A 94
High View Rd. Dow —1C 100
Highview Rd. Min S —5K 219
High View Rd. Sidc —9K 57
Highway, The. E1 & E14 —2D 5
Highway, The. Orp —6L 85 (2B 14)
Highwood. Short —6H 69
Highwood Clo. Orp —3E 84
Highwood Dri. Orp —3E 84
Highwoods Clo. High —9G 64
High Woods La. Tun W —3K 157 (in two parts)
Hilary Clo. Eri —8C 52
Hilary Clo. H Bay —3K 195
Hilary Gdns. Roch —1K 93
Hilbert Clo. Tun W —9J 151
Hilbert Rd. Tun W —8J 151
Hilborough Way. Orp —6F 84
Hilda May Av. Swan —5F 72
Hilda Rd. Chat —9D 80
Hilda Rd. Min S —6E 218
Hilda Vale Clo. Orp —5D 84
Hilda Vale Rd. Orp —5C 84
Hilden Av. Hild —3F 144
Hildenborough. —1D 144 (3E 25)
Hildenborough Cres. Maid —2M 125
Hildenborough Gdns. Brom —2H 69

Hildenborough Ho.—Hook Farm Rd.

Hildenborough Ho. Beck —3C 68
(off Bethersden Clo.)
Hildenborough Rd. Leigh —5N 143 (4D 25)
Hildenborough Rd. S'brne —4D 132 (3E 25)
Hilden Dri. Eri —7J 53
Hildenlea Pl. Brom —5H 69
Hilden Park. —2F 144
Hilden Pk. Rd. Hild —3F 144
Hilders Clo. Eden —3B 184
Hildersham Clo. Broad —8J 209
Hilders La. Eden —3A 184
Hillary Av. N'fleet —8D 62
Hillary Rd. Maid —2D 126
Hill Av. S'wll —2D 220
Hillborough. —3N 195 (2A 22)
Hillborough Av. Sev —4L 119
Hillborough Bus. Pk. H Bay —3N 195
Hillborough Dri. H Bay —1N 195
Hillborough Gro. Chat —8D 94
Hillborough Rd. H Bay —2J 195
Hill Brow. Bear —4K 127
Hill Brow. Brom —4N 69
Hill Brow. Dart —4G 59
Hill Brow. Sit —9E 98
Hillbrow Av. H Bay —5J 195
Hillbrow Av. Sturry —4E 168
Hill Brow Clo. Bex —9E 58
Hillbrow La. Afrd —9D 158
Hillbrow Rd. Brom —3H 69
Hillbrow Rd. Ram —4H 211
Hillbury Rd. Whyt —4D 13
Hill Chase. Chat —8B 94
Hill Clo. Chst —1D 70
Hill Clo. Grav —3D 76
Hill Clo. St Mc —8J 213
Hill Ct. Chatt —9C 66
Hill Cres. Aysm —2C 162
Hill Cres. Bex —6D 58
Hill Cres. Len —7E 200
Hillcrest. Four E —3B 24
Hill Crest. Maid —3C 138
Hill Crest. Sev —4H 119
Hillcrest. Sidc —5J 57
Hillcrest. Tun W —6H 151
Hillcrest Clo. Beck —9C 68
Hillcrest Clo. Kenn —4J 159
Hill Crest Dri. Cux —1G 92
Hillcrest Dri. Grnh —3G 61
Hillcrest Dri. Tun W —7K 151
Hillcrest Gdns. Deal —8K 177
Hillcrest Rd. Big H —4D 164
Hillcrest Rd. Brom —1K 69
Hillcrest Rd. Chat —1C 94
Hillcrest Rd. Dart —5F 58
Hillcrest Rd. Eden —3C 184
Hillcrest Rd. Hythe —5J 197
Hillcrest Rd. Kgdn —5M 199
Hillcrest Rd. L'brne —2K 173
Hillcrest Rd. Orp —3J 85
Hillcrest View. Beck —9C 68
Hillcroft Rd. H Bay —4J 195
Hillcroome Rd. Sutt —3B 12
Hillcross Av. Mord —2A 12
Hillden Shaw. Maid —9D 126
Hilldown Rd. Brom —2H 83
Hill Dri. E'try —2K 183
Hilldrop Rd. Brom —2L 69
Hillend. SE18 —8C 50
Hill End. Orp —3H 85
Hiller Clo. Broad —7L 209
Hill Farm Clo. H Hals —2H 67
Hillfield Rd. Dun G —2F 118
Hillgarth. Tun W —6G 151
Hill Green. —1E 112 (3A 18)
Hill Grn. Rd. S'bry —1D 112 (3A 18)
Hillgrove Rd. NW6 —1B 4
Hill Hoath. —9C 142
Hill Ho. Rd. Dart —5C 60
Hilliers La. Croy —2C 13
Hillingdale. Big H —6B 164
Hillingdon Av. Sev —3K 119
Hillingdon Rise. Sev —4L 119
Hillingdon Rd. Bexh —9D 52
Hillingdon Rd. Grav —7G 62
Hill La. Peene —3B 188 (2E 41)
Hillman Av. H Bay —3B 194
Hillmarton Rd. N7 —1C 5
Hillmore Ct. SE13 —1G 54
(off Belmont Hill)
Hillmore Gro. SE26 —1B 68
Hill Park. —5D 116
Hillreach. SE18 —5B 50 (3A 6)
Hill Rise. Dart —1D 74
Hill Rd. Dart —7M 59
Hill Rd. Folk —3K 189 (2A 42)
(in two parts)
Hill Rd. Roch —1L 93
Hill Rd. Woul —6J 93
Hillsgrove Clo. Well —7L 51
Hillshaw Cres. Roch —7H 79
Hillside. —4D 52
Hillside. NW10 —2A 4
Hillside. Dart —1E 74
Hillside. Eri —4E 52
Hillside. F'ham —1N 87
Hillside. Roch —1L 93
Hillside. S'gte —8E 188
Hillside. Tonb —8G 144
Hillside. W'hm —1B 226
Hillside Av. Cant —1J 171
Hillside Av. Grav —7J 63
Hillside Av. Queen —9A 218
Hillside Av. Roch —4M 79
Hillside Cotts. Cha —8E 170
Hillside Ct. Hythe —6K 197
Hillside Ct. Roch —5L 79
Hillside Ct. Swan —7H 73
Hillside Ct. W'bury —1C 136
Hillside Dri. Grav —7J 63
Hillside La. Brom —3J 83
(in two parts)
Hillside Rd. Brom —6J 69 (1E 13)
Hillside Rd. Chat —8D 80
Hillside Rd. Dart —4H 59
Hillside Rd. Dover —2F 180
Hillside Rd. Kems —8N 103
Hillside Rd. Min S —5J 219
Hillside Rd. Sev —5L 119
Hillside Rd. Stal —2D 29
Hillside Rd. Tats —7E 164
Hillside Rd. Whits —4J 225
Hillside St. Hythe —6J 197
Hillside, The. Orp —9K 85
Hills La. Knat —4B 104 (3D 15)
Hill's Ter. Chat —9C 80
Hill Street. —4C 31
Hill St. Tun W —9H 151
Hill St. Bottom. H'lgh & Bod —4C 31
Hill, The. Char —2K 175 (3D 29)
Hill, The. C'brk —8D 176
Hill, The. L'brne —2K 173 (1A 32)
Hill, The. N'fleet —4B 62 (4A 8)
Hill Top. —5N 153
Hill Top. C'brk —1D 37
Hilltop. Hunt —5H 137 (3C 27)
Hilltop. Tonb —8H 145
Hill Top Cotts. Langl —6B 138
Hilltop Gdns. Dart —3N 59
Hilltop Gdns. Orp —3G 84
Hill Top Rd. H Bay —2J 195
Hilltop Rd. Min S —7H 219
Hilltop Rd. Roch —3N 79
Hill View. Afrd —6G 159
Hillview. Bor G —5M 121
(Basted)
Hill View. Bor G —2N 121
(Borough Green)
Hillview. Mgte —6B 208
Hillview Clo. Bor G —2N 121
Hill View Cres. Orp —2H 85
Hill View Dri. Well —9G 50
Hillview Ho. Grav —6H 63
Hillview Rd. Cant —9J 167
Hillview Rd. Chst —1C 70
Hill View Rd. Hild —2F 144
Hill View Rd. Long —6A 76
Hill View Rd. Orp —2G 85
Hill View Rd. Tun W —1C 156
Hillview Rd. Whits —5F 224
Hill View Way. Chat —6B 94
Hillworth. Beck —5E 68
Hillydeal Rd. Otf —6K 103
Hillyfield Clo. Roch —3K 79
Hillyfield Rd. Afrd —1E 160
Hilly Fields Cres. SE4 —1D 54
Hillyfields Rise. Afrd —9E 158
Hilton Dri. Sit —5C 98
Hilton Ho. SE4 —2A 54
Hilton Rd. Afrd —8D 158
Hilton Rd. Cli —6M 65
Hinchliffe Way. Mgte —5H 209
Hind Clo. Dym —7B 182
Hind Cres. N Hth —6E 52
Hinde Clo. Sit —4G 98
Hindsley's Pl. SE23 —7A 54
Hines Ter. Chat —2F 94
Hinksey Path. SE2 —3M 51
Hinstock Rd. SE18 —6E 50
Hinton Clo. SE9 —6A 56
Hinton Cres. Hem —5K 95
Hinton Rd. SE24 —4C 5
Hinxhill. —1B 40
Hinxhill Rd. W'boro —1N 161 (1B 40)
Hirst Clo. Dover —9G 178
Historic Dockyard, The. —5C 80 (1E 17)
Hitchen Hatch La. Sev —6H 119
Hither Chantlers. L'tn G —3A 156
Hitherfield. Char —3J 175
Hither Green. —4H 55 (4E 5)
Hither Grn. La. SE13 —3F 54 (4E 5)
Hive La. N'fleet —4A 62
Hive, The. N'fleet —4A 62
Hoad Common. —4J 133
Hoaden. —3B 22
Hoades Wood Rd. Sturry —4F 168
Hoadleys La. Crowb —3C 35
Hoads Wood Gdns. Afrd —4C 158
Hoath. —2A 22
Hoath Clo. Gill —4L 95
Hoath Corner. —3C 148 (1C 34)
Hoath Hill. M'fld —3B 44
Hoath La. Gill —4L 95 (2E 17)
Hoath Meadow. Horsm —2C 198
Hoath Rd. Hoath —4G 168
Hoath Rd. Sturry —3E 21
Hoath Way. Gill —4L 95 (2E 17)
Hobart Cres. Dover —1G 181
Hobart Gdns. Sit —7D 98
Hobart Rd. Ram —3E 210
Hobbs La. Beckl —2E 45
Hoblands End. Chst —2G 71
Hockenden. —6B 72 (1C 14)
Hockenden La. Swan —6B 72 (1C 14)
Hockeredge Gdns. Wgte S —3L 207
Hockers Clo. Det —1K 127
Hockers La. Weav —3J 127 (1E 27)
Hockley. —2E 29
Hoddesdon Rd. Belv —5B 52
Hode La. Bri —6D 172 (2E 31)
Hodges Gap. Mgte —2G 208
Hodgson Cres. Snod —1E 108
Hodgson Rd. Sea —6A 224
Hodsoll Ct. Orp —8M 71
Hodsoll Street. —9C 90 (3A 16)
Hodsoll St. Sev —9C 90 (3A 16)
Hodson Cres. Orp —8M 71
Hoever Ho. SE6 —9F 54
Hogarth Clo. H Bay —2M 195
Hogarth La. W4 —3A 4
Hogarth Roundabout. (Junct.) —3A 4
Hogbarn La. H'shm —2B 28
Hogben Clo. Lym —7C 204
Hogben's Hill. —1A 30
Hogbrook Hill La. Alk —1B 42
Hogg La. Grays —3A 8
Hogg La. Up Hard —3D 31
Hog Green. Elham —7N 183
Hog Hill. Bear —5L 127
Hoghole La. Lam —3B 36
Hognore La. Sev —5C 106
Hogs La. Grav —8C 62
Hogs Orchard. Swan —4J 73
Hogtrough Hill. Bras —2H 117 (1B 24)
Holbeach Gdns. Sidc —4H 57
Holbeach Rd. SE6 —5E 54
Holbeam Rd. Stal —2E 29
Holborn. —2C 5
Holborn. EC1 —2C 5
Holborn La. Chat —7C 80
Holborn Viaduct. EC1 & EC4 —2C 5
Holborough. —9E 92 (3C 17)
Holborough M. Snod —1E 108
Holborough Rd. Snod —2E 108 (3C 17)
Holbourn Clo. H Bay —7J 195
Holbrook Dri. Ram —3F 210
Holbrook Ho. Chst —4F 70
Holbrook La. Chst —3F 70
Holbrook Way. Brom —9B 70 (2A 14)
Holburne Rd. SE3 —8A 50
Holcombe Rd. Chat —1C 94
Holcombe Rd. Roch —9N 79
Holcote Clo. Belv —3N 51
Holdenby Rd. SE4 —3B 54
Holden Corner. Tun W —5E 150
Holdenhurst. Afrd —3C 160
Holden Pk. Rd. Tun W —6F 150
Holden Rd. Tun W —5E 150 (1E 35)
Holder Clo. Chat —5F 94
Holding St. Gill —2B 96
Hole La. Eden —1A 184 (3A 24)
Holford St. Tonb —6H 145
Holiday Sq. Mgte —2C 208
Holland. —3A 24
Holland Av. Sutt —3B 12
Holland Clo. Broad —3L 209
Holland Clo. Brom —3J 83
Holland Clo. S'ness —3C 218
Holland Dri. SE23 —8B 54
Holland Ho. Roch —8A 80
Holland La. Oxt —3A 24
Holland Pk. Av. W11 —2A 4
Holland Park Roundabout. (Junct.) —3B 4
Holland Rd. W14 —3A 4
Holland Rd. Chat —7B 94
Holland Rd. Maid —4D 126 (1E 27)
Holland Rd. Oxt —3A 24
Hollands Av. Folk —4M 189
Hollands Clo. Shorne —1C 78
(in two parts)
Holland Way. Brom —3J 83
Hollicondane. —3H 211
Hollicondane Rd. Ram —4H 211
Hollies Av. Sidc —7H 57
Hollies, The. Grav —2J 77
Hollies, The. Long —6B 76
Holligrave Rd. Brom —4K 69
Hollin Clo. Tun W —1F 156
Hollingbourne. —6G 129 (2B 28)
Hollingbourne Av. Bexh —8A 52
Hollingbourne Hill. Holl —6H 129 (2B 28)
Hollingbourne Rd. Gill —9M 81
Hollingrove. —3A 44
Hollington Ct. Chst —2D 70
Hollington Pl. Afrd —7G 158
Hollingworth Rd. Maid —3J 139
Hollingworth Rd. Orp —1D 84
Hollingworth Way. W'ham —8F 116
Holloway. —1C 4
Holloway Rd. N19 & N7 —1C 4
Hollow La. Cant —4L 171 (1D 31)
Hollow La. D'land & E Grin —1A 34
Hollow La. H'lip —6G 96 (2B 18)
Hollow La. Snod —3D 108 (3C 16)
Hollowmede. Cant —4L 171
Hollow Rd. Hoath —2A 22
Hollows Trees Dri. Leigh —5A 144
Hollow Street. —3A 22
Hollow Wood Rd. Dover —4D 180
Holly Bank. Bchly —6N 153
Hollybank Hill. Sit —7F 98
Hollybrake Clo. Chst —3F 70
Holly Bush Clo. Sev —6K 119
Holly Bush Ct. Sev —6K 119
Hollybushes. —1C 29
Holly Bush La. Orp —7B 86
Holly Bush La. Sev —6K 119
Hollybush La. Stod —8K 169 (4A 22)
Hollybush Rd. Grav —7H 63
Holly Clo. Broad —1G 210
Holly Clo. Chat —2F 94
Holly Clo. E'try —3L 183
Holly Clo. Folk —4L 189
Holly Clo. Gill —6H 81
Holly Ct. Sidc —9K 57
(off Sidcup Hill)
Holly Cres. Beck —8C 68
Hollycroft. Cux —1G 92
Hollydale Dri. Brom —4B 84
Hollydown Way. E11 —1E 5
Holly Farm Rd. Otham —2M 139
Hollyfield Rd. Surb —2A 12
Holly Gdns. Mgte —3G 209
Holly Hedge Ter. SE13 —3G 54
Holly Hill. —3B 16
Holly Hill. Elham —4E 31
Holly Hill Rd. Belv & Eri —5C 52
Holly Hill Rd. Dunk —2N 165
Holly Hill Rd. Meop —8L 91 (3B 16)
Holly Ho. S'ness —2C 218
Holly La. Bans —4B 12
Holly La. Mgte —3G 209
Hollymeoak Rd. Coul —4C 12
Holly Rd. Dart —6L 59
Holly Rd. Orp —8J 85
Holly Rd. Ram —4J 211
Holly Rd. Roch —6J 79
Holly Rd. St Mar —2E 214
Holly Rd. Wain —2A 80
Hollyshaw Clo. Tun W —3J 157
Hollytree Av. Swan —5F 72
Hollytree Clo. Kgswd —6G 140
Hollytree Dri. High —1F 78
Holly Tree Ho. SE4 —1C 54
(off Brockley Rd.)
Hollytree Pde. Sidc —2L 71
(off Sidcup Hill)
Holly Vs. Bear —5M 127
(off Street, The)
Holly Vs. W Far —2H 137
Hollywood La. Wain —2N 79 (1D 17)
Hollywood La. W King —2F 104
Hollywood Way. Eri —7J 53
Holman M. Cant —3N 171 (1D 31)
Holmbury Gro. Croy —8C 82
Holmbury Mnr. Sidc —9J 57
Holmbury Pk. Brom —3A 70
Holm Ct. SE12 —8L 55
Holmcroft Way. Brom —8B 70
Holmdale Rd. Chst —1E 70
Holmdene Clo. Beck —5F 68
Holme Lacey Rd. SE12 —4J 55
Holme Oak Clo. Cant —4M 171
Holmes Clo. H Hals —2H 67
Holmesdale Clo. Loose —5C 138
Holmesdale Hill. S Dar —4C 74 (1E 15)
Holmesdale Rd. Bexh —9M 51
Holmesdale Rd. Sev —5L 119
Holmesdale Rd. S Dar —4C 74 (1E 15)
Holmes Dale Ter. Folk —7K 189
(off Sandgate Rd.)
Holmesley Rd. SE23 —4B 54
Holmestead Village. Ram —7G 210
Holmestone Rd. Dover —3D 180
Holmewood Ridge. L'tn G —2M 155
Holmewood Rd. Tun W —7J 151
Holmhurst Clo. Tun W —1F 156
Holmhurst Rd. Belv —5C 52
Holmlea Clo. W'boro —9J 159
Holmleigh Av. Dart —3K 59
Holm Mill La. H'shm —2K 141 (2B 28)
Holm Oak Gdns. Broad —9K 209
Holmoaks. Gill —1A 96
Holmoaks. Maid —4F 126
Holmoaks Ho. Beck —5F 68
Holmscroft Rd. H Bay —2L 195
Holmsdale Gro. Bexh —9F 52
Holmshaw Clo. SE26 —9B 54
Holmside. Gill —1H 95
Holmside Av. Min S —6E 218
Holmwood Rd. Afrd —2C 160
Holness Rd. Ah —4C 216
Holstein Way. Eri —3M 51
Holters La. Cant —9M 167
Holt Hill. —1H 125
Holton Clo. Birch —5F 206
Holt Rd. E16 —1A 50
Holt St. Non —4F 162 (3B 32)
Holt Wood Av. Ayle —1H 125
Holtwood Clo. Gill —6N 95
Holtye. —2B 34
Holtye Cres. Maid —7E 126
Holtye Rd. E Grin —2A 34
Holwood Pk. Av. Orp —5B 84
Holy Ghost All. S'wch —5M 217
(off St Peter's St.)
Holyoake Mt. Grav —6J 63
Holyoake Ter. Sev —6H 119
Holyrood Dri. Min S —7H 219
Holywell Av. Folk —3J 189
Holywell Ho. Folk —3J 189
Holywell La. Upc —8J 223 (2B 18)
Home Cotts. Cha —7D 170
Homedean Rd. Chip —4D 118 (2C 25)
Home Farm Clo. Leigh —4A 144
Home Farm Ct. Frant —9J 157
Home Farm La. Tun W —6L 151
Homefern Ho. Mgte —2D 208
(off Cobbs Pl.)
Homefield Av. Deal —4L 177
Homefield Clo. St P —7K 71
Homefield Clo. Swan —6G 72
Homefield Dri. Rain —1D 96
Homefield Ho. SE23 —8A 54
Homefield M. Beck —4D 68
Homefield Rise. Orp —2J 85
Homefield Rd. Brom —4M 69 (1A 14)
Homefield Rd. Sev —4F 118
Homefield Rd. S at H —5N 73
Homefield Row. Deal —4L 177
Homefleet Ho. Ram —5K 211
(off Wellington Cres.)
Home Gdns. Dart —4D 7
Home Hill. Swan —3G 73
Home Lea. Orp —6H 85
Homeleigh Rd. SE15 —3A 54
Homeleigh Rd. Ram —1F 210
Homemead. Grav —5G 63
Homemead. Grnh —4H 61
Home Mead Clo. Grav —5G 63
Homemead Rd. Brom —8B 70
Home Orchard. Dart —4M 59
(in two parts.)
Home Pk. Rd. SW19 —4B 4
Home Peak. Hythe —6J 197
(off Bartholomew St.)
Homer Clo. Bexh —8D 52
Homer Rd. Croy —9A 68
Homerton. —1D 5
Homerton High St. E9 —1D 5
Homerton Rd. E9 —1E 5
Homesdale Rd. Brom —7M 69 (1A 14)
Homesdale Rd. Orp —1G 84
Homeside Farm. Bos —3D 31
Homespire Ho. Cant —1N 171 (4D 21)
(off Knott's La.)
Homestall Ct. Cant —7J 167
Homestall Farm. —6M 187 (3A 20)
Homestall Rd. SE22 —4D 5
Homestall Rd. Ash W —2A 34
Homestall Rd. Good —6M 187 (3A 20)
Homestead. Afrd —1B 160
Homestead Clo. Mgte —4D 208
Homestead La. E Stu —3C 33
Homestead Rd. SW6 —3B 4
Homestead Rd. Eden —2B 184
Homestead Rd. Orp —8K 85
Homestead, The. Dart —3F 58
(off Crayford High St.)
Homestead, The. Dart —4K 59
(West Hill Dri.)
Homestead View. B'den —9C 98
Homevale Houses. S'gte —8E 188
Home View. Sit —7J 99
Homewards Rd. Allh —4J 201 (3A 10)
Homewood Av. Sit —8E 98 (3C 18)
Homewood Cres. Chst —2G 71
Homewood Rd. L'tn G —2N 155
Homewood Rd. Sturry —5F 168
Homewood Rd. Tent —6C 222
Homing Leisure Pk. Sea —8C 224
Honduras Ter. Maid —2D 126
Hone St. Roch —4M 79
Honeyball Wlk. Tey —2K 223
Honey Bee Glade. Gill —6A 96
Honeybourne Way. Orp —2F 84
Honey Clo. Hem —6K 95
Honeycrest Ind. Est. S'hrst —6J 221
Honeycrock Hill. S'bry —2H 113 (3B 18)
Honeyden Rd. Sidc —2N 71
Honeyfield. Afrd —9C 158
Honey Hill. —4F 166 (3C 21)
Honey Hill. Whits —2E 166 (3C 21)
Honey La. Otham —2L 139 (2E 27)
Honeypot Clo. Roch —4M 79
Honeypot La. Eden —4A 24
Honeypot La. Hods —9B 90
Honeypot La. Kems —1C 120 (1D 25)
Honeysuckle Clo. Chat —7B 94
Honeysuckle Clo. Hem —7J 95
Honeysuckle Clo. Mgte —5A 208
Honeysuckle Ct. Sit —6J 99
Honeysuckle Gdns. Croy —1A 82
Honeysuckle Rd. Ram —4K 211
Honeysuckle Way. H Bay —5L 195
Honeywell Parkwell. Dover —8G 178
Honeywood Clo. Cant —9A 168
Honeywood Clo. Lymp —5B 196
Honeywood Rd. Whitf —7F 178 (4C 33)
Honfleur Rd. S'wch —6L 217
Honiton Rd. Well —9H 51
Honley Rd. SE6 —5E 54
Honor Oak. —4A 54 (4D 5)
Honor Oak Pk. SE23 —4A 54 (4D 5)
Honor Oak Park. —5B 54 (4E 5)
Honor Oak Rd. SE23 —4D 5
Honywood Rd. Len —8D 200
Hoo. —7J 205 (2C 22)
Hoo Comn. Chatt —9D 66
Hood Av. Orp —8K 71
Hook Clo. Chat —6B 94
Hook Clo. Folk —6F 188
Hook Farm Rd. Brom —8N 69

Iron Bar La.—Kent Kraft Ind. Est.

Iron Bar La. Cant —2N 171 (1D 31)
Iron Mill La. Dart —2F 58 (4C 7)
Iron Mill Pl. Dart —2G 58
Ironside Clo. Chat —3D 94
Ironstones. L'tn G —2B 156
Irvine Dri. Mgte —5G 209
Irvine Rd. High —1F 78
Irvine Way. Orp —1H 85
Irving Wlk. Swans —5L 61
Irving Way. Swan —5E 72
Irwin Av. SE18 —7G 51
Irwin Pk. Min S —3H 219
Isabella Dri. Orp —5E 84
Isard Ho. Hay —2L 83
Isis Clo. Lymp —5B 196
Island Rd. Sturry —6E 168 (3E 21)
Island Wall. Whits —4E 224
Island Way W. Chat —3E 80
Isla Rd. SE18 —6E 50
Isledon Rd. N7 —1C 5
Islehurst Clo. Chst —4C 70
Islingham Farm Rd. Chatt —1A 80
Islington. —2C 5
Islington Pk. St. N1 —1C 5
Ismays Rd. Ivy H —7H 121
Ismays Rd. Sev —2E 25
Istead Rise. —4E 76 (1A 16)
Istead Rise. Grav —3E 76
Itchingwood Common. —3A 24
Itchingwood Comn. Rd. Oxt —3A 24
Ivanhoe Rd. H Bay —4H 195
Ivanhoe Rd. Wgte S —2K 207
Iveagh Ct. Beck —6F 68
Ivedon Rd. Well —9L 51
Ivens Way. H'shm —2M 141
Iverhurst Clo. Bexh —3M 57
Iversgate Clo. Gill —1B 96
Iverson Rd. NW6 —1B 4
Ivers Way. New Ad —8E 82
Ives Ga. S'wch —5M 217
Ives Rd. Tonb —6F 144
Ivor Gro. SE9 —6D 56
Ivory Clo. Fav —3E 186
Ivorydown. Brom —9K 55
Ivy Bower Clo. Grnh —3H 61
Ivybridge Ct. Chst —4C 70
(off Old Hill)
Ivychurch. —2D 47
Ivychurch Gdns. Clift —3J 209
Ivychurch Rd. Bztt —2C 47
Ivy Clo. Dart —4A 60
Ivy Clo. Etch —2E 41
Ivy Clo. Grav —8H 63
Ivy Clo. Kgswd —6F 140
Ivy Cottage Hill. Ram —2D 23
Ivy Cotts. Afrd —8E 158
Ivy Cotts. Gt Cha —1A 160
Ivy Ct. Tent —8C 222
Ivy Ct. T Hill —5L 167
Ivydale Rd. SE15 —1A 54 (4D 5)
Ivy Hatch. —8H 121 (2E 25)
Ivy Ho. La. Sev —9E 102 (4C 15)
Ivy Ho. Rd. Whits —4H 225
Ivy La. Cant —2N 171 (1D 31)
Ivy La. Knock —7N 101
Ivy La. Ram —6H 211
Ivy M. Kgswd —6G 140
Ivy Pl. Cant —3L 171
Ivy Pl. Deal —3N 177
Ivy Pl. Roch —1L 93
Ivy Rd. SE4 —2C 54
Ivy St. Gill —3B 96
Ivy Vs. Grnh —3G 61
Ivy Way. Folk —4L 189
Iwade. —8C 198 (1C 19)
Iwade Rd. N'tn —4L 97 (2B 18)
Izane Rd. Bexh —2A 58

Jackass La. Kes —6L 83 (2A 14)
Jacklin Clo. Chat —9C 94
Jackson Av. Roch —3B 94
Jackson Clo. Gill —2M 95
Jackson Clo. Grnh —3F 60
Jackson Rd. Brom —3B 84
Jackson Rd. Win I —3L 171
Jacksons La. Tent —8B 222
Jackson St. SE18 —6C 50
Jackson's Way. Croy —4D 82
Jackson Way. Bene —3A 38
Jacob Clo. Mgte —6C 208
Jacob Ho. Eri —2M 51
Jacob's Ho. S'ness —2D 218
Jacob's La. Hoo —7L 67 (4E 9)
Jacobs La. Hort K —6C 74
Jacob Yd. Fav —5H 187
(off Preston St.)
Jade Hill. Hall —5E 92
Jaffa Ct. Whits —5F 224
Jaffray Rd. Brom —7N 69
Jaggard Way. S'hrst —8J 221
Jagger Clo. Dart —5C 60
Jago Clo. SE18 —6E 50
Jail La. Big H —3D 164 (4A 14)
Jamaica Rd. SE1 & SE16 —3D 5
Jamaica Ter. Maid —2D 126
James Alchin Dri. Kenn —6K 159
James Allchin Gdns. Kenn —6K 159
James Clo. Ah —4C 216
James Clo. Lym —7C 204
James Ct. Folk —7G 188
James Ct. Mgte —3F 208
James Hall Gdns. Walm —7M 177
James Haney Dri. Kenn —5K 159
James Newham Ct. SE9 —8C 56
James Rd. Cux —1F 92
James Rd. Dart —5H 59
James St. W1 —2C 4
James St. Afrd —8E 158
James St. Beck —6C 68
James St. Chat —8C 80
(in two parts)
James St. Folk —4L 189
James St. Gill —6F 80 (1E 17)
James St. Maid —4D 126
James St. Ram —6H 211
James St. Roch —8N 79
James St. S'ness —2E 218
James Whatman Way. Maid —4C 126
Jane Grn. M. Cant —9A 168
Jane Seymour Ct. SE9 —5F 56
Janton Clo. Cli —6M 65
Japonica Clo. Chat —9F 94
Jarlen Rd. Lydd —3B 204
Jarman's Field. Wye —2N 159
Jarrett Av. Wain —2N 79
Jarrett Ho. Folk —7J 189
Jarretts Ct. Sit —7J 99
(off Wykeham Rd.)
Jarvis Brook. —4D 35
Jarvis Dri. W'boro —2L 161
Jarvis Ho. Maid —2C 126
Jarvis La. Goud —7M 185 (2D 37)
Jarvis Pl. St Mic —4C 222
Jarvist Pl. Kgdn —3N 199
Jashoda Ho. SE18 —5C 50
(off Connaught M.)
Jasmin Ct. SE12 —4K 55
Jasmine Clo. Chat —7C 94
Jasmine Clo. E Mal —1D 124
Jasmine Clo. Orp —3D 84
Jasmine Gdns. Croy —4E 82
Jasmine Pl. W'hm —2B 226
Jasmine Rd. E Mal —1D 124
Jason Wlk. SE9 —9C 56
Jasper Av. Roch —1N 93
Javelin Rd. W Mal —6L 123
Jay Gdns. Chst —9B 56
Jaynes Ind. Est., The. Dover —4D 180
Jayne Wlk. Whits —7D 224
Jefferson Clo. Afrd —9D 158
Jefferson Dri. Gill —2M 95
Jefferson Rd. S'ness —3E 218
Jefferson Wlk. SE18 —6C 50
Jefferstone Gdns. St Mar —2D 214
Jefferstone La. St Mar —3B 214 (2E 47)
Jeffery. Sidc —1K 71
Jeffery Clo. S'hrst —7J 221
Jeffery St. Gill —6F 80 (1E 17)
Jeffrey Row. SE12 —3L 55
Jeffrey St. Maid —4D 126
Jeffries Cotts. Maid —5H 137
Jeken Rd. SE9 —2M 55
Jellicoe Av. Grav —8H 63
Jellicoe Av. W. Grav —8H 63
Jellicoe Clo. W'boro —2L 161
Jellicoe Pavilion. Roy B —1K 125
Jemmett La. Mer —5N 161 (2B 40)
Jemmett Rd. Afrd —2E 160
Jenkins Dale. Chat —9C 80
Jenkins Dri. Maid —3H 139
Jenner Rd. Roch —8N 79
Jenner's Way. St Mar —3D 214
Jenner Way. Eccl —4K 109
Jennifer Ct. Hoo —8H 67
Jennifer Gdns. Mgte —5G 209
Jennifer Rd. Brom —8J 55
Jenningtree Rd. Eri —7J 53
Jenningtree Way. Belv —2D 52
Jenton Av. Bexh —9N 51
Jermyn St. SW1 —2C 4
Jerome Rd. Lark —6D 108
Jerrard St. SE13 —1E 54
Jersey Clo. Kenn —2G 159
Jersey Dri. Orp —9F 70
Jersey La. P'hm —2D 31
Jersey Rd. Roch —5L 79
Jeskyns Rd. Cob & Sole S —6H 77
Jeskyns Rd. Meop & Grav —1B 16
Jesmond St. Folk —5K 189
Jessamine Pl. Dart —5C 60
Jesse's Hill. Kgtn —3E 31
Jessett Clo. Eri —4E 52
Jessica M. Cant —1A 172
Jessica M. Sit —4F 98
Jesson Ct. Cvn. Pk. St Mar —2E 214
Jessup Clo. SE18 —4E 50
Jesuit Clo. Cant —7N 167
Jetty Rd. Hoo —6N 67
Jetty Rd. S'ness —1A 218
Jetty Rd. Ward —4K 203 (1A 20)
Jevington Way. SE12 —6L 55
Jewell Gro. Mard —3L 205
Jewels Hill. Warl —3A 14
Jewry La. Cant —2M 171 (1D 31)
Jeyes Rd. Gill —8F 80
Jezreels Rd. Gill —1G 94
Jillian Way. Afrd —2C 160
Jim Bradley Clo. SE18 —4C 50
Jiniwin Rd. Roch —4A 94
Joan Cres. SE9 —5N 55
Jockey La. C'brk —7D 176
Jodrell Rd. E9 —1E 5
Johanesburg Rd. Dover —9H 179
Johannesburg Ho. Maid —3H 139
John Badger Clo. Kenn —5J 159
John Graham Ct. Cant —4N 171
John Hall Ct. Fav —2F 186
John Islip St. SW1 —3C 4
John Nash Clo. Lyn —4J 223
John Newton Ct. Well —1K 57
John's Cross. —3B 44
John's Cross Rd. Rob —3A 44
John's Grn. S'wch —8K 217
John's Hole. —5D 60
Johnson Av. Chat —5E 80
Johnson Clo. N'fleet —8C 62
Johnson Clo. W'boro —2L 161
Johnson Ct. Fav —3F 186
Johnson Rd. Brom —8N 69
Johnson Rd. Sit —7E 98
Johnson's Av. Badg M —1C 102
Johnsons Ct. Seal —3N 119
Johnson's Way. Grnh —4J 61
Johnson Way. Min S —5H 219
John's Rd. Meop —8E 76
John's Rd. Tats —8D 164
Johnstone Ho. SE13 —1G 54
(off Belmont Hill)
John St. Broad —9M 209
John St. Maid —3D 126
John St. Roch —8N 79
John St. Tun W —9G 150
John Tapping Clo. Walm —9L 177
John Wilson Bus. Pk. Ches —4K 225
John Wilson St. SE18 —3C 50 (3A 6)
John Woolley Clo. SE13 —2H 55
Joiners Ct. Chat —1E 94
Jointon Rd. Folk —7H 189
Jonas La. Dur —3A 36
Jordan Clo. Maid —3H 139
Jordan Ho. SE4 —2A 54
(off St Norbert Rd.)
Joseph Conrad Ho. Cant —1K 171
Joseph Wilson Ind. Est. & Retail Pk. Whits —6H 225
Joss Gap Rd. Broad —4M 209 (1E 23)
Joyce Clo. C'brk —8C 176
Joyce Green. —2N 59 (4D 7)
Joyce Grn. La. Dart —2N 59
Joyce Grn. Wlk. Dart —2N 59
Joydens Wood. —9E 58 (1C 15)
Joydens Wood Rd. Bex —9E 58
Joyes Clo. Folk —4L 189
Joyes Clo. Whitf —6G 178
Joyes Rd. Folk —4K 189 (2A 42)
Joyes Rd. Whitf —6F 178
Joy La. Whits —6C 224 (2C 20)
Joy Rd. Grav —6H 63
Jubilee Clo. Grnh —4J 61
Jubilee Clo. Hythe —8E 196
Jubilee Cotts. B'le —8A 216
Jubilee Cotts. F'wch —7E 168
Jubilee Cotts. Sev —2J 119
Jubilee Ct. Broad —9M 209
(off Oscar Rd.)
Jubilee Ct. Dart —5L 59
(off Spring Vale S.)
Jubilee Cres. Grav —7K 63
Jubilee Cres. Igh —3J 121
Jubilee Cres. Queen —7A 218
Jubilee Dri. Walm —7N 177
Jubilee Fields. Wit —2A 46
Jubilee Rise. Seal —3N 119
Jubilee Rd. L'brne —2L 173 (1A 32)
Jubilee Rd. Orp —7B 86 (3C 14)
Jubilee Rd. S'wch —6L 217
Jubilee Rd. Worth —9N 217 (2D 33)
Jubilee St. E1 —2D 5
Jubilee St. Sit —6F 98
Jubilee Ter. Gill —6F 80
Jubilee Way. SW19 —1B 12
Jubilee Way. Chess —2A 12
Jubilee Way. Sidc —7J 57
Jubilee Way. Whitf —4C 33
Judd Rd. Fav —5E 186
Judd Rd. Tonb —8H 145
Judd St. WC1 —2C 5
Judeth Gdns. Grav —1K 77
Judkins Clo. Chat —5F 94
Jug Hill. Big H —4D 164
Juglans Rd. Orp —2J 85
Julian Rd. Folk —6H 189
Julian Rd. Orp —7J 85
Julians Clo. Sev —9H 119
Julians Way. Sev —9H 119
Julie Clo. Broad —7L 209
Julien Pl. W'boro —1L 161
Juliette Way. S Ock —2N 53
Jumper's Town. —3B 34
Junction App. SE13 —1F 54
Junction Rd. N19 —1C 4
Junction Rd. Bdm —2B 44
Junction Rd. Dart —4L 59
Junction Rd. Gill —8G 81
Junction Rd. H Bay —5D 194
Juniper Clo. Afrd —8C 158
Juniper Clo. Big H —5E 164
Juniper Clo. Cant —4N 171
Juniper Clo. Chat —7D 94
Juniper Clo. Maid —3M 125
Juniper Clo. Tun W —5K 151
Juniper Clo. Whits —4H 225
Juniper Wlk. Swan —5E 72
Jury's Gap. —4C 46
Jury's Gap. Jur G —4C 46
Jury's Gap Rd. Lydd —4A 204 (4C 47)
Jury St. Grav —4G 62
Jutland Clo. Allh —5L 201
Jutland Rd. SE6 —5F 54

Kake St. Walt —3C 31
Kale Rd. Eri —2N 51
Kane Hythe Rd. Batt —4A 44
Kangley Bri. Rd. SE26 —1C 68
Kangley Bus. Cen. SE26 —1C 68
Karen Ct. Brom —4J 69
Kashgar Rd. SE18 —4H 51
Katherine Ct. Chat —9E 94
Katherine Gdns. SE9 —2N 55
Katherine Rd. E7 & E6 —1A 6
Katherine Rd. Eden —7C 184
Katie Gdns. Dart —2A 60
Kaysland Cvn Pk. W King —8E 88
Kays La. Hern —3B 20
Kay St. Well —8K 51
Kearsney. —9C 178 (4C 32)
Kearsney Av. Dover —9D 178
Kearsney Ct. Temp E —9B 178
Keary Rd. Swans —5L 61
Keat Farm Clo. H Bay —2N 195
Keats Ho. Cray —3F 58
(off Bexley La.)
Keats Rd. Belv —3D 52
Keats Rd. Lark —7D 108
Keats Rd. Well —8G 51
Kechill Gdns. Brom —1K 83
Keddow's Clo. Hythe —8E 196
Kedleston Dri. Orp —8H 71
Keedonwood Rd. Brom —1H 69
Keefe Clo. Chat —1A 110
Keel Ct. Roch —4A 80
Keel Gdns. Tun W —6E 150
Keeling Rd. SE9 —3N 55
Keemor Clo. SE18 —7C 50
Keepers Cotts. Det —3M 127
Keeper's Hill. Pat —7H 173 (2E 31)
Keepers La. Folk —1E 41
Keightley Dri. SE9 —6E 56
Keith Av. Ram —4E 210
Keith Av. S at H —2B 74
Keith Pk. Cres. Big H —2A 164
Kelbrook Rd. SE3 —9A 50
Kelby Path. SE9 —8D 56
Kelchers La. Gold G —2E 146
Kellaway Rd. Chat —9D 94
Kellerton Rd. SE13 —3H 55
Kelley Dri. Gill —5F 80
Kelling Rd. SE9 —3N 55
Kellner Rd. SE28 —3H 51
Kelly Ho. Roch —4N 93
Kelsey Ga. Beck —5E 68
Kelsey La. Beck —5D 68
Kelsey Pk. Av. Beck —5E 68
Kelsey Pk. Rd. Beck —5D 68
Kelsey Rd. Orp —5K 71
Kelsey Sq. Beck —5D 68
Kelsey Way. Beck —6D 68
Kelso Dri. Grav —9L 63
Kelvedon Rd. SW6 —3B 4
Kelvedon Rd. Walm —8M 177
Kelvin Clo. Tonb —9K 133
Kelvington Clo. Croy —1B 82
Kelvington Rd. SE15 —3A 54
Kelvin Pde. Orp —2G 84
Kelvin Rd. Well —1J 57
Kemble Clo. Tun W —7L 151
Kemble Dri. Brom —4A 84
Kemble Rd. SE23 —6A 54
Kembleside Rd. Big H —6C 164
Kemerton Rd. Beck —5E 68
Kemnal Rd. Chst —3E 70
Kemp All. Whits —4F 224
(off Middle Wall)
Kemp Clo. Chat —7B 94
Kempe's Corner. —4A 30
Kemp Rd. Whits —3L 225
Kemps Gdns. SE13 —3F 54
Kempthorne St. Grav —4G 62
Kemps Wharf Rd. Gill —2A 18
Kempton Clo. Chat —8F 94
(in two parts)
Kempton Clo. Eri —6D 52
Kempton Wlk. Croy —9B 68
Kempt St. SE18 —6C 50
Kemsdale Rd. Hern —1J 165 (3B 20)
Kemsing. —8B 104 (4D 15)
Kemsing Clo. Bex —5N 57
Kemsing Clo. Brom —3J 83
Kemsing Gdns. Cant —7A 168
Kemsing Rd. Sev —8G 104 (4E 15)
Kemsley. —2G 98 (2C 19)
Kemsley Clo. Grnh —4H 61
Kemsley Clo. N'fleet —9E 62
Kemsley Down. —2J 99
Kemsley Rd. Tats —7D 164
Kemsley Street. —1N 111 (3A 18)
Kemsley St. Rd. Bred —9L 95 (3E 17)
Kenardington. —3E 39
Kenardington Rd. App —4D 39
Kenbrook. Kenn —3G 159
Kencot Way. Eri —2A 52
Kendal Clo. Ram —6E 210
Kendal Clo. Tonb —5J 145
Kendal Dri. Tonb —5J 145
Kendale Rd. Brom —1H 69
Kendall Av. Beck —5B 68
Kendall Ct. Sidc —8J 57
Kendall Rd. Beck —5B 68
Kendal Pk. Tun W —9E 150
Kendal Pl. Maid —9F 126
Kendal Rise. Broad —8L 209
Kendal Rd. NW10 —1A 4
Kendal Way. Gill —3N 95
Kender St. SE14 —3D 5
Kendon Bus. Pk. Roch —4A 80
Kenfield Rd. P'hm —2C 31
Kengate Ind. Est. Hythe —7G 197
Kenia Wlk. Grav —8L 63
Kenilworth Clo. St Mb —7K 213
Kenilworth Ct. Dart —4B 60
(off Bow Arrow La.)
Kenilworth Ct. Sit —6D 98
Kenilworth Dri. Gill —4N 95 (2A 18)
Kenilworth Gdns. SE18 —9D 50
Kenilworth Gdns. Gill —4N 95
Kenilworth Ho. Maid —7M 125
Kenilworth Rd. SE20 —4A 68
Kenilworth Rd. Orp —9E 70
Kenley. —4D 13
Kenley Airfield. —4D 13
Kenley Clo. Bex —5B 58
Kenley Clo. Chst —6G 71
Kenley La. Kenl —4D 13
Kenley Rd. King T —1A 12
Kenmere Rd. Well —9L 51
Kennard Clo. Roch —1K 93
Kennard St. E16 —1B 50
Kennedy Clo. Fav —4H 187
Kennedy Clo. Orp —2F 84
Kennedy Ct. Beck —9C 68
Kennedy Ct. Croy —9C 68
Kennedy Dri. Walm —8L 177
Kennedy Gdns. Sev —4L 119
Kennedy Ho. Grav —8D 62
Kennedy Ho. Ram —5K 211
(off Newcastle Hill)
Kennel Barn Rd. S'bry —6K 113 (4B 18)
Kennel Hill. Eyt —4L 185 (3C 32)
Kennelling Rd. Char —3D 29
Kennet La. Stanf —8N 215 (2D 41)
Kennet Rd. Dart —1H 59
Kennett Ct. Swan —6F 72
(off Oakleigh Clo.)
Kennett Dri. Deal —8K 177
Kenninghall Rd. E5 —1D 5
Kennington. —3H 159 (4A 30)
Kennington Clo. Gill —8M 81
Kennington Clo. Maid —1J 139
Kennington La. SE11 —3C 5
Kennington Oval. SE11 —3C 5
Kennington Oval. (Junct.) —3C 5
Kennington Pk. Rd. SE11 —3C 5
Kennington Pl. Kenn —3H 159
Kennington Rd. SE1 & SE11 —3C 5
Kennington Rd. W'boro —8L 159 (1A 40)
Kensal Green. —2A 4
Kensal Rise. —2A 4
Kensal Rd. W10 —2A 4
Kensal Town. —2B 4
Kensington. —3B 4
Kensington Av. T Hth —1C 13
Kensington Chu. St. W8 —2B 4
Kensington Gore. SW7 —3B 4
Kensington High St. W14 & W8 —3B 4
Kensington Ho. Maid —7L 125
Kensington Palace. —2B 4
Kensington Pk. Rd. W11 —2B 4
Kensington Rd. SW7 —3B 4
Kensington Rd. Cant —7B 168
Kenswick Ct. SE13 —3E 54
Kent Av. Afrd —7F 158
Kent Av. Cant —2B 172
Kent Av. Maid —8F 126
Kent Av. Min S —6H 219
Kent Av. Sit —8E 98
Kent Av. Well —3H 57
Kent Clo. Orp —7G 84
Kent Clo. Pad W —9M 147
Kent Clo. Roch —3N 93
Kent County Cricket Ground. —1D 31
Kent County Showground. —7M 111 (4A 18)
Kent & East Sussex Railway. —7B 222 (3B 38)
Kent Gdns. Birch —4E 206
Kent Garden Vineyard. —2A 28
Kent Ga. Way. Croy —7C 82 (3E 13)
Kent Hatch. —3A 24
Kent Hatch Rd. Oxt & Crock H —2A 24
Kent Ho. Folk —7H 189
Kent Ho. Maid —6D 126
Kent Ho. La. Beck —1B 68 (1E 13)
Kent Ho. Rd. SE20 & SE26 —1D 13
Kent Ho. Rd. SE26 & Beck —1B 68
Kent International Bus. Pk. Ram —9J 207 (2C 23)
Kentish Gdns. Tun W —5E 156
Kentish Rd. Belv —4B 52
Kentish Town. —1C 4
Kentish Town Rd. NW1 & NW5 —1C 4
Kentish Way. Brom —5K 69 (1A 14)
Kent Kraft Ind. Est. N'fleet —3M 61

Kent La.—Knock Rd.

Kent La. B'ling —3A 44
Kentmere Av. Ram —5D 210
Kentmere Rd. SE18 —4G 51
Kenton Ct. SE26 —9B 54
(off Adamsrill Rd.)
Kenton Gdns. Min —7M 205
Kenton Rd. E9 —1D 5
Kent Pl. Ram —6K 211
Kent Rd. Dart —4L 59
Kent Rd. Folk —4E 188
Kent Rd. Grav —6F 62
Kent Rd. Hall —5E 92 (2C 17)
Kent Rd. Long —5K 75
Kent Rd. Mgte —5F 208
Kent Rd. Orp —2B 14
Kent Rd. S'ness —3C 218
Kent Rd. Snod —4E 108
Kent Rd. St M —9L 71
Kent Rd. Tun W —8G 150
Kent Rd. W Wick —2E 82
Kent Street. —7L 123 (2B 26)
Kent St. Mere —7K 123 (2B 26)
Kent St. Sed —4C 44
Kent St. Whits —5F 224
Kent Ter. High —6H 65
Kent Ter. Meop —4F 90
Kent Ter. Ram —6K 211
(off Harbour Pde.)
Kent View Dri. E'chu —7C 202
Kentwell Clo. SE4 —2B 54
Kenward. —3C 26
Kenward Ct. Hdlw —8D 134
Kenward Rd. SE9 —3M 55
Kenward Rd. Maid —4N 125
Kenward Rd. Yald —4C 136 (3C 26)
Kenwood Av. Chat —7D 94
Kenwood Av. Long —6B 76
Kenwood Dri. Beck —6F 68
Kenworthy Rd. E9 —1E 5
Kenwyn Rd. Dart —3L 59
Kenya Ter. Maid —2D 126
Kenyon Wlk. Gill —8L 95
Kersey Gdns. SE9 —9A 56
Kerton Rd. Lydd S —4E 47
Kesteven Clo. Hall —6E 92
Kestlake Rd. Bex —4L 57
Kestner Ind. Est. Grnh —2G 60
Keston. —6M 83 (2A 14)
Keston Av. Kes —6M 83
Keston Clo. Well —7L 51
Keston Gdns. Kes —5M 83
Keston Mark. —5A 84 (2A 14)
Keston Mark. (Junct.) —4A 84 (2A 14)
Keston Pk. Clo. Kes —4B 84
Keston Postmill. —6N 83 (2A 14)
Kestrel Clo. Eden —4C 184
Kestrel Clo. Sit —9H 99
Kestrel Ct. Dover —1G 181
Kestrel Ho. Gill —7E 80
(off Marlborough Rd.)
Kestrel Rd. Chat —9F 94
Kestrel Way. New Ad —9G 83
Keswick Av. Sit —8K 99
Keswick Clo. Tonb —5J 145
Keswick Ct. Short —7J 69
Keswick Dri. Maid —4M 125
Keswick Rd. Bexh —8B 52
Keswick Rd. Orp —2H 85
Keswick Rd. W Wick —3H 83
Kettle Corner. —1J 137
Kettle Hill. E'Ing —2E 29
Kettle Hill Rd. E'Ing —1E 29
(in two parts)
Kettle La. E Far —3J 137 (2D 27)
Kettlewell Ct. Swan —5G 72
Kevin Dri. Ram —6F 210
Kevington. —9N 71 (2C 14)
Kevington Clo. Croy —1B 82
Kevington Clo. Orp —7H 71
Kevington Dri. Chst & Orp —7H 71
Kew. —3A 4
Kew Bridge. (Junct.) —3A 4
Kew Bri. Bren & Rich —3A 4
Kew Bri. Rd. Bren —3A 4
Kew Gdns. Rd. Rich —3A 4
Kewlands. Maid —3F 126
Kew Rd. Rich —3A 4
Keycol. —6N 97 (2B 18)
Keycol Hill. N'tn —6N 97 (2B 18)
Keyes Av. Chat —1C 94
Keyes Gdns. Tonb —8F 144
Keyes Pl. Folk —3L 189
Keyes Rd. Dart —2N 59
Keymer Clo. Big H —4C 164
Keynsham Gdns. SE9 —3A 56
Keynsham Rd. SE9 —3N 55
Key's Green. —2B 36
Key Street. —6B 98 (2C 18)
Key St. Sit —6B 98 (2C 18)
Keyworth Clo. Pad W —9L 147
Keyworth M. Cant —9A 168
Khalsa Dri. Grav —5H 63
Khartoum Pl. Grav —4H 63
Khartoum Rd. Chat —7C 80
Khartoum Sq. Whitf —8F 178
Khyber Rd. Chat —5D 80
Kibbles La. Tun W —5E 150 (1E 35)
Kidbrooke. —3A 6
Kidbrooke Est. SE3 —1M 55
Kidbrooke La. SE9 —2A 56
Kidbrooke Park. —3A 34
Kidbrooke Park. —3A 34
Kidbrooke Pk. Rd. SE3 —1M 55 (3A 6)
Kidd Pl. SE7 —5A 50
Kidd's Hill. Cole H —3B 34
Kilbride Ct. Ram —3K 211
Kilburn. —2B 4
Kilburn High Rd. NW6 —1B 4
Kilburn Ho. Maid —4D 126
Kilburn La. W10 & W9 —2A 4
Kilburn Pk. Rd. NW6 —2B 4
Kilburn Priory. NW6 —2B 4
Kilgour Rd. SE23 —4B 54
Killearn Rd. SE6 —6G 54
Killewarren Way. Orp —9L 71
Killick Clo. Dun G —2F 118
Killick Rd. Hoo —8G 67
Killigarth Ct. Sidc —9J 57
Kilmorie Rd. SE23 —6B 54
Kiln Barn Rd. Dit & E Mal —1G 124 (1C 27)
Kiln Clo. C'lck —8D 174
Kiln Clo. Sit —8H 99
Kilndown. —3C 37
Kilndown. Grav —2J 77
Kilndown Clo. Afrd —3C 160
Kilndown Clo. Maid —2N 125
Kilndown Gdns. Cant —7N 167
Kilndown Gdns. Clift —3J 209
Kilndown Rd. Kiln —2C 37
Kiln Field. Tent —8D 222
Kilnfields. Orp —7B 86
Kiln La. Beth —3L 163 (2D 39)
Kiln La. Leigh —6N 143
Kiln Rd. Adgtn —3B 40
Kiln Way. Pad W —1M 153
Kilnwood. Hals —4A 102
Kimberely Rd. Beck —5A 68
Kimberley Av. SE15 —4D 5
Kimberley Clo. Dover —1H 181
Kimberley Ct. Wgte S —2K 207
(off Sea Rd.)
Kimberley Dri. Sidc —7M 57
Kimberley Ga. Brom —3H 69
Kimberley Gro. Sea —7B 224
Kimberley Rd. Beck —5A 68
Kimberley Rd. Gill —9G 80
Kimberley Rd. Ram —3E 210
Kimberley Ter. Lym —7D 204
Kimberley Wlk. Dover —9H 179
Kimbolton Clo. SE12 —4J 55
Kimmeridge Gdns. SE9 —9A 56
Kimmeridge Rd. SE9 —9A 56
Kincraig Dri. Sev —5H 119
King Alfred Av. SE6 —9D 54
(in two parts)
King Arthur Rd. C'snd —5B 210
King Arthurs Dri. Roch —3K 79
King Charles Ct. Walm —8N 177
King Charles Rd. Surb —2A 12
Kingcup Clo. Croy —1A 82
King Edward Av. Broad —9L 209
King Edward Av. Dart —4L 59
King Edward Av. H Bay —3J 195
King Edward Ct. H Bay —3J 195
King Edward Rd. Birch —5E 206
King Edward Rd. Chat —1C 94
King Edward Rd. Deal —2N 177 (2E 33)
King Edward Rd. Gill —6J 81
King Edward Rd. Grnh —3G 60
King Edward Rd. Maid —7C 126
King Edward Rd. Ram —6G 210
King Edward Rd. Roch —7N 79
King Edwards Rd. Bark —2B 6
King Edward St. Whits —4F 224
Kingfisher Av. Hythe —8D 196
Kingfisher Clo. Iwade —8C 198
Kingfisher Clo. Mgte —4N 207
Kingfisher Clo. Orp —7M 71
Kingfisher Clo. Svgtn —2L 161
Kingfisher Clo. Whits —6E 224
Kingfisher Ct. Dover —2G 181
(off Maresfield Clo.)
Kingfisher Ct. H Bay —4E 194
Kingfisher Ct. W King —8E 88
Kingfisher Dri. Chat —4F 94
Kingfisher Gdns. Hythe —8D 196
Kingfisher Ho. S'ness —2B 218
(off Sheppey St.)
Kingfisher M. SE13 —2E 54
Kingfisher Pl. S Dar —5C 74
Kingfisher Rd. Lark —8D 108
Kingfisher Wlk. Broad —8K 209
Kingfisher Way. Beck —8A 68
King George V Hill. Tun W —9J 151
King George Rd. Chat —8B 94 (3D 17)
King George VI Av. Big H —4D 164
King Harolds Way. Bexh —7M 51 (3B 6)
King Henry M. Orp —6H 85
King Henry's Dri. New Ad —9E 82 (3E 13)
King Hill. W Mal —5L 123 (2B 26)
King John's Wlk. SE9 —6N 55
King Lear's Way. Dover —7G 181
King & Queen Clo. SE9 —9A 56
Kings Acre. Down —8J 127
Kingsand Rd. SE12 —7K 55
King's Av. SW12 & SW4 —4C 4
King's Av. Afrd —8E 158
King's Av. Birch —3C 206
King's Av. Broad —8M 209
Kings Av. Brom —2J 69
Kings Av. Ram —3F 210
King's Av. Roch —9N 79
King's Av. S'wch B —1D 33
King's Av. Whits —4G 225
King's Bank. —3D 45
King's Bank La. Beckl —3D 45
Kings Bastion. Gill —7D 80
King's Bri. Cant —2M 171 (1D 31)
Kingsbridge Ct. Folk —6L 189
(off Harbour Way)
King's Clo. Dart —2F 58
King's Clo. Kgdn —4M 199
Kings Cotts. Leeds —2B 140
King's Cotts. Nett —2B 136
King's Cotts. Yald —7D 136
Kings Ct. Walm —7N 177
(off King St.)
Kings Cross. (Junct.) —2C 5
King's Cross Rd. WC1 —2C 5
Kingsdale Ct. Chat —2F 94
Kingsdale Ct. Swans —4L 61
Kingsdale Rd. SE18 —7H 51
Kingsdale Rd. SE20 —3A 68
Kingsdown. —4N 199 (3E 33)
(nr. Deal)
Kingsdown. —6M 115 (4D 19)
(nr. Sittingbourne)
Kingsdown Clo. Grav —6L 63
Kingsdown Clo. Hem —7K 95
Kingsdown Clo. Maid —5B 126
Kingsdown Hill. Kgdn —4M 199 (4E 33)
Kingsdown Park. —2H 225
Kingsdown Pk. Whits —2C 21
Kingsdown Rd. Kgdn —7J 115 (4C 19)
Kingsdown Rd. St Mc —7J 213
Kingsdown Rd. Walm —8N 177 (3E 33)
Kingsdown Way. Brom —9K 69
Kings Dri. Grav —8G 63
Kings Farm. —8H 63 (4B 8)
Kingsferry Bridge. —1C 19
Kingsfield Ho. SE9 —8N 55
Kingsfield Rd. H Bay —5J 195
Kingsfield Ter. Dart —3L 59
Kingsford Clo. Mer —7M 161
Kingsford Ct. Dover —3G 181
Kingsford St. Mer —7L 161 (1B 40)
Kingsford Ter. Afrd —3E 160
Kingsgate. —4K 209 (1E 23)
Kingsgate Av. Broad —4K 209
Kingsgate Bay Rd. Broad —3M 209 (1E 23)
Kingsgate Clo. Bexh —8N 51
Kingsgate Clo. Maid —5N 125
Kingsgate Clo. Orp —5L 71
Kingsground. SE9 —5N 55
Kingshall M. SE13 —1F 54
Kings Hall Rd. Beck —3B 68 (1E 13)
Kings Head All. S'ness —1B 218
King's Head La. Hythe —6K 197
(off Dental St.)
King's Highway. SE18 —6G 51 (3B 6)
Kings Hill. —6M 123 (2B 26)
Kings Hill Av. King H —5M 123 (2B 26)
Kingshill Dri. Hoo —7G 67
(in two parts)
King's Hill Village. —8M 123
Kingsholm Gdns. SE9 —2N 55
Kingshurst Rd. SE12 —5K 55
Kingsingfield Clo. W King —8E 88
Kingsingfield Rd. W King —9E 88
Kings Keep. Brom —6H 69
Kingsland. —1D 5
Kingsland Cotts. Westw —2D 158
Kingsland Gdns. Walm —1L 199
Kingsland Gro. H'crn —3L 193
Kingsland High St. E8 —1D 5
Kingsland Hollow. St Mar —2F 214
Kingsland La. Eger —4C 29
Kingsland La. Westw —3C 158 (4E 29)
Kingsland Rd. E2 & E8 —2D 5
Kings La. Mard —4C 27
Kingsleigh Wlk. Brom —7J 69
Kingsley Av. Dart —3A 60
Kingsley Ct. Bexh —3B 58
Kingsley M. Chst —2D 70
Kingsley Rd. Maid —6D 126
Kingsley Rd. Orp —8H 85
Kingsley Rd. Whits —5G 224
Kingsley Wood Dri. SE9 —8B 56
Kingsman Pde. SE18 —3B 50
Kingsman St. SE18 —3B 50
Kingsmarsh La. Old R —3D 47
Kingsmead. Big H —4D 164
Kingsmead. Folk —3H 189
Kingsmead Clo. Sidc —7J 57
Kingsmead Cotts. Brom —2A 84
Kings Meadow. Kenn —3J 159
Kingsmead Pk. Allh —4M 201
Kingsmead Rd. Cant —9N 167 (4D 21)
King's M. Cant —1N 171
Kings Mill Clo. Sit —6F 98
Kingsmill Down. E Bra —1C 41
Kingsnorth. —6E 160 (2E 39)
(nr. Ashford)
Kingsnorth. —7N 67 (4A 10)
(nr. Hoo St Werburgh)
Kingsnorth Clo. Hoo —7H 67
Kingsnorth Ct. Folk —6H 189
Kingsnorth Gdns. Folk —6H 189
Kingsnorth Ind. Est. Afrd —3F 160
Kingsnorth Ind. Est. Hoo —6N 67
Kingsnorth Rd. Afrd —4E 160 (1A 40)
Kingsnorth Rd. Fav —6G 186
Kingsnorth Rd. Gill —8M 81
King's Orchard. SE9 —4A 56
Kings Orchard. Roch —7N 79
Kings Pde. Afrd —8F 158
(off High St. Ashford,)
Kings Pk. Cant —1A 172
Kings Pk. Tun W —2K 157
King's Pl. Ram —6J 211
(off Abbot's Hill)
Kingsridge Gdns. Dart —4L 59
King's Rd. SW6, SW10 & SW3 —3B 4
Kings Rd. Aysm —2D 162
Kings Rd. Big H —4C 164
Kings Rd. Birch —5F 206
Kings Rd. Chat —2G 94
Kings Rd. Dover —5F 180
King's Rd. Fav —6G 186
Kings Rd. Folk —5D 188
Kings Rd. H'crn —3K 193 (4A 28)
Kings Rd. H Bay —3G 194 (2E 21)
King's Rd. King T —1A 12
Kings Rd. Min S —5L 219
King's Rd. Orp —5H 85
King's Rd. Ram —4H 211
King's Rd. Tonb —8J 145
King's Rd. Wclf S —1B 10
Kings Ropewalk. Dover —7G 181
Kings Row. Maid —8D 126
Kings Standing Bus. Pk. Tun W —5M 151
Kings St. Stan H —2C 8
Kingstanding Way. Tun W —4M 151
Kingsthorpe Rd. SE26 —9A 54
Kings Toll Rd. Pem —8E 152 (1B 36)
Kingston. —3E 31
Kingston Av. Maid —9D 126
Kingston Av. Mgte —4N 207
Kingston Clo. H Bay —2N 195
Kingston Clo. Ram —2F 210
Kingston Clo. River —1E 180
Kingston Ct. N'fleet —3A 62
Kingston Cres. Beck —4C 68
Kingston Cres. Chat —7E 94
Kingstone Ct. Folk —7H 189
Kingston Hill. King T —1A 12
Kingston Rd. SW15 —4A 4
Kingston Rd. SW20 & SW19 —1A 12
Kingston Rd. Eps —3A 12
Kingston Rd. King T & N Mald —1A 12
Kingston Rd. Wor Pk & Eps —2A 12
Kingston upon Thames. —1A 12
Kingston Vale. —4A 4
Kingston Vale. SW15 —1A 12
King St. W6 —3A 4
King St. Blue T —2B 218
King St. B'Ind & Bztt —2B 46
King St. Cant —1M 171 (4D 21)
King St. Chat —8D 80
King St. Deal —4N 177
King St. Dover —5J 181
King St. F'wch —7F 168 (4E 21)
King St. Gill —7F 80
King St. Grav —4G 63
King St. Maid —5D 126 (2E 27)
King St. Mgte —2C 208 (1D 23)
King St. Ram —6J 211 (2E 23)
King St. Roch —7N 79
King St. S'wch —5M 217
King St. Sit —6F 98
King St. Walm —7N 177
King St. W Mal —1A 124
Kingsway. WC2 —2C 5
Kingsway. Chat —2G 95
(in three parts)
Kingsway. Dym —6C 182
Kingsway. Orp —8F 70
Kingsway. W Wick —4H 83 (2E 13)
Kingswear Gdns. Strood —5N 79
Kingswood. —6G 140 (3B 28)
Kingswood. Kenn —5H 159
Kingswood. W'wd —3E 31
Kingswood Av. Belv —4A 52
Kingswood Av. Brom —7H 69
Kingswood Av. Chat —1C 94
Kingswood Av. Swan —7G 73
Kingswood Clo. Dart —4K 59
Kingswood Clo. Orp —1F 84
Kingswood Clo. Tun W —2J 157
Kingswood Dri. SE19 —1D 13
Kingswood Pl. SE13 —2H 55
Kingswood Rd. Ayle —2A 110
Kingswood Rd. Brom —7G 69
Kingswood Rd. Dun G —2F 118
Kingswood Rd. Gill —7G 80
Kingswood Rd. Tun W —2J 157 (2E 35)
Kings Wood St. Dover —4K 181
Kingswood Vs. Dover —2F 180
Kingsworth Clo. Beck —8B 68
King William Rd. Gill —5F 80
King Wood Hill. B Oak —4D 45
Kinlet Rd. SE18 —8E 50
Kinnaird Av. Brom —2J 69
Kinnaird Clo. Brom —2J 69
Kinnings Row. Tonb —5J 145
Kinross Clo. Chat —4E 94
Kinveachy Gdns. SE7 —5A 50
Kipling Dri. Lark —6D 108
Kipling Rd. Afrd —8F 158
Kipling Rd. Bexh —8N 51
Kipling Rd. Dart —3B 60
Kipping's Cross. —9F 152 (2B 36)
Kippington. —8H 119 (2C 25)
Kippington Clo. Sev —6G 119
Kippington Dri. SE9 —6N 55
Kippington Grange. Sev —9H 119
(off Grange Rd.)
Kippington Rd. Sev —6H 119
Kirby Clo. C'brk —8D 176
Kirby Ct. L'tn G —2A 156
Kirby Rd. Chatt —8C 66
Kirby Rd. Dart —5D 60
Kirby's La. Cant —1M 171 (4D 21)
Kirkcourt. Sev —5H 119
Kirkdale. SE26 —4D 5
Kirkdale. Loose —3C 138
Kirkdale Clo. Chat —9G 94
Kirkdale Cotts. Maid —3C 138
Kirkdale Rd. Maid —2C 138
Kirkdale Rd. Tun W —1H 157
Kirk Gdns. Walm —8L 177
Kirkham St. SE18 —6G 50
Kirkins Clo. Horsm —2C 198
Kirkland Clo. Sidc —4G 56
Kirk La. SE18 —6E 50
Kirkstone Av. Ram —5D 210
Kirkstone Pl. Maid —2C 138
Kirkstone Way. Brom —3H 69
Kirkwood Av. Wdchu —8B 226
Kirtley Rd. SE26 —9B 54
Kitchener Av. Chat —2C 94
Kitchener Av. Grav —9H 63
Kitchener Clo. B'hm —8C 162
Kitchener Rd. C'den —4D 9
Kitchener Rd. Chatt —8C 66
Kitchener Rd. Dover —5F 180
Kitchener Rd. Roch —4L 79
Kitchener Sq. Folk —3L 189
Kitchenour La. Beckl —3E 45
Kite Farm. Whits —2M 225
Kite La. Bchly —8M 153 (1B 36)
Kitewell La. Lydd —1D 204
Kither Rd. Afrd —2E 160
Kit Hill. Sell —1B 30
Kit Hill Av. Chat —8B 94
Kit's Coty. —3A 110 (3D 17)
Kit's Coty House. —4N 109 (3D 17)
Kittington La. Evtn —1J 185 (2B 32)
Kitto Rd. SE14 —3D 5
Klondyke Ind. Est. Queen —7A 218
Knapmill Rd. SE6 —7D 54
Knapmill Way. SE6 —7E 54
Knares, The. Bas —1C 8
Knatchbull Way. Bra L —8K 165
Knatts La. Knat —2D 104 (3E 15)
Knatts Valley. —1D 104 (3E 15)
Knatts Valley Rd. Knat —7D 88 (3E 15)
Knaves Acre. H'crn —3L 193
Knaves Acre Ct. Gill —6N 95
Knave's Ash. —3E 21
Knave Wood Rd. Kems —8M 103
Knee Hill. SE2 —4L 51 (3B 6)
Kneehill Cres. SE2 —4L 51
Kneller Rd. SE4 —2B 54
Knight Av. Cant —2J 171
Knight Av. Gill —6G 81
Knight Clo. Pem —7C 152
Knighton Pk. Rd. SE26 —1A 68
Knighton Rd. Otf —7F 102
Knightrider St. Maid —6D 126
Knightrider St. S'wch —6M 217
Knight Rd. Roch —7L 79 (1D 17)
(in two parts)
Knights All. Whits —3F 224
(off Middle Wall)
Knight's Av. Broad —7M 209
Knightsbridge. —3B 4
Knightsbridge. SW1 —3B 4
Knightsbridge Clo. Tun W —9F 150
Knights Clo. Hoo —8H 67
Knights Ct. Brom —8J 55
Knights Croft. New Ash —4M 89
Knightsfield Rd. Sit —5E 98
Knights Hill. SE27 —1C 13
Knights Mnr. Way. Dart —3N 59
Knights Pk. Tun W —6M 151
Knights Pk. Ind. Est. Roch —6L 79
Knight's Pl. Pem —7C 152
Knights Ridge. Orp —6K 85
Knights Ridge. Pem —7C 152
Knights Rd. Dover —4K 181
Knights Rd. Hoo —8G 66
Knights Templar. Dover —6H 181
Knights Templar Church. —6H 181
Knights Way. Dover —1F 180
Knight's Way. H'crn —3L 193
Knightswick Rd. Can I —2E 9
Knockhall. —3J 61 (4E 7)
Knockhall Chase. Grnh —3H 61
Knockhall Rd. Grnh —4J 61 (4E 7)
Knock Hill. Stne —2A 46
Knockholt. —8K 101 (4B 14)
Knockholt Main Rd. Knock —1H 117 (4B 14)
Knockholt Pound. —6N 101 (4C 14)
Knockholt Rd. SE9 —3N 55
Knockholt Rd. Clift —2J 209 (1E 23)
Knockholt Rd. Hals —5A 102 (3C 14)
Knockmill. —3E 104 (3E 15)
Knock Mill La. Sev —4G 104 (3E 15)
Knock Rd. Afrd —2E 160

Knockwood La.—Laws La.

Knockwood La. Mol —3A 30
Knockwood Rd. Tent —6D 222
Knold Pk. Mgte —5C 208
Knole. —8L 119 (2D 25)
Knole Clo. Weald —6J 131
Knole Ga. Sidc —8G 57
Knole House & Park. —8M 119
Knole La. Sev —8K 119
Knole Park. —7L 119
Knole Rd. Chat —8F 94
Knole Rd. Dart —5H 59
Knole Rd. Sev —5L 119
Knole, The. SE9 —9C 56
Knole, The. Fav —5F 186
Knole, The. Grav —3D 76
Knole Way. Sev —7K 119
Knoll Hill. Adgtn —3B 40
Knoll Ho. Folk —7J 189
Knoll La. Afrd —2C 160 (1E 39)
Knoll Pl. Walm —9M 177
Knoll Rise. Orp —2H 85
Knoll Rd. Bex —5B 58
Knoll Rd. Sidc —1K 71 (1B 14)
Knoll, The. Beck —4E 68
Knoll, The. Brom —2K 83
Knoll, The. E'try —2K 183
(off Woodnesborough La.)
Knoll Way. Ward —4J 203
Knott Ct. Maid —3D 126
Knott Cres. W'boro —2L 161
Knott's La. Cant —1N 171 (4D 21)
Knotts La. St Mc —7J 213
Knotts Pl. Sev —6H 119
Knotts Sq. Afrd —8G 158
(off North St.)
Knowle Av. Bexh —7N 51
Knowle Clo. L'tn G —2M 155
Knowle Hill. —3B 28
(nr. Kingswood)
Knowle La. Pad W —1C 36
Knowle Rd. Bchly —1C 36
Knowle Rd. Brom —3B 84
Knowle Rd. Maid —3D 126
Knowle Rd. Woul —7G 93 (3C 17)
Knowler Way. H Bay —2K 195
Knowles Gdns. H'crn —3L 193
Knowles Hill Cres. SE13 —3G 54
Knowles Wlk. S'hrst —7K 221
Knowles Way. Folk —6J 189
Knowle, The. —1C 36
Knowlton. —2B 32
Knowlton Gdns. Maid —7M 125
Knowlton Grn. Brom —8J 69
Knowlton Wlk. Cant —1A 172
Knowsley Way. Hild —1D 144
Knox Bridge. —1E 37
Knught Rd. Tonb —1L 145
Kohima Pl. B Hts —2L 181
Kon Tiki. Mard —3L 205
Koonowla Clo. Big H —3D 164
Kowlam Pl. Gus —1L 181
Kydbrook Clo. Orp —1E 84
Kyetop Wlk. Gill —5N 95
Kymbeline Ct. Deal —6L 177
Kynaston Rd. Brom —1K 69
Kynaston Rd. Orp —1K 85

La Belle Alliance Sq. Ram —5J 211
Labour in Vain Rd. Wro —4K 105 (3E 15)
Laburnham Pl. Sit —7F 98
Laburnum Av. Dart —6K 59
Laburnum Av. S'wch —6L 217
Laburnum Av. Swan —6E 72
Laburnum Clo. Dover —9D 178
Laburnum Dri. Lark —8E 108
Laburnum Gdns. Croy —2A 82
Laburnum Gro. Min S —3H 219
Laburnum Gro. N'fleet —5C 62
Laburnum Ho. Brom —4H 69
Laburnum Ho. S'ness —2C 218
(off Russell St.)
Laburnum La. Sturry —4G 168
Laburnum Rd. Roch —7J 79
Laburnum Way. Brom —1C 84
Labworth Clo. Min S —6E 218
Lacarno Av. Gill —1K 95
Lacebark Clo. Sidc —5H 57
Lacey Clo. Langl —4A 140
Laceys La. Lin —8N 137 (3D 27)
Lachlan Way. S'gte —8F 188
Lackenden Cotts. L'brne —4J 173
Lacton Oast. W'boro —1M 161
Lacton Way. W'boro —1L 161
Ladbroke Gdns. W11 —2B 4
Ladbroke Gro. W10 & W11 —2A 4
Ladbrooke Cres. Sidc —8M 57
Ladbrooke Ho. Maid —4D 126
Laddingford. —3C 26
Ladds La. Snod —8B 92
Ladds La. Up Hall —3C 16
Ladds Way. Swan —7E 72
Lade. —8A 212 (3E 47)
Lade Fort Cotts. Lydd S —8A 212
Lade Fort Cres. Lydd S —8A 212
Ladesfield. Whits —6E 224
Ladham Rd. Goud —7L 185 (2D 37)
Ladies Mile. With —9D 154 (3C 35)
Lady Amherst's Dri. Ide H —4C 130
Ladyclose Av. Cli —6L 65
Ladycroft Gdns. Orp —6E 84
Ladycroft Rd. SE13 —1E 54
Ladycroft Way. Orp —6E 84
Ladyfields. H Bay —5L 195
Ladyfields. N'fleet —9E 62
Lady Garne Rd. W Hou —1B 42
Ladygrove. Croy —9B 82
Lady Oak La. Flim & Kiln —3C 37
Lady's Gift Rd. Tun W —6F 150
Ladysmith Gro. Sea —7B 224
Ladysmith Rd. SE9 —4C 56
Ladysmith Rd. Whits —8D 224
Lady's Wlk. Sev —6G 120
Lady Vane Clo. S'brne —3J 133
Ladywell. —3E 54 (4E 5)
Ladywell Clo. SE4 —3D 54
Ladywell Heights. SE4 —4C 54
Ladywell Ho. Dover —4J 181
(off Park St.)
Ladywell Pk. Pl. Dover —4J 181
Ladywell Rd. SE13 —3D 54 (4E 5)
Ladywood Av. Orp —8G 71
Ladywood Rd. Cux —1F 92
Ladywood Rd. Dart —1E 74
Ladywood Rd. Sturry —4E 168
Lady Wootton's Grn. Cant —2N 171 (1D 31)
Lagonda Way. Dart —2K 59
Lagoon Rd. Orp —8L 71
Lagos Av. Ram —3E 210
Lake Av. Brom —2K 69
Lakedale Rd. SE18 —6G 50 (3B 6)
Lake Dri. High —7G 65
Lake Footpath. SE2 —2M 51
Lake Ho. Rd. E11 —1A 6
Lakelands. H'shm —2N 141
Lakelands. Maid —1D 138
Lakemead. Afrd —1C 160
Lake Rd. Croy —3C 82
Lake Rd. Quar W —2J 125
Lake Rd. Tun W —1E 156
Laker Rd. Roch —5N 93
Lakeside. SE2 —3M 51
Lakeside. Beck —6E 68
Lakeside. Snod —4D 108
Lakeside Av. SE28 —2J 51
Lakeside Clo. Bough B —3A 142
Lakeside Clo. Sidc —3L 57
Lakeside Dri. Brom —4A 84
Lakeside Pk. Roch —5B 80
Lakes Rd. Kes —6M 83
Lake St. Mark X —4E 35
Lakeswood Rd. Orp —9E 70
Lakeview Clo. Snod —4E 108
Lake View Rd. Sev —5H 119
Lakeview Rd. Well —2K 57
Lakewood Dri. Gill —5M 95
Laking Av. Broad —6L 209
Laleham Gdns. Mgte —3F 208
Laleham Rd. SE6 —5F 54
Laleham Rd. Mgte —4F 208 (1E 23)
Laleham Wlk. Mgte —4F 208
Lambarde Av. SE9 —9C 56
Lambarde Clo. Hall —7E 92
Lambarde Dri. Sev —5H 119
Lambarde Rd. Sev —4H 119
Lambardes. New Ash —4M 89
Lambardes Clo. Prat B —2L 101
Lambard Ho. Maid —4D 126
Lambarton Rd. Dover —3F 180
Lambden Rd. P'ley —4D 29
Lamberden. —2D 45
Lamberhurst. —2D 200 (2B 36)
Lamberhurst Clo. Orp —2M 85
Lamberhurst Quarter. —2B 36
Lamberhurst Rd. Gill —9L 81
Lamberhurst Rd. Horsm —4A 198 (2C 36)
Lamberhurst Rd. Maid —2M 125
Lamberhurst Vineyards. —3C 200 (3B 36)
Lamberhurst Way. Clift —2K 209
Lambersart Clo. Tun W —5K 151
Lambert Clo. Big H —4D 164
Lambert Ct. Eri —6D 52
(off Park Cres.)
Lambert Ho. Deal —7L 177
Lambert M. Snod —2E 108
Lamberts Pl. Horsm —3D 198
Lamberts Rd. Tun W —6K 151 (1E 35)
Lambert's Yd. Tonb —6H 145
Lambes Ct. Gill —6N 95
Lambeth. —3C 5
Lambeth Bri. SW1 & SE1 —3C 5
Lambeth Clo. Chat —7E 94
Lambeth Pal. Rd. SE1 —3C 5
Lambeth Rd. SE1 —3C 5
Lambeth Rd. Cant —7B 168
Lambourne Dri. King H —7L 123
Lambourne Pl. Gill —1C 96
Lambourne Rd. Bear —7J 127
Lambourne Wlk. Cant —2B 172
(off Sturmer Clo.)
Lambourn Way. Chat —8F 94
Lambourn Way. Tun W —4K 157
Lambs Bank. Tonb —8H 145
Lambscroft Av. SE9 —8M 55
Lamb's Cross. —3E 27
Lambsfrith Gro. Hem —8L 95
Lambs Mobile Home Pk. Pad W —7M 147
Lambs Wlk. Whits —7E 224
Lamerock Rd. Brom —9J 55
Laming Rd. Birch —5G 206
Lamkin Wall. Stod —5N 169 (3A 22)
Lammas Dri. Mil R —5F 98
Lammas Ga. Fav —4H 187
Lamorbey. —6H 57
Lamorbey Clo. Sidc —6H 57
Lamorna Av. Grav —7J 63
Lamorna Clo. Orp —1J 85
Lampington Row. L'tn G —2M 155
Lampits Hill. Corr —1C 9
Lamplighters Clo. Dart —4N 59
Lamplighters Clo. Hem —6J 95
Lampmead Rd. SE12 —2J 55
Lamport Clo. SE18 —4B 50
Lanain Ct. SE12 —5J 55
Lanbury Rd. SE15 —2A 54
Lancashire Rd. Maid —1H 139
Lancaster Av. SE27 —4C 5
Lancaster Av. Cap F —2B 174
Lancaster Clo. Brom —7J 69
Lancaster Ct. Gill —4M 95
Lancaster Ct. Grav —8H 63
Lancaster Gdns. Birch —5E 206
Lancaster Gdns. H Bay —2L 195
Lancaster Ho. Deal —5K 177
Lancaster Ho. Dover —5J 181
(off Lancaster Rd.)
Lancaster Pl. WC2 —2C 5
Lancaster Rd. NW10 —1A 4
Lancaster Rd. SE25 —1D 13
Lancaster Rd. Cant —4M 171
Lancaster Rd. Dover —5J 181
Lancaster St. SE18 —7G 50
Lancaster Way. W Mal —6L 123
Lance Croft. New Ash —3M 89
Lancelot Av. Roch —6J 79
Lancelot Clo. Roch —6J 79
Lancelot Ct. Orp —3K 85
Lancelot Rd. Well —2J 57
Lances Clo. Meop —1F 90
Lancester Clo. Ram —3F 210
Lancet La. Maid —2C 138
Lancet Pl. Maid —2C 138
Lancey Clo. SE7 —4A 50
Lanchester Clo. H Bay —4B 194
Lancing Rd. Orp —3J 85
Landale Gdns. Dart —5K 59
Landau Way. Eri —5L 53
Landbury Wlk. Afrd —6D 158
Landgate. Rye —3A 46
Landon Rd. H Bay —2K 195
Landor Ct. Hem —8K 95
Landrail Rd. Lwr Hal —8L 223
Landseer Av. N'fleet —8C 62
Landseer Clo. Tonb —1L 145
Landstead Rd. SE18 —7F 50
Land Way. High —9H 65
Landway. Seal —2N 119
Landway, The. Bear —6J 127 (2E 27)
Landway, The. Bor G —2M 121
Landway, The. Kems —8A 104
Landway, The. Orp —6L 71
Landway, The. Sev —4D 15
Lane Av. Grnh —4J 61
Lane End. —9D 60 (1E 15)
Lane End. Bexh —1C 58
Lane End. H Bay —2E 194
Lanes Av. N'fleet —8E 62
Laneside. Chst —1E 70
Lanes, The. Min —2C 23
Lane's Wlk. Whits —3F 224
Lane, The. SE3 —1K 55
Lane, The. Gus —7K 179 (4D 33)
Lanfranc Gdns. Harb —1J 171
Lanfranc Rd. Deal —2M 177
Langafel Clo. Long —5L 75
Langbrook Rd. SE3 —1N 55
Lang Ct. Whits —2L 225
Langdale. Afrd —9C 158
Langdale Av. Ram —5E 210
Langdale Clo. Gill —2M 95
Langdale Clo. Orp —4D 84
Langdale Cres. Bexh —7B 52
Langdale Rise. Maid —4N 125
Langdale Wlk. N'fleet —8D 62
Langdon Av. Ah —5D 216
Langdon Clo. St Mc —8J 213
Langdon Rd. Brom —6L 69
Langdon Rd. Folk —4D 188
Langdon Rd. Roch —8N 79
Langdon Shaw. Sidc —1H 71
Langford Pl. Sidc —8J 57
Langham Clo. Mgte —2N 207
Langham Gro. Maid —5N 125
Langholm Rd. Afrd —2E 160
Langholm Rd. L'tn G —1N 155
Langhorne Gdns. Folk —7J 189
(off Leas, The)
Langhurst. —3A 24
Langland Gdns. Croy —3C 82
Langlands Dri. Dart —1E 74
Langley. —4M 139 (3A 28)
Langley Bottom. —4A 12
Langley Gdns. Brom —7M 69
Langley Gdns. Clift —2J 209
Langley Gdns. Orp —9D 70
Langley Gro. N Mald —1A 12
Langley Heath. —4A 140 (3A 28)
Langley Pk. Farm Cotts. Langl —4L 139
Langley Rd. Beck —7B 68
Langley Rd. Sit —5G 98
Langley Rd. S Croy —9A 82
Langley Rd. Well —6L 51
Langley Vale Rd. Eps —4A 12
Langley Way. W Wick —2G 82
Langmore Ct. Bexh —1M 57
Langney Dri. Afrd —3B 160
Langport Rd. New R —3D 212
Langthorne Ct. Brom —9F 54
Langthorne Rd. E11 —1E 5
Langton Cliffs Viewpoint. —3M 181
Langton Clo. Deal —2M 177
Langton Clo. Maid —4F 126
Langton Green. —2M 155 (2D 35)
Langton La. Cant —6N 171
Langton Rd. L'tn G & Tun W —3L 155 (2D 35)
Langton Rd. Speld —9N 149 (1D 35)
Langworth Clo. Dart —8L 59
Lanier Rd. SE13 —4G 54
Lankester Parker Rd. Roch —5N 93
Lankton Clo. Beck —4F 68
Lannoy Rd. SE9 —6E 56
Lanridge Rd. SE2 —3M 51
Lansbury Cres. Dart —3A 60
Lansdell Rd. Mitc —1C 12
Lansdown Cotts. Cant —3N 171
Lansdowne Av. Bexh —7M 51
Lansdowne Av. Maid —2F 138
Lansdowne Av. Orp —2D 84
Lansdowne Ct. Chat —8C 80
Lansdowne Dri. E8 —1D 5
Lansdowne Rd. Brom —3K 69
Lansdowne Rd. Chat —1B 94
Lansdowne Rd. Sev —4L 119
Lansdowne Rd. Tonb —4H 145
Lansdowne Rd. Tun W —1H 157 (2E 35)
Lansdowne Sq. N'fleet —4E 62
Lansdowne Sq. Tun W —1H 157
Lansdown Pl. N'fleet —6E 62
Lansdown Rd. Cant —3N 171
Lansdown Rd. Grav —6E 62
Lansdown Rd. Sidc —8K 57 (4B 6)
Lansdown Rd. Sit —7K 99
Lanterns Shop. Cen., The. Folk —7K 189
Lanthorne Rd. Broad —6L 209 (1E 23)
Lapins La. King H —7L 123
Lapis Clo. Grav —6N 63
La Providence. Roch —7N 79
Lapwing Clo. Eri —7J 53
Lapwing Dri. Lwr Hal —8L 223
Lapwing Rd. Isle G —3C 190
Lapwings. Long —6A 76
Lapwings, The. Grav —7J 63
Lapworth Clo. Orp —3L 85
Lara Clo. SE13 —4F 54
Larch Clo. Broad —9H 209
Larch Clo. Lark —8F 108
Larch Cres. Tonb —1J 145
Larchcroft. Chat —7D 94
Larch Dene. Orp —3C 84
Larches, The. Fav —4E 186
Larches, The. High —1G 79
Larches, The. Whits —5E 224
Larches Viewpoint, The. —8J 111
Larch Gro. Pad W —9L 147
Larch Gro. Sidc —6H 57
Larch Ho. Brom —4H 69
Larch Rd. Dart —5L 59
Larch Rd. Evtn —2J 185
Larch Ter. S'ness —4B 218
Larch Tree Way. Croy —4D 82
Larch Wlk. Kenn —4G 159
Larch Wlk. Swan —5E 72
Larch Way. Brom —1C 84
Larch Wood Clo. Chat —1G 110
Larchwood Rd. SE9 —7D 56
Largo Wlk. Eri —8F 52
Larkbere Rd. SE26 —9B 54
Larkey View. Cha —9E 170
Larkfield. —8E 108 (4C 17)
Larkfield. Five G —8F 146
Larkfield Av. Gill —8H 81
Larkfield Av. Sit —5F 98
Larkfield Clo. Brom —3J 83
Larkfield Clo. Lark —9E 108
Larkfield Rd. Lark —9E 108
Larkfield Rd. Sev —5D 118
Larkfield Rd. Sidc —8H 57
Larkfields. N'fleet —8D 62
Larkfield Trad. Est. Lark —5F 108
Larkin Clo. Roch —2M 79
Larks Field. Hart —7M 75
Larksfield Rd. Fav —3G 187
Larkspur Clo. E Mal —9E 108
Larkspur Clo. Orp —3L 85
Larkspur Lodge. Sidc —8K 57
Larkspur Rd. Chat —7B 94
Larkspur Rd. E Mal —9D 108
Larkstore Pk. S'hrst —6J 221
Larkswood Clo. Eri —8H 53
Larkwell La. Hart —7M 75
Larner Rd. Eri —7F 52
Lascelles Rd. Dover —6F 180
Laser Quay. Roch —5A 80
Lashenden. —1B 38
Lashenden (Headcorn) Airfield. —1B 38
Lassa Rd. SE9 —3A 56
Last La. Dover —5J 181
(off Queen La.)
Latchgate. S'gte —8C 188
Latchmere Rd. SW11 —3B 4
La-Tene. Deal —8L 177
Latham Clo. Big H —4C 164
Latham Rd. Bexh —3B 58
Lathe Barn. —2C 182
Lathe Barn Farm. —3C 41
Lathe Barn Farm Museum. —2C 182
Lathkill Ct. Beck —4C 68
Latimer Clo. H Bay —5C 194
Latimer Pl. Gill —5F 80
Latona Dri. Grav —1L 77
La Tourne Gdns. Orp —4E 84
Latters Flats. Hdlw —8D 134
Latymers. Pens —2J 149
Lauderdale Rd. W9 —2B 4
Launcelot Rd. Brom —9K 55
Launder's La. Rain —2D 7
Launder Way. Maid —7B 126
Laundry Rd. Min —2C 23
Laura Dri. Swan —3H 73
Laura Pl. Roch —1K 93
Laureate Clo. Mgte —3F 208
Laurel Av. Grav —7H 63
Laurel Av. St Mar —3D 214
Laurel Bank. Tun W —7H 151
Laurelbrook. SE6 —8H 55
Laurel Clo. Dart —6K 59
Laurel Clo. Folk —5E 188
Laurel Clo. Sidc —8J 57
Laurel Cres. Croy —4D 82
Laurel Gro. SE26 —9A 54
Laurel Gro. Kgswd —6F 140
Laurel Ho. Brom —4H 69
Laurel La. I'ham —4E 45
Laurel Rd. Gill —5F 80
Laurel Rd. Tun W —7K 151
Laurels, The. Brom —6K 69
Laurels, The. Dart —8K 59
Laurels, The. H Hal —7H 193
Laurels, The. Long —6C 76
Laurels, The. Maid —7N 125
Laurels, The. Mils —6G 115
Laurel Wlk. Gill —5A 96
Laurel Way. Tun W —7K 151
Laureston Pl. Dover —4K 181
Laurie Gray Av. Chat —1A 110
Lauriston Clo. Ram —7E 210
Lauriston Mt. Broad —8L 209
Lauriston Rd. E9 —1D 5
Lausanne Rd. SE15 —3D 5
Lausanne Rd. Mgte —3D 208
Lavenda Clo. Hem —7K 95
Lavender Av. Mitc —1B 12
Lavender Clo. Brom —9A 70
Lavender Clo. Chat —7B 94
Lavender Clo. Ches —3L 225
Lavender Clo. E Mal —1D 124
Lavender Clo. Mgte —5A 208
Lavender Ct. Sit —8H 99
Lavender Ct. Tun W —4E 156
Lavender Hill. SW11 —4B 4
Lavender Hill. Swan —6E 72
Lavender Hill. Tonb —7J 145
Lavender Rd. E Mal —1D 124
Lavenders Rd. W Mal —3A 124 (1C 26)
Lavender Wlk. E Mal —1D 124
Lavender Way. Croy —9A 68
Lavernock Rd. Bexh —9B 52
Laverstoke Rd. All —1N 125
Lavidge Rd. SE9 —7A 56
Lavinia Rd. Dart —4N 59
Lavisham Ho. Brom —1L 69
Lawford Gdns. Dart —3K 59
Lawley Clo. Ram —3G 211
Lawn Clo. Brom —2L 69
Lawn Clo. Chat —1E 94
Lawn Clo. Swan —5D 72
Lawn Clo. Tent —8A 222
Lawn Pk. Sev —9J 119
Lawn Rd. Beck —3C 68
Lawn Rd. Broad —8L 209
Lawn Rd. Grav —3B 62
Lawn Rd. Tonb —7H 145
Lawn Rd. Walm —9M 177
Lawnside. SE3 —2J 55
Lawns, The. SE3 —1J 55
Lawns, The. Bchly —6N 153
Lawns, The. Ram —5K 211
Lawns, The. Sidc —9L 57
Lawn Ter. SE3 —1H 55
Lawn Vs. Ram —6J 211
(off Guildford Lawn)
Lawrance Sq. N'fleet —7E 62
Lawrence Av. Ram —7F 210
Lawrence Clo. Folk —5F 188
Lawrence Clo. Maid —1D 138
Lawrence Ct. Folk —5L 189
Lawrence Dri. Cob —7M 77
Lawrence Gdns. H Bay —3K 195
Lawrence Hill Gdns. Dart —4K 59
Lawrence Hill Rd. Dart —4K 59
Lawrence Rd. Eri —7C 52
Lawrence Rd. Tonb —1L 145
Lawrence Rd. W Wick —5K 83
Lawrence St. Gill —7F 80
Lawrie Pk. Av. SE26 —1D 13
Lawrie Pk. Rd. SE26 —1D 13
Laws La. Mer —2B 40

Lwr. Rainham Rd.—Maltings, The

Lwr. Rainham Rd. Gill & Rain —6K 81 (1E 17)
Lwr. Range Rd. Grav —5K 63
Lwr. Richmond Rd. SW13 & SW15 —3A 4
Lwr. Richmond Rd. Rich & SW14 —4A 4
Lower Rd. SE16 & SE8 —3D 5 (in two parts)
Lower Rd. Bap & Fav —4A 186 (3D 19) (Bysing Wood Rd.)
Lower Rd. Bap & Fav —7N 99 (3D 19) (Hempstead La.)
Lower Rd. Belv & Eri —3C 52 (3C 6)
Lower Rd. Fav —5E 186 (3A 20)
Lower Rd. Maid —7E 126
Lower Rd. Min S —8F 218 (1D 19)
Lower Rd. N'fleet —2L 61
Lower Rd. Orp —2B 14
Lower Rd. River —9C 178 (1C 42)
Lower Rd. Shorne —7C 64 (4C 8)
Lower Rd. S'le —8A 216 (1B 32)
Lower Rd. St M —9K 71
Lower Rd. Stne —1A 46
Lower Rd. Sutt —2B 12
Lower Rd. Sut V —9A 140 (3A 28)
Lower Rd. Swan —3G 73 (1C 15)
Lower Rd. Temp E —8C 178 (1C 42)
Lower Rd. Til —2F 62
Lower Rd. Tilm —3C 33
Lower Rd. W Far & E Far —2G 137 (2C 27)
Lower Rd. Wdchu —8C 226 (3D 39)
Lower Road Estate. —5D 186
Lwr. Rochester Rd. High —7H 65 (4C 9)
Lwr. Rochester Rd. Roch —9L 65
Lwr. Sandgate Rd. Folk —8H 189
Lower Sands. Dym —5D 182
Lwr. Santon La. Pres —3B 22
Lower Shorne. —9C 64 (4C 8)
Lwr. Sloane St. SW1 —3B 4
Lwr. Station Rd. Cray —4F 58
Lower Stoke. —8K 201 (3A 10)
Lwr. Stone St. Maid —5D 126
Lower St. Broom —3F 140 (2A 28)
Lower St. E'try —3K 183 (2C 33)
Lower St. Hild —2M 143 (3D 25)
Lower St. Leeds —2C 140 (2A 28)
Lower Sydenham. —9A 54 (1D 13)
Lwr. Sydenham Ind. Est. SE26 —1C 68
Lower Ter. NW3 —1B 4
Lwr. Thames St. EC3 —2D 5
Lwr. Tovil. Tovil —7B 126 (2D 27)
Lower Twydall. —7M 81 (2A 18)
Lwr. Twydall La. Gill —8M 81 (1A 18)
Lower Upnor. —1D 80 (1E 17)
Lwr. Vicarage Rd. Kenn —3G 159
Lwr. Wall Rd. Burm —3B 40
Lwr. Wall Rd. W Hyt —9A 196
Lower Walmer. —7M 177
Lwr. Warren Rd. Chat —4A 110
Lwr. Woodlands Rd. Gill —6J 81
Lowfield Rd. Min S —6F 218
Lowfield St. Dart —5M 59 (4D 7)
Low Meadow. Hall —6E 92
Lownds Ct. Brom —5K 69
Lowslip Hill. W Hou —6A 180 (1B 42)
Lowther Hill. SE23 —5B 54
Lowther Rd. Dover —4G 181
Loxford. —1B 6
Loxford La. Ilf —1B 6
Loxley Clo. SE26 —1A 68
Loxton Rd. SE23 —6A 54
Loxwood Clo. Orp —3M 85
Loxwood Clo. Whitf —6G 178
Lubbock Clo. Maid —3H 139
Lubbock Rd. Chst —3B 70 (1A 14)
Lubbock Wlk. Gill —6N 95
Lucas Ct. SE26 —1B 68
Lucas Rd. Snod —3C 108
Lucerne Ct. Eri —3N 51
Lucerne Ct. Sea —7B 224
Lucerne Dri. Sea —7B 224
Lucerne La. Mart M —4D 33
Lucerne Rd. Orp —2H 85
Lucerne St. Maid —4D 126
Lucilina Dri. Eden —7C 184
Luckhurst Gdns. Clift —2J 209
Luckhurst Rd. Dover —1D 180
Luckhurst Rd. W'boro —2L 161
Lucknow Clo. B Hts —1L 181
Lucknow Rd. Pad W —7M 147
Lucknow St. SE18 —7G 50
Luck's Hill. W Mal —1A 124 (1C 26)
Lucks La. Cha S —3E 27
Lucks La. Pad W —6M 147 (4B 26)
Luck's Way. Mard —2J 205
Lucorn Clo. SE12 —4J 55
Lucy Av. Folk —4G 189 (2A 42)
Lucy's Av. Hythe —6L 197
Lucys Hill. Hythe —6J 197
Luddenham. —1C 186 (3E 19)
Luddenham Clo. Afrd —3D 160
Luddenham Clo. Maid —3F 126
Luddesdon Rd. Eri —7B 52
Luddesdown. —2L 91 (2B 16)
Luddesdown Rd. Ludd —2M 91 (2B 16)
Ludgate Hill. EC4 —2C 5
Ludgate La. Lyn —6M 115 (4D 19)
Ludley Hill. Peas —3D 45
Ludlow Clo. Brom —6K 69
Ludpit La. E'ham —2A 44
Luffield Rd. SE2 —3K 51
Luffman Rd. SE12 —8L 55
Lughorse La. Yald & Hunt —7E 136 (3C 27)
Lukes Clo. Dover —3G 180
Lukin Ho. Hythe —7G 196
Lullarook Clo. Big H —4C 164
Lullenden. —1A 34
Lullingstone. —5K 87 (2D 15)
Lullingstone Av. Swan —6G 72
Lullingstone Castle. —6K 87 (2D 15)
Lullingstone Clo. Hem —8L 95
Lullingstone Clo. Orp —3K 71
Lullingstone Ct. Cant —2M 171 (1D 31) (off St John's La.)
Lullingstone Cres. Orp —3J 71
Lullingstone La. SE13 —4G 54
Lullingstone La. Eyns —4K 87 (2D 15)
Lullingstone Park Visitor Centre. —3D 15
Lullingstone Rd. Belv —6A 52
Lullingstone Rd. Maid —2N 125
Lullingstone Roman Villa. —4J 87 (2D 15)
Lullington Garth. Brom —3H 69
Lulworth Rd. SE9 —7A 56
Lulworth Rd. Well —9H 51
Lumley Clo. Belv —5B 52
Lumsden Ter. Chat —8B 80
Lunar Clo. Big H —4D 164
Lunedale Rd. Dart —6C 60
Lunghurst Rd. Wold —4E 13
Lunsford. —6D 108 (4C 16)
Lunsford La. Lark —9D 108 (4C 16)
Lunsford Park. —6E 108 (4C 17)
Lupin Clo. Croy —2A 82
Lupton Clo. SE12 —8L 55
Lupus St. SW1 —3C 4
Lurkins Rise. Goud —9J 185
Luscombe Ct. Short —5H 69
Lushington Rd. SE6 —9E 54
Lushington Rd. Maid —2B 126
Lusted Hall La. Tats —8B 164 (1A 24)
Lusted Rd. Sev —2F 118
Luton. —1F 94 (2E 17)
Luton Av. Broad —1K 211
Luton Ct. Broad —1K 211
Luton High St. Chat —1F 94 (2E 17)
Luton Rd. Chat —9E 80 (2E 17)
Luton Rd. Fav —5J 187
Luton Rd. Sidc —8L 57
Lutwyche Rd. SE6 —7C 54
Luxfield Rd. SE9 —6A 56
Luxford La. Crowb —4D 35
Luxford Rd. Crowb —4D 35
Luxon Rd. Ludd —7K 91 (3B 16)
Luxted. —5C 100 (3A 14)
Luxted Rd. Orp —3C 100 (3A 14)
Lyall Way. Gill —7A 96 (in two parts)
Lychfield Dri. Roch —3L 79
Lych Ga. Ct. Eden —6C 184
Lych Ga. Rd. Orp —2J 85
Lyconby Gdns. Croy —1B 82
Lydbrook Clo. Sit —7E 98
Lydd. —3C 204 (3D 47)
Lydd Airport. —3E 47
Lydd Clo. Sidc —8G 57
Lydden. —9C 208 (2D 23)
Lydden Hill. Lyd —4B 32
Lydden Motor Circuit. —4A 32
Lydd-on-Sea. —4E 47
Lydd Rd. Bexh —7A 52
Lydd Rd. Cmbr —4B 46
Lydd Rd. Chat —6E 94
Lydd Rd. New R —3A 212 (2D 47)
Lydd Town Museum. —3C 204
Lydens La. Hever —9F 184 (4B 24)
Lydford Ct. Dart —4B 60 (off Clifton Wlk.)
Lydia Cotts. Grav —5G 62
Lydia Rd. Eri —6G 53
Lydia Rd. Walm —8K 177
Lydos Clo. Lydd S —9A 212
Lydstep Rd. Chst —9C 56
Lye Green. —3C 35
Lyell Clo. Hythe —7H 197
Lyell Ct. Birch —4E 206 (off Lyell Rd.)
Lyell Rd. Birch —3E 206
Lyewood Common. —2C 35
Lyford St. SE7 —4A 50
Lyle Clo. Roch —3M 79
Lyle Ct. Maid —5N 125
Lyle Pk. Sev —5J 119
Lymbridge Green. —4D 31
Lymden La. Wallc —4B 36
Lyme Farm Rd. SE12 —2K 55
Lyme Rd. Well —8K 51
Lyminge. —8D 204 (1E 41)
Lyminge Clo. Gill —1M 95
Lyminge Clo. Sidc —9H 57
Lyminge Way. Mgte —4G 208
Lymington Ct. Maid —4J 139
Lymington Rd. NW6 —1B 4
Lymington Rd. Wgte S —4J 207
Lympne. —5B 196 (3C 41)
Lympne Castle. —6A 196 (3C 41)
Lympne Hill. Lymp —6B 196 (3D 41)
Lympne Rd. Adgtn —2B 40
Lynden Way. Swan —6D 72
Lyndhurst Av. Gill —4M 95
Lyndhurst Av. Mgte —3F 208
Lyndhurst Clo. Bexh —1C 58
Lyndhurst Clo. Cant —8L 167
Lyndhurst Clo. Orp —5D 84
Lyndhurst Dri. Sev —6F 118
Lyndhurst Gro. Sit —9E 98
Lyndhurst Rd. Bexh —1C 58
Lyndhurst Rd. Broad —7L 209
Lyndhurst Rd. Dym —7B 182
Lyndhurst Rd. Maid —9F 126
Lyndhurst Rd. Ram —5K 211
Lyndhurst Rd. River —2D 180
Lyndhurst Way. Grav —4D 76
Lyndon Av. Sidc —3H 57
Lyndon Rd. Belv —4B 52
Lyndon Way. Lym —7D 204
Lynette Av. Roch —3L 79
Lyngate Ct. Clift —3H 209
Lyngs Clo. Yald —8D 136
Lynmead Clo. Eden —3B 184
Lynmere Rd. Well —9K 51
Lynmouth Dri. Min S —5K 219
Lynmouth Rise. Orp —7K 71
Lynne Clo. SE23 —5C 54
Lynne Clo. Orp —7H 85
Lynors Av. Roch —3L 79
Lynsore Bottom. —3E 31
Lynstead Clo. Beck —5B 68
Lynsted. —3D 19
Lynsted Clo. Afrd —3D 160
Lynsted Clo. Bexh —3C 58
Lynsted Clo. Brom —5M 69
Lynsted Ct. Beck —5B 68
Lynsted Gdns. SE9 —2N 55
Lynsted Ho. Maid —8L 125
Lynsted La. Lyn —4J 223 (3D 19)
Lynsted Rd. Gill —9L 81
Lynsted Rd. Min S —5F 218
Lynton Av. Orp —7K 71
Lynton Dri. Chat —8E 94
Lynton Pl. Bri —8H 173
Lynton Rd. W3 —2A 4
Lynton Rd. Grav —6F 62
Lynton Rd. Hythe —7K 197
Lynton Rd. S. Grav —6F 62
Lynwood. Folk —4J 189
Lynwood. Groom —7K 155
Lynwood Gro. Orp —1G 85
Lynwood Rd. Eps —3A 12
Lyons Cres. Tonb —5J 145
Lyons Wharf. Tonb —5J 145 (off Lyons Cres.)
Lyoth Rd. Orp —3E 84
Lypeat Ct. Cant —7J 167
Lysander Clo. Bek —6K 173
Lysander Clo. Pys R —1G 211
Lysander Rd. W Mal —6L 123
Lysander Way. H'nge —8C 192
Lysander Way. Orp —4E 84
Lytchet Rd. Brom —3L 69
Lytham Av. H Bay —6E 194
Mabel Rd. Swan —2H 73
Maberley Rd. Beck —6A 68
Mabledon Av. Afrd —9H 159
Mabledon Pl. WC1 —2C 4
Mabledon Rd. Tonb —7G 145
McAlpine Cres. Loose —5C 138
Macaulay Clo. Lark —6E 108
Macaulay Way. SE28 —1K 51
McAuley Clo. SE9 —3C 56
Macbean St. SE18 —3D 50
McCabe Clo. S'hrst —9J 221
McCall Cres. SE7 —5A 50
McCarthy Av. Sturry —4E 168
McCudden Rd. Dart —1N 59
McCudden Row. Gill —9D 80
McDermott Rd. Bor G —2M 121
Macdonald Ct. Pad W —9M 147
Macdonald Pde. Sea —7C 224
McDonald Rd. Dover —3F 180
Macdonald Rd. Gill —6G 80
Mace Ind. Est. Afrd —7G 159
Mace La. Afrd —8G 159 (1A 40)
Mace La. Cud —4F 100
McIntyre Ct. SE18 —4A 50 (off Prospect Vale)
Mackenders Clo. Eccl —4L 109
Mackenders Grn. Eccl —4L 109
Mackenders La. Eccl —4L 109
McKenzie Clo. Roy B —1K 125
Mackenzie Dri. Folk —6D 188
Mackenzie Rd. N7 —1C 5
Mackenzie Rd. Beck —5A 68 (1D 13)
Mckenzie Rd. Chat —8D 94
Mackenzie Ter. Dover —1G 181 (off Selkirk Rd.)
Mackenzie Way. Grav —2J 77
Mackerel Hill. Peas —2E 45
Mackeson Ct. Hythe —6J 197 (off Military Rd.)
McKinlay Ct. Birch —3C 206 (off Parade, The)
Macklands Way. Gill —1C 96
Maclean Rd. SE23 —4B 54
McLeod Rd. SE2 —4K 51 (3B 6)
McMillan Clo. Grav —9H 63
Macmillan Gdns. Dart —2A 60
McMillan Ho. SE4 —1B 54 (off Arica Rd.)
Macoma Rd. SE18 —6F 50
Macoma Ter. SE18 —6F 50
McPhie Ho. Maid —2C 126
Madan Rd. W'ham —7F 116
Mada Rd. Orp —4D 84
Madden Av. Chat —6B 94
Madden Clo. Swans —4K 61
Maddocks Clo. Sidc —1N 71
Madeira Av. Brom —3H 69
Madeira Ct. Folk —8H 189
Madeira Pk. Tun W —3G 157
Madeira Rd. L'stne —4F 212 (2E 47)
Madeira Rd. Mgte —3E 208
Madeira Rd. Mitc —1B 12
Madeira Wlk. Ram —6J 211 (2E 23)
Madginford. —7K 127 (2E 27)
Madginford Clo. Bear —7K 127
Madginford Rd. Bear —7J 127
Madison Cres. Bexh —7L 51
Madison Gdns. Bexh —7L 51
Madison Gdns. Brom —6J 69
Madison Way. Sev —5G 119
Madras Ho. Maid —3H 139
Maesmaur Rd. Tats —9D 164
Mafeking Rd. Chat —8C 94
Magazine Rd. Afrd —7F 158 (1A 40)
Magdala Rd. Broad —7J 209
Magdala Rd. Dover —3G 181
Magdalen Clo. Hem —7K 95
Magdalen Ct. Broad —7L 209
Magdalen Ct. Cant —3N 171
Magdalen Gro. Orp —5K 85
Magdalen Rd. SW18 —4B 4
Magness Rd. Deal —8K 177
Magnolia Av. Clift —3H 209
Magnolia Av. Gill —6L 95
Magnolia Clo. Tonb —8J 145
Magnolia Dri. Big H —4D 164
Magnolia Ho. Barm —6L 125 (off Springwood Rd.)
Magnolia Rise. H Bay —5L 195
Magpie Bottom. Shor & Knat —4L 103 (3D 15)
Magpie Clo. Lark —9E 108
Magpie Ct. Min S —6H 219
Magpie Grn. Eden —4C 184
Magpie Hall Clo. Brom —9A 70
Magpie Hall La. Brom —1A 84 (2A 14)
Magpie Hall La. Stu X —6B 160 (2E 39)
Magpie Hall Rd. Chat —3C 94 (2D 17)
Magpie La. ME9 —3A 18
Magpie La. Det —1A 112
Magpie La. R Min —8J 183 (1D 41)
Magpie Lodge. Dover —2G 180 (off Mayfield Av.)
Magwitch Clo. Roch —8M 79
Maida Rd. Belv —3B 52
Maida Rd. Chat —1E 94
Maida Vale. —2B 4
Maida Vale. W9 —2B 4
Maida Vale Rd. Dart —3H 59
Maiden Erlegh Av. Bex —6N 57
Maiden La. Cant —4K 171
Maiden La. Dart —2H 59
Maidstone. —5C 126 (2D 27)
Maidstone Ind. Cen. Maid —4C 126
Maidstone Museum & Art Gallery. —4C 126
Maidstone Rd. Afrd —3A 158
Maidstone Rd. Blue B & W'slde —1A 110 (in two parts)
Maidstone Rd. B'den —1J 113 (3B 18)
Maidstone Rd. Bor G —2M 121 (1A 26)
Maidstone Rd. Char —1H 175 (3D 29)
Maidstone Rd. Chat —4B 94 (2D 17)
Maidstone Rd. Chi —9H 175 (2B 30)
Maidstone Rd. E Peck & Nett (in two parts) —8M 135 (3B 26)
Maidstone Rd. Gill —3A 18
Maidstone Rd. Hdlw —8E 134 (3A 26)
Maidstone Rd. H'crn —1J 193 (4A 28)
Maidstone Rd. Hem —9L 95 (3E 17)
Maidstone Rd. Horsm —2C 198 (1C 37)
Maidstone Rd. Hoth —4E 29
Maidstone Rd. Langl —6N 139 (3A 28)
Maidstone Rd. Len —7D 200 (2C 28)
Maidstone Rd. Mard —2L 205 (4D 27)
Maidstone Rd. Matf —9G 152 (1B 36)
Maidstone Rd. Pad W —9L 147
Maidstone Rd. Pem —6C 152 (1A 36) (in two parts)
Maidstone Rd. Roch —9N 79 (2D 17)
Maidstone Rd. Seal —3A 120 (1D 25)
Maidstone Rd. Sev —4F 118
Maidstone Rd. Sidc —2M 71 (1B 14)
Maidstone Rd. S'hrst —4E 27
Maidstone Rd. W'slde —3D 17
Mailyns, The. Gill —4M 95
Maine Clo. Dover —1G 180
Main Ga. Rd. Chat —5C 80
Mainridge Rd. Chst —9C 56
Main Rd. Westf —4C 45
Main Rd. Big H —3B 164
Main Rd. Chatt —9C 66
Main Rd. Crock —9E 72 (2C 15)
Main Rd. Crock H —3A 24
Main Rd. Eden —1B 184 (3A 24)
Main Rd. F'ham —3C 88
Main Rd. Hex —3G 73 (1C 15)
Main Rd. Hoo —6N 67
Main Rd. I'ham —4E 45
Main Rd. Long —5K 75 (1E 15)
Main Rd. Orp —6L 71 (1B 14)
Main Rd. Queen —7B 218 (4C 11)
Main Rd. Sev —2B 24
Main Rd. S'ness —1B 218
Main Rd. Sidc —8F 56 (4B 6)
Main Rd. Sund —6M 117
Main Rd. S at H —2B 74 (1D 15)
Main Rd. W'ham & Brom —3A 14
Main St. Beckl —2D 45
Main St. Iden —3A 46
Main St. N'iam —2D 45
Main St. P'mrsh —3E 45
Maison Dieu. —4J 181 (Dover)
Maison Dieu. —6E 186 (3A 20) (Faversham)
Maison Dieu Gdns. Dover —4J 181
Maison Dieu Pl. Dover —4J 181
Maison Dieu Rd. Dover —4J 181 (1C 43)
Maitland Ct. Fav —3F 186
Maitland Rd. SE26 —2A 68
Majendie Rd. SE18 —5F 50
Majestic Pde. Folk —7J 189
Majors Hill. Crowb —3D 35
Major York's Rd. Tun W —2E 156 (2E 35)
Makenade Av. Fav —7H 187
Malan Clo. Big H —5E 164
Malcolm Sargent Rd. Afrd —3F 160 (1A 40)
Malden Cres. NW1 —1C 4
Malden Dri. Maid —1C 126
Malden Green. —2A 12
Malden Junction. (Junct.) —2A 12
Malden Rd. NW5 —1B 4
Malden Rd. N Mald & Wor Pk —2A 12
Malden Rd. Sutt —2A 12
Malden Way. N Mald —2A 12
Malham Rd. SE23 —6A 54
Mallard Clo. Dart —3N 59
Mallard Ct. Min S —6H 219
Mallard Path. SE28 —3F 50 (off Goosander Way)
Mallards. W'boro —2H 161
Mallard Wlk. Beck —8A 68
Mallard Wlk. Lark —8D 108
Mallard Wlk. Sidc —2L 71
Mallard Way. Down —8K 127 (2E 27)
Mallard Way. Eden —4C 184
Mallard Way. Lwr Sto —8J 201
Mallet Rd. SE13 —4G 55
Mallingdene Clo. Cli —5M 65
Malling Rd. King H —5C 108 (3C 16)
Malling Rd. Maid —2B 26
Malling Rd. Mere —9K 123 (2B 26)
Malling Rd. Snod —4D 108 (3C 16)
Malling Rd. Tstn —7D 124 (2C 26)
Mallings Dri. Bear —5M 127
Mallings La. Bear —5M 127
Malling Ter. Maid —5N 125
Malling Way. Brom —1J 83
Mallory Clo. SE4 —2B 54
Mallory Clo. Ram —2G 211
Mallow Clo. Croy —2A 82
Mallow Clo. N'fleet —9D 62
Mallows, The. Maid —2B 126
Mallow Way. Chat —7C 94
Mall, The. Bexh —2B 58
Mall, The. Brom —6K 69
Mall, The. Dover —4H 181
Mall, The. Fav —6G 187 (3A 20)
Mall, The. Swan —6F 72
Mallys Pl. S Dar —4C 74
Malmains Clo. Beck —7G 68
Malmains Rd. Dover —5F 180
Malmains Rd. P'ley —4D 29
Malmains Way. Beck —7F 68
Malmaynes Hall Rd. H Hals —2L 67
Malmaynes Hall Rd. Up Stok —9H 201 (4A 10)
Malpas Rd. SE4 —1C 54 (3E 5)
Malta Av. Chat —4D 94
Malta Ter. Maid —2D 126
Maltby Clo. Orp —2J 85
Malthouse Clo. Len —8E 200
Malthouse Cotts. W'bury —2B 136 (off Maidstone Rd.)
Malthouse Hill. Hythe —6J 197
Malthouse Hill. Loose —4C 138
Malthouse La. Shorne —1C 78
Malt Ho. La. Tent —8B 222
Malthouse La. W'hrne —6A 190 (3E 39)
Malthouse Rd. Cant —9M 167
Malthouse Rd. Stans —1M 105 (3A 16)
Malthus Path. SE28 —1L 51
Maltings. Nett —2B 136
Maltings Clo. Hdlw —8D 134
Maltings M. Sidc —8J 57
Maltings, The. Cant —2N 171 (1D 31) (off Longport)
Maltings, The. Fav —4H 187
Maltings, The. Gill —3C 96
Maltings, The. Grav —4F 62 (off Clifton Rd.)
Maltings, The. Hdlw —8D 134
Maltings, The. Langl —4E 138
Maltings, The. L'brne —3L 173
Maltings, The. Orp —2H 85
Maltings, The. Walm —1L 199

Maltings, The—Martindown Rd.

Maltings The. Weav —4H 127
Maltman's Hill. —1C 39
Malt M. Roch —7N 79
Malton M. SE18 —6G 51
Malton St. SE18 —6G 51
Malton Way. Tun W —7M 151
Malt Shovel Cotts. Eyns —4L 87
Malus Clo. Chat —1D 110
Malvern Av. Bexh —7N 51
Malvern Cotts. Kear —9D 178
Malvern Ho. Grav —4C 62
(off Laburnum Gro.)
Malvern Meadow. Temp E —8D 178
Malvern Pk. H Bay —3L 195
Malvern Rd. Afrd —6F 158
Malvern Rd. Dover —5H 181
Malvern Rd. Gill —1H 95
Malvern Rd. Orp —5K 85
Malvern Rd. Temp E —8D 178
Malvina Av. Grav —7G 63
Malyons Rd. SE13 —3E 54
Malyons Rd. Swan —3G 72
Malyons Ter. SE13 —3E 54
Mamignot Clo. Bear —4J 127
Manchester Clo. Chat —5F 94
Manchester Dri. Lgh S —1B 10
Manchester Rd. E14 —3E 5
Manciple Clo. Cant —3J 171
Mandeville Ct. Maid —4D 126
Mandeville Rd. Cant —9L 167
Mandeville St. E5 —1D 5
Manford Ind. Est. Eri —6J 53
Manger's La. Dover —2F 180
Mangers Pl. Dover —1F 180
Mangold Way. Eri —3M 51
Mangravet. —1F 138
Mangravet Av. Maid —1F 138
Manister Rd. SE2 —3J 51
Manitoba Gdns. Grn St —7H 85
Manitoba Ho. Dover —1H 181
(off Winnipeg Clo.)
Manley Clo. Whitf —6F 178
Manley Ho. Whitf —6F 178
Mannering Clo. River —1E 180
Manningham Ho. E Mal —3E 124
Manning Rd. Orp —8M 71
Mannock Ho. Cant —1A 172
Mannock Rd. Dart —1N 59
Manns Hill. Bos —3D 31
Mann Sq. Tonb —8K 145
Manor Av. Deal —6L 177
Manor Brook. SE3 —2K 55
Manor Clo. Bear —6L 127
Manor Clo. Cant —5J 171
Manor Clo. Cray —2E 58
Manor Clo. Deal —6K 177
Manor Clo. Grav —7N 63
Manor Clo. H Bay —1N 195
Manor Clo. Queen —9A 218
Manor Clo. Tun W —1E 156
Manor Clo. Wilm —8H 59
Manor Cotts. E Sut —8E 140
Manor Cotts. Langl —3M 139
Manor Ct. Bear —6L 127
Manor Ct. Bexh —3C 58
Manor Ct. Cant —3M 171
Manor Ct. Sole S —8J 77
Manor Ct. W Wick —2E 82
Manor Dri. Birch —5E 206
Manor Dri. Hart —9N 75
Manor Farm. F'ham —9N 73
Manor Farm Cotts. Sev —3G 121
Manorfield. Afrd —1C 160
Manor Field. Shorne —1C 78
Manorfields Clo. Chst —6H 71
Manor Forstal. New Ash —4M 89
Manor Gdns. Chat —8C 94
Manor Gro. Beck —5E 68
Manor Gro. Sit —8E 98
Manor Gro. Tonb —4J 145
Manor Ho. Fawk —4D 88
Manor Ho. Gill —6D 80
Manor Ho. Cotts. Bear —5M 127
(off Green, The)
Manor Ho. Dri. Maid —6A 126
Manor Ho. Gdns. Eden —6C 184
Manor La. SE13 & SE12 —3H 55 (4E 5)
Manor La. Fawk & Sev —1J 89 (2E 15)
Manor La. Hart —9N 75
Manor La. Roch —9K 79
Manor La. Ter. SE13 —2H 55
Manor Lea Rd. St N —9E 214
Manor Leaze. Sme —8L 165
Manor M. R'wld —4J 199
Manor Park. —1A 6
Manor Pk. SE13 —2G 55
Manor Pk. Chst —5F 70
Manor Pk. Eri —6H 53
(off Turpin La.)
Manor Pk. Tun W —2E 156
Manor Pk. Clo. W Wick —2E 82
Manor Park Country Park. —2N 123
Manor Pk. Pde. SE13 —2G 55
(off Lee High Rd.)
Manor Pk. Rd. NW10 —2A 4
Manor Pk. Rd. Chst —4E 70 (1B 14)
Manor Pk. Rd. W Wick —2E 82 (2E 13)
Manor Pl. Chst —5F 70
Manor Pl. Dart —6M 59
Mnr. Pound La. Bra L —6K 165 (1C 40)
Manor Rise. Bear —5L 127
Manor Rise. Dover —6F 180
Manor Rd. E15 —1E 5
Manor Rd. E16 & E15 —2E 5
Manor Rd. SE25 —1D 13
Manor Rd. Beck —5E 68 (1E 13)
Manor Rd. Bex —6C 58
Manor Rd. Broad —9K 209
Manor Rd. Chat —8C 80
Manor Rd. Dart —2F 58 (4C 7)
Manor Rd. Deal —6K 177 (3E 33)
Manor Rd. Dover —6F 180
Manor Rd. E'chu —2H 203
Manor Rd. Eden —6B 184
Manor Rd. Eri —6G 52 (3C 7)
Manor Rd. Folk —7J 189
Manor Rd. Grav —4G 63
Manor Rd. H Bay —1N 195
Manor Rd. Long —8B 76 (2A 16)
Manor Rd. Mils —8F 114 (4C 19)
Manor Rd. Mitc —1C 12
Manor Rd. Queen —9A 218
Manor Rd. Rich —4A 4
Manor Rd. Rust —1C 156
Manor Rd. Sidc —8J 57
Manor Rd. Sole S & Grav —8H 77
Manor Rd. S'boro —5E 150
Manor Rd. St N —8E 214 (2B 22)
Manor Rd. Sund —6M 117
Manor Rd. Swans —4K 61 (4E 7)
Manor Rd. Tats —8E 164
Manor Rd. Wall —2C 12
Manor Rd. W Wick —3E 82
Manor Rd. Whits —2J 225
Manor Row. Tent —8B 222
Manorside Clo. SE2 —4L 51
Manor St. Gill —6D 80
Manor View. Hart —9N 75
Manor Way. SE3 —2J 55
Manor Way. Afrd —6D 158
Manor Way. Beck —5D 68
Manor Way. Bex —6B 58
Manor Way. Bexh —1E 58
Manor Way. Brom —9A 70
Manor Way. E'chu —2H 203
Manor Way. Folk —7J 189
Manor Way. Grav —2N 61
Manor Way. Ley S —6M 203
Manor Way. Orp —7E 70
Manor Way. Rain —2C 7
Manor Way. Swans —2K 61
Manorway, The. Stan H —2C 8
Manover Ct. Fav —4F 186
Manse Field. Bra L —8K 165
Mansel Dri. Roch —1L 93
Mansell La. Sels —1A 42
Mansell St. E1 —2D 5
Mansen Rd. Grav —1J 77
Manse Pde. Swan —7H 73
Mansergh Clo. SE18 —7A 50
Manse Way. Swan —7H 73
Mansfield Clo. Orp —1M 85
Mansfield Ct. Bri —8H 173
Mansfield Rd. NW3 —1B 4
Mansfield Rd. Swan —2F 72
Mansfield Wlk. Maid —7B 126
Mansion Cotts. Maid —6H 127
Mansion Gdns. Whitf —9F 178
Mansion Ho. Clo. Bidd —7K 163
Mansion Row. Gill —6D 80
Mansion St. Mgte —2C 208
Manston. —3B 210 (2D 23)
Manston Airport. —2D 23
Manston Camping & Cvn. Pk. Mans —2A 210
Manston Ct. Rd. Mans —3A 210 (2D 23)
Manston Rd. Birch —7G 206 (2C 23)
Manston Rd. Mans —9M 207 (2D 23)
Mantelow Ct. Broad —2K 211
Manthorp Rd. SE18 —5E 50
Mantle Rd. SE4 —1B 54 (4E 5)
Mantles Hill. Ripp —3D 33
Manton Rd. SE2 —4J 51
Manwarings, The. Horsm —2C 198
Manwood Av. Cant —8M 167
Manwood Clo. Sit —9G 98
Manwood Rd. SE4 —3C 54 (4E 5)
Manwood Rd. S'wch —6M 217
Manwood St. E16 —1B 50
Mapesbury Rd. NW2 —1B 4
Maple Av. Gill —7H 81
Maple Av. Maid —3N 125
Maple Clo. Afrd —8C 158
Maple Clo. Lark —8E 108
Maple Clo. Orp —8F 70
Maple Clo. R Comn —8H 167
Maple Clo. Swan —5F 72
Maple Clo. Tun W —4G 156
Maple Cotts. Beth —3K 163
Maple Ct. SE6 —6E 54
Maple Ct. Grnh —5E 60
Maple Ct. Her —3K 169
Maple Cres. Sidc —4J 57
Mapledene. Chst —1E 70
Maple Dri. H'nge —7E 192
Maple Dri. St Mar —3E 214
Maple Ho. R Comn —8H 167
Maplehurst. Brom —5H 69
Maple Leaf Clo. Big H —4D 164
Maple Leaf Dri. Sidc —6H 57
Maple Rd. SE20 —1D 13
Maple Rd. Dart —7K 59
Maple Rd. Grav —9H 63
Maple Rd. Roch —6K 79
Maplescombe. —6C 88 (2D 15)
Maplescombe La. F'ham —4A 88 (2D 15)
Maplesden Clo. Maid —6K 125
Maples, The. Broad —9H 209
Maples, The. Long —5A 76
Maples, The. Min S —6J 219
Maple St. S'ness —3D 218
Maple Ter. Cant —2M 171
Mapleton Clo. Brom —9K 69
Mapleton Rd. W'ham & Eden —2B 24
Maple Way. Can I —2E 9
Maplin Ho. SE2 —2M 51
(off Wolvercote Rd.)
Maplins Clo. Rain —2B 96
Maplin Way. Sth S —1D 11
Maplin Way N. Sth S —1D 11
Mara Ct. Chat —2C 94
Maran Way. Eri —3M 51
Marathon Paddock. Gill —8G 81
Marble Arch. (Junct.) —2B 4
Marbrook Ct. SE12 —8M 55
Marcellina Way. Orp —4H 85
Marcet Rd. Dart —3K 59
Marcilly Rd. SW18 —4B 4
Marconi Rd. N'fleet —8C 62
Marcus Rd. Dart —5H 59
Mardale Clo. Gill —2C 96
Mardell Rd. Croy —8A 68
Marden. —2L 205 (4D 27)
Marden Av. Brom —9K 69
Marden Av. Ram —4F 210
Marden Beech. —1D 37
Marden Cres. Bex —3D 58
Marden Rd. C'brk —2D 37
Marden Rd. Roch —3N 79
Marden Rd. S'hrst —7H 221 (4E 27)
Marden's Hill. —3C 34
Mardens Hill. Crowb —3C 34
Marden Thorn. —1E 37
Mardol Rd. Kenn —5G 158
Marechal Niel Av. Sidc —8F 56
Marechal Niel Pde. Sidc —8F 56
(off Main Rd.)
Maresfield Clo. Dover —2G 181
Mare St. E8 —2D 5
Margaret Barr Row. Swans —5L 61
Margaret Ct. H Bay —3G 195
Margaret Gardner Dri. SE9 —7B 56
Margaret Rd. Bex —4M 57
Margaret St. Folk —6L 189
Margate. —3C 208 (1D 23)
Margate Clo. Gill —6H 81
Margate Hill. Acol —8G 207 (2C 23)
Margate Lighthous. —2C 208
Margate Rd. Broad —2E 23
Margate Rd. Broom —4J 195 (2E 21)
Margate Rd. H Bay —5K 195 (2E 21)
Margate Rd. Mgte —8E 208
Margate Windmill. —4E 208 (1E 23)
Margery St. WC1 —2C 5
Margetts La. Bur —3C 17
Margetts La. Burh —1H 109
Margetts Pl. Lwr U —1D 80
Marian Av. Min S —5H 219
Marian Sq. S'hrst —7K 221
Marigold Way. Croy —2A 82
Marilyn Cres. Birch —4G 207
Marina Clo. Brom —6K 69
Marina Ct. Deal —2N 177
Marina Dri. Dart —6A 60
Marina Dri. Min S —5H 219
Marina Dri. N'fleet —5E 62
Marina Dri. Well —9G 51
Marina Esplanade. Ram —6K 211
Marina Rd. Ram —5K 211
Marina, The. Deal —1N 177 (2E 33)
Marine Av. Dym —4E 182
Marine Av. Wclf S —1B 10
Marine Ct. Dover —5K 181
Marine Ct. Eri —7G 53
Marine Cres. Folk —7K 189
Marine Cres. Whits —2K 225
Marine Dri. SE18 —4B 50
Marine Dri. Broad —2L 209
Marine Dri. Mgte —3C 208 (1D 23)
Marine Gap. Whits —4E 224
Marine Gdns. Mgte —3C 208
Marine Pde. Dover —5K 181 (1D 43)
(in two parts)
Marine Pde. Folk —7K 189 (3A 42)
Marine Pde. Hythe —7K 197
Marine Pde. Lgh S —1A 10
Marine Pde. L'stne —4F 212 (2E 47)
Marine Pde. S'ness —2E 218 (4D 11)
Marine Pde. Sth S —1C 10
Marine Pde. Whits —2H 225 (2C 21)
Marine Pde. M. Folk —7L 189
Marine Point. Folk —8G 189
Marine Promenade. Folk —7K 189
Marine Rd. Walm —6N 177
Mariners Ct. Grnh —2H 61
Mariners, The. Roch —8M 79
Mariners Wlk. Eri —6G 53
Mariners Wlk. Oare —2F 186
Marine Ter. Folk —7L 189 (3A 42)
Marine Ter. Mgte —3B 208 (1D 23)
Marine Ter. Whits —4E 224
Marine Town. —3E 218 (4D 11)
Marine View. St Mi —3E 80
Marine Wlk. Folk —8H 189
Marine Wlk. S. Hythe —6K 197
Marion Clo. Chat —9D 94
Marion Cres. Maid —8E 126
Marion Cres. Orp —8J 71
Marischal Rd. SE13 —1G 54
Maritime Av. H Bay —3K 195
Maritime Clo. Grnh —3H 61
Maritime Clo. Roch —4A 80
Maritime Museum. —4N 177
Maritime Way. Chat —4D 80
Marjan Clo. Dover —3F 180
Mark Av. Ram —7F 210
Markbeech. —1B 34
Mark Clo. Bexh —8N 51
Mark Cross. —4E 35
Marke Clo. Kes —5A 84
Market All. Grav —4G 63
Market Bldgs. Afrd —8F 158
(off Godinton Rd.)
Market Bldgs. Maid —5C 126
Market Hill. SE18 —3C 50
Market Hill. Hythe —6K 197
Market La. Afrd —8F 158
(off Queen St.)
Market Meadow. Orp —7L 71
Market Pde. Sidc —9K 57
Market Pl. Aysm —2D 162 (2A 32)
Market Pl. Bexh —2B 58
Market Pl. Char —3K 175
Market Pl. Chat —8D 80
Market Pl. Dart —5M 59
Market Pl. Fav —5H 187
Market Pl. Folk —6K 189
Market Pl. Mgte —2C 208
(off Market St.)
Market Pl. S'hrst —6K 221
Market Pl. Tun W —3G 156
Market Rd. N7 —1C 5
Market Sq. Brom —5K 69 (1A 14)
Market Sq. Dover —5J 181
Market Sq. Tun W —1H 157
Market Sq. W'ham —8F 116 (2B 24)
Market St. SE18 —4C 50
Market St. Dart —5M 59 (4D 7)
Market St. Deal —4N 177
Market St. Dover —5J 181
Market St. Fav —5H 187
Market St. H Bay —2G 195
Market St. Maid —5C 126
Market St. Mgte —2C 208
Market St. S'wch —5L 217
(in two parts)
Market St. Tun W —3G 156
Market View. Aysm —2D 162
Market Way. Cant —9N 167
Market Way. W'ham —8F 116
Markham Cotts. Maid —2J 137
Markland Rd. Dover —5E 180
Mark La. Grav —5K 63
(in two parts)
Marks Sq. N'fleet —9E 62
Mark Way. Swan —8H 73
Marlborough Clo. Broad —1J 211
Marlborough Clo. L'stne —2E 212
Marlborough Clo. Orp —9H 71
Marlborough Clo. Tun W —1E 156
Marlborough Ct. Folk —7H 189
(off Earls Av.)
Marlborough Ct. Hythe —7L 197
Marlborough Ct. W'ham —9E 116
(off Croydon Rd.)
Marlborough Cres. Sev —6F 118
Marlborough Pde. Maid —7K 125
Marlborough Pk. Av. Sidc —5J 57
Marlborough Rd. N19 —1C 4
Marlborough Rd. Bexh —1M 57
Marlborough Rd. Brom —7M 69
Marlborough Rd. Dart —4K 59
Marlborough Rd. Deal —8K 177
Marlborough Rd. Dover —5E 180
Marlborough Rd. Gill —8E 80
Marlborough Rd. Mgte —4C 208
Marlborough Rd. Ram —6H 211
Marlborough St. Whits —8F 224
Marlborough Way. Kenn —3K 159
Marle Place Gardens. —2B 36
Marle Pl. Rd. Bchly —9N 153 (1B 36)
Marler Ho. Eri —9G 52
Marler Rd. SE23 —6B 54
Marler Rd. Folk —5E 188
Marley. —3E 31
(nr. Barham)
Marley. —2D 33
(nr. Eastry)
Marley Av. Bexh —6M 51
Marley Ct. Cant —7J 167
Marley La. Batt —4B 44
Marley La. Fin —2D 33
Marley La. Hoath —2A 22
Marley La. Kgtn —6A 162 (3E 31)
Marley Rd. H'shm —2N 141 (2B 28)
Marley Rd. Hoo —7G 67
Marley Way. Roch —1N 93
Marlhurst. Eden —3B 184
Marlings Clo. Chst —7G 71
Marlings Pk. Av. Chst —7G 71
Marling Way. Grav —2K 77
Marlow Clo. Whits —4K 225
Marlow Copse. Chat —1C 110
Marlowe Arc. Cant —2M 171 (1D 31)
Marlowe Av. Cant —2M 171
Marlowe Clo. Chst —2F 70
Marlowe Ct. Cant —1M 171 (4D 21)
(off King St.)
Marlowe Gdns. SE9 —4C 56
Marlowe Meadows. F'wch —7E 168
Marlowe Rd. Afrd —8F 158
(off Norwood Gdns.)
Marlowe Rd. Dover —1G 180
Marlowe Rd. Lark —7D 108
Marlowe Rd. Mgte —5G 208
Marlowes, The. Dart —2E 58
Marlow Ho. Birch —4G 206
(off Sutherland Dri.)
Marlow Rd. SE20 —1D 13
Marlpit. —6H 139
Marlpit Clo. Eden —3C 184
Marlpit Hill. —3B 184 (3B 24)
Marlpit La. Coul —4C 13
Marlwood Clo. Sidc —7G 56
Marmadon Rd. SE18 —4H 51
Marne Av. Well —1J 57
Marnock Rd. SE4 —3C 54
Maroons Way. SE6 —1D 68
Marquis Dri. Hem —8L 95
Marrabon Clo. Sidc —6J 57
Marr Clo. Min S —6G 219
Marriett Ho. SE6 —9F 54
Marriott Rd. Dart —5N 59
Marriotts Wharf. Grav —3G 62
Marrose Av. Ram —1F 210
Marsala Rd. SE13 —2E 54
Marsden Way. Orp —4H 85
Marshall Cres. Broad —9J 209
Marshall Cres. Queen —9A 218
Marshall Gdns. Hdlw —7D 134
Marshall Ho. Eri —2M 51
Marshall Rd. Gill —4M 95
Marshalls Gro. SE18 —4A 50
Marshalls Land. St Mic —4B 222
Marshall St. Folk —4K 189
Marsham Clo. Chst —1D 70
Marsham Clo. H'shm —2N 141
Marsham Cres. Cha S —7L 139
Marsham M. Cant —1A 172
(off Clement Clo.)
Marsham St. SW1 —3C 4
Marsham St. Maid —5D 126
Marsham Way. Hall —6E 92
Marshborough. —6F 216 (1C 33)
Marshborough Rd. M'boro & Wdboro —6E 216 (1C 33)
Marshbrook Clo. SE3 —1N 55
Marsh Cres. H Hals —1H 67
Marsh Cres. New R —3C 212
Marsh Farm Rd. Min —9M 205 (3C 23)
Marshfoot Rd. Grays —3A 8
Marshgate La. E15 —1E 5
Marshgate Path. SE18 —3E 50
Marsh Green. —4A 24
Marsh Grn. Rd. M Grn —9C 184 (1A 34)
Marsh Hill. E9 —1E 5
Marshlands. Dym —9A 182
Marshlands Clo. Dym —8A 182
Marshland View. Lwr Sto —7K 201
Marsh La. Cli —2C 176
Marsh La. Shol —4J 177
Marsh Quarter La. Sand —4L 215 (2C 45)
Marsh Rd. Hall —6E 92
Marsh Rd. Hams —8D 190 (3A 40)
Marsh Rd. Ruck —3A 40
Marshside. —2A 22
Marsh St. Dart —1A 60
(in two parts)
Marsh St. Strood —5M 79
Marsh View. Hythe —8D 196
Marsh Wall. E14 —3E 5
Marsh Way. Lark —6E 108
Marshwood Clo. Cant —8B 168
Marstan Clo. Upc —9H 223
Marston Clo. Chat —8B 94
Marston Dri. Maid —4E 126
Marston Wlk. Chat —8B 94
Martello Cotts. Hythe —7F 196
Martello Dri. Hythe —7G 196
Martello Ind. Est. Folk —5M 189
Martello Rd. Folk —5L 189
(Dover Rd.)
Martello Rd. Folk —8D 188
(West Rd.)
Martello Ter. S'gte —8F 188
Martello Tower. —4C 41
Martello Tower Number 24. —8B 182
Marten Rd. Folk —6H 189
Martens Av. Bexh —2C 58
Martens Clo. Bexh —2D 58
Martens La. H Hal —7N 193 (2C 39)
Martha Clo. Folk —4H 189
Martin. —2N 179 (4D 33)
Martin Bowes Rd. SE9 —1B 56
Martin Ct. Hem —8L 95
Martindale Av. Orp —6J 85
Martindale Clo. Cant —3N 171
Martin Dale Cres. Mart H —4D 33
(off Lucerne La.)
Martin Dene. Bexh —3A 58
Martindown Rd. Whits —7E 224

Martin Dri.—Meteor Av.

Martin Dri. Stone —4C 60
Martin Hardie Way. Tonb —2L 145
Martin Ho. Grav —8F 62
Martin Mill. —4D 33
Martin Rise. Bexh —3A 58
Martin Rd. Dart —8K 59
Martin Rd. Roch —4M 79
Martins Clo. High —7H 65
Martins Clo. Orp —6M 71
Martin's Clo. Ram —2G 211
Martins Clo. Tent —7D 222
Martins Clo. W Wick —3G 83
Martin's Dri. Leigh —8L 143
Martins La. E Peck —7K 135 (3B 26)
Martin Sq. Lark —8E 108
(in two parts)
Martin's Rd. Brom —5J 69
Martins Shaw. Chip —4D 118
Martins, The. H Hal —6M 193
Martin's Way. Hythe —8E 196
Martin Way. SW20 & Mord —1A 12
Marton Clo. SE6 —8D 54
Martyrs Field. —3L 171
Martyr's Field Rd. Cant —3L 171
Marvels Clo. SE12 —7L 55
Marvels La. SE12 —7L 55 (4A 6)
Marvillion Ct. E Peck —1L 147
Marwell. W'ham —8D 116
Marwell Clo. W Wick —3J 83
Marwood Clo. Well —1K 57
Mary Ann Cotts. Folk —4E 188
(off Ashley Av.)
Mary Bank. SE18 —4B 50
Mary Burrows Gdns. Kems —8B 104
Mary Day's. Goud —9K 185
Mary Dukes Pl. Maid —6E 126
Maryfield Clo. Bex —8F 58
Mary Grn. Wlk. Cant —9A 168
Maryland Ct. Gill —6A 96
Maryland Ct. Hythe —5L 197
Maryland Dri. Maid —7K 125
Maryland Gro. Cant —4A 172
Maryland Rd. Tun W —4K 157
Marylebone. —2C 4
Marylebone Flyover. (Junct.) —2B 4
Marylebone High St. W1 —2C 4
Marylebone Rd. NW1 —2B 4
Mary Magdalene Ho. Tonb —7H 145
Maryon Gro. SE7 —4A 50
Maryon Rd. SE7 —4A 50
Maryon Rd. SE18 —4A 50
Mary Rd. Deal —7K 177
Maryville. Well —9H 51
Mascalls. —1B 36
Mascall's Ct. La. Pad W —2N 153 (1B 36)
Mascall's Ct. Rd. Pad W —1M 153 (4B 26)
Mascalls Pk. Pad W —1L 153
Masefield Clo. Eri —8G 53
Masefield Dri. Cli —5M 65
Masefield Rd. Dart —3B 60
Masefield Rd. Lark —6D 108
Masefield Rd. N'fleet —8C 62
Masefield View. Orp —4E 84
Masefield Way. Tonb —7F 144
Mason Clo. Bexh —1C 58
Masons Hill. SE18 —4D 50
Masons Hill. Brom —6K 69 (1A 14)
Masons Rise. Broad —8L 209
Masons Rd. Dover —3G 180
Master Gunners Pl. SE18 —7A 50
Masters La. Birl —5N 107
Masthead Clo. Dart —2C 60
Matchless Dri. SE18 —7C 50
Matfield. —6J 153 (1B 36)
Matfield Clo. Brom —8K 69
Matfield Cres. Maid —4F 126
Matfield Rd. Belv —6B 52
Matilda Clo. Gill B —2L 95
Matterdale Gdns. Barm —7J 125
Matthews Clo. Deal —4M 177
Matthews Ct. Gill —7G 80
Matthews La. Hdlw —3E 134 (3A 26)
Matthew's Pl. Dover —3H 181
Matthews Rd. H Bay —5D 194
Matthias Rd. N16 —1D 5
Mattinson Pl. W'hll —1B 28
Matts Hill Rd. H'lip —9N 95 (3A 18)
Maud Cashmore Way. SE18 —3B 50
Maude Rd. Swan —2H 73
Maudslay Rd. SE9 —1B 56
Maugham Ct. Whits —5F 224
Maunders Clo. Chat —3F 94
Maunsell Pl. Afrd —2H 161
Maureen Ct. Beck —5A 68
Maury Rd. N16 —1D 5
Mavelstone Clo. Brom —4A 70
Mavelstone Rd. Brom —4N 69
Maxey Rd. SE18 —4E 50
Maximfeldt Rd. Eri —5F 52
Maximilian Dri. Hall —7F 92
Maxim Rd. Dart —3F 58
Maxim Rd. Eri —4E 52
Maxine Gdns. Broad —8K 209
Maxted Ct. H Bay —3K 195
Maxted Street. —4D 31
Maxted St. S Min —4D 31
Maxton. —1C 42
Maxton Clo. Bear —4J 127
Maxton Ct. Dover —6F 180
Maxton Rd. Dover —6F 180
Maxwell Dri. Maid —3M 125
Maxwell Gdns. Orp —4H 85
Maxwell Pl. Deal —6M 177
Maxwell Rd. Bromp —7D 80
Maxwell Rd. Well —1H 57
May Av. N'fleet —6E 62
May Av. Orp —8K 71
May Av. Ind. Est. N'fleet —6E 62
(off May Av.)
Mayberry Ct. Beck —3C 68
Maybrook Ind. Est. Cant —8B 168
Maybury Av. Dart —6C 60
Maybury Clo. Orp —8D 70
Maycotts La. Matf —5J 153 (1B 36)
Mayday Gdns. SE3 —9A 50
Maydowns Rd. Ches —3M 225
Mayerne Rd. SE9 —3N 55
Mayers Rd. Walm —9K 177
Mayes Clo. Swan —7H 73
Mayeswood Rd. SE12 —9M 55
Mayfair. —2C 4
Mayfair. Roch —3N 79
Mayfair Av. Bexh —8M 51
Mayfair Av. Maid —9D 126
Mayfair Clo. Beck —4E 68
Mayfair Rd. Dart —3L 59
Mayfield. Bexh —1A 58
Mayfield Av. Dover —2G 181
Mayfield Av. Orp —2H 85
Mayfield Clo. Chat —1D 110
Mayfield Clo. Gill —1A 96
Mayfield Cotts. Bear —5M 127
Mayfield Ct. Dover —2G 181
Mayfield Gdns. Dover —2H 181
Mayfield La. Dur —4A 36
Mayfield Rd. W3 —2A 4
Mayfield Rd. Belv —4D 52
Mayfield Rd. Brom —8A 70
Mayfield Rd. Frant —3E 35
Mayfield Rd. Grav —5E 62
Mayfield Rd. H Bay —4H 195
Mayfield Rd. Lym —8D 204 (1E 41)
Mayfield Rd. Mark X —4E 35
Mayfield Rd. Roth —4D 35
Mayfield Rd. S Croy —3D 13
Mayfield Rd. Tun W —1F 156
Mayfield Rd. Whitf —7F 178
Mayfields. Swans —4L 61
Mayfly Clo. Orp —7M 71
Mayfly Dri. H'nge —8C 192
Mayford Clo. Beck —6A 68
Mayford Rd. Chat —9G 95
Mayforth Gdns. Ram —6F 210
Maygrove Rd. NW6 —1B 4
Mayhew Clo. Afrd —1E 160
Maylam Ct. Tonb —3J 145
Maylands Dri. Sidc —8M 57
Maymills Cotts. E'try —3J 183
Maynard. H Hal —7J 193
Maynard Av. Mgte —3N 207
Maynard Clo. Eri —7G 52
Maynard & Cotton's Spital. Cant
(off Hospital La.) —2M 171 (1D 31)
Maynard Pl. Chat —1G 95
Maynard Rd. Win I —3K 171
Maynards. Mard —3K 205
Mayor's La. Dart —9K 59
Mayor's Pl. Tent —8B 222
(off Woodbury Gdns.)
Mayow Rd. SE26 & SE23 —9A 54 (1D 13)
Maypits. Afrd —1D 160
May Pl. Sole S —8J 77
Mayplace Av. Dart —2H 59
Mayplace Clo. Bexh —1C 58
Mayplace La. SE18 —7D 50
Mayplace Rd. E. Bexh & Dart —1C 58 (4C 6)
Mayplace Rd. W. Bexh —2B 58 (4C 6)
Maypole. —6F 58
(nr. Bexley)
Maypole. —9M 195 (2A 22)
(nr. Herne Bay)
Maypole. —7B 86 (3C 14)
(nr. Orpington)
Maypole Cres. Eri —6L 53
Maypole La. Goud —8K 185 (2D 37)
Maypole La. Hoath —8M 195 (2A 22)
Maypole Rd. Ash W —2A 34
Maypole Rd. Cant —9M 195 (2E 21)
Maypole Rd. Grav —6L 63
Maypole Rd. Orp —6A 86 (2C 14)
May Rd. Dart —9N 59
May Rd. Gill —8F 80
May Rd. Roch —9N 79
May's Cotts. Maid —4L 137
Mays Hill Rd. Brom —5H 69
May's Rd. Ram —6G 211
May St. Cux —1F 92
Maystreet. H Bay —3N 195
(in two parts)
May St. Snod —2F 108
May Ter. Gill —5D 80
Maytham Rd. Rol —3K 213 (4B 38)
Mayton La. B Oak —2A 168 (3E 21)
Maytree Cotts. W'boro —4M 161
May Tree Ho. SE4 —1C 54
(off Wickham Rd.)
Maytum's Cotts. Lin —8A 138
Mayville Rd. Broad —7J 209
Mayweed Av. Chat —7B 94
Maywood Clo. Beck —3E 68
Maze Hill. SE10 & SE3 —3E 5
Mead Clo. Swan —8H 73
Mead Cres. Dart —6L 59
Meades Clo. Mard —2J 205
Meade, The. H'nge —8B 192
Meadfield Rd. Meop —3F 90
Mead Grn. Chat —8F 94
Meadow Av. Croy —9A 68
Meadow Bank. SE3 —1J 55
Meadow Bank. Leigh —6N 143
Meadow Bank. W Mal —1A 124
Meadow Bank Clo. W King —9F 88
Meadowbank Rd. Chat —8E 80
Meadowbrook. S'gte —7E 188
Meadowbrook Av. Gill —6H 81
Meadowbrook Clo. Kenn —4H 159
Meadowbrook Ct. S'gte —7E 188
Meadowbrook Rd. Kenn —4H 159
Meadow Clo. SE6 —1D 68
Meadow Clo. Bexh —3A 58
Meadow Clo. Bri —8H 173
Meadow Clo. Chat —6C 94
Meadow Clo. Chi —8M 175
Meadow Clo. Chst —1D 70
Meadow Clo. H Bay —3K 195
Meadow Clo. Iwade —8B 198
Meadow Clo. Sev —5H 119
Meadow Clo. Up H'lng —7C 92
Meadow Ct. Wnhgr —2C 196
Meadowcourt Rd. SE3 —2J 55
Meadow Cres. Up H'lng —7C 92
Meadowcroft. Brom —6B 70
Meadowdown. Weav —5H 127
Meadowdown Clo. Hem —7K 95
Meadow Dri. Ches —5M 225
Meadow Gro. S'ndge —9K 215
Meadow Hill Rd. Tun W —2H 157
Meadowlands. Seal —2N 119
Meadow La. Culv —1E 106
Meadow La. Eden —3B 184
Meadow La. New Ash —3M 89
Meadow Lawn. —7G 145
Meadow Rise. Iwade —8B 198
Meadow Rd. Afrd —7E 158
Meadow Rd. Brom —4H 69
Meadow Rd. Cant —9J 167
Meadow Rd. Grav —7F 62
Meadow Rd. Groom —6K 155
Meadow Rd. Mgte —2N 207
Meadow Rd. N'fleet —6B 62
Meadow Rd. Rust —1C 156 (2E 35)
Meadow Rd. S'boro —5F 150
Meadow Rd. Sturry —5E 168
Meadow Rd. Tonb —7G 145
Meadow Rd. Tun W —1G 157
Meadows Ct. Sidc —2K 71
Meadowside. SE9 —2M 55
Meadowside. Dart —6M 59
Meadows, The. Bidd —7K 163
Meadows, The. Hals —4A 102
Meadows, The. H Bay —5K 195
Meadows, The. Hild —3D 144
Meadows, The. Orp —7L 85
Meadows, The. Sit —9G 98
Meadows, The. Tovil —7B 126
Meadowsweet View. St Mi —2E 80
Meadow, The. Chst —2E 70
Meadow, The. Pem —6C 152
Meadow View. Hoth —4E 29
Meadow View. Orp —6L 71
Meadow View. Sev —9E 102
Meadow View. Sidc —5K 57
Meadowview Rd. SE6 —1C 68
Meadowview Rd. Bex —4N 57
Meadow View Rd. Bou M —5E 138
Meadow View Rd. S'wll —1D 220
Meadow Wlk. Dart —9K 59
Meadow Wlk. Maid —6E 126
Meadow Wlk. Snod —3D 108
Meadow Wlk. Whits —6E 224
Meadow Way. Dart —5C 60
Meadow Way. Mard —2L 205
Meadow Way. Orp —4C 84
Mead Rd. Chst —2E 70
Mead Rd. Dart —6L 59
Mead Rd. Eden —8D 184
Mead Rd. Folk —5K 189
Mead Rd. Grav —7G 62
Mead Rd. W'boro —2J 161 (1A 40)
Meads Av., The. Sit —4E 98
Meadside Clo. Beck —4B 68
Meadside Wlk. Chat —5C 94
Meads, The. C'brk —3D 37
Meads, The. Tun W —3J 157
Meads Way. St Mar —3D 214
Mead, The. Beck —4F 68
Mead, The. Leyb —8C 108
Mead, The. New Ash —3L 89
Mead, The. W Wick —2G 82
Mead Wlk. Afrd —1C 160
(in two parts)
Mead Wall. Cli —1A 176
Meadway. Beck —4F 68
Mead Way. Brom —9J 69 (2E 13)
Mead Way. Cant —1L 171 (4D 21)
Mead Way. Coul —4C 13
Mead Way. Croy —3B 82
Meadway. Dover —1C 180
Meadway. Hals —4A 102
Meadway. Hild —2E 144
Meadway, The. Orp —7K 85
Meadway, The. Sev —4G 119
Meath Clo. Orp —8K 71
Medbury Rd. Grav —6L 63
Medebourne Clo. SE3 —1K 55
Mede Ho. Brom —1L 69
Medfield St. SW15 —4A 4
Medhurst Cres. Grav —7L 63
Medhurst Gdns. Grav —8L 63
Medhurst Row. —4B 24
Median Rd. E5 —1D 5
Medina Av. Whits —6D 224
Medina Ho. Eri —7F 52
Medina Rd. Dit —9G 109
Medina Rd. Tonb —1J 145
Medlar Clo. Bre —4B 114
Medlar Gro. Hem —7K 95
Medlar Ho. Sidc —8J 57
Medlars, The. Maid —3G 126
Medlars, The. Meop —9F 76
Medlar St. SE5 —3D 5
Medusa Rd. SE6 —4E 54
Medway Av. H Hals —1H 67
Medway Av. Yald —7D 136
Medway City Est. Roch —6B 80
Medway Clo. Sit —7E 98
Medway Enterprise Cen. Roch —4A 80
Medway Gdns. Chat —5C 80
Medway Heritage Centre. —7C 80
Medway Ho. Maid —9G 126
Medway Meadows. E Peck —1M 147
Medway Pl. Snod —1F 108
Medway Pl. Woul —7G 93
Medway Rd. Dart —1H 59
Medway Rd. Gill —5F 80 (1E 17)
(in two parts)
Medway Rd. S'ness —3C 218
Medway Rd. Tun W —9H 151
Medway St. Chat —7C 80 (1D 17)
Medway St. Maid —5C 126
Medway Ter. W'bury —2B 136
(off Maidstone Rd.)
Medway Trad. Est. Maid —6C 126
Medway Tunnel. Roch —4C 80
Medway Valley Pk., The. Roch —8K 79
Medway View. Gold G —2F 146
Medway View. Mid S —9K 201
Medway Vs. Maid —1M 137
Meehan Rd. G'stne —5F 212
Meehan Rd. S. G'stne —6F 212
Meerbrook Rd. SE3 —1M 55
Meeres Ct. La. Sit —6K 99
Meesons Clo. E'lng —1E 29
Meeting Ho. La. Chat —8C 80
Meeting St. Ram —5J 211
Megby Clo. Gill —5N 95
Meggett La. Alk —1B 42
Megone Clo. H'nge —8C 192
Megrims Hill. Sand —2J 215
Melanda Clo. Chst —1B 70
Melanie Clo. Bexh —8N 51
Melbourne Av. Dover —8G 179 (4C 33)
Melbourne Av. Ram —4E 210
Melbourne Clo. Orp —1G 85
Melbourne Ct. Grav —3G 62
Melbourne M. SE6 —5F 54
Melbourne Rd. Chat —9D 80
Melbury Clo. Chst —2B 70
Melbury M. New R —1D 212
Meldrum Clo. Orp —9L 71
Melfield Gdns. SE6 —9F 54
Melford Dri. Maid —5M 125
Melfort Rd. T Hth —1C 13
Meliot Rd. SE6 —7G 55
Mellanby Rd. Birch —5F 206
Melliker La. Meop —9E 76 (2A 16)
Melling St. SE18 —6G 51
Mellor Row. Kem —2G 98
Mells Cres. SE9 —9B 56
Melody Clo. Gill —7M 95
Melody Clo. Ward —4K 203
Melody Rd. Big H —6C 164
Melon La. Ivy —2D 47
Melrose Clo. SE12 —6K 55
Melrose Clo. Maid —1D 138
Melrose Cres. Orp —5F 84
Melrose Rd. Big H —4C 164
Melsetter Clo. Birch —4G 206
Melthorpe Gdns. SE3 —8A 50
Melton St. NW1 —2C 4
Melville Ct. Chat —6C 80
Melville Lea. Wdboro —7H 217
Melville Rd. Maid —6D 126
Melville Rd. Sidc —7L 57
Memel Pl. Ram —6H 211
Memess Path. SE18 —6C 50
Mendfield St. Fav —5G 186
Mendip. Afrd —6F 158
Mendip Rd. Bexh —8F 52
Mendip Wlk. Tun W —9K 151
Menin Rd. Kem —2G 98
Mentmore Ho. Ram —1G 210
Mentmore Rd. Ram —1G 210
Menzies Av. Walm —9L 177
Menzies Ct. Min S —7H 219
Meopham. —3F 90 (2B 16)
Meopham Cotts. Weald —5J 131
Meopham Green. —4F 90 (2B 16)
Meopham Station. —8F 76 (2A 16)
Meopham Windmill. —4E 90 (2A 16)
Mera Dri. Bexh —2B 58
Merantun Way. SW19 —1B 12
Merbury Clo. SE13 —3G 54
Merbury Rd. SE28 —2G 50
Mercator Rd. SE13 —2G 55
Mercer Dri. H'shm —6A 200
Mercers. Hawkh —6L 191
Mercers. L'tn G —2A 156
Mercers Clo. Pad W —9K 147
Mercers Pl. King H —7M 123
Mercer St. Tun W —9H 151
Mercer Way. Cha S —7L 139
Mercery La. Cant —2M 171 (1D 31)
Merchant Pl. Mard —3K 205
Merchants Way. Cant —3J 171
Merchiston Rd. SE6 —7G 54
Merchland Rd. SE9 —6E 56
Mercia Gro. SE13 —2F 54
Mercury Way. Roch —1L 93
Mercy Ter. SE13 —3E 54
Mere Clo. Orp —3C 84
Meredith M. SE4 —2C 54
Mere End. Croy —1A 82
Mere Ga. Mgte —4C 208
Meresborough. —6B 96 (2A 18)
Meresborough La. Gill —6C 96 (2A 18)
Meresborough Rd. Gill —8B 96 (3A 18)
Mere Side. Orp —3C 84
Meretone Clo. SE4 —2B 54
Merewood Clo. Brom —5C 70
Merewood Rd. Bexh —9D 52
Mereworth. —9J 123 (2B 26)
Mereworth Clo. Brom —8J 69
Mereworth Clo. Gill —9K 81
Mereworth Dri. SE18 —7D 50
Mereworth Rd. Maid —2B 26
Mereworth Rd. Tun W —8G 151
Mereworth Rd. W Peck —2G 134
Merganser Gdns. SE28 —3F 50
Meriden Clo. Brom —3N 69
Meridian Ct. Afrd —2C 160
Meridian Ct. Maid —5B 126
Meridian Pk. Roch —5B 80
Merifield Rd. SE9 —2M 55
Merino Pl. Sidc —4J 57
Merivale Gro. Chat —7E 94
Merland Rise. Eps & Tad —4A 12
Merleburgh Dri. Kem —3G 99
Merle Common. —3A 24
Merlewood. Sev —5J 119
Merlewood Dri. Chst —4B 70
Merlewood Pl. SE9 —4B 56
Merlin Av. Lark —8D 108
Merlin Clo. Sit —8H 99
Merlin Clo. Tonb —3L 145
Merlin Ct. Short —6J 69
Merlin Gdns. Brom —8K 55
Merlin Gro. Beck —7C 68
Merlin Rd. Roch —3L 79
Merlin Rd. Well —2J 57
Merlin Rd. N. Well —2J 57
Mermaid Clo. Chat —5D 94
Mermerus Gdns. Grav —9L 63
Merrals Wood Rd. Roch —7H 79
Merriams Farm Cotts. Leeds —9N 127
Merrilees Rd. Sidc —5G 56
Merrimans View. Chat —9F 80
Merriments Gardens. —2A 44
Merriments La. Hrst G —1B 44
Merrion Clo. Tun W —7H 151
Merrion Way. Tun W —7H 151
Merritt Rd. SE4 —3C 54
Merritt Rd. G'stne —7E 212
Merrow Way. New Ad —7F 82 (3E 13)
Merry Boys Cotts. Cli —5N 65
Merryboys Rd. Cli —5M 65 (4D 9)
Merrydown Way. Chst —4A 70
Merryfield Ct. Tonb —7H 145
Merryfield Ho. SE9 —8M 55
(off Grove Pk. Rd.)
Merryfields. Strood —3L 79
Merryfields Clo. Hart —7M 75
Merryfields Way. SE6 —5E 54
Merry Hill. —5H 91
Merryhills Clo. Big H —4D 164
Merryweather Clo. Dart —4N 59
Merrywood Gro. H Bay —5L 195
Mersey Rd. Tonb —2H 145
Mersham. —8M 161 (2B 40)
Merston Ct. High —1G 78
Merton. —1B 12
Merton Av. Hart —7L 75
Merton Cotts. Cant —5N 171
Merton Ct. Well —9K 51
Merton Gdns. Orp —8D 70
Merton High St. SW19 —1B 12
Merton La. Cant —6L 171 (2D 31)
Merton La. N. Cant —7N 171
Merton Park. —1B 12
Merton Rd. SW18 —4B 4
Merton Rd. SW19 —1B 12
Merton Rd. Bear —7J 127
Merttins Rd. SE15 & SE4 —3A 54 (4D 5)
Mervyn Av. SE9 —8E 56
Meryl Gdns. Walm —9M 177
Mesne Way. Shor —3G 102
Messent Rd. SE9 —3M 55
Messeter Pl. SE9 —4C 56
Metcalfe M. Cant —9A 168
Meteor Av. Whits —6D 224

Meteor Rd.—Monarch Rd.

Meteor Rd. W Mal —6L 123
Methuen Rd. Belv —4C 52
Methuen Rd. Bexh —2A 58
Metro Bus. Cen., The. Beck —2C 68
Metro Cen. Orp —9K 71
Metropole Arts Centre. —8H 189
(off Metropole Rd. E.)
Metropole Rd. E. Folk —8H 189
Metropole Rd. W. Folk —8H 189
Metropole, The. Folk —8H 189
Meverall Av. C'snd —7B 210 (2D 23)
Mews End. Big H —6D 164
Mewshurst. —4B 24
Mews, The. Hart —6L 75
Mews, The. Maid —4B 126
Mews, The. Pem —8B 152
Mews, The. Roch —5K 79
Mews, The. Sev —5K 119
(St John's)
Mews, The. Sev —6H 119
(Sevenoaks)
Mews, The. Sidc —9J 57
Mews, The. Sit —9G 98
Mews, The. Tun W —2H 157
Mews, The. Yald —7D 136
Meyer Rd. Eri —6E 52
Meyrick Rd. S'ness —2D 218
Miall Wlk. SE26 —9B 54
Micawber Clo. Chat —1D 110
Michael Av. Ram —4L 211
Michael Gdns. Grav —1K 77
Michael's Clo. SE13 —2H 55
Michaels La. Fawk & Sev —3H 89 (2E 15)
Micheldever Rd. SE12 —4J 55
Michele Cotts. High —7G 64
Michelle Gdns. Mgte —3M 207
Mickleburgh Av. H Bay —4J 195
Mickleburgh Hill. H Bay —3H 195 (2E 21)
Mickleham Clo. Orp —5H 71
Mickleham Rd. Orp —4H 71
Mickleham Way. New Ad —8G 82
Mid Comp Cotts. Platt —3E 122
Mid Comp Cotts. Sev —3E 122
Middelburg Sq. Folk —3A 42
Middleburg Ho. Folk —5D 188
Middleburg Sq. Folk —7K 189
Middle Clo. Gt Cha —9A 158
Middle Deal. —5M 177
Middle Deal Rd. Deal —5K 177 (2E 33)
Middlefield. Pem —6D 152
Middle Field. Tun W —1C 156
Middlefields. Croy —9B 82
Middlefields. Gill —3C 96
Middleham Ct. Dart —4B 60
(off Osbourne Rd.)
Middle Hill Rd. E Mal —2D 124
Middle La. Seal —3N 119
Middle Mead. Folk —4H 189
Middle Pk. Av. SE9 —4N 55 (4A 6)
Middle Quarter. —2C 38
Middle Rd. Bells Y —8N 157
Middle Roe. Afrd —8G 158
(off High St. Ashford,)
Middle Row. Fav —5H 187
Middlesex Rd. Maid —1G 139
Middle Stoke. —9K 201 (4A 10)
Middle St. Afrd —8F 158
(off Bank St.)
Middle St. Deal —4N 177
Middle St. Gill —6D 80
Middleton Av. Sidc —2K 71
Middleton Clo. Gill —7A 96
Middleton Ct. Sit —7F 98
Middleton Rd. Mord & Cars —2B 12
Middleton Way. SE13 —2G 55
Middletune Av. Sit —4F 98
Middle Wlk. Tun W —6L 151
Middle Wall. Whits —3F 224
Middle Way. Eri —3M 51
Middleway. Sit —8J 99
Middlings Rise. Sev —7G 119
Middlings, The. Sev —7G 119
Middlings Wood. Sev —7G 119
Midfield Av. Bexh —1D 58
Midfield Av. Swan —2H 73
Midfield Pl. Bexh —1D 58
Midfield Way. Orp —4K 71 (1B 14)
Midholm Rd. Croy —3B 82
Midhurst Ct. Maid —6D 126
Midhurst Hill. Bexh —4B 58
Mid Kent Bus. Pk. Maid —3M 125
Mid Kent Bus. Pk. Snod —3F 108
Mid Kent Shop. Cen., The. Maid —2N 125
Midland Rd. NW1 —2C 4
Midley Clo. Maid —2N 125
Midsummer Hill. Kenn —4H 159
Midsummer Rd. Snod —2C 108
Midway, The. Tun W —3D 156
Midwinter Clo. Well —1J 57
Mierscourt Clo. Gill —3C 96
Mierscourt Rd. Gill —7A 96 (3A 18)
(Meresborough Rd.)
Miers Ct. Rd. Gill —5A 96
(Nightingale Clo.)
Mike Spring Ct. Grav —9J 63
Milborough Cres. SE12 —4H 55
Milbourne Gro. Sit —4F 98
Milburn Rd. Gill —5F 80
Mildmay Gro. N1 —1D 5
Mildmay Pk. N1 —1D 5
Mildmay Pl. Shor —2G 102
Mildred Clo. Dart —4A 60
Mildred Cotts. Folk —4F 188
Mildred Rd. Eri —5F 52
Milebush. —4D 27
Milebush La. Mard —4D 27
Mile End. —2E 5
Mile End Green. —4K 75
Mile End Rd. E1 & E3 —2D 5
Mile La. Goud —7N 185 (2D 37)
Mile Oak. —1C 36
Mile Oak Rd. Bchly —5N 153 (1B 36)
Mile Oak Rd. Pad W —4C 26
Miles Ct. W'hm —2B 226
Miles Pl. Roch —9A 80
Milestone Clo. Folk —4G 189
Milestone Green. (Junct.) —4A 4
Milestone Rd. Dart —4B 60
Miles Way. Birch —4E 206
Mile Town. —2C 218 (4C 11)
Mile Town Ind. Pk. S'ness —3B 218
Milford Clo. SE2 —6N 51
Milford Clo. Maid —4N 125
Milford Gdns. Croy —8A 68
Milford Towers. SE6 —5E 54
Military Rd. Cant —1N 171 (4D 21)
Military Rd. Chat —8C 80
Military Rd. Dover —5J 181
Military Rd. Folk —6D 188 (2E 41)
Military Rd. Hythe —6H 197 (3D 41)
Military Rd. Ram —6J 211
Military Rd. Rye —3A 46
Milk Ho. Cotts. Siss —8C 220
Milking La. Kes —3A 14
Milking La. Orp —3A 100
Milk St. E16 —1D 50
Milk St. Brom —2L 69
Milkwood Rd. SE24 —4C 5
Millais Rd. Dover —3H 181
Millbank. SW1 —3C 5
Mill Bank. H'crn —2K 193 (4A 28)
Mill Bank. Lydd —3B 204
Millbank. —8M 195 (2A 22)
Millbank La. Old R —2C 47
Millbank Rd. Kgnt —4D 160 (1E 39)
Millbank Way. SE12 —3K 55
Mill Bay. Folk —6K 189
Millbro. Swan —4H 73
Millbrook. Hythe —5L 197
Millbrook. Leyb —9B 108
Millbrook Av. Well —2F 56
Millbrook Clo. Maid —8C 126
Millbrook Meadow. Afrd —9C 158
Mill Brook Rd. St M —7L 71 (1B 14)
Mill Bus. Pk., The. Hoth —3B 158
Mill Clo. Dover —2E 180
Mill Clo. Len —8D 200
Mill Clo. Roch —3M 79
Mill Clo. S'wch —4K 217
Mill Clo. Wickh —4A 22
Mill Corner. —3D 45
Mill Cotts. Ram —6G 211
Mill Cotts. Temp E —8C 178
Mill Ct. Hort K —5C 74
Mill Ct. Sit —8H 99
Mill Cres. Tonb —5J 145
Millcroft Ho. SE6 —9E 54
(off Melfield Gdns.)
Millcroft Rd. Cli —4C 176
Milldale Clo. Deal —6L 177
Millennium Experience Exhibition Site. —2E 5
Millen Rd. Sit —6F 98
Miller Av. Cant —2K 171
Miller Clo. Deal —2M 177
Miller Clo. Kem —3H 99
Miller Ct. Bexh —1C 58
Miller Ct. Min S —7H 219
Miller Rd. Grav —7M 63
Millers Ct. Whits —6F 224
Miller's Hill. Westf —4C 45
Millers La. Monk —2C 22
Millers Meadow Clo. SE12 —3J 55
Millers Wlk. Meop —3F 90
Millers Wharf. Maid —7A 126
Miller Way. Wain —2N 79
Mill Farm Cotts. Hoo —7F 66
Mill Field. Ah —5D 216
Millfield. Afrd —9B 158
Mill Field. Broad —8K 209
Mill Field. Folk —7J 189
Millfield. H'nge —6E 192
Millfield. H Hal —7J 193
Millfield. New Ash —3L 89
Millfield. Sit —8G 99
Millfield. St Mc —6J 213
Millfield Clo. H'nge —7D 192
Millfield Cotts. Orp —7K 71
Millfield Dri. N'fleet —7D 62
Millfield La. New Ash —3L 89
Millfield Mnr. Whits —4G 224
Millfield Rd. Fav —5J 187
Millfield Rd. Ram —1F 210
Millfield Rd. W King —7D 88
Millfields. Chat —9G 95
Millfields. S'wll —3D 220
Millfields Clo. St M —7K 71
Millfields Rd. E5 —1D 5
Mill Fields Rd. Hythe —6G 197
Mill Gdns. H Hal —7J 193
Mill Grn. E'try —3J 183
Mill Grn. Rd. Mitc —2B 12
Millhall. —8H 109
Millhall. Ayle —8H 109
Mill Hall Bus. Est. Ayle —8H 109
Mill Hall Cen. Ayle —8H 109
Mill Hall Rd. Ayle —8H 109
Mill Hill. —7K 177 (3E 33)
Mill Hill. W3 —3A 4
Mill Hill. Deal —8K 177 (3E 33)
Mill Hill. Eden —7D 184 (4B 24)
Millhill. O'nge —9L 183
Mill Hill. Tovil —2D 27
Mill Hill La. Shorne —1B 78 (1C 16)
Mill Hill Rd. SW13 —3A 4
Mill Ho. Clo. Eyns —2M 87
Millhouse Dri. Ram —6N 205
Mill Ho. La. Adtn —7J 107
Mill La. NW6 —1B 4
Mill La. SE18 —5C 50
Mill La. B'hm —9D 162 (3A 32)
Mill La. Birch —5E 206
Mill La. Blue B —1A 110
Mill La. Blue H —3D 17
Mill La. Bon —2B 40
Mill La. Bri —9E 172 (2E 31)
Mill La. Cant —1M 171 (4D 21)
Mill La. C'lck —7C 174
Mill La. Chat —2F 94
Mill La. Chi —8L 175
Mill La. Cox —5A 138
Mill La. Dover —5K 181
Mill La. E'try —3J 183 (2C 33)
Mill La. Eyns —2M 87
Mill La. Frit —1A 38
Mill La. Grays —3E 7
Mill La. Harb —2J 171
Mill La. H'lip —5G 96 (2B 18)
Mill La. H'nge —8D 192 (1A 42)
Mill La. H Bay —6J 195 (2E 21)
Mill La. Hild —9B 132 (3D 25)
Mill La. Hoath —2A 22
Mill La. Hythe —5L 197
Mill La. I'hm —9N 195
Mill La. Igh —4K 121 (1E 25)
Mill La. Kenn —4A 30
Mill La. Lyn —3D 19
Mill La. Maid —3C 126
Mill La. Mgte —3C 208
Mill La. Non —2B 32
Mill La. N'brne —3D 33
Mill La. Orp —1C 100 (3A 14)
Mill La. Ors —2A 8
Mill La. Oxt —3A 24
Mill La. P'mrsh —3E 45
Mill La. Pres —3B 22
Mill La. Sev —3K 119
Mill La. S'wll —3D 220 (3B 32)
Mill La. Shor —1G 103
Mill La. Siss —8B 220 (2E 37)
Mill La. Smar —2J 221 (1B 38)
Mill La. Snod —2F 108
Mill La. S Min —4D 31
Mill La. Tent —6C 222
Mill La. Tonb —5J 145
Mill La. Under —5B 132 (3D 25)
Mill La. W'bury —9B 124
Mill La. W'ham —9E 116
Mill La. Westf —4C 45
Mill La. Whitf —5F 178
Mill La. Worth —2D 33
Mill La. Yald —9E 136 (3C 27)
Mill La. N. H Bay —4J 195
Millmead Av. Mgte —4H 209
Millmead Gdns. Mgte —4H 209
Millmead Rd. Mgte —4F 208 (1E 23)
Mill Meads. —2E 5
Mill M. Deal —6L 177
Mill or Manor La. Holl —6G 128
Mill Pl. Chst —4D 70
Mill Pl. Dart —2H 59
Mill Pl. Fav —4H 187
Millpond Clo. Roch —4M 79
Mill Pond Clo. Sev —3L 119
Mill Pond Cotts. W'bury —1B 136
Millpond La. Tent —3B 38
Mill Pond Rd. Dart —4M 59 (4D 7)
Mill Rd. SE13 —1F 54
Mill Rd. Ave —2E 7
Mill Rd. B'le —9A 216 (1B 32)
Mill Rd. Beth —2K 163 (1D 39)
Mill Rd. Dart —9N 59
Mill Rd. Deal —6L 177 (3E 33)
Mill Rd. Dun G —2F 118
Mill Rd. Dym —8A 182 (1E 47)
Mill Rd. Eps —3A 12
Mill Rd. Eri —7D 52
Mill Rd. Gill —1E 17
Mill Rd. Hythe —6L 197
Mill Rd. Lydd —3D 204
Mill Rd. N'fleet —5D 62
Mill Rd. Roch —3M 79
Mill Rd. Sturry —7D 168 (4E 21)
Mill Rd. W'hm W —1A 32
Mill Row. Bex —5C 58
Mill Row. Birch —5E 206
Mills Clo. Min S —6G 219
Mills Cres. Seal —1N 119
Millside Ind. Est. Dart —2L 59
Mills Rd. Quar W —2J 125
Mills Ter. Chat —9D 80
Millstock Ter. Maid —7B 126
Mill Stone Clo. S Dar —5C 74
Mill Stone M. S Dar —4C 74
Millstone Rd. Deal —5L 177
Millstream Clo. A'st —3E 154
Millstream Clo. Fav —5G 186
Millstream Clo. Whits —4G 224
Mill Street. —2D 124 (1C 26)
Mill St. E Mal —2D 124 (1C 26)
Mill St. I Grn —4E 37
Mill St. Loose —3C 138 (2E 27)
Mill St. Maid —5C 126
Mill St. Sit —6F 98
Mill St. Snod —2F 108
Mill St. Temp E —8C 178
Mill St. W'ham —9F 116
Millstrood Rd. Whits —5G 224 (2C 21)
Mill Ter. Cha —7D 170
Mill Vale. Brom —5J 69
Mill View. Hdlw —7C 134
Mill View. W'boro —1K 161
Mill View. Wdchu —6B 226
Mill View Gdns. Croy —4A 82
Mill View Rd. H Bay —6H 195
Mill Wlk. Maid —6L 125
Millwall. —3E 5
Mill Wall. S'wch —6M 217
Millwall F.C. —3D 5
Mill Wall Pl. S'wch —6M 217
Mill Way. Sit —6F 98 (2C 19)
Millwood Rd. Orp —6L 71
Mill Yd., The. W Mal —1A 124
Milman Rd. NW6 —2A 4
Milne Gdns. SE9 —3A 56
Milne Ho. SE18 —4B 50
(off Ogilby St.)
Milne Memorial. —3B 34
Milner Clo. Evtn —2J 185
Milner Ct. Sturry —6E 168
Milner Cres. Aysm —2C 162
Milner La. Sturry —6E 168
Milne Rd. W'boro —1K 161
Milner Rd. Evtn —2J 185
Milner Rd. Gill —5G 81
Milner Rd. Sea —7C 224
Milner Wlk. Sidc —7F 56
Milroy Av. N'fleet —7D 62
Milstead. —8F 114 (4C 18)
Milstead Clo. Maid —4F 126
Milstead Clo. S'ness —5C 218
Milstead Cotts. Leeds —2B 140
Milton. —5J 63 (4B 8)
Milton Av. Badg M —1C 102
Milton Av. Cli —5M 65
Milton Av. Grav —6H 63
Milton Av. Mgte —4D 208
Milton Clo. Cant —4B 172
Milton Clo. Dover —9G 179
Milton Ct. Grav —6H 63
Milton Dri. Tun W —7K 151
Milton Gdns. Tonb —8F 144
Milton Hall Rd. Grav —6J 63
Milton Lodge. Sidc —9J 57
Milton Pl. Grav —4H 63
Milton Regis. —5F 98 (2C 18)
Milton Rd. Afrd —8E 158
Milton Rd. Belv —4B 52
Milton Rd. Cant —4N 171
Milton Rd. Dover —9G 179
Milton Rd. Dun G —3F 118
Milton Rd. Gill —8F 80
Milton Rd. Grav —4G 63 (4B 8)
(in two parts)
Milton Rd. Sit —7F 98 (3C 19)
Milton Rd. Swans —4L 61 (4A 8)
Milton Rd. Well —8H 51
Milton Rd. Wclf S —1B 10
Milton Sq. Mgte —4D 208
(off Shakespeare Rd.)
Milton St. Maid —7N 125
Milton St. Swans —4K 61 (4E 7)
Milverton Ho. SE6 —8B 54
Milverton Way. SE9 —9C 56
Milward Wlk. SE18 —6C 50
Mimms Ter. Pad W —8M 147
Mimosa Clo. Orp —3L 85
Minard Rd. SE6 —5H 55
(in two parts)
Mincers Clo. Chat —9F 94
Mineral St. SE18 —4G 50
Minerva Av. Dover —2H 181
Minerva Clo. Sidc —8G 57
Minerva Ho. Ram —5H 211
(off High St. Ramsgate,)
Minerva Rd. Roch —4L 79
Ministry Way. SE9 —7B 56
Minnis La. Dover —3A 180 (1B 42)
Minnis Rd. Birch —3C 206 (1C 22)
Minnis Ter. Dover —2F 180
Minnis, The. New Ash —4M 89
Minnis, The. S Min —4D 31
Minnis Way. Worth —9N 217
Minor Canon Row. Roch —7N 79
Minor Cen., The. Weav —4H 127
Minories. EC3 —2D 5
Minshaw Ct. Sidc —9J 57
Minshull Pl. Beck —3D 68
Minster. —8N 205 (2C 23)
(nr. Ramsgate)
Minster. —6L 219 (4D 11)
(nr. Sheerness)
Minster Abbey. —8N 205 (2C 23)
Minster Clo. Broad —2L 211
Minster Dri. H Bay —3E 194
Minster Dri. Min S —4J 219
Minster Rd. Acol —9G 207 (2C 23)
Minster Rd. Brom —3L 69
Minster Rd. Fav —5J 187
Minster Rd. Gill —9M 81
Minster Rd. Min S —6F 218 (4D 11)
Minster Rd. Ram —7F 210 (2E 23)
Minster Rd. Wgte S —3K 207 (1D 23)
Mintching Wood Rd. Mils —7G 114 (4C 19)
Minter Av. Dens —5B 192
Minter Clo. Dens —5B 192
Minterne Av. Sit —9E 98 (3C 18)
Minters Orchard. Platt —2A 122
Mintres Ind. Est. Deal —4M 177
Mint, The. Harb —1J 171
Miranda Ct. S'ness —3C 218
Miriam Rd. SE18 —5G 50
Mirror Path. SE9 —8M 55
Miskin Rd. Dart —5K 59
Miskin Rd. Hoo —8H 67
Miskin Way. Grav —2J 77
Misling La. S Min —4D 31
Missenden Ct. Folk —6K 189
(off Clarence St.)
Mistletoe Clo. Croy —2A 82
Mitcham. —1B 12
Mitcham La. SW16 —1C 12
Mitcham Rd. SW17 —1B 12
Mitcham Rd. Croy —2C 13
Mitcham Rd. Dym —7B 182
Mitchell Av. Chat —1C 94
Mitchell Av. N'fleet —7C 62
Mitchell Clo. SE2 —4L 51
Mitchell Clo. Belv —3D 52
Mitchell Clo. Dart —7M 59
Mitchell Clo. Len —7D 200
Mitchell Rd. Orp —5H 85
Mitchell Rd. W Mal —7L 123
Mitchell St. Folk —5D 188
Mitchell Wlk. Swans —5L 61
Mitchell Way. Brom —4K 69
Mitchem Clo. W King —8E 88
Mitchley Av. Purl & S Croy —3D 13
Mitchley Hill. S Croy —3D 13
Mitre Clo. Brom —5J 69
Mitre Ct. Tonb —5J 145
Mitre Rd. Roch —8M 79
Mittel Ct. Lydd —3B 204
Moat Clo. Chip —5C 118
Moat Clo. Orp —7H 85
Moat Ct. SE9 —4B 56
Moat Ct. Sidc —8H 57
Moat Croft. Well —1L 57
Moat Dri. Afrd —1B 160
Moat Farm Tun W —6G 156
Moat Farm Clo. Folk —4J 189
Moat Farm Rd. Folk —4J 189
Moat Farm Rd. St Mh —3A 10
Moat Field Meadow. Kgnt —5F 160 (2A 40)
Moat La. Ah —5C 216 (4C 22)
Moat La. Cowd —8A 148 (1B 34)
Moat La. Eri —8H 53
Moat La. F'wch —8E 168 (4E 21)
Moat La. R Comn —7H 167
Moat La. Sed —4C 44
Moat Rd. E Grin —2A 34
Moat Rd. H'crn —3H 193 (4A 28)
Moat Sole. S'wch —5L 217 (4D 23)
Moat, The. Char —3K 175
Moat Way. Queen —7B 218
Mockbeggar. —8L 65 (4D 9)
Mockbeggar. R Min —4D 31
Mockbeggar La. Bidd —2A 38
Mockett Ct. Sit —7F 98
(off Hawthorn Rd.)
Mockett Dri. Broad —6K 209
Mockford All. Tent —8B 222
(off High St. Tenterden,)
Mock La. Afrd —3A 160 (1E 39)
Model Farm Clo. SE9 —8A 56
Modest Corner. —5E 150 (1E 35)
Moira Rd. SE9 —2B 56
Molash. —3A 30
Molash Rd. Orp —7M 71
Molehill Rd. Ches —6M 225 (2D 21)
Molescroft. SE9 —8E 56
Molescroft Way. Tonb —8F 144
Moles Mead. Eden —5C 184
Molesworth St. SE13 —1F 54 (4E 5)
Moliner Ct. Beck —3D 68
Molineux Rd. Min —7M 205
Molland Clo. Ah —4B 216
Molland La. Ah —5B 216 (4C 22)
(in two parts)
Molland Lea. Ah —4B 216
Molland Rd. Cant —4N 171
Mollison Dri. Wall —3C 13
Mollison Rise. Grav —1K 77
Molloy Rd. Shad —2E 39
Molyneux Ct. Tun W —1F 156
Molyneux Pk. Gdns. Tun W —1F 156
Molyneux Pk. Rd. Tun W —1E 156
Monarch Clo. Chat —5D 94
Monarch Clo. W Wick —5J 83
Monarch Hill. Up H'ng —7C 92
Monarch Rd. Belv —3B 52

Monastery St.—Nelgarde Rd.

Monastery St. *Cant* —2N **171** (1D **31**)
Monckton's Dri. *Maid* —2B **126**
Monckton's La. *Maid* —3B **126**
Moncrif Clo. *Bear* —5L **127**
Monds Cotts. *Sund* —6N **117**
Mongeham Chu. Clo. *Gt Mon* —3D **33**
Mongeham Rd. *Deal* —7H **177** (3D **33**)
Monica James Ho. *Sidc* —8J **57**
Monins Rd. *Dover* —5G **180**
Monivea Rd. *Beck* —3C **68**
Monkdown. *Down* —8K **127**
Monkery La. *C'lck* —8A **174** (3E **29**)
Monks Clo. *SE2* —4M **51**
Monks Clo. *Cant* —9N **167**
Monk's Clo. *Fav* —4F **186**
Monk's Hill. —1B 38
Monkshill Rd. *Hern* —3B **20**
Monks La. *Cous W* —3B **36**
Monks La. *Eden* —3A **24**
Monks Orchard. —1B 82 (2E 13)
Monks Orchard. *Dart* —7L **59**
Monks Orchard Rd. *Beck* —2D **82** (2E **13**)
Monk St. *SE18* —4C **50**
Monks Wlk. *Char* —3K **175**
Monks Wlk. *S'fleet* —2N **75**
Monks Wlk. *Tonb* —7H **145**
Monks Way. *Beck* —9D **68**
Monks Way. *Dover* —1F **180**
Monks Way. *Orp* —2E **84**
Monkton. —6H 205 (2C 22)
Monkton Ct. La. *Eyt* —4L **185** (3C **32**)
Monkton Gdns. *Clift* —2J **209**
Monkton Mnr. *Ram* —2B **22**
Monkton Pl. *Ram* —5H **211**
Monkton Rd. *Bor G* —2M **121**
Monkton Rd. *Min* —7J **205** (2C **22**)
Monkton Rd. *Well* —9H **51**
Monkton's Av. *Maid* —2B **126**
Monkton St. *Monk* —6H **205** (2C **22**)
Monkwood Clo. *Roch* —3M **93**
Monmouth Clo. *Gill* —1N **95**
Monmouth Clo. *Well* —2J **57**
Monmouth St. *WC2* —2C **5**
Mons Ct. *Kem* —2G **98**
*Monson Colonnade. Tun W —1H **157***
(off Monson Rd.)
Monson Ho. *Tun W* —1H **157**
Monson Rd. *Tun W* —1H **157** (2E **35**)
Monson Way. *Tun W* —1H **157**
Mons Way. *Brom* —9A **70**
Montacute Gdns. *Tun W* —3F **156**
Montacute Rd. *SE6* —5C **54**
Montacute Rd. *New Ad* —9F **82**
Montacute Rd. *Tun W* —4G **156** (2E **35**)
Montague Av. *SE4* —2C **54**
Montague Ct. *Folk* —7H **189**
Montague Ct. *S'ness* —3C **218**
Montague Ct. *Sidc* —8J **57**
Montague Pl. *WC1* —2C **4**
Montague Pl. *Swan* —7G **72**
Montague Rd. *Ram* —4J **211**
Montague St. *H Bay* —2F **194**
Montague Ter. *Brom* —6J **69**
Montargis Way. *Crowb* —4D **35**
Montbelle Rd. *SE9* —8D **56**
Montbretia Clo. *Orp* —7L **71**
Montcalm Clo. *Brom* —9K **69**
*Montcalm Ter. Dover —1H **181***
(off Winnipeg Clo.)
Montefiore Av. *Ram* —3K **211** (2E **23**)
Montefiore Cotts. *Ram* —4K **211**
Monteith Clo. *L'tn G* —2A **156**
Montem Rd. *SE23* —5C **54**
Monterey Clo. *Bex* —7D **58**
Montfort Clo. *Afrd* —2D **160**
Montfort Clo. *Cant* —7N **167**
Montfort Rd. *Chat* —9B **94**
Montfort Rd. *Kems* —8M **103**
Montfort Rd. *Roch* —5L **79**
Montgomery Av. *Chat* —4D **94**
Montgomery Clo. *Sidc* —4H **57**
Montgomery Cotts. *Up H'ng* —6C **92**
Montgomery Rd. *Gill* —8F **80**
Montgomery Rd. *S Dar* —4D **74**
Montgomery Rd. *Tun W* —7H **151**
Montgomery Way. *Folk* —3K **189**
Montpelier Av. *Bex* —5M **57**
Montpelier Av. *Whits* —8F **224**
Montpelier Bus. Pk. *Afrd* —9D **158**
Montpelier Ga. *Maid* —4M **125**
Montpelier Row. *SE3* —3E **5**
Montreal Clo. *Dover* —1G **181**
Montreal Rd. *Sev* —5F **118**
Montreal Rd. *Til* —1F **62**
Montrose Av. *Sidc* —5J **57**
Montrose Av. *Well* —1F **56**
Montrose Clo. *Well* —1H **57**
Montrose Way. *SE23* —6A **54**
Monument Gdns. *SE13* —3F **54**
Monument Way. *Afrd* —3J **161**
Monypenny. *Rol* —3K **213**
Moon Ct. *SE12* —2K **55**
Moon Hill. *S'wll* —3D **220**
Moon's Green. —2E 45
Moonstone Dri. *Chat* —9E **94**
Moorcroft Gdns. *Brom* —8A **70**
Moorden La. *Chid C* —6H **143** (4D **25**)
Moordown. *SE18* —8C **50**
Moore Clo. *Bztt* —2C **47**
Moore End. *S'ness* —3C **218**
Moorehead Way. *SE3* —1L **55**
Mooreland Rd. *Brom* —3J **69**
Moore Rd. *Swans* —4L **61**
Moore's La. *Beckl* —3D **45**
Moore St. *Roch* —4L **79**
Moorfield. *Cant* —7M **167**
Moorfield Rd. *Orp* —1J **85**
Moorgate. *EC2* —2D **5**
Moorhen Clo. *Eri* —7J **53**
Moor Hill. *Hawkh* —7K **191** (1B **44**)
Moorhouse. —9B 116 (2A 24)
Moorhouse Bank. —2A 24
Moorhouse Rd. *Oxt & W'ham* —3A **24**
Mooring Rd. *Roch* —2A **94**
Moorings, The. *Con* —2E **19**
Moorings, The. *Sand* —4J **215**
Moorland Rd. *S'wll* —3C **220**
Moorlands. —3C **34**
Moor La. *D'land & Eden* —1A **34**
Moor La. *Chess* —2A **12**
Moor La. *Ivy* —2C **47**
Moor La. *Westf* —4C **45**
Moor La. *Wdchu* —9A **226** (3D **39**)
Moor Pk. Clo. *Gill* —3C **96**
Moor Rd. *Sev* —2J **119**
Moor Rd. *Westf* —4C **45**
Moorside Ct. *Cant* —1K **171**
Moorside Rd. *Brom* —8H **55**
Moorstock. —7J 215 (2C 41)
Moorstock La. *S'ndge* —8J **215** (2C **41**)
Moor Street. —3D 96 (2A 18)
Moor St. *Rain* —3D **96** (2A **18**)
Moor, The. —7K 191 (1B 44)
Moor, The. *Hawkh* —7K **191** (1B **44**)
Moorwell Dri. *S'wll* —2C **220**
Morants Ct. Rd. *Dun G & Sev* —9D **102** (4C **15**)
Moray Av. *Birch* —3E **206**
Mordaunt Av. *Wgte S* —3K **207**
Morden. —1B 12
Morden Ct. Rd. *Roch* —8N **79**
Morden Hall Rd. *Mord* —1B **12**
Morden Park. —2B 12
Morden Rd. *SW19* —1B **12**
Morden Rd. *Mitc* —1B **12**
Morden St. *Roch* —8N **79**
Mordred Rd. *SE6* —7H **55**
Morehall. —2A 42
Morehall Av. *Folk* —5F **188**
Moreland St. *EC1* —2C **5**
Morel Ct. *Sev* —4J **119**
Morella Wlk. *Len* —7D **200**
Morello Clo. *Swan* —7E **72**
Morello Clo. *Tey* —2K **223**
Moremead Rd. *SE6* —9C **54**
Morement Rd. *Hoo* —7G **66**
Morena St. *SE6* —5E **54**
Moreton Almshouses. *W'ham* —8F **116**
Moreton Clo. *Swan* —5F **72**
Moreton Ct. *Dart* —1G **58**
Moreton Ind. Est. *Swan* —7J **73**
Morewood Clo. *Sev* —5G **119**
Morewood Clo. Ind. Est. *Sev* —5H **119**
Morgan Dri. *Grnh* —5E **60**
Morgan Kirby Gdns. *Shel L* —1A **30**
Morgan Rd. *Brom* —3K **69**
Morgan Rd. *Roch* —4L **79**
Morgan St. *SE18* —3D **50**
Morhen Clo. *Snod* —3C **108**
Morland Av. *Dart* —3J **59**
Morland Dri. *Lam* —2D **200**
Morland Dri. *Roch* —3L **79**
Morland Rd. *SE20* —2A **68**
Morland Rd. *Croy* —2D **13**
Morley Clo. *Orp* —3D **84**
Morley Ct. *Short* —7J **69**
Morley Dri. *Horsm* —2C **198**
Morley Hill. *Stan H* —1C **8**
Morley Rd. *SE13* —2F **54**
Morley Rd. *Chst* —4E **70**
Morley Rd. *Tonb* —6K **145**
Morley's Rd. *Weald* —6K **131** (3D **25**)
Morning Cross Cotts. *Cli* —4C **176**
Morning La. *E9* —1D **5**
Mornington Av. *Brom* —6M **69**
Mornington Clo. *Big H* —5D **164**
Mornington Ct. *Bex* —6E **58**
Morris Av. *H Bay* —3A **194**
Morris Clo. *Croy* —8B **68**
Morris Clo. *E Mal* —9D **108**
Morris Clo. *Orp* —6G **84**
Morris Ct. Clo. *Bap* —9L **99**
Morris Gdns. *Dart* —3A **60**
Morrison Rd. *Folk* —5L **189**
Morris Rd. *E14* —2E **5**
Morry La. *E Sut* —9F **140** (3A **28**)
Morse Ho. *Sit* —8K **99**
Morston Gdns. *SE9* —9B **56**
Mortgramit Sq. *SE18* —3C **50**
Mortimer Clo. *Afrd* —2F **160**
Mortimer Rd. *NW10* —2A **4**
Mortimer Rd. *Big H* —2B **164**
Mortimer Rd. *Dover* —4L **181**
Mortimer Rd. *Eri* —6E **52**
Mortimer Rd. *Orp* —2J **85**
Mortimers Av. *Cli* —5L **65**
Mortimer St. *W1* —2C **4**
Mortimer St. *H Bay* —2G **194**
Mortlake. —4A 4
Mortlake High St. *SW14* —3A **4**
Mortlake Rd. *Rich* —3A **4**
Morvale Clo. *Belv* —4A **52**
Morval Rd. *SW2* —4C **5**
Moselle Rd. *Big H* —6E **164**
Mosquito Rd. *W Mal* —6L **123**
Mossbank. *Chat* —8D **94**
Mossdown Clo. *Belv* —4B **52**
Moss End M. *Ram* —2J **211**
Moss Gdns. *S Croy* —8A **82**
Mosslea Rd. *Brom* —8N **69**
Mosslea Rd. *Orp* —4E **84**
Mossy Glade. *Gill* —5A **96**
Mostyn Rd. *Maid* —5F **126**
Mosul Way. *Brom* —9A **70**
Mosyer Dri. *Orp* —3M **85**
Mote Av. *Maid* —6E **126**
Mote Rd. *Maid* —6D **126** (2E **27**)
Mote Rd. *S'brne & Ivy H* —4F **132** (2E **25**)
Mote, The. *New Ash* —3M **89**
Motherwell Way. *Grays* —3E **7**
Motney Hill. —1A 18
Motney Hill Rd. *Gill* —2A **18**
Motspur Park. —2A 12
Motspur Pk. *N Mald* —2A **12**
Mottingham. —7A 56 (4A 6)
Mottingham Gdns. *SE9* —6N **55**
Mottingham La. *SE12 & SE9* —6M **55** (4A **6**)
Mottingham Rd. *SE9* —7A **56** (4A **6**)
Mottins Hill. *Crowb* —4D **35**
Mottisfont Rd. *SE2* —3J **51**
Mott's Down. —3C 35
Mott's Mill. —3D 35
Mouchotte Clo. *Big H* —2A **164**
Moultain Hill. *Swan* —7H **73**
Mound, The. *SE9* —8C **56**
Mountain Bungalows. *Hams* —9E **190**
*Mountain Clo. Wro —7M **105***
(off West St.)
Mountain Street. —2B 30
Mountain St. *Chi* —9J **175** (2B **30**)
*Mt. Arlington. Short —5H **69***
(off Park Hill Rd.)
Mount Av. *Yald* —7E **136**
Mountbatten Av. *Chat* —4D **94**
Mountbatten Av. *High* —9G **64**
Mountbatten Clo. *SE18* —6G **50**
Mountbatten Gdns. *Beck* —7B **68**
Mountbatten Way. *Bra L* —7K **165**
Mt. Castle La. *Len H* —3C **29**
Mt. Charles Wlk. *Bri* —9E **172**
Mount Clo. *Brom* —4A **70**
Mount Clo. *Sev* —5G **119**
Mount Cotts. *Bear* —5L **127**
Mount Ct. *W Wick* —3H **83**
Mt. Culver Av. *Sidc* —2M **71**
Mount Dri. *Bear* —5L **127**
Mount Dri. *Bexh* —3N **57**
Mt. Edgecombe Rd. *Tun W* —2G **156**
Mt. Ephraim. *Tun W* —2F **156** (2E **35**)
Mount Ephraim Gardens. —2L **165** (3B **20**)
Mt. Ephraim Rd. *Tun W* —1G **157**
Mount Farm. —3A **36**
Mountfield. —3B 44
Mountfield. *Bor G* —2N **121**
Mount Field. *Fav* —6F **186**
Mount Field. *Queen* —7B **218**
Mountfield Clo. *Meop* —9E **90**
Mountfield Gdns. *Tun W* —2H **157**
Mountfield Ind. Est. *New R* —3D **212**
Mountfield La. *M'fld* —3A **44**
Mountfield Pk. *Tonb* —7J **145**
Mountfield Rd. *New R* —3D **212**
Mountfield Rd. *Tun W* —2H **157**
Mountfield Row. *New R* —3D **212**
Mountfield Way. *Orp* —7L **71**
Mountfield Way. *Wgte S* —5J **207**
Mt. Green Av. *C'snd* —7B **210**
Mountgrove Rd. *N5* —1D **5**
Mt. Harry Rd. *Sev* —5H **119** (2D **25**)
Mount Hill. *Knock* —8J **101**
Mounthurst Rd. *Brom* —1J **83**
Mountjoy Clo. *SE2* —2K **51**
Mount La. *Bear* —5L **127**
Mount La. *H'lip* —8F **96** (3A **18**)
Mount Pleasant. —2C 23
Mt. Pleasant. *Adgtn* —2B **40**
Mt. Pleasant. *Ayle* —7L **109**
Mt. Pleasant. *Big H* —5D **164**
Mt. Pleasant. *Blean* —5G **166**
Mt. Pleasant. *Chat* —8E **80**
Mt. Pleasant. *Crowb* —4D **35**
Mt. Pleasant. *Hild* —1D **144**
Mt. Pleasant. *Lam* —1A **200** (2B **36**)
Mt. Pleasant. *Oare* —2F **186**
Mt. Pleasant. *Pad W* —9L **147**
Mt. Pleasant. *Tent* —7D **222**
Mt. Pleasant Av. *Tun W* —2H **157**
Mt. Pleasant Clo. *Lym* —7D **204**
Mt. Pleasant Ct. *Hild* —1D **144**
Mt. Pleasant Dri. *Bear* —4K **127**
Mt. Pleasant La. *Lam* —1A **200** (2B **36**)
Mt. Pleasant Pl. *SE18* —4F **50**
Mt. Pleasant Rd. *SE13* —4E **54**
Mt. Pleasant Rd. *Dart* —4N **59**
Mt. Pleasant Rd. *Folk* —6K **189**
Mt. Pleasant Rd. *Tun W* —2G **157** (2E **35**)
Mt. Pleasant Rd. *Weald* —6J **131**
Mt. Pleasant Wlk. *Bex* —3D **58**
Mount Rd. *Bexh* —3M **57**
Mount Rd. *Cant* —4B **172**
Mount Rd. *Chat* —9C **80**
Mount Rd. *Dart* —4G **59**
Mount Rd. *Dover* —7F **180**
Mount Rd. *Roch* —1L **93**
Mounts Clo. *Deal* —5K **177**
Mountsfield Clo. *Maid* —4A **126**
Mountsfield Ct. *SE13* —4G **54**
Mounts Hill. *Bene* —3E **37**
Mt. Sion. *Tun W* —3G **157**
Mounts La. *Rol* —4L **213** (4B **38**)
Mounts Rd. *Grnh* —3H **61** (4E **7**)
Mount St. *SE18* —4D **50**
Mount St. *Batt* —4B **44**
Mount St. *Hythe* —6K **197**
Mount, The. *Bexh* —3C **58**
Mount, The. *Chat* —8C **80**
Mount, The. *Fav* —6F **186**
Mount Top. *R Min* —7J **183** (1D **41**)
Mountview. *B'den* —9C **98**
Mt. View Rd. *H Bay* —5H **195**
Mountview Rd. *Orp* —1J **85**
(in two parts)
Mount Vs. *Yald* —7E **136**
Movers Lane. (Junct.) —2B **6**
Movers La. *Bark* —2B **6**
Mowshurst. —3D 184
Moyes Clo. *C'snd* —7B **210**
Moyle Clo. *Gill* —7N **95**
Moyle Ct. *Hythe* —7K **197**
Moyle Tower Rd. *Hythe* —7K **197**
Mozart Ct. *Chat* —9B **80**
Mucking. —2C 8
Muckingford. —3B 8
Muckingford Rd. *W Til & Linf* —3B **8**
Mucking Wharf Rd. *Stan H* —2C **8**
Muddy La. *Sit* —9J **99**
Muggins La. *Shorne* —9A **64**
Muirkirk Rd. *SE6* —6F **54**
Muir Rd. *Maid* —6D **126**
Muir Rd. *Ram* —4K **211**
Muir St. *E16* —1A **50**
Mulberry Clo. *Hem* —7K **95**
Mulberry Clo. *Meop* —9G **76**
Mulberry Clo. *Ram* —4K **211**
Mulberry Clo. *Tun W* —5K **151**
Mulberry Cotts. *Old L* —1C **175**
Mulberry Ct. *Cant* —2M **171** (1D **31**)
Mulberry Ct. *L'stne* —4F **212**
Mulberry Ct. *Maid* —4E **126**
Mulberry Dri. *Purf* —4N **53**
Mulberry Fld. *S'wch* —5L **217**
Mulberry Hill. *Chi* —8L **175** (2B **30**)
Mulberry Ho. *Short* —5H **69**
Mulberry Rd. *N'fleet* —8D **62**
Mulberry Way. *Belv* —2D **52**
Mulgrave Rd. *Sutt* —3B **12**
Mullender Ct. *Grav* —6M **63**
Multon Rd. *W King* —7E **88**
Muncies M. *SE6* —7F **54**
Munday Works Est. *Tonb* —6J **145**
Mundy Bois. —4C 29
Mundy Bois La. *P'ley* —4C **29**
Mundy Bois Rd. *Eger* —4C **28**
Munford Dri. *Swans* —5L **61**
Mungo Pk. Rd. *Grav* —1J **77**
Mungo Pk. Rd. *Rain* —1D **7**
Mungo Pk. Way. *Orp* —1L **85**
Munnery Way. *Orp* —4C **84**
Munn's La. *H'lip* —5G **96** (2B **18**)
Munsgore La. *B'den* —1N **113** (3B **18**)
Munster Rd. *SW6* —3B **4**
Murchison Av. *Bex* —6M **57** (4B **6**)
Murillo Rd. *SE13* —2G **55**
Murrain Dri. *Down* —8K **127**
Murray Av. *Brom* —6L **69**
Murray Bus. Cen. *Orp* —6K **71**
*Murray Ho. SE18 —4B **50***
(off Rideout St.)
Murray Rd. *Orp* —6K **71**
Murray Rd. *Roch* —3N **79**
Murston. —7J 99
Murston Rd. *Sit* —8J **99** (3C **19**)
Murthwaite Ct. *Min S* —7H **219**
Murton. —2C 19
Murton Neale Clo. *Hawkh* —5L **191**
Murton Pl. *G'ney* —3B **20**
*Muscovy Ho. Eri —2N **51***
(off Kale Rd.)
Museum Av. *Maid* —4C **126**
Museum of Artillery in the Rotunda. —5B **50**
Museum of Carriages. —6D **126**
Museum Of Kent Life. —9A **110** (4D **17**)
Museum St. *Maid* —5C **126**
Musgrave Clo. *Mans* —9L **207**
Musgrave Rd. *Sit* —5G **98**
Musgrove. *Afrd* —1E **160**
Musket La. *Holl* —7C **128** (2A **28**)
(in two parts)
Mussenden La. *Hort K & Fawk* —8C **74** (2E **15**)
Mustang Rd. *W Mal* —6L **123**
Mustards Rd. *Ley S* —6J **203**
Mutrix Gdns. *Mgte* —2M **207**
Mutrix Rd. *Mgte* —3N **207**
Mutton Hill. *D'land* —1A **34**
Mutton La. *Osp* —7E **186** (3A **20**)
Mymms Clo. *Ches* —5L **225**
Mynn Cres. *Bear* —5K **127**
Myra St. *SE2* —4J **51**
Myron Pl. *SE13* —1F **54**
Myrtle Clo. *Eri* —7F **52**
Myrtle Cotts. *St Mic* —4C **222**
Myrtle Cres. *Chat* —6C **94**
Myrtledene Rd. *SE2* —5J **51**
Myrtle Pl. *Dart* —5D **60**
Myrtle Rd. *Crowb* —4C **35**
Myrtle Rd. *Croy* —4D **82**
Myrtle Rd. *Dart* —6L **59**
Myrtle Rd. *Folk* —5L **189**
Mystole La. *Cha* —9C **170** (2C **30**)
Mystole La. *Chi* —8N **175**

Naccolt. —4B 30
Naccolt Rd. *Brook* —4B **30**
Nacholt Clo. *Whits* —3J **225**
Nackington. —8N 171 (2D 31)
Nackington Ct. *Cant* —4A **172**
Nackington Rd. *Cant* —9N **171** (2D **31**)
Nagpur Ho. *Maid* —3H **139**
Nag's Head. (Junct.) —1C **5**
Nags Head La. *Roch* —8A **80**
Nags Head La. *Well* —1K **57**
Nailbourne Clo. *Kgtn* —3E **31**
Nailbourne Ct. *Lym* —7D **204**
Naildown Clo. *Hythe* —8A **188**
Naildown Rd. *Hythe* —8A **188**
Nairne Clo. *Shad* —2E **39**
Namur Pl. *B Hts* —2L **181**
Nansen Rd. *Grav* —9J **63**
Napchester. —2H 179 (4C 33)
Napchester Rd. *Whitf* —5F **178** (4C **33**)
Napier Clo. *Sit* —7D **98**
Napier Ct. *Maid* —2C **126**
Napier Gdns. *Hythe* —7K **197**
Napier Rd. *Belv* —4A **52**
Napier Rd. *Broad* —7J **209**
Napier Rd. *Brom* —7L **69**
Napier Rd. *Dover* —1G **181**
Napier Rd. *Gill* —8G **80** (2E **17**)
Napier Rd. *N'fleet* —6E **62**
Napier Rd. *Tun W* —3K **157**
Napleton Ct. *Ram* —6G **211**
Napleton Rd. *Fav* —5G **186**
Napleton Rd. *Ram* —6G **210**
Napoleon Dri. *Mard* —3L **205**
Napoleon Wlk. *Len* —7C **200**
Napwood Clo. *Gill* —5N **95**
Nares Rd. *Gill* —7N **95**
Nargate Clo. *L'brne* —2M **173**
Nargate St. *L'brne* —2L **173** (1A **32**)
Narrabeen Rd. *Folk* —5K **188**
Narrowbush La. *Old R* —2C **47**
Narrow La. *Warl* —4D **13**
Narrow Way. *Brom* —9A **70**
Naseby Av. *Folk* —6D **188**
Naseby Ct. *Sidc* —9H **57**
Nash. —7L 83 (2A 14)
Nash Bank. *Meop* —5E **76** (1A **16**)
Nash Clo. *Chat* —9F **94**
Nash Ct. Cotts. *Westw* —1C **158**
Nash Ct. Gdns. *Mgte* —5C **208**
Nash Ct. Rd. *Mgte* —5D **208**
Nash Croft. *N'fleet* —9D **62**
Nashenden Farm La. *Roch* —2K **93**
Nashenden La. *Roch* —1K **93**
Nash Gdns. *Broad* —9M **209**
Nash Grn. *Brom* —2K **69**
Nash Hill. *Lym* —8D **204**
Nash La. *Kes* —8K **83** (3E **13**)
Nash La. *Mgte* —6D **208**
Nash Rd. *SE4* —2B **54**
Nash Rd. *Mgte* —5C **208** (1D **23**)
Nash Street. —5F 76 (1B 16)
Nash St. *Meop* —5F **76**
Nasmyth Rd. *Birch* —3F **206**
Nassau Path. *SE28* —1L **51**
Natal Rd. *Chat* —1D **94**
Natal Rd. *Dover* —9H **179**
Nathan Way. *SE28* —4G **50** (3B **6**)
National Maritime Museum. —3E **5**
National Recreation Centre. —1D **13**
(Crystal Palace)
Nativity Clo. *Sit* —7F **98**
Nats La. *Brook* —4B **30**
Nautilus Clo. *Min S* —7H **219**
Nautilus Dri. *Min S* —7H **219**
Naval Ter. *S'ness* —1B **218**
Naval Wlk. *Brom* —5K **69**
Nayland Ho. *SE6* —9F **54**
Naylands. *Mgte* —4B **208**
Naylor's Cotts. *Gill* —1L **111**
Neale St. *Chat* —1C **94**
Neal Rd. *W King* —7E **88**
Neal's Pl. Rd. *Cant* —9J **167**
Neame Rd. *Birch* —4F **206**
Neames Forstal. —1B 30
Neasden. —1A 4
Neasden Junction. (Junct.) —1A **4**
Neasden La. *NW10* —1A **4**
Neasden La. N. *NW10* —1A **4**
Neason Ct. *Folk* —5M **189**
Neason Way. *Folk* —5M **189**
Neath Ct. *Maid* —9H **127**
Neats Ct. *Queen* —9B **218**
Neills Rd. *Free H* —3B **36**
Neills Rd. *Lam* —3A **200**
Nelgarde Rd. *SE6* —5D **54**

Nellington Ct.—N. Audley St.

Nellington Ct. Rust —1B 156
Nellington Rd. Tun W —9A 150 (1D 35)
Nelson Av. Min S —6L 219
Nelson Av. Tonb —6G 144
Nelson Clo. Big H —5E 164
Nelson Clo. S'ness —4B 218
Nelson Clo. W'boro —1M 161
Nelson Ct. Birch —3D 206
Nelson Ct. Chat —2F 94
Nelson Ct. Eri —7G 53
(off Frobisher Rd.)
Nelson Cres. Ram —6J 211
Nelson Gdns. Fav —6G 187
Nelson Ho. Grnh —3K 61
Nelson Ho. Maid —3J 139
Nelson Mandella Rd. SE3 —1M 55
Nelson Park. —9J 199
Nelson Pk. Rd. St Mc —9H 199
Nelson Pl. Broad —8M 209 (1E 23)
Nelson Pl. Sidc —9J 57
Nelson Rd. Belv —5A 52
Nelson Rd. Brom —7M 69
Nelson Rd. Dart —4K 59
Nelson Rd. Gill —8G 80 (2E 17)
Nelson Rd. Mgte —8B 208
Nelson Rd. N'fleet —7E 62
Nelson Rd. Sidc —9J 57
Nelson Rd. Tun W —3K 157
Nelson Rd. Whits —4E 224
Nelson Rd. Woul —7G 92
Nelson St. Deal —3N 177
Nelson St. Fav —6G 187
Nelson Ter. Chat —2F 94
Nelson Ter. Dover —1G 181
(off Alberta Clo.)
Nelson Ter. Fav —6G 187
Nelson Wlk. Sit —6C 98
Nepicar Farm. —9C 106 (4A 16)
Nepicar La. Wro —6B 106 (4A 16)
Neptune Bus. Ct. Roch —5B 80
Neptune Clo. Roch —5B 80
Neptune Ct. Eri —7G 53
(off Frobisher Rd.)
Neptune Ter. S'ness —2E 218
Neptune Way. Roch —6B 80
Nesbit Rd. SE9 —2N 55
Nesbit Rd. St Mar —2E 214
Nesbitt Clo. SE3 —1H 55
Ness Rd. Eri —6L 53
Ness Rd. Lydd —3C 204 (3D 47)
Ness Rd. Shoe —1D 11
Ness, The. Cant —5A 172
Nestor Ct. Tstn —9E 124
Nether Av. L'stne —3E 212
Nethercourt. —5F 210
Nethercourt Circ. Ram —6F 210
Nethercourt Farm Rd. Ram —5F 210
Nethercourt Hill. Ram —6F 210 (2E 23)
Netherfield. —4A 44
Netherfield Hill. Batt —4A 44
Netherfield Rd. Batt —4B 44
Netherfield Rd. Neth —4A 44
Nethergong Hill. Ups —3A 22
Netherhale Farm Rd. St N —7A 206
Nethersole Clo. Cant —7N 167
Nethersole Rd. W Vil —3A 32
Nethewode Ct. Belv —3C 52
(off Lwr. Park Rd.)
Netley Clo. Maid —3G 126
Netley Clo. New Ad —8F 82
Nettlefield. Kenn —5J 159
Nettlepole La. L Char —4D 29
Nettlestead. —2B 136 (2B 26)
Nettlestead Clo. Beck —3C 68
Nettlestead Green. —6A 136 (3B 26)
Nettlestead La. Mere —2M 135 (2B 26)
Neuchatel Rd. SE6 —7C 54
Nevill Ct. Tun W —3D 156
Nevill Ct. W Mal —9A 108
Neville Clo. Maid —1E 126
Neville Clo. Sidc —9H 57
Neville M. Deal —5N 177
Neville Rd. Chat —1B 94
Nevill Gdns. Walm —9L 177
Nevill Ga. Tun W —4H 157
Nevill Pk. Tun W —2D 156
Nevill Pl. Meop —8F 76
Nevill Pl. Snod —3E 108
Nevill Ridge. Tun W —2D 156
Nevill Rd. Snod —3E 108
Nevill St. Tun W —3G 156
Nevill Ter. Tun W —3F 156
New Addington. — 8F 82 (3E 13)
Newark Ter. Roch —5M 79
Newark Yd. Roch —5M 79
New Ash Green. —3M 89 (2A 16)
New Barn. —6A 76 (1A 16)
New Barn La. W'ham & Cud —9E 100 (4B 14)
New Barn Rd. H'lgh —4C 30
New Barn Rd. H'bury —4A 28
New Barn Rd. Long & S'fleet —6A 76 (1A 16)
New Barn Rd. Swan —4F 72 (1C 15)
New Barns Rd. Maid —1D 126
New Barn St. E13 —2A 6
New Beach Holiday Cen. Dym —9D 182
New Beckenham. —2C 68 (1E 13)
Newbery Rd. Eri —8G 52
New Bond St. W1 —2C 4
Newborough Ct. Tonb —1H 145
Newbridge. —3B 34
New Bri. Dover —5K 181
Newbridge Av. Sit —4F 98
Newbridge Point. SE23 —8A 54
(off Windrush La.)
New Bri. St. EC4 —2C 5
New Bri. Way. St Mar —3D 214
Newbury. —3D 19
Newbury Av. Maid —2N 125
Newbury Clo. Birch —5G 207
Newbury Clo. Cli —5M 65
Newbury Clo. Dover —5E 180
Newbury Clo. Folk —6D 188
Newbury Ct. Sidc —9H 57
Newbury La. Cous W —3B 36
Newbury Rd. Brom —6K 69
Newbys Pl. Mgte —3C 208
New Camden Pk. Tun W —3J 157
Newcastle Hill. Ram —5J 211
Newcastle La. Ewe M —1B 42
New Cavendish St. W1 —2C 4
Newce Wlk. Cant —9A 168
New Charlton. —3A 6
Newchurch. —4B 40
Newchurch La. Ivy —1D 47
New Chu. Rd. SE5 —3D 5
Newchurch Rd. Maid —8D 126
New City Rd. E13 —2A 6
New Clo., The. Bri —8F 172
New College Of Cobham. —7L 77 (1B 16)
Newcomen Rd. S'ness —2D 218
Newcomen Rd. Tun W —9G 150
New Convenant Pl. Roch —8A 80
(off New Rd.)
New Cotts. Rod —3G 115
New Cotts. S'wch —5L 217
New Cotts. Tonge —1M 115
New Ct. Tonb —5J 145
New Covenant Pl. Roch —8A 80
New Cross. —3E 5
New Cross. (Junct.) —3E 5
New Cross Gate. —3D 5
New Cross Gate. (Junct.) —3D 5
New Cross Rd. SE14 —3D 5
New Cross St. Mgte —3C 208
New Cut. —4C 45
New Cut. Chat —8C 80
New Cut. E Far —1A 138 (2D 27)
New Cut. M'fld —3B 44
New Cut Rd. Chi —6H 175
New Cut Rd. Sell & Chi —2B 30
New Cut Rd. Weav —5G 126 (2E 27)
New Delhi Ho. Maid —3H 139
New Dover Rd. Cant —3N 171 (1D 31)
New Dover Rd. Cap F —4A 174 (2B 42)
Neweden Clo. Maid —3F 126
New Eltham. —7E 56 (4B 6)
Newenden. —2D 45
Newenden Clo. Afrd —3C 160
Newenden Rd. Wain —2N 79
New England La. Sed —4C 44
New England Rd. Tun W —7G 151
New Farm Av. Brom —7K 69
New Forest La. Old L —2B 30
Newgardens. Tey —2K 223
Newgate Gap. Mgte —2E 208
(off Percy Rd.)
Newgate Lwr. Promenade. Mgte —2E 208
Newgate Promenade. Mgte —2E 208
New Hall Clo. Dym —7B 182
New Hall Farm La. Allh —6H 201 (3A 10)
Newham Way. E16 & E6 —2E 5
Newhaven Gdns. SE9 —2N 55
Newhouse. —8J 203
(nr. Leysdown-on-Sea)
New House. —8E 62 (4A 8)
(nr. Northfleet)
New Ho. Clo. Cant —6L 171
New Ho. La. Cant —9J 171 (2D 31)
New Ho. La. Grav —8E 62 (4A 8)
Newhouse La. H'crn —4J 193 (1A 38)
New Ho. La. P'ley —1C 39
Newhouse La. Shel —1A 30
New Ho. La. Wro —7L 105
New Hythe. —6G 108 (4C 17)
New Hythe Bus. Pk. Lark —7F 108
New Hythe Ho. Lark & Ayle —6F 108
New Hythe La. Lark & Ayle —9E 108 (4C 17)
Newick Clo. Bex —4C 58
Newing Clo. L'brne —2K 173
Newingreen. —3C 196 (2D 41)
Newing Grn. Brom —3N 69
Newington. —4A 188 (2E 41)
(nr. Folkestone)
Newington. —3F 210 (2E 23)
(nr. Ramsgate)
Newington. —5K 97 (2B 18)
(nr. Sittingbourne)
Newington Butts. SE11 —3C 5
Newington Causeway. SE1 —3C 5
Newington Enterprise Cen. N'tn —3L 97
Newington Grn. N16 —1D 5
Newington Grn. Rd. N1 —1D 5
Newington Ind. Est. H'lip —5H 97
Newington Meadow. Hythe —5L 197
Newington Rd. N'tn —4A 188 (2E 41)
Newington Rd. Ram —3F 210 (2E 23)
Newington Wlk. Maid —3F 126
New Inn Cotts. E Far —1N 137
(off Forge La.)
Newitt Rd. Hoo —8H 67
New Kent Rd. SE1 —3D 5
New King's Rd. SW6 —3B 4
Newland Green. —4C 29
Newland Grn. La. Eger —4C 28
Newland Rd. S'ness —5A 218
Newlands. —3A 54
Newlands. Afrd —3B 160
Newlands. L'tn G —2A 156
Newlands. St Mar —3D 214
Newlands. Whitf —7G 178
Newlands Av. Sit —7C 98
Newlands Ct. SE9 —4C 56
Newlands Dri. Walm —1L 199
Newlands Farm La. H Hals —1L 67 (3E 9)
Newlands Ho. Ram —2J 211
Newlands La. Broad —1H 211
Newlands La. Meop —1D 106 (3A 16)
Newlands Pk. SE26 —1A 68 (1D 13)
Newlands Rise. Tun W —8G 151
Newlands Rd. Char —3D 29
Newlands Rd. Ram —3H 211
Newlands Rd. Tun W —8G 151
Newland St. E16 —1A 50
Newlands Vs. Tey —4M 223
Newlands Way. Tun W —7H 151
Newlands Wood. New Ad —9C 82
New La. Lydd —3C 204
New Lincoln Houses. Folk —3K 189
New Lydd Rd. Cmbr —4B 46
Newlyn Ct. Maid —5D 126
Newlyn Dri. S'hrst —6K 221
Newlyn Rd. Well —9H 51
Newlyns Meadow. Alk —1B 42
New Malden. —1A 12
Newman Ct. Hythe —7J 197
Newman Dri. Kem —3G 98
Newman Rd. Aysm —2C 162
Newman Rd. Brom —4K 69
Newmans Rd. N'fleet —7E 62
Newmarket Grn. SE9 —5N 55
New Mill Rd. Orp —4L 71
Newnham. —1D 29
Newnham Clo. Gill —1M 95
Newnham La. N'tn —1D 29
Newnham Lodge. Belv —5B 52
Newnhams Clo. Brom —6B 70
Newnham St. Chat —9E 80
New North Rd. N1 —1D 5
New Oxford St. WC1 —2C 4
New Pk. Rd. SW2 —4C 5
New Pl. New Ad —7D 82
New Plaistow Rd. E15 —2E 5
New Pond Rd. Bene —3A 38
Newport Ct. Cant —4A 172
Newports. Swan —1E 86
New Pound. —7G 123
New Pound La. Mere —7G 123 (2B 26)
Newquay Rd. SE6 —7E 54
New Rectory La. Kgnt —5F 160
New Rents. Afrd —8F 158
New Rd. E1 —2D 5
New Rd. SE2 —4M 51 (3B 6)
New Rd. Bur —2D 17
New Rd. Burh —1K 109
New Rd. Cant —9B 166
New Rd. Chat —8C 80 (2D 17)
New Rd. Cli —4B 176
New Rd. C'brk —8B 176
New Rd. Dag & Rain —2C 6
New Rd. Dit —1G 108 (4C 17)
New Rd. E Mal —1E 124 (1C 27)
New Rd. Eger —4C 29
New Rd. Elham —7N 183 (1E 41)
New Rd. Eyt —4K 185
New Rd. Grav —4F 62
New Rd. Grays —3A 8
(in two parts)
New Rd. H'crn —3L 193
New Rd. Hex —3G 72
New Rd. Hythe —7J 197
New Rd. Langl —2M 139 (2A 28)
New Rd. Lgh S —1A 10
New Rd. Limp —2A 24
New Rd. Meop —8E 76
New Rd. Min S —6K 219
New Rd. N'iam —3D 45
New Rd. Orp —1J 85
New Rd. Pad W —9M 147
New Rd. Pens —5H 149 (1D 35)
New Rd. Rain —1N 53
New Rd. Roch —8A 80
New Rd. Rye —3A 46
New Rd. Salt —4J 197
New Rd. S'ness —4B 218 (4C 11)
New Rd. S Dar —5C 74
New Rd. Sund —6M 117 (2B 24)
New Rd. Swan —6G 73
New Rd. Well —9K 51
New Rd. Av. Chat —8B 80 (2D 17)
New Rd. Bus. Est. Dit —1F 124
New Rd. Hill. Bon —3B 40
New Rd. Hill. Kes & Orp —9A 84 (3A 14)
New Rd. Ind. Est. S'ness —3B 218
New Romney. —3B 212 (2E 47)
New Romney Cvn. Site. L'stne —4F 212
New Romney Pl. S'wch —6L 217
New Ruttington La. Cant —1N 171
New Stairs. Chat —6C 80
Newstead Av. Orp —4F 84
Newstead Rd. SE12 —5J 55
New Street. —6C 90 (2A 16)
New St. Ah —5D 216 (4C 22)
New St. Afrd —8F 158 (1A 40)
New St. Chat —9B 80
New St. Deal —3N 177
New St. Dover —5J 181
New St. Folk —6K 189
New St. H Bay —2G 195
New St. Lydd —3C 204
New St. Mgte —3C 208
New St. S'wch —5M 217 (4D 23)
New St. S'ness —3C 218
New St. St D —1L 171
New St. W'ham —9E 116
New St. Whits —3F 224
New St. Win —3L 171
New St. Hill. Brom —1L 69
New St. Rd. Meop & Hods —4B 90 (2A 16)
New Swan Yd. Grav —4G 63
New Tavern Fort. —4H 63
Newton Abbot Rd. N'fleet —7E 62
Newton Av. Tonb —9K 133
Newton Clo. Chat —9F 94
Newton Clo. Maid —6B 126
Newton Gdns. Pad W —8L 147
Newton Ho. SE20 —4A 68
Newton Rd. Fav —6H 187 (3A 20)
Newton Rd. Til —1F 62
Newton Rd. Tun W —1H 157
Newton Rd. Well —1J 57
Newton Rd. Whits —3K 225
Newtons Ct. Dart —2D 60
Newton's Hill. —3B 34
Newtons Hill. Hartf —3B 34
Newton Ter. Brom —9N 69
Newton Willows. Groom —6K 155
New Town. —1H 161
(nr. Ashford)
New Town. —4A 60 (4D 7)
(nr. Dartford)
New Town. —5E 92
(nr. Halling)
New Town. —1M 123
(nr. West Malling)
New Town Grn. Afrd —1H 161
Newtown Rd. Afrd —9G 159 (1A 40)
New Town St. Cant —9N 167
New Town St. Cha H —5C 170 (1C 31)
New Vs. Maid —1N 137
New Wlk. Wro —7M 105
New Wharf Rd. Tonb —6H 145
New Winchelsea Rd. Rye —4A 46
New Years La. Knock —7H 101 (4B 14)
Niagara Ho. Dover —1G 181
(off Toronto Clo.)
Nicholas Clo. Barm —6L 125
Nicholas Dri. C'snd —7B 210
Nicholas Rd. Kenn —3E 158
Nichol La. Brom —3K 69
Nicholls Av. Broad —2K 211
Nicklaus Dri. Chat —8C 94
Nickleby Clo. Roch —1N 93
Nickleby Rd. Grav —6M 63
Nickle La. Cha —5A 170
Nickley Wood Rd. Shad —2E 39
Nicola Ter. Bexh —8N 51
(off Long La.)
Nicolson Rd. Orp —1M 85
Nicolson Way. Sev —4L 119
Niddle St. Deal —3N 177
Niederwald Rd. SE26 —9B 54
Nightingale Av. Hythe —8E 196
Nightingale Av. Whits —7D 224
Nightingale Clo. Big H —3C 164
Nightingale Clo. Cha H —4C 170
Nightingale Clo. Gill —5A 96
Nightingale Clo. Lark —8D 108
Nightingale Clo. N'fleet —8D 62
Nightingale Clo. Svgtn —2M 161
Nightingale Corner. Orp —7M 71
Nightingale Ct. Dover —2G 181
(off Maresfield Clo.)
Nightingale Ct. Short —5H 69
Nightingale Gro. SE13 —3G 54
Nightingale Gro. Dart —2A 60
Nightingale Heights. SE18 —6D 50
Nightingale Ho. SE18 —5C 50
(off Connaught M.)
Nightingale La. SW12 & SW4 —4B 4
Nightingale La. Brom —5M 69 (1A 14)
Nightingale La. Ide H —3C 130 (3C 24)
Nightingale La. Non —3B 32
Nightingale Pl. SE18 —6C 50 (3A 6)
Nightingale Rd. Cars —2B 12
Nightingale Rd. Dover —2H 181
Nightingale Rd. Fav —5G 186
Nightingale Rd. Kems —8L 103
Nightingale Rd. Orp —9E 70
Nightingales, The. Bidd —2A 38
Nightingale Vale. SE18 —6C 50
Nightingale Way. Swan —6F 72
Nile Path. SE18 —6C 50
Nile Rd. Gill —8F 80
Nineacres. Kenn —5G 159
Nine Acres Rd. Cux —9F 78
Nine Ash La. Bou B —9N 187 (4B 20)
Nine Elms. —3C 4
Nine Elms Gro. Grav —5F 62
Nine Elms La. SW8 —3C 4
Ninehams Rd. Tats —9C 164
Nineveh La. Bene —3E 37
Ninhams Wood. Orp —5C 84
Ninn Cotts. Afrd —9A 158
Ninn La. Gt Cha —9A 158 (1E 39)
Nita Ct. SE12 —6K 55
Nithdale Rd. SE18 —7D 50
Niven Clo. Wain —2N 79
Nixon Av. Ram —2G 210
Nizels. —3D 25
Nizels La. Hild —7M 131 (3D 25)
Noah's Ark. —1B 120 (1D 25)
Noah's Ark. Kems —9A 104 (4D 15)
Noah's Ark Rd. Dover —4F 180
Noah's Ark Ter. Dover —4G 181
Noakes Meadow. Afrd —1D 160
Nobel Clo. Tey —2K 223
Nobel Ct. Fav —5F 186
Noble Ct. Mgte —3M 207
Noble Gdns. Mgte —3M 207
Noble Tree Rd. Hild —1B 144 (3D 25)
Noel Rd. W3 —2A 4
Noel Ter. Sidc —9K 57
Noke Street. —9N 65
No Name St. S'wch —5L 217
Nonington. —3B 32
Nonington Ct. Non —2B 32
Nonsuch Clo. Cant —2B 172
Nook, The. Ram —1G 211
Nook, The. Yald —6D 136
Norah La. High —9F 64
Norbiton. —1A 12
Norbury. —1C 13
Norbury Av. SW16 & T Hth —1C 13
Norbury Cres. SW16 —1C 13
Nordenfeldt Rd. Eri —5E 52
Noreen Av. Min S —6H 219
Norfield Rd. Dart —9D 58
Norfolk Clo. Chat —8F 94
Norfolk Clo. Dart —3A 60
Norfolk Clo. Gill —1N 95
Norfolk Cres. Sidc —5G 56
Norfolk Dri. Afrd —8E 158
Norfolk Gdns. Bexh —8A 52
Norfolk Pl. Well —9J 51
Norfolk Rd. Cant —4L 171
Norfolk Rd. Flete —8B 208
Norfolk Rd. Grav —4J 63
(in two parts)
Norfolk Rd. Maid —9F 126
Norfolk Rd. Mgte —3F 208
Norfolk Rd. Tonb —6G 145
Norfolk Rd. Tun W —3H 157
Norfolk St. Whits —5F 224
Norham Ct. Dart —4B 60
(off Osbourne Rd.)
Norheads La. Warl & Big H —7A 164 (4A 14)
Nork. —4A 12
Norlands Cres. Chst —4D 70
Norman Clo. Gill —7L 95
Norman Clo. Kems —8L 103
Norman Clo. Maid —3E 126
Norman Clo. Orp —4E 84
Norman Clo. Roch —8K 79
Norman Ct. Eden —5B 184
Normandy Way. Eri —8F 52
Normanhurst Av. Bexh —8M 51
Normanhurst Rd. Bor G —2N 121
Normanhurst Rd. Orp —5K 71
Norman Rise. C'brk —8D 176
Norman Rd. DA17 —1C 52
Norman Rd. SE10 —3E 5
Norman Rd. Afrd —2F 160 (1A 40)
Norman Rd. Belv —3C 52
Norman Rd. Broad —7J 209
Norman Rd. Cant —3M 171
Norman Rd. Dart —6M 59
Norman Rd. E'chu —2F 202
Norman Rd. Fav —5G 187
Norman Rd. Ram —6F 210
Norman Rd. Snod —4E 108
Norman Rd. St Mb —7L 213
Norman Rd. Tun W —1H 157
Norman Rd. Wgte S —2L 207
Norman Rd. W Mal —9M 107 (4B 16)
Norman Rd. Whits —5F 224
Norman's Clo. Grav —5F 62
Norman St. Dover —4J 181
Norman Tailyour Ho. Deal —5N 177
(off Hope Rd.)
Normanton St. SE23 —7A 54
Normanwood Ct. S'ness —2E 218
(off Unity St.)
Norreys Rd. Gill —4A 96
Norrie Rd. Birch —5F 206
Norrington Mead. Folk —4G 189
Norrington Rd. Maid —2D 138
Norris Way. Dart —1G 59
Norstead Gdns. Tun W —7H 151
Norsted La. Prat B —3J 101 (3B 14)
North Acton. —2A 4
N. Acton Rd. NW10 —2A 4
Northall Rd. Bexh —9D 52 (3C 7)
N. Ash Rd. New Ash —4L 89 (2A 16)
N. Audley St. W1 —2C 4

Oakwood Rise—Ottawa Way

Oakwood Rise. Long —6L 75
Oakwood Rise. Tun W —6L 151
Oakwood Rd. Maid —6N 125 (2D 27)
Oakwood Rd. Orp —3E 84
Oakwood Rd. Sturry —4F 168
Oare. —2F 186 (3A 20)
Oare Rd. Fav —2F 186 (3A 20)
Oasis, The. Brom —5M 69
Oast Clo. Tun W —7K 151
Oast Cotts. Cant —3L 171
Oast Cotts. Sev —4H 119
Oast Cotts. W'hm —3B 226
Oast Ct. Mgte —5D 208
Oast Ct. Sit —9F 98
Oast Ct. Yald —7D 136
Oasthouse Field. Ivy —2D 47
Oasthouse Way. Orp —7K 71
Oast La. Throw —2E 29
Oast La. Tonb —3G 144
Oast Meadow. W'boro —9K 159
Oast, The. Cant —4A 172
Oast View. Horsm —2C 198
Oastview. Rain —3C 96
Oast Way. Hart —9L 75
Oaten Hill. Cant —3N 171 (1D 31)
Oaten Hill Pl. Cant —3N 171 (1D 31)
Oates Clo. Brom —6G 69
Oatfield Clo. C'brk —7C 176
Oatfield Dri. C'brk —7C 176
Oatfield Rd. Orp —2H 85
Occupation La. SE18 —8D 50
Occupation Rd. Wye —2N 159
Ocean Clo. Birch —3G 207
Ocean Ter. Ley S —6J 203
Ocean Ter. Min S —5L 219
Ocean View. Broad —3L 211
Ocean View. H Bay —1M 195
Ocelot Ct. Chat —9E 80
Ockendon Rd. Upm —1E 7
Ockham. —2C 44
Ockham Dri. Orp —3J 71
Ockley. —4L 191
Ockley Ct. Sidc —8G 57
Ockley La. Hawkh —3L 191
Ockley Rd. Hawkh —5L 191
Octavia Ct. Chat —8E 94
Octavian Dri. Lymp —5B 196
Odiham Dri. Maid —2N 125
Odo Rd. Dover —4H 181
Offenham Rd. SE9 —9B 56
Offen's Dri. S'hrst —8J 221
Offham. —2J 123 (1B 26)
Offham Rd. W Mal —2L 123 (1B 26)
Officer's Rd. Chat —4E 80
Officers Ter. Chat —6C 80
(off Church La.)
Offley Clo. Mgte —4G 209
Offord Rd. N1 —1C 5
Ogilby St. SE18 —4B 50
Ogilvy Ct. Broad —6J 209
Okehampton Clo. Kenn —3K 159
Okehampton Cres. Well —8K 51 (3B 6)
Okemore Gdns. Orp —7L 71
Olantigh Ct. Birch —4F 206
Olantigh Rd. Wye —2N 159 (4B 30)
Olave Rd. Mgte —4E 208
Old Ash Clo. Kenn —5G 158
Old Ashford Rd. Char —3K 175
Old Ashford Rd. Len —7E 200 (2C 29)
Old Badgins Rd. Shel —1A 30
Old Bakery Clo. St Mar —2E 214
Old Barn Clo. Hem —5J 95
Old Barn Clo. Kems —8A 104
Old Barn Clo. Tonb —7F 144
Old Barn Rd. Leyb —8B 108
Old Barn Way. Bexh —2E 58
Old Bethnal Grn. Rd. E2 —2D 5
Old Bexley. —5C 58 (4C 6)
Old Bexley Bus. Pk. Bex —5C 58
Old Bexley La. Bex & Dart —7E 58 (4C 7)
(in two parts)
Old Billet La. E'chu —3B 202
Old Boundary Rd. Wgte S —2L 207
Old Bri. Rd. Whits —4G 224 (2C 21)
Old Bromley Rd. Brom —1G 69
Old Brompton Rd. SW5 & SW7 —3B 4
Oldbury. —3H 121 (1E 25)
Oldbury. —4G 120
Oldbury Clo. Igh —4H 121
Oldbury Clo. Orp —7L 71
Oldbury Cotts. Sev —3H 121
Oldbury La. Igh —3H 121 (1E 25)
Oldbury Vs. Igh —4H 121
Old Carriage Way, The. Gill —7J 95
Old Carriageway, The. Sev —4D 118
Old Castle Wlk. Gill —7N 95
Old Chapel Rd. Swan —1D 86 (2C 15)
Old Charlton Rd. Dover —2J 181 (1C 43)
Old Chatham Rd. Blue B —3A 110 (4D 17)
Old Chatham Rd. S'lng —5B 110 (3D 17)
Oldchurch Ct. Maid —6B 126
Old Chu. Hill. Lang H —1B 8
Old Chu. La. NW9 —1A 4
Old Chu. La. E Peck —3K 135
Old Chu. Rd. Burh —9G 92 (3C 17)
Old Chu. Rd. Mere —3J 135
(in two parts)
Old Chu. Rd. Pem —4C 152 (1A 36)
Old Chu. Rd. Ton —2B 26
Old Coach Rd. Wro —5L 105
Old Cotts. Maid —7B 126
Old Cotts. Sev —4H 121
Old Coulsdon. —4C 13
Old Ct. Hill. Aysm —1F 162 (2B 32)
Old Courtyard, The. Brom —4L 69
Old Crossing Rd. Mgte —2N 207
Old Cryals. —1B 36
Old Dairy Clo. Ram —5K 211
Old Dartford Rd. F'ham —9N 73
Old Dover Rd. SE3 —3A 6
Old Dover Rd. Cant —3N 171 (1D 31)
Old Dover Rd. Cap F —3B 174 (2B 42)
Old Downs. Hart —8L 75
Old Dri. Maid —2C 138
Old Farley Rd. S Croy & Warl —3D 13
Old Farm Av. Sidc —6F 56
Old Farm Clo. Whits —7E 224
Old Farm Gdns. Swan —6G 72
Old Farm Rd. Birch —4C 206
Old Farm Rd. E. Sidc —7J 57
Old Farm Rd. W. Sidc —7H 57
Old Ferry Rd. Iwade —7C 198 (1C 19)
Oldfield Clo. Brom —7B 70
Oldfield Clo. Gill —3N 95
Oldfield Clo. Maid —8H 127
Oldfield Rd. Bexh —9N 51
Oldfield Rd. Brom —7B 70
Oldfields Rd. Sutt —2B 12
Old Fold. Ches —5L 225
Old Folkestone Rd. Dover —8F 180
Old Ford. —2E 5
Old Ford. (Junct.) —2E 5
Old Ford Rd. E2 & E3 —2D 5
Old Forge La. S Grn —6H 113 (4B 18)
Old Forge Way. Sidc —9K 57
Old Gdns. Clo. Tun W —5H 157
Old Garden, The. Sev —5E 118
Old Ga. Rd. Fav —5F 186
Old Grn. Rd. Broad —6K 209
Old Grn. Rd. Mgte —4G 208
Old Hadlow Rd. Tonb —3L 145
Old Hall Dri. C'snd —7A 210
Old Ham La. Len —9B 200 (3C 28)
Old Harrow La. W'ham —1E 116
Oldhawe Hill. H Bay —7K 195
Old Hay. Bchly —1C 36
Old High St., The. Folk —6K 189
Old Hill. Chst —4C 70 (1A 14)
Old Hill. Orp —7F 84 (3B 14)
Old Hockley Rd. Stal —2E 29
Old Homesdale Rd. Brom —7M 69
Old Hook Rd. Min S —9N 219
Oldhouse La. B'Ind —2C 46
Old Ho. La. Ford —1K 155 (2D 35)
Old Ho. La. H'lip —7G 96 (3B 18)
Old Kent Rd. SE1 & SE15 —3D 5
Old Kent Rd. Pad W —9L 147
Old Kingsdown Clo. Broad —1J 211
Old Lain. H'shm —6A 200
Old La. Igh —5H 121
Old La. St Jhn —4D 35
Old La. Tats —8D 164 (1A 24)
Old Laundry, The. Chst —4E 70
Old Lenham Rd. Wich & Dod —2C 29
Old Lodge La. Purl —3C 13
Old London Rd. Badg M —9A 86 (3C 14)
Old London Rd. Eps —4A 12
Old London Rd. Hythe —6F 196
Old London Rd. Knock —6N 101 (4C 14)
Old London Rd. Sidc —3B 72
Old London Rd. Tonb —4J 145
Old London Rd. Wro —6M 105 (4A 16)
Old Loose Clo. Loose —4C 138
Old Loose Hill. Loose —4C 138 (3D 27)
Old Maidstone Rd. Sidc —3A 72 (1C 14)
Old Malden. —2A 12
Old Malden La. Wor Pk —2A 12
Old Manor Cotts. Bear —5M 127
(off Green, The)
Old Mnr. Dri. Grav —6H 63
Old Mnr. Way. Bexh —9E 52
Old Mnr. Way. Chst —1B 70
Old Marylebone Rd. NW1 —2B 4
Old Mead. Folk —4G 189
Old Mill Clo. Eyns —2M 87
Old Mill Cotts. Holl —8B 128
Old Mill La. Ayle —7N 109
Old Mill Rd. SE18 —6F 50
Old Mill Rd. Holl —9B 128 (2A 28)
Old Oak Common. —2A 4
Old Oak Comn. La. NW10 & W3 —2A 4
Old Oak La. NW10 —2A 4
Old Oak Rd. W3 —2A 4
Old Oast Bus. Cen., The. Ayle —9L 109
Old Orchard. Afrd —1B 160
Old Orchard. Charc —4H 143
Old Orchard. Sand —3J 215
Old Orchard La. Leyb —9B 108
Old Orchard, The. Rain —2C 96
Old Otford Rd. Sev —8J 103
(in two parts)
Old Pal. Rd. Pat —7H 173 (2E 31)
Old Park. —8F 178
Old Pk. Av. Cant —9B 168
Old Pk. Av. Dover —1F 180
Old Pk. Clo. Whitf —9F 178
Old Pk. Ct. Cant —9B 168
Old Pk. Hill. Dover —1F 180
Old Pk. Rd. SE2 —5J 51
Old Pk. Rd. Dover —2G 180
Old Parsonage Ct. W Mal —2A 124
Old Parsonage Yd., The. Hort K —7C 74
Old Pattens La. Roch —9A 80
Old Perry St. Chst —2G 70
Old Perry St. N'fleet —7D 62
Old Polhill. Sev —5D 102
Old Pond Rd. Afrd —9D 158
Old Rectory Clo. H'nge —8D 192
Old Regent Dri. Rol —3J 213
Old Rd. SE13 —2H 55
Old Rd. Chat —8C 80
Old Rd. Dart —3E 58 (4C 7)
Old Rd. E Peck —1L 147 (3B 26)
Old Rd. Elham —7N 183 (1E 41)
Old Rd. Sarre —2B 22
Old Rd. W'bury —1N 135 (2B 26)
Old Rd. E. Grav —6G 63 (4B 8)
Old Rd. W. Grav —6E 62 (4A 8)
Old Roman Rd. Mart H —4D 33
Old Romney. —2D 47
Old Royal Observatory. —3E 5
Oldroyd Ho. Cant —1K 171
Old Ruttington La. Cant —1N 171 (4D 21)
Old Ryarsh La. W Mal —9N 107
Old Saltwood La. Salt —4J 197
Old School Clo. Beck —5B 68
Old School Clo. Burh —1K 109
Old School Clo. Len —8E 200
Old School Ct. Chatt —9C 66
Old School Ct. Eger —4C 29
Old School Ct. Folk —7H 189
Old School Ct. Sev —4K 119
Old School Gdns. Mgte —4E 208
Old School Ho. Eden —6C 184
Old Schoolhouse La. Old R —2D 47
Old School La. Rya —6L 107
Old School M. Cha —8C 170
Old Soar Manor. —8A 122
Old Soar Rd. Plax —9A 122 (2A 26)
Oldstairs Rd. Kgdn —7M 199 (4E 33)
Old Station Rd. Wadh —3A 36
Oldstead Rd. Brom —9F 54
Old St. EC1 —2D 5
Old Street. (Junct.) —2D 5
Old Surrenden Mnr. Rd. Beth —2K 163 (1D 39)
Old Tannery Clo. Tent —8A 222
Old Terry's Lodge Rd. Sev —7F 104 (4E 15)
Old Tovil Rd. Maid —7C 126 (2D 27)
Old Town. SW4 —4C 4
Old Town. Croy —2C 13
Old Town Gaol. —4J 181
Old Trafford Clo. Maid —3M 125
Old Tree. —2A 22
Old Tree La. Bou M —5F 138 (3E 27)
Old Tree Rd. Hoath —9M 195 (2A 22)
Old Tye Av. Big H —4E 164
Old Valley Rd. B'hm —8D 162
Old Vicarage, The. Wdboro —7H 217
Old Vinters Rd. Maid —5E 126
Old Wlk., The. Otf —8K 103
Old Watling St. Grav —1F 76
Old Watling St. Roch —4F 78 (1C 17)
Old Way. App —1B 46
Old Well Ct. Maid —7B 126
Old Wives Lees. —6K 175 (2B 30)
Old Yews, The. Long —6A 76
Oleander Clo. Orp —6F 84
Olive Gro. Ram —4K 211
Oliver Clo. Chat —1E 94
Oliver Ct. SE18 —4E 50
Oliver Cres. F'ham —1N 87
Olive Rd. Dart —6L 59
Oliver Rd. E10 —1E 5
Oliver Rd. Grays —3E 7
Oliver Rd. S'hrst —7J 221
Oliver Rd. Swan —6E 72
Olivers Cotts. Bear —5M 127
Olivers Mill. New Ash —3L 89
Oliver Twist Clo. Roch —8M 79
Olivine Clo. Chat —2D 110
Olliffe Clo. Chat —9C 94
Olron Cres. Bexh —3M 57
Olven Rd. SE18 —6E 50
Olyffe Av. Well —8J 51
Olyffe Dri. Beck —4F 68
(in two parts)
Olympia. —3B 4
Omer Av. Clift —3G 209
O'Neill Path. SE18 —6C 50
One Tree Hill. Stan H & Bas —1C 8
One Tree Hill. —1C 132
Ongley La. Bidd —7H 163 (2A 38)
Onslow Cres. Chst —4D 70
Onslow Dri. Sidc —7M 57
Onslow Rd. Roch —9A 80
Onslow Sq. SW7 —3B 4
Ontario Way. Dover —1G 181
Opal Grn. Chat —9E 94
Openshaw Rd. SE2 —4K 51
Orache Dri. Weav —4H 127
Orange Ct. La. Orp —9C 84
Orangery La. SE9 —3B 56
Orange St. Cant —2M 171 (1D 31)
Orange Ter. Roch —7A 80
Orbital One. Dart —7B 60
Orbital One Ind. Est. Dart —7A 60
Orbital Pk. W'boro —3K 161
Orbit Clo. Chat —2D 110
Orchard Av. Ayle —9J 109
Orchard Av. Belv —6N 51
Orchard Av. Croy —2B 82 (2E 13)
Orchard Av. Dart —5J 59
Orchard Av. Deal —5L 177
Orchard Av. Grav —1G 76
Orchard Av. Roch —3K 79
Orchard Bank. Cha S —7L 139
Orchard Bus. Cen. SE26 —1C 68
Orchard Bus. Cen. All —1N 125
Orchard Bus. Cen. Tonb —6L 145
Orchard Bus. Cen. Tun W —6K 151
Orchard Bus. Pk. Five G —9H 147
Orchard Cvn. Pk. Burm —3C 182
Orchard Clo. Bexh —8N 51
Orchard Clo. Cant —7M 167
Orchard Clo. Cox —5N 137
Orchard Clo. Eden —5B 184
Orchard Clo. Horsm —2B 198
Orchard Clo. Langl —4A 140
Orchard Clo. L'brne —3L 173
Orchard Clo. Long —5A 76
Orchard Clo. Maid —6D 126
Orchard Clo. Mer —9M 161
Orchard Clo. Min —6M 205
Orchard Clo. Ram —1F 210
Orchard Clo. Sev —2K 119
Orchard Clo. Whitf —5E 178
Orchard Clo. Whits —2H 225
Orchard Clo. W'hm —3B 226
Orchard Cotts. Bou B —3K 165
Orchard Cotts. Maid —9L 125
Orchard Ct. Bene —3A 38
Orchard Ct. H Bay —6G 195
Orchard Cres. Horsm —2C 198
Orchard Dri. Afrd —6D 158
Orchard Dri. Dover —1D 180
Orchard Dri. Eden —5B 184
Orchard Dri. Hythe —7J 197
Orchard Dri. Meop —8E 76
Orchard Dri. N'tn —6J 97
Orchard Dri. Tonb —2L 145
Orchard Dri. Weav —6H 127
Orchard Dri. Wye —3N 159
Orchard Field. Beth —2J 163
Orchard Fields. Hythe —2D 41
Orchard Flats. Cant —3C 172
Orchard Gdns. Mgte —2M 207
Orchard Glade. H'crn —3L 193
Orchard Grn. Orp —3G 85
Orchard Gro. Croy —1B 82
Orchard Gro. Dit —8F 108
Orchard Gro. Min S —6K 219
Orchard Gro. Orp —3H 85
Orchard Heights. Afrd —5D 158
Orchard Hill. Dart —3F 58
Orchard Ho. E'try —2K 183
Orchard Ho. Eri —8G 52
Orchard Ind. Est. Maid —5J 139
Orchard La. C'lck —7D 174
Orchard La. Kenn —4K 159
Orchard La. St N —9E 214 (2B 22)
Orchard Lea. Hild —2F 144
Orchard Lea. S'fleet —1M 75
Orchard M. Deal —5N 177
Orchard Pk. Homes. H Bay —3L 195
Orchard Pl. Fav —5H 187
Orchard Pl. Maid —6B 126
Orchard Pl. Orp —6L 71
Orchard Pl. Sit —8H 99
Orchard Pl. Sund —6N 117
Orchard Rise. Croy —2B 82
Orchard Rise. Groom —7J 155
Orchard Rise E. Sidc —3H 57
Orchard Rise W. Sidc —3G 56
Orchard Rd. SE18 —4F 50
Orchard Rd. Belv —4B 52
Orchard Rd. Brom —4M 69
Orchard Rd. E Peck —1M 147
Orchard Rd. E'try —2K 183
Orchard Rd. Farn —6D 84
Orchard Rd. H Bay —4G 195
Orchard Rd. L'stne —3F 212
Orchard Rd. Mgte —3M 207
Orchard Rd. N'fleet —7B 62
Orchard Rd. Otf —7G 102
Orchard Rd. Prat B —1L 101
Orchard Rd. Sev —4F 118
Orchard Rd. Sidc —9G 57
Orchard Rd. St Mar —2F 214
Orchard Rd. St Mic —4B 222
Orchard Rd. Swans —3L 61
Orchard Rd. Well —1K 57
Orchard Row. H Bay —7H 195
Orchards, The. Dart —4M 59
Orchards, The. Elham —7N 183
Orchard St. Cant —1L 171 (4D 21)
Orchard St. Dart —4M 59
Orchard St. Gill —4A 96
Orchard St. Maid —6D 126
Orchard, The. Bear —5L 127
Orchard, The. Dun G —3F 118
Orchard, The. Swan —5E 72
Orchard Theatre, Dartford. —4M 59
Orchard Valley. —5H 197
Orchard Valley. Hythe —6H 197
Orchard View. Ah —5E 216
Orchard View. Tey —1K 223
Orchard Vs. Chat —9C 80
Orchard Vs. Sturry —6E 168
Orchard Way. C'brk —8B 176
Orchard Way. Croy & Beck —1B 82 (2E 13)
Orchard Way. Dart —8L 59
Orchard Way. E'chu —7C 202
Orchard Way. Horsm —3C 198
Orchard Way. Kems —8A 104
Orchard Way. Snod —3D 108
Orchid Clo. Roch —6G 78
Orchidhurst Tun W —7K 151
Orchid Pk. Roch —9A 80
Orchids, The. Mer —8M 161
Ordnance Cres. SE10 —3E 5
Ordnance Rd. SE18 —6C 50
Ordnance Rd. Grav —4H 63
Ordnance St. Chat —9B 80
Ordnance Ter. Chat —8B 80
Oregon Sq. Orp —2F 84
Orford Ct. Dart —4B 60
(off Osbourne Rd.)
Orford Rd. SE6 —8E 54
Organ Crossroads. (Junct.) —3A 12
Orgarswick Av. Dym —8A 182
Orgarswick Way. Dym —8B 182
Oriel Ho. Roch —7N 79
Oriel Rd. Afrd —6D 158
Orient Pl. Cant —1M 171
Oriole Way. Lark —8D 108
Orion Rd. Roch —4N 93
Orion Way. W'boro —1J 161
Orissa Rd. SE18 —5G 50
Orlestone. —3E 39
Orlestone Gdns. Orp —6N 85
Orlick Rd. Grav —6N 63
Ormonde Av. Orp —3E 84
Ormonde Ct. Hythe —7K 197
Ormonde Rd. Folk —5L 189
Ormonde Rd. Hythe —7K 197
Ormsby Grn. Gill —8A 96
Orpines, The. W'bury —1D 136
Orpington. —2J 85 (2B 14)
Orpington By-Pass. Orp —3K 85
Orpington By-Pass Rd. Orp & Bad M —9B 86 (3C 14)
Orpington Retail Pk. Orp —7L 71
Orpington Rd. Chst —6G 71 (1B 14)
Orsett. —2A 8
Orsett Heath. —2B 8
Orsett Rd. Grays —3A 8
Orsett Rd. Ors & Stan H —2B 8
Orwell Clo. Lark —7D 108
Orwell Ho. Maid —9H 127
Orwell Spike. W Mal —4M 123
Osberton Rd. SE12 —3K 55
Osborne Clo. Beck —7B 68
Osborne Gdns. H Bay —2L 195
Osborne Rd. Belv —5A 52
Osborne Rd. Broad —9K 209 (2E 23)
Osborne Rd. W'boro —9J 159
Osborne Ter. Mgte —4D 208
Osborn La. SE23 —5B 54
Osborn Ter. SE3 —2J 55
Osbourn Av. Wgte S —3K 207
Osbourne Dri. Det —8M 111
Osbourne Rd. Dart —4B 60
Osbourne Rd. Gill —7G 80
Osbourne Rd. Kgdn —3M 199
Oscar Rd. Broad —9M 209
Osgood Av. Orp —6H 85
Osgood Gdns. Orp —6H 85
Osier Field. Kenn —3J 159
Osier Rd. Tey —1M 223 (3E 19)
Oslac Rd. SE6 —1E 68
Osmers Hill. Spar G —3A 36
Osney Ho. SE2 —2M 51
Osney Way. Grav —7L 63
Osprey Clo. Whits —6E 224
Osprey Ct. Beck —3D 68
Osprey Ct. Dover —2G 181
Osprey Ct. Sit —8H 99
Osprey Wlk. Lark —9D 108
Ospringe. —6E 186 (3A 20)
Ospringe Pl. Fav —6F 186
Ospringe Pl. Tun W —8M 151
Ospringe Rd. Fav —6E 186 (3A 20)
Ospringe St. Fav —6E 186 (3A 20)
Ostend Ct. Kem —2G 98
Osterberg Rd. Dart —2N 59
Osterley Clo. Orp —4J 71
Ostlers Clo. Snod —2E 108
Ostlers Ct. High —7G 64
Ostlers La. Sarre —2B 22
Oswald Pl. Dover —2G 180
Oswald Rd. Dover —2G 180
Osward. Croy —9C 82
Otford. —7J 103 (4D 15)
Otford Clo. Bex —4C 58
Otford Clo. Brom —6C 70
Otford Cres. SE4 —4C 54
Otford La. Hals —3A 102 (3C 14)
Otford Rd. Sev —1J 119 (1D 25)
Otham. —1L 139 (2E 27)
Otham Clo. Cant —7N 167
Otham Hole. —2M 139 (2A 28)
Otham La. Bear —7M 127 (2A 28)
Otham St. Otham & Bear —1L 139 (2E 27)
Otlinge Clo. Orp —7M 71
Ottawa Cres. Dover —1H 181
Ottawa Way. Dover —1G 181
(off Selkirk Rd.)

Parsonage Cotts.—Pikefields

Parsonage Cotts. *Wdboro* —7G **216**
Parsonage Ct. *W Mal* —1A **124**
Parsonage Farm. —4E **31**
Parsonage Fields. *Monk* —2C **22**
Parsonage La. *Bob* —3A **98** (2C **18**)
Parsonage La. *Bre* —5A **114**
Parsonage La. *Lam* —1D **200** (2B **36**)
Parsonage La. *Roch* —3N **79**
Parsonage La. *Sidc* —9A **58** (1C **14**)
Parsonage La. *S at H* —2B **74**
Parsonage La. *Westf* —4C **45**
Parsonage Manorway. *Belv* —6B **52** (3C **6**)
Parsonage Rd. *H Bay* —4H **195**
Parsonage Rd. *Tun W* —9B **150**
Parsonage Stocks Rd. *Throw* —2E **29**
Parsonage, The. St Mc —7J **213**
(off High St. St Margaret's At Cliffe,)
Parsonage Vs. *Chu H* —7B **180**
Parsons Green. —3B 4
Parson's Grn. La. *SW6* —3B **4**
Parsons La. *Dart* —8J **59** (4D **7**)
Parsons La. *Stans* —1L **105**
Parsons Mead. *Croy* —2C **13**
Parsons Way. *Dover* —1F **180**
Partridge Av. *Lark* —7D **108**
Partridge Dri. *Orp* —4E **84**
Partridge Grn. *SE9* —8C **56**
Partridge La. *Fav* —4H **187**
Partridge Rd. *Sidc* —9G **56**
Partridges La. *Wadh* —3A **36**
Pascoe Rd. *SE13* —3G **54**
Pashley Manor. —1A **44**
Pashley Rd. *Tic* —4C **36**
Pasley Rd. *Gill* —6D **80**
Pasley Rd. E. *Chat* —5E **80**
Pasley Rd. N. *Chat* —5E **80**
Pasley Rd. W. *Chat* —5D **80**
Passage, The. Mgte —2D **208**
(off Zion Pl.)
Passey Pl. *SE9* —4B **56**
Passfields. *SE6* —8F **54**
Paston Cres. *SE12* —5L **55**
Pasture Rd. *SE6* —6J **55**
Pasture, The. *Kenn* —4H **159** (4A **30**)
Patch, The. *Sev* —4F **118**
Patchways. *Newch* —4B **40**
Pathway, The. *Broad* —8M **209**
Patience Cotts. *Weald* —6J **131**
Patmos Rd. *SW9* —3C **5**
Patricia Ct. *Chst* —4F **70**
Patricia Ct. *Well* —7K **51**
Patricia Way. *Pys R* —1G **211**
Patrixbourne. —7G 173 (2E 31)
Patrixbourne Av. *Gill* —1M **95**
Patrixbourne Rd. *Bri* —8H **173** (2E **31**)
Patrol Pl. *SE6* —4E **54**
Pattenden Gdns. *E Peck* —9M **135**
Pattenden La. *Mard* —1J **205** (4D **27**)
Pattenden Rd. *SE6* —6C **54**
Pattens Gdns. *Roch* —1A **94**
Pattens La. *Chat* —1A **94**
Pattens La. *Roch* —2D **17**
Pattens Pl. *Roch* —1A **94**
Patterdale Clo. *Brom* —2J **69**
Patterdale Rd. *Dart* —6D **60**
Patterson Clo. *Deal* —6K **177**
Patterson Ct. *Dart* —3A **60**
Pattison Farm Clo. *Adgtn* —2B **40**
Pattison Wlk. *SE18* —5E **50**
Paulinus Clo. *Orp* —5L **71**
Paul's Pl. *Dover* —3H **181**
Paul St. *EC2* —2D **5**
Pavement, The. *St Mic* —4C **222**
Pavilion Clo. *Deal* —2M **177**
Pavilion Ct. *Folk* —7L **189**
Pavilion Dri. *Kem* —2G **98**
Pavilion Gdns. *Sev* —6J **119**
Pavilion La. *Mere* —9M **123**
Pavilion Meadow. *Dover* —9D **178**
Pavilion Rd. *Folk* —5K **189** (2A **42**)
Pavings, The. *Holl* —7E **128**
Pavilion, The. *Tonb* —6H **145**
Pawsons Rd. *Croy* —2D **13**
Paxton Ct. SE26 —9B **54**
(off Adamsrill Rd.)
Paxton Rd. *SE23* —8B **54**
Paxton Rd. *Brom* —3K **69**
Payden Street. —2C 29
Payden St. *Wich & War S* —2D **29**
Payers Pk. *Folk* —6K **189**
Paygate Rd. *Sed* —4C **44**
Paynell Ct. *SE3* —1H **55**
Paynes Cotts. *Sev* —9E **102**
Paynesfield Rd. *Tats* —9C **164**
Payne's La. *Maid* —1D **138**
Pay St. *Dens* —5B **192** (1A **42**)
Payton Clo. *Mgte* —7E **208**
Payton M. *Cant* —1A **172**
Peace Cotts. *Maid* —9H **137**
Peace St. *SE18* —6C **50**
Peach Croft. *N'fleet* —8C **62**
Peacock M. *Maid* —5B **126**
Peacock St. *Grav* —5H **63**
Peafield Wood Rd. *Blad* —4E **31**
Peak Dri. *E'try* —2K **183**
Pea La. *Upm* —1E **7**
Peal Clo. *Hoo* —8H **67**
Peal Ter. *Tonb* —3L **145**
Pean Ct. Rd. *Whits* —3C **21**
Pean Hill. *Whits* —1D **166** (3C **21**)
Peareswood Rd. *Eri* —8G **52**
Pearfield Rd. *SE23* —8B **54**
Pearmain Wlk. Cant —3B **172**
(off Fiesta Way)
Pearman Clo. *Gill* —2C **96**
Pearse Pl. *Lam* —2D **200**
Pearsons Cotts. *Whits* —3F **224**
Pearson's Green. —1C 36
Pearson's Grn. Rd. *Bchly* —1C **36**
Pearson's Way. *Broad* —6J **209**
Pearson Way. *Dart* —7N **59**
Pear Tree All. Sit —6F **98**
(off St Paul's St.)
Pear Tree Av. *C'brk* —9D **176**
Pear Tree Av. *Dit* —9G **109**
Pear Tree Clo. *Broad* —9G **209**
Peartree Clo. *Eri* —8E **52**
Pear Tree Clo. *Swan* —5E **72**
Pear Tree Ho. *SE4* —2C **54**
Pear Tree La. *Dym* —6C **182**
Pear Tree La. *Hem* —3H **95**
Pear Tree La. *H'std* —2E **17**
Pear Tree La. *Maid* —2E **138**
Peartree La. *Shorne* —3C **78** (1C **16**)
Peartree Pl. *High* —1F **78**
Peartree Rd. *H Bay* —5J **195**
Pear Tree Row. *Langl* —3L **139**
Pear Tree Wlk. *N'tn* —6J **97**
Pease Hill. *As* —7L **89** (3A **16**)
Peasley La. *Goud* —2C **37**
Peasmarsh. —3E 45
Peatfield Clo. *Sidc* —8G **57**
Peat Way. *Isle G* —2A **190**
Peckham. —3D 5
Peckham Bush. —8K 135 (3B 26)
Peckham Clo. *Roch* —4N **79**
Peckham Ct. *E Peck* —1L **147**
Peckham High St. *SE15* —3D **5**
Peckham Hill St. *SE15* —3D **5**
Peckham Hurst. —1E 134
Peckham Hurst Rd. *Rough* —2D **134**
Peckham Hurst Rd. *W Peck* —2A **26**
Peckham Pk. Rd. *SE15* —3D **5**
Peckham Rd. *SE5 & SE15* —3D **5**
Peckham Rye. *SE15 & SE22* —4D **5**
(in two parts)
Peckham Wlk. Av. *Plax* —1K **133**
Pedding Hill. *W'hm* —1D **226** (4B **22**)
Pedham Pl. Ind. Est. *Swan* —9H **73**
Pedlinge. —4E 196 (3D 41)
Peel Dri. *Sit* —7K **99**
Peel Rd. *Orp* —6E **84**
Peel St. *Maid* —3D **126**
Peel St. Hedges. *Maid* —2D **126**
Peene. —3B 188 (2E 41)
Peene Cotts. *Peene* —2B **188**
Peening Quarter. —1E 45
Peens La. *Bou M* —8F **138** (3E **27**)
Pegasus Ct. *Grav* —8H **63**
Peggoty Clo. *High* —1F **78**
Pegley Gdns. *SE12* —7K **55**
Pegwell. —7E 210 (2E 23)
Pegwell Av. *Ram* —7E **210**
Pegwell Bay Cvn. Pk. *Ram* —7E **210**
Pegwell Clo. *Ram* —7E **210**
Pegwell Ct. *Ram* —7F **210**
Pegwell Rd. *Ram* —7E **210** (2E **23**)
Pegwell St. *SE18* —7G **50**
Pelham Cotts. *Bex* —6C **58**
Pelham Ct. *Sidc* —8J **57**
Pelham Gdns. *Folk* —7G **188**
Pelham Pl. Est. *Swan* —8H **73**
Pelham Rd. *Bexh* —1B **58**
Pelham Rd. *Grav* —6E **62** (4A **8**)
Pelham Rd. S. *Grav* —6E **62** (4A **8**)
Pelham St. *SW7* —3B **4**
Pelham Ter. *Grav* —5E **62**
Pelican Clo. *Roch* —6G **78**
Pelican Ct. *W'bury* —1C **136**
Pelinore Rd. *SE6* —7H **55**
Pell Green. —3B 36
Pell Grn. *Spar G* —3B **36**
Pellipar Gdns. *SE18* —5B **50**
Pells La. *W King* —3G **104** (3E **15**)
Pemberton Ct. *S'gte* —8B **188**
Pemberton Gdns. *Swan* —6F **72**
Pemberton Rd. *Afrd* —8H **159**
Pemberton Sq. *Roch* —4N **79**
Pemble Rd. *Five G* —8F **146**
Pembles Cross. —4C 28
Pembridge Rd. *W11* —2B **4**
Pembridge Vs. *W11 & W2* —2B **4**
Pembroke. *Chat* —4D **80**
Pembroke Av. *Mgte* —2N **207**
Pembroke Ct. *Folk* —5L **189**
Pembroke Ct. Ram —5J **211**
(off Hardres St.)
Pembroke Gdns. *Gill* —7A **96**
Pembroke M. *New R* —1D **212**
Pembroke M. *Sev* —7J **119**
Pembroke Pl. *S at H* —4B **74**
Pembroke Rd. *W8* —3B **4**
Pembroke Rd. *Brom* —5M **69**
Pembroke Rd. *Chat* —1E **17**
Pembroke Rd. *Cox* —5M **137**
Pembroke Rd. *Eri* —5D **52** (3C **7**)
Pembroke Rd. *Sev* —7J **119** (2D **25**)
Pembroke Rd. *Tonb* —6F **144**
Pembury. —8C 152 (1A 36)
Pembury By-Pass. *Pem* —1A **36**
Pembury Clo. *Brom* —1J **83**
Pembury Clo. *Pem* —7C **152**
Pembury Ct. Sit —7F **98**
(off Pembury St.)
Pembury Cres. *Sidc* —7N **57**
Pembury Gdns. *Maid* —6A **126**
Pembury Grange. *Tun W* —8N **151**
Pembury Gro. *Tonb* —7J **145**
(in two parts)
Pembury Hall Rd. *Tud & Pem* —3B **152** (1A **36**)
Pembury Northern By-Pass. *Pem* —7A **152** (1A **36**)
Pembury Rd. *E5* —1D **5**
Pembury Rd. *Bexh* —7N **51**
Pembury Rd. *Tonb* —7H **145** (4E **25**)
Pembury Rd. *Tun W* —1J **157** (2E **35**)
Pembury St. *Sit* —7F **98**
Pembury Walks. *Tonb* —4N **151** (1A **36**)
Pembury Way. *Gill* —1A **96**
Penberth Rd. *SE6* —7F **54**
Pencester Ct. *Dover* —4K **181**
Pencester Rd. *Dover* —4J **181** (1C **43**)
Pencroft Dri. *Dart* —5K **59**
Penda Rd. *Eri* —7C **52**
Pendennis Rd. *Orp* —3L **85**
Pendennis Rd. *Sev* —5J **119**
Penderel Ct. Tent —7C **222**
(off Ashford Rd.)
Penderel M. *Tent* —7C **222**
Penderry Rise. *SE6* —7G **54**
Pendragon Rd. *Brom* —8J **55**
Pendrell St. *SE18* —6F **50**
Penenden. *New Ash* —3M **89**
Penenden Ct. *Maid* —2E **126**
Penenden Heath. —2F 126 (1E 27)
Penenden Heath Rd. *Maid* —2F **126** (1E **27**)
Penenden St. *Maid* —3D **126**
Penerley Rd. *SE6* —6E **54**
Penfield La. *Rod* —7H **115**
Penfold Clo. *Chat* —4E **94**
Penfold Clo. *Maid* —3H **139**
Penfold Gdns. *S'wll* —2C **220**
Penfold Hill. *Leeds* —9D **128** (2A **28**)
Penfold La. *Bex* —7M **57**
(in two parts)
Penfold Rd. *Folk* —5L **189**
Penfolds Clo. *Tonb* —2J **145**
Penfold Way. *Maid* —2C **138**
Penford Gdns. *SE9* —1N **55**
Pengarth Rd. *Bex* —3M **57**
Penge. —1D 13
Penge High St. *SE20* —3A **68**
Penge La. *SE20* —3A **68**
Penge Rd. *SE25 & SE20* —1D **13**
Penguin Clo. *Roch* —6H **79**
Penhill Rd. *Bex* —4L **57** (4B **6**)
Penhurst. —4A 44
Penhurst Clo. *Weav* —4J **127**
Penhurst La. *P'hst* —4A **44**
Penhurst Place. —2J **149**
Penlee Clo. *Eden* —5C **184**
Penlee Point. *Kenn* —5H **159**
Penmon Rd. *SE2* —3J **51**
Pennant Rd. *Roch* —4N **93**
Penn Clo. *Sit* —9J **99**
Penney Clo. *Dart* —5L **59**
Penn Gdns. *Chst* —5D **70**
Penn Hill. *Afrd* —3C **160**
Pennine Wlk. *Tun W* —9K **151**
Pennine Way. *Afrd* —6F **158**
Pennine Way. *Bexh* —8F **52**
Pennine Way. *Down* —8K **127**
Pennine Way. *N'fleet* —8D **62**
Pennington Clo. *W'bre* —4H **169**
Pennington Mnr. *Tun W* —4G **150**
Pennington Pl. *Tun W* —4H **151**
Pennington Rd. *Tun W* —4F **150**
Pennington Way. *SE12* —7L **55**
Pennis La. *Fawk* —9K **75**
Penn La. *Bex* —3M **57**
Penn's Yd. *Pem* —8B **152**
Pennycroft. *Croy* —9B **82**
Pennyfields. *C'brk* —8D **176**
Pennypot. —7G 197
Pennypot Ind. Est. *Hythe* —7G **197**
Penny Pot La. *Sole S* —3C **30**
Penpool La. *Well* —1K **57**
Penrith Clo. *Beck* —4E **68**
Penrose Ct. *Hythe* —7K **197**
Penruddocke Ho. *Tonb* —3J **145**
Penryn Mnr. Gill —6F **80**
(off Skinner St.)
Pensand Ho. *Hythe* —7L **197**
Penshurst. —2J 149 (1D 35)
Penshurst Av. *Sidc* —4J **57**
Penshurst Clo. *Cant* —8N **167**
Penshurst Clo. *Gill* —1A **96**
Penshurst Clo. *Long* —5C **76**
Penshurst Clo. *W King* —7E **88**
Penshurst Gdns. *Clift* —3K **209**
Penshurst Grn. *Brom* —8J **69**
Penshurst Place. —4D **25**
Penshurst Rise. *Fav* —4F **186**
Penshurst Rd. *Bexh* —8A **52**
Penshurst Rd. *Bidb* —3L **149** (1D **35**)
Penshurst Rd. *Pens* —9H **143** (4D **25**)
Penshurst Rd. *Ram* —5K **211**
Penshurst Rd. *Speld* —6M **149** (1D **35**)
Penshurst Vineyards. —4G **148** (1C **35**)
Penshurst Wlk. *Brom* —8J **69**
Penshurst Way. *Orp* —7L **71**
Penstocks, The. *Maid* —7A **126**
Pentagon Cen. *Chat* —8C **80**
Penton Ho. *SE2* —1M **51**
Penton St. *N1* —2C **5**
Pentonville Rd. *N1* —2C **5**
Pentvale Clo. *Folk* —5G **189**
Pen Way. *Tonb* —2L **145**
Penwith Rd. *SW18* —4B **4**
Pepingstraw Clo. *Off* —2J **123**
Pepper All. *Maid* —1B **126**
Pepper Hill. —8B 62
Pepperhill. *N'fleet* —8B **62**
Pepperhill La. *N'fleet* —7B **62**
Peppermead Sq. *SE13* —3D **54**
Pepys Av. *S'ness* —2C **218** (4C **11**)
Pepys Clo. *Dart* —2A **60**
Pepys Clo. *N'fleet* —8C **62**
Pepys Rise. *Orp* —2H **85**
Pepys Rd. *SE14* —1A **54** (3D **5**)
Pepy's Way. *Roch* —5K **79**
Perch La. *Lam* —2B **36**
Percival Rd. *Orp* —3D **84**
Percival St. *EC1* —2C **5**
Percival Ter. *Dover* —5G **181**
Percy Av. *Broad* —4K **209**
Percy Rd. *SE20* —4A **68**
Percy Rd. *Bexh* —9N **51**
Percy Rd. *Broad* —8K **209**
Percy Rd. *Clift* —2E **208**
Percy Rd. *Ram* —4H **211**
Peregrine Ct. *Well* —8H **51**
Peregrine Dri. *Sit* —8H **99**
Peregrine Gdns. *Croy* —3B **82**
Peregrine Rd. *King H* —7M **123**
Peri Ct. *Cant* —4L **171**
Perie Row. Gill —6D **80**
(off Middle St.)
Perimeter Rd. *Lark* —7G **108**
Periton Rd. *SE9* —2N **55**
Periwinkle Clo. *Sit* —6F **98**
Perkins Av. *Mgte* —5D **208**
Perkins Clo. *Grnh* —3F **60**
Perks Clo. *SE3* —1H **55**
Perpins Rd. *SE9* —4G **56**
Perran Clo. *Hart* —7M **75**
Perries Mead. *Folk* —4H **189**
Perrott St. *SE18* —4E **50**
Perry. —4B 22
Perryfield St. *Maid* —3C **126**
Perry Gro. *Dart* —2A **60**
Perry Hall Clo. *Orp* —1J **85**
Perry Hall Rd. *Orp* —9H **71** (2B **14**)
Perry Hill. *SE6* —8C **54** (4E **5**)
Perry Hill. *Cli* —4N **65** (4D **9**)
Perry Rise. *SE23* —8B **54** (4E **5**)
Perry Rd. *W'hm* —4B **22**
Perrys La. *Prat B* —4K **101** (3B **14**)
Perry Street. —6E 62 (4A 8)
Perry St. *Chat* —9B **80**
Perry St. *Chst* —3F **70** (1B **14**)
Perry St. *Dart* —2F **58** (4C **7**)
Perry St. *Maid* —3C **126**
Perry St. *N'fleet* —6E **62** (4A **8**)
Perry St. Gdns. *Chst* —2G **71**
Perry St. Shaw. *Chst* —3G **71**
Perry Vale. *SE23* —7A **54** (4D **5**)
Perrywood. —2A 30
Persant Rd. *SE6* —7H **55**
Perth Gdns. *Sit* —7D **98**
Perth Rd. *Beck* —5F **68**
Perth Way. *Dover* —1H **181**
Pescot Av. *Long* —6N **75**
Pested. —3A 30
Pested Bars Rd. *Bou M* —3F **138** (2E **27**)
Pested La. *C'lck* —6E **174** (3A **30**)
Petchell M. Cant —9A **168**
(off Teddington Clo.)
Peterborough Gdns. *Roch* —6G **79**
Peters Clo. *Well* —9G **51**
Petersfield. *Pem* —7D **152**
Petersfield Dri. *Meop* —1E **106**
Peter's Green. —2B 44
Petersham Dri. *Orp* —5H **71**
Petersham Gdns. *Orp* —5H **71**
Peterstone Rd. *SE2* —3K **51**
Peter St. *Deal* —3N **177**
Peter St. *Dover* —4H **181**
Peter St. *Folk* —6L **189**
Peter St. *Grav* —5G **63**
Peters Works. *Woul* —8G **92**
Petfield Clo. *Min S* —6K **219**
Petham. —3D 31
Petham Grn. *Gill* —9M **81**
Petherton Rd. *N5* —1D **5**
Petley Ct. Almshouses. Tonb —7H **145**
(off Pembury Rd.)
Pett Bottom. —2E 31
Pett Bottom Rd. *Bos* —3E **31**
Pett Bottom Rd. *Bri* —9D **172** (3E **31**)
Petten Clo. *Orp* —2M **85**
Petten Gro. *Orp* —2L **85**
Petteridge. —8L 153 (1B 36)
Petteridge La. *Matf & Brchly* —8K **153** (1B **36**)
Pettfield Hill Rd. *Stal* —2E **29**
Pett Hill. *Bri* —9E **172** (2E **31**)
Pettings. —8A 90 (3A 16)
Pettitts Row. *Fav* —5F **186**
Pett La. *Char* —2K **175** (3D **29**)
Pett La. *I'ham* —4E **45**
Pett La. *S'bry* —2J **113** (3B **18**)
Pett Level Rd. *W'sea B* —4A **46**
Pettman Clo. *H Bay* —4G **195**
Pettman Cres. *SE28* —3F **50** (3B **6**)
Pettmans M. *Whits* —4E **224**
Petts Cres. *Min* —8M **205**
Petts La. *W'hm* —1A **226**
Pett St. *SE18* —4A **50**
Petts Wood. —8E 70 (2B 14)
Petts Wood Rd. *Orp* —8E **70** (2B **14**)
Petworth Rd. *Bexh* —3B **58**
Peverel Dri. *Bear* —5J **127**
Peverel Grn. *Gill* —7N **95**
Peverell Rd. *Dover* —9G **178**
Peveril Ct. Dart —4B **60**
(off Clifton Wlk.)
Pharos, The. —4L **181**
Pheasant La. *Maid* —1E **138** (2E **27**)
Pheasant Rd. *Chat* —1F **94**
Pheasants' Hall Rd. *Kgtn* —3E **31**
Phelps Clo. *W King* —7E **88**
Philimore Clo. *SE18* —5G **51**
Philip Av. *Swan* —7E **72**
Philip Corby Clo. *Clift* —3F **208**
Philip Gdns. *Croy* —3C **82**
Philipot Path. *SE9* —4B **56**
Philippa Gdns. *SE9* —3N **55**
Philippa Ho. *Folk* —5M **189**
Philippine Village Craft Centre. —2B **46**
Philip Rd. *Folk* —5E **188**
Phillippa Ct. *Mil R* —4F **98**
Phillips Clo. *Dart* —4J **59**
Phillips Ct. *Gill* —1L **95**
Phillips Rd. *Birch* —5F **206**
Philpots La. *Hild* —2L **143**
Philpots La. *Leigh* —3D **25**
Phineas Pett Rd. *SE9* —1A **56**
Phoebeth Rd. *SE4* —3D **54**
Phoenix Cen. *Brom* —7L **69**
Phoenix Clo. *W Wick* —3G **83**
Phoenix Cotts. W'bury —2B **136**
(off Maidstone Rd.)
Phoenix Dri. *Kes* —5N **83**
Phoenix Dri. *W'bury* —1C **136**
Phoenix Ind. Est. *Strood* —5A **80**
Phoenix Pk. Bus. Cen. *Maid* —4J **139**
Phoenix Pl. *Dart* —5L **59**
Phoenix Rd. *Chat* —9E **94**
Phoenix Wharf. *Roch* —5A **80**
Picardy Manorway. *Belv* —3C **52** (3C **6**)
Picardy Rd. *Belv* —5B **52** (3C **6**)
Picardy St. *Belv* —3B **52** (3C **6**)
Piccadilly. *W1* —2C **4**
Pickelden La. *Mys* —8M **175** (2C **30**)
Pickering Ct. Dart —4B **60**
(off Osbourne Rd.)
Pickering St. *Maid* —3D **138**
Pickford Clo. *Bexh* —9N **51**
Pickford La. *Bexh* —1N **57** (3C **6**)
Pickford Rd. *Bexh* —1N **57**
Pickhurst Grn. *Brom* —1J **83**
Pickhurst La. *W Wick & Brom* —8H **69** (2E **13**)
Pickhurst Mead. *Brom* —1J **83**
Pickhurst Pk. *Brom* —9H **69**
Pickhurst Rise. *W Wick* —2G **82**
Pickle's Way. *Cli* —2B **176**
Pickmoss La. *Off* —7H **103**
Pickneybush La. *St Mm & Newch* —1D **47**
Pickwick Cres. *Roch* —1N **93**
Pickwick Gdns. *N'fleet* —8C **62**
Pickwick Ho. *Grav* —8C **62**
Pickwick Way. *Chst* —2E **70**
Picton Rd. *Ram* —6G **211**
Piedmont Rd. *SE18* —5F **50**
Pie Factory Rd. *F'hm* —3B **32**
Pier App. *Broad* —9M **209**
Pier App. Rd. *Gill* —5G **80**
Pier Av. *H Bay* —2F **194**
Pier Av. *Whits* —2J **225**
Pierce Mill Rd. *Gold G* —2G **146**
Pierce Mill Rd. *Hdlw* —3B **26**
Pier Chine. *H Bay* —3F **194**
Piermont Pl. *Brom* —5A **70**
Pier Pde. E16 —1C **50**
(off Pier Rd.)
Pier Pl. *Roch* —1D **80**
Pierpoint Rd. *Whits* —6F **224**
Pierremont Av. *Broad* —9L **209**
Pier Rd. *E6* —3A **6**
Pier Rd. *E16* —2B **50**
Pier Rd. *Eri* —6F **52**
(in two parts)
Pier Rd. *Gill* —5G **80** (1E **17**)
Pier Rd. *Grnh* —2H **61**
Pier Rd. *N'fleet* —4E **62**
Pier Rd. *Queen* —6A **218**
Pier Rd. Ind. Est. *Gill* —5G **80**
Pier, The. *Whitf* —5E **178**
Pier Way. *SE28* —3F **50**
Pigdown La. *Hever* —1B **34**
Pigeon Hoo La. *Tent* —3C **39**
Pigeon La. *H Bay* —5H **195**
Pigsdean Rd. *Ludd* —1N **91**
Pigs Pass. *Hawkh* —5L **191**
Pigtail Corner. —4E 11
Pike Clo. *Brom* —1L **69**
Pike Clo. *Folk* —4G **189**
Pikefields. *Gill* —1M **95**

Poundsbridge—Queens Rd.

Poundsbridge. —6L 149 (1D 35)
Poundsbridge Hill. Ford —8L 149 (1D 35)
Poundsbridge La. Pens —4L 149 (1D 35)
Pound St. Cars —2B 12
Pound, The. E Peck —1L 147
Pound Way. Chst —3E 70
Pound Way. Folk —7K 189
Pounsley Rd. Dun G —3F 118
Pout Rd. Snod —3D 108
Poverest. —7J 71 (2B 14)
Poverest Rd. Orp —8H 71 (2B 14)
Povey Av. Wain —2N 79
Powder Mill Clo. Tun W —6J 151
Powdermill La. Batt —4B 44
Powder Mill La. Dart —7M 59
Powder Mill La. Leigh —5A 144 (4D 25)
(in two parts)
Powdermill La. Sed —4C 44
Powder Mill La. Tun W —7G 151 (1E 35)
Powder Mills. —5D 144 (4E 25)
Powell Clo. Ayle —7L 109
Powell Cotton Dri. Birch —5G 206
Powell Cotton Museum. —6G 207
Power Ind. Est. Eri —8H 53
Powerscroft Rd. E5 —1D 5
Powerscroft Rd. Sidc —2L 71
Power Sta. Rd. Min S —5F 218
Powis St. SE18 —3C 50
Powlett Rd. Roch —3N 79
Powster Rd. Brom —1K 69
Powys Clo. Bexh —6M 51
Poynders Rd. SW4 —4C 4
Poynings Clo. Orp —3L 85
Poyntell Cres. Chst —4F 70
Poyntell Rd. S'hrst —7K 221
Poynters La. Shoe —1D 11
Praed St. W2 —2B 4
Pragnell Rd. SE12 —7L 55
Prall's La. Matf —4K 153
Pratling Street. —7N 109 (4D 17)
Pratling St. Ayle —7M 109 (4D 17)
Pratt's Bottom. —1L 101 (3B 14)
Pratt's Bottom. (Junct.) —9L 85 (3B 14)
Pratt St. NW1 —2C 4
Prebend St. N1 —2D 5
Precincts, The. Cant —1N 171 (4D 21)
Precinct, The. Roch —7N 79
Precinct Toy Collection, The. —5M 217
(off Harnet St.)
Premier Pde. Ayle —9J 109
Prendergast Rd. SE3 —1H 55
Prentis Clo. Sit —6D 98
Prentis Quay. Sit —6F 98
Prescott Av. Orp —9D 70
Prescott Clo. Gus —7K 179
Prescott Ho. New R —2B 212
Prestbury Sq. SE9 —9B 56
Prestedge Av. Ram —2J 211
Preston. —6H 187 (3A 20)
Preston Av. Fav —7J 187
Preston Av. Gill —2H 95
Preston Ct. Sidc —9H 57
(off Crescent, The)
Preston Dri. Bexh —8M 51
Preston Gro. Fav —6H 187
Preston Hall Gdns. Ward —4J 203
Preston Hill. W'hm —1C 226 (4B 22)
Preston La. Fav —6G 187
(in two parts)
Preston La. Tent —8F 222 (3C 39)
Preston La. W'hm —4B 22
Preston Malthouse. Fav —6H 187
Preston Pde. Sea —6A 224
Preston Pk. Fav —6H 187
Preston Rd. Mans —1B 210 (2D 23)
Preston Rd. N'fleet —6D 62
Preston Rd. Pres —3B 22
Preston Rd. Tonb —6G 145
Preston Rd. W'hm —1C 226 (4B 22)
Prestons Rd. Brom —4K 83 (2E 13)
Preston St. Fav —6G 187 (3A 20)
Preston Way. Gill —1M 95
Prestwood Clo. SE18 —7J 51
Pretoria Ho. Eri —7F 52
Pretoria Ho. Maid —3H 139
Pretoria Rd. Cant —2A 172
Pretoria Rd. Chat —1C 94
Pretoria Rd. Gill —9G 80
Prettymans La. Eden —3F 184 (4B 24)
Price's Av. Mgte —3E 208
Price's Av. Ram —6G 210
Prices Cotts. Cli —5N 65
Prickley Wood. Brom —2J 83
Pridmore Rd. Snod —2D 108
Priest Av. Cant —2J 171
Priestfield. Roch —2D 17
Priestfield Rd. SE23 —8B 54
Priestfield Rd. Gill —7H 81
Priest Fields. H Bay —2N 195
Priestfields. Roch —9M 79
Priestlands Pk. Rd. Sidc —8H 57
Priestley Dri. Lark —6D 108
Priestley Dri. Tonb —9K 133
Priestly Hill. Elham —4E 31
Priests Bri. SW14 & SW15 —4A 4
Priest Wlk. Grav —7M 63
Priest Wlk. Whits —2L 225
Priestwood. —6H 91 (2B 16)
Priestwood Green. —6H 91 (2B 16)
Priestwood Rd. Meop —7G 91 (3B 16)
Primmers Grn. Spar G —3A 36
Primmett Clo. W King —7E 88
Primrose Av. Gill —6L 95
Primrose Clo. SE6 —1F 68
Primrose Clo. Chat —4B 94
Primrose Cotts. Maid —9L 127
Primrose Cotts. Cvn. Pk. Whits —6H 225
Primrose Dri. Dit —9H 109
Primrose Dri. Kgnt —5F 160
Primrose Hill. —2B 4
Primrose Hill. Cha H —3A 170 (1C 30)
Primrose Hill Rd. NW3 —1B 4
Primrose La. Bre —5B 114 (3C 18)
Primrose La Croy —2A 82
Primrose Pl. Dover —3G 180
Primrose Rd. Dover —3F 180
Primrose Rd. Up H'lng —6C 92
Primrose Ter. Grav —6H 63
Primrose Way. Ches —4L 225
Primrose Way. C'snd —7A 210
Prince Albert Rd. NW8 & NW1 —2B 4
Prince Andrew Rd. Broad —6J 209
Prince Arthur Rd. Gill —6E 80 (1E 17)
Prince Charles Av. Chat —7E 94 (3E 17)
Prince Charles Av. Min S —6K 219
Prince Charles Av. Ors —2B 8
Prince Charles Av. Sit —9J 99
Prince Charles Av. S Dar —5D 74
Prince Charles Rd. SE3 —3E 5
Prince Charles Rd. Broad —6J 209
Prince Consort Dri. Chst —4F 70
Prince Edward's Promenade. Ram —7F 210
Prince Henry Rd. SE7 —7A 50
Prince Imperial Rd. SE18 —8B 50
Prince Imperial Rd. Chst —4D 70 (1A 14)
Prince John Rd. SE9 —3A 56
Prince of Wales Dri. SW11 —3B 4
Prince of Wales Residential Mobile Home Pk. Hythe —8F 196
Prince of Wales Rd. NW5 —1C 4
Prince of Wales Rd. SE3 —3E 5
Prince of Wales Roundabout. Dover —6J 181
Prince of Wales Ter. Deal —5N 177 (2E 33)
Prince Regent La. E13 & E16 —2A 6
Prince Rupert Rd. SE9 —2B 56
Princes Av. Chat —8D 94 (3E 17)
Princes Av. Dart —6B 60
Princes Av. Min S —5L 219
Princes Av. Orp —8G 70
Prince's Av. Ram —3F 210
Princes Clo. Birch —4C 206
Princes Clo. Sidc —8M 57
Princes Cres. Mgte —3D 208
Prince's Gdns. Mgte —3G 208
Princes Pde. Hythe —7L 197 (3E 41)
Princes Park. —5E 94 (3E 17)
Prince's Plain. Brom —1A 84
Princes Rd. SE20 —2A 68
Princes Rd. Dart —4H 59 (4D 7)
Princes Rd. Grav —8H 63
Prince's Rd. Ram —4H 211 (2E 23)
Princes Rd. S'wch B —4D 23
Princes Rd. Swan —3H 73
Princes Road Interchange. (Junct.) —6B 60 (4D 7)
Princess Anne Rd. Broad —6J 209
Princess Clo. Whits —2L 225
Princesses Pde. Dart —3F 58
(off Waterside)
Princess Margaret Av. Clift —3H 209 (1E 23)
Princess Margaret Av. Ram —3E 210
Princess Margaret Rd. Linf & E Til —3B 8
Princess Mary Av. Chat —5E 80
Princess Of Wales Royal Regiments & Museum. —4K 181
Princess Pde. Orp —4C 84
Princess Rd. Whits —2L 225
Princess St. Folk —5L 189
Princes St. Bexh —1A 58
Princes St. Deal —3N 177
Princes St. Dover —5J 181
Princes St. Grav —4G 62
(in two parts)
Princes St. Maid —4D 126
Princes St. Mgte —3D 208
Prince's St. Ram —6J 211
Prince's St. Roch —8N 79
Princes St. Tun W —2J 157
Princes Ter. Hythe —7G 196
Princes View. Dart —6A 60
Princes Vs. Mard —2L 205
Prince's Wlk. Clift —2J 209
Princes Way. Cant —1K 171
Princes Way. Det —9K 111
Princes Way. W Wick —5J 83
Princethorpe Rd. SE26 —9A 54
Prince William Ct. Deal —3N 177
Printstile. —1D 35
Prinys Dri. Gill —7M 95
Prioress Rd. Cant —2K 171
Prioress Wlk. Dover —1F 180
Prior Rd. G'stne —7A 212
Priors Dean Clo. Barm —8J 125
Priorsford Av. Orp —7J 71
Priors Ga. Roch —7N 79
Priors Heath. —3C 37
Prior's Lees. Folk —7K 189
Prior's Way. Cowd —1B 34
Priory Av. Orp —9F 70
Priory Clo. Beck —6B 68
Priory Clo. Broad —1K 211
Priory Clo. Chst —4B 70
Priory Clo. Dart —3L 59
Priory Clo. E Far —9M 125
Priory Clo. New R —3A 212
Priory Ct. Dart —4L 59
Priory Ct. Gill —1K 95
Priory Dri. SE2 —5M 51
Priory Fields. Eyns —3N 87
Priory Gdns. Dart —3L 59
Priory Gdns. Folk —7K 189
Priory Ga. Maid —4D 126
Priory Ga. Rd. Dover —4H 181
Priory Gro. Dit —9H 109
Priory Gro. Dover —4H 181
Priory Gro. Tonb —7H 145
Priory Hill. Dart —4L 59
Priory Hill. Dover —4H 181
Priory Hill Holiday Camp. Ley S —7N 203
Priory La. SW15 —4A 4
Priory La. Eyns —2N 87
Priory La. H Bay —4H 195
Priory La. S'ndge —6K 215 (2C 41)
Priory Leas. SE9 —6A 56
Priory of St Jacob. Cant —4L 171
Priory Pk. SE3 —1J 55
Priory Pl. Dart —4L 59
Priory Pl. Dover —4J 181
Priory Pl. Fav —3G 186
Priory Rd. NW6 —2B 4
Priory Rd. Bils —3B 40
Priory Rd. Dart —2L 59
(in two parts)
Priory Rd. Dover —4J 181 (1C 43)
Priory Rd. Fav —4F 186 (3A 20)
Priory Rd. F Row —3A 34
Priory Rd. Gill —1K 95
Priory Rd. Maid —6D 126
Priory Rd. Ram —6H 211
Priory Rd. Roch —6L 79 (1D 17)
Priory Rd. Sutt —2A 12
Priory Rd. Tonb —7H 145 (4E 25)
Priory Row. Fav —4G 186 (3A 20)
Priory Shop. Cen. Dart —4L 59
Priory Sta. App. Rd. Dover —4H 181
Priory St. Dover —4J 181 (1C 43)
Priory St. Tonb —7H 145
Priory, The. SE3 —2J 55
Priory, The. E Far —9N 125
Priory Wlk. Tonb —7H 145
Priory Way. Tent —8D 222
(in two parts)
Pristling La. S'hrst —1E 37
Pritchard's Rd. E2 —2D 5
Procter Rd. Lydd —2C 204
Progress Est., The. Maid —3K 139
Promenade. Birch —3E 206
Promenade. Deal —1N 177
Promenade. Dover —5K 181
Promenade. Mgte —2C 208
Promenade. Walm —7N 177
Promenade. Whits —2H 225
(in three parts)
Promenade, The. Broad —1M 211
Promenade, The. Ley S —6M 203
Promenade, The. Mgte —2E 208
Proscect Ter. Elham —6N 183
Prospect Av. Roch —4M 79
Prospect Clo. Belv —4B 52
Prospect Clo. Wgte S —4K 207
Prospect Corner. Lydd —3C 204
(off Queens Rd.)
Prospect Cotts. Beth —2K 163
Prospect Cotts. S'wll —3C 220
Prospect Gdns. Min —6M 205
Prospect Gro. Grav —5J 63
Prospect Hill. H Bay —2H 195
Prospect M. Hythe —6K 197
Prospect Pk. S'boro —5F 150
Prospect Pl. App —8C 190
Prospect Pl. Broad —9M 209
Prospect Pl. Brom —6L 69
Prospect Pl. Cant —3N 171
Prospect Pl. Dart —4M 59
Prospect Pl. Dover —3G 180
Prospect Pl. Grav —5J 63
(in two parts)
Prospect Pl. Maid —6B 126
Prospect Pl. Roch —1L 93
Prospect Pl. St N —9D 214
Prospect Rd. Birch —4E 206 (1C 22)
Prospect Rd. Broad —9M 209
Prospect Rd. Hythe —6J 197 (3E 41)
Prospect Rd. Min —7M 205
Prospect Rd. S'gte —8D 188
Prospect Rd. Sev —5K 119
Prospect Rd. S'boro —5F 150
Prospect Rd. Tun W —2H 157 (2E 35)
Prospect Row. Chat —9D 80
Prospect Row. Gill —6D 80
Prospect Ter. Ram —6J 211
Prospect, The. Broad —9M 209
(off Parade, The)
Prospect Vale. SE18 —4A 50
Prospect Way. Bra L —7K 165
Provender La. Osp —3E 19
Provender Way. Weav —4H 127
Providence Cotts. Gill —2K 111
Providence Cotts. High —2F 78
Providence La. Hythe —6K 197
(off Dental St.)
Providence Pl. Woul —7G 93
Providence Row. Cant —4L 171
Providence St. Afrd —1G 160
Providence St. Grnh —3G 61
Prudence Cotts. Weald —6J 131
Prudhoe Ct. Dart —4B 60
(off Osbourne Rd.)
Puckle La. Cant —4N 171
Puddingcake La. Rol —1N 213
Pudding La. Ah —5C 216
Pudding La. Maid —5C 126
Pudding La. Seal —3N 119
Pudding Rd. Rain —3B 96
Puddledock. —2F 72 (3B 24)
Puddledock La. Dart —1F 72 (1C 15)
Puddledock La. W'ham —3B 24
Puffin Clo. Beck —8A 68
Puffin Rd. Isle G —3C 190
Pullington Cotts. Bene —3A 38
Pullman Clo. Ram —3G 211
Pullman Pl. SE9 —3A 56
Pulton Ho. SE4 —2B 54
(off Turnham Rd.)
Pump Clo. Leyb —9B 108
Pump La. Gill —2M 95 (2A 18)
(in two parts)
Pump La. Mgte —3D 208
Pump La. Orp —6C 86
Pump St. Horn H —2B 8
Punch Croft. New Ash —4L 89
Purbeck Rd. Chat —1B 94
Purcell Av. Tonb —1M 145
Purchas Ct. Cant —7J 167
Purelake M. SE13 —1G 54
(off Marischal Rd.)
Purfleet. —3D 7
Purfleet By-Pass. Purf —3D 7
Purfleet Ind. Pk. Ave —2N 53
Purfleet Rd. Ave —3D 7
Purland Rd. SE28 —2H 51
Purley. —3C 13
Purley Cross. (Junct.) —3C 13
Purley Downs Rd. Purl & S Croy —3D 13
Purley Way. Croy & Kenl —2C 13
Purneys Rd. SE9 —2N 55
Purrett Rd. SE18 —5H 51
Purser Way. Gill —5F 80
Putney. —4B 4
Putney Bri. SW15 & SW6 —4B 4
Putney Bri. Rd. SW15 & SW18 —4B 4
Putney Heath. —4A 4
Putney Heath. SW15 —4A 4
Putney High St. SW15 —4A 4
Putney Hill. SW15 —4A 4
Puttenden Rd. S'brne —4M 133 (3A 26)
Puttney Dri. Kem —3H 99
Pychers Pl. Pem —8C 152
Pye All. La. Whits —9F 224
Pye All. Rd. York —3C 21
Pye Corner. —3B 28
Pym Ho. Char —3L 175
Pym Orchard. Bras —6L 117
Pynham Clo. SE2 —3K 51
Pyott M. Cant —1A 172
Pyrus Clo. Chat —2E 110
Pyson's Rd. Ram —2G 210 (2E 23)
Pyson's Rd. Ind. Est. Broad —1H 211

Quadbrook. —3B 34
Quadrant, The. Bexh —7M 51
Quaggy Wlk. SE3 —2K 55
Quain Ct. Folk —7J 189
Quaker Clo. Sev —5L 119
Quaker Dri. C'brk —6D 176
Quaker La. C'brk —6D 176 (2E 37)
Quakers Clo. Hart —6L 75
Quakers Hall La. Sev —4K 119 (1D 25)
Quantock Clo. Tun W —9K 151
Quantock Dri. Afrd —7F 158
Quantock Gdns. Ram —1F 210
Quantock Rd. Bexh —9F 52
Quarries, The. —4F 138
Quarries, The. Bou M —4F 138 (3E 27)
Quarrington La. W Bra —1B 40
Quarry Av. Hythe —5J 197
Quarry Bank. Tonb —8G 144
Quarry Cotts. Langl —4E 138
Quarry Cotts. Sev —5H 119
Quarry Farm Rural Experience. —2B 44
Quarry Gdns. Tonb —7G 145
Quarry Hill. Sev —5L 119
Quarry Hill Pde. Tonb —7H 145
Quarry Hill Rd. Bor G —3M 121 (1A 26)
Quarry Hill Rd. Tonb —9G 145 (4E 25)
(in two parts)
Quarry La. Hythe —5J 197
Quarry Rise. Tonb —8G 145
Quarry Rd. Maid —7D 126
Quarry Rd. Tun W —9H 151 (1E 35)
Quarry Sq. Maid —4D 126
Quarry View. Afrd —2B 160
Quarry Wlk. Hythe —8A 188
Quarry Wood. Adgtn —2B 40
Quarry Wood Ind. Est. Ayle —1J 125
Quarter, The. —4C 28
Quay La. Fav —4H 187 (3A 20)
Quay La. Grnh —2H 61
Quay La. S'wch —5M 217
Quayside. Chat —4E 80
Quay, The. Rye —3A 46
Quay, The. S'wch —5M 217 (4D 23)
Quebec Av. W'ham —8F 116
Quebec Cotts. W'ham —9F 116
Quebec House. —8F 116 (2B 24)
Quebec Sq. W'ham —8F 116
Quebec Ter. Dover —1G 181
(off Winnipeg Clo.)
Queen Anne Av. Brom —6J 69 (1E 13)
Queen Anne Rd. Maid —5D 126
Queen Anne's Ga. Bexh —1M 57
Queen Bertha Rd. Ram —6G 210
Queen Bertha's Av. Birch —3H 207
Queenborough. —7B 218 (4C 11)
Queenborough Bus. Cen. Queen —9B 218
Queenborough Dri. Min S —5J 219
Queenborough Gdns. Chst —2F 70
Queenborough Rd. Min S —7C 218 (4D 11)
Queen Ct. Roch —8N 79
Queendown Av. Gill —6N 95
Queen Elizabeth Av. Mgte —4H 209 (1E 23)
Queen Elizabeth Pl. Til —2F 62
Queen Elizabeth Rd. Dover —4L 181
Queen Elizabeth's Dri. New Ad —9G 82
Queen Elizabeth II Bri. Dart & Grays —1D 60
Queen Elizabeth Sq. Maid —2G 138
Queen Mother Ct., The. Roch —8M 79
Queens Arms Yd. Mgte —2C 208
(off Market St.)
Queen's Av. Birch —4C 206
Queen's Av. Broad —7M 209
Queens Av. Cant —1K 171
Queens Av. Dover —5E 180
Queens Av. Folk —5B 188
Queens Av. H Bay —2L 195
Queen's Av. Maid —4A 126
Queen's Av. Mgte —4C 208 (1D 23)
Queen's Av. Ram —4F 210
Queen's Av. Snod —2E 108
Queensbridge Dri. H Bay —2D 194
Queensbridge Rd. E8 & E2 —1D 5
Queen's Ct. Afrd —7G 158
Queen's Ct. Eden —6D 184
Queens Ct. Hawkh —5L 191
Queen's Ct. H Bay —3H 195
Queens Ct. Hythe —7J 197
(off Albert Ct.)
Queens Ct. Mgte —2E 208
Queenscroft Rd. SE9 —3N 55
Queensdown. —8L 207
Queensdown Rd. Kgdn —5M 199
Queensdown Rd. Wdchu —7L 207
Queens Dri. W3 —2A 4
Queens Dri. Sev —2K 119
Queen's Farm Rd. Shorne —7C 64 (4C 8)
Queen's Gdns. Broad —1M 211
Queens Gdns. Dart —6B 60
Queens Gdns. Dover —4J 181
Queens Gdns. H Bay —2G 195
Queen's Gdns. Mgte —2E 208
Queen's Gdns. Tun W —8H 151
Queens Ga. SW7 —3B 4
Queensgate Gdns. Chst —4F 70
Queen's Ga. Rd. Ram —5G 211 (2E 23)
Queens Ho. Maid —6M 125
Queensland Ho. E16 —1C 50
(off Rymill St.)
Queens Mead Rd. Brom —5J 69 (1E 13)
Queens M. Deal —4N 177
Queen's Pde. Clift —2E 208 (1E 23)
Queens Pde. S'ness —4B 218
Queens Park Rangers F.C. —2A 4
Queens Pas. Chst —2D 70
Queens Ride. SW13 & SW15 —4A 4
Queen's Rise. R'wld —4J 199
Queens Rd. SE15 & SE14 —3D 5
Queens Rd. SW19 —1B 12
Queen's Rd. Ah —4C 216 (4C 22)
Queens Rd. Afrd —7G 159
Queens Rd. Aysm —2D 162
Queens Rd. Beck —5B 68
Queen's Rd. Broad —9L 209 (2E 23)
Queens Rd. Brom —5K 69
Queens Rd. Chat —1G 94
Queens Rd. Chst —2D 70
Queens Rd. Crowb —4C 35
Queens Rd. Croy —2C 13
Queen's Rd. Eri —6F 52 (3C 7)
Queens Rd. Fav —5F 186
Queens Rd. Gill —8F 80
Queens Rd. Grav —8H 63
Queen's Rd. Hawkh —5L 191 (4E 37)
Queen's Rd. King T —1A 12
Queen's Rd. L'stne —3D 212
Queens Rd. Lydd —3C 204 (3D 47)
Queen's Rd. Maid —6M 125 (2D 27)
Queens Rd. Min S —5L 219
Queen's Rd. Ram —5K 211
Queen's Rd. Rich —4A 4
Queen's Rd. Snod —2E 108
Queen's Rd. Tun W —9G 151 (1E 35)
Queen's Rd. Well —9K 51
Queens Rd. Wgte S —3L 207

Queens Rd.—Remston M.

Queens Rd. Whits —3H 225 (2C 21)
Queens Rd. W'boro —9L 159
Queensthorpe Rd. SE26 —9A 54
Queenstown Rd. SW8 —3C 4
Queen Street. —4C 26
Queen St. Afrd —8F 158
Queen St. Bexh —1A 58
Queen St. Chat —8D 80
Queen St. Deal —4M 177 (2E 33)
Queen St. Dover —5J 181
Queen St. Eri —6F 52
Queen St. Folk —6L 189
Queen St. Grav —4G 63
Queen St. H Bay —2G 194
Queen St. Mgte —3C 208 (1D 23)
Queen St. Pad W —4C 26
Queen St. Ram —6J 211 (2E 23)
Queen St. Roch —8N 79
(in two parts)
Queen St. Sand —2J 215
Queens View. Sea —6B 224
Queensway. W2 —2B 4
Queensway. Allh —3L 201
Queensway. Det —9K 111
Queensway. Dym —5C 182
Queens Way. Lydd —3C 204
Queensway. Orp —8E 70 (2B 14)
Queen's Way. S'ness —4B 218 (4C 11)
Queensway. Sth S —1C 10
Queensway. W Wick —4H 83
Queenswood Rd. SE23 —8A 54
Queenswood Rd. Ayle —3A 110
Queenswood Rd. Sidc —3H 57
Queen Victoria. (Junct.) —2A 12
Queen Victoria St. EC4 —2C 5
Quentin Pl. SE13 —1H 55
Quentin Rd. SE13 —1H 55
Quentins Dri. Berr G —7D 100
Quernmore Clo. Brom —2K 69
Quernmore Rd. Brom —2K 69
Quern Rd. Deal —7K 177
Querns Pl. Cant —2A 172
Querns Rd. Cant —2B 172
Quern, The. Maid —8B 126
Quested Rd. Folk —5E 188
Quested Way. H'shm —2L 141
Quetta Rd. Ram —3D 210
Quex Ct. Birch —5G 206
(off Powell Cotton Dri.)
Quex House. —6G 207 (1C 23)
Quex Rd. NW6 —2B 4
Quex Rd. Wgte S —3L 207
Quex View Rd. Birch —5E 206
Quickbourne La. N'iam —2D 45
Quickrells Av. Cli —3C 176
Quicks, The. Ah —4C 216
Quickthorn Cres. Chat —6B 94
Quiet Nook. Brom —4N 83
Quilter Gdns. Orp —2L 85
Quilter Rd. Orp —2L 85
Quilter St. SE18 —5H 51
Quince Orchard. Hams —7D 190
Quincewood Gdns. Tonb —9H 133
Quinell St. Gill —2A 96
Quinion Clo. Chat —2C 110
Quinton Clo. Beck —6F 68
Quinton Rd. Mil R —4D 98 (2C 18)
Quixote Cres. Roch —3M 79

Rabbit Hole. B'hm —9D 162 (3A 32)
Rabbit's Cross. —4E 27
Rabbits Rd. S Dar —5D 74 (1E 15)
Racecourse Rd. Ling —1A 34
Racefield Clo. Shorne —3C 78
Radcliffe Ct. Hythe —6J 197
Radcot Point. SE23 —8A 54
Radfall. —7L 225 (2D 21)
Radfall Hill. Whits —7L 225
Radfall Ride. Whits —8L 225
Radfall Rd. Whits —7L 225 (2D 21)
(in two parts)
Radfield. —3D 19
Radfield Way. Sidc —5F 56
Radford Rd. SE13 —4F 54
Radleigh Gdns. Chat —2B 94
Radley Clo. Broad —7L 209
Radley Ho. SE2 —2M 51
(off Wolvercote Rd.)
Radnor Av. Well —3K 57
Radnor Bri. Rd. Folk —6L 189 (2A 42)
Radnor Cliff. Folk —8G 188
Radnor Cliff Cres. Folk —8G 188
Radnor Clo. Chst —2G 71
Radnor Clo. H Bay —6J 195
Radnor Cres. SE18 —7J 51
Radnor M. Cant —9A 168
Radnor Pk. Av. Folk —5H 189
Radnor Pk. Cres. Folk —6J 189
Radnor Pk. Gdns. Folk —5J 189
Radnor Pk. Rd. Folk —6J 189 (2A 42)
Radnor Pk. W. Folk —6H 189
Radnor St. Folk —6L 189
Radnor Wlk. Croy —9B 68
Raeburn Av. Dart —3J 59
Raeburn Av. Surb —2A 12
Raeburn Clo. Tonb —1L 145
Raeburn Pl. Swans —3L 61
Raeburn Rd. Sidc —4G 57
Rafford Way. Brom —5L 69
Raggatt Pl. Maid —7E 126
Ragge Way. Seal —2N 119
Raggleswood. Chst —4C 70
Rag Hill Clo. Tats —9E 164
Rag Hill Rd. Tats —9D 164 (1A 24)
Raglan Ct. SE12 —3K 55
Raglan Pl. Broad —9M 209
Raglan Rd. SE18 —5E 50
Raglan Rd. Belv —4A 52
Raglan Rd. Brom —7M 69
Ragstone Ct. Dit —1G 125
Ragstone Hollow. Adgtn —2B 40
Ragstone Rd. Bear —7K 127
Railmania Museum. —4F 224 (2C 21)
(off High St.)
Railton Rd. SE24 —4C 5
Railway App. E Grin —2A 34
Railway App. Tonb —6H 145
Railway Av. Whits —4G 224 (2C 21)
Railway Cotts. Mard —2L 205
Railway Hill. B'hm —9B 162 (3E 31)
Railway Pl. Belv —3B 52
Railway Pl. Grav —4G 63
Railway Rd. S'ness —2C 218 (4C 11)
Railway St. Chat —8B 80 (2D 17)
Railway St. Gill —7G 80 (1E 17)
Railway St. N'fleet —3N 61
Railway St. Ind. Est. Gill —6G 81
Railway Ter. SE13 —3E 54
Railway Ter. Mgte —4B 208
Railway Ter. Queen —7B 218
Railway Ter. W'ham —7F 116
Rainbow La. Stan H —2C 8
Rainham. —3B 96 (2A 18)
Rainham Clo. SE9 —4G 56
Rainham Clo. Maid —8C 126
Rainham Hall. —2D 7
Rainham Rd. Dag —1C 7
Rainham Rd. Gill —2E 17
Rainham Rd. Rain & Horn —1C 7
Rainham Rd. N. Dag —1C 6
Rainham Shop. Cen. Rain —2B 96
Raleigh Clo. Chat —5D 94
Raleigh Clo. Eri —6G 53
Raleigh Clo. W'boro —1L 161
Raleigh Ct. Beck —4E 68
Raleigh Ct. Eri —7G 53
Raleigh M. Orp —6H 85
Raleigh Rd. SE20 —3A 68
Raleigh Way. Min S —6F 218
Ralph Grimshaw Ct. Wgte S —3K 207
Ralph Perring Ct. Beck —7D 68
Ramillies Clo. Chat —6D 94
Ramillies Rd. Sidc —4K 57
Ram Lane. —4E 29
Ram La. L Char —4D 29
Rammell M. C'brk —8D 176
Rampart Rd. Hythe —6J 197
Rampion Clo. Weav —4H 127
Ramsden. —2L 85 (2B 14)
Ramsden Clo. Orp —2L 85
Ramsden La. I Grn —4A 38
Ramsden Rd. Eri —7E 52
Ramsden Rd. Orp —2K 85
Ramsey Clo. Cant —1L 171
Ramsey Ho. Cant —3M 171 (1D 31)
(off Station Rd. E.)
Ramsgate. —5J 211 (2E 23)
Ramsgate Maritime Museum.
—6K 211 (2E 23)
Ramsgate Motor Museum. —7H 211
Ramsgate Museum. —6J 211 (2E 23)
Ramsgate Rd. Broad —1K 211 (2E 23)
Ramsgate Rd. Mgte —4D 208 (1D 23)
Ramsgate Rd. S'wch & C'snd
—5M 217 (4D 23)
Ramsgate Royal Harbour Lighthouse.
—7J 211
Rams Hill. —1C 37
Ramslye. —4D 156 (2E 35)
Ramslye Rd. Tun W —4D 156
Ramstone Clo. Sme —8K 165
Ram St. SW18 —4B 4
Ramuswood Av. Orp —6G 84
Rancliffe Gdns. SE9 —2A 56
Rancliffe Rd. E6 —2A 6
Rancorn Rd. Mgte —4A 208
Randall Clo. Eri —6D 52
Randall Hill Rd. Wro —7M 105
Randall Rd. Chat —2B 94
Randalls Row. Loose —3C 138
Randall St. Maid —3C 126
Randisbourne Gdns. SE6 —8E 54
Randlesdown Rd. SE6 —9D 54
(in two parts)
Randles La. Knock —5M 101
Randles La. Sev —4B 14
Randolph Clo. Bexh —1D 58
Randolph Clo. Cant —4N 171
Randolph Cotts. Roch —3M 79
Randolph Gdns. Kenn —5J 159
Randolph Ho. Gill —7F 80
Randolph Rd. Brom —2B 84
Randolph Rd. Dover —3G 180
Randolph Rd. Gill —7F 80
Randolphs. Bidd —9L 163
Randolph's La. W'ham —8D 116
Randolph Sq. Mgte —2D 208
Ranelagh Gdns. Broad —8J 209
Ranelagh Gdns. N'fleet —5E 62
Ranelagh Gro. Broad —8J 209
Ranelagh Rd. Deal —5N 177
Ranelagh Rd. S'ness —2D 218
Rangefield Rd. Brom —1H 69
Range Rd. E'chu —7C 202
Range Rd. Grav —5K 63
Range Rd. Hythe —7J 197
Range Rd. Ind. Est. Hythe —7J 197
Rangers House. —3E 5
Rangeworth Pl. Sidc —8H 57
Rankine Rd. Tun W —7K 151
Ranleigh Gdns. Bexh —7A 52
Ranmore Path. Orp —7J 71
Ranscombe Clo. Roch —7H 79
Ransley Grn. Ruck —3A 40
Ransome Way. Birch —5F 206
Ranters La. Goud —9H 185 (3C 37)
Ranworth Clo. Eri —9F 52
Raphael Ct. Hild —9D 132
Raphael Rd. Grav —5J 63
Rapier Clo. Purf —4N 53
Rashleigh Way. Hort K —7C 74
Raspberry Hill La. Iwade
—6A 198 (1C 18)
Ratcliffe Clo. SE12 —5K 55
Ratcliffe Highway. C'den —4E 9
Ratcliffe Highway. Chatt —8D 66 (4E 9)
Rathfern Rd. SE6 —6C 54
Rathmore Rd. Grav —5G 62
Ratling. —2B 32
Ratling Rd. Aysm —1D 162 (2A 32)
Rattington St. Cha —8D 170 (2C 31)
Raven Clo. Lark —9E 108
Ravenlea Rd. Folk —6G 189
Ravensbourne Av. Beck & Brom
—3G 68
Ravensbourne Av. H Bay —5J 195
Ravensbourne Ct. SE6 —5D 54
Ravensbourne Ho. Brom —1G 68
Ravensbourne Pk. SE6 —5D 54 (4E 5)
Ravensbourne Pk. Cres. SE6 —5C 54
Ravensbourne Rd. SE6 —5C 54
Ravensbourne Rd. Brom —6K 69
Ravensbourne Rd. Dart —1H 59
Ravensbury Rd. Orp —7H 71
Ravenscar Rd. Brom —9H 55
Ravens Clo. Brom —5J 69
Ravenscourt Gro. Horn —1D 7
Ravenscourt Rd. Deal —5M 177
Ravenscourt Rd. Orp —6J 71
Ravenscourt Rd. R Comn —8H 167
Ravenscroft Cres. SE9 —8B 56
Ravenscroft Rd. Beck —5A 68
Ravens Dane Clo. Down —8K 127
Ravenshill. Chst —4D 70
Ravensleigh Gdns. Brom —1L 69
Ravensmead Rd. Brom —3G 69
Ravens M. SE12 —3K 55
Ravensquay Bus. Cen. Orp —8K 71
Ravens Way. SE12 —3K 55
Ravenswood. Bex —6N 57
Ravenswood Av. Roch —4M 79
Ravenswood Av. Tun W —9J 151
Ravenswood Av. W Wick —2F 82
Ravenswood Cres. W Wick —2F 82
Ravensworth Rd. SE9 —9B 56
Ravensworth Rd. W Wick —2E 13
Ravine Gro. SE18 —6G 50
Rawdon Rd. Maid —6D 126
Rawdon Rd. Ram —6F 210
Rawlings Clo. Orp —6H 85
Rawling St. Mils —8F 114 (4C 19)
Rawlins Clo. S Croy —8C 82
Rawlinson Ho. SE13 —2G 55
(off Mercator Rd.)
Rawsthorne Clo. E16 —1B 50
Rayfield Clo. Brom —9A 70
Rayford Av. SE12 —5J 55
Rayford Clo. Dart —3K 59
Rayham Rd. Whits —5J 225
Ray Lamb Way. Eri —6J 53
Rayleas Clo. SE18 —8D 50
Raymere Gdns. SE18 —7F 50
Raymer Rd. Maid —1E 126
Raymond Av. Cant —4N 171
Raymond Rd. Beck —7B 68
Raymoor Av. St Mar —2F 214
Raymouth Rd. SE16 —3D 5
Rayner's Ct. Grav —4B 62
Rayners Hill. Len —3C 29
Raynes Park. —1A 12
Rays Hill. Hort K —7C 74 (1D 15)
Rays Rd. W Wick —1F 82
Reach Clo. St Mc —7J 213
Reachfields. Hythe —7H 197
Reach Meadow. St Mc —7K 213
Reach Rd. St Mc —8J 213 (4D 33)
Readers Bri. Rd. St Mic —3A 222 (3B 38)
Readers La. Iden —3A 46
Reading Clo. Walm —9L 177
Reading Ho. Maid —3J 139
Reading Rd. Dover —5E 180
Reading Street. —6L 209 (1E 23)
Reading St. Broad —5K 209 (1E 23)
Reading St. Tent —4D 39
Reading St. Rd. Broad —1E 23
Reading St. Rd. Mgte —4J 209
Readscroft Rd. Gill —6N 95
Read Way. Grav —1J 77
Rebecca Ct. Mgte —3F 208
Rebecca Ct. Sidc —9K 57
Recreation Av. Snod —2E 108
Recreation Clo. Maid —3E 126
Recreation Ground Rd. Tent —8C 222
Recreation Rd. SE26 —9A 54
Recreation Rd. Brom —5J 69
Recreation Rd. Sidc —8G 57
Rectory Bus. Cen. Sidc —9K 57
Rectory Clo. Dart —2F 58
Rectory Clo. Sidc —9K 57
Rectory Clo. Snod —2E 108
Rectory Clo. Wdchu —7B 226
Rectory Clo. Woul —6G 93
Rectory Cotts. Eyt —3K 185
Rectory Ct. Whits —3M 225
Rectory Dri. Bidb —3C 150
Rectory Fields. C'brk —7D 176
Rectory Gdns. Beck —4D 68
Rectory Gdns. Whits —3M 225
Rectory Grange. Roch —1N 93
Rectory Grn. Beck —4C 68
Rectory Gro. Lgh S —1A 10
Rectory La. SW17 —1C 12
Rectory La. Bans —4B 12
Rectory La. B'hm —7D 162 (3A 32)
Rectory La. Barm —8K 125 (2D 27)
Rectory La. Beckl —2D 45
Rectory La. Bras —6L 117 (2B 24)
Rectory La. Cha S —9M 139
Rectory La. C'brk —7D 176
Rectory La. H'shm —3N 141
Rectory La. Hever —4B 24
Rectory La. Igh —4J 121 (1E 25)
Rectory La. Lym —8D 204
Rectory La. Salt —4J 197
Rectory La. Sev —8K 119
Rectory La. Sidc —9K 57 (1B 14)
Rectory La. Sut V —9A 140 (3A 28)
Rectory La. W'ham —5A 116 (2A 24)
Rectory La. W'sea —4A 46
Rectory La. N. Leyb —8C 108
Rectory La. S. Leyb —8C 108
Rectory Meadow. S'fleet —2N 75
Rectory Pk. S Croy —3D 13
Rectory Pk. Rd. Horsm —2C 37
Rectory Pl. SE18 —4C 50
Rectory Rd. N16 —1D 5
Rectory Rd. As —6A 90 (2A 16)
Rectory Rd. Beck —4D 68 (1E 13)
Rectory Rd. Broad —8M 209
Rectory Rd. Cli —2L 65 (4D 9)
Rectory Rd. Deal —6J 177 (3D 33)
Rectory Rd. Grays —3A 8
Rectory Rd. Kes —8N 83
Rectory Rd. Ors —2B 8
Rectory Rd. Sit —9J 99
Rectory Rd. St Mm —1A 214
Rectory Rd. Swans —5L 61
Rectory Rd. W Til —3B 8
Rectory Way. Kenn —5G 158
Reculver. —1A 22
Reculver Av. Birch —3D 206
Reculver Clo. H Bay —2N 195
Reculver Dri. H Bay —2M 195
Reculver La. H Bay —1A 22
Reculver Rd. H Bay —4K 195 (2E 21)
Reculvers Rd. Wgte S —4L 207
Reculver Towers. —1A 22
Reculver Wlk. Maid —1J 139
Redan Pl. S'ness —2E 218
Redbank. Leyb —8C 108
Red Barracks Rd. SE18 —4B 50
Redbridge Clo. Chat —6F 94
Redbrook St. H Hal —7N 193 (2D 39)
Redbrooks Way. Hythe —5G 197
Red Cedars Rd. Orp —1G 84
Redcliffe Gdns. SW10 —3B 4
Redcliffe La. Maid —2D 126
Redcot La. Sturry —4G 168
Red Cotts. Maid —1B 126
Redding. Sidc —2K 71
Reddons Rd. Beck —3B 68
Reddy Rd. Eri —6G 52
Rede Ct. Rd. Strood —4H 79 (1D 17)
Rede Wood Rd. Maid —6J 125
Redfern Av. Gill —7H 81
Redfern Rd. SE6 —5F 54
Redgate Dri. Brom —3L 83
Redgates. H Bay —2H 195
Redgates Dri. Whits —3H 225
Red Hill. —8D 124 (2C 26)
Red Hill. Chst —1D 70 (1A 14)
Red Hill. W'bury —9C 124 (2C 26)
Redhill Rd. New Ash —5L 89 (2E 15)
Redhill Rd. Wgte S —3K 207
Redhill Wood. New Ash —4N 89
Redhouse Bungalows. Deal —1L 177
Red Ho. Cotts. Sev —7K 119
Red Ho. Gdns. W'bury —1A 136
Red Ho. La. Bexh —2M 57
Redhouse La. Deal —1L 177
Redhouse La. Str E —2D 31
Redhouse Rd. Tats —9C 164
Redhouse Wall. Deal —1L 177
Redington. Afrd —7G 159
Redlands Ct. Brom —3J 69
Redlands Ct. Dover —9D 178
Redland Shaw. Roch —2B 94
Redlands Rd. Sev —6G 119
Redlands, The. Beck —5E 68
Red La. Oxt —3A 24
Redleaf Clo. Belv —6B 52
Redleaf Clo. Tun W —8K 151
Red Lion Clo. Orp —9L 71
Red Lion La. SE18 —7C 50 (3A 6)
Red Lion La. Whits —3F 224
Red Lion Pl. SE18 —8C 50
Red Lion Rd. Surb —2A 12
Red Lion Sq. Hythe —6J 197 (3D 41)
Red Lion St. WC1 —2C 5
Red Lodge. W Wick —2F 82
Red Lodge Cres. Bex —8E 58
Red Lodge Rd. Bex —8E 58
Red Lodge Rd. W Wick —2F 82 (2E 13)
Redmans La. Sev —7D 86 (3C 15)
Redmill Clo. Folk —6E 188
Red Oak. Hawkh —7J 191
Red Oak Clo. Orp —4D 84
Redought Way. Dym —9E 182
Redpoll Wlk. Pad W —1M 153
Redpoll Way. Eri —3M 51
Red Post Hill. SE24 —4D 5
Redriff Rd. SE16 —3D 5
Red Rd. Cant —1N 165
Redroofs Clo. Beck —4E 68
Red Rover. (Junct.) —4A 4
Redruth Mnr. Gill —6F 80
(off Cross St.)
Redsells Clo. Down —8K 127
Redstreet. —2A 76
Red St. S'fleet —1N 75 (1A 16)
Redsull Av. Deal —7K 177
Red Tree Orchard. Afrd —2C 160
Redvers Cotts. Kear —8D 178
Redvers Rd. Chat —1D 94
Redwall La. Hunt —9L 137 (3D 27)
Redwall La. Lin —9B 138
Redwell Cotts. Sev —5J 121
Redwell La. Igh —5H 121 (2E 25)
Redwing Clo. Lark —7D 108
Redwing Path. SE28 —3F 50
Redwing Rd. Chat —5E 94
Redwings La. Pem —5C 152 (1A 36)
Redwood Clo. Cant —9L 167
Redwood Clo. Chat —9E 94
Redwood Clo. Sidc —5J 57
Redwood Ct. Dart —4A 60
(off Norfolk Clo.)
Redwood Pk. Five G —1F 152
Redyear Ct. W'boro —9L 159
Reece Adams Ho. Cap F —3A 174
Reed Av. Cant —9B 168
Reed Av. Orp —4G 84
Reed Clo. SE12 —3K 55
Reed Cres. Afrd —6G 160
Reede Rd. Dag —1C 6
Reedham Cres. Cli —6N 65
Reedland Cres. Fav —4G 186
Reedmace Clo. Afrd —1B 160
Reed Mill La. W'wd —3E 31
Reeds Clo. H Bay —3K 195
Reeds Ct. Maid —7A 126
Reeds La. S'brne —3L 133 (2E 25)
Reeds Mill La. Kgtn —3E 31
Reeds Mill Rd. Kgtn —6A 162 (3E 31)
Reed St. Cli —2C 176 (3D 9)
Reeves All. Whits —4F 224
(off Middle Wall)
Reeves Clo. S'hrst —7J 221
Reeves Cres. Swan —6E 72
Reeves Rd. SE18 —6D 50
Reform Rd. Chat —1E 94
Regency Clo. Gill —8M 95
Regency Clo. S'ness —1B 218
Regency Clo. W King —7E 88
Regency Clo. Whits —6G 225
Regency Ct. Sit —7E 98
Regency Hall. Tun W —3G 156
Regency M. Beck —4F 68
Regency Pl. Cant —9A 168
Regency Wlk. Croy —9B 68
Regency Way. Bexh —1M 57
Regent Dri. Maid —9D 126
Regent Pl. Tun W —2K 157
Regent Rd. Gill —8F 80
Regents Ct. Afrd —8F 158
(off Regents Pl.)
Regents Ct. Brom —3J 69
Regents Ct. Grav —3G 62
Regents Dri. Kes —6N 83
Regent's Park. —2B 4
Regent's Pk. Rd. NW1 —2B 4
Regents Pl. Afrd —8F 158
Regents Pl. S'ness —2C 218
Regent Sq. Belv —4C 52
Regent St. W1 & SW1 —2C 4
Regent St. Rol —2J 213 (4B 38)
Regent St. Whits —3F 224
Regents Wlk. H Bay —2L 195
Regina Ct. Tun W —1F 156
Regina Ho. SE20 —4A 68
Reginald Av. Cux —9G 78
Reginald Rd. Maid —6B 126
Regis Cres. Sit —5F 98
Regis Pk. S'ness —3B 218
Reidhaven Rd. SE18 —4G 51
Reigate Av. Sutt —2B 12
Reigate Rd. Brom —8J 55
Reigate Rd. Eps & Tad —3A 12
Reinden Gro. Down —8J 127
Reinickendorf Av. SE9 —3E 56
Rembrandt Clo. Tonb —1L 145
Rembrandt Dri. N'fleet —8C 62
Rembrandt Rd. SE13 —2H 55
Remston M. Cant —9A 168

Renault Clo.—Romily Gdns.

Renault Clo. H Bay —3B 194
Rendezvous St. Folk —6K 189
Rendezvous, The. Mgte —2C 208
Rennell St. SE13 —1F 54
Rennets Clo. SE9 —3G 56
Rennets Wood Rd. SE9 —3F 56
Renown Rd. Chat —9F 94
Renshaw Clo. Belv —6A 52
Rentain Rd. Cha —8D 170
Renton Dri. Orp —1M 85
Renwick Rd. Bark —2B 6
Replingham Rd. SW18 —4B 4
Repository Rd. SE18 —6B 50 (3A 6)
Repton Clo. Broad —7K 209
Repton Ct. Beck —4E 68
Repton Mnr. Rd. Afrd —7E 158
Repton Rd. Orp —4J 85
Repton Way. Chat —7C 94
Reservoir Cotts. Up H'lng —7C 92
Reservoir Rd. Whits —3G 224
Resolution Clo. Chat —6D 94
Resolution Wlk. SE18 —3B 50
Restavon Cvn. Site. Berr G —7D 100
Restharrow. Shel L —1A 30
Restharrow Rd. Weav —5H 127
Restons Cres. SE9 —4F 56
Retreat Cvn. Pk., The. Nett —2B 136
Retreat Club & Cvn. Pk., The. E'chu —2E 202
Retreat, The. Birch —3G 206
Retreat, The. Orp —7K 85
Retreat, The. Ram —4F 210
Retreat, The. Sev —6J 119
Revell Rise. SE18 —6H 51
Revelon Rd. SE4 —2B 54
Revenge Rd. Chat —1F 110
Reventlow Rd. SE9 —6E 56
Reynard Clo. SE4 —1B 54
Reynard Clo. Brom —6C 70
Reynolds Clo. H Bay —3J 195
Reynolds Clo. Tonb —1L 145
Reynolds Fields. High —7G 65
Reynolds La. Tun W —7F 150 (1E 35)
Rhee Wall. Bztt & Old R —2C 47
Rheims Ct. Cant —1K 171
Rheims Way. Cant —1K 171 (1D 31)
Rhodaus Clo. Cant —3M 171 (1D 31)
Rhodaus Town. Cant —3M 171 (1D 31)
Rhode Common. —1B 30
Rhode Ct. Sit —6D 98
Rhodes Gdns. Broad —7L 209
Rhodes Minnis. —9H 183 (1D 41)
Rhode St. Chat —8D 80
Rhodeswell Rd. E14 —2E 5
Rhodewood Clo. Down —8K 127
Rhododendron Av. Meop —8F 90
Ribblesdale Rd. Dart —6C 60
Ribston Clo. Brom —2B 84
Ribston Gdns. Pad W —8K 147
Ricardo Path. SE28 —1L 51
Riccards La. What —4B 44
Rice Pde. Orp —8F 70
Richard Clo. SE18 —4A 50
Richard Ct. Mgte —3F 208
Richards Clo. Chid C —5G 143
Richardson Clo. Grnh —3F 60
Richardson Rd. Tun W —8G 151
Richardson Way. C'snd —6A 210
Richard St. Chat —8C 80
Richard St. Roch —9N 79
Richborough Bus. Pk. S'wch —3M 217
Richborough Castle. —1K 217 (3D 23)
Richborough Clo. Orp —7M 71
Richborough Dri. Strood —3L 79
Richborough Port. —3D 23
Richborough Rd. Cant —1J 217
(in two parts)
Richborough Rd. S'wch —3C 23
Richborough Rd. Wgte S —4L 207
Richborough Roman Amphitheatre. —4D 23
Richdore Rd. Walt —3C 31
Rich Ind. Est. Dart —3G 58
Richmer Rd. Eri —7H 53
Richmond Av. Mgte —4F 208
Richmond Clo. Big H —7B 164
Richmond Clo. Chat —7E 94
Richmond Clo. Upnor —3C 80
Richmond Ct. Dover —3J 181
Richmond Dri. Grav —7K 63
Richmond Dri. H Bay —3M 195
Richmond Dri. New R —1C 212
Richmond Dri. Sit —4F 98
Richmond Gdns. Cant —9J 167
Richmond Pde. Roch —9A 80
Richmond Pl. SE18 —4E 50
Richmond Rd. E8 —1D 5
Richmond Rd. Gill —6F 80 (1E 17)
Richmond Rd. Ram —6H 211
Richmond Rd. Whits —4K 225
Richmond St. Folk —5D 188
Richmond St. H Bay —2G 194
Richmond St. S'ness —2E 218 (4D 11)
Richmond Way. Maid —9D 126
Richmount Gdns. SE3 —1K 55
Rickard M. Lam —2D 200
Ricketts Hill Rd. Tats —6D 164 (4A 14)
Rickyard Path. SE9 —2A 56
Riddlesdale Av. Tun W —8G 151
Riddlesdown. —3D 13
Riddlesdown Rd. Purl —3D 13
Riddles Rd. Sit —8D 98 (3C 18)
Riddons Rd. SE12 —8M 55
Rideout St. SE18 —4B 50
Rider Clo. Sidc —4G 56
Ridge Av. Dart —4G 58
Ridgebrook Rd. SE3 —1N 55
Ridgecroft Clo. Bex —6D 58
Ridgelands. Bidb —2C 150
Ridge La. Meop —8F 90
Ridgemount Av. Croy —2A 82
Ridge Rd. Sutt —2B 12
Ridge Row. —3B 192 (1A 42)
Ridge, The. Bex —5A 58
Ridge, The. Groom —7H 155
Ridge, The. Kenn —4J 159
Ridge, The. Orp —3F 84
Ridge, The. Wold & Warl —2A 24
Ridgeway. Brom —3K 83
Ridge Way. Cray —4G 58
Ridgeway. Dart —1E 74
Ridge Way. Eden —3C 184
Ridgeway. Hawkh —7H 191
Ridgeway. Lymp —5B 196
Ridgeway. Pem —7C 152
Ridgeway. Whits —4K 225
Ridgeway Av. Grav —8G 63
Ridgeway Bungalows. Shorne —3D 78
Ridgeway Cliff. H Bay —2D 194
Ridgeway Cres. Orp —4G 84
Ridgeway Cres. Tonb —3K 145
Ridgeway Cres. Gdns. Orp —4G 85
Ridgeway Dri. Brom —9L 55
Ridgeway E. Sidc —3G 57
Ridgewaye, The. Tun W —5G 151
Ridgeway Rd. H Bay —8H 195 (2E 21)
Ridgeway Ter. Bra L —8H 165
Ridgeway, The. Bou B —3K 165
Ridgeway, The. Broad —1K 211
Ridgeway, The. Chat —4B 94 (2D 17)
Ridgeway, The. Gill —6F 80
Ridgeway, The. Mgte —4F 208
Ridgeway, The. River —2D 180
Ridgeway, The. Shorne —3C 78 (1C 16)
Ridgeway, The. Sme —8H 165 (1B 40)
Ridgeway, The. Tonb —2J 145 (4E 25)
Ridgeway, The. Wclf S —1B 10
Ridgeway Wlk. H Bay —8H 195
Ridgeway W. Sidc —3G 57
Ridgewell Clo. SE26 —9C 54
Ridgewood. Long —5B 76
Ridgway. SW19 —1A 12
Ridgway. Maid —7M 125
Ridgy Field Clo. Wro —8N 105
Ridham Av. Kem —2G 99 (2C 19)
Riding Hill. Kenn —4G 159
Riding La. Hild —1D 144 (3E 25)
Riding Pk. Hild —9D 132
Ridings, The. Big H —5E 164
Ridings, The. Cant —1A 172
Ridings, The. Ches —4M 225
Ridings, The. Clift —2J 209
Ridings, The. Pad W —8M 147
Ridings, The. Tun W —8M 151
Ridlands La. Oxt —2A 24
Ridley. —7A 90 (3A 16)
Ridley Clo. H Bay —7H 195
Ridley Rd. Brom —6J 69
Ridley Rd. Roch —8M 79
Ridley Rd. Well —8K 51
Riefield Rd. SE9 —2E 56 (4B 6)
Rigden Rd. Afrd —2F 160
Rigden's Ct. Sit —6F 98
Riggs Way. Wro —7M 105
Rigshill Rd. O'den —2D 29
Riley Av. H Bay —3A 194
Ring Clo. Brom —3L 69
Ringden Av. Pad W —1K 153
Ringers Rd. Brom —6K 69
Ringle Grn. Sand —3L 215
Ringlestone. —2B 126 (1D 27)
Ringlestone Cres. Maid —1C 126
Ringlestone Rd. H'shm —4K 129 (1B 28)
Ringmer Way. Brom —8A 70
Ringold Av. Ram —4E 210
Ringshall Rd. Orp —6J 71
Rings Hill. Hild —1B 144 (3D 25)
Ringsloe Ct. Birch —3C 206
(off Parade, The)
Ringstead Rd. SE6 —5E 54
Ringwood Clo. Beck —3B 68
Ringwood Av. Orp —1L 101
Ringwood Clo. Cant —8L 167
Ringwood Clo. Gill —3N 95
Ringwood Rd. Maid —9F 126
Ringwould. —4J 199 (3E 33)
Ringwould Rd. Dover & R'wld —5H 199 (4D 33)
Ringwould Rd. Kgdn —4K 199 (3E 33)
Ripley Clo. Brom —8B 70
Ripley Clo. New Ad —7F 82
Ripley Rd. Belv —4B 52
Ripley Rd. W'boro —1L 161
Ripleys Museum of Rural Life. —3A 44
Ripon Av. Gill —2K 95
Ripon Clo. Gill —9N 81
Ripon Rd. SE18 —6D 50
Ripper's Cross. —1D 39
Rippersley Rd. Well —8J 51
Ripple. —3D 33
Ripple La. Crun —3B 30
Ripple Rd. Bark & Dag —2B 6
Ripple Rd. Gt Mon —3H 199 (3D 33)
Ripple Road Junction. (Junct.) —2B 6
Rippolson Rd. SE18 —5H 51
Ripton Cotts. Tstn —1E 136
Risborough La. Folk —7D 188 (2E 41)
(in two parts)
Risborough Way. Folk —5E 188 (2A 42)
Risden La. Hawkh —8N 191 (1B 44)
Risdon Clo. Sturry —5E 168
Risedale Rd. Bexh —1D 58
Riseden. —2C 37
(nr. Kilndown)
Riseden. —4A 36
(nr. Wadhurst)
Riseden Rd. Wadh —4A 36
Riseldine Rd. SE23 —4B 54
Rise, The. Afrd —2C 160
Rise, The. Bex —5L 57
Rise, The. B'den —9C 98
Rise, The. Dart —2G 59
Rise, The. Grav —9K 63
Rise, The. Hem —8K 95
Rise, The. Kgdn —4M 199 (3E 33)
Rise, The. Min S —7D 218
Rise, The. Roch —9A 80
Rise, The. Sev —1K 131
Rise, The. St Mb —7L 213
Rising Rd. Afrd —9E 158
Ritch Rd. Snod —2C 108
Ritter St. SE18 —6C 50
River. —1D 180 (1C 42)
River Clo. E Far —1M 137
River Ct. Cha —3H 170
River Ct. Dover —2E 180
River Ct. Sev —4F 118
Riverdale. SE13 —1F 54
Riverdale. Dover —1E 180
Riverdale Est. Tonb —7K 145
Riverdale Rd. SE18 —5H 51
Riverdale Rd. Bex —5A 58
Riverdale Rd. Cant —9A 168
Riverdale Rd. Eri —5C 52
River Dri. Dover —2E 180
River Dri. Roch —5J 79
River Gro. Pk. Beck —4C 68
River Hall Rd. Bidd —6N 163 (2B 38)
Riverhead. —4F 118 (1C 25)
Riverhead Clo. Maid —3A 126
Riverhead Clo. Mgte —4F 208
Riverhead Clo. Sit —8D 98
River Hill. Sev & TN15 —3L 131 (2D 25)
Riverhill House Gardens. —4M 131 (2D 25)
River Lawn Rd. Tonb —6H 145
River Meadow. Dover —1E 180
River Pde. Riv —4F 118
River Pk. Gdns. Brom —3G 69
River Pk. View. Orp —1K 85
River Rd. Bark —2B 6
Rivers Clo. W'bury —1C 136
Rivers Ct. Min —8N 205
Riversdale. N'fleet —8D 62
Riversdale Rd. Afrd —2G 160
Riversdale Rd. Ram —3E 210
Riverside. Cha —7C 170
Riverside. Eden —6C 184
Riverside. Eyns —3L 87 (2D 15)
Riverside Bus. Pk. Afrd —8H 159
Riverside Cvn. Pk. E Far —9L 125
Riverside Clo. Bri —8H 173
Riverside Clo. Kgnt —6E 160
Riverside Clo. Orp —5L 71
Riverside Cotts. Cha —7C 170
Riverside Country Park. —7M 81
Riverside Ct. SE3 —2J 55
Riverside Ct. Cant —1M 171 (4D 21)
Riverside Ct. Eden —7D 184
Riverside Ct. Tonb —6J 145
Riverside Est. Roch —6B 80
Riverside Ind. Est. Cant —8A 168
Riverside Ind. Est. Dart —3M 59
Riverside Ind. Est. W Hyt —7C 196
Riverside M. Bri —8H 173
Riverside Retail Pk. Sev —1K 119
Riverside Rd. Sidc —8N 57
Riverside View. Ayle —8M 109
Riverside Wlk. W Wick —2E 82
Riverside Way. Dart —3M 59
Rivers Rd. Tey —2L 223
River St. Dover —1D 180
River St. Gill —6D 80
Rivers Wlk. Len —7D 200
Riverview. Afrd —9C 158
River View. Dart —2A 60
(off Henderson Dri.)
River View. Gill —9N 81
River View. Grays —3A 8
River View. Maid —7C 126
River View. Queen —9A 218
River View. Sturry —4E 168
Riverview Park. —9L 63 (1B 16)
Riverview Pk. SE6 —7D 54
Riverview Rd. Grnh —3G 61
River Wlk. Tonb —6H 145
(in two parts)
River Way. Lark —6E 108
River Wharf Bus. Pk. Belv —1E 52
Riverwood La. Chst —4F 70
Riviera Ct. S'gte —8E 188
Riviera, The. S'gte —8F 188
Roach St. Roch —5L 79
Road of Remembrance. Folk —7K 189 (3A 42)
Roan Ct. Roch —4K 79
Roberton Dri. Brom —4M 69
Robertsbridge. —3A 44
Robertsbridge Aeronautical Museum. —2A 44
Roberts Clo. SE9 —6F 56
Roberts Clo. Orp —8L 71
Roberts Clo. Sit —4E 98
Roberts M. Orp —2J 85
Roberts Orchard Rd. Maid —6K 125
Roberts Rd. Belv —5B 52
Roberts Rd. Gill —3A 96
Roberts Rd. G'stne —7F 212
Roberts Rd. Sea —7B 224
Roberts Rd. Snod —2D 108
Robert St. E16 —1D 50
Robert St. NW1 —2C 4
Robert St. SE18 —5F 50
(in two parts)
Robert St. Deal —3N 177
Robeshaw. Mils —8F 114
Robhurst. —3D 39
Robina Av. Grav —5C 62
Robina Clo. Bexh —2M 57
Robina Ct. Swan —7H 73
Robin Hill Dri. Chst —2A 70
Robin Hood. (Junct.) —4A 4
Robin Hood Grn. Orp —8J 71
Robin Hood La. Bexh —3N 57
Robin Hood La. Lydd —4C 204 (3D 47)
Robin Hood La. W'slde —9C 94 (3D 17)
Robin Hood La. Lwr. W'slde —9B 94
Robin Hood La. Up. Blue B —1A 110
Robin Hood Way. SW15 & SW20 —1A 12
Robin La. Lydd —3C 204
Robins Av. Len —8D 200
Robin's Clo. Hythe —8D 196
Robins Clo. Len —8D 200
Robins Ct. SE12 —8M 55
Robin's Ct. Beck —5G 68
Robins Gro. W Wick —4K 83
Robin Way. Orp —6K 71
Robinwood Dri. Seal —1N 119
Robson Av. NW10 —2A 4
Robson Dri. Ayle —8H 109
Robson Dri. Hoo —8G 66
Robson Rd. SE27 —4C 5
Robus Clo. Lym —7D 204
Robus Ter. Lym —7D 204
Robyns Croft. N'fleet —9D 62
Robyns Way. Eden —7D 184
Robyns Way. Sev —4G 119
Rocfort Rd. Snod —2E 108 (3C 17)
Rochdale Rd. SE2 —5K 51
Rochdale Rd. Tun W —9J 151
Rochester. —6N 79 (1D 17)
Rochester Airport. —2D 17
Rochester Av. Brom —5L 69 (1A 14)
Rochester Av. Cant —3A 172
Rochester Av. Roch —4A 80
Rochester Castle. —6N 79 (1D 17)
Rochester Cathedral. —6N 79
Rochester Clo. SE3 —1M 55
Rochester Clo. Sidc —4K 57
Rochester Ct. Cant —4A 172
Rochester Ct. Roch —4B 80
Rochester Cres. Hoo —7G 67
Rochester Dri. Bex —4A 58
Rochester Ga. Roch —7A 80
Rochester Guildhall Museum. —6N 79
(off High St.)
Rochester Ho. Maid —1G 138
Rochester Rd. Ayle —7L 109 (4D 17)
Rochester Rd. Burh —8H 93 (3D 17)
Rochester Rd. Cux —2F 92 (2C 17)
(in two parts)
Rochester Rd. Dart —5A 60
Rochester Rd. Grav —5K 63 (4B 8)
Rochester Rd. Roch & Chat —5N 93 (2D 17)
Rochester Rd. Tonb —3K 145
Rochester Rd. Woul —6G 93 (2C 17)
Rochester Row. SW1 —3C 4
Rochester St. Chat —1B 94
Rochester Vistor Information Cen. —6N 79
Rochester Way. SE3 & SE9 —1M 55 (4A 6)
Rochester Way. Dart —5E 58 (4C 7)
Rochester Way Relief Rd. SE3 & SE9 —3A 6
Rock Av. Gill —8F 80 (2E 17)
Rockbourne M. SE23 —6A 54
Rockbourne Rd. SE23 —6A 54
Rockdale. Sev —7J 119
Rockdale Gdns. Sev —7J 119
Rockdale Pleasance. Sev —8J 119
Rockdale Rd. Sev —7K 119
Rockfield Rd. Oxt —2A 24
Rock Hill. Orp —7C 86 (3C 14)
Rock Hill. Stapl —3C 44
Rock Hill Rd. Eger —4C 28
Rockingham Pl. H Bay —5J 195
Rockmount Rd. SE18 —5H 51
Rock Rd. Bor G —2M 121 (1A 26)
Rock Rd. Maid —2D 126
Rock Rd. Sit —8F 98
Rockrobin. —3A 36
Rocks Clo. E Mal —3E 124
Rocks Hill. Frit —2E 37
Rocks Hill. Rob —2B 44
Rock's Hill. Westf —4C 45
Rocks La. SW13 —4A 4
Rocks Rd., The. E Mal —3E 124 (1C 27)
Rockstone Way. Ram —3E 210
Rock Villa Rd. Tun W —1G 157
Rocky Bourne Rd. Adgtn —2B 40
Rocky Hill. Maid —5B 126
Rocky Hill Ter. Maid —5B 126
Rocque La. SE3 —1J 55
Rodmell Rd. Tun W —3G 157
Rodmer Clo. Min S —4K 219
Rodmersham. —2L 115 (3C 19)
Rodmersham Green. —3J 115 (3C 19)
Rodmersham Grn. Rod —3J 115 (3C 19)
Rodney Av. Tonb —3L 145
Rodney Gdns. W Wick —5K 83
Rodney Rd. SE17 —3D 5
Rodney St. Ram —6H 211
Rodway Rd. Brom —4L 69
Roebourne Way. E16 —1C 50
Roebuck Rd. Fav —5E 186
Roebuck Rd. Roch —7N 79
Roedean Clo. Orp —5K 85
Roedean Rd. Tun W —4G 157
Roehampton. —4A 4
Roehampton Clo. Grav —5K 63
Roehampton Dri. Chst —2E 70
Roehampton High St. SW15 —4A 4
Roehampton La. SW15 —4A 4
Roehampton Lane. (Junct.) —4A 4
Roehampton Vale. SW15 —4A 4
Roethorne Gdns. Tent —7C 222
Roffen Rd. Roch —1N 93
Rogers Ct. Swan —7H 73
Rogersmead. Tent —8A 222
Rogers Rough Rd. Kiln —3C 37
Rogers Wood La. Fawk —5G 89 (2E 15)
Rogues Hill. Pens —2J 149 (1D 35)
Rojack Rd. SE23 —6A 54
Rokell Ho. Beck —1E 68
(off Beckenham Hill Rd.)
Rokesby Clo. Well —9F 50
Rokesley Rd. Dover —8G 178
Rolfe La. New R —1C 212 (2E 47)
Rolinsden Way. Kes —6N 83
Rolleston Av. Orp —9D 70
Rolleston Clo. Orp —1D 84
Rollo Rd. Swan —3G 72
Roll's Av. E'chu —7A 202
Rolls Rd. SE1 —3D 5
Rolvenden. —3J 213 (4B 38)
Rolvenden Av. Gill —9M 81
Rolvenden Dri. Sit —6C 98
Rolvenden Gdns. Brom —3N 69
Rolvenden Hill. Rol —1M 213 (3B 38)
Rolvenden Layne. —4B 38
Rolvenden Rd. Bene —3A 38
Rolvenden Rd. Tent —8A 222 (3B 38)
Rolvenden Rd. Wain —2N 79
Roly Ecknoff Ho. Dover —1G 181
Roman Amphitheatre. —2K 217
Roman Clo. Blue B —1A 110
Roman Clo. Deal —4L 177
Roman Ct. Bor G —1M 121
Roman Heights. Maid —3F 126
Romanhurst Av. Brom —7H 69
Romanhurst Gdns. Brom —7H 69
Roman Museum. —2N 171
(off Butchery La.)
Roman Painted House. —5J 181
(off New St.)
Roman Rd. E2 & E3 —2D 5
Roman Rd. Adgtn —2B 40
Roman Rd. Afrd —7K 161 (2A 40)
Roman Rd. Dover —2J 181 (1C 43)
Roman Rd. E Stu —1H 179 (3C 33)
Roman Rd. Fav —5G 187 (3A 20)
Roman Rd. M Grn —4B 24
Roman Rd. N'fleet —8B 62
Roman Rd. Ram —2F 210
Roman Rd. Snod —2D 108
Roman Sq. SE28 —1J 51
Roman Sq. Sit —8G 98
Roman Villa Rd. Dart —1C 74 (1E 15)
Roman Way. Croy —2C 13
Roman Way. Dart —3F 58
Roman Way. Evtn —1J 185
Roman Way. Folk —5C 188
Roman Way. Kgnt —5F 160 (2A 40)
Roman Way. Roch —8K 79
Roman Way. St Mc —8J 213
Romany Ct. Chat —1G 94
Romany Rise. Orp —2E 84
Romany Rd. Gill —1L 95
Romborough Gdns. SE13 —3F 54
Romborough Way. SE13 —3F 54
Romden. —3N 221 (1C 38)
Romden Rd. Smar —4L 221 (1C 38)
Rome Rd. New R —3B 212
Romero Sq. SE3 —2M 55
Rome Ter. Chat —8C 80
Romford. —7E 152 (1B 36)
Romford Rd. E15, E7 & E12 —1E 5
Romford Rd. Ave —2D 7
Romford Rd. Pem —7D 152 (1A 36)
Romily Gdns. Ram —2G 211

Romney Av.—Ryland Ct.

Romney Av. Folk —6F 188 (2A 42)
Romney Clo. Bear —6K 127
Romney Clo. Birch —4F 206
Romney Ct. Sit —6E 98
Romney Dri. Brom —3N 69
Romney Gdns. Bexh —8A 52
Romney, Hythe & Dymchurch Railway. —3D 212 (3E 47)
Romney Marsh Ho. Dym —8B 182
Romney Marsh Rd. Afrd (in two parts) —5E 160 (1A 40)
Romney Pl. Maid —5D 126
Romney Rd. SE10 —3E 5
Romney Rd. Chat —6E 94
Romney Rd. Hams —8D 190
Romney Rd. Lydd —1D 204 (3D 47)
Romney Rd. N'fleet —8D 62
Romney Rd. W'boro —9J 159
Romney Sands Holiday Village. G'stne —8E 212
Romney Street. —3A 104 (3D 15)
Romney St. Knat —2A 104 (3D 15)
Romney Toy & Model Museum, The. —3F 212 (2E 47)
Romney Way. Hythe —7G 196
Romney Way. Tonb —2L 145
Romsey Clo. Orp —5D 84
Romsey Clo. Roch —4J 79
Romsey Clo. W'boro —9L 159
Rom Valley Way. Romf —1C 7
Ronald Clo. Beck —8C 68
Ronalds Ct. Sit —7H 99
Ronalds Rd. Brom —4K 69
Ronaldstone Rd. Sidc —4G 57
Ronfearn Av. Orp —8M 71
Ronley Ct. Sev —3K 119 (off Hillingdon Av.)
Ronver Rd. SE12 —6J 55
Roodlands La. Four E —4B 24
Rookdean. Chip —4D 118
Rookery Clo. Bre —4B 114 (in two parts)
Rookery Clo. Kenn —3H 159
Rookery Cres. Cli —2C 176
Rookery Dri. Chst —4C 70
Rookery Gdns. St M —8L 71
Rookery Hill. Corr —2C 9
Rookery La. Brom —9N 69
Rookery Lodge. Cli —3C 176
Rookery Rd. Orp —1B 100 (3A 14)
Rookesley Rd. Orp —1M 85
Rook La. Bob —6N 97 (2B 18)
Rookley Clo. Tun W —3K 157
Rooks Hill. Under —3C 132
Roonagh Ct. Sit —9F 98
Roopers. Speld —7A 150
Roosevelt Av. Chat —4C 94
Roosevelt Rd. Dover —1G 180
Rooting Street. —4D 29
Ropemakers Ct. Chat —2D 94
Roper Clo. Cant —1L 171
Roper Clo. Gill —8M 95
Roper Rd. Cant —1L 171 (4D 21)
Roper Rd. Tey —1L 223
Roper's Ga. Tun W —4E 156
Roper's Grn. La. H Hals —5K 67
Roper's La. High H —4E 9
Roper's La. Hoo —5J 67
Roper St. SE9 —3B 56
Rope Wlk. Chat —7C 80
Ropewalk. C'brk —7C 176
Rope Wlk. M. S'wch —5L 217
Rope Wlk., The. Sand —3K 215
Rope Yd. Rails. SE18 —3D 50
Roseacre. —5K 127 (2E 27)
Roseacre Clo. Cant —1L 171
Roseacre Ct. Mgte —3J 209
Roseacre Gdns. Bear —5K 127
Roseacre La. Bear —6K 127 (2E 27)
Rose Acre Rd. L'brne —3L 173
Roseacre Rd. Well —1K 57
Rose Av. Grav —6K 63
Rosebank Wlk. SE18 —4A 50
Roseberry Gdns. Dart —5K 59
Roseberry Gdns. Orp —4G 84
Rosebery Av. EC1 —2C 5
Rosebery Av. H Bay —2M 195
Rosebery Av. Ram —3K 211
Rosebery Av. Sidc —5G 56
Rosebery Clo. Sit —7L 99
Rosebery Ct. N'fleet —6E 62
Rosebery Rd. Chat —1B 94
Rosebery Rd. Gill —5G 80
Rose Cottage. H Bay —4L 195
Rose Cotts. Loose —3C 138 (off Old Loose Hill)
Rose Cotts. Roch —4F 78
Rosecroft Clo. Big H —6F 164
Rosecroft Clo. Orp —9L 71
Rosecroft Pk. L'tn G —1A 156
Rose Dale. Orp —3D 84
Rosedale Clo. SE2 —3K 51
Rosedale Clo. Dart —5B 60
Rosedale Rd. Mgte —4E 208
Rosedene Ct. Dart —5K 59
Rosefield. Sev —6H 119
Rose Gdns. Birch —5E 206
Rose Gdns. Eyt —4L 185
Rose Gdns. H Bay —3K 195
Rose Gdns. Min —7M 205
Rosegarth. Grav —4D 76
Rosehill. —2B 12
Rose Hill. Chill —2D 32
Rose Hill. Ram —6J 211
Rose Hill. Stne —2A 46
Rose Hill. Sutt —2B 12
Rosehill Rd. Big H —5C 164
Rose Hill Roundabout. (Junct.) —2B 12
Rosehill Wlk. Tun W —2G 156
Roseholme. Maid —7A 126
Roselands. Walm —9M 177
Roselands Gdns. Cant —9K 167
Rose La. Bis —2E 31
Rose La. Cant —2M 171 (1D 31)
Rose La. Len H —3C 29
Roselawn Gdns. Mgte —3N 207
Roselea Av. H Bay —4G 195
Roseleigh Av. Maid —5N 125
Roseleigh Rd. Sit —1E 114
Rosemary Av. Broad —2K 211
Rosemary Av. Min S —6E 218
Rosemary Clo. Chat —7C 94
Rosemary Gdns. Broad —2K 211
Rosemary Gdns. Whits —5J 225
Rosemary La. Cant —2M 171 (1D 31)
Rosemary La. Hods —9C 90 (3A 16)
Rosemary La. Smar —4B 28
Rosemary La. Tic —3C 37
Rosemary Rd. Bear —6K 127
Rosemary Rd. E Mal —9D 108
Rosemary Rd. Well —8H 51
Rosemead Gdns. H'crn —2J 193
Rosemount Clo. Loose —4C 138
Rosemount Ct. Roch —3L 79
Rosemount Dri. Brom —7B 70
Rosemount Point. SE23 —8A 54
Rosendale Rd. SE21 —4D 5
Roseneath Clo. Orp —8L 85
Rosenthal Rd. SE6 —4E 54
Rosenthorpe Rd. SE15 —3A 54
Rosery, The. Croy —9A 68
Rose St. N'fleet —4A 62
Rose St. Roch —9A 80
Rose St. S'ness —2C 218
Rose St. Tonb —7J 145
Rose Ter. Fav —7H 187 (off Canterbury Rd.)
Rosetower Ct. Broad —5K 209
Roseveare Rd. SE12 —9M 55
Rose Vs. Afrd —1F 160 (off Lwr. Denmark Rd.)
Rose Vs. Dart —5B 60
Rose Vs. New R —3C 212
Rose Wlk. W Wick —3F 82
Rose Way. SE12 —3K 55
Rosewood. Dart —9F 58
Rosewood Clo. Sidc —8L 57
Rosewood Ct. Brom —4M 69
Rose Yd. Maid —5D 126
Rosher Ho. Grav —4E 62
Rosherville. —4D 62 (4A 8)
Rosherville Way. Grav —5D 62
Rosiers Ct. Cant —1L 171
Roslin Way. Brom —1K 69
Ross Ct. Afrd —3E 160
Rossdale. Tun W —9K 151
Rossendale Ct. Folk —5L 189 (off Dover Rd.)
Rossendale Gdns. Folk —5L 189
Rossendale Rd. Folk —5L 189
Rossetti Rd. Birch —3E 206
Ross Gdns. R Comn —8G 167
Rossland Clo. Bexh —3C 58
Rossland Rd. Ram —4E 210
Rosslare Clo. W'ham —7F 116
Rosslyn Clo. W Wick —4J 83
Rosslyn Grn. Maid —4M 125
Rosslyn Hill. NW3 —1B 4
Rossmore Rd. NW1 —2B 4
Ross Rd. Dart —4H 59
Ross St. Roch —8A 80
Ross Way. SE9 —1A 56
Ross Way. Folk —7E 188
Rothbrook Dri. Kenn —3G 158
Rothbury Rd. E9 —1E 5
Rotherfield. —4D 35
Rotherfield Rd. Crowb —4D 35
Rotherhithe. —3D 5
Rotherhithe New Rd. SE16 —3D 5
Rother Ho. Maid —9G 127
Rothermere Clo. Bene —3A 38
Rother Rd. Tonb —2H 145
Rother Vale. Chat —8F 94
Rother Valley Railway Museum. —3A 44
Rothesay Ct. SE12 —8L 55
Rothley Clo. Tent —7C 222
Rothsay Ct. Ram —3K 211
Rouge La. Grav —5G 63
Rough Common. —8H 167 (4D 21)
Rough Comn. Rd. R Comn —1G 171 (4D 21)
Roughetts Rd. Rya —6L 107 (4B 16)
Roughway. —2A 134 (2A 26)
Roughway La. D Grn & Rough —2N 133 (2A 26)
Round Ash Way. Hart —9L 75
Roundel Clo. SE4 —2C 54
Roundel Clo. Tey —2L 223
Roundell Way. Mard —3K 205
Roundels, The. Lyn —4H 223
Roundel, The. Sit —9G 98
Round Green. —2D 37
Round Grn. La. C'brk —2D 37
Round Gro. Croy —1A 82
Roundhay. Leyb —9B 108
Roundhay Clo. SE23 —7A 54
Roundhill Rd. Tun W —4K 157
Roundlyn Gdns. St M —7K 71
Roundshaw. —3C 13
Round Street. —7J 77 (1B 16)
Round St. Sole S —6H 77 (1B 16)
Roundtable Rd. Brom —8J 55
Roundway. Big H —4C 164
Roundwell. Bear —5N 127 (2A 28)
Roundwood. Chst —5D 70
Roundwood Rd. NW10 —1A 4
Rover Rd. Chat —9E 94
Rowan Clo. Afrd —8C 158
Rowan Clo. Meop —9G 76
Rowan Clo. Pad W —1L 153
Rowan Clo. S'le —1B 32
Rowan Clo. Sturry —5E 168
Rowan Cres. Dart —6K 59
Rowan Ho. Hay —5H 69
Rowan Ho. Maid —6L 125
Rowan Ho. S'ness —2C 218 (off Pepys Av.)
Rowan Ho. Sidc —8H 57
Rowan Lea. Chat —3E 94
Rowan Rd. SW16 —1C 12
Rowan Rd. Bexh —1N 57
Rowan Rd. Swan —6E 72
Rowans Clo. Long —5K 75
Rowan Shaw. Tonb —1K 145
Rowans, The. Min S —5J 219
Rowan Tree Rd. Tun W —4E 156
Rowan Wlk. Brom —4B 84
Rowan Wlk. Chat —9B 80
Rowanwood Av. Sidc —6J 57
Rowbrocke Clo. Gill —8N 95
Rowden Rd. Beck —4B 68
Rowdow. Otf —7L 103 (4D 15)
Rowdow La. Sev & Knat —4L 103 (3D 15)
Rowdown Cres. New Ad —9G 83
Rowena Rd. Wgte S —2K 207
Rowe Pl. Eccl —4K 109
Rowetts Way. E'chu —5C 202 (1E 19)
Rowfield. Eden —4D 184
Rowhill Rd. Swan & Dart —2G 73
Rowland Av. Gill —1H 95
Rowland Clo. Maid —6B 126
Rowland Cotts. Lymp —5A 196
Rowland Cres. H Bay —2M 195
Rowland Dri. H Bay —5D 194
Rowlatt Clo. Dart —9K 59
Rowlatt Rd. Dart —9K 59
Rowley Av. Sidc —5K 57
Rowley Rd. Ors —2B 8
Rowling Street. —2A 40
Rowman Ct. Broad —8L 209
Rowntree Path. SE28 —1K 51
Row, The. Eden —3B 184
Row, The. Elham —7N 183 (4E 31)
Row, The. New Ash —3M 89
Rowton Rd. SE18 —7E 50
Rowzill Rd. Swan —2G 72
Roxborough Rd. Wgte S —2L 207
Roxley Rd. SE13 —4E 54
Roxton Gdns. Croy —6D 82
Royal Albert Way. E16 —2A 6
Royal Artillery Museum. —5B 50 (3A 6)
Royal Artillery Way. Sth S —1C 11
Royal Av. Tonb —7J 145
Royal Av. Whits —8E 224
Royal British Legion Village. —9K 109 (1D 27)
Royal Chase. Tun W —1F 156
Royal Clo. Broad —9K 209
Royal Ct. S'ness —2D 218
Royal Cres. Mgte —3B 208
Royal Cres. Ram —7H 211
Royal Docks Rd. E6 & Bark —2A 6
Royal Eagle Clo. Roch —5B 80
Royal Engineers Museum. —5E 80 (1E 17)
Royal Engineers Rd. S'lng —9B 110
Royal Engineers Way. Maid —1D 27
Royal Esplanade. Mgte —2L 207 (1D 23)
Royal Esplanade. Ram —7F 210
Royal Herbert Pavilions. SE18 —8B 50
Royal Hill. SE10 —3E 5
Royal Hospital Rd. SW3 —3B 4
Royal Military Av. Folk —6D 188 (2E 41)
Royal Military Rd. Hythe —7A 196
Royal Military Rd. W'sea —4A 46
Royal Mint St. E1 —2D 5
Royal Museum & Art Gallery, The. —2M 171
Royal Oak Hill. Knock —9H 101
Royal Oak Rd. Bexh —3A 58
Royal Oak Ter. Grav —6H 63 (off Constitution Hill)
Royal Pde. SE3 —3E 5
Royal Pde. Chst —3E 70 (1B 14)
Royal Pde. Ram —7J 211 (2E 23)
Royal Pde. M. Chst —3E 70 (off Royal Pde.)
Royal Pier M. Grav —4G 63
Royal Pier Rd. Grav —4G 63
Royal Rd. Dart —1A 74
Royal Rd. Ram —6H 211 (2E 23)
Royal Rd. S'ness —2D 218
Royal Rd. Sidc —8M 57
Royal St George's Golf Course. —4D 23
Royal Sovereign Av. Chat —5E 80
Royal Star Arc. Maid —5C 126
Royal Tunbridge Wells. —1G 157 (2E 35)
Royal Tunbridge Wells Bus. Pk. Tun W —5L 151
Royal Victoria Pl. Dover —4J 181 (off High St. Dover,)
Royal Victoria Pl. Tun W —1H 157
Royal W. Kent Av. Tonb —3K 145
Royal West Kent Regiment Museum. —4C 126
Roydene Rd. SE18 —6G 50
Roydon Hall Rd. E Peck —3K 135 (3B 26)
Royds Rd. W'boro —3H 161
Royston Gdns. St Mc —7J 213
Royston Rd. SE20 —4A 68
Royston Rd. Bear —6K 127
Royston Rd. Dart —4G 58
Roystons Clo. Gill —1B 96
Roystons, The. Surb —2A 12
Royton Av. Len —7E 200
Rubens St. SE6 —7C 54
Rubery Drove. R'boro —3C 23
Ruckholt Rd. E10 —1E 5
Ruckinge. —3A 40
Ruckinge Rd. Bils —3A 40
Ruckinge Rd. Hams —8D 190 (3A 40)
Ruckinge Way. Gill —9M 81
Ruck La. Horsm —2C 36
Ruddstreet Clo. SE18 —4D 50
Rudge Clo. Chat —9G 94
Rudgwick Ct. SE18 —4A 50 (off Woodville St.)
Rudland Rd. Bexh —1C 58
Ruffets Wood. Grav —2H 77
Rugby Clo. Broad —8K 209
Rugby Clo. Chat —7C 94
Rugby Gdns. Afrd —1G 160
Rugby Rd. Dover —6F 180
Ruggles Clo. H Hals —2H 67
Ruins Barn Rd. Tun —6D 114
Rule Ct. S'ness —4C 218 (4C 18)
Rumania Wlk. Grav —8L 63
Rumfields Rd. Broad —9G 209 (2E 23)
Rumstead La. S'bry —8E 112 (4A 18)
Rumstead Rd. S'bry —6F 112 (4A 18)
Rumwood Ct. Langl —3M 139
Runcie Ho. Cant —3M 171 (1D 31) (off Station Rd. E.)
Runcie Pl. Cant —1K 171
Runciman Clo. Orp —1L 101
Runham La. H'shm —6N 141 (3B 28)
Running Horse Roundabout. S'lng —9B 110
Runnymede Ct. Dart —6C 60
Runnymede Gdns. Maid —9D 126
Rural Ter. Wye —2M 159
Rural Vale. N'fleet —5D 62
Ruscombe Clo. Tun W —4F 150
Rusham Rd. Shtng —1D 226 (4B 22)
Rushbrook. P'ley —4D 29
Rushbrook Rd. SE9 —7E 56
Rush Clo. Chat —8D 94
Rush Clo. Dym —9A 182
Rushdean Rd. Roch —7H 79
Rushdene. SE2 —3M 51 (in two parts)
Rushdene Wlk. Big H —5D 164
Rushenden. —9A 218 (1C 19)
Rushenden Ct. Queen —9A 218
Rushenden Rd. Queen —9A 218 (1C 19)
Rushet Rd. Orp —5K 71
Rushett. —3A 24
Rushett La. Nor —3E 19
Rushetts. L'tn G —1N 155
Rushetts Rd. W King —8E 88
Rushey Grn. SE6 —5E 54 (4E 5)
Rushey Mead. SE4 —3D 54
Rushford Clo. H'crn —3K 193
Rushford Rd. SE4 —4C 54
Rushgrove St. SE18 —4B 50
Rushley Clo. Kes —5N 83
Rushlye Clo. Bells Y —8M 157
Rushmead Clo. Cant —9K 167
Rushmead Dri. Maid —1D 138
Rushmere Ct. Igh —2K 121
Rushmore Clo. Brom —6A 70
Rushmore Hill. Orp & Knock —9L 85 (3B 14)
Rushymead. Kems —9A 104
Ruskin Av. Well —1J 57
Ruskin Clo. E Mal —1D 124
Ruskin Dri. Orp —4G 84
Ruskin Dri. Well —1J 57
Ruskin Gro. Dart —4A 60
Ruskin Gro. Well —9J 51
Ruskin Rd. Belv —4B 52
Ruskin Rd. Cars —2B 12
Ruskin Ter. Dover —1G 181
Ruskin Wlk. Brom —9B 70
Rusland Av. Orp —4F 84
Rusling Rd. Bor G —2N 121
Russell Clo. Beck —6F 68
Russell Clo. Bexh —2B 58
Russell Clo. Dart —2H 59
Russell Clo. Sit —8D 98
Russell Ct. Chat —9E 80
Russell Courtyard. Chst —4C 70
Russell Dri. Whits —3M 225
Russell Pl. Oare —1F 186
Russell Pl. S at H —4A 74
Russell Rd. Ayle —3A 110
Russell Rd. Folk —5K 189
Russell Rd. Grav —4J 63
Russell's Av. Gill —3C 96
Russell Sq. Long —6K 75
Russell St. WC1 —2C 5
Russell St. Dover —5K 181
Russell St. S'ness —2C 218
Russell Ter. Hort K —7C 74
Russet Av. Fav —7J 187
Russet Clo. Roch —4J 79
Russet Ct. Cox —5N 137
Russet Dri. Croy —2B 82
Russets, The. Ches —4M 225
Russets, The. Maid —4M 125
Russets, The. Meop —9F 76
Russett Clo. Ayle —1J 125
Russett Clo. Orp —6K 85
Russett Rd. Cant —3B 172
Russett Rd. E Peck —1L 147
Russett Way. Swan —5E 72
Russet Way. King H —7L 123
Rusthall. —1C 156 (2E 35)
Rusthall Grange. Tun W —1D 156
Rusthall Pk. Tun W —1D 156 (in two parts)
Rusthall Pl. Tun W —2D 156
Rusthall Rd. Tun W —1C 156 (2E 35)
Ruston Rd. SE18 —3A 50
Rustwick. Tun W —1D 156
Rutherford Rd. Kenn —5F 158
Rutherford Way. Tonb —9K 133
Rutherglen Rd. SE2 —6J 51
Ruth Ho. Maid —4B 126
Rutland Av. Mgte —3F 208
Rutland Av. Sidc —5J 57
Rutland Clo. Bex —7M 57
Rutland Clo. Dart —5L 59
Rutland Cotts. Leeds —3A 140
Rutland Ct. SE9 —7E 56
Rutland Ct. Chst —4C 70
Rutland Gdns. Birch —4E 206
Rutland Gdns. Clift —3G 208
Rutland Ga. Belv —5C 52
Rutland Ga. Brom —7J 69
Rutland Ho. Cant —3N 171 (1D 31)
Rutland Pk. SE6 —7C 54
Rutland Pl. Gill —8M 95
Rutland Rd. Cant —3C 172
Rutland Rd. Dover —1G 180
Rutland Wlk. SE6 —7C 54
Rutland Way. Maid —9H 127
Rutland Way. Orp —9L 71
Ruxley. —3N 71 (1C 14)
Ruxley Clo. Sidc —2M 71
Ruxley Corner Ind. Est. Sidc —2M 71
Ruxley La. Eps —3A 12
Ruxton Clo. Swan —6F 72
Ruxton Ct. Swan —6F 72
Ryan Clo. SE3 —2M 55
Ryarsh. —6L 107 (4B 16)
Ryarsh Cres. Orp —5G 85
Ryarsh La. W Mal —9N 107
Ryarsh Rd. Birl —5N 107 (3B 16)
Rycault Clo. Maid —6B 126
Rycaut Clo. Gill —8N 95
Rycroft La. Sev —3F 130 (2C 25)
Rydal Av. Ram —5E 210
Rydal Clo. Tun W —9E 150
Rydal Dri. Bexh —8B 52
Rydal Dri. Tun W —9E 150
Rydal Dri. W Wick —3H 83
Rydal Ho. Maid —1G 139
Ryde Clo. Chat —3E 94
Rydens Ho. SE9 —8M 55
Ryder Clo. Brom —1L 69
Ryders. L'tn G —2A 156
Ryder's Av. Wgte S —3J 207
Ryde St. Cant —1L 171
Rydons Clo. SE9 —1A 56
Rye. —3A 46
Rye Clo. Bex —4C 58
Rye Ct. Afrd —2B 160
Rye Cres. Orp —2L 85
Ryecroft Rd. SE13 —3F 54
Ryecroft Rd. Orp —9F 70
Ryecroft Rd. Otf —7H 103
Rye Field. Orp —2M 85
Rye Foreign. —3E 45
Ryegrass Clo. Chat —5F 94
Rye Harbour. —4A 46
Rye Hill. P'den —3A 46
Ryelands Cres. SE12 —4M 55
Rye La. SE15 —3D 5
Rye La. Dun G & Otf —2G 118 (1C 25)
Rye Rd. SE15 —2A 54
Rye Rd. B'lnd —2C 46 (in two parts)
Rye Rd. Hawkh —5L 191 (4E 37)
Rye Rd. Rye F —3E 45
Rye Rd. Sand —1H 215 (1C 45)
Rye Rd. Wit —2A 46
Rye Wlk. H Bay —5K 195
Ryewood Cotts. Dun G —2G 118
Ryland Ct. Folk —6L 189 (off Ryland Pl.)

Ryland Pl.—St Matthew's Dri.

Ryland Pl. Folk —6L 189
Rylands Rd. Kenn —4H 159
Rymers Clo. Tun W —7K 151
Rymill St. E16 —1C 50
Rype Clo. Lydd —4C 204
(in two parts)
Rysted La. W'ham —8E 116
Ryswick M. New R —1D 212

Sabre Ct. Gill B —2K 95
Sackett's Gap. Clift —2G 209
Sacketts Hill. Broad —7F 208
Sackville Av. Brom —2K 83
Sackville Clo. Hoth —4E 29
Sackville Clo. Sev —4J 119
Sackville College. —2A 34
Sackville Cres. Afrd —8E 158
Sackville Rd. Dart —7M 59
Saddington St. Grav —5G 63
Saddlers Clo. Weav —4H 127
Saddlers Hill. Good —2B 32
Saddlers M. Ches —4M 225
Saddler's Pk. Eyns —4L 87
Saddlers Wall La. B'lnd —2B 46
Saddlers Way. Afrd —5F 160
Saddleton Gro. Whits —5F 224
Saddleton Rd. Whits —5F 224
Sadlers Clo. Chat —9A 94
Saffron's Pl. Folk —6L 189
Saffron Way. Chat —6C 94
Saffron Way. Sit —4G 99 (2C 19)
Sahara Clo. Farn —6F 84
Sail Field Ct. Chat —5C 80
Sail Lofts, The. Whits —3F 224
Sailmakers Ct. Chat —1E 94
St Agnes Gdns. S'ness —3D 218
St Aidan's Way. Grav —8K 63
St Albans Clo. Gill —5H 81
St Alban's Clo. Grav —8J 63
St Albans Downs Rd. Non —3B 32
St Alban's Gdns. Grav —8J 63
St Alban's Rd. Dart —4N 59
St Albans Rd. Her —2K 169
St Alban's Rd. Roch —6H 79
St Alban Wlk. Chat —9B 80
St Alphege Clo. Whits —6D 224
St Alphege La. Cant —1M 171 (4D 21)
St Alphege Rd. Dover —3H 181
St Ambrose Grn. Wye —2M 159
St Amunds Clo. SE6 —9D 54
St Andrews. Folk —6L 189
St Andrew's Clo. Barm —7L 125
St Andrews Clo. Cant —3L 171 (1D 31)
St Andrew's Clo. H Bay —3H 195
St Andrew's Clo. Mgte —6D 208
St Andrew's Clo. Pad W —9M 147
St Andrew's Clo. Whits —6G 224
St Andrews Ct. Grav —4G 63
(off Queen St.)
St Andrews Ct. Swan —6F 72
St Andrews Ct. Tun W —5G 150
St Andrew's Dri. Orp —9K 71
St Andrews Gdns. Dover —2G 180
St Andrew's Gdns. S'wll —2D 220
St Andrews Ho. Maid —6L 125
St Andrews Lees. S'wch —6M 217
St Andrew's Pk. Rd. Tun W —5G 150
St Andrew's Rd. Deal —4M 177
St Andrews Rd. Gill —5G 80
St Andrew's Rd. Grav —5G 63
St Andrew's Rd. L'stne —3E 212 (2E 47)
St Andrew's Rd. Maid —7L 125
St Andrew's Rd. Pad W —9M 147
St Andrew's Rd. Sidc —8M 57
St Andrew's Rd. Til —1E 62 (3A 8)
St Andrew's Wlk. Allh —4L 201
St Andrews Way. Tilm —3C 33
St Andrew Ter. Dover —2F 180
St Anne Ct. Maid —5B 126
St Anne's Ct. H Bay —2F 194
St Anne's Ct. W Wick —5H 83
St Anne's Dri. H Bay —3E 194
St Anne's Gdns. Mgte —5D 208
St Anne's Rd. Afrd —2D 160
St Anne's Rd. Whits —2H 225 (2C 21)
St Ann's Green. —4D 27
St Ann's Grn. La. Mard —4D 27
St Ann's Hill. SW18 —4B 4
St Ann's Rd. Dym —8A 182
St Ann's Rd. Fav —6F 186
St Anns Way. Berr G —7D 100
St Anthony's Way. Mgte —4G 208
St Asaph Ho. Maid —1G 139
St Asaph Rd. SE4 —1A 54 (4D 5)
St Aubyn's Clo. Orp —4H 85
St Aubyn's Gdns. Orp —3H 85
St Audley Av. Bexh —9B 52
St Augustine's Abbey. —2A 172 (1D 31)
St Augustine's Av. Brom —8A 70
St Augustine's Av. Mgte —5D 208
St Augustines Bus. Pk. Whits —3N 225
St Augustine's Ct. Cant —2A 172
St Augustine's Cres. Whits —2M 225
St Augustine's Pk. Ram —6G 210
St Augustine's Rd. Belv —4A 52 (3C 6)
St Augustine's Rd. Cant —3A 172
St Augustine's Rd. Deal —6J 177
St Augustine's Rd. Ram
—7H 211 (2E 23)
St Barnabas Clo. All —1N 125
St Barnabas Clo. Afrd —2D 160
St Barnabas Clo. Beck —5F 68
St Barnabas Clo. Gill —9G 81
St Barnabas Clo. Tun W —9H 151
St Barnabas Rd. Sutt —2B 12
St Bartholomews. S'wch —6M 217
St Bartholomews La. Roch —8B 80
St Bartholomews Ter. Roch —8B 80
St Bart's Rd. S'wch —6L 217 (1D 33)
St Benedict Rd. Snod —3C 108
St Benedict's Av. Grav —8K 63
St Benedict's Lawn. Ram —7H 211
St Benets Ct. Tent —7C 222
St Benet's Rd. Wgte S —4K 207
St Benets Way. Tent —7C 222
St Benjamins Dri. Prat B —9L 85
St Bernards Rd. Tonb —1J 145
St Blaise Av. Brom —5L 69 (1A 14)
St Botolph Rd. Grav —8C 62
St Botolph's Av. Sev —6H 119
St Botolph's Rd. Sev —6J 119 (2D 25)
St Brides Clo. Eri —2M 51
St Catherine's. Old R —2D 47
(off Swamp Rd.)
St Catherines Ct. Ram —3J 211
St Catherine's Dri. Fav —6H 187
St Catherine's Gro. Mans —3B 210
St Catherines Hospital. Roch —8A 80
St Chad's Dri. Grav —8K 63
St Chads Rd. Til —3B 8
St Christopher Clo. Mgte —5H 209
St Christopher's Grn. Broad —8K 209
St Clare Rd. Walm —9M 177 (3E 33)
St Clements. S'wch —6M 217
St Clements Clo. Ley S —6J 203
St Clement's Clo. N'fleet —8E 62
St Clements Ct. Broad —8J 209
St Clements Ct. Folk —6M 189
St Clement's Ct. H Bay —4H 195
St Clements Ho. Roch —7A 80
St Clements Rd. Ward —5K 203
St Clements Rd. Wgte S —2K 207
St Clere Hill Rd. W King —3F 104 (3E 15)
St Columba's Clo. Grav —8J 63
St Cosmus Clo. C'lck —9D 174
St Crispin's Rd. Wgte S —4K 207
St David's Av. Dover —8F 180
St David's Bri. C'brk —8D 176 (3E 37)
St David's Clo. Birch —3G 207
St David's Clo. W Wick —1E 82
St David's Clo. Whits —6G 225
St David's Cres. Grav —9J 63
St David's Rd. Allh —4L 201
St David's Rd. Deal —4M 177
St David's Rd. Ram —3K 211
St Davids Rd. Swan —2G 72 (1C 15)
St David's Rd. Tun W —8H 151
St Denys Rd. H'nge —7D 192
St Dunstan's. —1K 171
St Dunstan's. (Junct.) —3B 12
St Dunstans Av. W3 —2A 4
St Dunstans Clo. Cant —1L 171
St Dunstan's Dri. Grav —8K 63
St Dunstan's Hill. Sutt —3B 12
St Dunstan's La. Beck —9F 68
St Dunstan's Rd. Mgte —3E 208
St Dunstan's St. Cant —1L 171 (4D 21)
St Dunstan's Ter. Cant —1L 171
St Dunstan's Wlk. C'brk —8D 176
St Eanswythe's Way. Folk —6K 189
St Edith Cotts. Sev —7H 105
St Edith's Farm Cotts. Kems —9B 104
St Edith's Rd. Kems —8A 104 (4D 15)
St Edmunds Clo. Eri —2M 51
St Edmund's Ct. W King —9F 88
St Edmunds Rd. Cant —2M 171 (1D 31)
St Edmund's Rd. Dart —2A 60
St Edmund's Rd. Deal —6H 177
St Edmunds Wlk. Dover —4J 181
(off Priory Rd.)
St Edmunds Way. Gill —2C 96
St Faith's La. Bear —5L 127
St Faith's St. Maid —5C 126
St Fidelis Rd. Eri —5E 52
St Fillans Rd. SE6 —6F 54
St Francis Av. Grav —9K 63
St Francis Clo. Deal —6J 177
St Francis Clo. Mgte —5H 209
St Francis Clo. Orp —9G 71
St Francis Rd. Eri —4E 52
St Francis Rd. Folk —5F 188
St Francis Rd. Meop —8G 91
St Georges Av. E'chu —6C 202
St George's Av. H Bay —3D 194
St George's Av. S'ness —4C 218 (4C 11)
St Georges Bus. Cen. Afrd —8D 158
St George's Cen. Cant
—2N 171 (1D 31)
St George's Cen. Grav —4G 62
St Georges Clo. Whits —6G 225
St Georges Ct. Dover —2F 180
St Georges Ct. S'ness —4C 218
St Georges Ct. Wro —7M 105
St Georges Cres. Dover —7G 180
St George's Cres. Grav —9J 63
St Georges Dri. SW1 —3C 4
St George's La. Cant —2M 171 (1D 31)
St George's Lees. S'wch —6M 217
(in two parts)
St George's M. Tonb —7H 145
St George's Pk. Tun W —5F 156
St George's Pas. Deal —4N 177
St George's Pl. Cant —2N 171 (1D 31)
St George's Pl. Hythe —8E 196
St Georges Pl. St Mc —7J 213
St George's Rd. SE1 —3C 5
St George's Rd. Beck —4E 68
St George's Rd. Broad —9L 209
St George's Rd. Brom —5B 70
(in two parts)
St George's Rd. Deal —4M 177
St Georges Rd. Folk —5F 188
St George's Rd. Gill —6F 80
St George's Rd. Orp —9F 70
St George's Rd. Ram —4K 211
St George's Rd. S'wch —6M 217 (1D 33)
St George's Rd. Sev —4J 119
St George's Rd. Sidc —2M 71
St Georges Rd. Swan —7G 72
St George's Rd. W. Brom —5A 70
St Georges Sq. Afrd —8F 158
(off Gilbert Rd.)
St Georges Sq. Grav —4G 62
St Georges Sq. Long —6L 75
St George's Sq. Maid —6A 126
St George's St. Cant —2N 171 (1D 31)
St George's Ter. Cant —2N 171 (1D 31)
St George's Ter. H Bay —2E 194
St George's Wlk. Allh —4L 201
St German's Rd. SE23 —6B 54
St Giles Clo. Dover —7G 180
St Giles Clo. Orp —6F 84
St Giles Rd. Dover —7G 180
St Giles Wlk. Dover —7G 180
St Gregory's Clo. Deal —6J 177
St Gregory's Ct. Cant —1A 172
St Gregory's Ct. Grav —7K 63
St Gregory's Cres. Grav —7K 63
St Gregory's Rd. Cant —1A 172
St Helen's Cotts. Maid —9J 125
St Helens La. E Far —9J 125 (2D 27)
St Helens Rd. Cli —3C 176
St Helen's Rd. Eri —2M 51
St Helen's Rd. S'ness —3E 218 (4D 11)
St Helier. —2B 12
St Helier Av. Mord —2B 12
St Helier's Clo. Maid —7M 125
St Hilda Rd. Folk —5E 188
St Hildas. Plax —9M 121
St Hildas Rd. Hythe —7J 197
St Hilda's Way. Grav —9J 63
St Jacob's Pl. Cant —4K 171
St James Av. Beck —6B 68
St James Av. Broad —8J 209
St Jame's Av. Ram —2F 210
St James Clo. SE18 —5E 50
St James Clo. E Mal —1D 124
St James Clo. Isle G —2C 190
St James Clo. Tonb —9K 133
St James Clo. Ward —4K 203
St James Ct. Grnh —4E 60
St James Ct. Tun W —1H 157
St James Gdns. Whits —5F 224
St James La. Dover —5K 181
St James La. Grnh —6E 60 (4E 7)
St James Oak. Grav —5F 62
St James Pk. Tun W —9J 151
St James Pk. Rd. Mgte —3M 207
St James Pl. Dart —4L 59
St James Rd. Isle G —3C 190
St James Rd. Kgdn —4N 199
St James Rd. Sev —4J 119
St James' Rd. Tun W —9J 151
St James's. —2C 4
St James's Av. Beck —6B 68
St James's Av. Grav —5F 62
St James's Dri. SW17 —4B 4
St James Sq. Long —6L 75
St James's Rd. SE1 & SE16 —3D 5
St James's Rd. Croy —2C 13
St James's Rd. Grav —4F 62
St James's St. SW1 —2C 4
St James's St. Grav —4F 62
St James's Ter. Birch —3G 207
(in two parts)
St James St. Dover —5K 181
St James Way. Sidc —1N 71
St Jean's Rd. Wgte S —4K 207
St John Fisher Rd. Eri —3M 51
St Johns. —3E 5
(nr. Lewisham)
St John's. —8G 150 (1E 35)
(nr. Tunbridge Wells)
St Johns. —4K 119 (1D 25)
(nr. Sevenoaks)
St John's Av. Ram —3D 210
St John's Av. Sit —8J 99
St John's Chu. Rd. Folk —5J 189
St John's Clo. Dens —5C 192
St John's Clo. Hart —8M 75
St John's Clo. High —9G 65
St John's Cotts. Beth —2J 163
St John's Ct. Cant —2M 171 (1D 31)
St John's Ct. Eri —5E 52
St John's Ct. Sev —4K 119
St Johns Cres. T Hill —4K 167
St John's Gro. N19 —1C 4
St John's Hill. SW11 —4B 4
St John's Hill. Sev —3K 119 (1D 25)
St John's Jerusalem. —3B 74
St John's Jerusalem Garden.
—3B 74 (1D 15)
St Johns La. Afrd —8G 158
St John's La. Cant —2M 171 (1D 31)
St John's La. Hart —9M 75
St Johns Pde. Sidc —9K 57
(off Sidcup High St.)
St John's Pk. Tun W —6G 150
St John's Pl. Cant —1N 171
St Johns Rise. Berr G —7D 100
St John's Rd. Crowb —4C 35
St John's Rd. Dart —5C 60
St John's Rd. Dover —5H 181
St Johns Rd. Evtn —1J 185
St John's Rd. Eri —5E 52
St John's Rd. Fav —6H 187
St John's Rd. Gill —9F 80
St John's Rd. Grav —5J 63
St John's Rd. High —9G 65
St Johns Rd. Hoo —7G 67
St John's Rd. Hythe —5H 197
St John's Rd. Mgte —3D 208
St John's Rd. New R —3B 212
St John's Rd. Orp —9F 70
St John's Rd. Sev —3J 119
St John's Rd. Sidc —9K 57
St John's Rd. Tun W —6G 150 (1E 35)
St John's Rd. Well —1K 57
St John's Rd. Whits —3M 225 (2D 21)
St John's St. Folk —6K 189
St John's St. Mgte —3D 208
St John's Ter. SE18 —6E 50
St John's Ter. Folk —5K 189
(off St John's Chu. Rd.)
St John St. EC1 —2C 5
St John's Way. Dens —5B 192
St Johns Way. Roch —1L 93
(in two parts)
St John's Wood. —2B 4
St John's Wood Rd. NW8 —2B 4
St Joseph's Clo. Orp —4H 85
St Joseph's Vale. SE3 —1G 55
St Julians Rd. Sev —2D 25
St Julian's Rd. Under —3M 131
St Julien Av. Cant —1C 172
St Justin Clo. St P —6M 71
St Katherine Rd. Min S —5F 218
St Katherine's La. Snod
—3D 108 (3C 16)
St Katherine's Rd. Eri —2M 51
St Keverne Rd. SE9 —9A 56
St Kilda Rd. Orp —2H 85
St Laurence Av. Maid —1M 125
St Laurence Clo. Orp —6M 71
St Lawrence. —5G 210 (2E 23)
St Lawrence Av. Bidb —3D 150
St Lawrence Av. Ram —6F 210
St Lawrence Clo. Bap —9L 99
St Lawrence Clo. Cant —4A 172
St Lawrence Ct. Cant —4A 172
St Lawrence Ct. Ram —5F 210
St Lawrence Forstal. Cant —4A 172
St Lawrence Ind. Est. Ram —4F 210
St Lawrence Pk. Rd. Ram
—5G 210 (2E 23)
St Lawrence Rd. Cant —4A 172 (1D 31)
St Lawrence Ter. Dover —1G 181
(off Montreal Clo.)
St Leonards Av. Chat —1C 94
St Leonard's Clo. Deal —6L 177
St Leonard's Clo. Well —1J 57
St Leonard's Ct. Hythe —7J 197
(off St Leonard's Rd.)
St Leonard's Rise. Orp —5G 84
St Leonards Rd. All —1N 125
St Leonard's Rd. Deal —6L 177 (3E 33)
St Leonard's Rd. Hythe —7J 197 (3D 41)
St Leonard's Street. —3N 123
St Leonard's St. W Mal
—3M 123 (1B 26)
St Louis Gro. H Bay —3D 194
St Lukes Av. Maid —4E 126
St Luke's Av. Ram —4H 211 (2E 23)
St Luke's Clo. Dart —1E 74
St Luke's Clo. Swan —5E 72
St Luke's Clo. Wgte S —3K 207
St Lukes Clo. Whits —6G 224
St Lukes Rd. Maid —4E 126
St Luke's Rd. Ram —4J 211
St Luke's Rd. Tun W —8H 151
St Lukes Wlk. H'nge —8B 192
St Luke's Way. Allh —4L 201
St Magnus Clo. Birch —3E 206
St Magnus Ct. Birch —3F 206
St Malo Ct. Folk —7J 189
(off Manor Rd.)
St Margarets. —3E 74
St Margaret's at Cliffe.
—7J 213 (4E 33)
St Margarets Av. Berr G —7D 100
St Margaret's Av. Sidc —8F 56
St Margarets Bank. Roch —8A 80
St Margarets Banks. Roch —7A 80
St Margaret's Clo. Maid —7M 125
St Margaret's Clo. Orp —5K 85
St Margarets Clo. Sea —7C 224
St Margarets Ct. Folk —6H 189
St Margaret's Ct. H Hals —2H 67
St Margaret's Cres. Grav —8K 63
St Margarets Dri. Gill —6M 95
St Margarets Dri. Walm —9L 177
St Margaret's Gro. SE18 —6E 50
St Margaret's M. Roch —7N 79
St Margaret's Pas. SE13 —1H 55
St Margaret's Rd. SE4 —2C 54
St Margarets Rd. N'fleet —6D 62
St Margarets Rd. S Dar & Grn St
—3E 74 (1E 15)
St Margaret's Rd. St Mc —8K 213
St Margarets Rd. St Mb —7K 199
St Margaret's Rd. Wgte S —4K 207
St Margarets Rd. Wdchu —8L 207
St Margaret's St. Cant
—2M 171 (1D 31)
St Margaret's St. Roch —8M 79 (2D 17)
St Margaret's Ter. SE18 —5E 50
St Margaret St. SW1 —3C 5
St Mark's Av. N'fleet —5D 62
St Marks Clo. Folk —6D 188
St Mark's Clo. N'tn —4L 97
St Mark's Clo. Whits —5G 225
St Marks Ct. Eccl —4K 109
St Mark's Ho. Gill —7F 80
St Mark's Rd. W10 —2A 4
St Mark's Rd. Brom —6L 69
St Marks Rd. Mitc —1B 12
St Mark's Rd. Tun W —5F 156 (2E 35)
St Martin's. —2A 172
St Martin's Av. Cant —2A 172
St Martin's Cvn. & Camp Site. Cant
—2D 172
St Martin's Clo. Cant —2A 172
St Martin's Clo. Det —9K 111
St Martin's Clo. Dover —7G 180
St Martin's Clo. Eri —2M 51
St Martin's Clo. N'tn —4L 97
St Martin's Ct. Cant —2A 172
St Martin's Dri. Eyns —4L 87
St Martins Gdns. Dover —5H 181
(off Clarendon Rd.)
St Martin's Hill. Cant —2A 172 (1E 31)
St Martins La. WC2 —2C 5
St Martins Meadow. Bras —5L 117
St Martin's Path. Dover —6H 181
St Martin's Pl. Cant —2A 172
St Martin's Plain. —5B 188
St Martin's Rd. Dart —4N 59
St Martin's Rd. Deal —6J 177
St Martins Rd. Folk —5D 188
St Martin's Rd. Gus —9K 179
St Martin's Rd. New R —3C 212
St Martin's Steps. Dover —6H 181
St Martin's Ter. Cant —2A 172
St Martin's View. H Bay —7H 195
St Mary Cray. —7L 71 (1B 14)
St Mary Hoo. —3A 10
St Mary in the Marsh.
—2A 214 (2E 47)
St Mary's Av. Brom —6H 69
St Mary's Av. Mgte —4H 209
St Mary's Bay. —2E 214 (2E 47)
St Mary's Clo. E'try —3L 183
St Mary's Clo. Grav —7H 63
St Mary's Clo. Hams —7D 190
St Mary's Clo. Non —2B 32
St Mary's Clo. Orp —5K 71
St Mary's Clo. Platt —2B 122
St Mary's Clo. Wdboro —8G 216
St Mary's Ct. St Mil —2L 171 (1D 31)
St Mary's Ct. W Mal —1N 123
St Mary's Dri. Sev —5F 118
St Mary's Gdns. Chat —5E 80
St Mary's Gdns. Ups —3A 22
St Mary's Ga. S'wch —5M 217
St Mary's Grn. Big H —6C 164
St Mary's Grn. Kenn —3J 159
St Mary's Gro. Big H —6C 164
St Mary's Gro. Sea —7A 224
St Mary's Gro. Tilm —3C 33
St Mary's-in-Castro Saxon Church.
—4L 181
St Mary's Island. —3E 80 (1E 17)
St Mary's La. Speld —6A 150
St Mary's La. Upm & Brtwd —1D 7
St Mary's Meadow. W'hm —2B 226
St Mary's Pas. Dover —4J 181
St Mary's Pl. SE9 —4C 56
St Mary's Pl. W'hm —2B 226
St Marys Platt. —1A 26
St Mary's Rd. SW19 —1B 12
St Mary's Rd. Bex —6D 58
St Mary's Rd. Broad —9M 209
St Mary's Rd. Elham —7N 183
St Mary's Rd. Fav —6H 187
St Mary's Rd. Gill —6F 80
St Mary's Rd. Grnh —3E 60
St Mary's Rd. Min —7M 205
St Mary's Rd. New R —1C 212 (2E 47)
St Mary's Rd. Pat —7G 173
St Mary's Rd. Roch —5M 79
St Mary's Rd. St Mm & Dym
—8A 182 (1E 47)
St Mary's Rd. Swan —7E 72
St Mary's Rd. Tonb —8H 145
St Mary's Rd. Walm —9M 177
St Mary's Rd. W Hyt —7C 196
St Mary's Rd. Wro —7N 105
St Mary's St. Cant —2M 171 (1D 31)
St Mary St. SE18 —4B 50
St Mary's View. N'tn —4L 97
St Mary's Wlk. Burh —1K 109
St Mary's Way. Long —6L 75
St Matthew's Clo. N'tn —4L 97
St Matthew's Dri. Brom —6B 70

St Matthews Dri.—School Field

St Matthews Dri. Roch —1L 93
St Matthews Rd. SW2 —4C 5
St Matthew's Way. Allh —4L 201
St Merryn Clo. SE18 —7F 50
St Merryn Ct. Beck —3D 68
St Michaels. —4C 222 (3B 38)
St Michaels All. Ram —6J 211
St Michael's Av. Mgte —5H 209
St Michael's Clo. Ayle —7N 109
St Michael's Clo. Brom —6A 70
St Michaels Clo. Chat —9C 80
St Michael's Clo. Eri —2M 51
St Michaels Clo. R Comn —1G 171
St Michaels Clo. Sit —7G 99
St Michael's Ct. Folk —6L 189 (off Harbour Way)
St Michaels Ct. Hild —9D 132
St Michaels Ct. Strood —4M 79
St Michael's Dri. Otf —7L 103
St Michael's Pl. Cant —9L 167
St Michaels Rise. Well —8K 51
St Michael's Rd. Cant —8L 167 (in two parts)
St Michael's Rd. Maid —6A 126
St Michael's Rd. Sit —7F 98 (3C 19) (in two parts)
St Michael's Rd. Tun W —7H 151
St Michael's Rd. Well —1K 57
St Michaels St. Folk —6L 189
St Michael's Ter. St Mic —4B 222
St Michael's Wlk. H'nge —8B 192
St Mildred's Av. Birch —4D 206
St Mildred's Av. Broad —9L 209
St Mildreds Clo. Tent —8B 222
St Mildreds Ct. Cant —2L 171 (1D 31)
St Mildreds Ct. Walm —9M 177
St Mildred's Ct. Wgte S —2L 207 (off Beach Rd.)
St Mildred's Gdns. Wgte S —2L 207
St Mildred's Pl. Cant —3L 171
St Mildreds Rd. SE12 —5J 55 (4E 5)
St Mildred's Rd. Mgte —3E 208
St Mildred's Rd. Min —8M 205
St Mildred's Rd. Ram —6G 210
St Mildred's Rd. Wgte S —2K 207 (1D 23)
St Monicas. Dover —5H 181
St Monica's Rd. Kgdn —3N 199
St Nicholas at Wade. —8E 214 (2B 22)
St Nicholas Cvn. & Camping Site. St N —8D 214
St Nicholas Clo. Deal —6J 177
St Nicholas Clo. Sturry —4E 168
St Nicholas Dri. Sev —8J 119
St Nicholas Gdns. Roch —5K 79
St Nicholas Ho. Aysm —2D 162 (off Queen's Rd.)
St Nicholas Rd. SE18 —5H 51
St Nicholas Rd. Cant —4J 171 (1D 31)
St Nicholas Rd. Fav —5E 186
St Nicholas Rd. Hythe —6H 197
St Nicholas Rd. L'stne —3E 212
St Nicholas Ter. Hythe —6J 197
St Nicholas Vineyard. —5C 216 (4C 22)
St Nicholas Way. Sutt —2B 12
St Nicolas La. Chst —4A 70
St Norbert Grn. SE4 —2B 54
St Norbert Rd. SE4 —3A 54 (4D 5)
St Pancras. —2C 5
St Pancras Way. NW1 —1C 4
St Patrick's Clo. Deal —4M 177
St Patricks Clo. Whits —6G 225
St Patrick's Ct. SE4 —3D 54
St Patrick's Gdns. Grav —8J 63
St Patrick's Rd. Deal —4M 177
St Patrick's Rd. Dover —8F 180
St Patricks Row. Rod —3J 115 (off Rodmersham Grn.)
St Paulinus Ct. Dart —2F 58 (off Manor Rd.)
St Paul's Av. NW2 —1A 4
St Paul's Av. Fav —5E 186
St Paul's Clo. Roch —7H 79
St Paul's Clo. Swans —5L 61
St Paul's Clo. Tonb —2K 145
St Paul's Ct. Folk —7E 188
St Paul's Cray. —5K 71 (1B 14)
St Paul's Cray Rd. Chst —4F 70 (1B 14)
St Pauls Cres. Bou B —3K 165
St Paul's Rd. N1 —1C 5
St Pauls Rd. Bark —2B 6
St Pauls Rd. Bou B —3K 165
St Paul's Rd. Clift —2E 208
St Paul's Rd. Eri —7D 52
St Paul's Sq. Brom —5J 69
St Paul's St. Sit —6F 98 (2C 19) (in two parts)
St Paul's St. Tun W —1C 156
St Paul's Ter. Cant —2N 171 (1D 31)
St Paul's Way. E3 —2E 5
St Paul's Way. Folk —7E 188
St Paul's Wood Hill. Orp —5G 71 (1B 14)
St Peter's. —8J 209 (1E 23)
St Peters Av. Berr G —7D 100
St Peter's Bri. Maid —5C 126
St Peter's Clo. Chst —3F 70
St Peter's Clo. Dit —9F 108
St Peter's Clo. Min S —6E 218
St Peter's Clo. Swans —5M 61
St Peter's Ct. Broad —7K 209
St Peter's Ct. Dit —9F 108
St Peter's Ct. Fav —5E 186
St Peter's Ct. Mgte —4D 208
St Peter's Gro. Cant —2M 171 (1D 31)
St Peter's La. Cant —1M 171 (4D 21)
St Peter's La. St P —4J 71
St Peter's Pk. Rd. Broad —8K 209 (1E 23)
St Peter's Path. Roch —7N 79
St Peter's Pl. Cant —2M 171 (1D 31)
St Peter's Pl. Eccl —4K 109
St Peters Rd. Bou B —3K 165
St Peter's Rd. Broad —8J 209 (1E 23)
St Peter's Rd. Croy —2D 13
St Peter's Rd. Dit —9F 108
St Peter's Rd. Mgte —4D 208 (1D 23)
St Peter's Rd. Whits —3F 224
St Peter's Row. Beth —2J 163
St Peter's Row. Ford —9J 149
St Peter's St. Cant —1M 171 (4D 21)
St Peter's St. S'wch —5M 217
St Peters St. Tun W —2J 157
St Peter St. Maid —4C 126 (2D 27)
St Peter St. Roch —8A 80
St Philip's Av. Maid —6E 126 (2E 27)
St Philips Ct. Tun W —8K 151
St Pier's La. Ling & Eden —1A 34
St Quentin Rd. Well —1H 57
St Quintin Av. W10 —2A 4
St Radigund's. —3F 180
St Radigund's Ct. Dover —3F 180
St Radigund's Pl. Cant —1N 171
St Radigund's Rd. Dover —3E 180
St Radigund's St. Cant —1M 171 (4D 21)
St Richard's Rd. Deal —6H 177 (3D 33)
St Richard's Wlk. Dover —8F 180
St Saviour's Clo. Fav —5J 187
St Saviours Clo. Folk —4K 189
St Saviours Rd. Maid —2G 139
Saint's Hill. —6H 149
Saints Hill. Pens —6H 149 (1D 35)
St Stephen's. —9M 167
St Stephen's Clo. Cant —9M 167
St Stephen's Clo. N'tn —4L 97
St Stephen's Cotts. Maid —2J 137
St Stephen's Ct. Cant —9M 167
St Stephens Ct. Tun W —9H 151
St Stephen's Fields. Cant —1M 171
St Stephens Grn. Cant —8M 167
St Stephens Gro. SE13 —1F 54
St Stephen's Hill. Cant —6L 167 (3D 21)
St Stephens M. Roch —3B 94
St Stephen's Pathway. Cant —9M 167
St Stephen's Rd. Cant —8M 167 (4D 21)
St Stephen's Sq. Maid —7B 126
St Stephen's St. Tonb —7H 145
St Stephen's Trad. Est. Cant —9M 167
St Stephen's Wlk. Afrd —2D 160
St Stephen's Way. Folk —7F 188
St Swithin's Rd. Whits —3K 225
St Swithun's Rd. SE13 —4G 54
St Theresa's Clo. Afrd —7F 158
St Thomas Ct. Bex —5B 58
St Thomas Dri. Orp —2E 84
St Thomas' Hill. Cant —8J 167 (4D 21)
St Thomas Rd. Belv —2D 52
St Thomas Rd. N'fleet —7D 62
St Thomas's Almshouses. Grav —6G 62
St Thomas's Av. Grav —6G 62
St Thomas's Hospital. S'wch —5L 217
St Thomas St. SE1 —3D 5
St Timothys M. Brom —4L 69
St Vincent Rd. St Mc —6H 213
St Vincents Av. Dart —3A 60 (4D 7)
St Vincent's Clo. L'brne —1L 173
St Vincents Clo. Whits —6G 225
St Vincent's La. Adtn —9F 106 (4A 16)
St Vincents Rd. Dart —4A 60 (4D 7)
St Vincents Vs. Dart —4M 59
St Welcume's Way. H'shm —2N 141
St Werburgh Ct. Hoo —8G 66
St Werburgh Cres. Hoo —8G 66
St Werburgh Ter. Hoo —8H 67
St William's Way. Roch —9A 80 (2D 17)
St Winifred Rd. Folk —5F 188
St Winifred's Rd. Big H —6F 164
Salamons Rd. Tun W —1C 156
Salcote Rd. Grav —1K 77
Salehurst. —2B 44
Salehurst Rd. SE4 —4C 54
Salem Pl. N'fleet —5C 62
Salem St. Maid —6D 126
Salisbury Av. Broad —1K 211
Salisbury Av. Gill —3N 95
Salisbury Av. Ram —4K 211
Salisbury Av. Swan —7H 73
Salisbury Clo. Sit —7K 99
Salisbury Clo. Tonb —2K 145
Salisbury Ho. Maid —1G 139
Salisbury Rd. Bex —6B 58
Salisbury Rd. Blue B —2A 110
Salisbury Rd. Brom —8A 70
Salisbury Rd. Cant —9L 167
Salisbury Rd. Chat —9D 80
Salisbury Rd. Dart —5C 60
Salisbury Rd. Dover —3J 181
Salisbury Rd. Folk —4E 188
Salisbury Rd. Grav —6E 62
Salisbury Rd. H Bay —2J 195
Salisbury Rd. L'tn G —2N 155
Salisbury Rd. Maid —3D 126
Salisbury Rd. St Mb —7L 213
Salisbury Rd. Tonb —3K 145
Salisbury Rd. Tun W —6J 151
Salisbury Rd. Walm —8L 177 (3E 33)
Salisbury Rd. Whits —5F 224
Salisbury Rd. Wor Pk —2A 12
Sallows Shaw. Sole S —8H 77
Sally Port. Gill —6D 80
Sally Port Gdns. Gill —6D 80
Salmestone Rise. Mgte —5C 208
Salmestone Rd. Mgte —5C 208
Salmon Cres. Min S —6G 219
Salmon La. E14 —2E 5
Salmon Rd. Belv —5B 52
Salmon Rd. Dart —1N 59
Salmons La. Whyt —4D 13
Salmons La. W. Cat —4D 13
Salmon St. NW9 —1A 4
Saltash Rd. Well —8L 51
Saltbox Hill. Big H —3A 164 (3A 14)
Salter Rd. SE16 —3D 5
Salters Cross. Yald —7F 136
Salters Hill. SE19 —1D 13
Salter's La. B'Ind —2B 46
Salters La. Fav —9H 187 (4A 20)
Saltford Clo. Eri —5F 52
Salthouse Clo. B'Ind —2C 46
Saltings Rd. Snod —3E 108
Saltings, The. L'stne —4F 212
Saltings, The. Whits —3F 224
Salt La. Cli —1J 65 (4D 9)
Saltmarsh La. Whits —4F 224
Salts Av. Loose —5C 138
Salts Clo. Whits —4F 224
Salts Dri. Broad —8J 209
Salts Farm Cotts. Maid —4D 138
Salts La. Loose —3D 138 (3E 27)
Saltwood. —4J 197 (3E 41)
Saltwood Clo. Orp —5K 85
Saltwood Gdns. Clift —3J 209
Saltwood Rd. Maid —8C 126
Salusbury Rd. NW6 —2B 4
Samara Clo. Chat —1D 110
Sambruck M. SE6 —6E 54
Samian Cres. Folk —5C 188
Samphire Clo. Weav —5H 127
Sampson Clo. Belv —3M 51
Samuel Clo. SE18 —4A 50
Samuel Palmer Ct. Orp —1J 85 (off Chislehurst Rd.)
Samuel St. SE18 —4B 50
Sancroft Av. Cant —1J 171
Sanctuary Clo. Broad —2K 211
Sanctuary Clo. Dart —4K 59
Sanctuary Rd. Gill —9K 81
Sanctuary, The. Bex —4M 57
Sandalwood Ho. Sidc —8H 57
Sandbach Pl. SE18 —4E 50
Sandbanks Hill. Bean —2H 75 (1E 15)
Sandbanks La. G'ney —1L 187 (3A 20)
Sandbourne Dri. Maid —9C 110
Sandby Grn. SE9 —1A 56
Sandcliff Rd. Eri —4E 52
Sanders Ct. Min S —7H 219
Sandersons Av. Badg M —1B 102
Sanderson Way. Tonb —6K 145
Sanderstead. —3D 13
Sanderstead Hill. S Croy —3D 13
Sanderstead Rd. Orp —9K 71
Sanderstead Rd. S Croy —3D 13
Sandfield Rd. Pens —7G 149 (1C 35)
Sandford Rd. Bexh —2N 57
Sandford Rd. Brom —7K 69
Sandford Rd. Sit —6C 98
Sandgate. —8E 188 (3A 42)
Sandgate Ct. Gill —7B 96
Sandgate High St. S'gte —8E 188 (3A 42)
Sandgate Hill. S'gte —8F 188 (3A 42)
Sandgate Rd. Folk —7G 189 (3A 42)
Sandgate Rd. Well —7L 51
Sandhawes Hill. E Grin —2A 34
Sandhill La. E Grn —3D 35
Sandhill La. High —7H 65 (4C 9)
Sandhurst. —3K 215 (1C 45)
Sandhurst Av. Pem —9D 152
Sandhurst Clo. Cant —7N 167
Sandhurst Clo. Gill —9M 81
Sandhurst Clo. Sand —4J 215
Sandhurst Clo. Tun W —7J 151
Sandhurst Cross. —4H 215 (2C 44)
Sandhurst La. Rol —4A 38
Sandhurst La. Cotts. Rol —2H 213
Sandhurst Pk. Tun W —8J 151
Sandhurst Rd. SE6 —6G 54 (4E 5)
Sandhurst Rd. Bex —3M 57
Sandhurst Rd. Bdm —2C 44
Sandhurst Rd. Clift —3K 209
Sandhurst Rd. Orp —4J 85
Sandhurst Rd. Sidc —8H 57
Sandhurst Rd. Tun W —7J 151 (1E 35)
Sandhurst Vineyards. —2N 215
Sandiland Cres. Brom —3J 83
Sandilands. Sev —4E 118
Sandilands. W'boro —9J 159
Sand La. Frit —2A 38
Sandle's Rd. Birch —4E 206
Sandlewood Dri. St N —9E 214
Sandling. —9C 110 (1D 27)
Sandling Clo. Afrd —3D 160
Sandling Ct. Maid —2E 126
Sandling La. S'lng —8B 110 (4D 117) (in two parts)
Sandling Rise. SE9 —8C 56
Sandling Rd. Hythe —2D 41
Sandling Rd. Maid —2C 126 (1D 27) (in two parts)
Sandling Rd. S'lng —1F 196 (2D 41)
Sandling Way. St Mi —3E 80
Sandown Clo. Deal —1N 177
Sandown Clo. Tun W —8M 151
Sandown Dri. Gill —4N 95
Sandown Dri. H Bay —3E 194
Sandown Gro. Tun W —8M 151
Sandown Lees. S'wch —6M 217
Sandown Park. —8M 151 (1A 36)
Sandown Rd. Deal —1N 177
Sandown Rd. Grav —2H 77
Sandown Rd. S'wch —5M 217 (4D 23)
Sandown Rd. W Mal —1N 123
Sandpiper Ct. Dover —2G 180
Sandpiper Ct. Mgte —2C 208 (off Fort Hill)
Sandpiper Dri. Eri —7J 53
Sandpiper Rd. Chat —9G 94
Sandpiper Rd. Whits —7D 224
Sandpipers, The. Grav —7J 63
Sandpiper Way. Orp —7M 71
Sandpit Hill. Ups —2A 22
Sandpit Pl. SE7 —5A 50
Sandpit Rd. Brom —1H 69
Sandpit Rd. Dart —2K 59
Sandpits Rd. Croy —5A 82
Sandringham Ct. Sidc —4H 57
Sandringham Dri. Well —9G 50
Sandringham Rd. E8 —1D 5
Sandringham Rd. Brom —1K 69
Sandringham Rd. Gill —7A 96
Sand Rd. Lam —3C 200 (3B 36)
Sandrock Pl. Croy —5A 82
Sandrock Rd. SE13 —1D 54
Sandrock Rd. Tun W —1J 157 (2E 35)
Sandrock Vs. Hawkh —4K 191
Sands End. —3B 4
Sandstone Ct. Folk —8G 189
Sandstone Rise. Chat —2F 110
Sandstone Rd. SE12 —7L 55
Sandway. —9C 200 (3C 28)
Sandway Path. St M —7L 71 (off Okemore Gdns.)
Sandway Rd. S'wy —3N 141 (3B 28)
Sandway Rd. St M —7L 71
Sandwich. —5M 217 (4D 23)
Sandwich Bay. —1E 33
Sandwich By-Pass. S'wch —6J 217 (1D 33)
Sandwich Clo. Folk —6F 188
Sandwich Folk Museum. —4K 217
Sandwich Guildhall Museum. —5L 217 (off Cattle Mkt.)
Sandwich Hill. W'hm —2C 226 (4B 22)
Sandwich Ind. Est. S'wch —5N 217
Sandwich La. F'hm —3B 32
Sandwich Leisure Pk. S'wch —5K 217
Sandwich Rd. Ah —5D 216 (4C 22)
Sandwich Rd. C'snd —9A 210 (3D 23)
Sandwich Rd. E'try —2L 183 (2C 33)
Sandwich Rd. Eyt —4K 185 (3C 32)
Sandwich Rd. Non —2B 32
Sandwich Rd. Shol —4H 177 (2D 33)
Sandwich Rd. Whitf —7F 178 (4C 33)
Sandwich Rd. Wdboro —7H 217 (1C 33)
Sandwich Windmill. —4K 217 (4D 23)
Sandwood Rd. Ram —3K 211
Sandwood Rd. S'wch —6L 217
Sandy Bank Rd. Grav —6G 63
Sandy Bury. Orp —4F 84
Sandycombe Rd. Rich —4A 4
Sandycroft. SE2 —6J 51
Sandycroft Rd. Roch —3K 79
Sandy Dell. Hem —8K 95
Sandy Hill Av. SE18 —5D 50
Sandy Hill Rd. SE18 —4C 50
Sandyhurst La. Afrd —4C 158 (4E 29)
Sandy La. Ave —2D 7
Sandy La. Bean —7J 61 (4E 7)
Sandy La. Bear —4L 127
Sandy La. Boxl —9F 110
Sandy La. Gt Cha —1D 39
Sandy La. Igh —6H 121
Sandy La. Ivy H —7H 121
Sandy La. Orp —1J 85
Sandy La. Rya —4B 16
Sandy La. S'gte —8B 188
Sandy La. Sev —5K 119 (2E 25)
Sandy La. Snod —4C 108
Sandy La. S Min —4D 31
Sandy La. St M & Sidc —1B 14
Sandy La. St P & Sidc —5M 71
Sandy La. Sutt —3B 12
Sandy La. Tent —8C 222
Sandy La. Wall —3C 12
Sandy La. W'ham —7F 116
Sandy La. W Mal —9M 107 (4A 16)
Sandy La. W'boro —9M 159
Sandy La. Wro H —9E 106
Sandy La. N. Wall —3C 12
Sandy La. S. Wall —3C 12
Sandy Mt. Bear —4L 127
Sandy Pl. Sme —8J 165
Sandy Ridge. Bor G —2N 121
Sandy Ridge. Chst —2C 70
Sandy Way. Croy —4C 82
Sanford St. SE14 —3E 5
Sanger Clo. Mgte —4C 208
Sangley Rd. SE6 —5E 54 (4E 5)
Sangro Pl. Cant —1C 172
Sanspareil Av. Min S —6G 219
Santon La. Stour —3B 22
Sapho Pk. Grav —9L 63
Saphora Clo. Orp —6F 84
Sappers Wlk. Gill —7F 80
Saracen Clo. Gill B —2K 95
Saracen Fields. W'slde —2F 110
Sara Cres. Grnh —2H 61
Sarah Gdns. Grav —7L 63
Sarah Gdns. Mgte —5H 209
Sara Ho. Eri —7F 52
Sara Pk. Grav —9K 63
Saras Ct. Whits —5E 224
Sark Clo. Dym —7B 182
Sarre. —2B 22
Sarre Ct. Sarre —2B 22
Sarre Pl. S'wch —6L 217
Sarre Rd. St M —8L 71
Sarre Windmill. —2B 22
Sarsen Heights. Chat —1C 110
Sarsens Clo. Cob —6L 77
Sartor Rd. SE15 —2A 54
Sassoon Clo. Lark —6E 108
Satins Hill. Siss —7C 220 (2E 37)
Satis Av. Sit —4F 98
Satmar. —1D 174 (2B 42)
Satmar La. Cap F —2B 42 (Capel St.)
Satmar La. Cap F & W Hou —1D 174 (2B 42) (Winehouse La.)
Saunders Clo. N'fleet —7D 62
Saunders La. Ah —5E 216 (4C 22)
Saunders Rd. SE18 —5H 51
Saunders Rd. Tun W —4E 156
Saunders St. Chat —9C 80
Saunders St. Gill —6F 80
Saunders Way. Dart —7N 59
Savage Rd. Chat —8E 94
Savernake Dri. H Bay —5J 195
Saville Clo. Tonb —9K 133
Saville Rd. E16 —1A 50
Saville Row. Brom —2J 83
Savill Ho. E16 —1D 50 (off Robert St.)
Savoy Rd. Dart —3L 59
Saw Lodge Field. Kgnt —5G 161
Sawpit Rd. Mils —7H 115 (4C 19)
Sawyers Ct. Chat —1E 94
Saxby's La. Ling —4A 24
Saxbys Rd. Sev —4D 120 (1E 25)
Saxby Wood. Leigh —6N 143
Saxon Av. Min S —6J 219
Saxon Clo. Hythe —6M 197
Saxon Clo. King H —7L 123
Saxon Clo. N'fleet —8B 62
Saxon Clo. Otf —8F 104
Saxon Clo. Roch —3K 79
Saxon Pl. Hort K —8C 74
Saxon Pl. Roch —7K 79
Saxon Rd. Bri —8H 173
Saxon Rd. Brom —3J 69
Saxon Rd. Dart —9M 59
Saxon Rd. Fav —5G 186
Saxon Rd. Ram —6F 210
Saxon Rd. Wgte S —2L 207
Saxons Clo. Deal —2M 177
Saxons Dri. Maid —2E 126
Saxon Shore. Whits —5E 224
Saxon Shore Way. Gill —5K 81
Saxon St. Dover —4J 181
Saxon Wlk. Sidc —2L 71
Saxton Clo. SE13 —1G 55
Saxton Rd. Lydd S —9A 212
Saxton St. Gill —7F 80
Saxville Rd. Orp —6K 71
Sayer Clo. Grnh —3G 60
Sayer Rd. Char —2K 175
Sayers La. Tent —8B 222
Sayes Ct. Rd. Orp —7J 71
Scabharbour La. Hild —3D 25
Scabharbour Rd. Weald —6K 131 (3D 25)
Scads Hill Clo. Orp —9H 71
Scagged Oak. —3A 18
Scanlons Bri. Rd. Hythe —6H 197
Scantlebury Av. Grav —5C 62
Scarborough. —9J 93 (3D 17)
Scarborough Clo. Big H —6C 164
Scarborough Dri. Min S —3J 219
Scarborough La. Burh —1G 109 (3C 17)
Scarlet Clo. St P —7K 71
Scarlet Rd. SE6 —8H 55
Scarlett Clo. Chat —6F 94
Scarsbrook Rd. SE3 —1N 55
Sceales Dri. C'snd —6B 210
Sceptre Way. Whits —6D 224
Scholars Rise. Roch —5H 79
Scholey Clo. Hall —7F 92
School App. Bor G —2N 121
School Av. Gill —8H 81
School Clo. Meop —1H 90
School Clo., The. Wgte S —2K 207
School Cres. Cray —2G 59
School Field. Eden —5C 184

School Hill—Shepherdswell Rd.

School Hill. Bod —4C **31**
School Hill. Chi —8J **175** (2B **30**)
School Hill. Lam —2D **200** (2B **36**)
School Ho. La. Horsm —2F **198** (1C **37**)
School La. Bap —8L **99** (3D **19**)
School La. Bean —9J **61** (1E **15**)
School La. Bek —6H **173** (2E **31**)
School La. Blean —4G **167**
School La. B'den —7A **98** (3B **18**)
School La. Bou B —3J **165** (2D **29**)
School La. F'wch —7F **168**
School La. Good —2B **32**
School La. Hdlw —7D **134**
School La. H Bay —7H **195** (2E **21**)
School La. High —1G **78** (1C **17**)
School La. Hoath —9M **195** (2A **22**)
School La. Hort K —7C **74** (1E **15**)
School La. I'hm —1A **32**
School La. Iwade —1A **98** (2B **18**)
(in two parts)
School La. Knat —3E **15**
School La. Lwr Hal —8L **223** (2B **18**)
School La. Lwr Har —2D **31**
School La. Maid —8H **127**
School La. Meop —9F **90**
School La. N'tn —4K **97** (2B **18**)
School La. Ors —2B **8**
School La. Peas —3E **45**
School La. Plax —1L **133** (2A **26**)
School La. P'den —3A **46**
School La. Ram —5J **211**
School La. Seal —3N **119** (1D **25**)
School La. S'ness —2B **218**
School La. S'le & Ah —1B **32**
School La. S'hrst —8K **221**
School La. St Jhn —4C **35**
School La. Sut V —9A **140**
School La. Swan —4J **73** (1D **15**)
School La. Tros —5F **106** (4A **16**)
School La. Well —1K **57**
School La. W King —3E **104**
School La. W Sto —3B **22**
School La. W'hm —3B **226**
School La. Woul —2C **17**
School Path. L'brne —3L **173**
School Rise. Tun W —4F **156**
School Rd. Acr —5A **192** (1A **42**)
School Rd. App —4D **39**
School Rd. Ah —4B **216**
School Rd. Beth —3J **163** (2D **39**)
School Rd. Char —2K **175** (3D **29**)
School Rd. Chst —4E **70**
School Rd. Fav —6F **186**
School Rd. Goud —7L **185** (2D **37**)
School Rd. Grav —8H **63**
School Rd. Hoth —4E **29**
School Rd. Hythe —3D **41**
School Rd. Salt —4J **197**
School Rd. S'wch —5L **217**
School Rd. Sit —8J **99**
School Rd. St Mm —2A **214** (2E **47**)
School Rd. Tilm —3C **32**
School Rd. Woul —6G **93**
School Ter. Hawkh —5K **191**
School View. Sit —2D **114**
School Vs. Nett —3B **136**
School Wlk. Eyt —3C **32**
Schooner Ct. Dart —2C **60**
Schreiber M. Gill —7G **81**
Scimitar Clo. Gill B —2K **95**
Scocles Rd. Min S —8J **219** (1D **19**)
Scoggers Hill. Wint —1B **30**
Scords La. Toy —3B **24**
Scotby Av. Chat —7E **94**
Scotch House. (Junct.) —3B **4**
Scotland La. Cob —6L **77**
Scotney Castle. —4F **200** (3C **36**)
Scotney Clo. Farn —5C **84**
Scotsdale Clo. Orp —7G **71**
Scotsdale Rd. SE12 —3L **55**
Scotshall La. Warl —4E **13**
Scott Av. Gill —3C **96**
Scott Clo. Dit —1G **124**
Scott Cres. Eri —8G **52**
Scotteswood Av. Chat —1C **94**
*Scott Ho. Belv —5A **52***
(off Albert Rd.)
Scotton St. Wye —2N **159** (4B **30**)
Scott Rd. Grav —1J **77**
Scott Rd. Tonb —7F **144**
Scotts Av. Brom —5G **69**
Scott's La. Brom —6G **68** (1E **13**)
Scotts Pas. SE18 —4D **50**
Scotts Rd. Brom —3K **69**
Scott's Ter. Chat —9C **80**
Scott St. Maid —3C **126**
Scotts Way. Sev —4F **118**
Scotts Way. Tun W —5E **156**
Scraces Cotts. Maid —9L **125**
Scragged Oak. —3N 111
Scragged Oak Cvn. Pk. Det —7L **111**
Scragged Oak Rd. Det —8L **111** (4A **18**)
Scragged Oak Rd. Huc —1E **128**
Scrapsgate. —3J 219 (4D 11)
Scrapsgate Rd. Min S —6H **219** (4D **11**)
Scratchers La. Fawk —3D **88** (2E **15**)
Scratton Fields. Sole S —8J **77**
Scratton Rd. Sth S —1B **10**
Screaming All. Ram —7H **211**
Scrooby St. SE6 —4E **54**
Scrubbs La. NW10 —2A **4**
Scrubbs La. Maid —5A **126**
Scudders Hill. Fawk —9H **75** (2E **15**)
Sea App. Broad —9M **209**
Sea App. Ward —4J **203**
Seabourne Clo. Dym —9A **182**
Seabourne Way. Dym —9A **182**
Seabrook. —9B 188
Seabrook Ct. S'gte —8B **188**
Seabrook Dri. W Wick —3H **83**
Seabrook Gdns. Hythe —9A **188**
Seabrook Gro. Hythe —9A **188**
Seabrook Rd. Hythe —6L **197** (3E **41**)
Seabrook Rd. Tonb —4G **144**
Seabrook Vale. Hythe —7B **188**
Seacliff Cvn. Pk. Min S —5M **219**
Seacourt Rd. SE2 —2M **51**
Seacroft Rd. Broad —3L **211**
Seadown Clo. Hythe —7A **188**
Seafield Ho. New R —3B **212**
Seafield Rd. Broad —9K **209**
Seafield Rd. Ram —5G **210**
Seafield Rd. Whits —2K **225**
Seaford Ct. Roch —8M **79**
Seafront. Allh —2K **201**
Seager Rd. Fav —3F **186**
Seager Rd. S'ness —2F **218**
Seagull Rd. Roch —6G **79**
Seal. —3N 119 (1D 25)
Sealand Ct. Roch —8M **79**
Seal Chart. —5C 120 (2E 25)
Seal Dri. Seal —3N **119**
Seal Hollow Rd. Sev —6K **119** (2D **25**)
Sea Life Centre. —1C **10**
Seal Rd. Sev —3K **119** (1D **25**)
Seamark Clo. Monk —2C **22**
Seamark Rd. B End —9D **206**
Seamark Rd. Monk —2C **22**
Seamew Ct. Roch —5G **79**
Seapoint Rd. Broad —1M **211**
Sea Rd. Hythe —6M **197**
(in three parts)
Sea Rd. Kgdn —3M **199**.
(in two parts)
Sea Rd. Wgte S —3G **207** (1C **23**)
Sea Rd. W'sea B —4A **46**
Seasalter. —6C 224 (2C 20)
Seasalter Beach. Sea —6C **224**
Seasalter Clo. Ward —4K **203**
Seasalter La. Sea —9B **224** (3C **20**)
Seasalter Rd. G'ney —3B **20**
Seaside Av. Min S —4K **219**
Sea St. H Bay —4C **194** (2D **21**)
Sea St. St Mc —7K **213** (4E **33**)
Sea St. Whits —3F **224** (2C **21**)
Seathorpe Av. Min S —5K **219**
Seaths Corner. W'hm —3B **226**
Seaton Av. Hythe —5J **197**
Seaton Rd. Dart —5H **59**
Seaton Rd. Gill —9H **81**
Seaton Rd. Well —7L **51**
Seaton Rd. Wickh —4A **22**
Seaview. Isle G —3C **190**
Sea View Av. Birch —3D **206**
Seaview Av. Ley S —7N **203**
Seaview Cvn. & Chalet Pk. Whits —1N **225**
Sea View Clo. Cap F —3B **174**
*Seaview Ct. Broad —1M **211***
(off W. Cliff Rd.)
Sea View Gdns. Ward —5K **203**
*Sea View Heights. Birch —3C **206***
(off Ethelbert Rd.)
Seaview Holiday Camp. Ley S —5K **203**
Sea View Rd. Birch —3D **206**
Sea View Rd. Broad —7L **209**
Seaview Rd. Can I —2A **10**
Sea View Rd. C'snd —6B **210**
Seaview Rd. Gill —8F **80**
Seaview Rd. G'stne —8E **212**
Sea View Rd. H Bay —2K **195** (1E **21**)
Sea View Rd. St Mb —9J **213**
Sea View Sq. H Bay —2G **194**
Sea View Ter. Dover —2F **180**
Sea View Ter. Mgte —3A **208**
Sea View Ter. S'gte —8D **188**
Seaville Dri. H Bay —2M **195**
Sea Wlk. S'gte —8E **188**
Sea Wall. Dym —8B **182**
Sea Wall. Whits —3F **224**
Seaway Cotts. Whits —4E **224**
Seaway Cres. St Mar —2E **214**
Seaway Gdns. St Mar —2E **214**
(in two parts)
Seaway Rd. St Mar —2E **214**
Second Av. Broad —3L **209**
Second Av. Chat —2E **94**
Second Av. Clift —2F **208**
Second Av. E'chu —3E **202**
Second Av. Gill —9H **81**
Second Av. S'ness —3C **218**
Secretan Rd. Roch —2M **93**
Sedcombe Clo. Sidc —9K **57**
Sedgebrook Rd. SE3 —1N **55**
Sedge Cres. Chat —7B **94**
Sedgehill Rd. SE6 —9D **54**
Sedgemere Rd. SE2 —3L **51**
Sedgeway. SE6 —6J **55**
Sedgewood Clo. Brom —1J **83**
Sedlescombe. —4C 44
Sedlescombe Organic Vineyard. —3B **44**
Sedley. S'fleet —2N **75**
Sedley Clo. Ayle —8K **109**
Sedley Clo. Cli —6N **65**
Sedley Clo. Gill —8M **95**
Seed. —1D 29
Seed Rd. Dod & Newn —1D **29**
Seeshill Clo. Whits —5G **225**
Sefton Clo. Orp —7H **71**
Sefton Rd. Chat —5F **94**
Sefton Rd. Orp —7H **71**
Segal Clo. SE23 —5B **54**
Segrave Cres. Folk —5M **189**
Segrave Rd. Folk —6M **189**
Selah Dri. Swan —4D **72**
Selborne Av. Bex —6N **57**
Selborne Rd. Mgte —4F **208**
Selborne Rd. Sidc —9K **57**
Selbourne Clo. Long —6C **76**
Selbourne Rd. Gill —5G **80**
Selbourne Ter. Dover —5H **181**
Selbourne Wlk. Maid —2J **139**
Selby Clo. Chst —2C **70**
Selby Clo. H Bay —3K **195**
Selby Rd. Maid —4J **139**
Selby's Cotts. Hild —3D **144**
Selgrove. —4A 20
Selhurst. —2D 13
Selhurst Rd. SE25 —2D **13**
Selkirk Dri. Eri —8F **52**
Selkirk Rd. Dover —1G **181**
Selbourne Pk. Frant —9J **157**
Sellindge. —8K 215 (2C 41)
Sellindge Clo. Beck —3C **68**
Selling. —1B 30
Selling Ct. Sell —1B **30**
Sellinge Grn. Gill —9M **81**
Selling Rd. Fav —7J **187** (4A **20**)
Selling Rd. Old L —6K **175** (2B **30**)
Selling Rd. Sell —1A **30**
Selsdon. —3D 13
Selsdon Pk. Rd. S Croy —9A **82** (3D **13**)
Selsdon Rd. S Croy —2D **13**
Selsea Av. H Bay —2E **194**
Selsey Cres. Well —8M **51**
Selson. —2J 183 (2C 33)
Selson Rd. E'try —1H **183** (2C **32**)
Selstead Clo. Gill —2M **95**
Selsted. —4A 32
Selway Ct. Deal —7L **177**
Selwood Clo. Min S —6F **218**
Selworthy Rd. SE6 —8C **54**
Selwyn Ct. SE3 —1J **55**
Selwyn Ct. Broad —8K **209**
Selwyn Cres. Well —1K **57**
Selwyn Dri. Broad —8K **209**
Selwyn Pl. Orp —6K **71**
Semaphore Rd. Birch —3E **206**
Semple Clo. Min —6N **205**
Semple Gdns. Chat —9B **80**
Senacre La. Maid —2H **139**
Senacres Cotts. Maid —2J **139**
Senacre Sq. Maid —1J **139**
Senacre Wood. —2H 139
Senator Wlk. SE28 —3F **50**
Sene Pk. Hythe —5L **197**
Senlac Clo. Ram —6F **210**
Senlac Rd. SE12 —6L **55**
Sennen Wlk. SE9 —8A **56**
Sennocke Ct. Sev —7J **119**
Sequoia Gdns. Orp —1H **85**
Serene Ct. Broad —9M **209**
*Serene Pl. Broad —9M **209***
(off Serene Ct.)
Sermon Dri. Swan —6D **72**
Serpentine Ct. Sev —4L **119**
Serpentine Rd. Sev —5K **119**
Serviden Dri. Brom —4N **69**
Sessions Ho. Sq. Maid —4C **126**
Setterfield Ho. Hythe —6L **197**
Setterfield Rd. Mgte —4D **208**
Settington Av. Chat —2F **94**
Sevastapol Pl. Cant —1C **172**
Sevenacre Rd. Fav —4G **186**
Seven Acres. New Ash —4L **89**
Seven Acres. Swan —9E **72**
Seven Mile La. Wro H, Sev & Mere
(in two parts) —1E **122** (1A **26**)
Sevenoaks. —7K 119 (2D 25)
Sevenoaks Bus. Cen. Sev —3K **119**
Sevenoaks By-Pass. Sev —5D **118** (2C **25**)
Sevenoaks Clo. Bexh —2C **58**
Sevenoaks Common. —2J 131 (2D 25)
Sevenoaks Museum & Art Gallery.
*(off Buckhurst La.) —7K **119** (2D **25**)*
Sevenoaks Museum & Library. —7K **119**
Sevenoaks Rd. SE4 —4B **54**
Sevenoaks Rd. Bor G —2L **121**
Sevenoaks Rd. Grn St & Hals —6H **85** (2B **14**)
Sevenoaks Rd. Igh —5F **120** (2E **25**)
(in two parts)
Sevenoaks Rd. Otf —4D **15**
Sevenoaks Rd. Sev —8H **85**
Sevenoaks Way. Orp —1B **14**
Sevenoaks Way. Sidc & Orp —3L **71**
Sevenoaks Way Ind. Est. Orp —6L **71**
Sevenoaks Weald. —6J 131 (3D 25)
Sevenoaks Wildfowl Reserve. —3G **119**
*Seven Post All. S'wch —5M **217***
(off St Peter's St.)
Seven Sisters Rd. N7, N4 & N15 —1C **5**
Seven Stones Dri. Broad —3L **211**
Severn Clo. Tonb —2J **145**
Severn Rd. Chat —6F **94**
Sevington. —3M 161 (1A 40)
Sevington La. Afrd & Svgtn —2A **40**
Sevington La. W'boro —1K **161** (2A **40**)
Sevington Pk. Maid —2C **138**
Seward Rd. Beck —5A **68**
Sewardstone Rd. E2 —2D **5**
Sewell Clo. Birch —5F **206**
Sewell Rd. SE2 —3J **51**
Sexburga Dri. Min S —4J **219**
Sextant Pk. Roch —6B **80**
Seymour Av. Mgte —2L **207**
Seymour Av. Whits —4G **225**
Seymour Clo. H Bay —4G **195**
Seymour Dri. Brom —2B **84**
Seymour Gdns. SE4 —1B **54**
Seymour Pl. W1 —2B **4**
Seymour Pl. Cant —3L **171**
Seymour Rd. Chat —9E **80**
Seymour Rd. N'fleet —6E **62**
Seymour Rd. Rain —3E **96** (2A **18**)
Seymour Rd. St Mc —9J **199**
Seymour's Cotts. Leeds —2A **140**
Seymour St. W1 —2B **4**
Seymour Wlk. Swans —5L **61**
Shab Hall Cotts. Sev —9D **102**
Shacklands Rd. Badg M —2C **102**
Shacklands Rd. Sev —3C **15**
Shackleton Clo. Chat —5E **94**
Shacklewell. —1D 5
Shacklewell La. E8 —1D **5**
Shades, The. Roch —5F **78**
Shadoxhurst. —2E 39
Shadoxhurst Rd. Wdchu —3D **39**
Shadwell. —2D 5
Shaftesbury Av. W1 & WC2 —2C **4**
Shaftesbury Av. Folk —4D **188** (2A **42**)
Shaftesbury Clo. E Mal —9D **108**
Shaftesbury Ct. Walm —8N **177**
Shaftesbury Dri. Maid —5N **125**
Shaftesbury La. Dart —2B **60**
Shaftesbury Rd. Beck —5C **68**
Shaftesbury Rd. Cant —8L **167**
Shaftesbury Rd. Her —2K **169**
Shaftesbury Rd. Tun W —8G **151**
Shaftesbury Rd. Whits —4F **224**
*Shaftsbury Ct. Eri —8G **52***
(off Selkirk Dri.)
Shaftsbury St. Ram —5K **211**
Shah Pl. Ram —5H **211**
Shakespeare Pas. Mgte —3B **208**
Shakespeare Rd. Bexh —8N **51**
Shakespeare Rd. Birch —3E **206**
Shakespeare Rd. Dart —2A **60**
Shakespeare Rd. Dover —6G **180**
Shakespeare Rd. Gill —8F **80**
Shakespeare Rd. Mgte —4D **208**
Shakespeare Rd. Sit —7H **99**
Shakespeare Rd. Tonb —7F **144**
Shakespeare Ter. Folk —7J **189**
Shalford Clo. Orp —5E **84**
Shalloak Rd. B Oak —6C **168** (3E **21**)
Shallons Rd. SE9 —9D **56**
Shallows Rd. Broad —7G **209**
Shalmsford Ct. Cha —8B **170**
Shalmsford Rd. Chi —6M **175** (2C **30**)
Shalmsford Street. —8B 170 (2C 30)
Shalmsford St. Cha —8A **170** (2C **30**)
Shambles, The. Sev —7K **119**
Shamel Bus. Cen. Roch —5N **79**
Shamley Rd. Chat —9G **94**
Shamrock Av. Whits —6D **224**
Shamrock Rd. Grav —5K **63**
Shandon Clo. Tun W —1J **157**
Shanklin Clo. Chat —3F **94**
Shannon Corner. (Junct.) —1A **12**
Shannon Way. Beck —2E **68**
Shapland Clo. H Bay —4K **195**
Shardeloes Rd. SE14 —1B **54** (3E **5**)
Share & Coulter Rd. Ches —4M **225**
Sharfleet Dri. Roch —5F **78**
Sharland Rd. Grav —7H **63**
Sharman Ct. Sidc —9J **57**
Sharnal La. Snod —3E **108**
Sharnal Street. —4K 67 (4E 9)
Sharnal St. H Hals —4K **67**
Sharnbrooke Clo. Well —1L **57**
Sharon Cres. Chat —7C **94**
Sharp's Field. H'crn —3M **193**
Sharp Way. Dart —1N **59**
Sharsted Hill. Newn —1D **29**
Sharsted Way. Bear —4L **127**
Sharsted Way. Hem —8K **95** (3E **17**)
Shatterling. —1F 226 (4B 22)
Shawbrooke Rd. SE9 —3M **55**
Shaw Clo. SE28 —1K **51**
Shaw Clo. Cli —5M **65**
Shaw Cross Kenn —5H **159**
Shawdon Av. S'wch B —1E **33**
Shawfield Pk. Brom —5N **69**
*Shaw Ho. E16 —1C **50***
(off Claremont St.)
*Shaw Ho. Belv —5A **52***
(off Albert Rd.)
Shaw Path. Brom —8J **55**
Shaw Rd. Brom —8J **55**
Shaw Rd. Tats —8C **164**
Shawstead Rd. Gill —4F **94** (2E **17**)
Shaws Way. Roch —9N **79**
Shaws Wood. Roch —3M **79**
Shaw, The. Tun W —3J **157**
Shaxton Cres. New Ad —9F **82**
Sheafe Dri. C'brk —7C **176**
Sheal's Ct. Maid —7D **126**
Sheal's Cres. Maid —7D **126** (2E **27**)
Shearers Clo. Weav —5H **127**
Shearman Rd. SE3 —2J **55**
Shears Grn. Ct. Grav —7F **62**
Shearwater. Long —6A **76**
Shearwater. Maid —4M **125**
Shearwater Av. Whits —6E **224**
Shearwater Clo. Roch —5G **78**
Shearwater Ct. S'ness —4B **218**
Shearwater Ho. St Mar —3F **214**
Shear Way. Burm —2B **182** (3C **41**)
Shearway Rd. Folk —3F **188**
Shearwood Cres. Dart —1G **59**
Sheen Comn. Dri. Rich —4A **4**
Sheen Ct. Mgte —3C **208**
Sheen La. SW14 —4A **4**
Sheen Rd. Orp —7H **71**
Sheen Rd. Rich —4A **4**
Sheepbarn La. Warl —3E **13**
Sheepcote La. Orp & Swan —8A **72** (2C **14**)
Sheepfold La. Kgnt —6G **161** (2A **40**)
Sheephurst La. Mard —4C **27**
Sheep Plain. Crowb —4C **35**
Sheepstreet La. Tic —1A **44**
Sheerness. —2D 218 (4D 11)
Sheerness Harbour Est. S'ness —1A **218**
*Sheerness Heritage Centre. —2D **218***
(off Rose St.)
Sheerness Rd. Lwr Hal —8M **223** (2B **18**)
Sheerstone. Iwade —8B **198**
Sheerwater Rd. Pres —3B **22**
Sheerways. Fav —5E **186**
Sheet Glass Rd. Queen —9B **218**
Sheet Hill. —7M 121 (2A 26)
Sheet Hill. Plax —7K **121** (2E **25**)
Sheffield Rd. Tun W —4F **150**
Sheilings, The. Seal —2N **119**
Shelbourne Pl. Beck —3D **68**
Shelbury Clo. Sidc —9J **57**
Sheldon Clo. SE12 —3L **55**
Sheldon Clo. Aysm —1D **162**
Sheldon Dri. Gill —3B **96**
(in two parts)
Sheldon Rd. Bexh —8A **52**
Sheldon Way. Lark —7E **108**
Sheldrake Clo. E16 —1B **50**
Sheldwich. —1A 30
Sheldwich Clo. Afrd —3D **160**
Sheldwich Lees. —1A 30
Sheldwich Ter. Brom —9A **70**
Shellbank La. Dart —1E **15**
Shellbank La. Grn St —2G **75**
Shell Clo. Brom —9A **70**
Shelldrake Clo. Isle G —3C **190**
Shelley Av. Cant —9B **168**
Shelley Clo. Orp —4G **85**
Shelley Dri. Well —8G **51**
Shelley Rd. Maid —7N **125**
Shelley Rd. Mgte —7B **208**
Shelleys La. Knock —7H **101** (4B **14**)
Shell Grotto. —3D **208**
Shellness Rd. Ley S —7N **203** (1A **20**)
Shellons St. Folk —6K **189** (3A **42**)
Shell Rd. SE13 —1E **54**
Shelton Clo. Tonb —2J **145**
Shelvingford Farm Rd. Hoath —2A **22**
Shelvin La. Woot —4A **32**
Shenden Clo. Sev —9K **119**
Shenden Way. Sev —1K **131**
Shenley Gro. S'ing —8C **110**
Shenley Rd. Dart —4A **60**
Shenley Rd. H'crn —1B **38**
Shenstone Clo. Dart —2E **58**
Shepherd Cotts. C'brk —7C **176**
Shepherd Dri. W'boro —1L **161**
Shepherdess Wlk. N1 —2D **5**
Shepherds Bush. —2A 4
Shepherd's Bush Grn. W12 —3A **4**
Shepherd's Bush Rd. W6 —3A **4**
Shepherd's Clo. Orp —4H **85**
Shepherd's Clo. Rd. Bri —2E **31**
Shepherds Ga. Cant —1M **171**
Shepherds Ga. Hem —6J **95**
Shepherdsgate Dri. H Bay —7H **195**
Shepherds Ga. Dri. Weav —4H **127**
Shepherds Grn. Chst —3F **70**
Shepherdsgrove La. Hamm —1A **34**
Shepherd's Hill. Cole H —3B **34**
Shepherd's La. Dart —6H **59** (4D **7**)
Shepherds Lea. SE9 —2E **56**
Shepherd St. N'fleet —5C **62**
Shepherds Wlk. Ches —5L **225**
Shepherds Wlk. Hythe —8F **196**
Shepherds Wlk. Tun W —1K **157**
Shepherds Way. Ches —5L **225**
Shepherds Way. Langl —4A **140**
Shepherds Way. Lwr Sto —8K **201**
Shepherds Way. S Croy —8A **82**
Shepherdswell. —2C 220 (4B 32)
Shepherdswell Rd. Col —4E **220** (4B **32**)

Shepherdswell Rd.—Snodland Rd.

Shepherdswell Rd. Eyt —1E 220 (3B 32)
Shepherds Well Rd. W Grn —1A 220 (3A 32)
Shepperton Clo. Chat —7F 94
Shepperton Rd. N1 —2D 5
Shepperton Rd. Orp —9E 70
Sheppey Beach Vs. Ley S —6N 203
Sheppey Clo. Birch —4F 206
Sheppey Clo. Eri —7J 53
Sheppey Holiday Camp. Ley S —6L 203
Sheppey Rd. Maid —1C 138
Sheppey St. S'ness —2B 218
Sheppey View. Whits —7E 224
Sheppey Way. Bob —6B 98 (2C 18)
Sheppey Way. Iwade & Min S —9E 218 (1C 19)
Sheppy Ct. Min S —5E 218
Sheppy Pl. Grav —5G 62
Shepway. —9G 126 (2E 27)
Shepway. Kenn —5J 159
Shepway Clo. Folk —5K 189
Shepway Ct. Maid —9F 126
Sherard Rd. SE9 —3A 56 (4A 6)
Sheraton Ct. Chat —1C 110
Sherborne Clo. Tun W —3K 157
Sherborne Rd. Orp —8H 71
Sherbourne Clo. W King —7E 88
Sherbourne Dri. Maid —7M 125
Sherbourne Dri. Strood —3L 79
Sherbrooke Clo. Bexh —2B 58
Sherenden La. Mard —1D 37
Sherenden Pk. Gold G —2F 146
(in two parts)
Sherenden Rd. Tud —9C 146 (4A 26)
Sherfield Rd. Grays —3A 8
Sheridan Clo. Chat —4F 94
Sheridan Clo. Maid —1B 126
Sheridan Clo. Swan —7G 72
Sheridan Ct. Dart —2A 60
Sheridan Ct. Hild —3F 144
Sheridan Ct. Roch —1L 93
Sheridan Cres. Chst —5D 70
Sheridan Lodge. Brom —7M 69
(off Homesdale Rd.)
Sheridan Rd. Belv —4B 52
Sheridan Rd. Bexh —1N 57
Sheridan Rd. Dover —1G 180
Sheridan Way. Beck —4C 68
Sheriff Dri. Chat —9D 94
Sheriffs Ct. La. Min —2C 22
Sheriff's La. Roth —4E 35
Sherlies Av. Orp —3G 84
Shermanbury Pl. Eri —7G 52
Sherman Clo. Gill —2L 95
Sherman Rd. Brom —4K 69
Shernden La. M Grn —9C 184 (4B 24)
Shernolds. Maid —1E 138
Sheron Clo. Deal —5K 177
Sherriffs Ct. La. Ram —8J 205
Sherway Clo. H'crn —3M 193
Sherway Rd. H'crn —4B 28
Sherwood Av. Chat —9D 94
Sherwood Av. Whits —7E 224
Sherwood Clo. Bex —4L 57
Sherwood Clo. Fav —3F 186
Sherwood Clo. H Bay —5K 195
Sherwood Clo. Kenn —3H 159
Sherwood Clo. Whits —7E 224
Sherwood Cotts. Tun W —8L 151
Sherwood Ct. Wgte S —2K 207
Sherwood Gdns. Ram —3J 211
Sherwood Ho. Chat —8C 94
Sherwood Park. —8L 151 (1A 36)
Sherwood Pk. Av. Sidc —5J 57
Sherwood Pk. Rd. Mitc —1C 12
Sherwood Rd. Birch —6E 206
Sherwood Rd. Tun W —8K 151
Sherwood Rd. Well —9G 50
Sherwood Way. Tun W —8K 151
Sherwood Way. W Wick —3F 82
Shieldhall St. SE2 —4L 51
Shifford Path. SE23 —8A 54
Shillingheld Clo. Bear —4J 127
Shinecroft. Otf —7H 103
(off Rye La.)
Shingle Barn La. W Far —5G 136 (3C 27)
Shinglewell Rd. Eri —7B 52
Shipbourne. —3J 133 (2E 25)
Shipbourne Rd. Tonb & Ship —4J 145 (4E 25)
Ship Clo. Dym —7B 182
Shipfield Clo. Tats —9C 164
Ship & Half Moon Pas. SE18 —3D 50
Ship Hill. Tats —9C 164 (1A 24)
Ship La. Ave & Purf —2E 7
Ship La. Roch —8B 80
Ship La. Swan & S at H —4L 73 (1D 15)
Shipley Ct. Maid —5D 126
Shipley Hills Rd. Meop —3C 90 (2A 16)
Shipley Mill Clo. Kgnt —5G 160
Shipman Av. Cant —2J 171
Shipman Rd. SE23 —7A 54
Shipman's Way. Dover —1F 180
Ship St. E Grin —2A 34
Ship St. Folk —6K 189
Shipwrights Av. Chat —2D 94
Ship Yd. Ah —5C 216
Shirebrook Rd. SE3 —1N 55
Shire Ct. Eri —3M 51
Shirehall Rd. Dart —1K 73 (1D 15)
Shire La. Kes & Orp —8B 84 (3A 14)
(in two parts)
Shire La. Orp —6G 85
Shire La. Stal —2D 29
Shires, The. Pad W —8M 147
Shireway Clo. Folk —4G 189
Shirkoak. —2D 39
Shirland Rd. W9 —2B 4
Shirley. —3A 82 (2D 13)
Shirley Av. Bex —5M 57
Shirley Av. Chat —6A 94
Shirley Av. Croy —2A 82
Shirley Av. Ram —2J 211
Shirley Chu. Rd. Croy —4A 82 (2D 13)
Shirley Clo. Dart —2K 59
Shirley Clo. Grav —6N 63
Shirley Cotts. Tun W —9G 151
Shirley Ct. Maid —3H 139
Shirley Cres. Beck —7B 68
Shirley Gdns. Tun W —1C 156
Shirley Gro. Tun W —9C 150
Shirley Hills Rd. Croy —6A 82 (2D 13)
Shirley Oaks. —2A 82 (2D 13)
Shirley Oaks Rd. Croy —2A 82
Shirley Rd. Croy —2D 13
Shirley Rd. Sidc —8G 57
Shirley Towermill. —2D 13
Shirley Way. Bear —6K 127
Shirley Way. Croy —4B 82 (2E 13)
Shoebury Comn. Rd. Shoe —1D 11
Shoeburyness. —1D 11
Sholden. —4J 177 (2D 33)
Sholden Back. Deal —6H 177
Sholden Gdns. Orp —8L 71
Sholden New Rd. Shol —4J 177 (2D 33)
Sholden Rd. Roch —3L 79
Shooters Hill. —8C 50 (3A 6)
Shooter's Hill. SE18 & Well —8C 50 (3A 6)
Shooter's Hill. Dover —3H 181
Shooters Hill. Eyt —3K 185 (3C 32)
Shooters Hill Rd. SE3 & SE18 —8A 50 (3E 5)
Shoot Up Hill. NW2 —1B 4
Shore Clo. H Bay —4C 194
Shore Ct. Birch —3C 206
(off Ethelbert Rd.)
Shoreditch. —2D 5
Shoreditch High St. E1 —2D 5
Shorefield Rd. Wclf S —1B 10
Shorefields. Rain —1C 96
Shoregate La. Upc —1B 18
Shoreham. —2G 103 (3C 15)
Shoreham Clo. Bex —6M 57
Shoreham La. Ewh G —3C 44
Shoreham La. Hals —3A 102 (3C 14)
Shoreham La. Orp —7B 86 (3C 14)
Shoreham La. Sev —4G 118
Shoreham La. St Mic —4B 222 (3C 38)
Shoreham Pl. Shor —3H 103
Shoreham Rd. Eyns —7K 87 (3D 15)
Shoreham Rd. Orp —4K 71
Shoreham Rd. Shor —2J 103 (3D 15)
Shoreham Wlk. Maid —1J 139
Shoreham Way. Brom —9K 69
Shorehill La. Knat —7N 103
Shore, The. N'fleet —3C 62
(in two parts)
Shorland Ct. Roch —8M 79
Shorncliffe Cres. Folk —6E 188
Shorncliffe Ind. Est. Folk —6E 188
Shorncliffe Rd. Folk —6E 188 (2A 42)
Shorndean St. SE6 —6F 54
Shorne. —1C 78 (1C 16)
Shorne Clo. Orp —7M 71
Shorne Clo. Sidc —4K 57
Shornefield Clo. Brom —6C 70
Shorne Ifield Rd. Shorne —2M 77 (1B 16)
Shornells Way. SE2 —5L 51
Shorne Ridgeway. —3C 78 (1C 16)
Shorne Wood Country Park. —3N 77
Shortlands. —5H 69 (1E 13)
Shortlands Clo. Belv —3A 52
Shortlands Gdns. Brom —5H 69
Shortlands Grn. Maid —3J 139
Shortlands Gro. Brom —6G 69
Shortlands Rd. Brom —6G 69 (1E 13)
Shortlands Rd. Sit —7H 99
Short La. Alk —1B 42
Short La. Bchly —1C 36
Short La. Gill —6K 81
Short La. Oxt —3A 24
Short La. Sev —5H 121
Short La. Snar —1C 46
Short Path. SE18 —6D 50
Short's Prospect. E'chu —8A 202
Short St. Chat —9E 80
Short St. Chill —2B 32
Short St. S'wch —5M 217
Short St. S'ness —2C 218
Shorts Way. Roch —9L 79 (2D 17)
Short Way. SE9 —1A 56
Shottendane Rd. Birch —6J 207 (1C 23)
Shottenden. —2B 30
Shottenden Rd. Bad —2A 30
Shottenden Rd. Gill —5G 80
Shottenden Rd. Shott —2A 30
Shottery Clo. SE9 —8A 56
Shover's Green. —4B 36
Showfields Rd. Tun W —4F 156
Shrapnel Clo. SE18 —7A 50
Shrapnel Rd. SE9 —1B 56
Shrewsbury La. SE18 —8D 50
Shrewsbury Rd. Beck —6B 68
Shrimp Brand Cotts. Grav —1F 76
Shrimpton Clo. Old L —2B 30
Shroffold Rd. Brom —9H 55
Shropshire Ter. Maid —1H 139
Shrubbery Rd. Grav —6G 63
Shrubbery Rd. S Dar —4D 74 (1E 15)
Shrubbery, The. B'hm —7C 162
Shrubbery, The. Walm —9M 177
Shrubcote. Tent —8D 222
Shrub Hill Rd. Ches —6M 225
Shrublands Av. Croy —4D 82
Shrublands Ct. Tonb —5K 145
Shrublands Ct. Tun W —1J 157
Shrubsall Clo. SE9 —6A 56
Shrubsole Av. S'ness —3D 218
Shrubsole Dri. S'lng —7C 110
Shuart La. St N —8E 214 (2B 22)
(in two parts)
Shurland Av. Ley S —7N 203
Shurland Av. Min S —6J 219
Shurland Av. Sit —1G 114
Shurland Cvn. Pk. E'chu —3D 202
Shurlock Av. Swan —5E 72
Shurlock Dri. Orp —5E 84
Shuttle Clo. Bidd —7L 163
Shuttle Clo. Sidc —5H 57
Shuttlemead. Bex —5A 58
Shuttle Rd. Broad —8M 209
Shuttle Rd. Dart —1H 59
Shuttlesfield. —1E 41
Shuttlesfield La. O'nge —1E 41
Sibert's Clo. S'wll —3E 220
Sibertswold. —2C 220 (4B 32)
Sibley Clo. Bexh —3N 57
Sibthorpe Rd. SE12 —4L 55
Sidcup. —9J 57 (4B 6)
Sidcup By-Pass. Chst & Sidc —8F 56 (1B 14)
Sidcup High St. Sidc —9J 57
Sidcup Hill. Sidc —9K 57 (1B 14)
Sidcup Hill Gdns. Sidc —1L 71
Sidcup Pl. Sidc —1J 71
Sidcup Rd. SE12 & SE9 —4M 55 (4A 6)
Sidcup Technical Cen. Sidc —2M 71
Siddons Rd. SE23 —7B 54
Side Hills. Dent —3A 32
Sidewood Rd. SE9 —6F 56
Sidings, The. Lym —7D 204
Sidmouth Ct. Dart —6B 60
(off Churchill Clo.)
Sidmouth Rd. NW2 —1A 4
Sidmouth Rd. Orp —8K 71
(in two parts)
Sidmouth Rd. Well —7L 51
Sidmouth St. WC1 —2C 5
Sidney. Sidc —2K 71
Sidney Clo. Tun W —5E 156
Sidney Gdns. Otf —8K 103
Sidney Rd. Beck —5B 68
Sidney Rd. Gill —5F 80
Sidney Rd. Roch —1L 93
Sidney St. E1 —2D 5
Sidney St. Folk —5L 189
Sidney St. Maid —7N 125
Signal Ct. Gill —2B 96
Silchester Ct. Maid —2F 126
Silecroft Ct. Afrd —9C 158
Silecroft Rd. Bexh —8B 52
Silk Clo. SE12 —3K 55
Silk Mills Clo. Sev —3K 119
Silvanus Ho. Ram —5H 211
(off High St. Ramsgate,)
Silver Av. Birch —5G 206
Silverbank. Chat —5D 94
Silver Birch Av. Meop —1E 106
Silver Birch Clo. SE28 —1J 51
Silver Birch Clo. Dart —9F 58
Silver Birches. Chat —8D 94
Silver Birches. Min S —3H 219
Silver Birch Gro. Kgnt —5F 160
Silver Clo. Tonb —9H 145
Silverdale. SE26 —9A 54
Silverdale. Hart —7M 75
Silverdale. Maid —7K 125
Silverdale Av. Min S —6H 219
Silverdale Dri. SE9 —7A 56
Silverdale Dri. Gill —4B 96
Silverdale Gro. Sit —8D 98
Silverdale La. Tun W —7H 151
Silverdale Rd. Bexh —9C 52
Silverdale Rd. Pet W —7E 70
Silverdale Rd. Ram —7E 210
Silverdale Rd. St P —6J 71
Silverdale Rd. Tun W —8H 151 (1E 35)
Silverden La. Sand —4H 215 (2C 44)
Silver Hill. —7A 128 (2B 44)
Silver Hill. Chat —9C 80
Silverhill. Hrst G —2B 44
Silver Hill. Roch —1K 93
Silver Hill. Tent —6C 222
Silver Hill Gdns. Chat —9C 80
Silver Hill Gdns. W'boro —9L 159
Silver Hill Rd. W'boro —9L 159 (1A 40)
Silverhurst Dri. Tonb —1J 145
Silverlands Rd. Lym —7C 204
Silverland St. E16 —1B 50
Silver La. W Wick —3G 82
Silvermere Rd. SE6 —5E 54
Silver Rd. Grav —7K 63
Silverspot Clo. Rain —4B 96
Silver Spring Clo. Eri —6C 52
Silverstead La. W'ham —3F 116 (1B 24)
Silvers, The. Broad —9G 208
Silver Street. —5A 114 (3B 18)
Silver St. SE13 —1E 54
Silver St. Bre —5A 114 (3B 18)
Silver St. Deal —3N 177
Silverthorne Rd. SW8 —3C 4
Silvertown. —3A 6
Silvertown Way. E16 —2E 5
Silver Tree Clo. Chat —1D 110
Silverweed Rd. Chat —7B 94
Silverwood Clo. Beck —3D 68
Silverwood Clo. Croy —9C 82
Silwood Clo. Tun W —8L 151
Simmonds Ct. Rust —1B 156
Simmonds Dri. Hart —8N 75
Simmonds La. Otham —2L 139
Simmonds Rd. Win I —3L 171 (1D 31)
Simmons Rd. SE18 —5D 50
Simnel Rd. SE12 —5L 55
Simon Av. Clift —3H 209
Simone Clo. Brom —4A 70
Simone Weil Av. Afrd —6E 158 (1A 40)
Simon's Av. Afrd —2D 160
Simpson Rd. Sit —6D 98
Simpson Rd. Snod —4E 108
Simpsons Rd. Brom —6K 69
Sims Wlk. SE3 —2J 55
Sinclair Clo. Gill —7A 96
Sinclair Way. Dart —9D 60
Sincoe Ter. Dover —1G 181
(off Toronto Clo.)
Sindal Shaw Ho. Chat —7B 94
Sindals La. Chat —1H 111
Singapore Dri. Gill —7D 80
Singer Av. H Bay —3C 194
Singledge Av. Whitf —7E 178
Singledge La. Col —2A 178 (4B 32)
Singles Cross La. Knock & Sev —5L 101 (3B 14)
Singles Cross La. Sev —3B 14
Single Street. —6D 100 (4A 14)
Single St. Berr G —6D 100 (4A 14)
Singleton. —2B 160 (1E 39)
Singleton Cen., The. Afrd —1B 160
Singleton Clo. Min —7M 205
Singleton Hill. Afrd —2A 160 (1E 39)
Singleton Rd. Gt Cha —9A 158
Singlewell. —1H 77 (1B 16)
Singlewell Rd. Grav —7G 62 (4B 8)
Sinkhurst Green. —1A 38
Sion Hill. Ram —6J 211
Sion Pas. Ram —6J 211
(off Sion Hill)
Sion Wlk. Tun W —3G 157
(off Mt. Sion)
Sirdar Strand. Grav —1L 77
Sir David's Pk. Tun W —5E 150
Sir Evelyn Rd. Roch —2M 93
Sir Hawkins Way. Chat —8C 80
Sir John Moore Av. Hythe —6H 197
Sir John Moore Ct. S'gte —8E 188
Sir Thomas Longley Rd. Roch —6B 80
Siskin Clo. H'nge —8A 192
Siskin Gdns. Pad W —1M 153
Siskin Wlk. Lark —8D 108
Sissinghurst. —8C 220 (2E 37)
Sissinghurst Castle. —2A 38
Sissinghurst Castle Garden. —7F 220
Sissinghurst Clo. Brom —1H 69
Sissinghurst Dri. Maid —5M 125
Sissinghurst Rd. Bidd —8H 163 (2A 38)
Sissinghurst Rd. Siss —9A 220 (2E 37)
Site of Battle of Hastings 1066. —4B 44
Sittingbourne. —7G 98 (3C 19)
Sittingbourne Ind. Est. Sit —6G 98
Sittingbourne & Kemsley Light Railway. —6F 98 (2C 19)
Sittingbourne Rd. Det & S'bry —8N 111 (4A 18)
Sittingbourne Rd. Maid —4E 126 (1E 27)
(in two parts)
Siviter Way. Dag —1C 6
Siward Rd. Brom —6L 69
Six Bells La. Sev —8K 119
Six Bells Pk. Wdchu —6B 226
Six Fields Path. Tent —8C 222
Sixmile. —4D 31
Sixth Av. E'chu —3G 202
Skeete. —1D 41
Skeete Rd. Lym —8A 204 (1D 41)
Skeet Hill La. Orp —3N 85 (2C 14)
Skene Clo. Gill —2C 96
Skeynes Rd. Eden —6B 184
Skibbs La. Orp —6N 85 (2C 14)
Skid Hill La. Warl —3E 13
Skinner Rd. Lydd —3C 204 (3D 47)
Skinners All. Whits —4F 224
(off King Edward St.)
Skinners Clo. Eccl —4L 109
Skinners Gdns. Siss —8C 220
Skinner's La. Eden —4D 184
Skinner's Ter. Tonb —7H 145
Skinner St. EC1 —2C 5
Skinner St. Chat —9C 80
Skinner St. Gill —7F 80
(in two parts)
Skinners Way. Langl —4A 140
Skinney La. Hort K —6D 74 (1E 15)
Skippers Clo. Grnh —3H 61
Skipton Ho. SE4 —2B 54
Skua Ct. Roch —5G 79
Skye Clo. Maid —1D 138
Slade. —2D 29
Sladebrook Rd. SE3 —1N 55
Slade Clo. Chat —9E 94
Sladedale Rd. SE18 —5G 50
Slade Gdns. Eri —8G 53
Slade Green. —8H 53 (3D 7)
Slade Grn. Rd. Eri —6J 53 (3D 7)
Slade Rd. War S & Dod —2D 29
Slades Clo. Ches —5L 225
Slades Dri. Chst —9E 56
Slade, The. SE18 —6G 50 (3B 6)
Slade, The. Lam —4C 200 (3B 36)
Slade, The. Tonb —5H 145
Slagrove Pl. SE13 —3D 54
Slaithwaite Rd. SE13 —2F 54
Slaney Rd. S'hrst —7K 221
Slatin Rd. Roch —4M 79
Sleepers Stile Rd. Free H —3B 36
Sleigh Rd. Sturry —5E 168
Slicketts Hill. Chat —8D 80
Slines New Rd. Wold —4D 13
Slines Oak Rd. Wold & Warl —4E 13
Slip La. Alk —1B 42
Slip Mill Rd. Hawkh —5J 191 (4D 37)
Slip Pas. Dover —5J 181
Slip, The. W'ham —8E 116
Slipway Rd. S'ness —1A 218
Sloane Gdns. Orp —4E 84
Sloane Sq. Long —6L 75
Sloane St. SW1 —3B 4
Sloane Wlk. Croy —9C 68
Sloe La. Broad —8F 208
Slough Rd. Mils —6H 115 (4C 19)
Smacks All. Fav —4H 187
Smallbridge Rd. Horsm —6H 185 (2C 37)
Small Grains. Fawk —4H 89
Small Hythe. —4C 38
Smallhythe Place. —4C 38
Smallhythe Rd. Tent —3C 38
Small Profits. Yald —4D 136 (3C 26)
Smarden. —3K 221 (1C 38)
Smarden Bell. —1H 221 (1B 38)
Smarden Clo. Belv —5B 52
Smarden Gro. SE9 —9B 56
Smarden Rd. Bidd —2B 38
Smarden Rd. H'crn —4M 193 (1B 38)
Smarden Rd. Smar & P'ley —4C 29
Smarts Cotts. Bear —5M 127
Smart's Hill. —1D 35
Smarts Hill. Pens —5H 149 (1D 35)
Smarts Rd. Grav —7H 63
Smeed Clo. Sit —7J 99
Smeed Dean Cen. Sit —7H 99
Smeeth. —9H 165 (2B 40)
Smetham Gdns. Roch —3M 79
Smitham Bottom La. Purl —3C 12
Smitham Downs Rd. Purl —3C 13
Smithers Clo. Hdlw —7D 134
Smithers Ct. E Peck —9M 135
Smithers La. E Peck —9M 135
Smithfield Rd. Isle G —3D 190
Smithies Rd. SE2 —4K 51
Smith Rd. Chat —8E 94
Smiths Est. S'lng —7B 110
Smith's Hill. W Far —4F 136 (3C 27)
Smith's Hospital Almshouses. Cant —2A 172
Smiths La. Crock H —3B 24
Smiths Orchard. Bre —5A 114
Smith St. Roch —6L 79
Smith St. Shoe —1D 11
Smithy Dri. Kgnt —5G 160
Smugglers. Hawkh —6L 191
Smugglers Wlk. Grnh —3H 61
Smugglers Way. Birch —3F 206
Smythe Clo. Tun W —3E 150
Smythe Rd. S at H —4A 74
Snag La. Cud —2F 100 (3B 14)
Snagshall. —2C 44
Snake Hill. E Grn —3D 35
Snakes Hill. Tilm —3C 33
Snakes Hill. W'hm W —1B 32
Snargate. —1C 46
Snargate La. Snar —2C 46
Snargate St. Dover —6J 181 (1C 43)
Snatts Hill. Oxt —2A 24
Snave. —1C 47
Snelgrove Ho. Dover —4J 181
Snell Gdns. H Bay —5C 194
Snelling Av. N'fleet —7D 62
Snipe Clo. Eri —7J 53
Snipe Clo. Pem —6D 152
Snipe Ct. Roch —5G 79
Snipeshill. —8K 99 (3D 19)
Snoad Hill. —1D 39
Snoad La. Mard —1E 37
Snode Hill. Dent —4A 32
Snodhurst Av. Chat —6B 94
Snodhurst Ho. Chat —4C 94
Snodland. —2E 108 (3C 17)
Snodland By-Pass. Snod —5D 108 (3C 17)
Snodland Clo. Orp —1C 100
Snodland Rd. Birl —4A 108 (3C 16)

Snoll Hatch—Spring Shaw Rd.

Snoll Hatch. —2K 147
Snoll Hatch Rd. *E Peck* —2K 147 (3B 26)
Snowbell Rd. *Kgnt* —5F 160
Snowdon Av. *Maid* —4E 126
Snowdon Clo. *Chat* —4E 94
Snowdon Pde. *Maid* —4F 126
Snowdown. —4E 162 (3B 32)
Snowdown Cvn. Site. *Snow* —3E 162
Snowdown Clo. *SE20* —4A 68
Snowdown Ct. *Aysm* —2D 162
Snowdrop Clo. *Folk* —3J 189
Snughorne La. *Smar* —1B 38
Sobraon Way. *Cant* —1C 172
Socket La. *Hay* —9L 69
Soho. —2C 4
Solefields. Sev —9K 119
(off Solefields Rd.)
Solefields Rd. *Sev* —1J 131 (2D 25)
Solent Gdns. *Chat* —3E 94
Soleoak Dri. *Sev* —9J 119
Soleshill Farm Cotts. *Chi* —8H 175
Soleshill Rd. *Shott* —8H 175 (2B 30)
Sole Street. —8J 77 (2B 16)
Sole St. *Crun* —3B 30
Sole St. *Grav* —8J 77
Sole St. *Meop & Grav* —2B 16
Sole St. *Sole S* —8J 77
Soloman Ho. *Deal* —7L 177
Solomon Rd. *Gill* —2B 96
Solomons La. *Fav* —5H 187
Solomon's La. *M'fld* —4B 44
Solomon's Rd. *Chat* —8C 80
Somerden Rd. *Orp* —1M 85
Somerfield Barn Ct. *S'ndge* —9J 215
Somerfield Clo. *Maid* —5A 126
Somerfield La. *Maid* —4A 126
Somerfield Rd. *Maid* —5A 126
Somerhill. —9M 145
Somerhill Av. *Sidc* —5K 57
Somerhill Rd. *Tonb* —7K 145
Somerhill Rd. *Well* —9K 51
Somerset Av. *Well* —2H 57
Somerset Clo. *Chat* —3F 94
Somerset Clo. *Sit* —7D 98
Somerset Clo. *Whits* —6D 224
Somerset Ct. *Broad* —9K 209
Somerset Ct. *Walm* —7L 177
Somerset Rd. *Afrd* —8G 158 (1A 40)
Somerset Rd. *Cant* —2C 172
Somerset Rd. *Dart* —4J 59
Somerset Rd. *Folk* —5E 188 (2A 42)
Somerset Rd. *Maid* —9F 126
Somerset Rd. *Orp* —1J 85
Somerset Rd. *Tun W* —8G 150
Somerset Rd. *Walm* —7M 177
Somersham Rd. *Bexh* —9N 51
Somers Town. —2C 4
Somertrees Av. *SE12* —7L 55
Somerville Gdns. *Tun W* —1F 156
Somerville Rd. *SE20* —3A 68
Somerville Rd. *Dart* —4N 59
Somme Ct. *Cant* —1C 172
Sommerville Clo. *Fav* —5J 187
Somner Clo. *Cant* —1K 171
Somner Wlk. *Maid* —4J 139
Somnes Av. *Can I* —1E 9
Sondes Clo. *H Bay* —5H 195
Sondes Rd. *Deal* —5N 177 (2E 33)
Sonnet Wlk. *Big H* —6B 164
Soper's La. *Hawkh* —3H 191
Sophurst Wood La. *Matf* —9H 153 (1B 36)
Sopwith Clo. *Big H* —4D 164
Sorrel Bank. *Croy* —9B 82
Sorrel Clo. *SE28* —1J 51
Sorrell Clo. *Eden* —4D 184
Sorrell Rd. *Chat* —7B 94
Sorrells, The. *Stan H* —2C 8
Sorrel Way. *N'fleet* —9D 62
Sortmill Rd. *Snod* —3F 108
Sotherton. *W'boro* —2J 161
Souberg Clo. *Deal* —2M 177
Sounds Lodge. *Swan* —9D 72
South Acton. —3A 4
South Alkham. —1B 42
Southall Clo. *Min* —6N 205
Southampton Rd. *NW5* —1B 4
Southampton Row. *WC1* —2C 5
Southampton Way. *SE5* —3D 5
South Ashford. —1F 160 (1A 40)
S. Ash Rd. *As* —1J 105 (3E 15)
S. Audley St. *W1* —2C 4
South Av. *Gill* —1K 95
South Av. *Sit* —8H 99 (3C 19)
South Av. *Snow* —4E 162
S. Aylesford Retail Pk. *Ayle* —1J 125
South Bank. *Cli* —3M 65
South Bank. *S'hrst* —9J 221
South Bank. *Sut V* —9A 140
South Bank. *W'ham* —8F 116
S. Barham Rd. *B'hm* —9C 162 (4E 31)
South Beddington. —3C 12
South Benfleet. —1E 9
Southborough. —9A 70 (2A 14)
(nr. Bromley)
Southborough. —4E 150 (1E 35)
(nr. Royal Tunbridge Wells)
Southborough Ct. *Tun W* —5F 150
Southborough La. *Brom* —8A 70 (2A 14)
Southborough Rd. *Brom* —6A 70 (2A 14)
Southbourne. *Afrd* —4C 160
Southbourne. *Brom* —1K 83
Southbourne Gdns. *SE12* —3L 55
Southbourne Gro. *Chat* —7D 94
Southbourne Gro. *Wclf S* —1B 10
S. Bourne Rd. *Folk* —6L 189
Southbridge Rd. *Croy* —2D 13
Southbrook M. *SE12* —4J 55
Southbrook Rd. *SE12* —4J 55 (4E 5)
S. Bush La. *Gill* —6D 96 (2A 18)
S. Camber Way. *Dover* —4N 181
S. Canterbury Rd. *Cant* —4N 171 (1D 31)
Southchurch. —1C 11
Southchurch Av. *Sth S* —1C 10
Southchurch Boulevd. *Sth S* —1C 11
Southchurch Hall. —1C 10
Southchurch Rd. *Sth S* —1C 10
S. Cliff Pde. *Broad* —3L 211
South Clo. *Bexh* —2M 57
South Clo. *Cant* —2N 171 (1D 31)
South Ct. *Deal* —4N 177
South Ct. *Maid* —8D 126
S. Court Dri. *W'hm* —3B 226
South Cres. *Cox* —5N 137
Southcroft Av. *Well* —1G 57
Southcroft Av. *W Wick* —3F 82
Southcroft Rd. *SW17 & SW16* —1C 12
Southcroft Rd. *Orp* —4G 84
S. Croxted Rd. *SE21* —4D 5
South Croydon. —3D 13
S. Dagenham Rd. *Dag & Rain* —1C 7
South Darenth. —4C 74 (1E 15)
Southdene. *Hals* —4A 102
Southdown Rd. *Min S* —6F 218
South Dri. *Orp* —6G 84
S. Eastern Rd. *Ram* —6G 211 (2E 23)
S. Eastern Rd. *Roch* —5N 79
S. Eden Pk. Rd. *Beck* —9E 68 (2E 13)
Southenay La. *S'ndge* —6H 215 (2C 40)
Southend. —9G 54 (1E 13)
South End. *Croy* —2D 13
Southend Clo. *SE9* —4D 56
Southend Cres. *SE9* —4D 56 (4A 6)
Southend La. *SE26 & SE6* —9C 54 (1E 13)
Southend-on-Sea. —1C 10
Southend Pier. —1C 10
S. End Rd. *NW3* —1B 4
Southend Rd. *Beck* —4D 68 (1E 13)
Southend Rd. *Corr* —1C 9
Southend Rd. *Grays* —3A 8
S. End Rd. *Rain & Horn* —2C 7
Southernden. —4B 28
Southernden Rd. *H'crn* —4B 28
Southern Pl. *Swan* —7E 72
Southernwood Rise. *Folk* —7F 188
Southey St. *SE20* —3A 68
Southey Way. *Lark* —6D 108
Southfield La. *Eger* —3D 29
Southfield Rd. *W4* —3A 4
Southfield Rd. *Chst* —6J 71
Southfield Rd. *Tun W* —8G 150
Southfields. —4B 4
Southfields. *Roch* —9M 79
Southfields. *Speld* —7A 150
Southfields. *Swan* —3F 72
Southfield Shaw. *Meop* —1G 106
Southfields Rd. *W King* —8F 88
Southfields Way. *Tun W* —6H 151
Southfleet. —1N 75 (1A 16)
Southfleet Av. *Long* —5A 76
Southfleet Rd. *Bean* —9J 61 (1E 15)
Southfleet Rd. *N'fleet* —6E 62
Southfleet Rd. *Orp* —4G 84
Southfleet Rd. *Swans* —5M 61 (4A 8)
South Foreland Lighthouse. —1E 43
Southgate Rd. *N1* —2D 5
Southgate Rd. *Tent* —8D 222
S. Gipsy Rd. *Well* —1M 57
S. Glade, The. *Bex* —6A 58
S. Goodwin Ct. *Deal* —2N 177
South Green. —5J 113 (3B 18)
South Grn. La. *S'bry* —3H 113 (3B 18)
South Gro. *Tun W* —3G 157
South Hackney. —2D 5
S. Hall Clo. *F'ham* —1N 87
South Hampstead. —1B 4
South Hill. *Chst* —2B 70
South Hill. *H'gh* —4C 30
South Hill. *Horn H* —2B 8
South Hill. *Lang H* —1B 8
S. Hill Rd. *Brom* —6H 69
S. Hill Rd. *Grav* —6H 63
South Hornchurch. —2C 7
Southill Ct. *Hay* —8J 69
Southill Rd. *Chat* —9C 80
Southill Rd. *Chst* —3A 70
South Kensington. —3B 4
S. Kent Av. *N'fleet* —4B 62
South Lambeth. —3C 5
S. Lambeth Rd. *SW8* —3C 5
Southland Rd. *SE18* —7H 51
Southlands Av. *Orp* —5F 84
Southlands Gro. *Brom* —6A 70
Southlands Rd. *Brom* —7N 69 (1A 14)
South La. *N Mald* —1A 12
South La. *Sut V* —9A 140 (3A 28)
South La. W. *N Mald* —1A 12
South Lea. *Kgnt* —6E 160
Southlees La. *S Grn* —7H 113 (4B 18)
South Lodge. *Whits* —2G 225
S. Lodge Av. *Mitc* —1C 13
S. Lodge Clo. *Whits* —2G 225
S. Lodge Hill. *S Min* —4E 31
S. Lodge Rd. *S Min* —4D 31
Southmead Clo. *Folk* —5G 189
S. Military Rd. *Dover* —7H 181 (1C 43)
South Motto. *Kgnt* —5F 160
South Norwood. —1D 13
South Norwood Country Park. —1D 13
S. Norwood Hill. *SE25* —1D 13
South Ockendon. —2E 7
South of England Farm Park. —8E 226
South of England Rare Breeds Centre. —3D 39
Southold Rise. *SE9* —8B 56
Southover. *Brom* —1K 69
South Pde. *W4* —3A 4
South Pk. *Sev* —7J 119
South Pk. Bus. Village. *Maid* —8D 126
South Pk. Ct. *Beck* —3D 68
South Pk. Cres. *SE6* —6J 55
S. Park Dri. *Ilf & Bark* —1B 6
S. Park Hill Rd. *S Croy* —2D 13
South Pk. Rd. *Maid* —8E 126
Southport Rd. *SE18* —4F 50
South Promenade. *Deal* —4N 177
S. Rise Way. *SE18* —4F 50
South Rd. *SE23* —7A 54
South Rd. *Chat* —5E 80
(Officers' Rd.)
South Rd. *Chat* —5D 80
(Wood St.)
South Rd. *Dover* —4G 181
South Rd. *Eri* —7G 52
South Rd. *Fav* —5G 186 (3A 20)
South Rd. *Folk* —8C 188
South Rd. *H Bay* —3H 195
South Rd. *Hythe* —7K 197 (3E 41)
South Rd. *Kgdn* —4N 199
South Rd. *Mard* —2M 205
South Rd. *S Ock* —2E 7
Southsea Av. *Min S* —3J 219
Southsea Dri. *H Bay* —3E 194
South Side. *Til* —2D 62
Southside Comn. *SW19* —1A 12
S. Side Three Rd. *Chat* —4E 80
Southspring. *Sidc* —5F 56
South Stifford. —3A 8
South Stour. —2A 40
S. Stour Av. *Afrd* —1G 160
South Street. —7E 90 (3B 16)
(nr. Meopham)
South Street. —4E 112 (3A 18)
(nr. Stockbury)
South Street. —1C 116 (1A 24)
(nr. Westerham Hill)
South Street. —6J 225 (2D 21)
(nr. Whitstable)
South St. *Barm* —8J 125 (2D 27)
South St. *Bou B* —9N 187 (4B 20)
South St. *Brom* —5K 69
South St. *Cant* —8B 168
South St. *Deal* —4N 177
South St. *Eps* —3A 12
South St. *Folk* —6L 189
South St. *Grav* —5G 63
South St. *Lydd* —3C 204
South St. *Meop* —7E 90 (3A 16)
South St. *Queen* —7A 218
South St. *Roth* —4D 35
South St. *Whits* —5J 225 (2D 21)
South St. Rd. *S'bry* —3C 112 (3A 18)
South Tankerton. —4J 225
South Trench. *Tonb* —2J 145
S. Undercliff. *Rye* —3A 46
South View. *Bear* —5M 127
South View. *Brom* —5M 69
South View. *Her* —3K 169
S. View Clo. *Bex* —4A 58
S. View Clo. *Swan* —7H 73
Southview Gdns. *S'ness* —4D 218
Southview Rd. *Brom* —9G 55
Southview Rd. *Crowb* —4C 35
S. View Rd. *Dart* —8L 59
S. View Rd. *Spar G* —3A 36
S. View Rd. *Tun W* —6H 151
S. View Rd. *Whits* —7F 224
Southviews. *S Croy* —9A 82
S. View Ter. *Goud* —8K 185
South Wlk. *W Wick* —4H 83
South Wall. *Deal* —2K 177 (2E 33)
Southwall Rd. *Deal* —4L 177 (2E 33)
Southwark. —2C 5
Southwark Bri. *SE1* —2D 5
Southwark Bri. Rd. *SE1* —3C 5
Southwark Pk. Rd. *SE16* —3D 5
Southwark Pl. *Brom* —6B 70
Southwark Rd. *Roch* —6H 79
Southwark St. *SE1* —2C 5
Southwater Clo. *Beck* —3E 68
South Way. *Croy* —4B 82
South Way. *Hay* —1K 83
South Way. *Wemb* —1A 4
South Ways. *Sut V* —9A 140
Southwell Rd. *Roch* —6G 79
South Willesborough. —2J 161 (1A 40)
South Wimbledon. —1B 12
Southwold Pl. *Wgte S* —4K 207
Southwold Rd. *Bex* —4C 58
Southwood. *Maid* —7K 125
Southwood Av. *Tun W* —8G 151
Southwood Clo. *Brom* —7B 70
S. Woodford to Barking Relief Rd. *E11, E12 & Bark* —1A 6
Southwood Gdns. *Ram* —5F 210
Southwood Rd. *SE9* —7D 56 (4A 6)
Southwood Rd. *SE28* —1K 51
Southwood Rd. *Ram* —5G 210
Southwood Rd. *Tun W* —9B 150
Southwood Rd. *Whits* —3K 225
Soval. —6B 180
Sovereign Boulevd. *Chat* —1H 95
Sovereign Ct. *Roch* —6G 78
Sovereign Ct. S at H —4A 74
(off Barton Rd.)
Sovereigns, The. *Maid* —5A 126
Sovereigns Way. *Mard* —2J 205
Sovereign Way. *Tonb* —6J 145
Sowell St. *Broad* —8K 209 (1E 23)
Sowerby Clo. *SE9* —3B 56
Spade La. *H'lip* —6E 96 (2A 18)
Spa Esplanade. *H Bay* —2D 194
Spa Hill. *SE19* —1D 13
Spa Ind. Pk. *Tun W* —6L 151
Spalding Ho. *SE4* —2B 54
Spaniards Rd. *NW3* —1B 4
Spanton Cres. *Hythe* —5H 197
Sparepenny La. *Eyns* —3L 87 (2D 15)
Sparkes. *Sidc* —1K 71
Sparkeswood. —3K 213
Sparkeswood Av. *Rol* —2K 213
Sparkeswood Clo. *Rol* —3K 213
Sparrow Castle. *Mgte* —4D 208
Sparrow Dri. *Orp* —2E 84
Sparrow's Green. —3B 36
Sparrows Grn. Rd. *Wadh* —3A 36
Sparrow's Herne. *Bas* —1C 9
Sparrows La. *SE9* —5E 56
Spa Valley Railway. —6K 155 (2D 35)
Speakman Ho. SE4 —1B 54
(off Arica Rd.)
Spearhead Rd. *Maid* —2C 126
Spearman St. *SE18* —6C 50
Spectrum Bus. Cen. *Roch* —4B 80
Spectrum Bus. Est. *Maid* —4J 139
Spectrum W. *Maid* —1A 126
Speedgate Hill. *Fawk* —3G 88 (2E 15)
Speedwell Av. *Chat* —7B 94
Speedwell Clo. *Eden* —4D 184
Speedwell Clo. *Gill* —7H 81
Speedwell Clo. *Weav* —5H 127
Speke Hill. *SE9* —8B 56
Speke Rd. *Broad* —7J 209
Spekes Rd. *Hem* —5L 95
Spelders Hill. *Brook* —1B 40
Speldhurst. —6A 150 (1D 35)
Speldhurst Clo. *Afrd* —4C 160
Speldhurst Clo. *Brom* —8K 69
Speldhurst Ct. *Maid* —5A 126
Speldhurst Gdns. *Clift* —2K 209
Speldhurst Hill. *Speld* —7A 150 (1D 35)
Speldhurst Rd. *L'tn G* —2M 155 (2D 35)
Speldhurst Rd. *Tun W* —6D 150 (1E 35)
Spelmonden Rd. *Horsm* —4B 198 (2C 36)
Spencer Clo. *Chat* —6D 94
Spencer Clo. *Orp* —3G 85
Spencer Ct. *Farn* —6E 84
Spencer Ct. *S'gte* —8C 188
Spencer Flats. *Chat* —3E 94
Spencer Gdns. *SE9* —3B 56
Spencer Ho. Folk —6F 188
(off Coolinge La.)
Spencer M. Tun W —3G 157
(off Berkeley Rd.)
Spencer Pk. *SW18* —4B 4
Spencer Rd. *Birch* —3E 206
Spencer Rd. *Brom* —3J 69
Spencers Cotts. *Bor G* —2N 121
Spencer Sq. *Ram* —6H 211
Spencer St. *EC1* —2C 5
Spencer St. *Grav* —5F 62
Spencer St. *Ram* —6H 211
Spencer Way. *Maid* —1H 139
Spendiff. —4B 66 (4D 9)
Spenlow Dri. *Chat* —1D 110
Spenny La. *Mard* —4C 27
Spenser Rd. *H Bay* —3F 194 (2E 21)
Speranza St. *SE18* —5H 51
Speyside. *Tonb* —2H 145
Spicers Ct. *Hythe* —7K 197
Spicer's Pl. *Wickh* —4A 22
Spielman Rd. *Dart* —2N 59
Spiers, The. *Gill* —7M 81
Spillett Clo. *Fav* —6F 186
Spillway, The. *Maid* —7A 126
Spindle Clo. *SE18* —3A 50
Spindle Glade. *Maid* —4F 126
Spindlewood Clo. *Chat* —8E 94
Spinel Clo. *SE18* —5H 51
Spinnaker Ct. *Roch* —2N 93
Spinners Clo. *Bidd* —7L 163
Spinney Clo. *Clift* —4J 209
Spinney La. *Aysm* —4B 162 (3A 32)
(in two parts)
Spinney Oak. *Brom* —5A 70
Spinneys, The. *Brom* —4B 70
Spinney, The. *Afrd* —7C 158
Spinney, The. *Dover* —2D 180
Spinney, The. *Maid* —7E 126
Spinney, The. *Sidc* —1N 71
Spinney, The. *Swan* —5F 72
Spinney, The. *Tonb* —8G 144
Spinney Way. *Cud* —2F 100
Spire Av. *Whits* —5H 225
Spire Clo. *Grav* —6G 63
Spires, The. *Cant* —1M 171
Spires, The. *Dart* —7L 59
Spires, The. *Maid* —5A 126
Spires, The. *Roch* —7H 79
Spitalfield La. *New R* —3A 212
Spitalfields. —2D 5
Spitals Cross. —4C 184 (4B 24)
Spitals Cross Estate. —4D 184
Spital St. *Dart* —4L 59
Spitfire Clo. *Chat* —5E 94
Spitfire & Hurricane Pavilion. —9M 207 (2D 23)
Spitfire Rd. *W Mal* —6L 123
Spivers Garden. —4A 198
Split Ho. *Dover* —3F 180
Split La. *S Min* —3D 31
Spode La. *Cowd* —1B 34
Sponden La. *Sand* —1J 215
(in two parts)
Spongs La. *Siss* —7C 220 (2E 37)
Sportsbank St. *SE6* —5F 54
Sportsfield. *Maid* —4E 126
Sportsmans Cotts. *King H* —4N 123
Spot Farm Cotts. *Maid* —1N 139
Spothouse La. *Wdchu* —6F 226 (3E 39)
Spot La. *Down* —7J 127 (2E 27)
(in three parts)
Spout Hill. *Croy* —6D 82 (2E 13)
Spout Hill. *Roth* —4E 35
Spout La. *Bchly* —9N 153 (1B 36)
Spout La. *Crock H* —3B 24
Spratling La. *Ram* —3D 210 (2D 23)
Spratling St. *Mans* —3B 210 (2D 23)
Spray Hill. *Lam* —2D 200 (3B 36)
Spray's La. *Sed* —4C 44
Spray St. *SE18* —4D 50
Sprig, The. *Bear* —5K 127
Springbank Rd. *SE13* —4G 55
Springbourne Ct. *Beck* —4F 68
(in two parts)
Spring Cotts. *Hams* —8C 190
Springcroft. *Hart* —9N 75
Spring Cross. *New Ash* —4N 89
Springett Almshouses. *Hawkh* —7J 191
Springett Clo. *Eccl* —4K 109
Springetts Hill. —3B 124
Springett Way. *Cox* —4A 138
Springfarm Rd. *Bztt* —1C 47
Springfield Av. *Maid* —2C 126
Springfield Av. *Swan* —7G 73
Springfield Clo. *Ram* —2J 211
Springfield Cotts. *Bek* —4F 172
Springfield Gdns. *Brom* —7B 70
Springfield Gdns. *W Wick* —3E 82
Springfield Ind. Est. *Hawkh* —4K 191
Springfield Pas. *Hythe* —6J 197
Springfield Rd. *Bexh* —2C 58
Springfield Rd. *Brom* —7B 70
Springfield Rd. *Clift* —2J 209 (1E 23)
Springfield Rd. *Dover* —2G 181
Springfield Rd. *Eden* —6B 184
Springfield Rd. *Gill* —6H 81
Springfield Rd. *Groom* —6K 155
Springfield Rd. *Lark* —7D 108
Springfield Rd. *Sit* —6E 98
Springfield Rd. *Tun W* —5F 150
Springfield Rd. *Well* —1K 57
Springfield Ter. *Chat* —8C 80
Springfield Ter. *S'ndge* —9K 215
Springfield Wlk. Orp —2G 84
(off Andover Rd.)
Springfield Way. *Hythe* —8B 188
Spring Gdns. *Big H* —6C 164
Spring Gdns. *Cant* —3L 171 (1D 31)
Spring Gdns. *Orp* —7K 85
Spring Gdns. *Tun W* —1B 156
Spring Gro. *Grav* —6G 63
Springhead. *Tun W* —9K 151
Springhead Enterprise Pk. *N'fleet* —6A 62
Springhead Rd. *Eri* —6G 53
Springhead Rd. *Fav* —3G 187
Spring Head Rd. *Kems* —8N 103
Springhead Rd. *N'fleet* —7B 62 (4A 8)
Spring Hill. *Ford* —8H 149 (1D 35)
Spring Hollow. *St Mar* —2F 214
Springholm Clo. *Big H* —6C 164
Spring Ho. Flats. Hythe —6K 197
(off Dental St.)
Springhouse La. *Corr* —2C 9
Springhouse Rd. *Corr* —2C 8
Springhurst Clo. *Croy* —5C 82
Spring La. *SE25* —2D 13
Spring La. *Bidb* —3C 150
Spring La. *Cant* —2A 172
Spring La. *F'wch* —7F 168
Spring La. *Hythe* —7A 188
Spring La. *Igh* —4H 121 (1E 25)
Spring La. *Oxt* —3A 24
Spring Park. —4D 82 (2E 13)
Spring Pk. Av. *Croy* —3A 82
Springpark Dri. *Beck* —6F 68
Spring Pk. Rd. *Croy* —3A 82
Springrice Rd. *SE13* —4G 54
Springshaw Clo. *Sev* —5E 118
Springshaw Ct. *Tun W* —8K 151
Spring Shaw Rd. *Orp* —4J 71

Stockdale Gdns.—Sunnyside Rd.

Stockdale Gdns. *Deal* —6M 177
Stockenbury. *E Peck* —1L 147
Stockers Brow. *Rod* —3H 115
Stocker's Head. —1N 175 (3E 29)
Stocker's Hill. *Bou B* —2H 165 (4B 20)
Stockers Hill. *Rod* —3H 115 (3C 19)
Stockett La. *Cox & E Far* —5N 137 (3D 27)
Stockett La. *E Far* —2D 27
Stockham. *Sels* —4A 32
Stockham Ct. *Folk* —4E 188
Stock Hill. *Big H* —4D 164 (4A 14)
Stockland Green. —5C 150 (1E 35)
Stockland Grn. Rd. *Tun W* —6B 150 (1D 35)
Stock La. *Dart* —8K 59
Stock La. *Sme* —2B 40
Stocks Green. —2B 144 (3D 25)
Stocks Grn. Rd. *Hild* —2B 144 (3D 25)
Stocks Rd. *Wit* —2A 46
Stocks, The. —2A 46
Stockton Clo. *Maid* —1E 126
Stockton Sq. *Brom* —6K 69
Stockwell. —3C 5
Stockwell Clo. *Brom* —5L 69
Stockwell La. *Fav* —4H 187
Stockwell Rd. *SW9* —3C 5
Stockwood Chase. *R Comn* —9G 167
Stockwood Hill. *R Comn* —9G 167
Stoddards La. *Beckl* —2D 45
Stoddart Rd. *Folk* —5E 188
Stodmarsh. —5N 169 (3A 22)
Stodmarsh Rd. *Cant & Stod* —2D 172 (4E 21)
Stofield Gdns. *SE9* —8N 55
Stoke. —9H 201 (4A 10)
Stoke Newington. —1D 5
Stoke Newington Chu. St. *N16* —1D 5
Stoke Newington High St. *N16* —1D 5
Stoke Newington Rd. *N16* —1D 5
Stoke Rd. *Hoo* —8H 67 (4E 9)
Stoke Rd. *Lwr Sto* —6K 201 (3A 10)
Stoke Rd. Bus. Cen. *Hoo* —8H 67
Stokesay Ct. Dart —4B 60
(off Osbourne Rd.)
Stokes Rd. *Croy* —9A 68
Stombers La. *Drel* —6E 192 (1A 42)
Stoms Path. *SE6* —1D 68
Stonar Clo. *Ram* —3J 211
Stonar Clo. *S'wch* —5M 217
Stonar Gdns. *S'wch* —4M 217
Stondon Pk. *SE23* —4B 54 (4E 5)
Stone. —3E 60 (4E 7)
Stoneacre. —1L 139 (2A 28)
Stoneacre Clo. *Gill* —6N 95
Stoneacre Cotts. *Maid* —1M 139
Stoneacre La. *Otham* —9L 127
Stone Barn Av. *Birch* —5F 206
Stonebridge. —2A 4
Stonebridge. *Brook* —4B 30
Stonebridge Green. —4C 29
Stonebridge Grn. Rd. *Eger* —4C 29
Stonebridge Rd. *N'fleet* —3N 61 (4A 8)
Stonebridge Vs. *New R* —2B 212
Stonebridge Way. *Fav* —5F 186
Stone Chapel. —5C 186 (3E 19)
Stonecot Hill. *Sutt* —2B 12
Stone Cotts. *E Far* —1K 137
Stone Cotts. *Langl* —4L 139
Stone Cotts. *Maid* —8G 127
Stone Ct. *Eri* —5G 52
Stone Ct. La. *Pem* —6D 152
Stonecroft. *Meop* —2F 106
Stonecroft Rd. *Eri* —7D 52
Stone Cross. —3H 155 (2C 35)
(nr. Ashurst)
Stone Cross. —7L 217 (1D 33)
(nr. Sandwich)
Stonecross Lea. *Chat* —2F 94
Stone Cross Lees. *S'wch* —7L 217
Stonecrouch. —3C 36
Stonedane Ct. *Fav* —4G 187
Stonefield Clo. *Bexh* —1B 58
Stone Gdns. *Broad* —8M 209
Stonegate. *Wye* —2M 159
Stonegate Clo. *Orp* —6L 71
Stonegate Rd. *Shov G* —4B 36
Stone Grn. *Stne* —2A 46
Stonehall. —4B 32
Stonehall Rd. *Lyd* —4B 32
Stoneheap Rd. *E Stu* —3C 33
Stone Hill. —2C 40
Stone Hill. *S'ndge* —2C 40
Stonehill Green. —3D 72
Stone Hill Rd. *Eger* —4C 29
Stonehill Woods Pk. *Sidc* —2C 72
Stonehorse Ct. *Roch* —1L 79
Stonehorse La. *Roch* —1L 79
Stone Ho. *Broad* —6M 209
Stonehouse La. *Hals* —9M 85 (3B 14)
Stonehouse La. *Purf* —3E 7
Stonehouse M. *Broad* —7M 209
Stonehouse Rd. *Hals* —1L 101
Stoneings La. *Knock* —9H 101 (1B 24)
Stone in Oxney. —2A 46
Stoneleigh. —2A 12
Stoneleigh Pk. Av. *Croy* —9A 68
Stone Lodge Farm Park. —4E 7
Stoneness Rd. *Grays* —3E 7
Stone Pk. Av. *Beck* —7D 68 (1E 13)
Stone Pit La. *Sand* —3N 215 (1C 45)
Stone Pl. Rd. *Grnh* —3E 60 (4E 7)
Stonequarry. —2A 34
Stone Quarry Rd. *Chel G* —4A 34
Stone Rd. *Broad* —8M 209 (1E 23)
Stone Rd. *Brom* —8J 69
Stone Row. *Ford* —9J 149
Stones Cross Rd. *Swan* —9D 72 (2C 15)
Stonestile Farm Rd. *Char* —3D 29
Stonestile Rd. *H'crn* —1H 193 (4A 28)
Stone Street. —7E 120 (2E 25)
Stone St. *C'brk* —7D 176 (2E 37)
Stone St. *Fav* —5G 187 (3A 20)
Stone St. *Grav* —4G 62
Stone St. *Lymp* —3D 41
Stone St. *N'grn* —5B 196
Stone St. *P'hm* —3D 31
Stone St. *Stanf* —2D 41
Stone St. *S Min* —4D 31
Stone St. *Tun W* —1H 157
Stone St. *Wnhgr* —3C 196 (2D 41)
(in two parts)
Stonestreet Green. —2B 40
Stone St. Rd. *Ivy H* —5C 120 (2D 25)
Stonewall Pk. Rd. *L'tn G* —2N 155
Stonewood. —8K 61
Stonewood. *Bean* —8J 61
Stonewood Rd. *Eri* —5F 52
Stoney All. *SE18* —9C 50
Stoneycroft Clo. *SE12* —5J 55
Stoney Hill. *Chat* —9E 80
Stoney Path. *Walm* —6N 177
Stoney Rd. *Dunk* —3L 165
Stony Corner. *Grav* —7D 76
Stony Corner. *Meop* —1A 16
Stonyfield. *Eden* —4D 184
Stony La. *Goud* —8K 185
Stony La. *Roch* —6M 93
Stonyway La. *Chu H* —7A 180 (1B 42)
Stopford Rd. *E13* —2A 6
Stopford Rd. *Gill* —8F 80
Store Rd. *E16* —2C 50
Storey St. *E16* —1C 50
Stornaway Strand. *Grav* —8L 63
Stour Clo. *Afrd* —9C 158
Stour Clo. *Cha* —8D 170
Stour Clo. *Kes* —5M 83
Stour Clo. *Roch* —5K 79
Stour Clo. *Tonb* —2H 145
Stour Ct. *Cant* —2M 171 (1D 31)
Stour Ct. *S'wch* —5L 217
Stour Cres. *Cant* —8C 168
Stour Ho. *Maid* —9G 126
Stourmouth Rd. *Pres* —3B 22
Stour Rd. *Cha* —8D 170
Stour Rd. *Dart* —1H 59
Stour St. *Cant* —2M 171 (1D 31)
Stour Valley Clo. *Ups* —3A 22
Stour Valley Ind. Est. *Cha* —7D 170
Stour Valley Wlk. *Chi* —9L 175
Stour View. *Cant* —9N 167
Stourville *Cant* —2M 171 (1D 31)
Stow Ct. *Dart* —5C 60
Stowe Rd. *Orp* —5K 85
Stowting. —1D 41
Stowting Common. —1D 41
Stowting Hill. *Stow* —1D 41
Stowting Rd. *Orp* —5G 84
Straight Hill. *Blad* —4E 31
Straight La. *B'lnd & Bztt* —2C 46
Straight Mile. *E'ham* —2A 44
Strait Rd. *E6* —2A 6
Strakers Hill. *E Stu* —3C 33
Strand. *WC2* —2C 5
Strand App. Rd. *Gill* —5H 81
Strand Clo. *Meop* —1F 90
Strand Ct. *SE18* —5G 51
Strandfield Clo. *SE18* —5G 51
Strand Hill. *W'sea* —4A 46
Strand St. *S'wch* —4L 217 (4D 23)
Strand, The. *Walm* —6N 177 (3E 33)
Strangers Clo. *Cant* —4J 171
Strangers La. *Cant* —4J 171 (1D 31)
Strangford Pl. *H Bay* —5J 195
Strangford Rd. *Whits* —3H 225
Strasbourg St. *Mgte* —7E 208
Stratford. —1E 5
Stratford Av. *Gill* —3N 95
Stratford Ho. Av. *Brom* —6A 70
Stratford La. *Gill* —3B 96
Stratford Marsh. —2E 5
Stratford New Town. —1E 5
Stratford Rd. *W Mal* —1M 123
Stratford St. *Tun W* —9J 151
Strathaven Rd. *SE12* —4L 55
Strathearn Rd. *SW19* —1B 12
Stratheden Rd. *SE3* —3A 6
Strath Ter. *SW11* —4B 4
Strathyre Av. *SW16* —1C 13
Stratton Clo. *Bexh* —1N 57
Stratton Rd. *Bexh* —1N 57
Stratton Ter. *W'ham* —9E 116
Strawberry Clo. *Tun W* —5E 156
Strawberry Fields. *Swan* —4F 72
Strawberry Hill. *Tun W* —7D 156 (2E 35)
Strawberry Vale. *Tonb* —7J 145
Straw Mill Hill. *Maid* —8B 126 (2D 27)
Stream Cotts. *S'ing* —9B 110
Streamdale. *SE2* —6K 51
Stream La. *Hawkh* —8K 191 (1B 44)
Stream La. *Sed* —4B 44
Streampit La. *Sand* —3K 215
Streamside. *Dit* —9F 108
Stream Side. *Tonb* —9K 133
Streamside Clo. *Brom* —7K 69
Stream, The. *Dit* —9G 108
Stream Wlk. *Whits* —3F 224
(in three parts)
Stream Way. *Belv* —6A 52
Streatfield. *Eden* —6D 184
Streatham. —1C 13
Streatham Common. —1C 13
Streatham Comn. N. *SW16* —1C 13
Streatham High Rd. *SW16* —4C 5
Streatham Hill. —4C 4
Streatham Hill. *SW2* —4C 5
Streatham Park. —1C 12
Streatham Pl. *SW2* —4C 5
Streatham Rd. *Mitc & SW16* —1C 12
Streatham Vale. —1C 12
Streatham Vale. *SW16* —1C 12
Streete Ct. *Wgte S* —3L 207
Streete Ct. Rd. *Wgte S* —3L 207
Street End. —2D 31
Street End. *Str E* —2D 31
Street End Rd. *Chat* —3E 94 (2E 17)
Street Farm Cotts. *Hoo* —7J 67
Streetfield. *H Bay* —6J 195
Streetfield. *Ulc* —9H 141
Streetfield M. *SE3* —1K 55
Streetfield Rd. *Gill* —2B 96
Street, The. *Abb* —1B 46
Street, The. *Acol* —8G 207 (2C 23)
Street, The. *Adm* —2A 32
Street, The. *Ah* —5B 216 (4C 22)
Street, The. *As* —6L 89 (2E 15)
Street, The. *Asht* —4A 12
Street, The. *Bap* —8L 99 (3D 19)
Street, The. *B'hm* —7D 162 (3A 32)
Street, The. *Bear* —5M 127 (2A 28)
Street, The. *Bene* —3A 38
Street, The. *Beth* —2J 163 (1D 39)
Street, The. *Bis* —2E 31
Street, The. *B'den* —9B 98 (3C 18)
Street, The. *Bou B* —3J 165 (4B 20)
Street, The. *Boxl* —8F 110 (4E 17)
Street, The. *Bre* —5A 114 (3B 18)
Street, The. *Bred* —1L 111 (3E 17)
Street, The. *Brook* —4B 30
Street, The. *Chi* —8J 175 (2B 30)
Street, The. *Cob* —7M 77 (1B 16)
Street, The. *Deal* —2D 33
Street, The. *Det* —9K 111 (1E 27)
Street, The. *Dod* —1D 29
Street, The. *E Bra* —1C 41
Street, The. *E Lan* —4M 179 (4D 33)
Street, The. *E'ing* —1E 29
Street, The. *Eger* —4C 29
Street, The. *Eyt* —4K 185 (3C 32)
Street, The. *Fin* —2D 33
Street, The. *Frit* —1A 38
Street, The. *F'hm* —3B 32
Street, The. *Godm* —3B 30
Street, The. *Good* —2B 32
Street, The. *Grav* —1B 16
Street, The. *Gt Cha* —9A 158 (1E 39)
Street, The. *Gus* —7K 179 (4D 33)
Street, The. *Hams* —8D 190 (3A 40)
Street, The. *H'lip* —7F 96 (3A 18)
Street, The. *H'lgh* —4C 30
Street, The. *H'nge* —7D 192 (1A 42)
Street, The. *High H* —4E 9
Street, The. *H Hals* —2H 67
Street, The. *Hort K* —7B 74 (1D 15)
Street, The. *Hoth* —4E 29
Street, The. *Hythe* —2D 41
Street, The. *I'hm* —1N 173 (4A 22)
Street, The. *Igh* —3K 121 (1E 25)
Street, The. *Iwade* —8C 198 (2C 19)
Street, The. *Kenn* —3J 159 (4A 30)
Street, The. *Kgtn* —6A 162 (3E 31)
Street, The. *L Char* —4D 29
Street, The. *Lwr Hal* —8L 223 (2B 18)
Street, The. *Lymp* —6A 196
Street, The. *Lyn* —4D 19
Street, The. *Maid* —2B 26
Street, The. *Mart* —2N 179 (4D 33)
Street, The. *Meop* —2F 90 (2B 16)
Street, The. *Mere* —1J 135
Street, The. *Mer* —8M 161 (2B 40)
Street, The. *Mol* —3A 30
Street, The. *N'tn* —4A 188
Street, The. *Newn* —1D 29
Street, The. *Non* —2B 32
Street, The. *Oare* —2F 186 (3A 20)
Street, The. *Pat* —7G 173 (2E 31)
Street, The. *P'hm* —3D 31
Street, The. *Plax* —9L 121 (2A 26)
Street, The. *P'ley* —4D 29
Street, The. *Pres* —3B 22
Street, The. *Rya* —6L 107 (4B 16)
Street, The. *Sed* —4C 44
Street, The. *Shad* —2E 39
Street, The. *Shol* —5J 177 (2D 33)
Street, The. *Shorne* —1C 78 (1C 16)
Street, The. *Siss* —8C 220 (2E 37)
Street, The. *S'le* —1B 32
Street, The. *St N* —8E 214 (2B 22)
Street, The. *S'bry* —2G 112 (3B 18)
Street, The. *Stne* —2B 46
Street, The. *Tstn* —1E 136 (2C 27)
Street, The. *Ulc* —9H 141 (3B 28)
Street, The. *Upc* —7H 223 (2B 18)
Street, The. *Up H'lng* —7C 92 (3C 16)
Street, The. *Up Stok* —9H 201 (4A 10)
Street, The. *W Hou* —1B 42
Street, The. *W Sto* —3B 22
Street, The. *Wickh* —4A 22
Street, The. *W'boro* —1M 161 (1B 40)
(in two parts)
Street, The. *Wit* —2E 45
Street, The. *Wdboro* —8G 217 (1C 33)
Street, The. *W'hll* —1B 28
Street, The. *Worth* —9M 217 (1D 33)
Strettit Gdns. *E Peck* —2L 147
Strickland Av. *Dart* —1N 59
(in two parts)
Strickland Way. *Orp* —5H 85
Stringer Dri. *Birch* —5F 206
Strode Cres. *S'ness* —2D 218
Strode Pk. Rd. *H Bay* —5H 195
Strond St. *Dover* —6J 181
Strongbow Cres. *SE9* —3B 56
Strongbow Rd. *SE9* —3B 56
Strood. —4L 79 (1D 17)
(nr. Rochester)
Strood. —1M 213 (3B 38)
(nr. Rolvenden)
Strouts Rd. *Afrd* —2B 160
Strover St. *Gill* —5F 80
Struttons Av. *N'fleet* —7E 62
Stuart Av. *Brom* —2K 83
Stuart Clo. *Maid* —3E 126
Stuart Clo. *Swan* —3G 73
Stuart Clo. *Tun W* —5F 156
Stuart Ct. *Cant* —4N 171
Stuart Ct. Dover —4H 181
(off Priory Ga. Rd.)
Stuart Cres. *Croy* —4C 82
Stuart Evans Clo. *Well* —1L 57
Stuart Ho. *Deal* —5L 177
Stuart Mantle Way. *Eri* —7F 52
Stuart Rd. *SE15* —2A 54
Stuart Rd. *Folk* —5L 189
Stuart Rd. *Gill* —9G 81
Stuart Rd. *Grav* —4F 62 (4B 8)
Stuart Rd. *Well* —8K 51
Stubbers La. *Upm* —1E 7
Stubb La. *Brede* —4D 45
Stubb's Cross. —6B 160 (2E 39)
Stubbs Hill. *Orp* —4L 101 (3B 14)
Stub Stairs. *Chu H* —7B 180
Studdal. —3C 33
Studd Hill. —3B 194 (2D 21)
Studds Cotts. *H Bay* —4B 194
Studfall Clo. *Hythe* —8E 196
Stud Farm La. *Blad* —4E 31
Studio Clo. *Kenn* —4H 159
Studios, The. New Ash —3M 89
(off Row, The)
Studland Clo. *Sidc* —8H 57
Studland Rd. *SE26* —1A 68
Studland St. *W6* —3A 4
Studley Ct. *Sidc* —1K 71
Studley Cres. *Long* —5B 76
Stumble Hill. *S'brne* —4J 133 (3E 25)
Stumble La. *Kgnt* —8F 160 (2A 40)
Stumps Hill La. *Beck* —2D 68
Stuppington Ct. Farm. *Cant* —6L 171
Stuppington La. *Cant* —6L 171 (2D 31)
Sturdee Av. *Gill* —8H 81
Sturdee Cotts. *Hoo* —7K 67
Sturdy Clo. *Hythe* —6L 197
Sturges Field. *Chst* —2F 70
Sturges Rd. *Afrd* —7F 158
Sturla Rd. *Chat* —1D 94
Sturmer Clo. *Cant* —3B 172
Sturmer Ct. *King H* —7M 123
Sturry. —6E 168 (3E 21)
Sturry Ct. M. *Sturry* —6E 168
Sturry Hill. *Sturry* —5E 168 (3E 21)
Sturry Rd. *Cant* —9A 168 (4D 21)
Sturry Way. *Gill* —1M 95
Styants Bottom. —4F 120 (1E 25)
Styants Bottom Rd. *Sev* —3F 120 (1E 25)
Style Clo. *Gill* —7A 96
Styles Clo. *Four E* —3B 24
Styles La. *Boxl* —7F 110
Styles Way. *Beck* —7F 68
Succombs Hill. *Warl* —4D 13
Sudbury Cres. *Brom* —2K 69
Sudbury Pl. *Wgte S* —4K 207
Suffolk Av. *Gill* —2B 96
Suffolk Av. *Wgte S* —4J 207
Suffolk Ct. *Gill* —2B 96
Suffolk Dri. *Afrd* —9E 158
Suffolk Gdns. *Dover* —5E 180
Suffolk Ho. SE20 —3A 68
(off Croydon Rd.)
Suffolk M. *Chat* —8C 80
Suffolk Rd. *Cant* —3C 172
Suffolk Rd. *Dart* —4M 59
Suffolk Rd. *Grav* —4J 63
Suffolk Rd. *Maid* —9G 126
Suffolk Rd. *Sidc* —2L 71
Suffolk St. *Whits* —5F 224
Suffolk Way. *Sev* —7K 119
Sugarloaf Hill. *Chat* —1G 94
Sugarloaf Wlk. *Folk* —3K 189
Sulby Ho. SE4 —2B 54
(off Turnham Rd.)
Sullivan Clo. *Dart* —4J 59
Sullivan Rd. *Tonb* —1L 145
Sultan Rd. *Chat* —1F 110
Sultan St. *Beck* —5A 68
Summer Clo. *Hythe* —6G 197
Summer Clo. *Tent* —6D 222
Summer Ct. *Harb* —1J 171
Summerfield. —2B 32
Summerfield Av. *Whits* —4H 225
Summerfield Rd. *Clift* —3J 209 (1E 23)
Summerfield St. *SE12* —5J 55
Summerhill. —1D 37
Summerhill. *Afrd* —3C 160
Summer Hill. *Chst* —5C 70 (1A 14)
Summer Hill. *Harb* —1J 171 (4D 21)
Summerhill. *H'crn* —2H 193 (4A 28)
Summerhill Av. *Tun W* —5F 150
Summerhill Clo. *Orp* —4G 84
Summerhill Cotts. *H Hal* —7H 193
Summerhill Pk. *W'boro* —2N 161
Summerhill Rd. *Dart* —5L 59
Summerhill Rd. *Mard* —4E 27
Summerhill Vs. *Chst* —4C 70
Summerhouse Dri. *Bex & Dart* —9E 58 (4C 7)
Summerlands Lodge. *Orp* —5C 84
Summer La. *T Hill* —5L 167
Summer Leeze. *W'boro* —1J 161
Summer Leeze Gdns. *W'boro* —1J 161
Summer Rd. *St N* —9D 214
Summerstown. —4B 4
Summerstown. *SW17* —4B 4
Summervale Rd. *Tun W* —4D 156
Summerville Av. *Min S* —7G 219
Sumner Clo. *Orp* —5E 84
Sumner Clo. *Rol* —3K 213
Sumner Rd. *Croy* —2C 13
Sump Cotts. *Afrd* —8F 160
Sumpter Way. *Fav* —5D 186
Sunbeam Av. *H Bay* —3A 194
Sunburst Clo. *Mard* —3L 205
Sunbury St. *SE18* —3B 50
Sun Ct. *Eri* —9G 53
Sundale Av. *S Croy* —9A 82
Sunderland Dri. *Rain* —3C 96
Sunderland Mt. *SE23* —7A 54
Sunderland Quay. *Roch* —6A 80
Sunderland Rd. *SE23* —6A 54 (4D 5)
Sundew Gro. *Ram* —4J 211
Sundridge. —2M 69 (1A 14)
(nr. Bromley)
Sundridge. —6N 117 (2C 24)
(nr. Sevenoaks)
Sundridge Av. *Brom & Chst* —4N 69 (1A 14)
Sundridge Av. *Well* —9F 50
Sundridge Clo. *Cant* —7N 167
Sundridge Clo. *Dart* —4A 60
Sundridge Dri. *Chat* —7D 94
Sundridge Hill. *Cux* —9G 79 (2C 17)
Sundridge Hill. *Knock* —9L 101
Sundridge Hill. *Sev* —4B 14
Sundridge La. *Knock* —8K 101
Sundridge La. *Sev* —4B 14
Sundridge Pde. *Brom* —3L 69
Sundridge Park. —3L 69
Sundridge Rd. *Chev* —2B 118
Sundridge Rd. *Ide H* —1C 24
Sunerland Clo. *Roch* —9L 79
Sun Hill. *Fawk* —4G 88 (2E 15)
Sunhill Ct. *Pem* —8B 152
Sun-in-the-Sands. (Junct.) —3A 6
Sunland Av. *Bexh* —2N 57
Sun La. *Grav* —7H 63
Sun La. *Hythe* —6K 197
Sun La. *St N* —8E 214
Sunningdale Av. *Folk* —4G 189
Sunningdale Clo. *Gill* —5N 95
Sunningdale Ct. *Maid* —5E 126
Sunningdale Dri. *Gill* —5N 95
Sunningdale Rd. *Brom* —7A 70
Sunningdale Wlk. *H Bay* —6E 194
Sunninghill. *Grav* —7D 62
Sunnings La. *Upm* —1E 7
Sunningvale Av. *Big H* —3C 164 (4A 14)
Sunningvale Clo. *Big H* —3D 164
Sunny Bank. *Eyt* —3J 185
Sunny Bank. *Hythe* —6G 197
Sunny Bank. *Murs* —6J 99
Sunnybank. *Warl* —4E 13
Sunnydale. *Orp* —3C 84
Sunnydale Rd. *SE12* —3L 55
Sunnydene St. *SE26* —9B 54
Sunnyfield Rd. *Chst* —6J 71
Sunnyfields Clo. *Gill* —3A 96
Sunnyfields Cri. *Min S* —6D 218
Sunnyhill Rd. *H Bay* —4D 194
Sunnymead. *T Hill* —4K 167
Sunnymead Av. *Gill* —7H 81
Sunnymead Cvn. Pk. *E'chu* —3E 202
Sunnyside. Bear —5M 127
(off Street, The)
Sunnyside. *Dod* —1D 29
Sunnyside. *Eden* —4B 184
Sunnyside Av. *Min S* —6H 219
Sunnyside Clo. *Ripp* —3D 33
Sunnyside Cotts. *Deal* —4M 177
Sunnyside Cotts. *Sturry* —6E 168
Sunnyside Gdns. *S'wch* —6K 217
Sunnyside Holiday Pk. *E'chu* —3D 202
Sunnyside Rd. *S'gte* —8D 188

Trafalgar Av.—Up. Stone St.

Trafalgar Av. SE15 —3D 5
Trafalgar Clo. Woul —6G 92
Trafalgar Ct. Eri —7G 53
(off Frobisher Rd.)
Trafalgar Pl. Min S —6J 219
Trafalgar Rd. SE10 —3E 5
Trafalgar Rd. Dart —7M 59
Trafalgar Rd. Grav —5F 62
Trafalgar Rd. St Mc —8J 199
Trafalgar Rd. Wdchu —8L 207
Trafalgar Sq. WC2 —2C 4
Trafalgar St. Gill —7F 80
Tram Rd., The. Folk —6L 189 (2A 42)
Tranquil Rise. Eri —5F 52
Tranquil Vale. SE3 —3E 5
Transfesa Rd. Pad W —7M 147
Transmere Clo. Orp —9E 70
Transmere Rd. Orp —9E 70
Transom Ho. Roch —2N 93
Transport Museum. —8F 178
Trapfield Clo. Bear —5M 127
Trapfield La. Bear —5M 127
(in two parts)
Trapham Rd. Maid —4A 126
Traps La. N Mald —1A 12
Travers Gdns. Bre —5A 114
Travers Rd. Deal —5K 177
Travertine Rd. Chat —1E 110
Treasury View. I'hm —1A 32
Trebble Rd. Swans —4L 61
Trebilco Clo. Tun W —7K 151
Treblers Rd. Crowb —4D 35
Tredegar Rd. E3 —2E 5
Tredegar Rd. Dart —7H 59
Tredwell Clo. Brom —7A 70
Treebourne Rd. Big H —6C 164
Tree La. Plax —9L 121 (2A 26)
Treetops. Grav —1G 77
Tree Tops. Tonb —8H 145
Treetops Clo. SE2 —5N 51
Treewall Gdns. Brom —9L 55
Trefoil Ho. Eri —2N 51
(off Kale Rd.)
Trefor Jones Ct. Dover —2G 180
Trelawn Cres. Chat —9E 94
Trellyn Clo. Maid —7K 125
Trenchard Clo. W'boro —1K 161
Trench Rd. Tonb —1H 145
Trench Wood. —1H 145 (3E 25)
Trentham Dri. Orp —7J 71
Trenton Clo. Maid —2M 125
Trent Rd. Chat —6E 94
Tresco Clo. Brom —2H 69
Tressillian Cres. SE4 —1D 54
Tressillian Rd. SE4 —2C 54
Trevale Rd. Roch —2M 93
Trevelyan Clo. Dart —2N 59
Trevenna Ho. SE23 —8A 54
(off Dacres Rd.)
Trevino Dri. Chat —8C 94
Treviso Rd. SE23 —7A 54
Trevithick Dri. Dart —2N 59
Trevor Clo. Brom —1J 83
Trevthick Dri. Dart —4D 7
Trewin Clo. Ayle —8H 109
Trewsbury Ho. SE2 —1M 51
Trewsbury Rd. SE26 —1A 68
Tribune Ct. S'ness —4C 218
Tribune Dri. Sit —5G 98
Trident Clo. Roch —5B 80
Trigg Gro. Afrd —8G 158
Triggs Row. Tey —2L 223
Trilby Rd. SE23 —7A 54
Trimworth Rd. Folk —5F 188
Trinity Clo. SE13 —2G 54
Trinity Clo. Brom —2A 84
Trinity Clo. Tun W —1K 157
Trinity Ct. Ayle —7L 109
Trinity Ct. Dart —6B 60
(off Churchill Clo.)
Trinity Ct. Deal —6K 177
Trinity Ct. Mgte —2D 208
Trinity Cres. Folk —7H 189
Trinity Gdns. Dart —4L 59
Trinity Gdns. Folk —7J 189
Trinity Hill. Mgte —2D 208 (1D 23)
Trinity Homes. Deal —9M 177
Trinity Pl. Bexh —2A 58
Trinity Pl. Deal —6K 177
Trinity Pl. Ram —5K 211
Trinity Pl. S'ness —2D 218
Trinity Rd. SW18 & SW17 —4B 4
Trinity Rd. Folk —7H 189
Trinity Rd. Gill —6F 80
(in two parts)
Trinity Rd. Grav —5H 63
Trinity Rd. Kenn —4F 158 (4A 30)
(in two parts)
Trinity Rd. S'ness —2D 218 (4D 11)
Trinity Rd. Sit —4G 98
Trinity Sq. Broad —6K 209
Trinity Sq. Mgte —2D 208 (1D 23)
Trinity Trad. Est. Sit —5G 99
Tristan Gdns. Tun W —1C 156
Tristan Sq. SE3 —1H 55
Tristram Rd. Brom —9J 55
Tritton Clo. Kenn —3K 159
Tritton Fields. Kenn —3J 159
Tritton Gdns. Dym —6C 182
Tritton La. New R —3C 212
Trivett Clo. Grnh —3G 60
Troodos Hill. Maid —1C 126
Trosley Av. Grav —7G 62
Trosley Country Park. —3F 106
Trosley Rd. Belv —6B 52
Trottiscliffe. —5F 106 (3B 16)
Trottiscliffe Rd. Adtn —7H 107 (4B 16)
Trotts Hall Gdns. Sit —8G 99
Trotts La. W'ham —9E 116
Trotwood Clo. Chat —2D 110
Trotwood Pl. Broad —9M 209
(off John St.)
Troubridge Clo. W'boro —2L 161
Troughton M. Mgte —4B 208
Troutbeck Ho. Dit —9G 108
Trove Ct. Ram —5K 211
(off Newcastle Hill)
Troy Ct. SE18 —4D 50
Troys Mead. Holl —7F 128
Troy St. SE18 —4D 50
Troy Town. —4A 24
(nr. Edenbridge)
Troy Town. —8A 80
(nr. Rochester)
Troy Town La. Brook —4B 30
Trubridge Rd. Hoo —8G 67
Trueman Clo. Blean —4G 166
Truggers La. Chid H —4B 148 (1C 34)
Trumpet Ho. Afrd —1F 160
Trundley's Rd. SE8 —3D 5
Trunks All. Swan —5C 72
Truro Clo. Gill —9N 81
Truro Ho. Maid —1G 139
Truro Rd. Grav —8J 63
Truro Rd. Ram —5K 211
Truro Wlk. Tonb —2K 145
Trycewell La. Igh —3K 121
Tryon. Sidc —2K 71
Tuam Rd. SE18 —6F 50
Tubbenden Clo. Orp —4G 84
Tubbenden Dri. Orp —5F 84
Tubbenden La. Orp —5F 84 (2B 14)
Tubbenden La. S. Orp —6F 84
Tubbs Rd. NW10 —2A 4
Tubs Hill. Sev —6J 119
Tubs Hill Ho. Sev —6H 119
Tubs Hill Pde. Sev —6H 119
Tubslake. —3E 37
Tudeley. —7B 146 (4A 26)
Tudeley Hale. —4A 26
Tudeley La. Tonb —8J 145 (4E 25)
(in two parts)
Tudor Av. Dym —6C 182
Tudor Av. Maid —3E 126
Tudor Byway. Kenn —4H 159
Tudor Clo. Birch —3G 207
Tudor Clo. Chst —4B 70
Tudor Clo. Dart —4J 59
Tudor Clo. N'fleet —6D 62
Tudor Cotts. Maid —4B 138
Tudor Ct. SE9 —2A 56
Tudor Ct. Big H —5E 164
Tudor Ct. Cant —7J 167
Tudor Ct. Crock —1D 86
Tudor Ct. Sidc —8J 57
Tudor Ct. Tun W —5E 156
Tudor Ct. Whits —2J 225
Tudor Cres. Otf —7K 103
Tudor Dri. King T —1A 12
Tudor Dri. Mord —2A 12
Tudor Dri. Otf —7K 103
Tudor End. Kenn —5H 159
Tudor Gdns. NW9 —1A 4
Tudor Gdns. W Wick —4F 82
Tudor Gro. Chatt —9C 66
Tudor Gro. Gill —3A 96
Tudor Ho. Deal —5K 177
Tudor House Museum. —2D 208
Tudor Rd. Beck —6F 68
Tudor Rd. Cant —3L 171
Tudor Rd. Folk —5D 188
Tudor Rd. Kenn —5H 159
Tudor Wlk. Bex —4N 57
Tudor Way. Orp —9F 70 (2B 14)
Tudway Rd. SE3 —1L 55
Tuesnoad. —1C 39
Tufa Clo. Chat —1E 110
Tuffs Cotts. Mid S —8K 201
Tufnail Rd. Dart —4N 59
Tufnell Park. —1C 4
Tufton Rd. Afrd —8H 159
Tufton Rd. Gill —2B 96
Tufton Rd. Hoth —4E 29
Tufton St. Afrd —8F 158
Tufton St. Maid —5D 126
Tufton Wlk. Afrd —8F 158
Tugboat St. SE28 —2G 50
Tugela St. SE6 —7C 54
Tugmutton Clo. Orp —5D 84
Tulip Clo. Croy —2A 82
Tulip Tree Clo. Tonb —7G 145
Tulse Clo. Beck —6F 68
Tulse Hill. —4C 5
Tulse Hill. SW2 —4C 5
Tumbledown Hill. Westw —4E 29
Tumblefield Rd. Stans —1M 105 (3A 16)
Tumblers Hill. Sut V —9B 140
Tunbridge Hill. —5M 67 (4A 10)
Tunbridge Wells. —1G 157 (2E 35)
Tunbridge Wells Museum & Art Gallery.
(off Mt. Pleasant Rd.) —1H 157
Tunbridge Wells Rd. Mark X —3E 35
Tunbridge Wells Rd. Tic —4B 36
Tunbury Av. Chat —8C 94
Tunbury Av. S. Chat —1C 110
Tunis Ct. Cant —1C 172
Tunis Rd. Broad —8M 209
Tunnel App. SE16 —3D 5
Tunnel Av. SE10 —3E 5
(in two parts)
Tunnel Rd. Tun W —1H 157
Tunstall. —3C 18
Tunstall Clo. Orp —5G 84
Tunstall Rd. Bre —3C 18
Tunstall Rd. Cant —7N 167
Tunstall Rd. Tun —2E 114
Tunstock Way. Belv —3A 52
Tupman Clo. Roch —8M 79
Turgis Clo. Langl —4A 140
Turketel Rd. Folk —6G 189
Turkey Ct. Maid —6F 126
Turks Hill. W'wd —3E 31
Turmine Ct. Min S —7H 219
Turnagain La. Cant —2M 171 (1D 31)
Turnberry Way. Orp —2F 84
Turnbull Clo. Grnh —5E 60
Turnden. —8B 176 (3E 37)
Turnden Gdns. Clift —3J 209
Turnden Rd. C'brk —9A 176 (3D 37)
Turner Av. C'brk —9D 176
Turner Clo. Kem —3G 99
Turner Ct. Dart —3K 59
Turner Ct. Folk —6F 188
Turner Ct. Mgte —3E 208
Turner Rd. Bean —8H 61
Turner Rd. Big H —2B 164
Turner Rd. Tonb —2L 145
Turners Av. Tent —7B 222
Turners Clo. S'ness —3D 218
Turners Ct. W King —8E 88
Turners Gdns. Sev —1K 131
Turner's Green. —3A 36
Turners Grn. Rd. Spar G —3A 36
Turners Meadow Way. Beck —4C 68
Turners Oak. New Ash —4L 89
Turners Pl. S Dar —4C 74
Turner St. Cli —3C 176
Turner St. Ram —6J 211
Turney Rd. SE21 —4D 5
Turnham Green. —3A 4
Turnham Grn. Ter. W4 —3A 4
Turnham Rd. SE4 —3B 54
Turnpike Clo. Hythe —6H 197
Turnpike Ct. Bexh —2M 57
Turnpike Dri. Orp —9L 85
Turnpike Hill. Hythe —5H 197
Turnpike La. W Til —3B 8
Turnstone. Long —6N 75
Turnstone Ct. St Mar —3E 214
(off Cedar Cres.)
Turnstone Rd. Chat —9F 94
Turnstones Ct. Wgte S —2J 207
(off Westgate Bay Av.)
Turnstones, The. Grav —7J 63
Turpington Clo. Brom —9A 70
Turpington La. Brom —1A 84 (2A 14)
Turpin La. Eri —6H 53
Tuscan Dri. Chat —1F 110
Tuscan Rd. SE18 —5F 50
Tutsham Farm. W Far —2F 136
Tutsham Way. Pad W —9K 147
Tutt Hill. —4E 29
Tuxford Rd. Tun W —9B 150
Tweed Rd. Tonb —2J 145
Tweed Ter. Hythe —6H 197
Tweedy Rd. Brom —4K 69 (1E 13)
Twelve Acres. —8H 109
Twelve Acres. W'boro —1J 161
Twelve Oaks. —3A 44
20/20 Ind. Est. All —1N 125
Twigg Clo. Eri —7F 52
Twisden Rd. E Mal —1D 124
Twiss Av. Hythe —6L 197
Twiss Gro. Hythe —6L 197
Twiss Rd. Hythe —6L 197 (3E 41)
Twistleton Ct. Dart —4L 59
Twitham. —4F 226 (1B 32)
Twitton. —7F 102 (4C 15)
Twitton La. Otf —6E 102 (4C 15)
Twitton Meadows. Otf —7F 102
Twitton Stream Cotts. Otf —7F 102
Two Chimneys Cvn. Pk. Birch —6J 207
Twogates Hill Cli & High —8K 65 (4D 9)
Two Post All. Roch —6N 79
Twydall. —9L 81 (2E 17)
Twydall Grn. Gill —9L 81
Twydall La. Gill —1L 95
Twyford Abbey Rd. NW10 —2A 4
Twyford Av. W3 —2A 4
Twyford Clo. Gill —1C 96
Twyford Ct. Maid —3G 126
Twyford Rd. Hdlw —7D 134
Twyne Clo. Sturry —5F 168
Twysden Cotts. Sand —4J 215
Tydeman Rd. Bear —7J 127
Tydemans Av. Ches —4L 225
Tye La. Orp —6E 84
Tyeshurst Clo. SE2 —5N 51
Tyland Barn. S'lng —7B 110 (4D 17)
Tyland Cotts. S'lng —7B 110
Tyland La. S'lng —7B 110 (4D 17)
Tyler Clo. Cant —8M 167
Tyler Clo. E Mal —1D 124
Tyler Dri. Gill —7A 96 (3A 18)
Tyler Gro. Dart —2N 59
Tyler Hill. —5L 167 (3D 21)
Tyler Hill Rd. Blean & T Hill —5G 167 (3D 21)
Tylers Grn. Rd. Swan —9D 72 (2C 15)
Tyler Way. Whits —2N 225
Tyler Way Ind. Est. Whits —2N 225
Tylney Rd. E7 —1A 6
Tylney Rd. Brom —5N 69 (1A 14)
Tyndale Pk. H Bay —3J 195
Tyndall Rd. Well —1H 57
Tyne Clo. Chat —6F 94
Tynedale Clo. Dart —6D 60
Tyne Ho. Maid —2H 139
Tynemouth Rd. SE18 —5G 51
Tyne Rd. Tonb —2H 145
Typhoon Rd. W Mal —6L 123
Tyrell Ho. Beck —1E 68
(off Beckenham Hill Rd.)
Tyrols Rd. SE23 —6A 54
Tyron Way. Sidc —9G 57
Tyrrell Av. Well —3J 57
Tyrwhitt Rd. SE4 —1D 54
Tysoe Ct. Min S —7H 219
Tyson Av. Mgte —2M 207
Tyson Rd. Folk —4L 189

Uckfield La. Hever —4B 24
Uckfield Rd. Crowb —4C 35
Uden Rd. Dym —9D 182
Udimore. —4E 45
Udimore Rd. B Oak & Rye —4D 45
Ufton Clo. Maid —8H 127
Ufton La. Sit —9F 98 (3C 19)
Ulcombe. —9H 141 (3B 28)
Ulcombe Gdns. Cant —8N 167
Ulcombe Hill. Ulc —9H 141 (3B 28)
Ulcombe Rd. H'crn —1K 193 (4A 28)
Ulcombe Rd. Langl —5A 140 (3A 28)
Ulley Cottage. Kenn —3J 159
(off Ulley Rd.)
Ulley Rd. Kenn —3H 159 (4A 30)
Ullswater Clo. Brom —3H 69
Ullswater Gdns. Aysm —1D 162
Ullswater Ho. Maid —1G 139
Ulster Rd. Mgte —5D 208
Ulundi Pl. Woul —6G 93
Undercliff. Maid —6C 126
Undercliff. S'gte —8E 188
Undercliffe Rd. Kgdn —4N 199 (3E 33)
Undercliff Rd. SE13 —1D 54
Underdown Av. Chat —2C 94
Underdown La. H Bay —4G 195
Underdown Pas. Cant —3L 171
Underdown Rd. Dover —5G 181
Underground Rd. H Bay —3G 195
Underhill Cotts. Peene —3B 188
Underhill Rd. Folk —6B 188
Underling Green. —4D 27
Underling La. Mard —4D 27
Underriver. —3B 132 (2D 25)
Underriver Ho. Rd. Under —5C 132 (3E 25)
Undershaw Rd. Brom —8J 55
Undertrees Farm Rd. Stod —3A 22
Underwood. H'nge —6E 192
Underwood. New Ad —6F 82
Underwood Clo. Cant —5N 171
Underwood Clo. Kenn —4H 159
Underwood Clo. Maid —7C 126
Underwood Gdns. Folk —8F 188
Underwood, The. SE9 —8B 56
Unicorn Wlk. Grnh —3F 60
Unicumes La. Maid —7N 125
Union Cres. Mgte —3D 208
Union Pk. Bus. Cen. Maid —4J 139
Union Pl. Cant —1N 171
Union Pl. Chat —8D 80
Union Rd. Bri —9E 172 (2E 31)
Union Rd. Brom —8N 69
Union Rd. Deal —4M 177
Union Rd. Min S —5K 219 (4D 11)
Union Rd. Ram —4K 211
Union Row. Mgte —3D 208
Union Sq. Broad —9M 209
Union Sq. Tun W —3F 156
Union Street. —4C 37
Union St. SE1 —3C 5
Union St. Cant —1N 171 (4D 21)
Union St. Chat —8D 80
Union St. Dover —6J 181 (1C 43)
Union St. Fav —5G 187
Union St. Flim —4C 37
Union St. Maid —5D 126
Union St. Ram —5J 211
Union St. Roch —7N 79
Union St. S'ness —2B 218
Unity Clo. New Ad —9E 82
Unity Pl. Ram —5K 211
Unity St. S'ness —2E 218
Unity St. Sit —8F 98
University Gdns. Bex —5A 58
University Pl. Eri —7D 52
University Rd. Cant —8K 167
University Way. Dart —2K 59 (4D 7)
Unwin Clo. Ayle —7L 109
Upbury Way. Chat —8D 80
Upchat Rd. Chatt —9B 66
Upchat Rd. Upnor & C'den —1D 17
Upchurch. —8H 223 (2B 18)
Upchurch Wlk. Mgte —4J 209
Updale Rd. Sidc —9H 57
Uphill. H'nge —8D 192
Upland Rd. Bexh —1A 58
Uplands. Beck —5D 68
Uplands. Cant —7M 167
Uplands Clo. Roch —6H 79
Uplands Clo. Sev —5G 118
Uplands Rd. Orp —2K 85
Uplands Way. Min S —7D 218
Uplands Way. Sev —5G 118
Uplees Rd. Oare —1E 186 (2E 19)
Upminster. —1E 7
Upminster Rd. Horn & Upm —1D 7
Upminster Rd. N. Rain —2D 7
Upminster Rd. S. Rain —2C 7
Upney La. Bark —1B 6
Upnor Castle. —2C 80 (1D 17)
Upnor Rd. Lwr U —1D 17
Upnor Rd. Upnor & Lwr U —4A 80
(in two parts)
Up. Abbey Rd. Belv —4A 52
Up. Approach Rd. Broad —1L 211
Up. Austin Lodge Rd. Eyns —5L 87 (2D 15)
Upper Av. Grav —4D 76
Up. Barn Hill. Hunt —5J 137 (3D 27)
Up. Beulah Hill. SE19 —1D 13
Up. Brents. Fav —4H 187
Up. Bridge St. Cant —2N 171 (1D 31)
Up. Bridge St. Wye —2M 159 (4B 30)
Up. Britton Pl. Gill —7E 80
Up. Brockley Rd. SE4 —1C 54
Upper Bush. —1D 92
Up. Bush Rd. Cux —1D 92
Up. Chantry Ct. Cant —3N 171 (1D 31)
Up. Chantry La. Cant —3N 171 (1D 31)
Up. Church Hill. Grnh —3E 60
Up. Clapton Rd. E5 —1D 5
Up. Corniche. S'gte —8C 188
Up. Cumberland Wlk. Tun W —4G 157
(in two parts)
Up. Dane Rd. Mgte —4E 208 (1E 23)
Upper Deal. —6J 177 (2E 33)
Up. Denmark Rd. Afrd —1F 160
Upper Dri. Big H —6C 164
Up. Dumpton Pk. Ram —4J 211
Up. Dunstan Rd. Tun W —8H 151
Up. East Rd. Chat —4E 80
Upper Elmers End. —8C 68 (2E 13)
Up. Elmers End Rd. Beck —7B 68 (1E 13)
Upper Eythorne. —4K 185
Up. Fant Rd. Maid —7N 125 (2D 27)
Up. Field Rd. Sit —6J 99
Up. Free Down. H Bay —5H 195
Upper Goldstone. —1D 216 (3C 22)
Up. Gore La. E'try —3J 183
Up. Green La. S'brne —3K 133
Up. Green Rd. S'brne —3J 133 (2E 25)
Up. Green W. Mitc —1B 12
Up. Grosvenor Rd. Tun W —1G 157 (1E 35)
Up. Grosvenor St. W1 —2C 4
Upper Grounds. Hoath —2A 22
Upper Gro. Mgte —3D 208
Up. Grove Rd. Belv —6A 52
Upper Hale. Birch —7B 206
Upper Halling. —6C 92 (2C 16)
Upper Harbledown. —1E 170 (4C 21)
Upper Hardres Court. —3D 31
Upper Hartfield. —3B 34
Upper Hayesden. —9C 144 (4E 25)
Up. Hayesden La. Tonb —9D 144 (4E 25)
Up. High St. Eps —3A 12
Up. Holly Hill Rd. Belv —5C 52
Up. Hunton Hill. E Far —6L 137 (3D 27)
Upper Lake. Batt —4B 44
Up. Luton Rd. Chat —9F 80 (2E 17)
Up. Malthouse Hill. Hythe —6J 197
Upper Mill. W'bury —9B 124
Up. Mulgrave Rd. Sutt —3B 12
Upper Nellington. L'tn G —1B 156
Up. North St. E14 —2E 5
Upper Norwood. —1D 13
Upper Olantigh. Wye —3B 30
Up. Park Rd. Belv —4C 52 (3C 6)
Up. Park Rd. Brom —4L 69
Upper Profit. L'tn G —2A 156
Up. Queens Rd. Afrd —7F 158
Up. Rainham Rd. Horn —1C 7
Up. Richmond Rd. SW15 —4A 4
Up. Richmond Rd. W. Rich & SW14 —4A 4
Upper Rd. E13 —2E 5
Upper Rd. Dover —3K 181 (1D 43)
Upper Rd. Maid —7E 126
Upper Rd. St Mc —9H 213
Upper Rodmersham. —4L 115 (3D 19)
Upper Ruxley. —3A 72
Up. St Ann's Rd. Fav —6F 186
Up. Selsdon Rd. S Croy —3D 13
Up. Sheridan Rd. Belv —4B 52
Upper Shirley. —5A 82 (2D 13)
Up. Shirley Rd. Croy —4A 82 (2D 13)
Up. Spring La. Igh —4H 121
Up. Stephens. L'tn G —2A 156
Up. Stone St. Maid —6D 126 (2E 27)

Waldens Clo.—Webb's All.

Waldens Clo. Orp —1M 85
Waldens Rd. Orp —1N 85 (2B 14)
Waldens, The. Kgswd —6G 140
Walder Chain. B'hm —3A 32
Waldershare Av. S'wch B —1E 33
Waldershare Rd. Ashl —3C 33
Walderslade. —8D 94 (3D 17)
Walderslade Bottom. —8D 94
Walderslade Cen. Chat —8D 94
Walderslade Rd. Chat —3C 94 (2D 17)
Walderslade Village By-Pass. Chat —9C 94
Walderslade Woods. Chat —8A 94 (3D 17)
Waldo Ind. Est. Brom —6N 69
Waldo Rd. Brom —6N 69
Waldram Pk. Rd. SE23 —6A 54 (4D 5)
Waldrist Way. Eri —2A 52
Waldron Dri. Maid —3C 138
Waldron Gdns. Brom —6G 69
Waldron Rd. Broad —2M 211
Walerand Rd. SE13 —1F 54
Wales Farm Rd. W3 —2A 4
Walham Green. —3B 4
Walkden Rd. Chst —1C 70
Walker Clo. SE18 —4E 50
Walker Clo. Dart —1G 58
Walker Pl. Igh —3K 121
Walker Way. Birch —3C 206
Walkhurst Rd. Bene —3A 38
Walkley Rd. Dart —3J 59
Walks, The. Groom —5K 155
Walk, The. Kgswd —6G 140
Wallace Clo. Tun W —5G 157
Wallace Gdns. Swans —4L 61
Wallace M. Folk —4K 189
Wallace Rd. Roch —3B 94
Wallace Way. Broad —9J 209
Wallbridge La. Gill —1F 96 (2A 18)
Wallbutton Rd. SE4 —1B 54
Wall Clo. Hoo —6G 66
Wallcrouch. —4B 36
Wallend. —2A 6
(nr. Barking)
Wall End. —3A 22
(nr. Upstreet)
Waller Rd. G'stne —7A 212
Wallers. New Ash —4M 89
Wallers Speld —7A 150
Wallers Cotts. Maid —4K 137
Wallers Rd. Fav —6E 186
Walleys Clo. Gill —2D 96
Wall Hill. —2A 34
Wall Hill Rd. Ash W & F Row —2A 34
Wallhouse Rd. Eri —7J 53
Wallington. —3C 12
Wallington Green. (Junct.) —2C 12
Wallis Av. Maid —3H 139 (2E 27)
Wallis Clo. Dart —8G 59
Wallis Field. Groom —7J 155
Wallis Pk. N'fleet —3A 62
Wallis Rd. Afrd —8H 159
Wall Rd. Afrd —7F 158
Wall, The. Sit —6F 98
Wallwood Rd. Ram —4K 211
Walmer. —9L 177 (3E 33)
Walmer Castle. —9N 177 (3E 33)
Walmer Castle Rd. Walm —9M 177
Walmer Clo. Farn —5F 84
Walmer Ct. Maid —4D 126
Walmer Ct. Walm —9L 177
Walmer Gdns. Deal —8K 177
Walmer Gdns. Ram —7B 210
Walmer Gdns. Sit —6E 98
Walmer Rd. Whits —5G 224
Walmers Av. High —9E 64
Walmer Ter. SE18 —4E 50
Walmer Way. Deal —8K 177
Walmer Way. Folk —6F 188
Walm La. NW2 —1A 4
Walmsley Ho. Folk —5L 189
(off Princess St.)
Walmsley Rd. Broad —8K 209
Walner Gdns. New R —2C 212
Walner La. New R —2C 212
Walnut Clo. Chat —3E 94
Walnut Clo. Eyns —4L 87
Walnut Clo. Kenn —4H 159
Walnut Clo. Pad W —9M 147
Walnut Hill Rd. Grav —6D 76 (1A 16)
Walnut Ridge. Adgtn —2B 40
Walnut Row. Dit —1F 124
Walnuts Rd. Orp —2J 85
Walnuts, The. Orp —2J 85
Walnut Tree Av. Dart —7M 59
Walnut Tree Av. Maid —3D 138
Walnut Tree Clo. Birch —4F 206
Walnut Tree Clo. Chst —4F 70
Walnut Tree Clo. Yald —7D 136
Walnut Tree Cottage. Yald —7D 136
Walnut Tree Cotts. Maid —3D 138
Walnut Tree Ct. Lark —9F 108
Walnut Tree Dri. Sit —7E 98
Walnut Tree La. Maid —3D 138
Walnut Tree La. W'bre —4J 169
Walnut Tree Rd. Dag —1C 6
Walnut Tree Rd. Eri —5F 52
Walnut Tree Way. Meop —9F 76
Walnut Way. Swan —5E 72
Walnut Way. Tun W —6K 151
Walpole Clo. E Mal —1D 124
Walpole Pl. SE18 —4D 50
Walpole Rd. Brom —8N 69
Walpole Rd. Mgte —2D 208
Walsby Dri. Kem —3H 99
Walsham Ho. Maid —3D 126
Walsham Rd. Chat —1C 110
Walshes Rd. Crowb —4D 35
Walsingham Clo. Gill —8N 95
Walsingham Ho. Maid —3D 126
Walsingham Pk. Chst —5F 70
Walsingham Rd. Orp —4K 71
Walsingham Wlk. Belv —6B 52
Walter Burke Av. Woul —6G 92
Walter's Farm Rd. Tonb —6J 145
Walter's Green. —8F 148 (1C 35)
Walters Grn. Rd. Ford —8F 148
Walters Grn. Rd. Pens —1C 35
Walters Rd. Hoo —7H 67
Walters Way. SE23 —4A 54
Walters Yd. Brom —5K 69
Walterton Rd. W9 —2B 4
Waltham. —3C 31
Waltham Clo. Clift —3J 209
Waltham Clo. Dart —4H 59
Waltham Clo. Orp —2M 85
Waltham Clo. W'boro —8L 159
Waltham Rd. Gill —9L 81
Waltham Rd. Walt —3C 31
Walton Cotts. E'try —2L 183
Walton Gdns. Folk —4K 189
Walton Grn. New Ad —9E 82
Walton Hall Farm Museum. —2B 8
Walton Mnr. Clo. Folk —3K 189
Walton Rd. Folk —5K 189
Walton Rd. Sidc —8K 57
Walton Rd. Tonb —1M 145
Walton's Hall Rd. Stan H —3B 8
Walworth. —3D 5
Walworth Rd. SE17 —3C 5
Walwyn Av. Brom —6N 69
Wanden. —4C 28
Wanden La. Eger —4C 28
Wandle Ho. Brom —1G 68
Wandle Rd. Mord —1B 12
Wandsworth. —4B 4
Wandsworth Bri. SW6 & SW18 —4B 4
Wandsworth Bri. Rd. SW6 —3B 4
Wandsworth Gyratory. (Junct.) —4B 4
Wandsworth High St. SW18 —4B 4
Wandsworth Rd. SW8 —4C 4
Wansbury Way. Swan —8H 73
Wanshurst Green. —4E 27
Wanstead Clo. Brom —5M 69
Wanstead Rd. Brom —5M 69
Wansum Ct. St N —8E 214
Wansunt Rd. Bex —6D 58
Wantage Rd. SE12 —3J 55
Wantsum Clo. H Bay —2N 195
Wantsume Lees. S'wch —4K 217
Wantsum M. S'wch —5L 217
Wantsum Way. St N —8D 214 (2B 22)
Wapping. —2D 5
Wapping High St. E1 —2D 5
Wapping La. E1 —2D 5
Wapping Way. E1 —2D 5
Wapses Roundabout. (Junct.) —4D 13
Warbler's Clo. Roch —5L 79
Ward Clo. Eri —6E 52
Warden. —4K 203 (1A 20)
Warden Bay Cvn. Pk. Ley S —6K 203
Warden Bay Holiday Camp. Ley S —6K 203
Warden Bay Rd. Ley S —5K 203 (1A 20)
Warden Clo. Maid —5N 125
Warden Ct. Dover —3H 181
Warden Ct. Maid —5A 126
Warden Mill Clo. W'bury —1C 136
Warden Rd. E'chu —5C 202 (1E 19)
Warden Rd. Roch —9N 79
Wardens Field Clo. Grn St —7H 85
Warden Spring Cvn. Pk. Min S —3J 203
Warden Ter. W'bury —2B 136
(off Maidstone Rd.)
Warden View Gdns. Ley S —7J 203
Warde's. Yald —6D 136
Warde's Cotts. Maid —9L 127
Wardona Ho. Swans —4M 61
Wardour Clo. Broad —9M 209
Wardour Ct. Dart —4B 60
(off Bow Arrow La.)
Wardour St. W1 —2C 4
Wardsbrook Rd. Tic —4C 36
Wards Hill Rd. Min S —4J 219 (4D 11)
Ward's La. Wallc —4B 36
Wardwell La. Lwr Hal —4L 97 (2B 18)
Ware. —3B 22
Wareham Wlk. Bene —3A 38
Warehorne. —9A 190 (3E 39)
Warehorne Rd. Hams —8C 190 (3E 39)
Warehorn Rd. Ah —3C 22
Warepoint Dri. SE28 —2F 50
Ware Street. —4K 127 (1E 27)
Ware St. Weav —1E 27
Warham Rd. Otf —7J 103
Warham Rd. S Croy —2C 13
Waring Clo. Orp —7H 85
Waring Dri. Orp —7H 85
Waring Rd. Sidc —2L 71
Warland Rd. SE18 —7F 50
Warland Rd. W King —9F 88
Warlingham. —4D 13
Warlingham Clo. Gill —2C 96
Warmlake. —7A 140 (3A 28)
Warmlake Ind. Est. Sut V —7A 140
Warmlake Rd. Cha S —7L 139 (3E 27)
Warne Pl. Sidc —4K 57
Warner Pl. E2 —2D 5
Warner Rd. Brom —3J 69
Warner St. Chat —9C 80
Warnett Ct. Snod —1E 108
Warnford Gdns. Maid —9D 126
Warnford Rd. Orp —6H 85
Warre Av. Ram —7G 210
Warren Av. Brom —3H 69 (1E 13)
Warren Av. Orp —6H 85
Warren Av. S Croy —8A 82
Warren Camp Site, The. Folk —4A 174
Warren Clo. Bexh —3B 58
Warren Clo. Folk —5M 189
Warren Clo. Sit —9J 99
Warren Ct. Beck —3D 68
Warren Ct. Sev —6K 119
Warren Dri. Broad —8J 209
Warren Dri. Orp —6K 85
Warren Dri., The. Wgte S —4J 207
Warren Farm La. E Grn —9A 156
Warren Gdns. Orp —6J 85
Warren Hastings Ct. Grav —4E 62
(off Pier Rd.)
Warren La. SE18 —3D 50
Warren La. Afrd —6E 158
Warren La. Ewe M —1B 42
Warren La. Grays —3E 7
Warren La. H'lip —8E 96 (3A 18)
Warren La. Oxt —3A 24
Warren Retail Pk., The. Afrd —6F 158
Warren Ridge. Frant —3E 35
Warren Rd. E10 —1E 5
Warren Rd. Bexh —3B 58
Warren Rd. Blue B —2A 110
Warren Rd. Blue H —3D 17
Warren Rd. Brom —3K 83 (2A 14)
Warren Rd. Chels —6H 85 (2B 14)
Warren Rd. Dart —8M 59
Warren Rd. Folk —5M 189
Warren Rd. L'stne —3E 212
Warren Rd. Ludd —9A 78 (2C 16)
Warren Rd. Purl —3C 13
Warren Rd. Sidc —8L 57
Warren Rd. S'fleet —1A 76 (1A 16)
Warrens, The. Hart —9M 75
Warren Street. —2D 29
Warren St. Len —2D 29
Warren St. Rd. Char —3D 29
Warren, The. —5E 158
Warren, The. Bra L —8K 165
Warren, The. Grav —9K 63
Warren, The. Pens —2H 149
Warren, The. Whits —7E 224
Warren View. Afrd —6D 158
Warren View. Shorne —1C 78
Warren Wood Clo. Brom —3J 83
Warren Wood Rd. Roch —4N 93
Warrington Rd. Pad W —9L 147
Warrior Av. Grav —9H 63
Warsop Trad. Est. Eden —7D 184
Warspite Rd. SE18 —3A 50
Warten Rd. Ram —3K 211
Warwick. Sidc —1K 71
Warwick Av. W9 —2B 4
Warwick Clo. Bex —5A 58
Warwick Clo. Orp —4J 85
Warwick Ct. Brom —5H 69
Warwick Ct. Eri —7G 52
Warwick Ct. Sev —7J 119
Warwick Cres. Roch —1K 93
Warwick Cres. Sit —6D 98
Warwick Dri. Ram —7F 210
Warwick Gdns. W14 —3B 4
Warwick Gdns. Meop —3F 90
Warwick Ho. Swan —7F 72
Warwick La. Rain & Upm —2D 7
Warwick Pk. Tun W —3G 156 (2E 35)
Warwick Pl. Maid —5B 126
Warwick Pl. N'fleet —3A 62
Warwick Rd. W14 & SW5 —3B 4
Warwick Rd. Cant —2B 172
Warwick Rd. Clift —3F 208
Warwick Rd. Kenn —5J 159
Warwick Rd. Sidc —1K 71
Warwick Rd. Tun W —3G 157
Warwick Rd. Walm —8N 177
Warwick Rd. Well —1L 57
Warwick Rd. Whits —3F 224
Warwick Ter. SE18 —6F 50 (3B 6)
Warwick Way. SW1 —3C 4
Washford Farm Rd. Afrd —4C 160
Washingstool Hill. E Grn —8C 156 (2E 35)
Washington Clo. Dover —1G 180
Washington Ho. Maid —3H 139
Washington La. Old R —2C 47
Washneys Rd. Orp —5J 101 (3B 14)
Washpond La. Warl —4E 13
Wassall La. Rol —1D 45
Wass Drove. Ware —3B 22
Wastdale Rd. SE23 —6A 54
Watchester Av. Ram —7G 211
Watchester La. Min —8M 205 (2C 23)
Watchgate. —1D 74
Watchgate. Dart —1D 74
Waterbank Rd. SE6 —8E 54
Waterbrook. —4L 161 (1A 40)
Waterbrook Av. Afrd —4K 161 (1A 40)
Watercress Clo. Sev —2K 119
Watercress Dri. Sev —2K 119
Watercress La. Afrd —1D 160
Watercroft Rd. Hals —1A 102 (3C 14)
Waterdale Rd. SE2 —6J 51
Waterdales. N'fleet —6C 62
Waterden Rd. E15 —1E 5
Waterditch La. Len —2D 29
Waterdown Rd. Tun W —4D 156
Water End. Temp E —8B 178
Waterer Ho. SE6 —9F 54
Waterfall La. Hoth —4E 29
Water Farm. Elham —7N 183
Waterfield. Tun W —6G 156
Waterfield Clo. SE28 —1K 51
Waterfield Clo. Belv —3B 52
Waterfield Gdns. SE28 —1K 51
Waterham. —3B 20
Waterham Rd. Hern —3B 20
Waterhead Clo. Eri —7F 52
Wateringbury. —1C 136 (2C 26)
Wateringbury Clo. Orp —6K 71
Wateringbury Rd. E Mal —7D 124 (2C 26)
Waterlakes. Eden —7C 184
Water La. E15 —1E 5
Water La. Cant —2M 171 (1D 31)
Water La. Eden —4A 24
Water La. Fav —5G 186
(off West St.)
Water La. H'shm —2J 141
Water La. Hawkh —1M 191 (3E 37)
Water La. H'crn —4H 193 (1A 38)
Water La. Hunt —9H 137
Water La. Ilf —1B 6
Water La. Kgswd —6H 141
Water La. Maid —5D 126
Water La. Osp —8D 186 (4E 19)
Water La. Shor —3G 102
Water La. Sidc —8A 58
(in two parts)
Water La. Smar —1H 221 (1B 38)
Water La. Sturry —6E 168 (4E 21)
Water La. T'hm —5N 127 (2A 28)
Water La. W'ham —9F 116
Water La. W Mal —1A 124 (1C 26)
Waterlock Cotts. W'hm —3B 226
Waterloo Bri. SE1 —2C 5
Waterloo Cotts. Bri —8H 173
Waterloo Cres. Dover —6J 181
Waterloo Hill. Min S —6K 219
Waterloo Mans. Dover —5J 181
Waterloo Pl. Ram —5K 211
Waterloo Pl. Tonb —7H 145
Waterloo Rd. SE1 —3C 5
Waterloo Rd. C'brk —7D 176 (2E 37)
Waterloo Rd. Eps —3A 12
Waterloo Rd. Folk —6D 188
Waterloo Rd. Gill —8F 80
Waterloo Rd. Sit —6E 98
Waterloo Rd. Tonb —7H 145
Waterloo Rd. Whits —3F 224
Waterloo St. Grav —5H 63
Waterloo St. Maid —6D 126
Waterloo Ter. S'ndge —8J 215
Waterlow Rd. Maid —3D 126
Waterlow Rd. Meop —3D 106 (3A 16)
Waterman Ho. Afrd —1F 160
Waterman Quarter. —1A 38
Waterman's La. Pad W —2M 153 (1B 36)
Watermead Clo. Afrd —2D 160
Watermeadow Clo. Hem —5J 95
Watermeadows. F'wch —7E 168
Watermead Rd. SE6 —9F 54
Watermill Clo. Maid —4M 125
Water Mill Clo. Roch —4N 79
Watermill La. Pett & I'ham —4E 45
Water Mill Way. S Dar —5B 74
Watermint Clo. Orp —7M 71
Waters Edge. Maid —7C 126
Waterside. —4A 24
Waterside. Beck —4C 68
Waterside. Dart —3F 58
Waterside. Maid —4C 126
Waterside. W'boro —1K 161
Waterside Ct. Hythe —6J 197
Waterside Ct. Leyb —7C 108
Waterside Ct. Roch —5B 80
Waterside Dri. Wgte S —2L 207
Waterside La. Gill —5J 81
Waterside M. W'bury —2B 136
Waterside View. Ward —4K 203
Water Slippe. Hdlw —7C 134
Waters Pl. Hem —5K 95
Waters Rd. SE6 —8H 55
Waterstone Pl. Fav —6E 186
Water St. Deal —3N 177
Waterton. Swan —7E 72
Waterton Av. Grav —5K 63
Waterworks Cotts. Bear —2J 127
Waterworks Cotts. Boxl —7F 110
Water Works Cotts. Roch —3L 93
Waterworks Hill. Mart —2N 179 (4D 33)
Waterworks La. Mart —2N 179
Waterworks Vs. Sev —8J 119
Watery La. Kems —3C 120 (1E 25)
Watery La. P'hm —2D 31
Watery La. Sidc —2K 71 (1B 14)
Watery La. Westw —2A 158 (4E 29)
Watkin Rd. Folk —5J 189
Watkins. Sidc —1K 71
Watkins Clo. S'hrst —6J 221
Watling Av. Chat —1G 95
Watling Pl. Sit —8H 99
Watlings Clo. Croy —9B 68
Watling St. Bexh —2C 58 (4C 7)
Watling St. Cant —2M 171 (1D 31)
Watling St. Chat —1G 95 (2E 17)
Watling St. Cob & Strd —1C 16
Watling St. Dart & Grav —5A 60 (4D 7)
Watlington Gro. SE26 —1B 68
Watney's Rd. Mitc —2C 12
Watson Av. Chat —6A 94
Watsons Clo. Afrd —2G 158
Watsons Hill. Sit —6F 98
Watts Almshouses. Roch —8N 79
Watts Av. Roch —8N 79 (2D 17)
Watts Bri. Rd. Eri —6G 52
Watts Clo. Snod —2F 108
Watts Cotts. Kenn —3G 159
Watt's Cross. —9B 132 (3D 25)
Watt's Cross Rd. Hild —1B 144 (3D 25)
Watts La. Chst —4D 70 (1A 14)
Watts' Pal. La. B Oak —3C 45
Watts' St. Chat —9B 80
Wat Tyler Rd. SE10 —3E 5
Wat Tyler Way. Maid —5D 126 (2E 27)
Wauchope Rd. Sea —7B 224
Wave Crest. Whits —4E 224
Wavell Dri. Sidc —4G 57
Waveney Ho. Maid —9H 127
Waveney Rd. Tonb —2H 145
Waverley Av. Min S —5J 219
Waverley Clo. Brom —8N 69
Waverley Clo. Chat —9G 95
Waverley Clo. Cox —6N 137
Waverley Cres. SE18 —5F 50 (3B 6)
Waverley Dri. Tun W —8M 151
Waverley Rd. SE18 —5F 50
Waverley Rd. Mgte —2N 207
Way. —2D 23
Wayborough Hill. Min —2C 23
Wayfares. S'wch —7L 217
Wayfield. —2D 17
Wayfield Link. SE9 —4F 56
Wayfield Rd. Chat —5C 94 (2D 17)
Way Hill. Min —2D 23
Waylands. Bear —5L 127
Waylands. Swan —7G 72
Waylands Clo. Knock —6N 101
Waylands Mead. Beck —4E 68
Wayne Clo. Broad —8J 209
Wayne Clo. Orp —4H 85
Wayne Ct. Roch —2A 80
Wayside. New Ad —7E 82
Wayside. St Mic —5C 222
Wayside Av. Tent —4C 222
Wayside Dri. Eden —4D 184
Wayside Flats. St Mic —5C 222
(off Ashford Rd.)
Wayside Gro. SE9 —9B 56
Wayville Rd. Dart —5B 60
Way Volante. Grav —9K 63
Weald Clo. Brom —3A 84
Weald Clo. Grav —3D 76
Weald Clo. Maid —2F 138
Weald Clo. Weald —6K 131
Weald Ct. Hild —1D 144
Weald Ct. Sit —9E 98
Wealden Av. Tent —5C 222
Wealden Clo. Hild —2E 144
Wealden Ct. Chat —9E 80
Wealden Forest Pk. H Bay —3E 21
Wealden Pl. Sev —3J 119
Wealden View. Goud —8K 185
Wealden View. H'crn —2J 193
Wealden Way. Quar W —2J 125
Wealdhurst Pk. St Pet —8H 209
Weald Rd. Sev —2J 131 (2D 25)
Weald, The. Afrd —7G 158
Weald, The. Chst —2B 70
Weald View. Bchly —1C 36
Weald View Rd. Tonb —8H 145
Wear Bay Cres. Folk —5M 189
Wear Bay Rd. Folk —6M 189 (2A 42)
Weardale Av. Dart —7C 60
Weardale Rd. SE13 —2G 55
Weare Rd. Tun W —6J 151
Wearside Rd. SE13 —2E 54
Weatherly Clo. Roch —8N 79
Weatherly Dri. Broad —2K 211
Weavering. —1E 27
Weavering Clo. Roch —2M 79
Weavering Cotts. Weav —6H 127
Weavering Street. —4J 127
Weavering St. Weav —6H 127 (2E 27)
Weavers Clo. Grav —6F 62
Weavers Clo. S'hrst —7K 221
Weavers La. Sev —3K 119
Weavers Orchard. S'fleet —2N 75
Weavers, The. Bidd —8L 163
Weavers, The. Maid —5M 125
Weavers Way. Afrd —2C 160
Weavers Way. Dover —1F 180
Webb Clo. Folk —4G 188
Webb Clo. Hoo —7G 66
Webber Clo. Eri —7J 53
Webb's All. Sev —7K 119

Webbs Meadow—West St.

Webbs Meadow. Sev —7K 119
Webster Rd. Gill —2B 96
Weddington. —3D 216 (4C 22)
Weddington La. Ah —4C 216 (4C 22)
(in two parts)
Wedgewood Clo. Maid —4M 125
Wedgewood Dri. Chat —4D 94
Wedgwoods. Tats —9C 164
Weeds Wood. —7C 94 (3D 17)
Weeds Wood Rd. Chat —7C 94
Weekes Ct. Queen —7B 218
(off Main Rd.)
Weekes La. W Bra —1C 40
Weeks La. Bidd —1B 38
Week St. Maid —4D 126
Weigall Pl. Ram —5G 210
Weigall Rd. SE12 —3K 55 (4A 6)
Weighbridge Cotts. Cant —1M 171
Weighbridge Way. Dover —3N 181
Weird Wood. Long —6B 76
Weir Rd. Bex —5C 58
Weirton Hill. Bou M —9G 139
Welbeck Av. Brom —9K 55
Welbeck Av. Sidc —6J 57
Welbeck Av. Tun W —6J 151
Welcombe Ct. Gill —3N 95
(off Derwent Way)
Weld Clo. S'hrst —7K 221
Wellan Clo. Sidc —3K 57
Welland Ct. SE6 —7C 54
(off Oakham Clo.)
Welland Ho. Maid —9H 127
Welland Rd. Tonb —3H 145
Wellands Clo. Brom —5B 70
Wellbrook Rd. Orp —5C 84 (2A 14)
Well Clo. Leigh —6N 143
Well Clo. Sturry —5F 168
Wellcome Av. Dart —2M 59
Well Cotts. Det —9K 111
Weller Av. Roch —1A 94 (2D 17)
Weller Pl. Orp —2C 100
Weller Rd. Tun W —1C 156
Wellers Clo. W'ham —9E 116
Weller's Town. —9E 142 (4C 25)
Wellesley Av. Walm —8M 177
Wellesley Clo. Broad —1K 211
Wellesley Clo. Wgte S —4K 207
Wellesley Rd. W4 —3A 4
Wellesley Rd. Afrd —8G 159 (1A 40)
(in two parts)
Wellesley Rd. Croy —2D 13
Wellesley Rd. Dover —5K 181
Wellesley Rd. Mgte —4F 208
Wellesley Rd. Wgte S —4K 207
Wellesley Ter. S'wch —6M 217
Wellesley Vs. Afrd —8G 159
(off Wellesley Rd.)
Well Field. Hart —7M 75
Wellfield Rd. Folk —6G 188
Well Hall Pde. SE9 —2B 56
Well Hall Rd. SE9 —1A 56 (4A 6)
Well Hall Roundabout. (Junct.)
—2A 56 (4A 6)
Well Hill. —7C 86 (3C 14)
Well Hill. Orp —7C 86 (2C 14)
Well Hill La. Orp —7C 86
Wellhouse La. Shott —2A 30
Wellhouse Rd. Beck —7D 68
Welling. —1K 57 (3B 6)
Welling High St. Well —1K 57 (4B 6)
Wellington Av. Sidc —4J 57
Wellington Clo. Wgte S —2K 207
Wellington Cotts. Hawkh —3J 191
Wellington Cotts. Meop —4F 90
Wellington Cres. Ram —6K 211 (2E 23)
Wellington Gdns. Dover —1G 180
Wellington Gdns. Mgte —2D 208
Wellington Ho. Maid —3H 139
Wellingtonia Way. Eden —5C 184
Wellington Pde. Sidc —3J 57
Wellington Pde. Walm —1N 199
Wellington Pl. Maid —3C 126
Wellington Pl. S'gte —8D 188
Wellington Rd. NW8 —2B 4
Wellington Rd. Belv —5A 52
Wellington Rd. Bex —3M 57
Wellington Rd. Brom —7M 69
Wellington Rd. Dart —4K 59
Wellington Rd. Deal —5N 177
Wellington Rd. Folk —6D 188
Wellington Rd. Gill —8F 80
Wellington Rd. Mgte —9B 208
Wellington Rd. Orp —9K 71
Wellington Rd. Sit —6C 98
Wellington Rd. Temp E —8C 178
Wellington Rd. Wgte S —4K 207
Wellington St. SE18 —4C 50 (3A 6)
Wellington St. WC2 —2C 5
Wellington St. Grav —5H 63 (4B 8)
Wellington St. Whits —8F 224
Wellington Ter. S'gte —8D 188
(off Esplanade, The)
Wellington Way. W Mal —6L 123
Welling Way. SE9 & Well —1E 56 (4B 6)
Wellis Gdns. Mgte —4A 208
Well La. Cant —8F 168 (4E 21)
Well La. Osp —9A 186 (4E 19)
Well La. St Mc —7J 213
Wellmeade Dri. Sev —9J 119
Wellmeadow Rd. SE13 & SE6 —4H 55
(in two parts)
Well Penn Rd. Cli —4C 176
Well Rd. Lym —8D 204 (1E 41)
Well Rd. Maid —4D 126 (1E 27)
Well Rd. Otf —7K 103
Well Rd. Queen —7B 218
Well Rd. R'den —9A 218
Wells Av. Cant —3A 172
Wells Clo. New R —3D 212
Wells Clo. Tent —7B 222
Wells Clo. Tonb —3K 145
Wells Clo. Tun W —2G 156
Wells Cotts. Hild —3D 144
Wells Cotts. Nett —6A 136
Wells Ct. Roch —7H 79
Wells Ct. W'boro —8J 159
Wells Farm Cotts. E'try —2K 183
Wells Ho. Brom —1L 69
Wells Ho. Maid —1G 139
Wells Ho. Sit —7J 99
Wellsmoor Gdns. Brom —6C 70
Wells Pk. Rd. SE26 —1D 13
Wells Rd. Brom —5B 70
Wells Rd. Folk —5F 188
Wells Rd. Roch —7H 79
Well Street. —3C 124 (1C 26)
Well St. E9 —1D 5
Well St. E Mal —3B 124 (1C 26)
Well St. Loose —5B 138 (3D 27)
Wells Way. SE5 —3D 5
Wells Way. Fav —3F 186
Wellwinch Rd. Sit —6E 98
Welsdene Rd. Mgte —3N 207
Welson Rd. Folk —6F 188
Welton Gdns. Tonb —8F 144
Welton Rd. SE18 —7G 50
Wembley Hill. Rd. Wemb —1A 4
Wembley Park. —1A 4
Wembley Pk. Dri. Wemb —1A 4
Wembley Stadium. —1A 4
Wemmick Clo. Roch —4A 94
Wemyss Way. Cant —1B 172
Wendover Clo. Hall —6F 92
Wendover Rd. SE9 —1N 55
Wendover Rd. Brom —6L 69
Wendover Way. Orp —9J 71
Wendover Way. Well —3J 57 (4B 6)
Wenham's La. Ivy —2D 47
Wennington. —2D 7
Wennington Rd. Rain —2D 7
Wensley Clo. SE9 —4B 56
Wentland Clo. SE6 —7G 55
Wentland Rd. SE6 —7G 55
Wents, The. Maid —5L 137
Went Woods. Weav —4J 127
Wentworth Av. Mgte —2M 207
Wentworth Clo. Grav —1F 76
Wentworth Clo. Hay —3K 83
Wentworth Clo. Lym —8D 204
Wentworth Clo. Orp —6G 84
Wentworth Ct. Sit —6J 99
Wentworth Dri. Cli —5M 65
Wentworth Dri. Dart —4H 59
Wentworth Dri. Gill —4A 96
Wentworth Dri. Ram —3E 210
Wentworth Dri. Sit —6D 98
Wentworth Gdns. H Bay —5E 194
Wenvoe Av. Bexh —9C 52
Wernbrook St. SE18 —6E 50
Wesley Clo. Maid —6K 125
Wesley Clo. Orp —6L 71
Wesley Ter. Lym —7D 204
Wessex Ct. Beck —4B 68
Wessex Dri. Eri —9F 52
West Acton. —2A 4
West App. Orp —8E 70
West Barnes. —2A 12
W. Barnes La. N Mald —1A 12
West Beach. Whits —4E 224
W. Beach Cvn. Pk. Whits —5D 224
Westbere. —4H 169 (3E 21)
Westbere La. W'bre —5G 168 (3E 21)
Westbere Rd. NW2 —1B 4
Westbourne. Afrd —3B 160
Westbourne Dri. SE23 —7A 54
Westbourne Gdns. Folk —7H 189
Westbourne Green. —2B 4
Westbourne Gro. W2 —2B 4
Westbourne Gro. W11 —2B 4
Westbourne Gro. Wclf S —1B 10
Westbourne Pk. W11 —2B 4
Westbourne Rd. N7 —1C 5
Westbourne Rd. SE26 —2A 68
Westbourne Rd. Bexh —7N 51
Westbourne St. Sit —7F 98
Westbourne Ter. SE23 —7A 54
(off Waldram Pk. Rd.)
Westbourne Ter. W2 —2B 4
Westbridge Rd. SW11 —3B 4
Westbrook. —4A 208 (1D 23)
Westbrook Av. Mgte —2L 207 (1D 23)
Westbrook Cotts. Mgte —4A 208
Westbrook Dri. Orp —2M 85
Westbrooke Clo. Chat —1D 94
Westbrooke Cres. Well —1L 57
Westbrooke Rd. Sidc —7F 56
Westbrooke Rd. Well —1K 57
Westbrook Gdns. Mgte
—4A 208 (1D 23)
Westbrook Ind. Est. H Bay —4C 194
Westbrook La. H Bay —4C 194
Westbrook Promenade. Mgte —2M 207
Westbrook Rd. Mgte —3A 208
Westbrook Ter. Tun W —4K 157
Westbury Cres. Dover —6G 180
Westbury Heights. Dover —6G 180
Westbury Rd. SE20 —4A 68
Westbury Rd. Beck —6B 68
Westbury Rd. Brom —4N 69
Westbury Rd. Dover —6G 180
Westbury Rd. Wgte S —3K 207
Westbury Ter. W'ham —9E 116
Westchurch Ho. Afrd —9F 158
West Cliff. Whits —5E 224
W. Cliff Arc. Ram —6J 211
W. Cliff Av. Broad —1M 211
Westcliff Av. Wclf S —1B 10
W. Cliff Ct. Broad —1L 211
(off W. Cliff Rd.)
W. Cliff Dri. H Bay —3C 194
Westcliff Dri. Min S —4L 219
West Cliffe. —4D 33
W. Cliff Gdns. Folk —7K 189
W. Cliff Gdns. H Bay —3C 194
Westcliff Gdns. Mgte —2N 207
Westcliff Ho. Folk —7K 189
(off W. Cliff Gdns.)
W. Cliff Mans. Ram —6J 211
(off Cliff St.)
W. Cliff M. Broad —1M 211
(off W. Cliff Rd.)
Westcliff-on-Sea. —1B 10
Westcliff Pde. Wclf S —1B 10
W. Cliff Promenade. Broad —2M 211
W. Cliff Promenade. Ram —7H 211
W. Cliff Rd. Broad —1L 211 (2E 23)
Westcliff Rd. Mgte —4A 208
W. Cliff Rd. Ram —6H 211 (2E 23)
W. Cliff Ter. Ram —7F 210
Westcliff Ter. Mans. Ram —7F 210
Westcombe Hill. SE3 —3A 6
West Comn. Rd. Brom —2A 14
West Comn. Rd. Hay & Kes —3K 83
Westcote Rd. SW16 —1C 12
Westcott Av. N'fleet —8F 62
Westcott Clo. Brom —8A 70
Westcott Clo. New Ad —9E 82
Westcourt. —7J 63 (4B 8)
West Ct. Maid —8D 126
West Ct. Downs. S'wll —2A 220 (3B 32)
Westcourt Farm La. Grav —6L 63
Westcourt La. S'wll —2A 220 (3B 32)
W. Court La. Woot —4A 32
Westcourt Pde. Grav —8L 63
Westcourt St. Gill —6D 80
West Cres. Rd. Grav —4G 63
West Cross. —2H 213 (4A 38)
West Cross. Tent —8B 222 (3B 38)
W. Cross Gdns. Tent —8A 222
W. Cross M. Tent —8A 222
Westdale Pas. SE18 —6D 50
Westdale Rd. SE18 —6D 50
Westdean Av. SE12 —6L 55
Westdean Clo. Dover —2D 180
West Down. H'gh —4C 30
Westdown Rd. SE6 —5D 54
West Dri. SW16 —1C 12
West Dri. Chat —6A 94
West Dri. E Sut —9D 140
West Dulwich. —4D 5
West Dumpton. —2J 211
W. Dumpton La. Ram —2J 211 (2E 23)
Wested La. Swan —1H 87 (2C 15)
West End. —2D 21
(nr. Chestfield)
West End. —2C 4
(nr. Westminster)
West End. Bras —7K 117
West End. Kems —8N 103 (4D 15)
West End. Mard —2K 205 (4D 27)
W. End La. NW6 —1B 4
Westenhanger. —2C 196 (2D 41)
Westergate Rd. SE2 —6N 51
Westergate Rd. Roch —3K 79
Westerham. —8F 116 (2B 24)
Westerham Clo. Cant —7N 167
Westerham Clo. Clift —4K 209
Westerham Clo. Gill —8L 81
Westerham Dri. Sidc —4K 57
Westerham Hill. —2C 116 (1A 24)
Westerham Hill. W'ham
—3D 116 (1A 24)
Westerham Lodge. Beck —3D 68
(off Park Rd.)
Westerham Rd. Kes —8N 83 (2A 14)
Westerham Rd. Oxt —9C 116 (2A 24)
Westerham Rd. Sev —5C 118 (2C 24)
Westerham Rd. Sit —8D 98
Westerham Rd. W'ham
—7H 117 (2B 24)
Westerhill Rd. Cox —3D 27
Westerhill Rd. Lin —7N 137
Westerhout Clo. Deal —2M 177
Westerley Cres. SE26 —1C 68
Western Av. UB6, W5 & W3 —2A 4
Western Av. Afrd —8E 158
Western Av. Bri —9E 172
Western Av. Hawkh —5K 191
Western Av. H Bay —3E 194 (2E 21)
Western Av. Min S —6E 218
Western Circus. (Junct.) —2A 4
Western Clo. Dover —6H 181
Western Cross Clo. Grnh —4J 61
Western Esplanade Broad —2M 211
Western Esplanade. Can I —2E 9
Western Esplanade. H Bay
—2C 194 (1E 21)
Western Esplanade. Wclf S —1B 10
Western Gdns. W'boro —1J 161
Western Heights. —6H 181 (1C 43)
Western Heights. —6H 181
Western Heights Roundabout. Dover
—7H 181
Western Ho. Deal —3M 177
Western Link. Fav —5D 186 (3E 19)
Western Rd. SW19 & Mitc —1B 12
Western Rd. Bor G —2M 121 (1A 26)
Western Rd. Crowb —4D 35
Western Rd. Deal —4M 177 (2E 33)
Western Rd. Hawkh —5K 191
Western Rd. Maid —7N 125
Western Rd. Mgte —5G 208
Western Rd. S'boro —5F 150
Western Rd. Tun W —9J 151
Western Undercliff. Ram —7F 210
Western Vs. Kenn —4H 159
Western Way. SE28 —2G 50 (3B 6)
West Ewell. —3A 12
West Farleigh. —2G 136 (2C 27)
Westferry Rd. E14 —2E 5
Westfield. —4C 45
Westfield. Blean —5G 166
Westfield. New Ash —5M 89
Westfield. Sev —4K 119
Westfield Bus. Cen. Roch —5N 79
Westfield Clo. Grav —1H 77
W. Field Clo. H Bay —5D 194
Westfield Cotts. F'wch —7E 168
Westfield Cotts. Lwr Hal —9K 223
Westfield La. Etch —2E 41
Westfield Rd. Beck —5C 68
Westfield Rd. Bexh —1D 58
Westfield Rd. Birch —4E 206
Westfield Rd. Mgte —3N 207
Westfields. P'ley —4D 29
Westfield Sole. —3F 110 (3E 17)
Westfield Sole Rd. Boxl —3E 17
Westfield Sole Rd. Chat —2F 110
Westfield St. SE18 —3A 50
Westfield Ter. C'brk —3D 37
Westgate Av. Wdchu —7M 207
Westgate Bay Av. Wgte S
—2J 207 (1D 23)
Westgate Clo. Cant —1J 171
Westgate Ct. SE12 —6K 55
(off Burnt Ash Hill)
Westgate Ct. Av. Cant —1J 171
Westgate Garden Flats. Cant
—2L 171 (1D 31)
Westgate Gro. Cant —1M 171 (4D 21)
Westgate Hall Rd. Cant
—1M 171 (4D 21)
West Gate Museum. —1M 171
Westgate on Sea. —2K 207 (1D 23)
Westgate Rd. Beck —4F 68
Westgate Rd. Dart —4L 59 (4D 7)
(in two parts)
Westgate Rd. Fav —5J 187
Westgate Ter. Whits —3G 224
W. Grn. Kem —2G 99
W. Hallowes. SE9 —6N 55
Westhall Rd. Warl —4D 13
West Ham. —2A 6
W. Ham La. E15 —1E 5
West Hampstead. —1B 4
West Ham United F.C. —2A 6
Westharold. Swan —6E 72
West Heath. —6M 51 (3B 6)
W. Heath Clo. Dart —4G 59
W. Heath Cotts. Sev —1J 131
W. Heath La. Sev —1J 131
W. Heath Rd. NW3 —1B 4
W. Heath Rd. SE2 —6M 51 (3B 6)
W. Heath Rd. Dart —4G 59
West Hill. —4B 4
West Hill. SW15 & SW18 —4B 4
West Hill. Dart —4K 59 (4D 7)
West Hill. E Grin —2A 34
West Hill. Eps —3A 12
West Hill. Orp —3B 100
West Hill. Oxt —2A 24
Westhill Clo. Grav —6G 63
W. Hill Dri. Dart —4K 59
W. Hill Rise. Dart —4L 59
W. Hill Rd. H Bay —2D 194
W. Hoathly Rd. E Grin —2A 34
W. Holme. Eri —8D 52
Westholme. Orp —1G 85
Westhorne Av. SE12 & SE9
—5K 55 (4A 6)
West Hougham. —1B 42
Westhurst Dri. Chst —1D 70
West Hythe. —7C 196 (3D 41)
W. Hythe Rd. W Hyt —8B 196 (3D 41)
W. India Dock Rd. E14 —2E 5
West Kensington. —3A 4
W. Kent Av. N'fleet —4B 62
West Kilburn. —2B 4
West Kingsdown. —7E 88 (3E 15)
W. Kingsdown Ind. Est. W King
—9E 88
Westland Dri. Brom —3J 83
Westland Ho. E16 —1C 50
(off Rymill St.)
Westlands Av. Sit —7C 98
Westlands Cvn. Pk. H Bay —9F 194
Westlands Rd. H Bay —4D 194
West La. Isle G —2B 190
West La. S'ness —2B 218
West La. Sit —7H 99
(Castle Rd.)
West La. Sit —7H 99
(East St.)
West La. Ter. Isle G —3B 190
W. La. Trad. Est. Sit —6H 99
West Langdon. —2K 179 (4C 33)
W. Lawn Gdns. S'gte —8D 188
West Lea. Deal —3M 177
Westlea Ct. Folk —8G 188
Westleigh Dri. Brom —4A 70
Westleigh Rd. Wgte S —3J 207
West Malling. —1A 124 (1B 26)
W. Malling By-Pass. W Mal —3A 124
W. Malling Ind. Est. W Mal —8K 107
Westmarsh. —3C 22
Westmarsh Clo. Maid —1J 139
Westmarsh Dri. Mgte —3J 209
Westmead. Lark —6G 108
Westmead Rd. Sutt —2B 12
Westmeads Rd. Whits —3G 224
West Mill. Grav —4E 62
W. Mill Rd. Lark —7G 108
West Minster. —4B 218 (4C 11)
Westminster Bri. SW1 & SE1 —3C 5
Westminster Bri. Rd. SE1 —3C 5
Westminster Rd. Cant —7B 168
Westminster Wlk. Ram —3G 210
Westmoat Clo. Beck —3F 68
West Moors. Afrd —3C 160
Westmore Grn. Tats —8C 164
Westmoreland Av. Well —2G 57
Westmoreland Dri. Lwr Hal —8L 223
Westmoreland Pl. Brom —6K 69
Westmoreland Rd. Brom
—8H 69 (2E 13)
Westmore Rd. Tats —9C 164
Westmorland Clo. Maid —1H 139
Westmorland Grn. Maid —1H 139
Westmorland Rd. Maid —1H 139
Westmount Av. Chat —8C 80
Westmount Rd. SE9 —9B 50 (3A 6)
W. Norman Rd. Dover —4K 181
West Norwood. —1D 13
West Oak. Beck —4G 68
Weston Av. Grays —3E 7
Weston Gro. Brom —4J 69
Weston Rd. Brom —3J 69
Weston Rd. Roch —5L 79
Westonville Av. Mgte —2N 207
Westover Gdns. Broad —6J 209
Westover Rd. Broad —6J 209 (1E 23)
Westow Hill. SE19 —1D 13
Westow St. SE19 —1D 13
West Pde. Hythe —8J 197 (3D 41)
West Pk. SE9 —7A 56 (4A 6)
W. Park Av. Mgte —4H 209
West Pk. Av. Tun W —5F 150
West Pk. Rd. Maid —7E 126
West Pas. S'ness —2B 218
(off West La.)
West Peckham. —2G 134 (2B 26)
West Pl. B'lnd —2C 46
West Pl. Cant —1L 171
Westree Ct. Maid —6B 126
Westree Rd. Maid —6B 126
West Ridge. Sit —8E 98
West Rise. Ram —3F 210
Westrise. Tonb —8G 144
West Rd. Chat —3D 80
(Dock Head Rd.)
West Rd. Chat —5D 80
(Wood St.)
West Rd. Folk —8C 188 (3E 41)
West Rd. Goud —8K 185 (2D 37)
West Rd. S Ock —2E 7
West Rd. Wclf S —1B 10
W. Roman Ditch. Dover —4L 181
West Shaw. Long —5K 75
West Side. E Lan —4M 179
(in two parts)
W. Side Comn. SW19 —1A 12
W. Smithfield. EC1 —2C 5
W. Station Flats. Afrd —8F 158
West Stourmouth. —3B 22
West Street. —3B 176 (3D 9)
West St. Afrd —8F 158 (1A 40)
West St. Bexh —1A 58
West St. Brom —4K 69
West St. Cars —2B 12
West St. Deal —4N 177 (2E 33)
West St. Dover —4H 181
West St. E Grin —2A 34
West St. Eri —4E 52 (3C 7)
West St. Fav —5G 186 (3A 20)
(in two parts)
West St. Gill —6G 80
West St. Grav —4F 62 (4B 8)
West St. Grays —3A 8
West St. H'shm —2L 141 (2B 28)
West St. Hoth —4E 29
West St. Hunt —3C 27
West St. Len —2C 29
West St. New R —3B 212
West St. Queen —7A 218
West St. Roch —3M 79

West St.—Willow Tree Clo.

West St. S'ness —2B 218
West St. Sit —7F 98 (3C 19) (in two parts)
West St. Sth S —1B 10
West St. Sutt —2B 12
West St. W Mal —1N 123 (1B 26)
West St. Wro —7M 105
West St. Yald & Hunt —8F 136
West Ter. Folk —7K 189
West Ter. Sidc —6G 57
West Thurrock. —3E 7
W. Thurrock Way. W Thur —3E 7
West Tilbury. —3B 8
West View. Folk —3K 189
W. View Cotts. Cha S —6M 139
W. View Rd. Crock —9E 72
W. View Rd. Dart —4N 59
W. View Rd. Swan —7H 73
West Wlk. Maid —6M 125
Westway. SW20 —1A 12
Westway. W12 —2A 4
Westway. Cox —5N 137
West Way. Croy —3B 82
Westway. Orp —8F 70
Westway. Pem —7C 152
West Way. W Wick —9G 69
West Way Gdns. Croy —3A 82
Westways. Eden —5C 184
Westways. W'ham —8E 116
Westwell. —4E 29
Westwell Clo. Orp —2M 85
Westwell Ct. Tent —8A 222
Westwell La. C'lck —9A 174
Westwell La. Char —4M 175 (3E 29)
Westwell La. Hoth —4E 29
Westwell La. Westw —1B 158 (4E 29) (in two parts)
Westwell Leacon. —4D 29
West Wickham. —2F 82 (2E 13)
West Wing Rd. Dover —3K 181
Westwood. —9F 208 (1E 23)
Westwood Clo. Brom —6N 69
Westwood Court. —9H 187
Westwood Hill. SE26 —1D 13
Westwood Ind. Est. Mgte —7E 208
Westwood La. Sidc —3J 57
Westwood La. Well —1H 57 (4B 6)
Westwood Pl. Fav —7H 187
Westwood Retail Pk. Broad —8F 208
Westwood Rd. Broad —9F 208 (2E 23)
Westwood Rd. E Peck —1K 147
Westwood Rd. Maid —1D 138
Westwood Rd. S'fleet —3L 75 (1E 15)
Westwood Rd. Tun W —9B 150
W. Wood Rd. Yel —3D 112 (3A 18)
W. Woodside. Bex —6N 57
Westwood Wlk. N'tn —4K 97
Westwood Way. Sev —4G 119
West Yoke. —4L 89 (2E 15)
West Yoke. As —2E 15
West Yoke. New Ash —3K 89
W. Yoke Rd. New Ash —4L 89 (2A 16)
Wetham Green. —6J 223 (1B 18)
Wetheral Dri. Chat —7E 94
Wetsted La. Swan —1H 87
Weybridge Clo. Chat —7F 94
Weyburn Dri. Ram —3E 210
Wey Clo. Chat —6F 94
Weyhill Clo. Maid —3F 126
Weymouth Clo. Folk —4D 188
Weymouth Rd. Folk —5D 188
Weymouth St. W1 —2C 4
Weymouth Ter. Folk —4D 188
Wey St. Snave & Ruck —4A 40
Wharfdale Rd. N1 —2C 5
Wharfedale Rd. Dart —6C 60
Wharfedale Rd. Mgte —4E 208
Wharf La. Cli —2C 176
Wharf Rd. Fob —2C 8
Wharf Rd. Grav —4K 63
Wharf Rd. Maid —7B 126
Wharf Way. Sit —6G 99
Wharncliffe Rd. SE25 —1D 13
Wharnecliffe. Grnh —4H 61
Wharton Gdns. W'boro —1J 161
Wharton Rd. Brom —4L 69
Whatcote Cotts. Platt —2B 122
Whateley Rd. SE20 —3A 68
Whatlington. —4B 44
Whatlington Rd. Batt —4B 44
Whatman Clo. Maid —3F 126
Whatman Rd. SE23 —5A 54
Whatmer Clo. Sturry —5F 168
Whatsole Street. —4C 31
Whatsole St. H'lgh —4C 31
Wheatcroft Clo. Murs —7J 99
Wheatcroft Gro. Gill —4B 96
Wheatear Way. Chat —4E 94
Wheatfield. Leyb —9C 108
Wheatfield Clo. C'brk —7C 176
Wheatfield Dri. C'brk —7C 176
Wheatfield Lea. C'brk —7C 176
Wheatfields. Chat —9G 95
Wheatfields. Weav —5G 127
Wheatfield Way. C'brk —7C 176
Wheatley Clo. Grnh —3G 60
Wheatley Rd. Ram —3G 210
Wheatley Rd. Whits —3G 224
Wheatley Ter. Rd. Eri —6G 53
Wheatsheaf Clo. Bou B —3K 165
Wheatsheaf Clo. Maid —9E 126
Wheatsheaf Farm Rd. Huc & Bic —9H 113 (1B 28)
Wheatsheaf Gdns. S'ness —3C 218
Wheatsheaf Hill. Hals —9A 86
Wheatsheaf Way. Tonb —1K 145
Wheelbarrow Pk. Est. Mard —2J 205
Wheelbarrow Town. —4D 31
Wheeler Rd. Char —2K 175
Wheeler's La. Lin —8A 138 (3D 27)
Wheelers, The. Gill —5L 95
Wheeler St. H'crn —3L 193 (4A 28)
Wheeler St. Maid —4D 126
Wheeler St. Hedges. Maid —3E 126
Wheel La. Westf —4C 45
Wheelwrights, The. H'shm —2M 141
Wheelwrights Way. E'try —3K 183
Whenman Av. Bex —7D 58
Whetsted. —7J 147 (4B 26)
Whetsted Rd. Five G —8G 147 (4B 26) (in two parts)
Whetynton Clo. Roch —6B 80
Whiffen's Av. Chat —7C 80
Whiffen's Av. W. Chat —7C 80
Whigham Clo. Afrd —1B 160
Whimbrel Clo. Sit —3G 98
Whimbrel Grn. Lark —8D 108
Whimbrels, The. St Mi —3E 80
Whimbrel Wlk. Chat —1F 110
Whinchat Rd. SE28 —3F 50
Whinfell Av. Ram —5D 210
Whinfell Way. Grav —9L 63
Whinless Rd. Dover —4F 180
Whinyates Rd. SE9 —1A 56
Whippendell Clo. Orp —4K 71
Whippendell Way. Orp —4K 71
Whistler Rd. Tonb —9K 133
Whiston Rd. E2 —2D 5
Whitbread Rd. SE4 —2B 54
Whitburn Rd. SE13 —2E 54
Whitby Clo. Big H —7B 164
Whitby Clo. Grnh —3G 60
Whitby Rd. SE18 —4B 50
Whitby Rd. Folk —5D 188
Whitby Ter. Dover —1G 181 (off Toronto Clo.)
Whitchurch Clo. Maid —5B 126
Whitcombe Clo. Chat —9F 94
Whiteacre Dri. Deal —1L 199
Whiteacre La. Walt —3C 31
White Av. N'fleet —8E 62
Whitebeam Av. Brom —1C 84
Whitebeam Dri. Cox —5M 137
White Bear Pas. Tun W —3G 156
Whitebine Gdns. E Peck —1M 147
Whitebread La. Beckl —2D 45
Whitechapel. —2D 5
Whitechapel Rd. E1 —2D 5
White City. —2A 4
White City. (Junct.) —2A 4
White Cliffs. Folk —7K 189
White Cliffs Bus. Pk. Whitf —7F 178
White Cliffs Experience, The. —5J 181 (off Market Sq.)
White Cliffs Pk. Cap F —2D 174 (in two parts)
Whitecliff Way. Folk —5M 189
White Cottage Rd. Tonb —1J 145
White Cotts. S'lng —9B 110
White Ct. S'gte —8E 188
Whitecroft. Swan —5F 72
Whitecroft Clo. Beck —7G 68
Whitecroft Way. Beck —8F 68
Whitedyke Rd. Snod —9B 92
Whitefield Clo. Orp —6L 71
Whitefield Rd. Tun W —8G 150
Whitefoot La. Brom —9F 54 (1E 13)
Whitefoot Ter. Brom —8J 55
White Friars. Sev —9H 119
Whitefriars Meadow. S'wch —6L 217
Whitefriars Shop. Cen. Cant —2M 171 (1D 31)
Whitefriars Way. S'wch —5L 217
White Ga. Roch —3K 79
Whitegate Clo. Tun W —6G 150
Whitegate Ct. Gill —6N 95
Whitegates. Hythe —7K 197
Whitegates Av. W King —7E 88
Whitegates La. Wadh —3A 36
Whitehall. —3G 210
Whitehall. SW1 —2C 5
Whitehall. B'lnd —2C 46
Whitehall Bri. Rd. Cant —1L 171 (1D 31)
Whitehall Clo. Cant —2L 171 (1D 31)
Whitehall Dri. Kgswd —6F 140
Whitehall Gdns. Cant —1L 171 (1D 31)
Whitehall La. Eri —9G 53 (3C 7)
Whitehall La. T'hm —2C 128
Whitehall Pde. Grav —8J 63
Whitehall Rd. Brom —8N 69
Whitehall Rd. Cant —3J 171 (1D 31) (in two parts)
Whitehall Rd. Ram —4F 210
Whitehall Rd. Sit —9F 98
Whitehall Rd. T'hm —2C 128
Whitehall Way. S'ndge —8K 215
White Hart Clo. Sev —1K 131
White Hart La. SW13 —3A 4
White Hart Mans. Mgte —2C 208 (off Parade, The)
White Hart Pde. Riv —4F 118
White Hart Rd. SE18 —4G 51
White Hart Rd. Orp —1J 85
White Hart Slip. Brom —5K 69
White Hart Wood. Sev —2K 131
Whitehaven Clo. Brom —7K 69
Whitehead Clo. Dart —8K 59
Whiteheads La. Bear —5L 127
Whitehill. —9E 186 (4A 20)
Whitehill. Wro —7A 106
White Hill Clo. Lwr Har —2D 31
Whitehill La. Grav —8H 63 (4B 8)
Whitehill Rd. Crowb —4C 35
Whitehill Rd. Dart —3H 59
White Hill Rd. Det —1N 111 (3A 18)
Whitehill Rd. Grav —7H 63 (4B 8)
Whitehill Rd. Long —5K 75 (1E 15)
Whitehill Rd. Meop —3G 90 (2B 16)
White Horse Hill. C'lck & Bou A —3A 30
Whitehorse Hill. Chat —9E 80
White Horse Hill. Chst —9C 56 (1A 14)
White Horse Hill. H'nge —9E 192 (2A 42)
White Horse La. E1 —2D 5
Whitehorse La. SE25 —1D 13
White Horse La. Cant —2M 171 (1D 31)
White Horse La. Otham —2K 139 (2E 27)
White Horse La. R Min —8H 183 (1D 41)
Whitehorse Rd. Croy & T Hth —2D 13
White Horse Rd. Meop —1H 107 (3B 16)
White House. Non —2B 32
Whitehouse Clo. Hoo —9H 67
Whitehouse Cres. Burh —2L 109
Whitehouse Drove. S'wch —3C 23
White Ho. La. Weald —3G 131
White Ho. Rd. Sev —2C 25
White Ho. Rd. Weald —4G 130
Whitelake Rd. Tonb —2J 145
White La. Oxt —2A 24
White Leaves Rise. Cux —1F 92
Whitelocks Clo. Kgtn —3E 31
White Lodge. Sev —1H 131
White Lodge. Tun W —1J 157
White Lodge Clo. Sev —5J 119
Whitemarsh Ct. Whits —3G 224
Whitenbrook. Hythe —8A 188
Whiteness Grn. Broad —4K 209
Whiteness Rd. Broad —4L 209 (1E 23)
White Oak Clo. Tonb —7H 145
Whiteoak Ct. Chst —2C 70
White Oak Ct. Swan —6F 72
White Oak Dri. Beck —5F 68
White Oak Gdns. Sidc —5H 57
White Oak Sq. Swan —6F 72 (off London Rd.)
White Post. —7E 148 (1C 35)
Whitepost Gdns. Ah —5D 216
White Post Hill. F'ham —1A 88
Whitepost La. Culv —9E 90 (3A 16)
White Post La. Meop —7G 76 (1B 16)
White Rd. Chat —2D 94
White Rock Ct. Maid —6B 126
White Rock Pl. Maid —6B 126
Whites Clo. Grnh —4J 61
Whites Dri. Brom —9J 69
Whites Hill. Tilm —3C 33
White's La. Hawkh —5L 191 (4E 37)
White's Meadow. Brom —7C 70
Whitewall Cen. Roch —4A 80
Whitewall Rd. Roch —4A 80
Whitewall Way. Roch —5A 80
Whiteway Rd. Queen —6A 218 (4C 11)
Whitewebbs Way. Orp —4H 71
Whitewell La. C'brk —6D 176 (2E 37)
Whitewood Cotts. Tats —8C 164
White Wood Rd. E'try —4K 183
Whitfeld Rd. Afrd —1F 160
Whitfield. —6F 178 (4C 33)
Whitfield Av. Broad —6J 209
Whitfield Av. Dover —2G 180 (1C 43)
Whitfield Cotts. Afrd —1G 160
Whitfield Hill. Dover —9D 178 (1C 42) (in two parts)
Whitfield Rd. Bexh —7A 52
Whitfield Roundabout. Whitf —7F 178
Whitgift Ct. Cant —1K 171
Whiting Cres. Fav —4E 186
Whitley Row. —2C 130 (2C 24)
Whitley Wlk. Whitf —6G 178
Whitmore Rd. Beck —6C 68
Whitmore St. Maid —7N 125
Whitney Wlk. Sidc —2N 71
Whitstable. —3F 224 (2C 21)
Whitstable Clo. Beck —4C 68
Whitstable Museum & Art Gallery. (off Oxford St.) —4F 224
Whitstable Rd. Blean —7H 167 (4D 21)
Whitstable Rd. Cant —9K 167
Whitstable Rd. Fav —5J 187 (3A 20)
Whitstable Rd. Good —6M 187 (3B 20)
Whitstable Rd. H Bay —4A 194 (2D 21)
Whitstable Vistor Information Cen. —4F 224
Whittaker St. Chat —8D 80
Whittington Ter. S'wll —3C 220
Whitworth Rd. SE18 —7C 50
Whitworth Rd. SE25 —1D 13
Whybornes Chase. Min S —5K 219
Whybourne Crest. Tun W —4J 157
Whydown Hill. Sed —4C 44
Whytecliffs. Broad —2L 211
Whyteleafe. —4D 13
Whyteleafe Hill. Whyt —4D 13
Whyteleafe Rd. Cat —4D 13
Wichling. —1C 29
Wichling Clo. Cant —8N 167
Wichling Clo. Orp —2M 85
Wickenden Cres. W'boro —1L 161
Wickenden Rd. Sev —4K 119
Wicken Ho. Maid —5B 126
Wicken La. Char —4M 175 (3E 29) (in two parts)
Wickens Cvn. Site. Dun G —1H 119
Wickens Meadow. Dun G —1G 119
Wickens Pl. W Mal —1A 124
Wickets, The. Weald —6K 131
Wickets, The. W'boro —2K 161
Wicket, The. Croy —6D 82
Wickham Av. Croy —3B 82
Wickham Av. Ram —4L 211
Wickhambreaux. —9N 169 (4A 22)
Wickham Chase. W Wick —2G 82
Wickham Clo. N'tn —5K 97
Wickham Ct. La. Wickh —7M 169 (4A 22)
Wickham Ct. Rd. W Wick —3F 82 (2E 13)
Wickham Cres. W Wick —3F 82
Wickham Field. Off —7G 102
Wickham Gdns. SE4 —1C 54
Wickham Gdns. Tun W —9D 150
Wickham La. SE2 & Well —5J 51 (3B 6)
Wickham La. I'hm —9N 169 (4A 22)
Wickham Pl. Len —7E 200
Wickham Rd. SE4 —2C 54 (4E 5)
Wickham Rd. Beck —5E 68 (1E 13)
Wickham Rd. Croy —3A 82 (2D 13)
Wickham Rd. Wickh —1N 173 (4A 22)
Wickham Rock La. W'sea —4E 45
Wickham St. Roch —9A 80
Wickham St. Well —9G 51 (3B 6)
Wickhams Way. Hart —8M 75
Wickham Way. Beck —7F 68 (1E 13)
Wickhurst. —3D 25
Wickhurst Rd. Weald —4G 130
Wick La. E3 —2E 5
Wick La. W Grn —3A 32
Wick Rd. E9 —1D 5
Wicks Clo. SE9 —9N 55
Wicksteed Clo. Bex —8E 58
Widbury. L'tn G —2N 155
Widecombe Rd. SE9 —8A 56
Wide Way. Mitc —1C 12
Widgeon Rd. Eri —7J 53
Widgeon Rd. Roch —6H 79
Widmore. —6M 69 (1A 14)
Widmore Green. —4M 69
Widmore Lodge Rd. Brom —5N 69
Widmore Rd. Brom —5K 69 (1A 14)
Widred Rd. Dover —4H 181
Wierton. —3E 27
Wierton Hill. Bou M —3E 27
Wierton Rd. Bou M —7H 139 (3E 27)
Wife of Bath Hill. Cant —2J 171
Wigeon Path. SE28 —3F 50
Wigmore. —7L 95 (3E 17)
Wigmore Cotts. Eyt —3K 185
Wigmore La. Eyt —3K 185 (3C 32)
Wigmore Rd. Gill —7L 95 (2E 17) (in two parts)
Wigmore St. W1 —2C 4
Wigwam Paddocks. Birch —3F 206
Wihtred Rd. Bap —9L 99
Wilberforce Rd. Cox —5A 138
Wilberforce Rd. S'gte —8E 188
Wilberforce Way. Grav —1J 77
Wilbrough Rd. Birch —4F 206
Wilcox Clo. Aysm —2B 162
Wildage. S Min —4E 31
Wilden Pk. Rd. S'hrst —1D 37
Wildernesse. —4M 119 (1D 25)
Wildernesse Av. Sev —4M 119
Wildernesse Mt. Sev —4L 119
Wilderness Hill. Mgte —3E 208
Wilderness Rd. Chst —3D 70
Wilde Rd. Eri —7C 52
Wilderwick Rd. Ling & E Grin —1A 34
Wildfell Clo. Chat —2F 110
Wildfell Rd. SE6 —5E 54
Wildish Rd. Fav —4E 186
Wildman Clo. Gill —8N 95
Wildwood Clo. SE12 —5J 55
Wildwood Clo. Kgswd —6G 140
Wildwood Glade. Hem —7L 95
Wildwood Rd. Sturry —5E 168
Wiles Av. New R —3C 212
Wiles Ho. New R —3C 212
Wilfred Rd. Ram —5G 211
Wilfred St. Grav —4G 63
Wilgate Green. —1E 29
Wilgate Grn. Rd. Throw —1E 29
Wilkes Rd. Broad —1J 211
Wilkie Rd. Birch —3F 206
Wilkinson Clo. Dart —2N 59
Wilkins Way. Bras —6K 117
Wilks Av. Dart —7N 59
Wilks Clo. Rain —1D 96
Wilks Gdns. Croy —2B 82
Will Adams Ct. Gill —6F 80
Willard's Hill. —2A 44
Will Crooks Gdns. SE9 —2N 55
Willement Rd. Fav —5F 186
Willenhall Rd. SE18 —5D 50
Willersley Av. Orp —4F 84
Willersley Av. Sidc —6H 57
Willersley Clo. Sidc —6H 57
Willesborough. —1L 161 (1A 40)
Willesborough Ct. W'boro —8M 159
Willesborough Ind. Pk. W'boro —9L 159
Willesborough Lees. —9L 159 (1A 40)
Willesborough Rd. Kenn —5K 159 (4A 30)
Willesborough Windmill. —9L 159 (1A 40)
Willesden. —1A 4
Willesden Green. —1A 4
Willesden La. NW2 & NW6 —1A 4
Willesley Gdns. C'brk —6D 176
Willett Clo. Orp —9G 70
Willetts Hill. Monk —6H 205 (2C 22)
Willetts La. Blac —1D 154
Willett Way. Orp —8F 70
William Av. Folk —4H 189 (2A 42)
William Av. Mgte —5G 209
William Baker Ho. Roy B —1K 125
William Barefoot Dri. SE9 —9C 56 (1A 14)
William Clo. SE13 —1F 54
William Cory Promenade. Eri —5F 52
William Gibbs Ct. Fav —5H 187
William Ho. Grav —5G 62
William Judge Clo. Tent —8E 222
William Luck Clo. E Peck —1K 147
William Nash Ct. St M —6L 71
William Pit Av. Deal —4L 177
William Pitt Clo. Hythe —6L 197
William Pl. St M —7L 71
William Rd. Afrd —1F 160
William Rd. Cux —1G 92
William Smith Ho. Belv —3B 52 (off Ambrooke Rd.)
Williamson Rd. Lydd S —8A 212
William St. Fav —5H 187
William St. Gill —2C 96
William St. Grav —5G 63
William St. H Bay —3G 195
William St. Sit —8F 98
William St. Tun W —9G 150
William St. Whits —3F 224
Willingdon. Afrd —4C 160
Willingdon Pl. Walm —9M 177
Willington. —9H 127 (2E 27)
Willington Grn. Maid —1H 139
Willington St. Maid —6J 127 (2E 27)
Willis Cotts. Gill —2K 111
Willis Ct. Min S —7G 219
Willis Rd. Eri —4E 52
Willop Way. Dym —4E 182
Willoughby Ct. Cant —2M 171 (1D 31)
Willow Av. Broad —9H 209
Willow Av. Fav —5E 186
Willow Av. Sidc —4J 57
Willow Av. Swan —7G 73
Willowbank Clo. St Mar —2F 214
Willowbank Dri. H Hals —1H 67
Willow Brook Rd. SE15 —3D 5
Willowby Gdns. Gill —7A 96
Willow Clo. SE6 —6J 55
Willow Clo. Bex —4A 58
Willow Clo. Brom —8B 70
Willow Clo. Cant —9N 167
Willow Clo. Hythe —7F 196
Willow Clo. Mgte —3G 209
Willow Clo. Orp —1K 85
Willow Cottage. Hall —5E 92
Willow Ct. Broad —8K 209
Willow Ct. Folk —7E 188
Willow Ct. Maid —2D 138
Willow Cres. Five G —8F 146
Willow Cres. S'hrst —6K 221
Willow Dri. Hams —8D 190
Willow Dri. St Mar —3E 214
Willow Grange. Hoo —9G 67
Willow Grange. Sidc —8K 57
Willow Gro. Chst —2C 70
Willow Ho. Brom —5H 69
Willow Ho. Chat —7C 94
Willow Ho. Maid —6L 125
Willow Ho. S'ness —2C 218 (off Hope St.)
Willow Ho. Sit —8J 99
Willow Ind. Est. Iwade —6B 198
Willow Industries. S'lng —7C 110
Willow La. Pad W —4C 26
Willow Lea. Tonb —9J 133
Willowmead. Leyb —8C 108
Willow Pk. Off —8G 103
Willow Rise. Down —8J 127
Willow Rd. Dart —6K 59
Willow Rd. Eri —8H 53
Willow Rd. Gt Mon —3D 33
Willow Rd. Lark —7D 108
Willow Rd. Roch —6J 79
Willow Rd. Whits —8E 224
Willows Ct. Cant —7J 167
Willowside. Snod —1E 108
Willow's, The. Afrd —7C 158
Willows, The. Beck —4D 68
Willows, The. Bidd —7L 163
Willows, The. Gill —1A 96
Willows, The. Kem —2G 98
Willows, The. Min S —3J 219
Willows, The. N'tn —5K 97
Willow Ter. Eyns —3M 87
Willow Tree Clo. H Bay —2L 195
Willow Tree Clo. W'boro —9K 159

Willow Tree Ct.—Wood Retreat

Willow Tree Ct. Sidc —1H 71
Willow Tree Farm Cvn. Pk. Hythe —8E 196
Willow Tree Rd. Tun W —4E 156
Willow Tree Wlk. Brom —4L 69
Willow Vale. Chst —2D 70
Willow Wlk. Dart —2K 59
Willow Wlk. Meop —8E 90
Willow Wlk. Orp —4D 84
Willow Wlk. Tun W —6L 151
Willow Way. Ches —5L 225
Willow Way. Maid —6E 126
Willow Way. Mgte —5A 208
Willow Waye. Eyt —4L 185
Willow Wents. Mere —8H 123 (2B 26)
Willow Wood Rd. Meop —9E 90
Willow Woods Rd. Ashl —3C 33
Willrose Cres. SE2 —5K 51
Willson's Rd. Ram —6G 211
Wilman Rd. Tun W —7G 151
Wilmar Gdns. W Wick —2E 82
Wilmar Way. Seal —2N 119
Wilmecote Ct. Gill —3N 95
Wilmerhatch La. Eps —4A 12
Wilmington. —8K 59 (1D 15)
Wilmington Av. Orp —3L 85
Wilmington Ct. Rd. Dart —8H 59
Wilmington Way. Gill —1L 95
Wilmot Rd. Dart —3H 59
Wilmott Pl. E'try —3K 183
Wilmount St. SE18 —4D 50
Wilsley Green. —6D 176
Wilsley Pound. —8A 220 (2E 37)
Wilson Av. Deal —7J 177
Wilson Av. Roch —2A 94
Wilson Clo. Hild —2E 144
Wilson Clo. Maid —1H 139
Wilson Clo. W'boro —9L 159
Wilson La. S Dar —5F 74 (1E 15)
Wilson Rd. Tonb —1L 145
Wilsons La. E Far —4L 137 (2D 27)
Wilson St. EC2 —2D 5
Wilson's Way. Meop —6E 90
Wiltie Gdns. Folk —6J 189
Wilton Clo. Deal —5L 177
Wilton Dri. Dit —1F 124
Wilton Rd. SE2 —4L 51
Wilton Rd. Folk —5H 189
Wilton Rd. Ram —3D 210
Wilton Ter. Sit —6C 98
Wiltshire Clo. Chat —3F 94
Wiltshire Clo. Dart —5D 60
Wiltshire Rd. Orp —1J 85
Wiltshire Way. Maid —9H 127
Wiltshire Way. Tun W —7K 151
Wimbledon. —1A 12
Wimbledon Hill Rd. SW19 —1B 12
Wimbledon Park. —4B 4
Wimbledon Pk. Rd. SW19 & SW18 —4B 4
Wimbledon Pk. Side. SW19 —4A 4
Wimbledon Rd. SW17 —1B 12
Wimbledon Tennis Courts. —1B 12
Wimborne Av. Orp & Chst —7H 71
Wimborne Clo. SE12 —3J 55
Wimborne Pl. Ram —4F 210
Wimborne Way. Beck —6A 68
Wimbourne Dri. Gill —5N 95
Wimpole Clo. Brom —7M 69
Winant Way. Dover —1G 180
Winch Clo. C'brk —9D 176
Winchcomb Gdns. SE9 —1N 55
Wincheap. Cant —4K 171 (1D 31)
Wincheap Grn. Cant —3M 171 (1D 31)
Wincheap Ind. Est. Cant —3K 171 (1D 31)
Winchelsea. —4A 46
Winchelsea Av. Bexh —7A 52
Winchelsea Beach. —4A 46
Winchelsea Ct. Dover —5H 181
Winchelsea La. W'sea —4E 45
Winchelsea Rd. NW10 —2A 4
Winchelsea Rd. Chat —5E 94
Winchelsea Rd. Dover —5G 181
Winchelsea Rd. Rye —3A 46
Winchelsea St. Dover —5G 181
Winchelsea Ter. Dover —5G 181
Winchester Av. Chat —7C 94
Winchester Clo. Brom —5G 69
Winchester Cres. Grav —8J 63
Winchester Gdns. Cant —4N 171
Winchester Gro. Sev —5J 119
Winchester Ho. Maid —1G 139
Winchester Pk. Brom —6J 69
Winchester Pl. Maid —4D 126
Winchester Rd. Bexh —9M 51
Winchester Rd. Brom —6J 69
Winchester Rd. Hawkh —5L 191
Winchester Rd. Orp —5L 85
Winchester Rd. Tonb —2K 145
Winchester St. W3 —3A 4
Winchester Way. Gill —2C 96
Winchet Hill. —1D 37
Winchfield Rd. SE26 —1B 68
Winch's Garth. S'hrst —6K 221
Wincliff Rd. Tonb —7H 145
Wincrofts Dri. SE9 —2F 56
Windermere. Fav —6J 187
Windermere Av. Ram —5D 210
Windermere Clo. Dart —6J 59
Windermere Clo. Orp —4D 84
Windermere Ct. Afrd —6G 158
Windermere Dri. Gill —4N 95
Windermere Gdns. Aysm —2D 162
Windermere Gro. Sit —8E 98
Windermere Ho. Maid —1G 139
Windermere Rd. Bexh —9D 52
Windermere Rd. W Wick —3H 83
Windfield Clo. SE26 —9A 54
Windham Av. New Ad —9G 83
Windhill. Char H —3D 29
Wind Hill La. Char H —3D 29
Windhover Way. Grav —9K 63
Winding Hill. Sell —1A 30
Windmill Av. Ram —1F 210
Windmill Clo. Bri —8H 173
Windmill Clo. Cant —2B 172
Windmill Clo. H Bay —5H 195
Windmill Clo. Roch —3M 79
Windmill Clo. W'boro —9L 159
Windmill Cotts. C'brk —6D 176
Windmill Cotts. Lwr Sto —7K 201
Windmill Cotts. Weald —6J 131
(off Hurst La.)
Windmill Ct. Langl —5E 138
Windmill Ct. Whits —6E 224
Windmill Dri. Kes —5M 83
Windmill Gdns. H'crn —3L 193
Windmill Heights. Bear —5L 127
Windmill Hill. Platt —3C 122
Windmill Hill. Sev —1A 26
Windmill Hill. Ulc —9J 141 (3B 28)
Windmill La. E15 —1E 5
Windmill La. Cous W —3B 36
Windmill La. Eps —3A 12
Windmill La. Cvn. Site. W Mal —4M 123
Windmill La. E. W Mal —3N 123
Windmill La. W. W Mal —4N 123
Windmill Pk. Wro H —2D 122
Windmill Quay Rd. Min S —9N 219
Windmill Rise. Min S —6M 219
Windmill Rd. SW18 —4B 4
Windmill Rd. Cant —2B 172
Windmill Rd. Croy —2C 13
Windmill Rd. Gill —9E 80
Windmill Rd. H Bay —5H 195
Windmill Rd. Mitc —1C 12
Windmill Rd. Sev —3J 131 (2D 25)
Windmill Rd. Sit —5E 98
Windmill Rd. Weald —6J 131 (3D 25)
Windmill Rd. Whits —6F 224
Windmill St. Grav —4G 63 (4B 8)
(in two parts)
Windmill St. Hythe —7J 197
Windmill St. Roch —3M 79
Windmill St. Tun W —2J 157
Windmill View. Mgte —5E 208
Windmill Wlk. Ram —3F 210
Windrush. SE28 —1K 51
Windrush La. SE23 —8A 54
Windsor Av. SW19 —1B 12
Windsor Av. Chat —1C 94
Windsor Av. Mgte —4F 208
Windsor Clo. Broad —8J 209
Windsor Clo. Chst —1D 70
Windsor Clo. Maid —3E 126
Windsor Ct. Mgte —4F 208
Windsor Ct. Walm —8M 177
Windsor Dri. Dart —4H 59
Windsor Dri. Orp —7J 85
Windsor Dri. Sit —9E 98
Windsor Gdns. H Bay —4C 194
Windsor Gdns. Ward —5J 203
Windsor Ho. Deal —5K 177
Windsor Ho. Dover —5J 181
(off Durham Clo.)
Windsor Ho. Whits —4F 224
Windsor M. SE6 —6F 54
Windsor M. SE23 —6B 54
Windsor M. New R —1D 212
Windsor Rd. Bexh —2N 57
Windsor Rd. Cant —4J 171
Windsor Rd. C'snd —5B 210
Windsor Rd. Gill —7G 81
Windsor Rd. Grav —8G 63
Windward Rd. Roch —2N 93
Windy Ridge. Brom —4A 70
Windyridge. Gill —2H 95
Winehouse La. Cap F —2B 42
Wine Pine Ho. Hythe —7H 197
Wineycock. N'tn —1D 29
Winfield La. Bor G —7L 121 (2E 25)
Wingate Hill. Harb —1G 170
Wingate Rd. Folk —4K 189
Wingate Rd. Sidc —2L 71
Wingfield Bank. N'fleet —7B 62
Wingfield Ct. Sidc —7H 57
Wingfield Rd. Grav —6G 63
Wingham. —2B 226 (1B 32)
Wingham Bird Park. —1D 226 (4B 22)
Wingham Clo. Gill —9M 81
Wingham Clo. Maid —1J 139
Wingham Ct. W'hm —3B 226
Wingham Green. —1A 32
Wingham Rd. L'brne —1A 32
Wingham Well. —1A 32
Wingham Well La. W'hm W —1A 32
Wingmore. —4E 31
Wing Rd. Ley S —7N 203
Wingrove Dri. Strood —4N 79
Wingrove Dri. Weav —4H 127
Wingrove Hill. Dover —2D 180
Wingrove Rd. SE6 —7H 55
Wings Clo. Broad —8M 209
Winifred Av. Ram —2G 210
Winifred Rd. Bear —6J 127
Winifred Rd. Dart —3J 59
Winifred Rd. Eri —5F 52
Winifred St. E16 —1B 50
Winkhurst Green. —9C 130 (3C 24)
Winkhurst Grn. Rd. Bough B —9C 130 (3C 24)
Winkle Clo. H Bay —4C 194
Winkworth Rd. Bans —3B 12
Winlaton Rd. Brom —9G 55
Winnipeg Clo. Dover —1H 181
Winnipeg Dri. Grn St —7H 85
Winn Rd. SE12 —6K 55 (4A 6)
Winns Comn. Rd. SE18 —6G 51
Winser Rd. Rol —4B 38
Winsford Rd. SE6 —8C 54
Winslade Way. SE6 —5E 54
Winstanley Cres. Ram —4H 211
Winstanley Rd. S'ness —2D 218
Winston Clo. Cant —3B 172
Winston Clo. Grnh —4F 60
Winston Ct. Birch —3F 206
Winston Ct. Brom —4L 69
Winston Dri. Wain —2A 80
Winston Gdns. H Bay —3L 195
Winston Ho. Folk —6F 188
Winston Rd. Roch —7H 79
Winston Scott Av. L'tn G —1M 155
Winston Way. Ilf —1A 6
Winterage La. Folk —5A 192 (1E 41)
Winterborne Av. Orp —4F 84
Winterbourne. —1B 30
Winterbourne Rd. SE6 —6C 54
Winterfield La. W Mal —1C 124 (1C 26)
Winter Gardens. —1E 9
Winters Croft. Grav —2J 77
Winterstoke Cres. Ram —4L 211
Winterstoke Rd. SE6 —6C 54
Winterstoke Undercliff. Ram —5L 211
Winterstoke Way. Ram —4K 211
Winterton Ct. W'ham —9F 116
(off Market Sq.)
Winton Ct. Swan —7F 72
Winton Rd. Orp —5D 84
Wireless Rd. Big A —3D 164
Wirrals, The. Chat —7D 94
Wirral Wood Clo. Chst —2C 70
Wiseacre. Lam —4C 200
Wises La. B'den —8B 98 (3C 18)
Wise's La. Stans —9K 89
Wish St. Rye —3A 46
Wish, The. Ken —3E 39
Wisley Green. —2E 37
Wisley Rd. Orp —3J 71
Wissenden. —1C 39
Wissenden La. Beth —2H 163 (1C 39)
Wistaria Clo. Orp —3D 84
Wisteria Gdns. Swan —5E 72
Wisteria Rd. SE13 —2G 54
Witches La. Sev —4E 118 (2C 25)
Witham Way. Roch —5K 79
Withens Clo. Orp —7L 71
Withersdane. —4B 30
Witherston Way. SE9 —7C 56
Withyham. —9C 154 (3C 34)
Withyham Rd. Groom —6G 155 (2D 35)
Witley Cres. New Ad —7F 82
Witney Path. SE23 —8A 54
Wittersham. —2A 46
Wittersham Clo. Chat —6E 94
Wittersham Rd. Brom —1J 69
Wittersham Rd. Iden —2A 46
Wittersham Rd. Rol & Wit —1E 45
Wittersham Rd. Wit —2A 46
Wittersham Windmill. —2A 46
Wivenhoe. Afrd —4C 160
Wivenhoe Clo. Rain —1C 96
Woburn Pl. WC1 —2C 5
Wodehouse Clo. Lark —6D 108
Wodehouse Rd. Dart —2A 60
Wold Chalet & Cvn. Pk., The. E'chu —2E 202
Woldham Pl. Brom —7M 69
Woldham Rd. Brom —7M 69
Woldingham Rd. Wold —4D 13
Wolds Dri. Orp —5C 84
Wolfe Clo. Brom —9K 69
Wolfe Cotts. W'ham —9F 116
Wolfe Rd. Maid —7M 125
Wolfram Clo. SE13 —3H 55
Wolf's Hill. Oxt —3A 24
Wolf's Rd. Oxt —2A 24
Wolf's Row. Oxt —2A 24
Wollaston Clo. Gill —8N 95
Wollaston Rd. Walm —6N 177
Wolseley Av. H Bay —3B 194
Wolseley Pl. Afrd —7F 158
Wolseley Rd. Tun W —7J 151
Wolseley Ter. Lydd —4C 204
Wolsey Cres. New Ad —9F 82
Wolsey M. Orp —6H 85
Wolsley Clo. Dart —3F 58
Wolvercote Rd. SE2 —2M 51
Wolverton. —1B 42
Wolverton Hill. Alk —1B 42
Wombwell Gdns. N'fleet —7D 62
Wombwell Park. —7C 62
Womenswold. —3A 32
Wood Av. Folk —4K 189
Woodbank Rd. Brom —8J 55
Woodbastwick Rd. SE26 —1A 68
Woodberry Dri. Sit —8J 99
Woodberry Gro. Bex —8E 58
Woodbine Rd. Sidc —6G 56
Woodbridge Dri. Maid —8B 126
Woodbrook. Char —3L 175
Woodbrook Rd. SE2 —6J 51
Woodbury Av. E Grin —2A 34
Woodbury Clo. Big H —6F 164
Woodbury Clo. Tun W —9G 151
Woodbury Gdns. Tent —8B 222
Woodbury La. Tent —8B 222
Woodbury Pk. Gdns. Tun W —9H 151
Woodbury Pk. Rd. Tun W —9G 151
Woodbury Rd. Chat —1B 110
Woodbury Rd. Hawkh —5L 191
Woodbury Rd. W'ham —6F 164
Woodchurch. —6M 207 (2D 23)
(nr. Acol)
Woodchurch. —7B 226 (3D 39)
(nr. Brattle)
Woodchurch Clo. Chat —6E 94
Woodchurch Clo. Sidc —8F 56
Woodchurch Cres. Gill —1M 95
Woodchurch Dri. Brom —3N 69
Woodchurch Ho. Gill —1M 95
Woodchurch Rd. App —4D 39
Woodchurch Rd. Shad —2E 39
Woodchurch Rd. Tent —7D 222 (3C 38)
Woodchurch Rd. Wdchu
(in two parts) —8L 207 (2D 23)
Woodchurch Windmill. —6B 226 (3D 39)
Wood Clo. Bex —8F 58
Wood Clo. Quar W —1J 125
Woodclyffe Dri. Chst —5C 70
Woodcock Gdns. H'nge —8B 192
Woodcock La. Graf G —3B 28
Woodcock La. I Grn —4A 38
Woodcote. —4A 12
(nr. Epsom)
Woodcote. —3C 12
(nr. Purley)
Woodcote. Ches —4M 225
Woodcote Dri. Orp —1F 84
Woodcote Green. —3C 12
Woodcote Grn. Wall —3C 12
Woodcote Grn. Rd. Eps —4A 12
Woodcote Gro. Rd. Coul —4C 12
Woodcote Rd. Eps —3A 12
Woodcote Rd. Wall & Kenl —3C 12
Woodcote Side. Eps —4A 12
Woodcote Valley Rd. Purl —3C 12
Wood Cottage La. Folk —4D 188
Woodcourt Clo. Sit —9F 98
Woodcroft. SE9 —8B 56
Woodcut Cotts. Holl —7B 128
Wood Dri. Chst —2A 70
Wood Dri. Sev —8G 119
Wood End. Swan —7E 72
Woodfall Dri. Dart —2F 58
Woodfalls Ind. Est. Ladd —3C 26
Woodfield Av. SW16 —4C 4
Woodfield Av. Folk —4E 188
Woodfield Av. Grav —6G 62
Woodfield Av. Hild —2E 144
Woodfield Clo. Folk —4D 188
Woodfield Ho. SE23 —8A 54
(off Dacres Rd.)
Woodfield Rd. Tonb —7H 145
Woodfields. Sev —5E 118
Woodfield Way. Chatt —9A 66
Woodford Av. Ram —3H 211
Woodford Ct. Birch —4F 206
Woodford Rd. E7 —1A 6
Woodford Rd. Maid —7M 125
Woodgate. Bis —3E 31
Woodgate Clo. Fav —4G 187
Woodgate La. B'den —9L 97
Woodgate Rd. Adtn —6H 107
Woodgate Rd. W Mal —4B 16
Woodgate Way. Tonb —8K 145 (4E 25)
Woodgers Gro. Swan —5G 73
Woodgrange Dri. Sth S —1C 10
Woodgrange Rd. E7 —1A 6
Woodhall Ter. Queen —7B 218
Woodham Rd. SE6 —8F 54
Woodhayes Rd. SW19 —1A 12
Woodhead Dri. Orp —4G 85
Woodhill. SE18 —4A 50
Woodhill. Meop —5H 91 (2B 16)
Wood Hill. T Hill —5L 167 (3D 21)
Woodhill Pk. Pem —8B 152
Woodhurst. Chat —7A 94
Woodhurst Av. Orp —9E 70
Woodhurst Clo. Cux —1F 92
Woodhurst La. Oxt —3A 24
Woodhurst Rd. SE2 —5J 51
Woodington Clo. SE9 —4C 56
Woodknoll Dri. Chst —4B 70
Woodland. —1D 41
Woodland Av. Aysm —2C 162
Woodland Av. Birch —5G 206
Woodland Av. Hart —8M 75
Woodland Clo. Dover —2D 180
Woodland Clo. Long —6B 76
Woodland Clo. Tun W —7J 151
Woodland Clo. W Mal —1M 123
Woodland Cotts. Lym —7C 204
Woodland Dri. Eden —4C 184
Woodland Dri. Min S —5J 219
Woodland Rise. Sev —5M 119
Woodland Rise. W Hyt —7B 196
Woodland Rd. H Bay —5C 194
Woodland Rd. Lym —7A 204 (1D 41)
Woodland Rd. Tun W —7J 151
Woodlands. —4D 104 (3E 15)
Woodlands. Chat —9D 94
Woodlands. Cox —5M 137
Woodlands. C'brk —6D 176
Woodlands. Dar —3B 20
Woodlands. Pad W —8L 147
Woodlands. Pem —7E 152
Woodlands. Short —7J 69
Woodlands Av. Sidc —6G 57
Woodlands Av. Snod —2D 108
Woodlands Clo. Brom —5B 70
Woodlands Clo. Maid —2D 126
Woodlands Clo. Swan —5G 72
Woodlands Clo. Tstn —9F 124
Woodlands Clo. Tun W —1K 157
Woodlands Cotts. H'shm —1N 141
Woodlands Ct. Brom —4J 69
Woodlands Ct. S'boro —4G 150
Woodlands Dri. Hythe —7A 188
Woodlands Est. Residential Pk. Blean —4F 166
Woodlands La. Shorne —3B 78 (1C 16)
Woodlands Pde. Dit —1H 125
Woodlands Pk. Bex —9E 58
Woodlands Rise. Swan —5G 73
Woodlands Rd. Adm —2A 32
Woodlands Rd. Bexh —1N 57
Woodlands Rd. Brom —5A 70
Woodlands Rd. Dit & Ayle —9G 108
Woodlands Rd. Gill —1J 95 (2E 17)
Woodlands Rd. Orp —7J 85
Woodlands Rd. Sit —8J 99
Woodlands Rd. Tonb —8G 145
Woodlands Rd. W'boro —6N 159
Woodlands St. SE13 —5G 55
Woodlands Ter. Gill —9J 81
Woodlands Ter. Swan —9C 72
Woodlands, The. SE13 —5G 54
Woodlands, The. Orp —7K 85
Woodlands, The. Tun W —1J 157
Woodlands View. Badg M —1C 102
Woodlands View. Wit —2E 45
Woodland Ter. SE7 —4A 50
Woodland Wlk. Brom —9H 55
(in two parts)
Woodland Way. SE2 —4M 51
Woodland Way. Bidb —2D 150
Woodland Way. Broad —4L 209
Woodland Way. Cant —7K 167
Woodland Way. Croy —2B 82
Woodland Way. Dym —9D 182
Woodland Way. Grnh —3H 61
Woodland Way. Maid —2E 126
Woodland Way. Orp —7E 70
Woodland Way. W Wick —5E 82
Woodland Way. Wdboro —8H 217
Wood La. W12 —2A 4
Wood La. Bene —3A 38
Wood La. Dag —1B 6
Wood La. Dart —9D 60
Wood La. Horn —1D 7
Wood La. W'slde —3D 17
Woodlawn St. Whits —3F 224
Woodlea. Afrd —7G 159
Woodlea. Leyb —8D 108
Woodlea. Long —6B 76
Woodlea Dri. Brom —8H 69
Woodleas. Maid —7K 125
Woodley Rd. Orp —3L 85
Wood Lodge Gdns. Brom —3A 70
Wood Lodge Grange. Sev —4K 119
Wood Lodge La. W Wick —4F 82
Woodman Av. Whits —3M 225
Woodman Pde. E16 —1C 50
(off Woodman St.)
Woodmans Green. —4B 44
Woodmansterne. —4B 12
Woodmansterne La. Bans & Cars
(Croydon La.) —3B 12
Woodmansterne La. Bans —4B 12
(Park Rd.)
Woodmansterne Rd. Cars —3B 12
Woodmansterne St. Bans —4B 12
Woodman St. E16 —1C 50
(in two parts)
Woodman Vs. Fawk —4H 89
Woodmere. SE9 —6B 56
Woodmere Av. Croy —1A 82
Woodmere Clo. Croy —1A 82
Woodmere Gdns. Croy —1A 82
Woodmere Way. Beck —8G 68
Woodmount. Swan —1E 86
Woodnesborough. —8G 217 (1C 33)
Woodnesborough La. E'try —2K 183 (2C 33)
Woodnesborough Rd. S'wch —7J 217 (1C 33)
Woodpecker Clo. Eden —4D 184
Woodpecker Glade. Gill —5N 95
Woodpecker Mt. Croy —9B 82
Woodpecker Rd. Lark —9D 108
Woodplace La. Coul —4C 12
Wood Retreat. SE18 —2D 50

HOSPITALS, HEALTH CENTRES and HOSPICES
covered by this atlas
with their map square reference

N.B. Where Hospitals, Health Centres and Hospices are not named on the map, the reference given is for the road in which they are situated.

ALEXANDRA BUPA HOSPITAL, THE
—2D **110**
Impton La., Chatham, Kent. ME5 9PG
Tel: (01634) 687 166

ALL SAINTS HOSPITAL —1D **94**
Magpie Hall Rd., Chatham,
Kent. ME4 5NG
Tel: (01634) 407311

Ashford Mental Health Centre —8F **158**
1 Elwick Rd., Ashford, Kent. TN23 1PD
Tel: (01233) 643407

Aylesham Health Centre —2C **162**
Boulevard Courrieres, Aylesham,
Kent. CT3 3DY
Tel: (01304) 840474

BECKENHAM HOSPITAL —5C **68**
379 Croydon Rd., Beckenham,
Kent. BR3 3QL
Tel: 020 8289 6600

BELVEDERE PRIVATE CLINIC —5L **51**
Knee Hill, Abbey Wood,
London. SE2 0AT
Tel: 020 8311 4464

BENENDEN HOSPITAL —3A **38**
Goddards Green Rd., Benenden,
Cranbrook, Kent. TN17 4AX
Tel: (01580) 240333

BETHLEM ROYAL HOSPITAL, THE
—1D **82**
Monks Orchard Rd., Eden Park,
Beckenham, Kent. BR3 3BX
Tel: 020 8777 6611

BEXLEY HOSPITAL —7F **58**
Old Bexley La., Bexley,
Kent. DA5 2BW
Tel: (01322) 526282

BLACKHEATH HOSPITAL —1J **55**
40-42 Lee Ter., Blackheath,
London. SE3 9UD
Tel: 020 8318 7722

Broadstairs Health Centre —9L **209**
The Broadway, Broadstairs,
Kent. CT10 3JB
Tel: (01843) 602654

BROMLEY HOSPITAL —7L **69**
Cromwell Av., Bromley, Kent. BR2 9AJ
Tel: 020 8289 7000

BUCKLAND HOSPITAL —3F **180**
Coombe Valley Rd., Buckland,
Dover. Kent. CT17 0HD
Tel: (01304) 201624

Canterbury Health Centre —3N **171**
Old Dover Rd., Canterbury,
Kent. CT1 3JB
Tel: (01227) 454435

Castlewood Therapy Centre —8C **50**
25 Shooter's Hill, London. SE18 4LG
Tel: 020 8856 4970

Central Lewisham Health Centre —4E **54**
410 Lewisham High St.,
London. SE13 6LL
Tel: 020 8690 9723

Chatham Mental Health Centre —1C **94**
Throwley Ho., 49 Maidstone Rd.,
Chatham, Kent. ME4 6DP
Tel: (01634) 845678

CHAUCER HOSPITAL, THE —6N **171**
Nackington Rd., Canterbury,
Kent. CT4 7AR
Tel: (01227) 455466

CHELSFIELD PARK HOSPITAL —6N **85**
Bucks Cross Rd., Chelsfield,
Orpington, Kent. BR6 7RG
Tel: (01689) 877855

Dartford East Health Centre —5B **60**
Pilgrims Way, Dartford, Kent. DA1 1QY
Tel: (01322) 274211

Dartford West Health Centre —4K **59**
17-19 Tower Rd., Dartford,
Kent. DA1 2HA
Tel: (01322) 622500

Deal Mental Health Centre —5L **177**
Bowling Grn. La., Deal,
Kent. CT14 9HF
Tel: (01304) 865464

Demelza House Childrens Hospice —5A **98**
Rook La., Bobbing, Sittingbourne,
Kent. ME9 8DZ
Tel: (01795) 843843

Dover Health Centre —4J **181**
Maison Dieu Rd., Dover,
Kent. CT16 1RH
Tel: (01304) 865500

Downham Health Centre —9J **55**
24 Churchdown, Downham,
Bromley, Kent. BR1 5PT
Tel: 020 8695 6644

EASTRY HOSPITAL —3K **183**
Mill La., Eastry, Sandwich,
Kent. CT13 0JU
Tel: (01304) 614110

EDENBRIDGE & DISTRICT WAR
MEMORIAL HOSPITAL —8C **184**
Mill Hill, Edenbridge, Kent. TN8 5DA
Tel: (01732) 863164

ERITH & DISTRICT HOSPITAL —6E **52**
Park Cres., Erith, Kent. DA8 3EE
Tel: 020 8302 2678

Erith Health Centre —6G **52**
2 Queen's St., Erith, Kent. DA8 1TT
Tel: (01322) 336661

FARNBOROUGH HOSPITAL —5C **84**
Farnborough Comn., Locksbottom,
Orpington, Kent. BR6 8ND
Tel: (01689) 814000

FAVERSHAM COTTAGE HOSPITAL
—5G **187**
Bank St., Faversham, Kent. ME13 8PS
Tel: (01795) 536621

Faversham Health Centre —5G **187**
Faversham Cottage Hospital,
Bank St., Faversham,
Kent. ME13 8QR
Tel: (01795) 536621

FAWKHAM MANOR HOSPITAL —2J **89**
Manor La., Fawkham,
Longfield, Kent. DA3 8ND
Tel: (01474) 879900

Folkestone Health Centre —6K **189**
15 Dover Rd., Folkestone,
Kent. CT20 1JY
Tel: (01303) 228888

GOLDIE LEIGH HOSPITAL —6L **51**
Bostall House, Lodge Hill,
Abbey Wood, London. SE2 0AY
Tel: 020 8319 7111

GRAVESEND & NORTH KENT HOSPITAL
—4F **62**
Bath St., Gravesend, Kent. DA11 0DG
Tel: (01474) 564333

Greenwich & Bexley Cottage Hospice
—5L **51**
185 Bostall Hill, Abbey Wood,
London. SE2 0QX
Tel: 020 8312 2244

HAWKHURST COTTAGE HOSPITAL
—5H **191**
High St., Hawkhurst, Kent. TN18 4PU
Tel: (01580) 753345

HAYES GROVE PRIORY HOSPITAL
—3K **83**
Prestons Rd., Hayes, Bromley,
Kent. BR2 7AS
Tel: 020 8462 7722

Heart of Kent Hospice —1K **125**
Preston Hall, Royal British Legion Village,
Aylesford, Kent. ME20 7NJ
Tel: (01622) 792200

HOMOEOPATHIC HOSPITAL —2G **156**
Church Rd., Tunbridge Wells,
Kent. TN1 1JU
Tel: (01892) 542977

Honor Oak Health Centre —2B **54**
20 Turnham Rd., London. SE4 2LA
Tel: 020 7639 8811

Hospice in the Weald —5D **152**
Maidstone Rd., Pembury, Kent. TN2 4TA

Jenner Health Centre —6B **54**
201 Stanstead Rd., London. SE23 1HU
Tel: 020 7771 4110

JOYCE GREEN HOSPITAL —9N **53**
Joyce Green La., Dartford,
Kent. DA1 5PL
Tel: (01322) 227242

Kennard Street Health Centre —1B **50**
1 Kennard St., North Woolwich,
London. E16 2HR
Tel: 020 7445 7150

KENT & CANTERBURY HOSPITAL
—5N **171**
Ethelbert Rd., Canterbury, Kent. CT1 3NG
Tel: (01227) 766877

KENT & SUSSEX HOSPITAL —1G **156**
Mount Ephraim, Tunbridge Wells,
Kent. TN4 8AT
Tel: (01892) 526111

KENT COUNTY OPHTHALMIC &
AURAL HOSPITAL —5D **126**
Church St., Maidstone, Kent. ME14 1DT
Tel: (01622) 673444

KEYCOL HOSPITAL —5N **97**
Keycol Hill, Bobbing, Sittingbourne,
Kent. ME9 8NG
Tel: (01795) 842222

Kingswood Mental Health Centre —5E **126**
180 Union St., Maidstone,
Kent. ME14 1EY
Tel: (01622) 673358

Lakeside Health Centre —2M **51**
Tavy Bri., Thamesmead,
London. SE2 9UQ
Tel: 020 8310 3281

Lee Health Centre —3J **55**
2 Handen Rd., London. SE12 8NE
Tel: 020 8318 4431

LEWISHAM HOSPITAL —3E **54**
Lewisham High St., Lewisham,
London. SE13 6LH
Tel: 020 8333 3000

Lions Hospice —9E **62**
Coldharbour Rd., Northfleet,
Gravesend, Kent. DA11 7HQ
Tel: (01474) 320007

LIVINGSTONE HOSPITAL —5N **59**
East Hill, Dartford, Kent. DA1 1SA
Tel: (01322) 622222

Lordswood Health Centre —9F **94**
Sultan Rd., Lordswood,
Chatham, Kent. ME5 8TJ
Tel: (01634) 660441

MAIDSTONE HOSPITAL, THE —5L **125**
Hermitage La., Maidstone,
Kent. ME16 9QQ
Tel: (01622) 729000

Marvels Lane Health Centre —7L **55**
37 Marvels La., Grove Park,
London. SE12 9PN
Tel: 020 8857 0042

MEDWAY HOSPITAL —8E **80**
Windmill La., Gillingham, Kent. ME7 5NY
Tel: (01634) 830000

MEMORIAL HOSPITAL —9C **50**
Shooters Hill, Woolwich,
London. SE18 3RZ
Tel: 020 8856 5511

NUNNERY FIELDS HOSPITAL —4M **171**
Nunnery Fields, Canterbury,
Kent. CT1 3LP
Tel: (01227) 766877

ORPINGTON HOSPITAL —5J **85**
Sevenoaks Rd., Orpington,
Kent. BR6 9JU
Tel: (01689) 815000

Parkwood Health Centre —6N **95**
Long Catlis Rd., Parkwood,
Rainham, Kent. ME8 9PR
Tel: (01634) 234400

PEMBURY HOSPITAL —6A **152**
Tonbridge Rd., Pembury,
Tunbridge Wells, Kent. TN2 4QJ
Tel: (01892) 823535

Pilgrims Hospice in Canterbury —1K **171**
56 London Rd., Canterbury,
Kent. CT2 8JY
Tel: (01227) 457766

Pilgrims Hospice Thanet —6D **208**
Ramsgate Rd., Margate,
Kent. CT9 4AD
Tel: (01843) 230277

Plumstead Health Centre —5G **51**
Tewson Rd., Plumstead,
London. SE18 1BH
Tel: 020 8855 9341

PRESTON HALL DAY HOSPITAL —9K **109**
London Rd., Aylesford,
Maidstone, Kent. ME20 7NJ
Tel: (01622) 710161

PRIORITY HOUSE —5M **125**
Hermitage La., Maidstone,
Kent. ME16 9PH
Tel: (01622) 725000

QUEEN ELIZABETH HOSPITAL —7A **50**
Stadium Rd., Woolwich,
London. SE18 4QH
Tel: 020 8856 5533

QUEEN ELIZABETH THE QUEEN MOTHER
HOSPITAL —5D **208**
St Peter's Rd., Margate,
Kent. CT9 4AN
Tel: (01843) 225544

QUEEN MARY'S HOSPITAL —2J **71**
Frognal Av., Sidcup,
Kent. DA14 6LT
Tel: 020 8302 2678

QUEEN VICTORIA MEMORIAL HOSPITAL
—3J **195**
King Edward Av., Herne Bay,
Kent. CT6 6EB
Tel: (01227) 373246

Rainham Health Centre —2A **96**
Holding St., Rainham, Kent. ME8 7JP
Tel: (01634) 374041

Rochester Health Centre —9A **80**
Delce Rd., Rochester, Kent. ME1 2EL
Tel: (01634) 401111

ROYAL VICTORIA HOSPITAL —5J **189**
Radnor Park Av., Folkestone,
Kent. CT19 5BN
Tel: (01303) 850202

ST BARTHOLOMEW'S HOSPITAL —8B **80**
New Rd., Rochester,
Kent. ME1 1DS
Tel: (01634) 402030

St Johns Health Centre —5K **119**
St Johns Rd., Sevenoaks,
Kent. TN13 3LR
Tel: (01732) 743222

St Mark's Health Centre —6D **50**
24 Wrottesley Rd., Plumstead,
London. SE18 3EP
Tel: 020 8317 3540

ST MARTIN'S HOSPITAL —2C **172**
Littlebourne Rd., Canterbury,
Kent. CT1 1TD
Tel: (01227) 459371

ST SAVIOUR'S BUPA HOSPITAL
—6N **197**
73 Seabrook Rd., Hythe,
Kent. CT21 5QW
Tel: (01303) 265581

SEVENOAKS HOSPITAL —3K **119**
Hospital Rd., Sevenoaks,
Kent. TN13 3PG
Tel: (01732) 455155

Sheerness Health Centre —2D **218**
7-10 Trinity Rd., Sheerness,
Kent. ME12 2PJ
Tel: (01795) 580528

SHEPPEY COMMUNITY HOSPITAL
—5L **219**
Wards Hill Rd., Minster,
Sheppey, Kent. ME12 2NL
Tel: (01795) 872116

Shepway Mental Health Centre —5J **189**
2-4 Radnor Park Av., Folkestone,
Kent. CT19 5BW
Tel: (01303) 222424

Sidcup Health Centre —9J **57**
43 Granville Rd., Sidcup,
Kent. DA14 4TA
Tel: 020 8302 7811

SITTINGBOURNE MEMORIAL HOSPITAL
—8G **98**
Bell Rd., Sittingbourne, Kent. ME10 4DT
Tel: (01795) 418300

SLOANE HOSPITAL, THE —4G **69**
125-133 Albemarle Rd., Beckenham,
Kent. BR3 5HS
Tel: 020 8466 6911

SOMERFIELD HOSPITAL —4A **126**
71 London Rd., Maidstone,
Kent. ME16 0DU
Tel: (01622) 686581

South Lewisham Health Centre —9F **54**
50 Conisborough Cres.,
London. SE6 2SP
Tel: 020 8698 8921

STONE HOUSE HOSPITAL —4C **60**
Cotton La., Dartford,
Kent. DA2 6AU
Tel: (01322) 227211

SUNDRIDGE HOSPITAL —9N **117**
Church Rd., Sundridge,
Sevenoaks, Kent. TN14 6AU
Tel: (01959) 562841

Sydenham Green Health Centre —9B **54**
26 Holmshaw Clo.,
London. SE26 4TH
Tel: 020 8778 1333

TONBRIDGE COTTAGE HOSPITAL
—9J **145**
Vauxhall La., Tonbridge,
Kent. TN11 0NE
Tel: (01732) 353653

TUNBRIDGE WELLS BUPA HOSPITAL,
THE —2K **155**
Fordcombe Rd., Fordcombe,
Tunbridge Wells, Kent. TN3 0RD
Tel: (01892) 740047

TUNBRIDGE WELLS NUFFIELD
HOSPITAL, THE —2J **157**
Kingswood Rd., Tunbridge Wells,
Kent. TN2 4UL
Tel: (01892) 531111

UPTON ROAD DAY HOSPITAL —2N **57**
14 Upton Rd., Bexleyheath,
Kent. DA6 8LQ
Tel: 020 8301 7900

VICTORIA HOSPITAL —5L **177**
London Rd., Deal, Kent. CT14 9UA
Tel: (01304) 865400

WESTERN AVENUE DAY HOSPITAL
—7E **158**
King's Av., Ashford, Kent. TN23 1LX
Tel: (01233) 623321

WEST HILL HOSPITAL —4L **59**
West Hill, Dartford, Kent. DA1 2HF
Tel: (01322) 223223

WEST VIEW HOSPITAL —9A **222**
Plummer La., Tenterden,
Kent. TN30 6TX
Tel: (01580) 763677

WHITSTABLE & TANKERTON HOSPITAL
—3J **225**
Northwood Rd., Whitstable,
Kent. CT5 2HN
Tel: (01227) 272225

Whitstable Health Centre —3G **224**
Harbour St., Whitstable,
Kent. CT5 1BZ
Tel: (01227) 263844

WILLIAM HARVEY HOSPITAL —9N **159**
Kennington Rd., Willesbrough,
Ashford, Kent. TN24 0LZ
Tel: (01233) 633331

Wisdom Hospice —1A **94**
High Banks, Rochester,
Kent. ME1 2NU
Tel: (01634) 830456

Woodlands Health Centre —8L **147**
Allington Rd., Paddock Wood,
Kent. TN12 6AX
Tel: (01732) 833331

Woodside Mental Health Centre —4A **126**
89 London Rd., Maidstone,
Kent. ME16 0EB
Tel: (01622) 756077

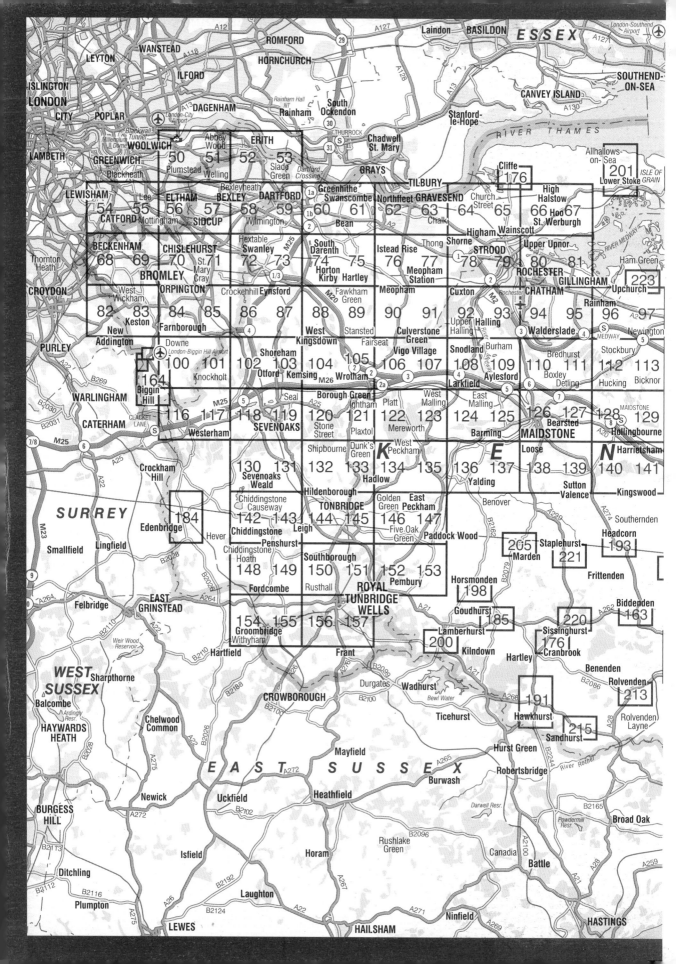